Wiltshire Record Society

(formerly the Records Branch of the Wiltshire
Archaeological and Natural History Society)

VOLUME 56

FOR THE YEAR 2000

Impression of 500 copies

A true Note and Terrier of the Glebe Lands Meadowes
Gardens Orchards Houses Implem.ts tenem.ts & Portents
& Tythes belonging to the Parsonage of Wyly made
forth & Delivered Ann regni R.ß Caroli Secundi nunc
Angliæ &c Regis nono Annoq dni 1677

Inp.s a Parsonage house w.th Barnes Stables Pigeon house and other
outhouses there vnto belonging Scituate neer London Road way
in Wyly Betwixt a tenem.t of W.m Pottrary on the North side and
the tenem.t of W.m Barnes on the South Side w.th Gardens and &c
Orchards Conteyning about One acre

Item four acres of Arrable Land Lying by Hindon Highway
Item three halues of Arrable Lying on Hindons way
Item other three Acres Lying in the East field by a Hedg Comonly
called the Parsonage Hedg

Item a Meadow formerly called Comb Stocks now comonly called
Bester Close or the Hay Close Conteyning neer about one Acre

Item three halues of Arrable Land about the said Close of the
same breadth as the Close is

Item a Plott of Meadow Called Pegnam or Parradice adjoyning
to the West Meades and abutting on the Waters side being about two
acres by Zugg

Item a little Plott of Meadow Called Scotland Lying at the East
end on the Waters side neer Hanging Langford Meadowes being about
one halue of Ground

Item Pasture for Six Kine and a Bull to feed in the farmers
on the Cowdownes and in the fields as farr foeth as the farmers

Item Pasture for Sixtie Sheep Barg and Ram going with the
farmers flock in the East end Downes and fields as farr foeth as
the farmers

Item the Tyth of Corn Acres in Dutnam &c &c a Meadow Comonly
called Dutnam Meade Conteyning by Estimacon Thirteen acres in
the whole Lying in the parish of Little Langford

Item the Tythes of all Corne Wooll Lamb Meadow Pasture
Oblacons and Adventons And all other kinds of Tythes due
by the Law both in Wyly and in Dotford only the farmer of
Wyly Claimes and hath as long as we remember gon free of
Three hundred Sheep of the farmes whole flock Consisting of
Eight hundred Running out at the Leate

John Stevens Rector

William Washon }
will.am .... } Church-
william Pottrary } wardens.
william ....
John Lock
Bridget Poticary
william ....

Wylye glebe terrier, 1677, no. **859** *(WSRO D1/24/234/3).*

WILTSHIRE GLEBE TERRIERS 1588–1827

EDITED BY

STEVEN HOBBS
Wiltshire & Swindon Record Office

TROWBRIDGE

2003

ISBN 0 901333 33 6

Typeset by John Chandler
Produced for the Society by
Salisbury Printing Company Ltd, Salisbury
Printed in Great Britain

CONTENTS

PREFACE

The project to publish Wiltshire's glebe terriers began just over thirty years ago. Susan Avery, working to a scheme of calendaring drawn up by Douglas Crowley, produced a manuscript comprising the earliest terrier of each parish with initial letter A–S in the bishop's series that could be photocopied. Work ceased but was begun again in 1995 by Steven Hobbs, and expanded to cover the whole collection of terriers. The analysis of the information on rectories and vicarage houses in the introduction has been contributed by Pamela Slocombe of the Wiltshire Buildings Record.

The Wiltshire Record Society acknowledges the permission of the bishop of Salisbury to publish these documents from the diocesan archives.

Mr Hobbs much appreciates the work of his predecessors in this project, and that of Christine Pictor and Elizabeth Hickerton for their expertise in producing a word-processed text. He acknowledges with thanks my assistance in bringing the work to press. He is particularly grateful to Dr Joseph Bettey for his advice on several matters to do with tithes and agricultural practice, and to Kenneth Rogers, whose enthusiasm for all aspects of Wiltshire's history is a constant source of inspiration and encouragement. He is also most grateful to his wife Shirley for her patience and support throughout the project. The line in Gray's *Elegy*, 'Their furrow oft the stubborn glebe has broke', has a particular resonance for Mr Hobbs as the glebe terriers did not always easily offer up their secrets.

JOHN CHANDLER

INTRODUCTION

Glebe terriers are descriptions of the property of benefices drawn up by incumbents and churchwardens, often with the assistance of knowledgeable parishioners, at the request of the bishop, archdeacon or ordinary of a peculiar jurisdiction for deposit in their respective registries.[1] Such property comprised glebe land, a house for the incumbent, tithes, offerings and endowments. The terriers recorded the sources of income of parish clergy, and in doing so they were aimed at protecting the property and rights of the clergy against encroachment and dispute. They were in effect the clergyman's title deeds. Their significance was exemplified in 1705 in the terrier for Rowde (**638**); it is to be preserved in the registry *in futuram rei memento*. The collection calendared here is deposited in the Wiltshire and Swindon Record Office (WSRO) and consists largely of the series compiled at the instruction of the various bishops of Salisbury. This covers almost 250 Wiltshire parishes and chapelries; the majority are represented by at least three terriers. They range between 1588 and 1783 although a few come after this date, the latest being 1827 (**712**). These terriers have the catalogue mark D1/24. They seem to have been filed in the bishop's registry by year, not alphabetically, and kept in ten files E, F, G, H and K for Wiltshire (A, B, C, D and J for Berkshire), although an endorsement to **149** 'South Wiltes terriers from 1588-1610', suggests that this arrangement may not have been applied throughout the collection. Then in the early or mid 18th century a catalogue was made (D1/24/369) in which the documents were arranged under the initial letter of the parish names, although not in strict alphabetical order, since each initial letter was subdivided by deanery. The old file reference symbol, consisting of the file letter plus a number, is given for each terrier, although in only a few cases was the date given. Probably shortly afterwards a new reference was created consisting of the initial letter of the parish plus a number, and no doubt at the same time the terriers themselves were arranged accordingly. They remained thus until the 1960s, when they were listed by Pamela Stewart, assistant diocesan archivist, who arranged them in strict alphabetical order (by the main component in the case of double-barrelled names), apart from chapelries which remained with the mother parish. This arrangement has been retained although in this volume parish names appear in natural order.

The dean of Salisbury exercised quasi-episcopal jurisdiction over nearly fifty Wiltshire parishes for which only about one-third have terriers, mostly singletons. They range in date between 1612 and 1674, and have the catalogue mark D5. A few can be found in the archives of 'peculiar' jurisdictions, two of which were inhibited by the dean, one not. They have the catalogue marks D9, D24 and D26. The terrier of Westbury (**792**), a peculiar of the precentor of the cathedral, found its way into the bishop's series. A few terriers survive only as copies in parish archives and have been included to fill the gaps. Furthermore, in order to be as inclusive as possible, terriers of impropriated benefices have also been calendared. Their inclusion is further justified by the fact that several terriers in the main series cover both vicarage and impropriated rectory and, in the cases of Calne (**122**) and Mere (**536**), the latter only.

The earliest reference to a call for terriers is found in Salisbury diocese. An article of enquiry of bishop Capon's visitation of 1550 (D1/43/1 f.6-8) acknowledging that 'myche controversye & dissencion dothe dailye arise', instructed parishes to draw up schedules of customs of tithes and offerings, ' by thadvyse of the parson, vicarr or curatt & the churchwardens of the parishe'. There is no evidence that this was implemented although since there was no requirement to place a copy in the registry the documents may have remained in the parishes to be discarded when superseded by later terriers. Continuing awareness of the need to protect the rights of the clergy led to a canon of 1571 directing bishops to collect terriers of the lands of benefices in their sees. Reaction to this in the diocese of Salisbury seems to have been somewhat tardy, as responses date from 1588, although they are more wide-ranging in that tithes and offerings are also included. This instruction was developed in Canon 87 of 1604 and provoked a swifter response in the diocese, as several terriers of 1605 and more from 1608/9 are in the collection. Subsequent terriers in the bishop's series generally fall into the years 1671, 1677, 1704 and 1783 or thereabouts. Apart from the 1783 terriers, for which detailed instructions as to their compilation were issued by Bishop Shute Barrington (see Figure 1) no evidence of instructions for new terriers to be drawn up at these dates has come to light. [Of the years in question visitation mandates survive only for 1677, and are silent on the matter. No visitation articles of enquiry are extant for these years.] However those for 1631, 1634 (a metropolitan visitation), 1695 and 1732 (D1/36/2, D1/55/1) sought only to determine whether terriers existed and were 'laid up' in the registry.

Only four parishes, Landford, Manningford Abbots, Mildenhall, and Stanton Fitzwarren appear to have full sets. Whether such a low count is due to parochial inaction in preparing new documents or carelessness on the part of registry officials in losing them needs to be considered. References to terriers missing from the registry for Bishopstone (S. Wilts.) (**58**) and Urchfont (**784**) and the fact that parts of the Steeple Langford (**457**) and Potterne terriers (**613**) were misplaced in the series and found among a series of unidentified fragments respectively point to the latter cause. That no terrier earlier than 1671 could be found for Great Chalfield (**129**) could have been due to either. Furthermore no terriers for Wiltshire parishes survive for the 1634 visitation by the archbishop of Canterbury while an almost complete new set survives in the registry of the archdeaconry of Berkshire. It seems improbable that the archdeaconries of Wiltshire and Salisbury were exempt from this requirement, although it is probably the case that the archdeacon of Berkshire wished to ensure that new terriers were drawn up while his counterparts in Wiltshire and Salisbury relied on old terriers. It is possible that the terriers were lost in their registries or that of the bishop during the hiatus of the Interregnum (1650-1660), when ecclesiastical administration above parish level was wound up. Loss so soon after compilation is suggested by the fact that no copies made for legal or administrative reasons have been found. The1671 terrier of Somerford Keynes (**679**) cites its1605 predecessor (**678**), suggesting that there was not one between those dates. This point is important, since it illustrates that the terriers were not consigned into oblivion in the registry. They were frequently consulted in the course of disputes, often over tithes. Several sets in the bishop's series were removed for chancery cases, as endorsements bear witness. The opportunities for loss and misfiling were present and undoubtedly explain some of the gaps.

     However, two sources for the 1704/5 and 1783 terriers suggest that blame for gaps did not generally lie with the registry and its officials. The visitation book listing clergy and churchwardens attending the bishop in October 1704 (D1/50/6) has a separate list indicating those parishes which had presented terriers. All the terriers presented then have survived; of the 54 who did not present one, only three subsequently sent into the registry terriers which are extant. Moreover the replies to a question as to whether the parish had a true terrier in the returns to Bishop Shute's visitation enquiries in 1783 (D1/56/1-2) provide further evidence of the natural inclination against reinventing the wheel.[2] Several ministers felt that the 1704/5 terriers accurately reflected the current position and did not need revision. Furthermore eighteen responses promised that new terriers would be drawn up although none is extant, and presumably they were never sent in. Concern for this is apparent by a note in the printed timetable for confirmations during the 1786 visitation urging those who had not yet presented a terrier to do so (D1/54/1). Grittleton stated that a new document had been sent; but it is not present in the collection. The 1783 terriers of Great Wishford (**835**) and Huish (**412**), and the1705 terriers of Foxley (**387**), Stratford Tony (**717**) and Wilcot (**802**) were merely reissues of earlier ones with new signatories. Clearly several parishes did not see the merit or necessity of producing a new terrier when the current one still reflected the situation satisfactorily. Such inaction could present problems however. At Purton the 1588 terrier was repeated each time up to 1711 and the drawback of this was noted by the vicar in 1728 (**630B**) as its failure to be updated had led to the loss of tithes on certain lands. However there may be sound reasons for not producing a terrier. In making his response to the bishop's enquiries in 1783 the rector of Tockenham claimed that since he disputed the outcome of an enclosure of land in 1699, which he claimed had seriously depleted the value of his living, he refused to commit himself to make a new one which could only be construed as endorsing that previous agreement.[3] The rector of Colerne was not alone in holding fire on producing a terrier in 1783 because an imminent enclosure of land would invalidate it (**202A**). Such concern did not prevent the rector of Kingston Deverill from producing one at that time. He merely omitted the glebe as it was as yet 'undefinable due to an imminent inclosure' (**264**). Clearly the attentiveness and inclination of the incumbent was often a crucial factor. A letter from Winchester college, patron of Downton, in 1786 stated that it was not possible to send as particular an account of the glebe lands there as required

DIRECTIONS

TO THE

Reverend the CLERGY of the Diocefe of SALISBURY,
and the CHURCHWARDENS of the fame,

FOR

Making and Difpofing their TERRIERS.

L ET there be Two original Inftruments, fairly written, containing
the fame Words, and figned by the fame Perfons.

Let them be figned by the Minifter and Churchwardens, and likewife by
as many as may be of the fubftantial Inhabitants of the Parifh.

Let One of them be delivered to my Regiftrar, at my Vifitation, which
I propofe (God willing) to hold this Year at the Time and Place appointed by the Book of Articles herewith fent: Let the other be affixed to
the Parifh Regifter-Book, or kept with it.

IN THE TERRIER.

1. Defcribe the Parfonage or Vicarage-Houfe; exprefs what Materials
it is built and covered with; how many Rooms it contains, and in what
Manner they are floored, wainfcotted, and cieled; or that they are not.
Add the Out-houfes, and the Dimenfions of each, and what they are built
and covered with.

2. Set forth the Glebe; the other Houfes, if any, upon it; the Quantity of Ground in the Whole; the Abuttals or Boundaries of each Parcel;
what inclofed, and what in common Fields; and how many Acres of Land
in each Inclofure, or lying together in the faid Fields, with the Diftinction
throughout of Orchard, Meadow, Pafture, Arable, Woods, Underwoods,
&c. and add an Article of the Right of Commoning, if any; how many
Beafts, Sheep, &c. it extends to; more particularly fet down the Quantity and Divifions of the Gardens, Yards, and Outlets, and the Nature of
their

Figure 1: Bishop Barrington's instructions for compiling glebe terriers, 1783 (WSRO D1/24

[2]

their feveral Fences, whether Walls or otherwife. Laftly, particularife any Number and Value of Timber, or other Trees, growing on the Church-yard, or any Part of the Glebe.

3. Set down what Tythes are due to the Minifter, and from what Townfhip.

4. Specify all Penfions, Augmentations, Gifts, or Bequefts made to the Church or Chapel, and their Minifters; and annex attefted Copies (if practicable) of the Deeds, Wills, or Claufes, by which they are given or fettled. On the other Hand, fignify, whether any Penfion be payable out of the Living, and to whom; .or Stipend or Allowance to the Minifter of a Chapel; or Cuftom eftablifhed to the Expence or Charge of the Incumbent, by Diftribution, Entertainment, or otherwife.

5. The Curates of Churches impropriate, and of Chapels that have Tythes, or Portions of Tythes, muft particularife the Lands, or other Things, tythable to them; adding (as before directed) the Penfions, Stipends, or other Maintenance, if any, and by whom payable.

6. Set forth the Furniture of.the Church or Chapel, and Chancel; the Bells, Clock, Utenfils, particularly the Communion Plate, with the Infcription upon it, and the Weight, if marked thereupon ; together with a Catalogue of the Books which have been left, or belong, to the Church, Parifh, or Chapel.

7. Lands, or Money in Stock, for Repair of the Church, Chapel, or Utenfils; Writings concerning the fame, and in whofe Cuftody.

8. Who are charged with the Repair of the Edifices and Church-yard Fence.

9. The Clerk's and Sexton's Wages, by Cuftom or otherwife; by whom paid, and who appoints them.

N. B. I earneftly recommend to you, that thefe TERRIERS be made as carefully and as accurately as poffible.

S.   S A R U M.

May 20, 1783.

because 'unity of possession, length of time and other circumstances render it difficult to ascertain the situation and boundaries of them'.[4] The rector of Baverstock in his response to the visitation queries of 1783 indicated that he would produce a terrier as soon as an accurate survey could be made 'To present at his Lordship's primary visitation is impossible'.[5]

The dean's series is far less complete, probably reflecting a different emphasis of administration, although interestingly it does include a couple of terriers produced as a result of the archbishop of Canterbury's visitation in 1634.

A pattern can be discerned in the compilation of the terriers. The earliest, in 1588, are almost all drawn up by the churchwardens, sidesmen and parishioners with, in several cases, the expressed support of the incumbents. Those of Enford (**319**), Hilmarton (**392**), and Steeple Langford (**457**) are examples of terriers which describe themselves as inquisitions, implying evidence produced by knowledgeable witnesses on behalf of the collective interest of the parish. Purton (**625**) and Rowde (**635**), drawn up by 'we the parishioners', refer to the information being 'reduced into writing', which gives a glimpse into the process of the collection of information gleaned from the testimonies and agreement of the parishioners. In fact the 1608 terrier of Milton Lilborne (**547**) resembles an extract from a church court deposition book, as it is composed solely of testimonies of individuals often repeating details in each other's account. It shows how terriers may have been produced; it being the rough version from which the finished article would be written, although in this case it was signed and handed in. North Wraxall (**830**) is written in the form of a churchwardens' presentment with absolutely no detail and could have been reduced to the phrase *Omnia bene* (All is well) often found in such documents. In subsequent terriers the incumbent generally emerges as the natural initiator albeit in conjunction with the churchwardens. In several cases, (e.g. **12**, **36**, **187** and **597**), the incumbents added notes after the terrier had been signed off by the parishioners querying aspects of its content. Nevertheless the process was supposed to be a joint effort agreed by all parties. Those of Aldbourne (**5**) and Marlborough St. Mary (**527**) were read out at parish meetings and they could not have been exceptional in this.

The main purpose of the terriers was to record sources of income of parish clergy and they are informative as to their economic condition. They show to what extent the incumbent relied on land, tithes, offerings or stipends. Those endowed with land which they might farm directly or lease out and tithes paid in kind were generally better off than clergy reliant on a stipend or money payments in lieu of tithes in kind which might be based on an ancient modus devalued by inflation. This probably lies behind the dispute noted in Lydiard Tregoze (**503**) whereby an earlier modus was rejected by the rector who reverted to claim tithe in kind because of a doubt in its validity. Tithes on Draycot farm in Wilcot were to be in kind unless the owner and the vicar agreed otherwise (**803**). A similar arrangement existed in Brinkworth (**102**). However there are many examples where compositions were in use. Payment in money solved the problem of dealing with quantities of produce, some of it perishable and much often surplus to the requirements of the incumbent's household. It reduced the chances of conflict – something which could also be achieved by leasing the tithes to a 'farmer'.

The value of most livings was dependent on land. Benefices might be endowed with little more than a few acres or, as in the case of the rectory of East Knoyle, a large estate comprising land and 19 tenements (**441**). Boyton was endowed with land and a chapel at Rodden, Somerset dedicated to St. Blaise, although it was not used for religious purposes at the time of the 1609 terrier (**73**). At the other end of the scale was the curacy of Imber, whose minister was dependent only on a discretionary stipend (**132**).

Concern at the plight of the clergy of less well endowed benefices led in 1704 to the creation of a fund known as the Queen Anne's Bounty (QAB). Those benefices with the 'clear improved value' of under £50 were to be discharged from payment of First Fruits and Tenths and were also to be eligible to receive help from the Bounty. The official valuation or *Valor Ecclesiasticus* was made in 1535 and was regarded as a most unreliable guide by then. In response to this inadequacy the terriers of 1704/5 provide valuations of both glebe and tithes.[6] Bishop Gilbert Burnet played an important part in the establishment of the QAB and it is probable that this issue prompted the drawing up of the terriers at this time.[7] The impact of the QAB in augmenting livings is evidenced in many terriers (see index), although several terriers record augmentations from other sources, principally private donation or episcopal gift.

Incumbents were entitled to offerings such as annual payments at Easter by adult parishioners and mortuaries, a payment on death to settle unpaid tithes. Scales of payment according to the value of the deceased's estate are given in a few terriers (**39, 92, 134, 637** and **638**). Tithes on poultry were also due at Easter, payment generally in eggs, two for a hen, three for a cock (eg **201**). Since the eating of eggs was forbidden during Lent, which preceded Easter, eggs were plentiful, making it a convenient time to pay tithe on poultry. In Latton (**466**) and Trowbridge (**766**), this was extended to include geese and turkeys. Other sources of income included payments for the churching of women (receiving new mothers into church), and in several 1783 terriers, fees for marriages by licence or banns (**705**), mortuaries and burial in the church. Examples of more unusual sources of income for annual sermons are found in Compton Chamberlayne (**318**), Enford (**322**) and Hullavington (**415**). The vicar of Fisherton Delamere received a cake and 1d. for saying a prayer or gospel at mills or near their wheat bins during Procession Week (**338**).

The customary payment of one tenth of the harvest of corn, hay and wood was a principal source of income of rectors; vicars received the tithes of lesser crops and the produce of livestock. The terriers provide much information about the local tithe customs which, as the examples from Highworth (**391**) Ludgershall (**495**) and Steeple Langford (**458**) reveal, could be fiendishly complicated. Such complexities created numerous opportunities for disagreement between minister and parishioners and emphasised the value of a terrier to protect the rights of the incumbent. In three cases, Norton Bavant (**576**), South Newton (**566**) and Potterne (**616**), tithe corn was claimed on any land that might in the future be converted to arable. Change in land use could have a serious impact on the incumbent's income; for instance conversion of grassland, supporting sheep, to arable replaced tithe on wool and lambs, payable to the vicar by tithe on corn which was due to the rector, clerical or lay. Hence the attention in enclosure awards to recompense incumbents with land for loss of tithes.

Land was not all necessarily liable to the payment of tithes. Some was exempt because it had formerly belonged to a monastic house. There are several examples of portions of tithes on properties being owed to different owners other than the lay rector (eg Fittleton **346**), and Horrell tithes that had formerly been due to Wherwell abbey and had passed into lay hands after the Dissolution (**381, 544, 546**). Furthermore a benefice might be entitled to tithes in another parish (see Donhead St.Andrew **280-283**), which might be a further complication.

For those parishes in which details of customs were not recorded but were covered by catch-all statements or lists of tithable produce, it can be assumed that similar customs pertained. However it is reasonable to infer that customs of those tithes of particular relevance and value in a parish might be given prominence in the terrier. Clergy were entitled to receive agistment money, due for animals from outside the parish brought in to feed for part of the year. Specific reference to this in a terrier probably indicates that movement of livestock into and through the parish might not have been at all uncommon there. The single reference to 'Welch' beasts (**722**) hints at the work of drovers.

Tithe customs for livestock, notably 'Cow white', which related to milk cows and calves and often young horses, were often referred to as Lammas dues because they were paid on 1 Aug (Lammas day). They might include provision for payment if sold (a tenth of the price), or killed (the left shoulder).

The difficulty of receiving the tithe of the young of livestock which were rarely produced conveniently in multiples or fractions of ten each year might be dealt with by the drive, whereby assessment was carried over to the following year as suitable numbers were reached. An alternative method in circumstances where between seven and nine young were produced was for the incumbent to take an animal and pay the owner a sum of money as set out in the custom (see Highworth **391**).

An interesting tithe custom for wool is described in a few terriers, in particular Wylye (**857**). Selection of sheep whose fleeces were to be tithed took place at shear time. The sheep who were presumably penned were allowed to run 'leate or aventure'. Those that ran were not tithed. Possibly this separated off the heavily fleeced sheep, less able to run as freely, who would be tithable. The element of chance inherent in such a method, however, meant that the advantage presumably balanced out between farmer and clergy over the years. Selecting sheep in this way occurs in many mid-16th century wills from the downland parishes of South Wiltshire as a method of dividing a flock among the beneficiaries.[8]

Such arrangements inevitably left much opportunity for conflict and dispute. In his study of the relationship between ministers and parishioners, Donald Spaeth found that over half of Wiltshire parishes experienced at least one tithe suit in the consistory or Exchequer court of Equity in the period 1660-1740.[9] Litigation enabled incumbents to make examples of those who withheld payment of tithes and discourage others from similar action. But since the threat of proceedings must have deterred many, the number of cases must have been far smaller than disputes that occurred throughout the county. Clergy faced a constant struggle between protecting their rights and those of their successors and alienating parishioners who felt they were over-zealous in claiming tithes. Religious dissension from the late-17th century exacerbated this as more parishioners objected to the principle of paying tithes, rather than to the details of tithe customs as before. These factors all emphasised the value of a reliable and credible glebe terrier that could form an important part of the basis of the relationship between the incumbent and his parishioners.

As life tenant of the glebe rural clergymen took their place alongside their neighbours in the agricultural life of the village. Their strips in the open fields or their enclosed fields lay alongside each other and they enjoyed the same common rights with regard to crops and livestock. The terrier for Little Cheverell (**149**) is a good example with regard to livestock. In East Knoyle the number of sheep allowed to be wintered by the rector was determined by him and the manor court jury (**439-40**). Consequently glebe terriers provide important evidence for agricultural history, and their countywide coverage makes them one of the most comprehensive sources in local Record Offices; likewise for topographical and local place name studies. In open field parishes descriptions of the incumbents' strips explain how the fields were laid out. They are informative as to the spread of enclosure, either implicitly by successive terriers listing first land in common fields then in enclosed fields, or explicitly by a specific reference to enclosure having taken place which might not be documented anywhere else. Good examples of this are Sutton Benger (**727**) and Stanton Fitzwarren (**690**). Glebe land in open fields was more susceptible to encroachment and the terriers were most important in protecting them. The view expressed in the 1783 terrier of Milton Lilbourne (**550**) that part of the glebe was so intermixed with land of a neighbour that it could not be accurately described illustrates the problem if not endorsing the solution offered by a terrier. It is possible that some clergy sought to avoid this by consolidating their land into closes within common fields, or even fields of individual land owners, and there are examples of this (see the Subject Index under Enclosure). There are other examples (also indexed) where glebe in common fields had been consolidated into blocks of three acres or more, which is not a usual feature of arable open field practice. Enclosure was not always as straightforward and clear-cut as might be imagined and those examples may also be the result of the lack of participation by all the relevant land holders rather than a conscious policy on the part of individual clergy. There are a few examples of land being enclosed into parks (see Index).

Several terriers refer to 'stean mead' and 'laines', and a terrier of Swindon (**739A**) uses these terms to distinguish grass. The precise meaning is unclear but it is likely that the distinction is between pasture in strips (laines) bounded by balks or low ditches in open fields which could easily be converted to arable by agreement or rotation and permanent pasture in fields marked out in lots by stone (stean) markers.[10]

The terriers are an important source for the study of parsonage and vicarage houses, particularly those of 1783 which often give details of the materials and dimensions. Again their county-wide scope adds to their value as a source.

Furthermore since it is reasonable to infer that in terms of style and construction they would not have differed much from the houses of the social equals of the clergy – gentlemen, yeomen and professional men – it is true to say that Goldsmith's 'village preacher's modest mansion' is an important model for studying the vernacular architecture of Wiltshire.

Building materials are often specified and they document, for instance, the change from timber-framing to building in brick during the 18th century throughout much of Wiltshire. By 1783 many houses had been re-built in brick, or it had been used to infill the timber panels replacing wattle and daub. Likewise clay tiles and slate were becoming increasingly common replacing thatch as the favoured roofing material. Stourton rectory, built in 1820, was covered in 'blue slate'(712). Materials also came from nearer to home as the terriers have several references to quarries (cleeves or quars) such as Yatton Keynell (866), and one tilepit at Monkton Farleigh (332). Floor materials are interesting: apart from the usual oak, elm and deal boards, ash, beech, sycamore and chestnut are sometimes encountered. As well as earthen floors, as in the 'ancient building' at Dauntsey in 1783 (256) other types include lime and sand floors (Hullavington 415), lime and ashes (Keevil 425) and mortar (West Kington 439). At the end of the 18th century wallpaper was common, with flock at Corsley (224) and wainscoting on the walls, unusually walnut at Fittleton (347).

Houses varied in size and appearance, largely reflecting disparities in the wealth of benefices. In 1609 the rectory at Codford St. Mary was a single bay (field) house while the barn had six bays (191). At Ashton Keynes the house was noted as newly built in 1611 and to this day still bears the date stone 1584 (18). The parsonage at Codford St. Peter in 1608 had one part 'now in building, the other old and ruinous' (196). In 1677 Rodbourne Cheney vicarage was described as being large with a wall, gate and gatehouse, suggesting a substantial property (633). The vicarage house at Erlestoke was said in the early-17th century to have been used by Sir William Brounker to keep hawks in (531). Detached kitchens, a medieval practice, were not uncommon. In 1671 East Knoyle had 'an outhouse called the old kitchen'(441), and at Stanton St. Bernard the kitchen was about 20 feet away from the house (690). Outdoor privies, usually called houses of office or, later, necessaries, are often mentioned. Melksham vicarage had a double necessary house in 1783 (530).

Rural vicarages and parsonages often had many farm buildings, usually barns, stables and cow stalls, which illustrate the agricultural links of the clergy. Stourton had a barn and wheelhouse, presumably a horse gin, in 1827 (712). Poulshot had a 'granary upon stavells' in 1705 (620). In 1783 barns on staddle stones were mentioned at Norton Bavant (528) and Donhead St. Andrew (283). In the same year Steeple Langford had a wagon house 'now building' (460). More primitive was the stable 'enclosed with hurdle work' at Tollard Royal also in 1783 (765). Some clergy, like the rector of Little Hinton in 1677, had their own facilities for malting and brewing (405). There was an oasthouse' for drying of malt' in 1704 at Sopworth (688). References to sheephouses (Baverstock 1609: 36), a vetch house (Orcheston St. Mary 1677: 591) and two hen or chicken houses adjoining the brewhouse at Great Somerford in 1671 (675) illustrate the variety of agricultural life.

The scope of the terriers of 1783 was far more comprehensive, reflecting the intention of Bishop Shute to gain a clear picture of the position of his parish clergy. This marked something of a change from the more *laissez faire* attitude prevalent in the Anglican church in the 18th century. But it should be noted that Salisbury was not at the forefront of the widening of the scope of terriers. Terriers of parishes in the archdeaconry of Cornwall for 1726/7 covered church furnishings, the maintenance of the church and appointment of clerks and sextons: they reflected the regulations for terriers issued by the bishop of Lincoln in 1706 for his diocese.[11] The Wiltshire terriers of 1783 should be seen in conjunction with the visitation returns collected in the same year and surveys of parsonage houses carried out between 1787 and 1789 in the bishop's peculiars and the archdeaconries of Salisbury and Wiltshire (D1/54/58, D2/9, D3/14/1). Although the primary function of the terriers remained as before, now information was required about the furnishings of the church, particularly the plate, responsibility for the maintenance of church, chancel and churchyards bounds as well as the appointment and salaries of the clerk and sexton. Church fabric was not covered in earlier terriers, although properties from which the churches were endowed at Chippenham in 1671 (**164**) and Marlborough St. Peter and St Paul in 1783 (**524**) were described. Often extremely detailed accounts of parsonage and vicarage houses were provided in order that their state of repair might be recorded, it being understood that suitable accommodation was vital to ensure a resident clergyman on hand to serve his parish. The value of timber is also recognised by its inclusion in the terriers, possibly as a source of material for building or repair of these houses. As with earlier terriers there was a variation in the amount of detail given although on the whole they are extremely informative. In at least two cases in particular, Sutton Benger (**727**) and Yatton Keynell (**869**) requirements were fortuitously exceeded. In the former the vicar provided a thumbnail sketch of the parish and the history of the endowment of the benefice. He also displayed a degree of candour in describing the church bells as unmusical. In Yatton Keynell the description of the fittings in the church noted that the Ten Commandments were put up in 1773 on two tablets of stone dug up in the parish.

The significance of glebe terriers had declined by the 19th century. They were revived in 1891 by Convocation, although the focus of their attention was directed towards the furnishings of the church and the responsibility for their compilation had fallen back to the churchwardens. Several developments had considerably reduced their importance. The Tithe Apportionment Act of 1836 introduced a standard assessment for the payment of tithes based on the price of corn, thus sweeping away local tithe customs. Its resulting maps and schedules became the authoritative record of titheable land including glebe. The management of glebe land itself was changed by a series of Acts between 1842 and 1888 which enabled the leasing and sale of glebe.[12] The Endowment and Glebe Measure 1976 brought the most fundamental change by handing over glebe to the respective Diocesan Boards of Finance for the general benefit of the diocesan stipends fund of each diocese. This came about, despite the efforts of some clergy, notably Revd. Edward Courtman, rector of Mildenhall until his death in 1979 who, under the auspices of the Parochial Clergy Association

which he founded and through his editorship of *Parson and Parish*, campaigned
to maintain 'the Parsons' Freehold'.

1. The best guides to glebe terriers are the introductions to *Ecclesiastical Terriers of
    Warwickshire Parishes*, vol. 1, by D.M. Barratt (Dugdale Society Publications vol.
    22, 1955); *Berkshire Glebe Terriers*, by Ian Mortimer (Berkshire Record Society
    vol. 2, 1995); and *A Calendar of Cornish Glebe Terriers*, by Richard Potts (Devon
    and Cornwall Record Society N.S. 19, 1974). See also *Short Guides to Records* no.
    13, by D.M. Barrett, ed. by L. Munby (Historical Association, 1994). For the uses of
    glebe terriers see M.W. Berresford, 'Glebe terriers and open field Leicestershire',
    Leics. Archaeological Society Transactions, vol. 24, 1948, pp. 77-26; 'Glebe Terriers
    and open field Yorkshire', *Yorks. Archaeological Journal*, vol. 38, 1950, pp. 325-368;
    and 'Glebe Terriers and open field Buckinghamshire,' *Records of Bucks.*, vol. 15 (5),
    1951-2, pp. 283-298, vol. 16 (1), 1953-4, pp. 5-28. See also David Dymond, 'The
    Parson's Glebe: Stable or Expanding or Shrinking', in C. Harper-Bill, C. Rawcliffe
    and R. Wilson (eds.) *East Anglia's history: Studies in Honour of Norman Scarfe*,
    Boydell & UEA, 2002.
2. Published in Wiltshire Record Society (WRS) vol. 27.
3. *op. cit.* p. 217.
4. Wiltshire and Swindon Record Office (WSRO) 490/959.
5. WRS vol. 27, p.32.
6. Certainly the need to revise the *Valor* led to a projected volume on the state of
    parish churches, and returns were requested to be endorsed on a brief issued for All
    Saints Oxford. Those returns, known as *Notitia Parochialis*, are at Lambeth palace.
    See 'Some Somerset parishes in 1705', by R. W. Dunning (*Somerset Archaeology
    and Natural History*, vol. 112 for 1968). Copies for 38 Wiltshire parishes are in the
    Benet of Pythouse archive (WSRO 413/450).
7. See *The foundation of the early years of Queen Anne's Bounty* by A. Savidge (1955)
    pp. 13-15. The editor is grateful to Donald Spaeth for this reference.
8. Between 1542 and 1558 48 wills in the registers of the archdeacon of Salisbury
    (WSRO P2/3Reg, P2/2Reg, P2/3Reg) refer to this method of selection of sheep,
    occasionally using the phrase 'run at the hurdle' and once, in the will of William
    Shayle of Rushall, 1558 the following 'one hundred of sheep to be delivered owt of
    the farme folde & they to runne of their owne accorde' (P2/3Reg/160B).
9. *The Church in an Age of Danger: Parsons and Parishioners 1660-1740*, by D.A.
    Spaeth (Cambridge 2000).
10. This interpretation of stean mead is borne out by a 1614 custumal of the manor of
    Christian Malford which states that a customary tenant may break up and plough
    any or all of his estate except 'stonemead' without licence or breaking
    custom. (*WANHM*, vol. 41, pp. 174-7). Customs of several manors belonging to the
    Hungerford family in west and north Wiltshire in the late 16th and early 17th
    centuries in describing the custom of the executor's year state that the executor of
    a copyholder might enjoy the whole tenement until 25 Mar next following; then
    the reversioner may enter the steanmead and fallow; then the whole tenement at
    Lammas (1 Aug) (WSRO 442/1-2).

11. See Potts, *op. cit.*
12. Several Acts relaxed the Ecclesiastical Leases Act 1571 (13 Eliz 1 c.10); the Ecclesiastical
    Leases Act 1842 (5&6 Vict c.27) made provision for the letting of glebe lands on
    agricultural leases by incumbents, generally on 14-year leases. The Ecclesiastical
    Leases Act 1842 (5&6 Vict c.108) allowed for the granting of building leases not
    exceeding 99 years. The Ecclesiastical Leasing act 1858 (21&22 Vict c.57) widened
    the scope of leases allowed under the second 1842 Act and enabled sales, exchanges
    and partitions. By the Glebe Lands Act 1888 (51&52 Vict c.20) the facilities for
    selling glebe were greatly extended. In 1887 there were 17,693 acres of glebe in the
    diocese of Salisbury. The editor is grateful to Philip M A Nokes of the Bath and
    Wells Diocesan Board of Finance, and a member of the WRS, for the later history of
    glebe land.

EDITORIAL METHOD

The nature of the terriers demands a detailed calendar. In fact only the headings
or opening sentences have been calendared together with sections or whole
documents substantially repeating another terrier (in these cases variations have
been noted in footnotes). Apart from these exceptions the sense and words of
the original have been retained as much as possible. Punctuation has been added
or altered to clarify meaning and spellings modernised, except surnames and
field-names, although standard elements in the latter have been altered when
they appear as separate words. Where a significant word or name is modernised
the original form is given in square brackets [ ] after its first appearance in the
document, as have Saints' days. Measurements of length, weight and area have
been abbreviated except where they are part of a field name. Points of the
compass have also been shortened. Phrases like '2 separate halves' (acres) have
been contracted to 2 x ½a. Signatories making their marks are indicated by [X].
Some standardisation of frequent words has been used, e.g: farndell for farundell,
farthingdale, farndale, farndeal, farundell and varndell; rother is used for rudder
and rou(w)ther; enclosure for inclosure; senior and junior for elder and younger;
arable for earable; coppice for copse, cops. Bays of or fields of building have
generally been reduced to bays or fields. Christian names of clergymen have
been provided where possible by consulting parish registers, bishop's transcripts
and ordination papers all in the WSRO. Dates of incumbencies are generally
taken from *Institutiones clericorum in comitatu Wiltoniensis*, by Sir Thomas
Phillipps (1825).

ABBREVIATIONS

a.   acre(s)
c.   containing, be it more or less.
d.   dwt., pennyweight
li   links

mrs.   Mistress
p.   pole(s), perch(es)
qtr.   quarter(s)
r.   rod(s), rood(s)
VCH   *Victoria County History: Wiltshire*
WAM   *Wiltshire Archaeological & Natural History Magazine*
wid.   widow
WRS   Wiltshire Record Society (formerly WA&NHS Records Branch)

GLOSSARY

This is based on the glossary produced by Eric Kerridge for his edition of the *Pembroke Estate Survey, 1631-2* (WRS vol. 9), with reference also to the *Oxford English Dictionary* and *Agrarian landscape terms: a glossary for historical geographers*, by I. H. Adams (Institute of British Geographers Special Publication 9, 1976). In cases where the meaning is not clear or a definition has been surmised by the editor the number of the terrier is given in order that the reader can easily refer to it.

Afterlease: pasture after the first crop of hay.
Aftermath: the second crop or shear of grass.
Agistment (injoicement, silement): the pasturing of animals from another district within the parish which are liable to tithe for the duration of the stay.
Arable or pasture: land subject to convertible husbandry.
Aventure: see *Leat*
Backside: a farmyard.
Barge: a hog or 2 year lamb.
Barton (barken): a farmyard.
Bay: the division of a building by a low wall or beam; see also *Field*.
Bayting, baiting land: a place for tethering animals for feeding.
Bolting house: a building in which bran or course meal is separated by sifting.
Borde, board land: Demesne land rented out by the lord of the manor.
Blade: the leaf of a crop.
Breach: the removal of dead hedges after the corn or hay harvest opening the land up for livestock.
Browsing (brousting): Feeding on young shoots and leaves of trees and shrubs.
Bury: a farm or manor house often an element in a place name.
Butt: a small piece of land.
Chick: ? a cheek, a piece of land on the side of a field.
Chilver: a year-old ewe.
Chrisom: a white robe worn by a child at baptism. Its estimated value was given as an offering at the mother's purification unless the child had died, in which case it was used as a shroud.
Composition: a payment in lieu of tithe agreed between the tithe owner and the payer.

Coney: a rabbit.
Cow white: tithe on milk and other dairy produce.
Crate: a small enclosure, possibly a sheep fold.
Croft (croft): a close frequently attached to a house.
Cub: a penning or stall.
Curative: pertaining to a curacy.
Custom acre: land whose size is determined by local custom as opposed to a statute acre. See also *Lug acre.*
Cut, cut end(coot): a lean to, penthouse or skilling.
Cut and go: meadow to which a right of enjoying the first cut of grass and nothing else applied.
Dotterel: a tree that has lost its top branches through decay.
Dredge: a mixture of oats and barley grown together.
Drive: to carry forward a tithe payment to the next year; most commonly when the number of titheable young animals made for a complicated calculation.
Dry beast: a cow which has ceased to produce milk.
Dry grounds: land not liable to flood and thus not restricted in its use.
Eared: a yard.
Ell ridge: equivalent to ½ a. in **31**; see *Ridge.*
fattening cattle: grazing animals.
Fellow; one of a pair.
Field of building: as bay.
Fleate, flat: a variant of furlong. (**694**)
Folding, manuring land by sheep in folds.
Foreacre, forehalf: a headland acre or halfacre.
Foreshear, foreshare; the first cut of hay; the right to choose the cut first.
Frowse: to cover or strew with.
Garson (garston): a grass enclosure or paddock.
Goad: a land measurement of 9 or 15 ft.
Grip(e) furrow: a draining furrow.
Groat: a coin worth 4 old pence.
Guisse: a rafter.
Ham: to enclose with a hedge.
Hamlet: ? a small pasture or meadow field. (**337**)
Haulier (haulier): a draught animal.
Headen: ? a piece of land in a headland.
Headlease or Roughlease: see *Rough lease thing.*
Headland: a strip running across the ends of the furlongs in an open field, on which the plough turned. It was later ploughed.
Hilary money: Dues owed by the parish to the bishop around 1Jan.
Hitching land: part of a field ploughed and sown in the year when the rest lay fallow.
Hocktide: the second Monday and Tuesday after Easter.
Hood: possibly a piece of land lying across the top of an acre or strip. (**109**)
Hook: a spit of land in a river bend.
Hookland: land ploughed and sown each year.

*Impropriate rectory :*one in lay hands managed as an estate with a vicar or
curate appointed to carry out the religious duties.

Ingrounds: often the best land regularly manured and continuously under
cultivation, often near to the farmstead.

*Intercommoning, intercomminers:*sharing commons especially pasture and those
who share.

*Lammas land:*land thrown open to common pasture after haymaking on Lammas
day (1 Aug).

Lanchard see linchett.

Lawn: strips of grass land like selions in a common arable field.

Layne, laine: meadow or pasture regularly ploughed and converted to arable. See
also *Ley.*

Lease, leaze: a right to keep an animal on common land.

Leasowe (leazesowe); a piece of pasture or meadow.

Lea(e)t, running at: a method of selecting sheep which are let to run freely;
(**545–6, 806, 857–8**). *Aventure* in **857**.

Ley, lay: meadow ploughed occasionally to improve the sward. See also *Layne.*

*Linchet, linch (lanchard, lanchet, linchyardes, lincherd:*a grass partition in an
arable field.

Litton: a churchyard.

Lug: a quarter of an acre; see also *Rod.*

Lug acre; a customary acre based on the local measurement of a lug.

Meal: the amount of milk given by a cow at one milking.

*Malm, maame:*The chalky clay loam found throughout the chalk area ofWiltshire.
It was used as a dressing for the land.

Mere: a strip of grassland forming a boundary.

Mere stones; boundary stones.

Midsty: the area by the door in the middle of a barn where corn is threshed.

Misceline; a mixture of wheat and rye grown together. See also *Dredge.*

Mixton (mixen): a dung or manure heap. (**571**)

Modus: a fixed money payment in lieu of tithe.

Mortuary: a payment to the incumbent at death to cover unpaid tithes.

Mound; a boundary.

Mowth, math: a cut of grass; the amount of meadow which could be mowed by
one man in a day.

Neate, neat: a cow shed; also a bullock.

Neccessary: a toilet.

Ollett: fuel made from cow dung or straw.

Outland: temporarily cultivated land as opposed to Inland or Ingrounds on
which crops are continually grown.

Oxgang: a medieval measurement of land, c.18– 20a.

Quartene: a quarter of a *Yardland.* (**381**)

Padhay: ? a small enclosure. (**381**)

Pane: a panel often of bricks; like a pane of glass.

Pasture or arable; land subject to convertible husbandry.

Pigscit; pigs cot, a pen.

Pit ridge: meaning not clear. (**141**)

INTRODUCTION xxiii

Plat: plot.

Pleck: a small plot of ground.

Prebend: the portions of the revenue of a cathedral granted as a stipend to a canon or prebendary.

Procession week: as *Rogation week.*

Pulse (poulse): edible seeds of leguminous plants like peas and beans.

Quarterdays: The principal feast and rent days 25 Mar, 24 Jun, 29 Sep, 25 Dec.

Questman: a sidesman.

Rag, rage: an odd piece of land in an open field. **(573)**.

Ride, wride: a temporary enclosure kept in tillage.

Ridge, rudge: a strip in a common field. la. in **570**; 35p.x 3p. in **141**.

Rogation week: 5th. week after Easter; often a time when perambulations of parishes took place.

Rope; a linear measurement equivalent to 20ft.

Rother ,rudder beasts: oxen.

Row ground: ? land on which crops are planted in rows e.g. a vegetable plot. **(450)**

Rough lease things (ancient head holds): probably a corrupt form of roofless tenements i.e. the original tenements within a manor which had become run down or lacked a house but to which any ancient manorial customs were still attached.**(221)**

Roweless tenement: see *Rough lease things.*

Runner: a young best running with the cows.

Rydd: to take.

Scrall, scrall; poorly grown corn.

Several; land, generally enclosed, held by the owner in his own right and not in common with others.

Shard: a broken gap in a hedge.

Shooting: running in a particular direction.

Shear: a crop of grass.

Spear: couch grass.

Skilling (skeeling): see *Cut.*

Stavell, staddle: a stone placed under each corner of a granary barn to prevent vermin gettmg in.

Stean(e), steine meadow: possibly meadow permanently divided by stones and thus not able to be converted as Laine.

Stinted land: land on which the numbers of animals allowed by holders of common rights are controlled.

Stitch: as *Ridge.*

Swarth (swayth): a portion of meadow, originally the width of a sweep of a scythe.

Thorough: a coin worth 6s. 8d., the equivalent of a Noble.

Thorough milk (white) cow: a proven milker as opposed to a heifer or new milker.

Tilepite: a stone tile quarry. **(332)**

Tining: an enclosure.

Tithe: great or predial; a tenth of the crops harvested directly from the soil due to the rector; grain, hay and timber. Small or mixed; a tenth of the produce indirectly from cultivation due to the vicar; the young of livestock, wool, honey and wax, garden produce (generally commuted to a money payment).

Toll dish: a dish used to measure out the toll of grain.

Trencher patch: ? a plot in which vegetables were grown for the table (**464**).

Unprofitable cattle: cattle not good for milking or draught (pail or plough) and not titheable.

Wale, weal: a bank or ridge of earth or stone.

Warden: an old variety of pear.

Wether sheep: a castrated ram.

Yard (yarden): a quarter of an acre.

Yardland: an area of land generally c.30a. in Wiltshire but varying in the terriers between 18½a. and 31a.

Yate, (eate): a gate.

Yeomath: a variant of *Aftermath*. Yea mead in **633**.

CALENDAR

ALDBOURNE vicarage

1   1609 (D1/24/1/1)

A vicarage house with a little close adjoining and 24a. of arable in the common fields, pasture for 60 sheep and 6 horses and beasts in the commons, as the rest of the parishioners. Another house in which the vicar now dwells with an orchard, garden, backside, barn, stable, and other buildings; 1a. of arable belonging to it called Bullocks acre. Tithe wool and lamb, underwood, and all other petty tithes. Tithe corn and hay, wool and lamb, and all tithes from the glebe land of the parsonage. The parsonage is to pay to the vicarage 40s. p. a., i. e. 20s. at Ladyday [25 Mar] and Michaelmas [29 Sep]. All tithes of Pickewood Farm, i. e. of corn, hay, wool and lamb, wood, and all other tithes.

John Webb, vicar, Thomas Collence, George Addams, churchwardens, John Knight, Robert Pears.

2   11 Sep 1671 (D1/24/1/2)

Terrier presented at the bishop's visitation at Marlborough 15 Sep 1671. A dwelling house, barn,[1] with garden, orchard and barton of c. 1a. One cottage in High street with a plot of meadow or pasture, c. ½a., adjoining. 25a. 3yds. of arable land in the common fields: 12a. in N. field; 2a. in W. field; 1a. in Windmill field; 3½a. in S. field; 3a. in Denacres; 4a. 1yd. in E. field. Commons for 60 sheep, 6 cows or horses or other cattle in the fields and other commonable places in Aldborne.

Tithe in kind of wool, lambs, wood, fruit, pigs, gardens, eggs, honey and wax, hops, calves, geese, pigeons, turkeys, and all minute and small tithes. All oblations at Easter; 1d. for every 'milchecow'; 1d. for every agistment sheep that is taken in of strangers into the parish and fed there during the summertime only; 2d. for every whether sheep of the inhabitants or strangers that feed there for the whole year whereof the tithe of wool is not paid.

All great and small tithes arising from the glebe lands of the impropriate rectory of Aldborne held by Oliver Nicholas esq. and certain tenements or parcels of land belonging to the glebelands now held by Joseph Goddard gent, Henry Neale, Stephen Knackston, Robert Wiat, Ann Browne wid., Ann Bankes wid., and Ruth Hill wid.[2] An annual pension of 40s. paid by the dean and chapter of Winchester (impropriate rector of Aldborne) in equal parts at Ladyday [25 Mar] and Michaelmas [29 Sep]. All great and small tithes on a farm anciently called Pickwood farm: viz. Pickwood Laynes held by the earl of Pembroke or his tenant John Collins;[3] Broadclose, Newmead or Newclose and a composition of £4 p. a. to be paid on Quarterdays for the herbage or feeding of Stockclose, all held by Thomas Hawles esq. or his tenant George Perkins by lease of the earl of Pembroke[4] but of which parcels of land are one entire farm but are let separately. All great and small tithes due on 4 closes called Pierce his closes held by Elizabeth Scory widow. A composition[5] of £3

p. a. to be paid on Quarterdays for the tithe of conies belonging to the N. Walk of Aldbourne chase.[6]
John Norris, vicar, William Neale, Robert Peirce [X], churchwardens.

1. Stable and carthouse, added in **3**.
2. John Elderfield gent., Henry Neale, Edward Witts, Robert Wyat, Ann Browne widow, Ruth Hill widow, and Robert Chamberlin, in **3**.
3. A modus of £3 paid on St Thomas Day (21 Dec), in **3**.
4. John Perkins, tenant of the earl of Pembroke, in **3**.
5. This composition not mentioned in **3**.
6. A third part of tithes of corn, grain, hay or grass (besides the privy tithes) arising from a parcel of land called Sandridg alias Sanderwitch Heartshoote and an adjoining plot held by the earl of Pembroke and his tenant Robert Peirce, added in **3**.

3   15 Sep 1677 (D1/24/1/3)
As **2** *with amendments in footnotes.* John Norris, vicar, William King, Thomas Collins [X], churchwardens, Robert Peirce [X].

4   1705 (D1/24/1/4)
One vicarage house with little close adjoining and 23a. 3yds. of arable in the common fields. Pasture for 60 sheep and 6 horses or beasts. A house in which the vicar dwells with an orchard, garden, backside, barn, stable, and other buildings, and 1a. of arable called Bullocks acre. Tithe wool, lambs, underwood, and all petty tithes in Aldborne. Tithe corn, hay, lambs, and all other tithes due from the glebe of the parsonage of Aldborne.

The parsonage [*impropriate rector*] is to pay 40s. p. a. as **2**. Tithe corn, hay, wool, lamb, wood, and all other tithes due from Pikewood farm now divided into two farms called Stock Closes and Laynes. All the same tithes due from Peirces close. A third part of tithe corn and hay due from Sandridge which was allowed by the parsonage to Mr Norris, the present vicar's predecessor, to the vicarage in lieu of the loss which the vicar sustained by the inclosing of Sandridge, it being before part of the common.

William Jackson, vicar, Edward Francis, Richard Scory.

5   1783 (526/2)[1]
Ancient residence of the vicars. A ground in High Street whereon stood a tenement, let by the vicar to William Mudge, with a garden and a close, ½a.; which tenement was burned down in the fire in 1771 and has not been rebuilt. The premises are bounded by John Bunce's house N., Mrs. Pizzie's S., Mr. Smith's premises E., the Street W.

The glebe 24 a.: 12a. in N. field, 2a. in W. field, 1a. in Windmill field, 3a. in S. field, 2a. in Demacres field, ?4a. 1yd. in E. field. 60 sheep and 6 beast commons.

The present residence of the house: There is an ancient house said to be formerly a religious house and given by the owners to the vicars. It is built of large timber covered with tile and the sides rough cast. The ground floor consists of a brewhouse and kitchen, a hall, a parlour, a pantry and a cellar: on the first floor, 5 chambers and 3 closets; above are garrets. None of the rooms are wainscotted. They are all plastered except the room over the kitchen which is hung with paper. The parlour and hall are c. 15ft. square and 8ft. high, the kitchen 12ft. square, the chambers over them are of the same dimensions. There is a kitchen garden, a barton, a barn c. 50ft. long and a stable for 5 horses. The whole premises are c. 1a. The N. and part of the E. fence is John Shepherd's, part of the E. fence to John Willis, the S. fence to Susan Packer, the W. fence to the vicar, the E. fence of the barton to Susan Packer.

Vicarial tithes: Tithe lamb, wool and all underwood; offerings at Easter 4d. from each house. Petty tithes or fruits of pigs, gardens, honey, wax, hops, calves, geese, pigeons and turkeys. For every milch cow 1d. For agistment sheep, that is sheep of other parishes, for the summer feed 1d. For every sheep feeding the whole year 2d.

Parsonage tithes: The parsonage held by William Shepherd on lease from the Dean and Chapter of Winchester gives to the vicar all the tithes of the [parsonage] glebe, as corn, hay, wool, lamb, etc. The Parsonage pays the vicar 40s. p. a. in equal payments at Ladyday [25 Mar] and Michaelmas [29 Sep].

All the tithes of Stock Close farm and Lane's farm occupied by Sir William Jones and William Read as of corn, woods, hay, wool and lambs belong to the vicar.

The Warren rented by Thomas Bunce pays tithes by composition but a modus is asserted by the tenant. All the tithes of Pierce's close as corn, hay, wool and lambs.

A third part of the tithe corn and hay upon a ground called Sandridge, allowed by the parsonage to Mr. Norris and to the vicars for ever, in lieu of the loss the vicar sustained by enclosing this ground, before common.

The church consists of a strong square gothic tower, a body in the shape of a cross, a chancel, walls stone, roof leaded. In the tower a peal of 6 bells, a town clock and a set of chimes. In the chancel: a communion oak table, a parish chest with 3 locks, and one with a single lock, an oak box and in it an extract of Goddard's will,[2] a poor box. Communion plate: a large silver flagon that contains above a gallon, a large silver chalice, a smaller silver chalice, gilt, a silver patten gilt, all given by Oliver Nicholas whose arms are engraved on the vessels, the cup [with] an inscription on the foot, weight not specified. Vestry: Pay table and forms, 5 forms, 2 surplices, communion cloth and napkin, a large bible imperfect, 2 folio prayer books, pulpit cushion red velvet laced, Fox's Martyrology and Jewel's Apology; torn, an old pall black cloth.

Church: A large fire engine[3] and pipes, a smaller one, 2 fire hooks, a ladder, 2 forms, grave boards, 12 old buckets in room over the porch.

No trees in the churchyard, the chancel is repaired by the lay impropriator, the church by the parish. No timber on the glebe. The churchyard fence is repaired by the parish except N. and W. sides. Churchways kept by the parish. The parish clerk: The salary used to be £3. Appointed by the vicar he has so much annually from every house, i. e. 4d. and dues from weddings and 30s. for minding the church clock. The sexton chosen by the parish; he has 1d. from every house and 2s. 6d. for burial.

This terrier was made from former terriers sent from the registry at Salisbury and from the information of the parishioners and was read in the vestry publicly

and consented to in 1783, being the primary visitation of the bishop.
James Neale, M.A., curate.
A copy of this terrier was sent to the registry [at Salisbury] by J. Neale.[4]

1. Copy in the parish register.
2. Thomas Goddard of Upham by his will of 1597 left money for the benefit of the poor of Aldbourne.
3. Aldbourne suffered from two serious fires in 1760 and 1771 and these arrangements although by no means unique were clearly believed to be of particular importance.
4. This copy has not survived.

ALDERTON rectory

6   14 Oct 1608 (D1/4/2/1)
A parsonage house for the residence of the curate, with a barn, little garden, and close adjoining, c. ½a., bounded E., W., and S. with the grounds of Mrs Wroughton and the churchyard, N. with the highway from Alderton to Sherston and other places. An enclosed pasture S. of Alderton called Old leaze, c. 12a., bounded N. with the common field, S. a ground called Cranhill, E. ground of Ralph Coxe and W. ground of Arthur Terrill of Alderton. Another enclosed pasture E. of Alderton called Arly, c. 12a., bounded E. and N. with the highway turning from the Fosse Way to Tetbury (Tedbury), W. with a ground of Mrs Wroughton and a common meadow called Broad mead belonging to the parishioners, S. with the leazes of George Emley and Arthur Terrill of Alderton. In Broad mead E. of Alderton certain portions of meadow ground in several parcels not enclosed, c. 4a. All the rest of the glebe is arable in the W. field scattered here and there, c. 18a.
    Samuel Dowlinge, clerk, Ralph Coxe, George Bullock, churchwardens, Thomas Bishopp, Arthur Terrill, John Watts [X], Richard Marshe.

7   23 Dec 1704 (D1/4/2/2)
Terrier consists solely of a note of the annual payment of £30 to the minister by the treasurer of the dean and chapter of Gloucester Cathedral [rector] out of the profits of the impropriate rectories of Sherston and Alderton.
    Richard Weeksy, minister, Daniel Holborrow, Samuel Latham, churchwardens.

ALLINGTON rectory

8   25 Sep [. . .] early 17th cent.[1] (D1/24/3/1)
Arable land in the W. side of the parish: 3a. in Sower land bottom abutting N. on the farm lands, and S. land of Henry Weeks;[2] 2a. adjoining on the W. with a lay bank between; 1a. by the stony linch abutting E. land of Richard Peryn[3] and W. land of Gwilbert Gwyne;[4] 3a. in the middle of the field abutting N. land of John Hatcheman,[5] S. of Stephen Rutt;[6] 1a. in Long Crookeborowe[7] abutting E. the farm lands and W. 2a. of the parsonage land; the said 2a. abutting N. land of

Richard Peryn[3] and S. the farm land; 1a. more in Long Crookeborowe above Gollinche abutting E. land of Henry Weeks[2] and W. the farm lands; 3 x ½a. in Short Crookeborowc above Gollinche abutting E. Newton field[8] and W. land of William Knappe;[9] 1a. in the same furlong next to Gollinche abutting E. Newton field[8] and W. land of William Knappe;[9] 2a. in Crosse Land abutting E. Newton field,[8] W. the parsonage land; 1a. in Gollinche furlong abutting E. the last 2a., W. the farm land; ½a. by Newton side abutting N. the land of John Hearne,[10] S. of Robert Knappe;[11] 3 x ½a. abutting N. the Down side, S. land of Stephen Rutt;[6] 3a. abutting N. land of Gwylbert Gwyne,[2] S. of John Hearne;[10] 5a. in Dytchland furlong abutting N. land of Gwylbert Gwyne,[2] S. of Henry Weeks;[2] 2a. in Small Path furlong abutting E. land of William Knappe,[9] W. the farm land; 1a. in Knoll Land furlong abutting E. the farm land, W. land of Gwylbert Gwyne;[2] 2a. in the same furlong abutting as the last; 3a. in Sheep Land furlong abutting E. land of Richard Peryn,[3] W. the farm land.

Arable land on the E. side: ½a. shooting on Andover way abutting E. Andover way, W. land of John Donnell;[12] ½a. abutting E. Andover way, W. land of John Goodale; 1a. in Leowe furlong abutting E. land of Henry Weeks,[2] W. of John Goodale;[2] ½a. in Lampitts abutting N. and S. land of Henry Weeks;[2] ½a. more in Shells furlong abutting E. land of John Donnell,[12] W. of John Hatcheman;[5] 3 x ½a. in Twenty acres furlong abutting N. land of John Dawe,[13] S. the Woodway; 1a. in Banners land abutting N. land of John Goodale and S. the Woodway; ½a. abutting E. land of Mrs Clifford[14] and W. of John Goodale; ½a. more under the linch abutting N. land of John Goodale, S. of Mrs Clifford;[14] 1a. above Cleve linch abutting N. land of John Goodale, S. of Mrs Clifford[15] being Boscombe woodway.

1a. common meadow abutting N. the portion of Henry Weeks[2] and John Goodale, S. of William Knap,[9] E. and W. bounded with quickset. A close at the N. end of the parish of 1a. Another close adjoining the parsonage house of 1a. 60 sheep leaze on the W. side, on the E. side 18 and a ram; on the W. side 2 horse and 2 cow leaze, on the E. 1 horse and 1 cow leaze; on the W. side 8 hogs to go in the stubble, 4 on the E.; a bull and a boar on the common of both sides. The dwelling house standing at the S. end of the parish consists of a quadrangle of which 3 sides are housing, the 4th is a fair new wall[16] to the W. N. of the house lies the garden streetward, W. the barn and next the fodder house, stable and cow house all in one. The whole tithe of 21½ yardlands being all the ground of the parish.

Nicholas Fuller MA, rector,[1] Nicholas Miller, farmer, William Knapp, Henry Weeks [X], William Jones [X], John Hearne [X], John Goodale [X].

1. Nicholas fuller signed the bishop's transcript for 1608 and was rector up to 1623.
2. Mr Samuel Heskins, rector of Cholderton in **9**; spelled Hiskins in **10**.
3. John Miller in **9**; John Puckredg in **10**.
4. John Gwynne in **9**; Samuel Hiskins in **10**.
5. Mr Punchardon Roberts in **9**; William Hearth/ Hearst in **10**
6. George Rutt in **9**; Stephen Brownjohn in **10**.
7. 'above Gollynch' added in **9**.
8. Newton Tony field in **9** and **10**.

9. Wid. Knapp in **9**; John Knapp in **10**.
10. William Childe senior in **9**; William Childe in **10**.
11. John Walker in **9**; Thomas Walker in **10**.
12. Christopher Gale in **9**; Richard Marsh in **10**.
13. Stephen Rut in **9**; William Dudds in **10**.
14. John Kent of Boscombe, esq. in **9** and **10**.
15. No owner mentioned in **9** and **10**.
16. Flint wall in **9** and **10**.

9   15 Oct 1677 (D1/24/3/2)
As 8 with amendments in footnotes. Nathanial Forster, rector, John Miller, farmer, William Childe senior, John Walker [X], Christopher Gale, Mary Knap wid. [X], John Goodall.

10   9 Jan 1705 (D1/24/3/3)
As 8 with amendments in footnotes. Thomas Cox, rector, John Knapp [X], Stephen Brownjohn, churchwardens, Edward Millar, Nicholas Miller.

ALTON BARNES rectory

11   n. d. late 16th cent. (D1/24/4/1)
7a. in one place W. of the parsonage, land of John Benger on one side, Henry Brown on the other; 3a. more adjoining the highway, 2a. of Henry Brown on the other side; 1a. at the end of the same furlong by the highway 1a. more, land of Henry Brown on the other side; 1a. more adjoining the lordship of Woodborough, land of William Benger on the other side; a several close N. of his house [*i. e. the rector's*] and next to a close of John Stone; 1a. to cut and go in the farmer's mead; a little paddock at Shaw between the farmer and John Benger; 1 church hay there; 1a. more in Shaw field, land of Mr Goddard on one side, Henry Brown the other. John Benger, Henry Brown, churchmen. *Names in the same hand*

12   n. d. early 17th cent.[1] (D1/24/4/2)
Parsonage house and other buildings;[2] a close, an orchard and a barton of 2a. 1a. bounded by meres or marks at the N. and S. ends of Long meadow.[3] A close of ½a.[4] adjoining on S. William Stone's severall, on N. the common field. A churchyard at Alton and another at Shaw lying in the farmers' severall at Shaw. A little parrock of 6 lugs at Shaw abutting E. Farmer Verne's close, W. John Bengar's close. 100 sheep leaze at Shaw. 7a. of glebe 'overgaynst' the Parson's field gate abutting John Benger's land N., Richard Hall's land S., 2 green meeres W. 1a. by Woodborough hedge abutting William Bengar's land S., shooting down upon Splot N.[5] 4a. towards the hill abutting Marlborough way W., Richard Hall's land E., and the little green mere dividing one from the other. 1a. above the said 4a. with the same bounds. 1a. of glebe in Shaw abutting Richard Hal's land W. and Sir William Button's land E., from which it is divided by a mere of green 'tincher'. Richard Hall, Edward Bengar, William Stone.

'This terryer is unperfect as shalbe proved by very honest and suffitient witnesses. There is no mention made in yt of the halfe that was taken out of the south syde and uppon the common felde on the north syde. This halfe is layde unto John Bengars barton. Lykewise there is no mention made of the hedlande that was taken from those 7 acres of glebe overagainst the field gate of the parson's home close. Lastly yt is doubted whether that parcell of glebe which lies over against the said field gate be 8 acres or not as the tenants say that is but 7 acres so they that have lived in Alton heretofore say that yt is 8.'

1. The postscript is in the same hand as the bishop's transcript for 1609 which was written by Robert Boxold, rector, who served between 1592 - 1614.
2. In a terrier 28 Oct. 1661, the parsonage, a kitchen and 2 barns are mentioned. *Progress notes of Warden Woodward...* (WRS vol. 13), pp. 87-8.
3. Described as a cut and go meadow in 1661 terrier see footnote 2
4. 1a. in 1661 terrier see footnote 2
5. 1a. by Woodborough sands shooting down upon Stantonmere called Splot in 1661 terrier see footnote 2.

AMESBURY donative curacy

13   25 Mar 1678 (D1/24/5/1)
Terrier ordered by bishop Seth Ward at his last visitation. £10 a quarter paid out of the parsonage by special order of the dean and canons of Windsor; also the profits from the churchyard herbage. The house[1] there to be kept in repair by the owner of the parsonage for the curate to dwell in. The Easter book and all offerings Tithes[2] of calves, cow white, gardens and eggs, with all accustomed dues for christenings, marriages, burials, and churching of women.
     Thomas Holland, curate.

1. Described as at the N. E. corner of the chancell 18yd. long 8yd. broad, in **14**.
2. Valued at £3 p. a. in **14**.

14   16 May 1705. (D1/4/5/2)
As **13** with amendments in footnotes. Thomas Holland, curate, William Reeves, John Jons.

ASHLEY rectory

15   1671 (D1/24/6/1)
The messuage[1] with outhouses, barns, stables and gardens; a little parcel of pasture[2] adjoining of c. 2a.;[3] a parcel of meadow called Splackett mead[4] between 2 meads of John Wake, of c. ¼a.; a piece of lot meadow in Crudd mead in the parish of Crudwell.
     15a. arable[5] in W. field: 1a. in Wayneshard furlong; 4a. in Woodcocks furlong; 6¼a. in the same furlong called Woodcocks piece; 1a. in the same furlong called

Clay acre; 1¾a. in the same furlong between the land of John Wake and John Sherborne; 2a. shooting on Rivye hedge, land of William Morse on one side and John Wake on the other. In E. field: [5] 1a. at Risden shard; 1a. shooting on Splacketts mead, land of Timothy Morse on both sides; 1a. shooting on the same meadow, land of John Sherborne on one side, Timothy Morse on the other. 6a. in Rowdowne piece: 2 head acres shooting on Hargroves; 2a. in Lynch furlong, land of John Wake on one side, John Sherborne the other; 2a. shooting on Hargroves, land of John Wake on one side and Timothy Morse the other.[6]

William Morse, churchwarden.

1. Called the parsonage house with a barn of 3 bays, an oxhouse and stable in **16**.
2. On E. side of the parsonage house in **17**.
3. A paddock called Bean Plot included in **16**.
4. Called Splackett Meadow Rowe in **16**, and Placket in **17**.
5. In N. and S. fields in **17**.
6. 3 beast leazes in the common called Town leaze in **16** and **17**, from 25 Mar to 1 Nov in **16**, from 3 May to 1 Nov in **17**. Described as formerly only for cows, oxen or young beasts in **16**.

16   1678 (D1/24/6/2)
*As **15** with amendments in footnotes. Bounds of lands in common fields not given.* All tithes and Easter offerings enjoyed by the rector. John Scawen, rector; John Wake, churchwarden. Note refers to a terrier of 1616 in which reference is made to mortuaries and a query to check the old register.

17   1704 (D1/24/6/3)
*As **15** with amendments in footnotes.* Tithes and Easter offerings enjoyed by the rector.

John Giles, rector, John Wake, churchwarden, Thomas Mosse.

ASHTON KEYNES vicarage

18   25 Mar 1611 (D1/24/7/1)
Terrier taken by Mr Anthony Ferris, yeo.; John Cove, yeo.; Maurice Chapperlayne, George Andros, and John Harding, husbandmen. Thomas Aubrey, doctor and professor in divinity, the vicar was himself present at the taking of the view.

Arable lands lying here and there dispersed in the W. field: 1 picked a. bounded Green way, N., Humphrey Kibble freeholder's land, S., Richard Bennett's headland, E., headland of Thomas Bastons *alias* Randall's freehold land, W.; 2a. bounded Vicar's Peele, E., 1a. of Mr Anthony Ferris and 1a. of Thomas Rowley, W., ½a. of Mr Anthony Ferris, S., 3 farndells of Thomas Haukins belonging to King's copyhold, N. In the furlong shooting upon the forenamed 2a. 1 farndell bounded ½a. of Francis Archard, S., 1a. of Thomas Rowlye, N.

In the furlong by the Vicar's Peele ½a. bounded 1a. of Giles Dryver, S., 1a. of William Jefferyes' wife, N.; ½a. shooting upon Mr Thomas Haukins' hedge on E., bounded 1a. of Humphrey Kebble's freehold, S., ½a. of Mr George Ferris,

N.; 1 farndell bounded 1 farndell of Thomas Packer's freehold, S., ½a. of Mr
George Ferris, N.A broad headland a. bounded Sheasie furlong, N., 1a. of Nicholas
Mackeley, S. In Sheasie furlong ½a. bounded ½a. of William Cox the farmer, E.,
½a. of John Cove, W. 2 x ½a., one coming cross the other, whereof one does
head Mr Thomas Haukins' short butts by the green way, the other bounded
with the butts of Thomas Randall and William Clifford, S., ½a. of Thomas Randle's
copyhold, N. 1 headland a. which heads Grassy furlong on N.; ½a. adjoining it,
bounded the forename headland, N., ½a. Mr George Ferris, S. In Gracy furlong
1a. bounded ½a. of William Clifford, E., 1 farndell of Raymond Telling, W.; 1½a.
together bounded 1 farndell of Raymond Telling, E., ½a. of William Clifford,
W.; ½a. bounded ½a. of Maurice Chapperlayne E., ½a. of John Harding, W. In
the furlong shooting upon Somerford hedge 2 broad butts together accompted
as 1a., bounded 1 farndell of Mr Anthony Ferris, S., 1a. of Thomas Packer, N.;
1a. bounded 1a. of Mr Barnard of Shorncott, S., ½a. of William Jefferies' wife, N.
In the furlong shooting upon Larte furlong on the home side 1a. bounded 1a. of
William Jefferyes' wife, W., 1a. of Francis Archard, E.; 1½a lying together bounded
½a. of Mr Thomas Haukins, E., 1a. of Giles Dryver, W. In the Linck furlong, 1
farndell bounded 3 farndells of Thomas Packer's freehold, S., 1 farndell of Walter
Wooley, N. In the furlong called the Long Lands 1½ headland a. bounded Mr
Thomas Haukins' Shornecott lands, W., land of William Cox, the farmer, E.; ½a.
bounded 1a. of Mr George Ferris, W., 1½a. of Mr Thomas Haukins, E. In Huckell
Staple ½a. bounded ½a. of wid. Ferris, N., (?½a.) of Giles Dryver, S.; 1a. [. . .]
bounded with ½a. of Giles Dryver [. . .] a piece of Mr Thomas Haukins' lands [.
. .]; in the same furlong 4 x ½a. [. . .] bounded 1a. of William Cox, N., ½a. of
Maurice Chapperlayne, S. On W. side of the Down, ½ headland a and ½a.
adjoining ½a. of Maurice Chapperlayne, W. In the furlong which the forenamed
½ headland a. heads ½a. bounded Mr Christopher Hynton, N., ½a. of Maurice
Chapperlayne, S.; 2 x ½a. together bounded ½a. of Maurice Chapperlayne, N.
½a. of Giles Dryver, S. Upon the top of the Down in Rye furlong, 1a. bounded
½a. of Giles Dryver, N. 1a. of William Carver al. Tayler, S. In Rye furlong 1a.
bounded 1a. of Christopher Hynton, N., ½a. Mr Anthony Ferris, S.; 1a. bounded
½a. Mr Anthony Ferris, N., ½a. of wid. Ferris, N. In the furlong shooting upon
S. side of the Down, 3 farndells bounded 1 farndell of Mr Anthony Ferris, W.,
½a. of William Clifford, E. At the upper end on E. side of the forenamed 3
farndells, 2 butts, in measure about 1 farndell, bounded 1 butt of John Harding,
E., 1 butt of wid. Ferris, W. In the furlong called Beetillgoe, ½a. bounded ½a. of
John Harding, E., 1a. of John Smith, W.; ½a. bounded ½a. of Humphrey Kybble's
freehold, E., ½a. Mr George Ferris, W.; ½a. bounded ½a. of Humphrey Kibble's
freehold, E., ½a. of Giles Dryver, W. In Odall furlong shooting upon Mr Thomas
Haukins' Down mead hedge ½a. bounded ½a. John Cove, N., ½a. Christopher
Hynton, S.; 1 farnedell bounded ½a. of Mr Anthony Ferris, N., 1 farnedell of John
Harding, S. In Odall by Bryarbush 1 gore bounded ½a. of Mr Anthony Ferris, E.,
1a. William Clifford, W.; ½a. bounded 1 farnedell of wid. George, W., ½a. of wid.
George, occupied by Thomas Carter her son-in-law, E. 1 headland farndell on E.
side of the Down, bounded ½a. W. Carter's widow, S. Total 31a. 3 farndells.

Arable land lying here and there dispersed in the N. field: In Odall furlong
shooting upon the Rixen ½a. bounded ½a. of John Cove, W., 1a. of Giles Dryver,

E.; 1 headland ½a. bounded ½a. of William Clifford, W., the whole furlong which belongeth to divers men, E. In the furlong shooting upon the left hand of Portway 1a. bounded ½a. of John Cove, N., 1a. of George Andros, S. In the furlong upon the right hand of Portway towards Cerney (*Sarney*) ½a. bounded green highway, S., ½a. of John Harding, N.; ½a. bounded 1a. of Mr Anthony Ferris, S., 1a. of Mr Thomas Haukins, N.; ½a. bounded ½a. of Mr Anthony Ferris, S., ½a. of Mr George Ferris, N.; ½a. bounded ½a. of John Harding, S., 1a. of John Cove, N. In ?King furlong ½a. in a little piece of lay ground upon the other side of Portway, bounded ½a. of Mr Edward Ferris, S., ½a. of Mr Anthony Ferris, N. In the furlong on the E. side of the Down, a farndell bounded a green ridge of Mr Anthony Ferris, S., ½a. of William Clifford, N.; a picked farndell bounded a farndell of Humphrey Kebble, S., ½a. of William Clifford, N.; 2 x ½a. together bounded ½a. of wid. Ferris, S., ½a. of John Cove, N.; ½a. bounded ½a. of William Bennett, S., ½a. of Maurice Chapperlayne, N. A headland farndell of lay ground beginning at John Woodward's ½a. and ending at 'myne owne' 2 x ½a. of furze; 2 x ½a. together whereupon furze grows, bounded ½a. of Mr Thomas Haukins, S., ½a. of Mr Anthony Ferris, N.; ½a. bounded ½a. Edmund Hall, S., ½a. of wid. Millard, N. In the furlong shooting down upon Tidmores ditch by the vicar's bridge 5 x ½a. together, bounded Nicholas Mackleye's ground, W., the highway to Cirencester [Cicester], E.; ½a. at the end [*?of these*] shooting along by the sand pits hard by the highway. In the furlong shooting upon Cerney ditch, 1a. bounded ½a. of Mr Thomas Haukins, N., ½a. of Francis Archard, S.; ½a. bounded ½a. of William Clifford, N., ½a. Thomas Packer's freehold which wid. Hushe has to her house, S.; 2 x ½a. together bounded 1a. of John Cove, N., ½a. of Richard Selbye, S.; ½a. bounded ½a. of Richard Selbye, N., ½a. of Mr George Ferris, S. A picked butt of 1 farndell of ground by Portway side, bounded 1 farndell of Mr George Ferris, W., ½a. of Mr Thomas Haukins, E. In Tetbury furlong 1a. bounded 1a. of Thomas Younge, N., ½a. of wid. George now in the tenure of Thomas Carter, S.; ½a. bounded ½a. of wid. George, N., 1a. of Mr Thomas Haukins lying unto King's copyhold, S.; 1a. bounded 1a. of wid. Ferris, N., ½a. of William Clifford, S. A picked ½a. by Portway side, bounded ½a. of young Henry Carter, W.; ½a. of John Harding, E. In the furlong without a name (nullius nominis) 1a. called the Squyer acre, bounded 1a. of Mr Thomas Haukins, N., 1a. of John Cove, S. In the furlong called the Blacklands, ½a. bounded ½a. of Mr Anthony Ferris, N., 1a. of Thomas Maslin's freehold, S. In the furlong called Broadway ½a. bounded a 3 farndells of wid. Ferris, N., ½a. of Mr Anthony Ferris, S. In the furlong by Broadway a 3 farndells headland, bounded 1a. of Mr Edward Ferris, E., John Cove's butts, W. In the Lyde [*furlong*] a farndell bounded ½a. of Mr Anthony Ferris, E., 3 farndells of Thomas Randoll alias Baston's copyhold land, W.; 1 farndell bounded 1 farndell of John Harding, E., a 3 farndells of Richard Wake's widow, W.; 3 farndells and 1 farndell adjoining, in all 1a. of ground bounded a 3 farndells of Mr Thomas Haukins, E., 1 farndell of Mr Anthony Ferris, W. Total of acres in the N. field, 21a. and 3 farndells.

Arable lands lying here and there dispersed in the E. field: 3a. together butting upon Mr Anthony Ferris' ham, bounded ½a. of John Smyth W.; 3 farndells of Richard Wakes' widow, E. A 3 farndells butting upon the foresaid ham, bounded a 3 farndells of Richard Wakes' widow, W., a 3 farndells of Mr Anthony Ferris, E.

In the furlong called Hallash ½a. bounded ½a. of John Harding, W., ½a. Humphrey Kibble's freehold, E.; a 3 farndells bounded ½a. of Humphrey Kibble's freehold, W., a 3 farndells of Mr Anthony Ferris, E.; a 3 farndells and 2 x ½a. adjoining together, bounded a 3 farndells of Mr Anthony Ferris, W. ½a. of John Giles, E.; ½a. bounded W. and E. with 2 farndells of Thomas Dorrell. In the furlong shooting down upon Water furlong, a 3 farndells bounded by a 3 farndells of wid. Jacson, S., a 3 farndells of Christopher Hynton, N.; ½a. bounded a 3 farndells of Mr Thomas Haukins, S., ½a. of John Harding, N. In the furlong called Northill, ½a. bounded ½a. of Humphrey Kibble's freehold, W., 3 sundry ½a. of John Cove, E.; 2a. together bounded ½a. of John Burges' freehold, W., ½a. of Christopher Hynton, E. In Water furlong, ½a. bounded by the green pack way by Hignells hedge, N., ½a. of William Clifford, S.; ½a. bounded ½a. of William Clifford, N., ½a. of wid. George, in the tenure of Thomas Carter her son-in-law, S.; 1a. bounded by ½a. of Humphrey Kibble's freehold, N. ½a. of Mr George Ferris, S. In Short Beare furlong, ½a. bounded by ½a. of Mr George Ferris, W., ½a. of John Edmund, E.; ½a. bounded ½a. of John Edmund, W., ½a. of Mr Anthony Ferris, E.; ½a. bounded by a 3 farndells of John Woodward, W., 3 farndells of John Harding, E.; ½a. bounded by a 3 farndells of John Harding, W., 1a. of wid. George in the tenure of Thomas Carter, E. In Lower Beare furlong, a headland a. lying along by William Clifford's meadow leaze. 1 farndell bounded by 1 farndell of Mr Anthony Ferris, W., 3 farndells of Maurice Chapperlayne, E.; ½a. bounded a 3 farndells of Maurice Chapperlayne, W., a 3 farndells of young Henry Carter, E.; a 3 farndells bounded a 3 farndells of John Cove, W., a farndell of Mr Edward Ferris, E.; ½a. bounded by a farndell of Mr Edward Ferris, W., a 3 farndells of young Henry Carter, E. In Winchcombe furlong, 2 x ½a. together, bounded a 3 farnedells of John Cove, N., 3 farnedells of Christopher Hynton, S.; a farndell bounded a 3 farndells of Christopher Hynton, N., ½a. of young Henry Carter, S.

In More furlong ½a. bounded ½a. of William Jeferye's widow, W., 1a. of George Andros, E.; ½a. bounded ½a. of wid. Ferris, W.; ½a. of Mr George Ferris, E. ½a. bounded 1a. of Mr Thomas Hawkins, W.; ½a. of Humphrey Kibble's freehold, E. 1a. bounded wid. Jacson's piece, W.; ½a. of Mr Anthony Ferris, E. 1 headland a. which heads Bleatch- mans furlong, bounded ½a. of Maurice Chapperlayne, E. Total 22a. 3 farndells.

The meadow grounds which are in several belonging unto the vicarage: In Fryday Yates lease, 5a. a farndell of lug measure or thereabouts. In a lease called the Oxham 5a. and ½ lug measure or thereabouts. In a lease called the Rixen ground, 6a. of lug measure, or better [?].

In a lease 2a. adjoining the Farmers Odd Croft on W. side and the Fosse [Forse] way towards Cirencester on E. side. In his [the vicar's] home lease called the Pigeon house leaze with garden, orchard, and other backsides, 3a.

The churchyard of Ashton Keynes, ½a. The church hey at Leigh chapel belonging to the vicar is accompted at ½a. Sum total of all these several acres are in the whole number 23a. and a farndell.

The meadow ground lying here and there dispersed in the great mead. 1 whole a. in the Brook mead shooting upon the river Thames, bounded on the lower side with one of the 3 doles belonging to the lord and tenants, and upon the further side with the farmer's Stonam acres.

In the said Brook mead 1 whole a. shooting upon the river Thames, bounded on lower side with the farmer's forenamed Stonam acres, on the further side with 1a. between Mr Edward Ferris and Maurice Chapperlyn. In Ditch Dole 1a. bounded ½a. of Christopher Hynton, N.; ½a. of Humphrey Kibble or Thomas Carter, S. In Ditch Dole ½a. bounded ½a. of John Cove, N.; ½a. of Mr Anthony Ferris, S.

Of the tenantry doles which lie there: In Eastlong Dole, 1 whole a., [*?bounded*] home side with 2 or 3 swathes of Nicholas Mackley; on the other side next towards and downwards a ham of William Clifford, which ham is tithe free and occupied by [. . .] Hubert. In Northlonge Dole 1a., [*?bounded*] lower side ½a. of Christopher Hynton, and on the further side with 3 farndells of George Andros. In the Swaths 6 swathes accompted at 1 farndell, [*?bounded*] lower side by a little ham which every second year is parted between Mr Edward Ferris and Leonard Telling's kinsmen and on the further side a patch of ground belonging to Mr Edward Ferris. The whole number of acres belonging unto the vicarage which lie in common in the great mead are 5a. 3 farndells.

The vicar has 3 kine and 1 bull which may be fed with the farmer's kine in the Rixen upon the N. part of the town. The farmer is to find a herdsman at his own cost and charge, to attend to the foresaid 3 kine and 1 bull, which are there to depasture for 11 weeks before Lammas [1 Aug] with the farmer's own kine, and to fair as they do.

The vicar has 8 kine and 1 bull to go and be fed with the farmer's kine in the Lammas ground towards Packer's bridge, from Lammas day unto the breach of the mead, which is upon Ladyday [25 Mar],[1] about 5 weeks together. The farmer is to find a herdsman at his own cost and charge, to attend and to look unto the foresaid 8 kine and 1 bull of the vicar's, which are there to depasture the whole forenamed time with the farmer's own kine and to faire as they do.

The vicar has 7 tenements belonging unto the vicarage, all of which are tenants at will. One of them, called Leonard Woodman, has beside his dwelling house his garden ground and orchard, 3a. of arable ground lying at the end of his house, bounded by a close of Giles Dryver, W., the horseway that goes to Cirencester E. The other 6 tenants besides their dwelling houses have each of them an orchard or garden or both.

The vicar has a barn of roughstone slated upon the top, being of 5 space beside the porch, every space being 10 feet in length. He has a stable and ox house of 10 spaces more or thereabouts being covered in thatch. He has a new mansion house which Dr Aubrey[2] built himself from the ground, of rough and free stone, and covered in slate, being 50ft. in length and 22ft. in height at the gable end. In the mansion house there is a hall, a parlour, a kitchen, a buttery, another little room. Over the hall and kitchen there are 2 fair chambers, a study between both, and over these 2 fair chambers and study there are 2 fair chambers more. At the end of the new building there are 3 upper and under rooms. There are 4 chimneys in the mansion house and 12 windows glazed with 5, 4, or 3 lights apiece.

1. This must be a mistake for Michaelmas [29 Sep] which although about 8 weeks after Lammas must represent the period described.
2. The house stands today and has a date stone Thomas Aubrey 1584: Wiltshire Buildings Record report B2337

19   16 Nov 1671 (D1/24/7/2)

As *21* apart from the tenants and rents: Thomas Weston, £1 2s.; John Slade, 8s.; John Darby, 8s.; Giles Chapperlin, 16s.; William Taylor alias Carver, 6s. 8d.; Francis Coulston, 10s.; George Blackford, 4s.; Humphrey Strange, 8s.

Maurice Chapperlyne, Thomas Carter, churchwardens, John Ferrers, Maurice Embry, sidesmen.

20   15 Dec 1677 (D1/24/7/3)

As *19*. Isaac Gwinnett, vicar Edward Hinton, Giles Cox, churchwardens, John Say, William Davis, sidesmen.

21   14 Dec 1683 (D1/24/7/4)

The meadow and pasture, 30a., divided and lying in Ashton Keynes common meadow, 5¾a.; one inclosed ground called Fridays ham, 6¼a.; one inclosed ground called Oxham, 6a.; one ground called Rixon close, 6a.; one little ground lying before the vicarage house, 2a.; one little close adjoining the backside to the house, 2a. The vicar has pasture for 3 kine and a bull in the farmer's Rixon, adjoining N. and W. fields, to be pastured and kept by the farmer's herdsman from the breach of the said Rixon until Lammas [1 Aug]. The vicar also has pasture for 8 kine and a bull in the farmer's Lammas meadow, to be kept by the farmer's herdsman, from the breach of the said meadow until the breach of the common meadow. An inclosed ground of 2a. in the possession of Maurice Chapperlin,[1] on the side of the down next the highway.

Arable land as it lies in every furlong in each field, 72¼a:

In E. field, in Hall Ash furlong, 3½a.; in the furlong right upon Water furlong, 1¼a.; in the furlong shooting on Burts ham, 3¼a.; upon North Hill, 2½a.; in Water furlong, 2a.; in Long Bear furlong, 1¼a.; in Short Bear furlong, 3½a.

In N. field, in Broadway Corner and the furlong by it, 1¼a.; in the Lyde, 1½a.; upon Portway and in Oadell, 4a.; in Blacklands 1½a.; in Herring furlong, ½a.; in Tedbury furlong, 3a.; in the furlong shooting on Cerny ditch, 3a.; on the down and the side, 4¼a.

In W. field, on the down side by Portway, ¼a.; in Rye furlong and about the down, 5¼a.; in Bittle gore and up the down, 2½a.; in Westham Oadle, 2¼a.; by the down-mead hedge, 3¼a.; in Huckle Staple, 2a.; in Longland furlong, 2a.; in Link furlong, ¼a.; in the furlong shooting on Summerford hedge, 2a.; in the furlong shooting on Link furlong, 2½a.; in the furlong shooting on the Vicar's headland, 3½a.; in Greenway furlong, 3¼a.; by the Greenway, 1½a.

The tithe of all the hay growing in the parish on inclosed grounds, uplands and meadow, except such grounds and meadows as are exempt from paying of tithe, viz: The vicar has but the 30th cock of hay in a certain ham of the farmer's called Tyth ham, and no tithe in any of the land 'that do or formerly did belong to the farmer'; 30th cock of hay growing in Esq. Dunch[2] his Oldburys. The following lands yield no tithe to the vicar; all Shorncott meadow that lies within the parish; 4a. in Ashton Keynes meadow in the possession of Ann Jones[3] of S. Cerney, widow; Durlingham; 20a. of meadow in the possession of Mrs Masters; a parcel of meadow called Fridays ham, and a little ground called Fridays ham, c. ½a., both in the possession of Edmund Hinton; a Lord's Close; Mill-ham in Ashton Keynes meadow.

Tithe corn: In E. field, ⅓ of the tithe belongs to the vicar, except for the tithe of Lower Breach furlong, Upper Breach furlong, and a furlong shooting on Hall close; 4a. in Moor furlong; 2a. in Water furlong. In N. field, ⅓ of the tithe corn belongs to the vicar, except for the tithes of Shorncott lands and the headlands shooting by Shire ditch occupied by Edmund Hinton, and the furlong shooting on it; Ten acres furlong with 4a. shooting on Portway (lately in the possession of James Jeffries). In W. field ⅓ of the tithe corn belongs to the vicar, except the tithes of Shorncott lands, which yield tithe to Shorncott; ⅓ of tithe corn on E. side of John Hawkins esq, called Boarn's piece, belongs to the vicar. The arable land belonging to the living occupied by George Driver in this and the other fields pays ⅔ of the tithe corn to the vicar.

Tithe wool and lambs: A third part belongs to the vicar. All tithe calves, pigs, geese, and such like. All lammas dues paid customarily as follows: 1d. for the fall of every colt; ½d. for every calf weaned; 2d. for the milk of every cow; 1½d. for the milk of every heifer; 1d. for every garden, tithes of apples, eggs, and all privy tithes.

Tenements and names of present tenants belonging to the vicar: Thomas Weston; Elizabeth Slade wid.; John Darby; Eleanor Chapperlin wid.; William Tayler alias Carver; Francis Coulstone; George Blackford senior, Dorothy Strange wid.

The churchyard at Ashton Keynes, 1a. A fair vicarage house with an orchard, garden, barn, and a stable. A church house belongs to the maintenance of the church; 2s. out of the rent is paid annually to the lord[4] of the manor. A little parcel of ground called the Butthay belongs to the church house.

Isaac Gwinnett, vicar, John Ferrers, John Tomes, churchwardens.

1. William Chapperlin in **22** and **23**.
2. Thomas Carter in **22** and **23**.
3. John Jones in **22** and **23**.
4. Lady in **22**.

22   17 Oct 1698 (D1/24/7/5)
As **21** with amendments in footnotes, apart from the tenants and rents: Thomas Weston, £1.; Elizabeth Slade wid., 8s.; William Darby, 8s.; Giles Chapperlin, 16s.; William Tayler alias Carver, 8s.; Francis Coulstone, 10s.; George Blackford senior, 4s.; Thomas Hobbs, 8s.

Isaac Gwinnett, vicar, Edmund Hinton, John Bennett, churchwardens, Giles Chapperlin, sidesman.

23   1704 (D1/24/7/6)
As **21** *with amendments in footnotes, apart from the tenants:* Richard Danby; Elizabeth Slade wid.; William Darby; Giles Chapperlin; William Tayler alias Carver; Francis Coulston; Thomas Hobbs; John Vincent.

Isaac Gwinnett, vicar, Olive Richmond, Robert Selby, churchwardens, Robert Chapperlin, Edmund Hinton.

ASHTON KEYNES: Leigh chapelry

24 16 Nov 1671 (D1/24/7/7)
All the tithes of hay, except of John Packer's Woodbreach[1] and Mrs Robins's meadow.[2] Another ground called Woodbreach held by John Deighton yields 1s. 4d. annually by ancient composition; also certain other grounds called Pips-Moors[3] yield 3s. 4d. annually. A third of all the tithes of corn except the Leigh furlong; ⅓ of all the tithes of wool and lambs; a row of houses called the Woodrow pays all whole tithes both of wool and lambs and other tithable things; the tithes of calves, pigs, and such like. All lammas dues are accustomed to be paid as follows:[4] the tenth penny for every calf sold; ½d. for every calf weaned; 2d. for the milk of every cow; 1½d. for the milk of every heifer; 1d. for every garden; tithes of apples, eggs, and all privy tithes.[5] A chapel yard[6] of c. ½a.

William Oatley, Thomas Roberts, chapelwardens, Thomas Williams, James Jeffris, sidesmen *Names in the same hand.*

1. Held by John and William Packer in **26**, and by William only in **27**. Both these terriers refer to payment of the 30th cock of hay to the vicar. No tithes mentioned in **25**.
2. Possibly called Oldburys, held by Thomas Carter in **26** and **27**, and paying the 30th cock of hay to the vicar. No tithe mentioned in **25**.
3. Possibly the ground belonging to Nicholas Painter in **26** and **27**.
4. The other terriers include 1d. for the fall of a colt.
5. An Easter offering of 2d. by every communicant over 16 years in **26** and **27**.
6. Described as ¼a. in **25** and **26**.

25 16 Nov 1677 (D1/24/7/8)
*As **24** with amendments in footnotes.* Isaac Gwinnett, vicar, Edward May, Charles Clarke, chapelwardens, John Packer.

26 18 Oct 1698 (D1/24/7/9)
*As **24** with amendments in footnotes.* Isaac Gwinnett, vicar, John Deighton, John Cowley, chapelwardens.

27 10 Dec 1704 (D1/24/7/10)
*As **24** with amendments in footnotes.* Isaac Gwinnett, vicar, Thomas Carter, William Bathe, chapelwardens, Nicholas Painter, Thomas Waldren, sidesmen, William Packer, John Packer, John Deighton, John Waldren.

STEEPLE ASHTON vicarage

28 25 Sep 1608 (D1/24/8/1)
A close of meadow adjoining the house of c. 1½a. An orchard plot with two gardens of in all c. ½a. 1a. meadow in Oathil field lying next but one at the E entrance into the field, and bordering the butts.

George Webb, vicar, Henry Long, John Ballard [X], churchwardens, Robert Hancock, Robert Bartlet, William Hancock, sidesmen.

29   1671 (D1/24/8/2)

Dwelling house, dove house, barn, stable, wood house, cart house, cow house, together with two orchards and a garden containing 2a. 1a. of glebe land in Oatehill and feeding for 12 beasts in Raydown and Laydown. In Moor field the tithes on 35½a. of arable land. The tithe of all groves and Southcrofts except 1a. in Mr Styleman's piece.

Tithes on the following lands: In the E. field and ground adjacent: in William Ballard's leaze next to the grove, 3a.; in Mr John Styleman's leaze next to the grove, 1½a.; in Sir Walter Long's leaze, 4½a.; in Robert Margerum's leaze, 3a.; in Robert Axford's leaze, 3a.; in Stephen Wilkin's leaze, 2a.; in William Ballard's leaze, 3a.; in the corner of Francis Long's Flipmead, 2a.; in William Ballard's Drove, 1a.; in Mr John Martin's ground let to Richard Ballard, 1a.; in Mrs Smyth's leaze and in Mrs Martyn's leaze, 1½a.; Mrs Styleman's leaze, ½a.; wid. Hancock's leaze, 2a. In the Lane: in the upper furlong the tithe of wid. Styleman's, 1a.; in the upper furlong Robert Axford's, 3a; in the lower furlong, 7a.; in Mr Roger Crook his ham, 1a.; in wid. Crook's Raydown leaze, 2a.; in Stephen Wilkins his leaze, 2a.; in the Standly field the tithe of arable land, 29a. In the ground adjacent: in Brook mead the wid. Crook's, 4a.; in Mr Beach his Pinnock, 1½a.; all the tithe of Mr Holford's Great and Little Pinnock and all of Mr. Hooper's Pinnock. In the Moor Crofts: in wid. Crook's Moorcroft, 2a.; in the Paddock adjoining it, ½a. In Oate Hill and grounds adjacent: in Mr Smyth's and Mr Martyn's leaze the tithes of 4a.; in Oatehill the tithe of 7a.; in William Long's leaze, 2a.; in Mr Roger Markes his leaze, ½a.; in Mr Roger Markes his leaze adjoining Oatehill, 3a.; in Windmill field the tithe of 20½a.; in William Long's Mudmead, 1a.; in Robert Margerum's Mudmead, 1a.; Mr Smyth's Mudmead, 1a.; Robert Jefferyes Mudmead, 1a.; Mr Edward Martyn's leaze, 2a.; Mr Henry Martyn's newleaze, 3a.; in wid. Styleman's leaze, 1a.; in John Jenning's leaze, 1a.; in Thomas Waterman's leaze, 1a. All the tithes of Rowd Ashton, West Ashton, and East Town, and of all the grounds at Blackball and Pole Barn which are within the parish of Steeple Ashton. The tithe of all the coppices in the parish. All privy tithes of Hinton, Littleton, Semington, and of all the said parish.

Peter Adams, vicar, Stephen Wilkins, George Hancocke, churchwardens.

30   28 Dec 1704 (D1/24/8/3)

In the tithing of Steeple Ashton: The vicarage house, as **28**. 1a. of glebe lately in the common field called Oatehill but now enclosed. The feeding or herbage of the churchyard. 12 beast leazes in Raydown and Laydown. All the privy tithes. The endowment of great tithes on 253a. 6s. 8d. due from the vicar of Hilperton each Easter for procurations; 4s. due from the vicar of Trowbridge each Easter for procurations; £1 due from the Churchwardens of Semington each Christmas. In the tithing of West Ashton: All great and small tithes. In the tithing of Hinton: All small tithes. All tithe coppices or underwoods in the parish. All mortuaries and customary offerings.

Thomas Bennetts, Thomas Wilkins, churchwardens, Stephen Palmer, Henry Lettell.

The chapel of Semington comprises the tithings of Semington and Littleton. The vicar has small tithes in both tithings; feeding or herbage of the churchyard.

A chamber for the curate in the Church house or 10s. per annum in lieu to be paid by the churchwardens. Mortuaries and offerings in each of the tithings as are due.

Bartholomew Martyn, vicar, William Stoakes [X], John Strobrigg, churchwardens of Semington, Robert Bisse, Matthew Bruges, Thomas Tucker.

AVEBURY vicarage

31   5 May 1682 (D1/24/9/1)

A dwelling house, stable, garden, and home close, c. 3yd. A churchyard, 3yd. A meadow bounded E with a ground of Mr Popham and W with the church meadow, 3yd. 20p. A ground by the bridge, 1yd. 20p. A plot of meadow called the Hooke by river side, ½a., the hay of which is to be cut and carried by Lammas [1 Aug], then it is common to the parish till Candlemas [2 Feb]. A plot of down on Windmill Hill, 2a. 3yd. 8a. 3yd. of arable in the N and W fields as follows: 1a. in Lambern furlong; ½a. in Lower Ditch furlong; ½a. in the middle of the W field bounded S with land of William Braye, N of John White; ½a. in Rudden furlong; ½a. in Foxul; ½a. in Middle Oar furlong; ½a. in the furlong shooting on Yatesbury meer in the N field; ½a. in the next furlong on this side; 1yd. in the same furlong; ½a. in Burrow furlong; 1a. called Short acre in the N field; 1a. in the furlong that shoots on Burrow furlong; ½a. in the same furlong; 2yd. in little Bittum; ½a. in White lands.

Keeping for 2 cows on the down called Hackpin, and feeding for 20 sheep in the N and W fields. The feeding of 2½a. bounded by ground of Thomas Phelps, N in the winter till Hocktide[1] one year, and 4a. in Lambern the other. A pension of £12 per annum due from the parsonage half yearly at Lady Day [25 Mar] and Michelmas [29 Sep].

All the tithes of E Brooke tithing except of hay on Col Stawel's farm, the parsonage close by Kennet lane, and the land mead by S mead. The tithes of Richard Phelps's ground called the New Inclosure now held by Thomas Mortimer, and the tithes of hay of John White's living where he now dwells. Tithe hay on Mr Popham's farm, on Higden's, Chesterman's, Juggins's, the wid. Phelps's Home close, and N Hayes, also the tithes of Lymour's Home close, except a little on the S. The tithes of Horslip and of 9½a. 1yd. 20p. on the S side of William Braye's great meadow; 2a. in Peter Griffin's meadow on the S side lately held by Thomas Pontinge; the Church mead; William Braye's picked close; c. 3yd. meadow by the river side toward Monkton belonging to Thomas Etwald's living; c. 50p. of meadow adjoining belonging to Mary Stephen's living; a plot of meadow on the E side of Selborrow hill of c. 50p.

There is a composition for cow white at 3d. the cow, 4d. for the fall of a calf, the tenth penny if sold, 2d. if weaned. If any beasts' leaze is sold the tenth penny. All small tithes and offerings except wool and lamb. The privilege of choosing, cutting, and carrying away 2 ell ridges of wheat as soon as it is ripe of c. 3yd. growing on Col. Stawel's farm in any of the pieces following: Thornhill; 30a. shooting on S mead; 20a. lying by the road; 2 pieces of 12a. outside Bar close; 30a. in the same field.[2] The same privilege on each of the 4 farms at Beckhampton

in any of the pieces there. The farmers there have declared that an ell ridge is
½a., so that there are 2a. due on the 4 farms each year.

These parcels of tithe in W Kennet: all the tithes of N mead except 3yd., ½a.
on the W and 1yd. on the E; Broad mead except ½a. on the S; the Marsh; the
lower part of Crates from the trees to the lane; Mr Grubbs' Lower Cow leaze, his
Upper Cow leaze from the bank to the river, his Bell close, his Broad close; Mr
Smith's Heel except the new enclosed dry ground, that which is tithable is *c.* 4a.
3yd. of his ham, being about ½a. of his little mead, ½a. of his Gason; Richard
Harding's mead on the W side of the river; Thomas Frye's 3 closes; 3yd. in
Richard Harding's mead on the E side of the river.

John White, vicar, Richard Smith, John Mills [X], churchwardens.

1. The second Monday and Tuesday after Easter.
2. Disputes arose over this particular right between the vicar, John White, and Sir John
   Holbrook from 1692, when he purchased Great Farm until 1701 and again in 1756
   between their respective successors, Revd James Mayo and Staynor Holbrook. The
   vicars claimed the right to payment in kind whereas the owners of the farm
   maintained that it was covered by a prescriptive annual payment of £4; £3 for the
   ell ridges of wheat and £1 for the small tithes. In 1756 the ell ridges were described
   being nearest to the church and consisting each of 60 lugs and together equalling 1
   tenantry a. They derived from 1275 when the vicarage was endowed with, among
   other things, the wheat crop of 1a. of the demesne of the prior of Amesbury. It was
   also claimed by Holbrook in 1756 that the 1682 terrier was not of any use in the
   case because since it was written several parcels of ancient glebe had been exchanged
   and were now 'so ploughed with other Property' as to render it obsolete (WSRO
   184/2 and VCH vol 12 p. 102).

BARFORD ST MARTIN rectory

32   26 Mar 1672 (D1/24/10/1)
The parsonage house with a court, garden, pigeon house, 2 barns, 2 stables, and
backside. All tithes and portions of tithes except of Dennis farm. A tenement
with a close and garden of *c.* 1yd. leased for 99 years at 13s. 4d. p. a., now held by
John Hatkins senior.[1] A meadow called Slovens bank, *c.* 2a. bounded W with a
marsh of Thomas London, E with Woolford mead. Heath close, 2a. bounded N
with a copse of Christopher Hibbert, W with a close of William Gravell, E with
Little field.

3a. arable in W field: 1a. bounded S with ½a. of James Carpenter, N with
1½a. of Nicholas Hollett; 1a. bounded W with 1a. of Walter Cowdrey, E with 1a.
of James Twogood; 1a. bounded N with 3a. of William Bowles, S with 1a. of
John Brooke.

8a. arable in Little field: 3a. bounded N with Hookland, S with a crate of
Nicholas Hayter; 1a. bounded W with 1a. of Stephen Hibbert, E with 1a. of
James Twogood; 1a. bounded E with 1a. of Mr Abbott, W with 2a. of John
Brook; 3a. bounded S with 2a. of John Green, S with 2a. of James Carpenter; 6a.
of arable in the N. field; 2a. bounded N. with ½a. of John London, 2a. of John

Scovell S.; 1a. bounded W with 1a. of Mr Abbott, E with 1a. of William Gravell; 2a. bounded W with 2a. of wid. Browen, E with a roadway in Parsonage bottom; ½a. bounded W with 1a. of Francis Due, E with 1a. of wid. Pavy; ½a. bounded W with ½a. of Mr Abbott, E with 1a. of John London.

6a. arable in W Cadworth: 2a. bounded W with 1a. of John London, E with 1a. of Mr Abbott; 2a. bounded W by 1a. of James Twogood, E with 1a. of Mr Rosington; 2a. bounded W by 2a. of Nicholas Hayter, E with 1a. of John Brook.

4a. arable in E Cadworth: 3a. bounded E with parsonage hedge, W with 1a. of Mr Rosington; 1a. bounded E with a common highway, W with 1a. of Mr Abbott.

7a. arable in the E field: 3a. bounded E with a highway commonly called Green way bottom, W with 5yd. of Thomas London; 2a. bounded E with 1½a. of John Scovell, W with 4a. of Stephen Hibbert; 2a. bounded W with 1a. of John Scovell, E with 2a. of William Gravell. Robert Clarke, rector, John Brooks, John Skoville, Steven Hebberd, Nicholas Hayter, John Cowdray, James Twogood.

1. John Atkins senior of Barford in **33**.

33   14 Sep 1690 (D1/24/10/2)
*As **34** with amendments in footnotes.* The glebe has been let and will still be let for £10. The tithes were let 2 years since and will still be let for £40. The incumbent is 31 years of age.

34   28 Dec 1704 (D1/24/10/3)
Arable and pasture glebe land: In the E field 3a. in Grinning Bottom; 2a. at Foxberyes in the middle of the field; 2a. besides the hills above the parsonage house. In the N field 3a. in Parsonage Bottom; 2a. at Carry Down Clitte; 1a. at the Butts. In the W field 1a. at the Lipgate; 1a. at Spitford Bottom; 1a. at Greens Hedge. In the Little field 3a. against the Gasson Corner; 1a. under the Coppice called Barford Heath; 1a. on Ratel Hill; 3a. by Rowles Hedge. In W Cadford (*field*) 2a. in the corner called Maper Gore; 2a. in Nettle Linch; 2a. on Sand Hills. In E Cadford (*field*) 3a. by Parsonage Hedge; 1a. at Lime Kilns. 2a. in the enclosures in the Marsh;[1] 2a. in the enclosures in the Heath.[2] The whole contains 38a.

A dwelling house, pigeon house, barn, stable, and outhouses. A tenement comprising a dwelling house and garden, 2a. in the heath and a close occupied by [. . .] Crouch senior of Barford St Martin. The whole amounts to £73 per annum.

Robert Clarke, rector, John London, Richard Fulford, churchwardens.

1. Marsh pasture in **33**
2. Heath underwood in **33**.

35   1 Aug 1783 (D1/24/10/4)
Parsonage house consists of hall, 2 parlours, pantry, kitchen, servants hall, scullery, and brewhouse, with offices for whetting knives, keeping coals, etc., 4 bed chambers, and a small study on the second floor with good garrets. 2 good barns, stabling for 10 horses. House covered with tile, the barn with thatch.

The glebe land consisting of 37½a. lies interspersed throughout the whole parish. N. B. the field acres in this parish do not in general measure more than between 90p. and 100p. Last year the glebe land was measured and contained 24a. 3r. E field: 3a. at Grinning Bottom adjoining the road to Salisbury, and bounded by the hedge dividing Barford and Burcombe; 2a. at the head of Foxbury; 2a. by Parsonage Hedge. N field: 1a. in Parsonage Bottom; 2a. in same; ½a. by Brimble Hill; 2a. across the Small Path; 1a. called the Woman acre. W field: 1a. called Hindon Way; 1a. called Spitford Bottom; 1a. that goes up to Greens Hedge; 1a. called Fowsand acre. Little field: 3a. in Garson Corner; 1a. under the Heath; 2a. called Heath Croft; 3a. called Littlefield Gap; 1a. on Rattle Hill.

£5 per annum paid to the churchwardens for the benefit of the church in compensation for a right which the inhabitants of Barford formerly claimed of going up to Groveley one day every year and bringing home as much wood as they could bring without the assistance of horse, mule, or any 'beast of burthen'.

BAVERSTOCK rectory

36   13 Jun 1609 (D1/24/11/1)[1]
Arable: 8a. in N field; 15a. in E field; 19½a. in W field; 3a. in Hooke land. 1 close lying N and S called Melledge, 5a.; 1 close at Barford Marsh, lying N and S, called Melledge, 5a.

Pasture: 1 close called Short lands, 3a.; 1 close bounding upon S side of the churchyard, of 2a.; the churchyard containing 1yd. of ground; 1 close called Fryth, 1½a.; 1 close called Colledge, 3a.

Meadow: 1 close W side of the house containing 1a.; 1 close E side of the house containing 1a.; Bell mead containing 3a.; ½a. in the common mead, only to share and be gone.

Housing: A mansion house with all the rooms belonging to it: hall, parlour, buttery, chambers, and other small rooms for necessary uses with garden. A kitchen severed from the dwelling house, with milk house, bolting house, malt loft. A barn of 7 rooms together with stalls, stables, sheep houses, cart house, with other houses for swine and poultry.

Common of pasture for 10 kine and 1 bull among the tenants at the woods and in the fields. In the fields commons for 2 horses. Common for 100 sheep upon the Downs and in the fields.

The tithes of Henry Jeffraye's house in Barford accruing yearly to the rectory of Baverstock.

Richard Byrckbeke, parson, Walter Fricker, Edward Stephens, churchwardens.

All this was put in after our hands were set to it, unto the which the churchwardens can say nothing: 1 head a. of arable in Eastley, occupied by Gyles Greene now of Baverstock, which shoots N and S; W the hedge; a ground of Henry Daniell which lies on the other side the hedge, being Dinton.

Stocks, implements, tenements: none.

2a. of arable occupied by Henry Jefferye in Barford St Martin, with the little field, E and W next unto the hedge; a meadow called Parckes lying on the other side of the said hedge, late in the tenure of Richard Careye of Wilton, clothier, now occupied by Thomas Gawen of Hurdcott [Hurdcourte] in Baverstock esq. The tithe of which 2a. as yearly grow by ancient custom to the parsonage of Baverstock, and from time to time has been by all persons there go enjoyed and carried away.

The tithe hay of ½a. of meadow which lies in Walveren mead within Barford St Martin, now belonging to Thomas Gawen of Hurdcott esq. appertains to the parson of Baverstock.

1. The document is written in green ink.

37   5 Dec 1693 (D1/24/11/2)
1 dwelling house, 1 orchard, with barn, stable, backside, outhouses.

In the High field: 3a. at W end; 2a. at E end; 3a. running down against the drove.

In the W field: 1a. running along by the Warminster road; 3 halves upon top of the hill; 1a. headland to the 3 halves; 2a. shooting upon the E field, 2a. shooting against Farmer Daniel's field; 1a. shooting against Farmer Daniel's field; 1a. shooting against the E field; 2a. shooting against the E field; 8a. near Farmer Daniel's hedge; 1a. more shooting against the E field; 2 hookland a. shooting against Farmer Daniel's hedge; 1a. of hookland shooting against the E field.

In the E field: 2a. lying 1a. breadth from the Down; 4a. in the middle of the field; 9a. lying against the W field. In the common meadow, ½a.

Enclosed grounds: A ground called the Millenge, adjoining Roger Lyde's ground, 5a. A square paddock adjoining Roger Lyde's, 3x ⅓a A ground called the College, 3a. A meadow called Bell meadow, 2½a. A croft [craught] running up by Joseph Abram's house, 8a. The Rick close, 1a. The churchyard close, 2a. The whole sum, 70a.

Matthew Bowles, rector, John Hayter, John Nicolas [X], churchwardens.

38   4 May 1705 (D1/24/11/3)
In the W field, 23½a.; in the Lower field, 15a.; in the High field, 8a.; Home Crate enclosure, arable land, 6a.; Church close, 2a.; Bell mead, 2½a.; Square paddock, 1a.; College pasture ground, 2a.; 1 ham in the common mead; Total, 64½a.

1 dwelling house, 2 barns, 1 stable, and outhouses, with 1 orchard and gardens.

R[obert] Clarke, rector, Steven Naish, John Rickets, churchwardens.

GREAT BEDWYN vicarage

39   15 Jul 1672 (D5/10/1/3)
A house and garden given by the ancestors of the duke of Somerset and the churchyard. 6d. a cow for cow white, for calves the tenth penny for a calf sold of the money it is sold for, the left shoulder if killed and 1½d. if weaned. For pigs, geese, apples, hops, honey and eggs as they are payable by the tithing table. The tithe of all turnips, carrots, parsnips, onions and all other garden fruits. Mortuaries as they are payable by the Canon: that is 10s. for anyone that is worth (at his

decease) £40 in goods and chattels, 6s. 8d. for anyone worth £30 and 3s. 4d. for £5 and 1 mark. 1s. to be paid by every woman that is churched for an offering and 1s. for burying a corpse.

No tithe corn, hay, wool nor lamb except ½d. a piece for every lamb under the number of 7 and so likewise for every odd lamb that remains over and above when the impropriator has taken his tithe.

Robert Randall, vicar, Francis Savage, John Hawkens, churchwardens, Robert Brunsdon, Robert Wallis.

LITTLE BEDWYN vicarage

39A   10 Apr 1672 (9/4/88)
Terrier[1] made according to a mandate of the dean of Sarum by Daniel Early and John Minoll junior, churchwardens.

A dwelling house, 1 barn, 1 stable and outhouses, 1 backside, 2 orchards, 2 gardens and the churchyard.

All small tithes throughout the whole parish except Chisbury farm, viz. tithe calves, cow white, for every cow 1d. p. a., pigs, geese, apples, hops, honey, for every garden 1d. for every colt 1d.; tithe for odd lambs exceeding 10 but not being 17 and in the same manner for greater numbers or being under 7 for every such odd lamb is due to the vicar ½d. Tithe corn and grain on Shortheade field and Church field both at Chisbury, and on arable lands in the tenure of Richard Carpenter in the fields belonging to Chisbury. On lands and meadows belonging to Burnwood's heath, viz. Hunts living, Clistons living, Earlys living, Batts living and also on George's living, Smith's living of Forebridge and the lands of the mill except Spaines and the lands which lie out of the parish. Tithe corn and hay on all lands, grounds and meadows in the tithing of Little Bedwyn except Parlour field, Crutch lands, Merrill Down and Millclose adjoining Slopers mill, E. meads below the bridge at Forebridge, 2 of which are in the tenure of John Bushell, one of Thomas Streete and 1 of Stephen Blandy, 4 meadows below Sloper's mill called E. (recte W.) meads in the tenure of Thomas Gregory, John Smith, John Bushell, and Stephen Blandy; Tithes of E. and W. meads the rector has held time out of mind; on Tithing meadow below E. Mead. Tithe wood on Mouchins coppice in the tenure of Thomas Skeate and Strokehedge coppice of Sir John Elwes and of the underwoods or coppice in Hunts leaze and Earlys coppice.

Endorsement; 17 Oct 1777 Stephen Wentworth says Mouchins coppice lies against E. field and he thinks belongs to the vicar – but admits Strokeheys coppice is Lord Ailesbury's tithe which shows that heed is to be given to this terrier. Hunts leaze and Earlys coppice he thinks are the vicars but claimed by Lord A.

1. A copy of the terrier was sent to Lord Ailesbury's steward by Dr. William Harrison, vicar, Aug. 1770 and copied into a survey book of the prebend of Little Bedwyn.

BEECHINGSTOKE rectory

40 1671 (D1/24/12/1)

A house of 2 bays, a barn, stable, and 2 skillings adjoining of 6 bays, a cart house of 2 bays, a backside, a garden, an orchard adjoining the house, c. 1a.

2 grounds called Ryuls, 10a., Little mead at the end, Thomas Hayward W, John Hayward E. A little meadow called N mead, Mr Cleevely W, Mrs Jane Lavington, wid., E. A little mead called Fowle mead, wid. Miles W, Francis Hayward E. A little lammas meadow called Scotchfull, wid. Miles S, Francis Hillier N.

1a. on Shill and half it heads it, Francis Hillier E, John Hayward W. 3a. in Holasorah, wid. Miles N, and it heads the farm land and the tenants S. 2a. at Townesend, John Hayward W, Francis Hayward E; ½a. in the same field, John Hayward N, Francis Hayward S. 2 butts at the Townesend moor in the same field, Thomas Hayward E, John Hayward W. In Drove furlong ½a. between John Hayward on E and W; 3x ½a in the same field, John Hayward E, Thomas Hayward W; 3a. in the same field, Thomas Hayward E and W. 1a. in Gouldhill, Thomas Hayward N, Francis Hillier S, ½a. against 3 helmes, Mrs Lavington E and W; 1a. in the same field, Thomas Hayward S; 2a. in the same field, Mr Raymond ?W, John Hayward ?E [both W. in MS]; ½a. in the same field, John Hayward E and W. ½a. at Greenes Slad, wid. Miles E, Thomas Hayward W. A ground called Hatfield, of 4½a., Mr Raymond N, Mr Cleevely S.

The tithes of Milmeade in Wilsford parish; of 1a. in Wilsford mead belonging to Mr Raymond; 1a. in Wilsford mead belonging to Mr Lavington of Marden; 1a. Mr Raymond has in Patney at Limber stone.

Offerings: 2d. for every person of age; 2d. for every yardland for fuel; 10 eggs to a yardland; 2d. for a cow white; 6d. a calf, or the 10th calf; 1d. a garden.

The tithe of a little plot in Patney of Thomas Hayward; of a little plot of Thomas Hayward in the same; of another little plot in the same meadow of Francis Hillier.

Thomas Easton, rector, John Hayward [X], Francis Hayward [X], churchwardens.

41 Mar 1705 (D1/24/12/2)

1 dwelling house containing 2 bays; 1 barn containing 5 bays; 1 stable; 1 carthouse with other little outbuildings; 1 orchard, 1a.

1 little plat called the hopyard lying next the street; 1 plat called the Withybed being something better than a yard of ground; 1 ground and a little meadow at the lower end of them called the N grounds, 10a.; N meadow lying below John Hayward's N ground, 3yd.; Hatefield, 4½a.; Foul, 1a.; 1 little plat of lammas [meadow] lying between wid. Harris' and John Hillier's plats. All these grounds are enclosed.

In the common field: 2 butts of ½a. running N and S, wid. Hayward E, Joseph Hayward W; 2a. running N and S, Joseph Hayward W, Francis Hayward E; ½a. running E and W, William Hayward N, Francis Hayward S; 3a. at Hollow furrow running E and W, wid. Harris N, the farm piece S; 1 little a. at the Elm running N and S, lying between Joseph Hayward W, John Hillier E; 1 little headland running E and W, lying by the wayside. In Drove furlong 3a. at the Bush running N and S, William Hayward W, wid. Hayward E; 3 halves running N and S, wid. Hayward W, John Hayward E. At Green Slade ½a. running N and S, wid. Hayward W, wid. Harris E. At 3 Elms furlong 3a. running N and S, Mr Raymond W, wid. Harris E; 1a. running N and S, John Hillier W, William Hayward E; ½a. running N and S, John Smith W, Mr Lavington E; 1a. on Gold Hill running E and W, wid. Hayward N, John Hillier S.

Tithe of 1 lammas meadow called Mill meadow, belonging to Mr Raymond's farm but lying in Wilsford. Tithe of 1 lammas meadow belonging to Mr Raymond's farm but lying in a meadow belonging to the parish of Wilsford. Tithe of 1a. of lammas meadow, belonging to the Little farm of Marden but lying in Wilsford meadow. Tithe of 1 little plat of lammas meadow belonging to John Hillier; same belonging to wid. Hayward; same belonging to John Hayward; all these 3 plats lie in a meadow belonging to Patney and in a meadow belonging to wid. Nash. Tithe of a very small plat of meadow in another meadow of wid. Nash belonging to the parish of Patney; the plat belongs to wid. Harris of Beechingstoke. Tithe of 1a. of lammas meadow belonging to Mr Raymond's farm lying at Limber Stone in the parish of Patney.

All tithe corn, hay, wool, lambs, calves, and all other tithes belonging to the rectory. Custom tithes, viz. 2d. for cow white; 2d. a yardland for fuel; 2d. a yardland for eggs; 1d. for a garden. 40 sheep leaze in the common field.

Thomas Easton, rector, Samuel Lavington, John Hellier, Henry Maish.

42   2 Jul 1808 (D1/24/12/3)
A brick-built dwelling house and 2 gardens. A barn with 2 floors, a stable, a farmyard and a rick yard. The churchyard and a small plat adjoining planted with Arbrals and other trees.

11¼a. of arable in the field, Mr Gilbert E, Mr Mayo W. An inclosure of arable called N ground, 10a., with a plantation of firs, etc., adjoining. An inclosure of arable called Drove Hatfield, 5¾a. Foul mead, 1a., Mr Hayward E, Mr Mayo W. N mead: 1a. on N side of N ground; in N mead ¾a., meadow of Mr Hayward W, Mrs Sawyer E.

All the great and small tithes. Tithe of a portion of meadow allotted to Puckshipton estate in Wilsford meadow; ¾a. of meadow on the Patney side of the brook at Limberstone. Tithe of 1a. of lammas meadow in Wilsford meadow belonging to the Little farm at Marden, property of Mr Gilbert. Tithe of small plot [plat] of lammas meadow held by wid. Sawyer. Tithe of 2 small plots of lammas meadow held by Richard Hayward senior; all these in a meadow called Scotchfield on the Patney side of the brook. *Custom tithes as* **41**.

It appears from a memorandum of Rev John Mayo,[1] late rector, that the rails between the churchyard and Mr Gilbert's meadow were erected at the expense of the parish.

Charles Mayo, rector, Joseph Hayward, John Gale, churchwarden, Joseph Gilbert.

1. John Mayo was incumbent 1737-1779.

BERWICK ST JAMES rectory

43 13 Jun 1609 (D1/24/13/1)

A barn with a backside or barton and a close of pasture of 1a. 3a. in Berwick meadow. Pasture for 9 kine and a bull in the common fields and marshes of the manor of Berwick; also common and feeding for 200 sheep in the common fields. Tithe of all kinds of corn or grain, hay and wool in the manor except the tithe corn of Kings farm and the bord lands.

48a. of arable in the common fields, as follows: in the N. Outfield 12a.; in the S. Outfield 10a.; in the N. Infield 10a.; in Marsh furlong 3a.; in Martins field 3a.; in the S. Infield 10a.

In Asserton 17a. arable in the common fields as follows: in the field next to Winterbourne Stoke 3a.; in the Outfield 3a.; in the Home field 11a.

Feeding and pasture for 60 sheep, 2 horses and 2 kine, in the common fields of Asserton. A close of enclosed pasture, c. ½a. The tithe corn and wool of half the manor of Asserton.

By me William Powell,[1] William Hayes, John Gilbert, [X], churchwardens.

1. William Powell was vicar; he signed the bishop's transcript for 1608.

43A Sep 1787 (D1/36/2/21)

A survey and valuation of the glebe and tithes. In N. field:[1] 1½a. (1a. 2r. 28p.) in London way; 1a. (1a. 19p.) in Sheeps Henge furlong; Parsonage Piece, 5a. (3a. 2r. 12p.), in Cakebread furlong; 2 x ½a. (2r. 12p., 1r. 21p.) in the furlong above Brown; 2a. (1a. 3r. 39p.) in Brown furlong; 1a. 91a. 27p.) in Cleaver furlong; 1a. (2r. 35p.) in Main Hide furlong. In S. field: 1½a. (1a. 34p.) in Windabout furlong; ½a. (2r. 32p.) in Lower Cow Drove furlong; ¼a. 1r. 8p.) in Middle Cow Drove furlong; 3 x ½a. (2r. 26p.), 3r. 34p., 3r. 31p.) in Middle Hill furlong; 1½a. (3r. 13p.) in the furlong above Frogland; ½a. 92r. 5p.) in Simmonds furlong; 1a. (3r. 11p.) in the furlong shooting on Headcombe. Total 21¾a. (19a. 2r. 16p.)

Criss Cross Croft, arable, 7a. 16p.; 1a. 3r. 16p. in Berwick Mead furlong. House, buildings and orchard, 1a. 10p. The foreshare of 5 parts out of 19 of the Up marsh and Church marsh water meadows, 34a. 15p., from 1 Jan to 12 Aug after which it is fed in common by all the the cows in the parish. Vicarage house, garden, 9p. Church and churchyard, 3r. 26p.

Tithe of arable, 513a. 1r. 22p., valued at £77 2d. Tithe of Berwick meads, 27a. 24p., valued at £3 7s. 10½d. Tithe of the water meadows of Berwick, 41a. 3r. 1p., valued at £10 8s. 9d. Tithe wool and lambs on sir James Harris' farm, 5 yardlands, 80 sheep or lambs a yardland, valued at £10.

Asserton glebe and commons of pasture as **43**. Great tithes of Asserton farm, the property of Mr. Biggs, belong in equal parts to Henry Penruddock Wyndham and lord Chedworth; Mr. Wyndham's part valued at £31 10s.

1. Statute acreages in N. and S. fields in ( ).

BERWICK ST JOHN rectory

44   20 May 1588 (D1/24/14/1)

2a. in Hewes field[1] abutting on the highway N, the lands of Mr Shelley W,[2] lord Pembroke[3] E. The Breach (3a.) in the W field, the highway at N and S, bounding the lands of Mr Shelley[2] E, and a hedge that parts 2 fields W. 3a. in Pytlande abutting on a landshard E and W, lands of lord Pembroke N and S. 4a. in the Farm field abutting at each end N and S,[4] lord Pembroke[3] on both sides E and W. 3 x ½a. arable in Chaw throsle[5] and *c.* 3 x ½a. meadow adjoining abutting E and W, lands of Mr Shelley[2] S, the watercourse on the N, of which the parson ought to scour half as far as the said land lies. 3a. arable at the nether end of Wollands abutting E and W, land of Mr Shellie[2] on both sides N and S. 2a. meadow in the E mead E and W, the lands of lord Pembroke[3] on both sides N and S. 5a. arable in the E field abutting N and S, Nortthington[6] mead E, lands of lord Pembroke[3] W. 6½a. arable[7] in the Middle field in Bredmore and in Rackesfield 7½a. adjoining together N and S, the highway W and the lands of Mr Udall E. 1a. arable in Pynne furlong on the hill in Bredmore abutting E and W, lands of Mr Udall N and the lands called Brockways S. A close of pasture of *c.* ½a. abutting on the Middle field W and the highway E. 1a. arable in Easton called Coose a. abutting N and S, the lands of Mr Shelley[2] W, and the highway E. A close of pasture at Combe of *c.* 5a.

Common of pasture for 50[8] sheep in Berwick common fields, and feeding for 9 rother beasts. On the farm ground of Bridmore pasture and feeding for 160[8] sheep at all times.

The parson has in consideration of his tithes of lord Pembroke 14a. wood; 5½a. wood in consideration of tithes in the manor of Bridmore (Mr Pinkney rector dissented since). Tithe wood in Cuttes and Ashcombe. 2 fleeces customarily paid out of Mr Shellie's[2] farm in Easton of the tithe wool. All the predial and privy tithes except the tithes of 100 sheep which are to be kept on the demesnes held by lease from lord Pembroke[9] free from payment of any tithes. For privy tithes the offering at Easter for the first time for everyone ½d. and after 2d.; for a garden 1d., a cow white 1d.; a heifer white 1d.; the fall of a colt 1d.; under 7 pigs and geese ¼d. each; lambs under the same number ½d. each; under 7 calves if they are weaned or killed ⅓d. each,[10] if sold 4d. (Mr Pinkney, rector, dissented since) [...] A house, orchard or garden [...].[11]

Robert Topp, William Lucas, churchwardens, Nicholas Mor, gent., John Vyncent, sidesmen. With the rest of the ancientest of the parish this bill was made.

1. Described as being at the Great lane in the Little W field commonly called Hawes field, in 1677.
2. Sir Charles Shelley in **45**.
3. The earl of Shaftesbury in **45**.
4. With the meadow added in **45**.
5. Chaw croft in **45**.
6. W mead in **45**.
7. 6½a. arable in Middle field in Breedmore and 1a. on E side exchanged for an a.

which the parson once had on the hill called Pynne furlong, which last 7½a. bounded land of lord Shaftesbury E and S, the parson's hedge N and W. The last 7½a. are always enclosed at the pleasure of the parsons. In **45** the foregoing replaces the section from 6½a. in Middle field to ½a. in Middle field in **44**.

8. The two totals have been reversed; see VCH. vol. 13 p. 26.
9. James Bennett in **45**.
10. If killed, the best shoulder, in **45**.
11. With appurtenances in 18th. cent. copy, (WSRO 1764/12)

45   17 Dec 1677 (D1/24/14/2)
*As **44** with alterations in footnotes.* John Gane, rector, James Vencent, William Cox, churchwardens, Bartholomew Gilbert, Robert Gould, sidesmen, John Bennett, Giles Jervase [X], John Vincent.

46   5 Aug 1783 (D1/24/14/3)
The parsonage house is very ancient solid and stone built fabric with stone and brick tile; has two oak-floored parlours, the smallest of them wainscotted, the lower partly wainscotted and partly papered; with a brick floored kitchen; five rooms on the second floor, all ceiled, but no garret; an adjoining brewhouse covered likewise with brick and tile. It has at a convenient distance two large thatched barns and stables with the usual and necessary conveniences of a farm yard.

The glebe consists of 21a. by computation of arable in the common fields, the boundaries of which are well known and ascertained. 21 computed a. of arable, meadow, and pasture consisting of 5 enclosed fields. 8a. by computation of meadow in the flat of the common field, subject to different customs in a round of every 4 years, which customs are well known and of which an exact record is kept.

Parsonage coppice 14a. and Staple-foot coppice 7a., both in Cranbourne Chase. A garden, a little field, a walled yard and the church yard of adjoining the parsonage house. Annual right of feed on the Downs and Common fields for 110 sheep; and for 3 horses, 12 cows, 1 bull in the Chase and the common fields.

There is no modus except that of 100 sheep belonging to Berwick farm paying no tithe from time immemorial. Excepting likewise the annual custom of ½ a buck which the rector receives in lieu of the tithe of pasture ground adjoining Rushmoor Lodge. An annual customary payment of 8s. is made to the earl of Shaftesbury, lord of the manor, on account of the exchange of the feed of 160 sheep, the rector formerly had on Berwick farm, for a tenement called Sangers, being the little enclosed field in front of the parsonage house. The rector had a little customary venison twice a year in common with the tenants of the manor, which includes part of the Chase.

The church has 5 bells, 1 clock, a silver chalice containing about a quart, a small silver cup for the communicants, and a silver plate for bread. There are no bequests or pensions made for the purposes of repairing the church or chancel.

The clerk's wage, £2 1s. 0d., is paid by the parish. He has the rent of a cottage given by a former rector for ringing an 8 o'clock bell every night for the winter half year. There is no sexton.

Edward Rolle, rector, Joseph Foot, William Foot, churchwardens, John Phelps, Thomas Wright.

BERWICK ST LEONARD rectory

47   12 Dec 1677 (D1/24/15/1)
A dwelling house with a barn, stable, outhouse, backside, garden and close adjoining of *c.* 2a. The wood growing on a parcel of ground of *c.* 3a. called the Parson's plot, the herbage of which belongs to the tenants of the manor. Tithes of wood of coppices belonging to the lord of the manor on the N side of Berwick customarily cut once in 2 years. All other great and small tithes. John Bracher, churchwarden.

Memorandum: Mr Samuel Stone rector was required to set his hand to this terrier by the churchwarden but refused. Dennis Sturges, Reuben Ford.

48   5 Jan 1705 (D1/24/15/2)
*As **47**, without the memorandum.* Samuel Stone, rector, Walter Kingman, churchwarden, John Sturges, Edward Grant.

BERWICK ST LEONARD: Sedgehill chapelry

49   3 Jan 1705 (D1/24/15/3)
A dwelling house, orchard and garden of *c.* ¼a.; the churchyard adjoining. For cow white every 14th day's milk skimmed and made in a cheese in a housewife manner, beginning the 3 May if a Monday, if not the Monday after, till the Monday after 6 Nov. All other great and small tithes.

Samuel Stone, rector, Peter Bownd, George Geffries, churchwardens, Thomas Grove, Henry Good, John King, Henry Jerard, John Collens, Edward Cowherd, Richard Oborn.

50   24 Mar 1734. (D1/24/15/4)
*As **49**.* William Nairn, rector, Henry Dyer, James Wigmor, churchwardens, James Bridle, Henry Dyer, overseers, John Woodhouse, Edmund Troubridge, Isaac Trowbridge, Edward Frowd, John King, Anthony Merywether, James Frowd, John King junior.

BIDDESTONE ST PETER rectory

51   7 Dec 1671 (D1/24/16/1)
A house with a backside of *c.* ½a. In the N field 3a.; in N More 1a. and in Long furlong 2a. In the W field 3½a.; 2½a. in Stanhills and 1a. in the same field called Blackslow. In Beckhill *c.* 2½a. All the tithes of corn and hay belonging to the farm of Thomas Mountjoy gent. The tithes of corn and hay of the tenement and lands of Thomas Dark, also of Bromley lands being *c.* 8a. held by Benjamin

Bristow. All the small or personal tithes in Biddestone St Peter, also all personal tithes in Biddestone St Nicholas and Slaughterford usually paid to the rector.

John Hort, Joseph Hakins, churchwardens, William Lytle, Thomas Wilsher, sidesmen.

52   29 Oct 1677 (D1/24/16/2)

A house with the backside and close adjoining, 1 farndell of ground. 2a. in Long furlong in N field. 3a. at Stonehills in W field; the end of one of the acres lies enclosed in a ground of Richard Frampton gent. 2a. of arable or pasture at Beckhill adjoining a copse of Mr Godward S. 1a. of arable at Black Slow in W field.

Tithe corn and hay belonging formerly to Thomas Mountjoy gent, and the tenements of John Darke lying dispersedly in several grounds, and also in the several common fields as have been exchanged by the predecessors of Thomas Mountjoy gent, and John Dark.

1a. of arable enclosed in N Moore owned by Richard Lewis. Small tithes due from Thomas Mountjoy, John Dark, and personal from Biddestone St Nicholas and Slaughterford.

John Ferris, rector, William Awste, Anthony Marish [X], churchwardens.

53   n. d. [1704x1705][1] (D1/24/16/3)

A parsonage house with ½a. of pasture adjoining. 1½a. in a ground called Backwell. 2a. in Slaughterford field shooting on a ground called Stonely. 2a. in Biddestone field shooting on a ground called Stannills. 1a. in W dry field shooting on Black Slow. 2a. in N field.

Thomas Tattersall, rector, Richard Wastfeld, John Borshar, churchwardens, inhabitants

1.   The churchwardens were recorded in the attended the bishop's visitation book, Oct 1704 (WSRO D1/50/6)

54   17 Jul 1783 (D1/24/16/5)

A cottage consisting of 1 dwelling room *c.* 10ft. square and 6ft. high paved with stones. A pantry or woodhouse of similar dimensions with an earth floor. 2 garrets over the whole covered with straw or thatch. Small garden and *c.* 1 farndell of land adjoining. The above never remembered to have been deemed a parsonage house, but inhabited by a cottager at *c.* 20s. a year. The yard or barton surrounding the ruinated chapel there.

2a. in Long furlong in N field. 2a. of arable in W field near Black Slow hedge. 3a. of arable in Slaughterford field, being part of an enclosure of which the other part belongs to William Mountjoy gent. Also a small quarry on the other side of the road nearly opposite to the mere of the glebe called Parson's Quarr. 2a. of pasture at Beckhill adjoining S a coppice of Edward Goddard esq., on which are growing 4 oak trees. *c.* 1 farndell of pasture adjoining the ruinated chapel at Slaughterford.

Tithe corn and hay of the several grounds and fields of William Mountjoy gent, and from all other lands lying severally in Biddestone St Peter, viz: 2 Home meads, c. 30a.; 1 mead called Redbrink, 6a.; 2 arable fields called Rudge Ways, 12a.; 1 pasture ground called Witch mead, 6½a.; 2 pasture grounds called Broad Heaths, 10a.; 1 pasture ground called Rowens, 8a.; Dukes Hill House and land, 1a.; Honey Brook House and garden; Bonds Hill House and land, 10a.; 3 houses and gardens near Witch Mead. The above all confessed to be in Biddeston St Peter. The following have been always so reputed by the oldest inhabitants: 2 called Ashtons, pasture, 5a.; Chalcroft, pasture, 10a.; Chalcroft, arable, 7a.; Squeak, pasture, 1a.; 2 called Pye Corners, arable, 12a.; Pye Corner, pasture, 3a.

All the small tithes of Biddeston St Peter, Biddestone St Nicholas, and Slaughterford, with a portion of Hartham. There is no modus.

Charles Page, rector, Aaron Little, John Edward, churchwardens, John Skeate, Matthew Mountjoy, William Davis [X]. Rowens being expressed as doubtful.

Endorsement: Furniture of the church: A decent pulpit cloth and cushion and a desk cloth. A green serge cloth for the communion table with white linen on proper occasions. A pewter flagon, one silver chalice and cover weight c. 8ozs. A small bell. Church and yard repaired by parish rate. Chancel by the impropriate or lessee. Clerk appointed by minister. Wages paid by voluntary subscription. Signed by rector and churchwardens as above.

BISHOPSTONE (North Wilts) rectory or prebend and vicarage.

55   14 Jul 1631 (D5/10/1/4)

The rectory or parsonage: A plot of ground whereon stands the dwellinghouse, a barn and stable, 4a. In Chipmead 2a. 3yd. In the Down field 14a. of arable; 11a. in the Parsons breach, 3a. at Common Sheard. 2a. shooting on the W. combe banks. 1a. by Woodway, 3a. by Ridgeway, 2a. in Waterslade, 2a. in White pits.

In the W. field: 2a. abutting upon Heywards ham. In the E. field: 1a. at Marwell stream; 3a. shooting upon Ridgeway above Ridgeway; 2a. at High bush; 2a. at Panstone.

The vicarage: A plot of ground whereon stands the dwelling house, a new built barn and stable, garden and orchard, 1½a. The churchyard, 2a.

Meadow: ½a. in the field above Crophill; ½a. over the drove at Vicarage stile; ½a. and 1 stitch in a furlong above the Sheephouse furlong; a close between Charles Younge and John Smith, ½a.; In Whiteland 1a. 1yd. between that a. and Blackland hedge.

Arable: W. side; in the Down field 3 ridges and 2 butts at Tylers bush, 2a.; In the Hitchins 3yd. on Ladder way. On Knil ½a.; ½a. below Ridgeway crossing Evillway; ½a. in Sherlands; ½a. at Hilmans hedge; ½a. the end shooting on Ridgeway; ½a. shooting between the 2 Green ways shooting on Waterslad; ½a. on Sanders hedge; ½a. at Upper Sanders hedge; ½a. at Vicars Batch; ½a. on Little Churchstead. East side: ½a. in Holy Dean furlong shooting on the Downs. In Panston furlong ½a.; at High bush ½a.; at Middle Sanders hedge ½a.; 1 picked a. shooting on Taylers headland; 1 broad a., shooting on Idston field; ½a. at Hilmans hedge by the way side; 2 little butts, ½a., on Sittles down; ½a. at Combe end; ½a. at Icleton way; ½a. in Heland; ½a. in Forty furlong.

John Wilson, vicar, Thomas Hull, Oliver Harding, churchwardens, John Hodges, Thomas Horton senior [X], John Smith [X], Charles Young.

56   16 Mar 1672 (D5/10/1/4)
Vicarage: Terrier made by John Hedges and Tobias Smith, churchwardens. The churchyard, c. 3r., bounded E. the E. brook with the trees growing on the bank belonging to the vicarage, S. the orchard and garden wall of Christopher Willoughby esq., W. the orchard and barn of John Butler, N. The vicarage, comprising a dwelling house containing 3 spaces or bays of building and some what more in the skilling adjoining and a well house on N. side, a stable on S. side. A barn of 3 bays with a penthouse adjoining, 2 orchards, one on W. side the other on the E. side of the dwelling house with a garden on E. side. It is bounded with the churchyard on E. and S. on W. with the highway and N. with E. brook and W. brook. The acres growing on the bank belong belong to the vicarage. The whole plot of ground on which the dwelling house stands is 1a.

1 yardland of glebe which has commons for horses, cows and sheep as any yardland in Bishopstone in all commonable place. 1 close of meadow in E. brook, ½a., belongs to this yardland, it is bounded N. and S. with the highways E. the dwelling house, backside and orchard of Edmund Young, W. the backside and close of Samuel Smith. Certain lands in the commons of Bishopstone belong to this yardland: viz. ½a. of meadow in the Down field beneath Horton's bush shooting E. and W., a land of Samuel Precey N., land of Margery Tayler S. One 3yd. of arable in the same field shooting E. to W., a land of Samuel Precey N., a land of Henry Keep S. On the other side of the hedge in the Down field 2a. of arable shooting N. and S., the land called the parsonage breach on E., lands of Christopher Willoughby esq. W.; ½a. of meadow shooting over the drove, a land of Charles Purton on N.

In the E. field. ½a. of meadow shooting E. and W., a land of William Norrice S.; a little plot of ground called a stitch shooting upon a ditch of Samuel Precey senior; 1yd. of meadow shooting E. and W., 1yd. of John Butler on N.; 1a. in a furlong called Whiteland shooting E. and W., a land of John Kent on S.; ½a. in Vorty furlong shooting N. and S., a land of the wid. Maton on E.; ½a. in Little mead shooting upon the quickset hedge of Thomas Collins; ½a. shooting on Ickleton way, a land of the wid. Spainswick on W.; ½a. at Combe foot, a land of Samuel Precy on N.; ½a. and a butt on the top of Sithedown shooting N. and S. upon a headland of John Horton; ½a. by Hellmans hedge shooting N., a land of Samuel Precey junior. W., a land of Oliver Hicks E.

Above Ridgeway on the E. side of Saunders hedge ½a. shooting on Idstone field, a land of the wid. Gybbs S. and a headland of Samuel Precey N.; ½a. shooting N. and S. upon Taylers headland; ½a. shooting upon Saunders hedge near Broad gap, a land of Samuel Precey N.; ½a. in Swindly furlong shooting towards Swindly; ½a. in Panstone furlong, the stone standing on the upperside of the middlemost short hedge; ½a. shooting on the upper end of Saunders hedge; ½a. in Churchsteed shooting upon the lands of William Norrice; ½a. shooting upon Saunders hedge, a land of Samuel Smith N.; ½a. near the Middle greenway's side, a land of Samuel Smith W., a land of John Horton E.

Beneath Ridgeway; ½a. shooting upon Ridgeway; ½a. shooting E. and W. by Hellmans hedge; ½a. shooting E. and W. over the way going up from the town, a headland of Samuel Smith N., a land of William Kent S.; ½a. on Knill a land of Henry Green N.; ½a. in ? Sheelands shooting N. and S., a land of Samuel Precey W., a land of Henry Keepe E.

Tithe corn, hay, wool and lamb of those 9 yard lands belonging to the parsonage of Bishopstone being the right of the late prebendary of Bishopstone, John Barnstone, DD. 4 marks to be paid yearly out of the parsonage on Quarterdays 6s. 8d. and 1 bushell of wheat to be paid yearly on the feast of St. Thomas [21 Dec] out of the mills of Bishopstone. For Easter dues 2d. for every communicant, 1d. for every garden, 3 eggs for every cock, 2 eggs for every hen. For Lammas day [1 Aug] 1½d. for every milk cow, 1d. for a thorough milk cow, 1d. for every calf that falls. Tithe calves, the left shoulder if they be killed at the age of 4 weeks or upward, the tenth penny if they be sold at that age, ½d. if they wean them. The tenth pig of every sow that fallows; if there be not 10, one of 7 allowing 1½d. for the rest or if under 7 then ½d. a pig for the rest. The tenth goose at Lammas [...] or if there be not so many one of 7s. 6d. for the churching of every woman; 1s. 6d. for every couple that are married in the church. On St. Mark's day [25 Apr] the tenth lamb of all ewes kept on the said 9 yard lands or if they have not 10 then one of 7, the vicar to allow ½d. for to make 10. Tithe honey of all stocks of bees or if they sell the stocks or honey then the tenth penny. The tithe and tenth of all apples, nuts, hops, hemp and pigeons. £12 p. a. to be paid out of the parsonage of Bishopstone at Lady day [25 Mar] and Michaelmas [29 Sep] being the bequest of Mr. Henry Kinnimond [Kinninmod], now prebendary of Bishopstone.[1]

John Rowland, vicar, John Hedges, Tobias Smith, churchwardens, William Kent, John Kent. Henry Keepe, Oliver Hickes.

1.   Kinnimond died in 1678; bequest here presumably meant a gift in his lifetime.

57   13 Jul 1671 (D5/10/1/4)
Rectory [prebend]: Terrier made by John Hedges and Tobias Smith, churchwardens. A parsonage house with a malthouse thereunto belonging, 2 barns, a stable, a carthouse, a little edifice for hogs, a backside adjoining to the highway on E., a garden adjoining to the dwelling house on N. E., a close of meadow adjoining to the dwellinghouse on W., 1a. 3yd. In Shipmead 2a. 3yd. of meadow, Thomas Hull laying on W., Elizabeth Hull wid. on E. In the Down field ? 3a. at Common [...] shooting E. and W., a land of John Tucker on N. In the same field 11 ?yd. of arable shooting N and S., John Rowland on W., Nicholas Horton on E. In the W. field 3a. shooting N. and S., Edward Pigott E., Hinton field W.; 2a. on W. shooting on the Coomb banks; 1a. under Woodway shooting N. and S.; 3a. under Ridgeway shooting E. and W., William West N.; 2a. in Waterslade, Hercules Purton between them; 2a. at White Pits shooting E. and W., Samuel Pressey senior on N.; 2a. shooting against Swindly, Henry Hedges S., John Rowland N.; 2a. shooting on Idstone field, John Horton S., the wid. Taylor N.; 3a. shooting upon Ridgeway Thomas Hull W.; 1a. at Marrill.

7 tenements[1] and 9 yardlands in Bishopstone, viz. 1 tenement with a barn and 1r. of ground in the possession of John Butler, bounded E. the churchyard, S. the fishpond of Christopher Willoughby esq., W. and N. the highway: a tenement

with a barn belonging to Frances Tucker wid. with an orchard and backside adjoining the house bounded E. and S. with the highway, W. with the backside of Thomas Morrant, N. the parsonage backside. 1 yardland belonging to it in the common fields, viz. In the Down field 2 x 3yd. at Broad Close stile,; 1a. in the middle of the same field; 2 x ½a. at Common Shord; ½a. of meadow in the E. field shooting against Middle drove, William Norrice N., Ann Gybbs wid, S.; 1a. shooting against Blackland hedge being a headland to Wool furlong; 1a. at Palmers gate; 1a. at Hither Saunders hedge; ½a. on Idstone field on Norrice's headland, John Kent on S. 1a. on Avenel, Edmund Young S., William Norrice N.; 1a. shooting on Ridgeway on Morrats hedge Elizabeth Hull S.; 1a. headland to Kents piece; 2a. shooting towards Ridgeway, the wid. Harding on both sides; ½a. by Hinton brook; 1a. by the wayside, 1a. shooting on the wayside acre, Edward Pigott N.

A tenement with barn belonging to Robert North alias Harding with a close, c. ½a., shooting upon the brook on W., a close of the wid. Harding N., a close belonging to Thomas [. . .] S.; with 1 yardland in the common fields, viz. In the Down field ½a. in Middle drove on Ladder way, the wid. Gybbs on S., John Spanswick N.; 1yd. or r. at Old Craft shooting N. and S. a land of [. . .] W., Thomas Collins E.; 1yd. of arable land the wid. [. . .] S., the wid. Harding N. In the E. field: ½a. in Sheephouse furlong, the wid. Maton, N., Martin S[. . .] S., 1yd. headland to Wool furlong, the wid. Harding N.; ½a. in Wool furlong, Thomas Collins E., Edward Pigott W.; ½a. in Ireland John Kent W., [. . .] Harwood E.; Arable: ½a. at Ickleton way Oliver Hicks E., John Harwood W.; ½a. at Sidlesdown, John Horton E., wid. Hill W.; 1a. at Sidlesdown William Norris N., Thomas Collins S.; a head a. at Coombe Foot, wid. Spanswick N.; ½a. at Ridgeway, wid. Maton E. Henry Hedges W.

Separate sheet stitched to terrier. ½a. at Taylers headland the wid. Maton W., Stephen Tayler E., ½a. at Sanders hedge John Butler S., Charles Pressey N.; ½a. in Flint furlong, the wid. Young on both sides. A headland ½a. in Flint furlong Henry Greene N., 1yd. [eardd] at Swinley Charles Purton S., Robert Noath N.; 1yd. in the Down field the wid. Gibbs S., wid. Hardinge N.; ½a. at Swindley Henry Hedges N., wid. Spanswick S.; ½a. at Mill John Hedges N., wid. Gibbs S.; ½a. at Helmans hedge Oliver Hicks N., Thomas Collins S.; ½a. at Ridgeway Edmund Young E., wid. Younge W.; ½a. Sanders hedge John Kent N., wid. Younge S.; ½a. at Sanders hedge wid. Gibbs N., wid. Hull S.; ½a. at Sanders hedge Edmund Young N., wid. Hull S.; ½a. in the middle of the field, wid. Gibbs W., Robert Noath E.; ½a. in Cheasted John Kent E., wid. Hull W.; ½a. in Crannell Martin Spanswick S., Charles Pressey N.; ½a. in Cannons Deane Martin Spanswick S., William Norris N.; ½a. at Helmans hedge wid. Gibbs S., wid. Hull N. Commons belonging to the 9 yardlands; 27 rother beasts, 18 horse beasts, 270 sheep. *Separate sheet ends*

A note of all the arable land belonging to Samuel Smyth's yardland: ½a. in Whiteland, John Greene S, Henry Green N.; ½a. at Little mead John Greene E, Henry Greene W.; ½a. at Ickleton way John Greene E., Henry Hedges W.; ½a. at Sidlesdown Henry Keepe N., the wid. Maton S.; ½a. at Sidlesdown Stephen Tayler N., Thomas Collins S.; ½a. above Ridgeway John Greene E., Thomas Collins W.; ½a. above Ridgeway Mr. Rowland E., John Horton W.; ½a. in Flint furlong John Kent E., Martin Spanswick W.; ½a. in Flint furlong John Greene on both sides; ½a., at High bush John Horton N., Martin Spanswick S.; ½a. at High Bush Henry Keepe N., John Greene S.; ½a. above Panstone Martin Spanswick S., John Kent N.; ½a. at Sanders hedge Mr. Rowland S., Thomas Butler N.; a. at Sanders hedge Hercules Purton S., Martin Spanswick N.; ½a. at Sanders hedge John Grene on both sides; ½a. lying between the Green ways Mr. Rowland E., John Horton W.; ½a. between Green ways John Greene both sides; ½a. below Ridgeway John Kent N.; ½a. headland Mr. Rowland S.; ½a. at Helmans hedge Mr. Rowland S., wid. Hull N.; ½a. at Helman's hedge John Greene both sides; ½a. at Nill the wid. Maton N., Oliver Hickes S.; ½a. lying Townsend Edmund Younge E., the wid. Gibbs W.; 1yd. lying on Sidlesdown Henry Keepe W., Mr. Rowland E.; 1yd. lying on Sidlesdown Martin Spanswick E., John Horton W.; ½a. lying on the drove hedge Martin Spanswick S., John Greene N. of meadow [sic]; 1a. at the Middle drove John Spanswick S., John Horton N.; ½a. lying over the Drove hedge John Horton S., William Norris N.; ½a. lying in Vorty furlong Isaac Purton W., William Norris E.; ½a. lying at Blackland hedge the wid. Goddard W., John Greene E., a dwelling house, barn, stable, backside, 2 horse commons, 3 rother beasts commons, 30 sheep commons.

Martin Spanswick's yardland: a dwelling house, barn, stable, cowhouse, the backside, an orchard. The meadow: ½a. lying in Ull furlong, John Harwood E., Samuel Pressey W.; ½a. lying at the Vicarage stile John Kent S., Mr. Rowland N.; ½a. lying in the Sheephouse furlong Robert North N., the wid. Younge S.; a rick barton; 1yd. lying in old Craft, Thomas Collins W., Samuel Pressi E.; 1yd. at Ladder John Kent W., Oliver Hicks E.; ½a. lying in Long Breach Stephen Taylor N., Samuel Pressey S. The arable land: 1yd. at Ladder the wid. Gibbs N., Samuel Pressey S.; ½a. lying in White land, the wid. Norris N., Oliver Hicks S.; ½a. lying at Little mead, the wid. Gibbs W., John Hull E.; ½a. lying at Craft Samuel Pressey N., John Kent S.; ½a. at Helmans hedge the wid. Gibbs N., the wid. Hull S.; ½a. lying by the wid. Goddard's headland, the wid. Gibbs W.; 1 headland lying above Ridgeway, the wid. Gibbs W.; ½a. lying at Sanderses hedge, Henry Hedges S., the wid. Gibbs W.; ½a. at Sanderses hedge Oliver Hicks N., Samuel Smith S.; ½a. lying next to the Greeneyou Samuel Pressey E.; 1a. lying in Crannel Samuel Pressey S., Robert North N.; 1yd. lying on Chestide the wid. Gibbs N., Samuel Pressey S.; ½a. lying in the Farm down William Kent S., Samuel Pressey N.; ½a. lying at the Farm down the wid. Norris N., the wid. Hull S.; ½a. lying at Sanders hedge Thomas Collins N., William Norris S.; ½a. at Idston field, Henry Hedges S., Samuel Smith N.; ½a. at Idston field Samuel Pressey S., John Kent N.; ½a. at High bush Robert North S., Samuel Smith N.; ½a. in Flint furlong Samuel Smith E., Henry Hedges W.; ½a. at Norris his headland John Harwood N., Charles Pressey S.; ½a. at Sanders hedge John Kent S., John Greene N.; ½a. above Ridgeway wid. Gibbs N., John Harwood S.; a headland below Ridgeway Samuel Pressey W.; 1yd. on Sidlesdown Oliver Hicks E., Samuel Smith W.; ½a. at Marwell John Harwood E., Samuel Pressey W.; ½a. at Nill the wid. Gibbs N., the wid. Taylor S.

A note of William Kent's yardland: a dwelling house, barn, stable, backside, orchard. The mead land: ½a. at Sharpland end John Harwood E.; ½a. at White land John Hedges S., Thomas Collins N.; ½a. in Ull furlong, John Kent E.,

Thomas Collins W.; ½a. lying overthwart Ladder way John Kent N., John Green
[...] John Greene S.; a stitch [...] Ladder, John Greene W. The arable land: ½a.
in Vorty furlong Martin Spanswick [...]; [...]a. at Ickleton way John Kent E.,
Thomas Collins W.; ½a. at Sidlesdown John Kent S., Thomas Collins N.; ½a. at
Sidlesdown John Kent W., John Greene E.; ½a. at Ridgeway John Kent E.,
Thomas Collins W.; ½a. at Sanders hedge wid. Goddard N., John Kent S.; ½a. at
Sanders hedge John Kent S., Henry Greene N.; ½a. at Norris his headland John
Kent N., Edmund Young S.; ½a. at Gibbings piece John Kent S., the wid. Goddard
N.; ½a. at Vickerses butts John Kent S., Thomas Collins N.; 1a. at Vickerses butts
John Kent N., Samuel Pressey S.; ½a. at the Green way John Hedges W.; 1yd. at
Short Chester John Kent E., John Greene W.; ½a. at White pitts John Greene S.,
John Wilson N.; ½a. in the middle of the field John Kent W., John Greene E.; ½a.
at Sanderses hedge John Kent N., wid. Harding S.; ½a. in Water slad John Kent
W., John Greene E.; ½a. at Sanders hedge John Kent N., Thomas Collins S.; 2a.
by the Farm field Hercules [Arculus] Purton W., the wid. Hull E.; ½a. at Nill
Martin Spanswick S., John Hedges N.; 1yd. below Ridgeway John Kent on
each side; ½a. at Nill Charles Pressey S., John Kent N.; ½a. at the Upper Hitchings
John Greene S., John Kent N.; a butt in the Combes John Kent E.

Samuel Pressey his land and housing; a dwelling house, barn, stable, cowhouse,
backside, orchard and a close; 3a. of arable above Ickleton way Martin Spanswick
S.; a head a. in the E. field John Tucker S.; a 3yd. [earden] upon Ladder way John
Kent N., Mr. Rowland S.; 3yd. at Ladder way John Hull N., Martin Spanswick
S.; 1yd. at Ladder way Martin Spanswick N., Thomas Collins S.; ½a. at Marwell
Martin Spanswick E., the wid. Tayler W.; ½a. at Marwell William Kent W., the
wid. Maten E.; ½a. at Combe foot William Kent N., Mr. Rowland S.; ½a. in the
Upper hitchings the wid. Gibbs N., wid. Younge S.; ½a. in the Combes John
Greene E., Henry Greene W.; a butt in the Combes John Kent E.; a butt in the
Combes John Harwood E.; ½a. below Ridgeway Mr. Rowland E., Stephen
Tayler W.; ½a. on Ridgeway Martin Spanswick E., Thomas Collins W.; ½a. at
Elcombe John Greene S., Henry Greene N.; headland ½a. above Ridgeway Mr.
Rowland S.; ½a. in the middle of the ? field Henry Greene N., John Greene S.;
½a. more Thomas Collins W., John Greene E.; ½a. at Broad Gap Mr. Rowland [.
..] wid. [...]; ½a. in Flint furlong John Butler S., Henry Hedges N.; ½a. at Short
hedges Henry Greene N., John Greene S.; a 3yd. in the same furlong John Kent
S., John Butler N.; ½a. at Upper Short hedge Henry Greene N., Martin Spanswick
S.; ½a. more the wid. Hull N., John Greene S.; ½a. more at the end of him
Martin Spanswick S., John Harwood N.; ½a. by Martin Spanswick N.; ½a. on
the Downs Henry Greene N., Mr. Rowland S.; ½a. in the Downs John Kent N.,
Martin Spanswick S.; ½a. at the Upper Short hedge John Greene S., Samuel
Kent N.; ½a. at the Downs Charles Purton N.; ½a. at the Downs John Greene S.,
Martin Spanswick N.; ½a. at the 2 short hedges Mr. Rowland S., John Harwood
N.; ½a. more Stephen Tayler N., Martin Spanswick S.; 1yd. in Chested William
Norris S., Martin Spanswick N.; a headland a. at White pitts the wid. Taylor E.;
1a. in Crannell Henry Hedges S., Martin Spanswick N.; ½a. in Crannell Charles
Pressey S., John Greene N.; ½a. in the bottom of the field Mr. Rowland E.; ½a.
at Sanders hedge John Greene on each side; ½a. at Sanders hedge Martin
Spanswick E., John Greene W.; ½a. at Water Slad Charles Purten E., Martin

Spanswick W.; ½a. on Ridgeway Mr. Rowland E., Martin Spanswick W.; ½a. on
Ridgeway John Greene W., Charles Pressey E.; ½a. at Ridgeway John Harwood
S., Robert Noath N.; ½a. at Helmans hedge Martin Spanswick S., John Greene
N.; ½a. in Shillands Henry Greene W., Mr. Rowland E.; ½a. in Nill John Greene
N., and S. Meadow: 2a. at Marwell John Kent E., John Butler W.; ½a. at Padpit
John Greene E., Henry Hedges W.; 1yd. in Helands Martin Spanswick on each
side; ½a. in Ull furlong John Horton W., wid. Maten E.; ½a. in Ull furlong
Martin Spanswick E., William Norris W.; ½a. in Black lands hedge John Greene
E., Edmund Younge W.; ½a. in Sheephouse furlong William Norris N., John
Hull S.; ½yd. Martin Spanswick N., wid. Maten S.; ½a. in Long breach Martin
Spanswick on each side; 1yd. in Old Craft Martin Spanswick W., Thomas Collins
E.; 1yd. at Ladder John Kent E., Thomas Morrant W.; ½yd. at Ladder the wid.
Hardinge E., John Harwood W.; ½a. at Horton's bush Mr. Rowland S., John
Kent N.

John Greene's land and housing; a dwelling house, barn, backside and orchard;
3yd. upon Ladder way Henry Greene N., John Hull S.; ½a. in the Drove Henry
Greene N., Samuel Smith S.; ½a. in Vorty furlong Martin Spanswick E., John
Kent W.; ½a. in Little mead Samuel Smith W., Martin Spanswick E.; ½a. overthirte
Ickleton way wid. Hull E., John Kent W.; ½a. next Idston field Samuel Smith W.;
½a. in the Upper Hitchings William Kent N., wid. Hill S.; ½a. in the Combes
Samuel Pressey W., Oliver Hicks E.; a butt in the Combes, a linch on each side;
½a. on Sidlesdown, the wid. Younge S., John Kent N.; ½a. on Sidlesdown John
Hull E., William Kent W.; a butt upon the Combe bank between 2 linches; ½a.
in Elcombe, John Kent S., Samuel Pressey N.; 3 x ½a. above Ridgeway in the
bottom of the field, Samuel Pressey N., John Horton S.; ½a. next Idston field
Samuel Smith W.; ½a. in the middle of the field, Henry Greene E., Charles
Pressey W.; ½a. at Sanderses hedge John Kent N., wid. Hull S.; ½a. at Sanders
hedge Robert Noath N., wid. Gibbs S.; ½a. at Sanders hedge John Hedges N.,
Martin Spanswick S.; 2 x ½a. in Flint furlong wid. Hull W., wid. Younge E.,
Samuel Smith between them; ½a. in the Broad furlong Robert Noath S., John
Kent N.; ½a. at High bush William Norris S., Samuel Smith N.; 3yd. at Vicarses
Butts Samuel Pressey N., Henry Greene S.; 1yd. in the same furlong Henry
Greene S.; ½a. in the same furlong Samuel Pressey N., wid. Hull S.; ½a. shooting
upon the Downs the wid. Hull N., John Kent S.; 1yd. at the Short hedge Martin
Spanswick N., wid. ... [S.]; ½a. in Cannons Dean Samuel Pressey N., John Kent
S.; 1yd. in Short Cheasted John Kent E., Martin Spanswick W.; ½a. at White Pits
William Kent N., the wid. Hull S.; 1yd. in Long Cheasted Robert Greene S.,
John Harwood N.; ½a. in the bottom of the field William Kent W., Martin
Spanswick E.; ½a. at the Crannell Thomas Collins N., Samuel Pressey S.; 2 x ½a.
at Broad gap the wid. Goddard N., John Kent S., Samuel Pressey between; ½a. in
Water slad Henry Greene E., Martin Spanswick W.; ½a. in the same furlong
Samuel Pressey E., William Kent W.; ½a. at Sanders hedge the wid. Young S.,
William Norris N.; 2 x ½a. at Sanders hedge the wid. Hull S., Thomas Collins
N., Samuel Smith between; 2 x ½a. betwixt the Green ways Henry Greene W.,
Martin Spanswick E., Samuel Smith between; ½a. at Ridgeway the wid. Goddard
W., Samuel Pressi E.; 2 x ½a. at Helman hedge the wid. Hull S., wid. Goddard
N., Samuel Smith between; a head a. at Helmans hedge Samuel Pressey S.; 2 x

½a. at Nill Henry Greene N., wid. Hull S., Samuel Pressey between. Meadow: ½a. at Ladder the wid. Gibbs E., William Norris W.; ½yd. at Ladder William Kent E., Henry Greene W.; ½a. overthirt Ladder way William Kent N., wid. Hull S.; ½a. at Ladder way William Kent N., wid. Hull S.; 1a. at Blackland hedge wid. Young E., Samuel Pressey W.; 1a. at Whiteland Samuel Smith N., Henry Hedges S.; a 3yd [earden] at Marwell Henry Greene E., Samuel Smith W.; 1a. at Padpit Samuel Pressey W., the wid. Hull E.; a close called Mannington the value of a yd. of ground.

Tobias Smith, John Hedges, churchwardens.

An addition to the terrier presented by John Rowland, vicar, Edward Pigott, Robert Harding and the two churchwardens present that the tithes of those 9 yardlands belonging to the prebend were given to the vicar of Bishopstone and his successors by Dr. John Barnston, prebend of Bishopstone,[2] and were confirmed by the present prebend, Mr. Henry Kinninmond, who added to this endowment £12 p. a. to be paid to the vicar and his successors by the fee farmer of the prebendary and they have heard that Mr. Henry Kinninmond heartily desires that his successors in the prebend would continue this. John Saintebarbe, notary public.

1. In fact 8 tenements are described; possibly the first two are counted as one.
2. Barnston was prebendary 1601–45.

BISHOPSTONE (South Wilts) rectory

58 1677 (D1/24/17/1)

Taken out of the terriers[1] in the Bishop's registry of 1588 and 1605 compared with the present occupancy. A parsonage and vicarage in one rector. 2 houses adjoining near the wall end of another, 3 barns, a dove house, 2 stables, a pigsty to fatten pigs adjoining the river set up by the present rector, 2 gardens, and an orchard with a small hop yard on the S., of the parsonage house. There is now no close of pasture of c. ½a. on the S. side of the parsonage house mentioned in the terrier of 1605.

Arable lands as follows: In Flamreston or Flamston: In W. field a close of c. 2a. tenant measure adjoining the highway one of which was changed for 1a. in Goddards close; 1a. in Cleyfield adjoining Robert Lanham's close now held by Thomas King; 1a. headland in the middle of the same field bounding the farmer's butts which is headland to that shooting on Stoakefield; ½a. between the farmland and Christopher Selwood's land now held by Thomas King; 1a. by the greenway to the down called Portway, those last 3 half a. running N. and S.; 1a. above Toplinch adjoining Robert Lanham now held by John Lanham shooting on Stoakfield lying E. and W.; another a. in the same field lying E. and W., William now wid. Pickland's land N. and the farmer's S.; another a. on the hill top next to the farmer's head ½a. shooting on Stoakfield lying E. and W.

In the N. field 6½a. as follows: 1a. in the nether bottom lying E. and W., the farm land on the N. and Christopher Selwood now Thomas King S.; 1a. in Ashden bush furlong, between the farm land and Robert now John Lanham running N. and S.; 1a. in the middle of the upper bottom between Robert now John Lanham and the farmer's land, running E. and W., 1a. in Lidland furlong between William now wid. Pickland and William Harwood now Richard Griffin, running N. and S.; 1a. running E. and W. between 1½a. held by Thomas Ovington, now James Willis, and the farm land; ½a. in the same furlong running E. and W. next to the farm land; ½a. in the Middle furlong on the hill top between the farm land and the land then held by Thomas Ovington, now James Willis, running E. and W.

In the Middle field 6½a. bounded as follows: 1a. below the way shooting towards the water running along Nettenhedge; 1a. shooting on the highway bounded by 1a. of Christopher Selwood now Thomas King E. and a stitch of land once held by Thomas Ovington now Francis Heighmor on the W.; 1a. in Stanch Chester bounded W. with John Shory's land and wid. now William Goddard E., running N. and S.; 1a. on the hill top running E. and W., a stitch of William now wid. Pickland S. and a stitch of wid. Baylye now Phil. Blake N.; 1a. running along the Cowway which lies on N. bounded by ½a. of Thomas Selwood S.; 1a. on the hill top, 1a. of William now wid. Pickland S. and 3 x ½a. of wid. now William Goddard on the N. running E. and W.; ½a. near the upper end of the field, William now wid. Pickland W. and wid. now William Goddard E. running N. and S. Common of pasture for 50 sheep, 4 rother beasts, 2 runners, 2 horses, all to common and feed as the tenants do.

Arable in Falderston or Faulston: In the demesne lands in Homefield in Stony furlong the 2a. of tenant measure running E. and W. so expressed in the terrier of 1605. This land is lately divided in tenants' hands, the rector has not, nor knows how to find them; 7a. in the Middle field running E. and W. of tenant measure in the rector's possession; in the same field 8½a. running N. and S. next to Throope without any common for sheep, beast or horse as far as the rector knows. Bishopstone contains 6 hamlets: Bishopstone Netton, Flamston [Flamerston], Croucheston [Crowston], Faulston and Throope. All tithes of corn and hay in kind, also of wool and lambs and all privy tithes in kind and Easter book.

R[anulph] Caldecott, rector, Geo. Button, John Spearinge, churchwardens.

1.   Sadly these early terriers are no longer extant.

BISHOPSTROW rectory

59   20 Apr 1631 (D/24/18/1)
9a. arable as follows: in the field next to Burton or Boreham 4½a. shooting E. and W. of which 2a. lie at the S. end under a great linch, only 1a. above the linch, between it and the highway having S. a ditch cast up at the end of the 2a. dividing it from Boreham field, N. 1a. belonging to a tenement now held by William Stokes of Bishopstrow; in the same field on the N. of the Bourne [Boren] 3 x ½a. together having S. 2a. belonging to a tenement lately held by William Shergell decd. in the same field 1a. not far from Lock furlongs, 1a. S. belonging to William Gifford of Boreham esq., N. 1a. belonging to a tenement

held by John Stokes of Bishopstrow. In the field on the hill 1a. called Amon acre shooting E. and W., having E. a green linchet dividing it from 2a. of Mr. William Gifford adjoining the farm field, and S. 1a. belonging to the tenement held by John Stokes. In the Middle field on the S. of the hill in the bottom among the picked lands is 1½a. shooting E. and W with 1a. S. belonging to a tenement held by Thomas Hinton of Bishopstrow, and on the other side 1a. of Mr. William Gifford, and the ½a. lies W. of Mr. Gifford's a. and is commonly called a butt, it shoots N. and S.; 2a. in the same field by Harpeway shooting N. and S., at the N. end runs the Bourne in wintertime. One of these has on W. 1a. belonging to a tenement held by wid. Bayly of Boreham and on E. 1a. belonging to a tenement held by John Stokes. The other has the same a. of John Stokes on W. and 1a. of William stokes on E. E. of the parsonage house a garden and meadow, c. 2a., S. the churchyard, W. 2 gardens, a barn and orchard, N. a backside and garden. A lammas ground called Samborne meadow, c. 2a., out of the parish, bounding the N. W. end of Henfords marsh, S. W. a little ground belonging to the farmer of Bishopstrow, John Temple.

The tithes of 2 grounds on the N. side of Samborne meadow, now held by Thomas Aldredge of Warminster, which lie in the hanging of a hill, a little highway N.; Great Damasks a close of arable near Warminster belonging to the farmer, but now held by Mrs. Ludlow [Ludlough] of Warminster; a ground bounding the S. W. side of Sutton common now held by Stephen Blake of Warminster, but belonging to the farm; 2a. at Moote hill bounded by 2 linchets having 2a. N. and 2a. S. now held by John Eldets of Moote hill; all meadow and such arable as belongs to Bishopstrow mill. For the tithes of toll corn 6s. 8d. p. a. at Easter. The tithes of all copses, pastures, arable lands and meadows called Hilwood adjoining Warminster heath belonging to the farmer of Bishopstrow; the moor and all the grounds at Leechcraft belonging to the farmer; Mr. Gifford's 4 grounds called the Berries, with the tithes of 2 meadows called Longclose and Culver close bounding on the water side N. and S. held by Mr. William Gifford; a little ground called Wynballs by the Berries on the W. of Mr. Francis Goodroofes new house; all grounds in Pit Meate belonging to the farm, or any tenement in the parish with the tithes of Raye Meate. The tithes of all corn, wool, lambs, hay, cow white, calves, orchards, gardens, and all other tithes. Mortuaries. Feeding for 15 sheep in the field. The tithes of 4a. in Spot Meate held by wid. Bayly but Mr. Gifford's.

Walter Bisse clerk, Thomas Hinton, Thomas Longely [X], churchwardens, John Temple, Christopher ?Greene.[1]

1. Christopher Greene signed the bishops transcript as churchwarden in 1672

60 1705 (D1/24/18/2)

In the field next Boreham field 2a. shooting E. and W. under the linch Mr. Hewlett's a. S., William Player's a. N. On the other side of the Bourn 1½a. shooting E. and W. bounded S. 2a of Mr. Gifford's, N. 1a. of Mr. Gifford; 1a. in the same furlong bounded S. 1a. of Mr. Gifford, N 1a. William Stoakes. In the next field nothing. In Almond land 1a. shooting E. and W. bounded N. Mr. Gifford's la., S. William Stoakes's a. In the Goar lands ½a. on the outside next

Slade furlong shooting almost N. and S. Mr. Gifford's a. between this ½a. and
another a. of the glebe. Christopher Hinton's a. on E. side of the a. 2a. shooting
to the highway and the Bourn ditch one bounded W. Mr. Hewlett's a., E. William
Stoak's a.; the other bounded on W. by the same a. of William Stoak and on E. by
William Player's a. W. 1 close of pasture 14a. at Henfords [Henfeild's] Marsh next
bounded S. closes of Mr. Temple, N. Mr. French. House, orchard and backside 7
beast leazes and 15 sheep leazes in the commons.

George Straight, rector, William Pryor, William Stokes, churchwardens

61   30 Jul 1783 (D1/24/18/3)
The parsonage is built, part with stone part with brick and part with lath and
plaster. It is tiled and thatched. 2 parlours on the ground floor, one floored with
oak, the other with deal, both stuccoed chair high, the other part papered and
ceiled. A pantry floored with brick, white washed walls and ceiled. A small cellar
under the staircase neither floored or ceiled. A brewhouse, the bottom part
brick part of stone, not ceiled. On the first floor 5 rooms, with a small closet 2
floored with oak, 2 and the closet with deal, one with aspen boards, all papered
and ceiled. 2 garrets, floored with elm, part papered, part whitewashed, ceiled.
Outhouses; a stable with room for 4 horses, with a small barn under the same
roof, the entrance to both at the same door, built with stone from the ground to
c. 2 ft. high, the remainder elm boards covered with thatch, 2 or 3 very small
places for ashes and other conveniences. 1 convenient outhouse covered with
tile, floored part with oak part with elm, ceiled.

The kitchen garden on the other side of the water to the house measures 50
lugs, part fenced with a live thorn hedge the remainder with boards and pales,
with a ditch the greatest part around it. The pleasure garden measures c. 30 lugs,
S. fenced by a live thorn hedge, N. and E. by the water, W. by the house. The
stable garden formerly called the yard measures nearly 40 lugs, including stable
and barn, fenced S. by a live elder hedge, N. by the water, W. by the barn stable
and some live hedge with a few rails and boards, E. by the house. A little meadow,
adjoining the kitchen garden on the other side the water, measures c. 78 lugs,
fenced W. and S. by the water, N. by the pales, E. by pales and a ditch.

A small court to the entrance of the house near 2 lugs, fenced part with a
wall, part with pales. The church yard, including the church, measures c. 80 lugs,
part fenced with a live thorn hedge and a ditch, part with rails and a small part
with a stone wall.

2a. of water meadow at Hillwood, fenced all round with a live hedge, E. and
W. sides belong to the rectory; bounded W. Mr. John Buckler, N. and S. Mr. John
Maskelyne, E. the road E.

Arable in Bishopstrow field: 2a. bounded Boreham field W, Mr. Buckler's
head a. E., a linchet S., Mrs. Temple N. 1½a. bounded Boreham field W., Mr.
Buckler E. and S., Mrs. Temple N. 1a. in the field next to Boreham, bounded
Boreham field W., Mr. Mondy's, commonly called Burrows N., Mr. Buckler S.
and E. In the Middle field no land. In the second Middle field 2a. bounded by
the bourne ditch N., Mrs. Temple E., Mr. Mondy's commonly called Burrows
W., by the old road S. ½a. called Goreland or Three cornered land, bounded Mr.
Buckler E., Mr. Hinton, Burrows, Mr. Buckler and Mr. Bayly W., Mr. Bayly N.,

to S. reduced to a point. 1a. bounded Mr. Buckler W., Mr. Hinton E., Mr. Bayly N. and S. On the other side the Hill called Harmon's land 1a. bounded Middleton field E., Mr. Buckler N., Mr. Mondy's called Burrows S., Mrs. Temple W.

The kitchen garden there are c. 50 elms, 5 out of 7 very small, 6 or 7 very small ash trees, c. 20 withys. In the little meadow adjoing this kitchen garden there are 20 elms, almost all very small, 2 pollard ash trees and 2 others very small. In the churchyard 14 elms, most very small. The largest elm of the premises does not measure more than 1 foot.

12 beast leaze, 15 sheep leaze. No pensions augmentations gifts or bequests made to this church or minister. The rector pays to the king a pension of 40s. p. a.

The church furniture consists of a mahogany table with a desk blue broad cloth, 1 white linen cloth, and 1 napkin, 1 flagon, c. 3 pints, 1 small cup, 1 very small thin plate, all of silver without either weight or inscription on them. There is only a bible, 2 common prayer books, 1 for the minister, 1 for the clerk. No lands or money in stock for the repair of the church or utensils. The church and steeple are repaired by the church rates. The estates of the parish are charged with the expense of the church yard fence unless it is that part which separates the churchyard from the rector's garden, which the rector provides for. The clerk's wages are paid by the church rates. The clerk is appointed by the rector.

Thomas Fisher, rector, Richard Hooper, Richard Sainsbury, churchwardens.

BLUNSDON ST. ANDREW rectory

62   29 Oct 1671 (D1/24/19/1)
Presented to the bishop's registry until a more perfect terrier can be found out. No house or land besides the churchyard. All tithes, offerings and other dues. The incumbent is allowed by the lord of the manor a house near the church without rent.

Henry Green, rector, Seth Harding, Giles Cleeve, churchwardens, William Mackley, John Mackley.

Endorsement: Chancery. Joseph Bell, complainant. Edward Read, Edward Church and Thomas Ayres, defendants. Shown to Thomas Pratt, witness, 1 Oct 1744.

63   18 Mar 1678 (D1/24/19/2)
As *62.* Thomas Browne A. M. curate, Seth Harding churchwarden, Gyles Cleeve, John Mackley. *Endorsement as 62.*

64   1704 (D1/24/19/3)
No glebe except the churchyard. The rector receives for his tithes each year £50 from Francis Leck esq., £8 from Mr. Edward Godringe or his tenants each year and £7 from Richard Harding.

Joseph Pullen, rector, Richard Harding, churchwarden.

BOSCOMBE rectory

65   30 Oct 1671 (D1/24/20/1)
24a. ploughed ground. 1½a. meadow and pasture, 60 sheep leaze, 2 cow leaze, 2 horse leaze, a garden.
John Hussey, Robert Eyres, churchwardens.

66   1705 (D1/24/20/2)
1a. bounding upon Church hill. 2a. bounded with land of Stephen Childs and Richard Ivey. 1a. bounded on both sides by land of Mr. Kent. 1a. bounded with Mrs. Harris and heads the furlong. 1a. between Mrs. Harris and Robert Freemantle. 2a. one by Mrs. Harris and one by Mr. Kent. 2a. bounded with Mrs. Harris and Stephen Child. 2a. bounded on each side by Mr. Kent. 2a. on the other side of the great linch bounded with Mrs. Harris. 2a. bounded with Mr. Kent and Stephen Childs. 1a. bounded with Mr. Kent and Mrs. Harris. 2a. bounded with Richard Ivey and Stephen Child. 3a. bounding on Salisbury way, Mrs. Harris on one side Robert Freemantle on the other. Meadow ground or Inground, c. 2a. bounded by Mr. Kent lying by the parsonage house.
Robert Wat, clerk, Thomas Penny, churchwarden.

BOX vicarage

67   Jun 1619 (D1/24/21/1)
Presentment of a terrier at the bishop's visitation held at Devizes. The vicarage house[1] with dove house[2] at the end of the same adjoining with the outhouses backhouses orchard gardens and churchyard. All the offerings and tithes of wool, lambs, cow white, coppices, wood, groves. Tithe of underwood and hedgerow, which are sold. All small tithes belonging to the rectory and hay tithes due from the glebe of the rectory due at cutting time. Composition for corn and grain as **69** described as 'cleane sweete and marchauntable[3]'.
Peter Webb, Clement Inglande [X], John Butler [X], Robert Butchar [X], all churchwardens, William Cottle [X], John Cottle [X], sidesmen.

1.   Described as of three bays in **68**.
2.   Described as adjoining the south end of the vicarage house in **68**.
3.   i. e. marketable.

68   24 Sep 1672 (D1/24/21/2)
*As **69** with amendments in footnotes to **67**.* William Grffry senior [X], John Wills, churchwardens.

69   11 Jan 1678 (D1/24/21/3)
The vicarage house with the outlets gardens and orchard. The use of 2 rooms called the church chambers over the N aisle of the church. A house at the SE side of the churchyard of 1 bay. A stable of 1 bay. The churchyard, the bounds and gates whereof are to be maintained by the parish.[1]

A right of commons throughout the parish. 10th cock of hay and of french grass called sainfoin [St Faen], or the seed of it. 3d. at Lammas [1Aug] for the cow white of every cow fed in the parish. 9d. at lammas for every calf fallen in the parish. If sold, tenth of the money; if killed by the owner 1 shoulder. ½d. for every calf weaned; if sold before they come to be milked or yoked tenth of the price. The tenth weight or tenth lb. or tenth of the locks of wool of all sheep kept in the parish. If sold before shearing for every sheep ¼d. for every month they have been kept within the parish paid at Ladyday [25 Mar], and so for all sheep taken in as agistments. The tenth, or if no more, the seventh lamb to be paid on St Marks day [25 Apr] for unprofitable cattle the tenth penny rent of their feeding. The tenth or seventh of all pigs. For every hen 1 egg for the cock 2 to be paid at Easter. The tithe of apples, pears and all other fruit. The tenth a. or tenth p. of all coppice woods. Of all hedgerows that are sold the tenth of the money. The tenth of all hedgerows reserved by the owner to his own use if they are above 1p. broad. The Easter offering of every communicant 2d. and for every garden 1d. For Pinchen's mill 5s. For Parker's mill[2] 5s. For Bollins mill[3] 1s. 4d. all to be paid at Our Lady day.

By a certain composition[4] between the monks of Farleigh, anciently the impropriator, and the vicar out of the parsonage the vicar is to be paid each year: 5 qtrs. of wheat, 5 qtrs. of barley, 2 qtrs. of oats, 3 qtrs. of dredge or misceline, viz of barley and oats. Since no misceline is now sowed in the parish the same is paid in 12 bushells of barley and 12 bushells of oats. The said 15 qtrs. to be paid in kind or in so much money as the grain yields in neighbouring markets as the impropriator and vicar can agree.

Jacob Filkes, vicar, William Pinchen, John Harding, churchwardens.

1   28 lime trees and no other trees in the churchyard in **70**.
2. Parker's alias Crooks mill in **70**. Drewett's mill in **71**.
3. Bollins mill destroyed and the payment ceased by in **71**.
4. This document described as dated 1227 and being in the Dean and Chapter archives in the cathedral in **71**.

70   23 Dec. 1704 (D1/24/21/4)
*As **69** with amendment in footnotes.* John Phillipps, vicar, John Rawlings, William Harding, churchwardens, Thomas Eyre gent., Samuel Webb gent., Thomas Bayly, Clement Harding, John Baylay, inhabitants of Box.

71   30 Jul 1783 (D1/24/21/5)
The vicarage house, 2 parlours, a kitchen, 3 pantries with bedchambers and garretts above. A brewhouse adjoining. A stable yard with stable, coach house, granary, coal house and 2 woodhouses. A walled garden *c.* 1a. A house on SE side of the churchyard with coal house and woodhouse. All buildings of stone and tiled and in good repair.

*The remainder of the terrier is as **69** with amendments in footnotes, apart from the fact that no details of tithes are given there other than that all tithes except corn and grain belong to the vicarage, and offering of 1d. from gardens is omitted.* Samuel Webb, vicar; William Brown, Stephen Bridges, churchwardens;

Humphrey Beak, Robert Reynolds, William Cottle, William Gibbons, Edward Lee, George Mullins.

A separate document signed by the same witnesses attached to the terrier lists the church furniture: A communion table and cloth of superfine cloth with silk fringe. Linen cloth and napkins used only when the sacrament is administered. 1 flagon, 1 chalice, 2 salvers, all of silver, each with the inscription, 'This plate was given to the parish of Box by Rd. Musgrave of Haselbury esq., and Dame Rachel Speke, his wife, who was the daughter of Sir William Windham, of Orchard Windham in the County of Somersett, Kt. and Barrt. An. Dom. 1707'. Pulpit cloth and cushion and moveable cloths for the minister's and clerk's reading desks, all of superfine cloth with silk fringe and 2 surplices. The church, vestry room and churchyard fence are to be maintained by the parish. The chancel and E end of the N aisle are repaired by the impropriator. The clerk is appointed by the vicar and his customary dues are paid by every householder in the parish at Easter, besides fees for marriages, funerals, etc.

BOYTON rectory

72   5 May 1588 (D1/24/22/1)
Note of glebe exhibited by Christopher Hinton and Robert Symmes, churchwardens. About the parsonage house *c.* ½a. enclosed ground. 1a. in the tenant's meadow in lying length S. and N. from the corn field to the river between the ground of John Smith W. and Richard Gibbes E. Arable: 16a. in the fields of Edmund Lambert esq., of which 3a. lie in Chatwell close N. and S., the linch W. and the hedge E.; 2a. in the Ovinger furlong lying E. and W. shooting on the Cleve hedge; 3a. [. . .] in the Ovinger bottom between the linches; above the Cleve 3a. E. and W. from the highway to the Cleve, and 1a. more lying S. and N. the mill W. and Mr. Lambert E.; 2a. at the fields end; 1a. at the end of the Middle furlong; 13½a. in the tenant's field of which 1a. lies at the lane end lying S. and N. from the way to the meadow; 2 x ½a. in the Marsh furlong butting on the meadow between the land of John Moodie E. and George Lacocke W.; 3 x ½a. picked land in Lancharde lying N. and S. between the land of George Lacocke E. and Richard Gibbes W.; ½a. in Staple furlong lying E. and W. between the land of John Modie M. and George Lacocke S.; ½a. at the towns end, the land of Tristram Moodie E. and John Moodie W.; a head ½a. athwart Holcomes furlong, the land of John Smith W.; ½a. in Claie lands lying N. and S. between the land of Robert Symes W. and George Lacocke E. ½a. in White lands furlong lying N. and S. having Sherrington field E. and Richard Gibbes W.; ½a. in the bottom between Sherrington field E. and Tristram Moody W.; ½a. in the same furlong between the land of wid. Harris W. and Tristram Modie E.; ½a. in Borrowe furlong lying E. and W between the land of wid. Harvie N. and Ric. Gibbes S.; ½a. at the Ashe furlong having the linch N. and John Smith S.; 1a. N. the head of the bottom between the 2 Cleves; ½a. at the lower end of the bottom having the land of George Lacocke N. and Will Modye S.; ½a. in the furlong on the S. of the White way between the land of John Modie N. and Tristram Moodye S.; 1a. in lying length from the White way to the hedge having the linch W. and John

Smith E.; 1½a. under the great linch above Mr. Lambert's house having the land of Robert Smithe N.; ½a. shooting on the E. hedge between the great linches; 3 x ½a. in Deadman having a linch S. and wid. Harvie N. All tithes accustomed to be paid. There is ground in Somerset belonging to the parsonage but what none in our parish know.

73   30 Jul 1609 (D1/24/22/2)
Terrier made by the view of Tristram Moody and John Hellier, churchwardens. Edward Wacombe, sidesman, John Henton senior of Corton, Robert Tucker of Rodden in Somerset, yet of the parish of Boyton, and William Mervin, parson.

A dwelling house with barn, orchard and garden all standing in a close and measuring 1½a. In the common meadow 1a. shooting N. and S. bounded E. 1½a. of Cicely Gibs wid.

In the common field 1a. of arable in Marsh furlong immediately without the hedge of the close by the highway. ½a. in the last furlong on W. side of ½a. of Simon Poticary. ½a in the last furlong on W. side of ½a. of Anthony Raishwoode. 1½a. in the last furlong shooting N. and S. ½a. in Townesdende furlong on W. side of 1a. of Tristram Moody. ½a. in Staple furlong on side of ½a. of Simon Poticary. ½a. in Clayland on W. side of ½a. of Simon Poticary. ½a. lying thwart a bottom, being headland to Clayland and Staple furlong. 1½a. in White land furlong on S. side of ½a. of Simon Poticary. 1½a. in Horsecombe bottom next to Sherrington field. ½a. in Horsecombe bottom on W. side of ½a. of Tristram Moody, which ½a. was admitted by Thomas Knapp, sometimes receiving the fruits of the parsonage under Sir. John Knight, farmer of the parsonage under Paul French[1] then incumbent by way of exchange for ½a. in Horsecombe furlong belonging to John Moody decd.; these being 2a. between these 2 x ½a., which exchange was made by consent of Edmund Lambert esq., patron and Thomas Knap and John Moody. 1½a. on Borrow hill on W. side of ½a. of Anthony Raishwoode which is a headland at N. end of Rowlande furlong. ½a. in Little Down furlong on N. side of ½a. of Simon Poticarie. 1a. at upper end of Holecombe bottom. ½a. in Holecombe bottom on S. side of ½a. of Simon Poticary. ½a. in Pitman's linch on N. side of ½a. of Tristram Moody. 1½a. in Deadmans furlong on N. side of ½a. of Simon Poticary. 1½a. running E. and W. against Mr. Lambert's hedge between 2 x ½a. of Tristram Moody. 1½a. under Great linch on S. side of 1½a. of Edmund Wacombe. 1a. in Cuny furlong on W. side of ½a. of Richard Poticary. Arable land in the Farm field: 3a. shooting S. and N. upon the W. land the W. side of which at Nead being the headland to the furlong shooting on Chapel Stile. 2a. in Cuniger field on E. side of ½a. of Anthony Raishwood. 3a. in the bottom shooting on Gespar hedge bounded W. a great linch. 2a. on S. Cleeve on W. side of a piece of 3a. 1a. on S. Cleeve. N. end of which is a headland to the Picked furlong. 1a. running E. and W. on S. side of 1½a. of Christopher Poticary of Stockton, clothier. 1a. under new broke land hedge being headland to a piece of 18a. 2a. running almost E. and W. on S. side of the last 18a. 1a. at W. end of the last 2a. having linches on both sides.

Without the parish are these particulars: There is a place commonly called Rodden in Somerset in the N. E. end of Frome Selwood from Walbridge which is over Frome water extending in length up to Corsley and to the top of Holman hill or to the Shire Stone where in times past were some six or seven householders but are of late increased to a far greater number. Herein there was sometimes a chapel of St. Blaise [Blaze] appropriate then to divine service but now turned and at this instant employed to profane use. Notwithstanding there are yet belonging to the principal and mother church and parsonage of Boyton: A chapel wholly standing and some part of a churchyard on S. side of the chapel but the limits thereof we cannot yet certainly find. A meadow on N. side of chapel; between these lies Rodden farm with a court garden adjoining and a leaze or pasture, formerly arable. On N. side of the leaze lies a meadow of 4a. running E. and W. and divided from the leaze by a hedge and ditch.

At the W. end of the meadow is a coppice of 3½a. divided only by a hedge without ditch, having at present in it a hedge or some suchlike partition. On N. side of the coppice at a distance of c. 2a. in breadth is another coppice of 2½a. A certain portion of the tithes of a house in the town of Frome occupied by Walter Barnes. Certain a. in the W. field of Frome appertain to this house yet are proper parcels of Rodden.

William Mervin, parson, John Henton, Tristram Moody, John Helliar, Walter Sly, John Smith, Robert Tucker.

1. Rector between 1565-1600.

74   1671 (D1/24/22/3)

A dwelling house with barn, stable adj., a carthouse, with a hog sty, a garden, orchard in all c. 1a. 16a. of arable in the farm fields of Thomas Lambert esq., viz. in Chatell field 3a. lying N. and S. adj. the close called Eight acres in the field called the Bottome; 3a. in the Cunnygar field; 2a., upon the Cleaves; 3a., in the corner; 1a. bounded with linchets on each side; 1a. in the piece beyond Warminster way lying under the hedge; 2a. in the same piece at the field end; 1a. beyond the sheephouse toward the field end.

In the common meadow 2a. in Halfacre furlong; 1½a. called Picked piece bounded with linchets on both sides; ½a. in the piece called Half an Acre lying in Whiteland; 2 x ½a. lying in Hoscombs Lynchetts; ½a. upon the Burrough Hill; ½a. upon Little Down; 1a. up the upper end of the bottom; 1a. at the lower end of the same; 1½a. in Deadman; 1a. next to Greenlynch; ½a. under Great-Lynch lying in Courtfield; ½a. called the Picked half lying in the same field.

Great and small tithes of corn, hay, wool, lamb and wood in Boyton and Corton which are all paid in kind, except for the tithes of grounds called the Chreight estimated at £30 p. a. according to an ancient composition paid at 4s. p. a. and for the fulling mill of Boyton 3s. 4d.

Thos. Lambert rector, John Moodie, Thomas Lacocke, churchwardens.

BRADFORD ON AVON vicarage

75   19 Oct 1608 (D1/24/23/1)

A mansion and dwelling house with gardens, orchards and other grounds, c. 2a., the churchyard E. and Barton orchard W. A little close, c. 1a., in the churchyard

[litton] reaching from the church gate to the garden.
    Thomas Read vicar, John Blanchard, Peter Godbee.

76   20 Dec 1704 (D1/24/23/2)
A mansion house where the vicar is resident, a stable or outhouse. A house
where the clerk lives. A house where the sexton lives. A house where one Cooper
lives. All these are built on the churchyard or glebe. A parcel of meadow or
pasture, *c.* 2a., now converted into a public garden with a house built on it. 3
other gardens. All other dues usually belonging to the vicarage.
    Thomas Lewis, vicar, John Shewell, Thomas Cater, churchwardens.

BRADFORD ON AVON: Holt rectory and vicarage

77   1609 (D1/24/23/3)
Parsonage: 2 little cottages, a little orchard, a little garden and a little close of
pasture, *c.* 1½a. 2a. in N. field. Tithe corn, hay, and lamb, and a barn. Vicarage: a
house for the minister, a garden and a little parrock with the churchyard, a
backside between the parson and the vicar. Tithe wool, calves, cow white, and all
kinds of fruit, all tithe wood, with all privy tithes.
    Thomas Davie curate, Richard Cheppenham, Robert Lawrance,
churchwardens, John Errle, Luke Steevenes; with the consent of Edward Longe
parson, and Thomas Read vicar. *Names in the same hand*

78   19 Dec 1704 (D1/24/23/4)
Glebe land and due pertaining to the bishop. 12 lugs of meadow called the
Paddock on E. side of the chapel, adjoining the chapel yard. 8 lugs in part of the
parsonage barton on N.W. side of the chapel adjoining the chapel yard.
    William Skammell curate, John Earle chapelwarden, Jonathan Godwin.

BRADFORD ON AVON: Winsley chapelry

79   1608 (D1/24/23/5)
A house with a garden of *c.* 1 lug of ground.
    Thomas Read; Bartholemew Tudgue, John Raynold, churchwardens.
Churchwardens' names in the same hand.

80   15 Apr 1678 (D1/24/23/6)
Terrier of tithes belonging to the curate. A little house with garden adjoining the
churchyard. Small tithes of coppice wood, pigs, wool, cow white, calves, apples,
hops, gardens, Easter dues. 2 mill thorowes. All which tithes do no exceed £10 p. a.
    William Kiftill, minister, Charles Bayly, Richard Wilshere, churchwardens.

81   21 Dec 1704 (D1/24/23/7)
A house of 2 bays by the churchyard and a garden of *c.* 6 lugs adjoining. The
churchyard bounds to be maintained by the parish. Every tenth lb. of wool. The
best shoulder of every calf killed and the tenth penny of every calf sold. 4d. for

summering every cow. If any young beast is sold before they come to pail or yoke the tenth of the price or value. Every tenth pig or if only 7 1½d. for one. Tithe of pears, apples, plums and all other fruit. Tenth acre or tenth lug of all coppices, hedgerows and borders above a lug except what grows on the parsonage. Tenth pound or tenth shilling of any land rented by a person not belonging to Winsley. For every mill thorough 6s. 8d. The tithe arising from all commons. The tenth quart or tenth lb. of all honey. 2d. for every man and his wife and his garden to be paid at Easter and for every cock 3 eggs and for every hen 2 eggs to be paid on Food Friday. 2d. to be paid for every one above 16s. 4d. for all women giving thanks after childbirth. 10s. for every person who dies worth £40 in goods and chattels, his debts being paid.

James Butter, minister, Robert Wilshere, churchwarden, John Curll, Richard Druce, William Tylie, Andrew Blatchly.

BRADFORD ON AVON: S. Wraxall chapelry

82   20 Nov 1704 (D1/24/23/8)
Belonging to the bishop a small dwelling house and garden, stable, and the churchyard. All small tithes, offerings and mortuaries, and all tithes except corn and hay. The value of the house, garden, stable, offerings, oblations, mortuaries and tithes amounts to about £15 p. a.

Thomas Sartain curate, John Keeping, Thomas Collett, sidesman.

BRADFORD ON AVON: Atworth vicarage

83   n. d. early 17th cent. (D1/24/23/9)
Parsonage: c. 10a. arable land in the W. field; c. 9a. arable land in the S. field; c. 8a. arable in a field called the Hammes; c. 2a. meadow and fallow in 2 fields called Leies amd Medlies; c. 1a. meadow in several. c. 1a. in a several close belonging to the farm called Sibly crafte. c. 1a. wood in several. An orchard, backside and barn of c. 1 farndell. Vicarage: a close of pasture on which the house stands, c. 1½a. The churchyard, c. 1a.

Thomas Feltham, John Stox churchwardens, Thomas Tayler, George Stret sidesmen, with the consent of Mr. John Yerbury [Herbury] the parsonage being impropriate, John Tit MA., Thomas Shepard and others.

84   12 Jul 1614 (D1/24/23/10)
A house of 2 fields being a hall and chamber with a room overhead. 1 ground, c. 2a., adjoining the houses, the ground of Thomas Mathew W, the ground of John Kyveton E., shooting on the highway N.

Owen Price minister, John Pinchin, Thomas Self [X], churchwardens, John Feltham, Henry Taylor, Thomas Tayler, John Woodman[X].

85   25 Dec 1704 (D1/24/23/11)
The vicarage house with a close of 2a. adjoining on the N.W. side of the side of the church. William Skammell, curate, J. Godwyn.

BRADFORD ON AVON: Westwood vicarage

86 29 Dec 1704 (D1/24/23/12)
The vicarage, garden, barn of 3 fields of building with 1a. ground adjoining. A close of pasture by the way side going to Rowley, c. 7a.; a little ground by the way side going to Bradford, c. ¼a. 2a. arable land in W. field near Iford; 3a. in the upper side of Westwood field between the land of Mr. Butcher S. and Tobias Garland N.; 1a. between the land of John Smith N. and S.; 1½a. between the land of Chas. Savage esq., N. and S.; 2a. between the land of Chas. Savage esq., S. and Mr. Shrapnell N.; 3 yd between the land of William Hayward N. and S.; 3yd. called the Head land; 3a. between the land of wid. Godwin W. and Mr. Seal, land of Wingfield parsonage and Robert Howell E., shooting to the highway from Trowbridge to Westwood; 3yd. between the land of Mr. Seal S. and Mr. Butcher N.; 1a. 1yd. in Freshford moor between the land of Mr. Shrapnell E. and Robert Harvy W.; 3 yd in the moor in Mr. Shrapnell's inclosure under the hedge, that was Edward Adams'; 2a. in a ground called Release, the land of Wingfield parsonage E., Mr. Butcher W.; 3yd. in Mr. Butcher's inclosure, the land of Mr. Butcher N. and S.; 3 yd near Daintons Grave.
Thomas Lewis, vicar, Richard Gardner, William Millard, chapelwardens.

BRADFORD ON AVON: Limpley Stoke vicarage

87 1608 (D1/24/23/13)
A house with an orchard adjoining of 1 lug (looge) of ground belonging to the vicarage. Thomas Read; William Walter, Felix Marshman, churchwardens. *Churchwardens' names in the same hand.*

88 29 Jan. 1705 (D1/24/23/14)
A dwelling house with a garden, c. 4 lugs adjoining. All tithes usually belonging to any vicarage except endowed.
Thomas Lewis vicar, Thomas Townsend, churchwarden, John Clarke.

MAIDEN BRADLEY rectory (impropriate)

89 13 Apr 1681 (1332 box9)[1]
A parsonage house[2] wherein is a dairy house and backhouse, brewhouse with divers lodging rooms. A barn and stable, now added to the barn containing 11 bays covered with slate in good reparation. A coach stable for 4 horses an a room for a coach to stand in, thatched. The quantity of ground on which these buildings with the backsides, gardens and courts stand contain 2a. 1r. 10p. a little garden, part of the court contains 7p.
The chancel[3] wainscotted within and 2 wainscott pews. The churchyard handsomely fenced on 2 sides next the parsonage yard with pale and the other 2 sides with wall. A cottage of 3 bays, a garden, little mead plott and a parcell of arable ground adjoining called Coles Parrock, 1¼a.; Stubbs close, near the

parsonage house, 4½a., the ground of Mr. Ralph Baily S., highway E. and W.; Little mead, 2½a., enclosed, lying in the midst of the field, John Shore S., Meadows Parrock E., the common field N., the parsonage ground, being common field, W.; Lamberts mead alias Knowles' close, 2a., which is in lieu of the tithe hay of the farm heretofore Lamberts lands, John Redish N. and W., John Molton part S., common field and highway E.; 1 close, 2a., in the tithing of Baycliffe near the pool, Mr. Clark S., and part N., Mr. Hollyday E. and part N., the pool W. end.

     Arable in the common fields of Bradley: In the W. field, a parcel of arable, 9a. 2r. 10p.; in W. ham adjoining Yarnfield; a parcel by Wiltshire bushes, 1a. 2r.; a parcel, 1a., in Brewham [Bruorn] Somerset, Lyppeatt E., land of Ralph Annerly N., Penny S., highway E. and W.; a piece on the top of Knowl, 3a., Little Knowl E., Great Knowl W.; a piece, 1a., bounding upon Longlinch, James Redish N. and E., John Shore W., wid. Wansey S.; 3yds. running N. and S., James Redish E., Penny and Shore N., Walters S., George Young and others W.; a parcel, 1yd., pointing from Longlinch westward towards Mere way; a parcel, 1a., near Mere way called Blacklands acre the S. end upon the last yd. N. upon Mere way; a parcel, 1a., lying over Mere way Blackland acres, Ralph Baily W., Mr. Redish N.; 1a. lying over Mere way, James Redish E., the last a. W., Mr. Redish N., George Moulton S.; 1½a. running N. and S., Wansey S. and E., James Redish W., James Redish and others N.; ½a. running by Redmead way E. and S., Edward Wansey N. and S.

     In the E. field: 2 parcels, 7a., one hedging the other, lying by Bitley corner, shooting E. and W., new mead of Joseph Gibbons W., Kingston field E., Anne Davis N., James Redish and others S.; a parcel by Kingston field, 3a., Kingston field S. and E., Philip Andrews, N., James Redish W.; 4 parcels in Gorsmarsh, 3a., Edward Wansey S., John Shore N., Edward Wansey and Richard Dunford E.; 3 x ½a. by the Burrough, 1a., the Borough W. end, Edward Wansey E., John Shore [Shole] N., John Parson S.; a parcel, 1a., going athwart Gorsmarsh, John Redish N., James Redish S., Henry Wansey E., William Baily W.; a parcel by Gibbons Hedge, ½a., Gibbons hedge E., William Penny S., Edward Wansey N., William Bayly W.; 1a. George Moulton N., John Redish S., Philip Andrews W., wid. Draper E.; 2a. at Hucklebreach gate Edward Wansey's enclosure W., highway E., Henry Wansey S. and N.

     In the Middle field: A parcel 1½a., by the pit; ½a. in the pit, John Shore E., Ralph Baily W., Edward Wansey N., Anne Davis S.; 1a. on the E. side of Little mead Philip Andrews N., wid. Ricketts E., wid. Shore W., John Shore S.; a parcel, 3a., on W. side of Little mead, the parsonage enclosure E., John Redish W., George Adria S., George Nunton N.; 1a., John Redish N., Edward Wansey E., Mary Shore W., Richard Dunford and others S.; 1a. shooting E. upon Edward Wansey, W. upon wid. Wansey, William Baily S., Edward Wansey N.; 1a. by Rodmead hedge shooting E. upon Edward Wansey, W. upon James Redish, S. upon Philip Andrews, Edward Wansey N.

     The customary tithes: For a grist mill 5s. p. a. For the priory house and grounds under which is comprehended Kate Bench and the lords wood 3s. p. a. For every communicant 2d. For a communicant the first time 1d. For a cow white 2d. For a thorough cow 1½d. For a heifer 1d. For a calf sold the tenth penny. For 5 calves, half of one. For 7 calves, one to the parson to the party [i. e.

owner] 1½d. paid by the parson. For a calf killed, the best shoulder. For a calf weaned ½d. For a garden 1d. For a colt 1d. For the cattle of strangers that are depastured in the liberty the tenth penny that is given for the herbage. The several lordships that pay tithe to this parsonage are the manor of Maiden Bradley, the manor of Yarnfield and the tithing of Little Horningsham occupied by Mr. Cooke being the inheritance of Thomas Thynne esq.

Robert Burscough, curate, Henry Whatman, John Redish, Thomas May, Henry Wansey, Nicholas Molton, Andrew Baily, Thomas Draper, Gabriel Draper, John Parsons.

1. This is attached to a lease of the same date of the rectory and is with a series of terriers for 1718, 1772 and 1818, in which the adjoining owner of almost all the glebe is Sir Edward Seymour in 1718, and the duke of Somerset in 1772 and 1818.
2. Subsequent terriers (see n. 1) mention a parsonage house but only a malt house with a slaughterhouse at the end covered with slate and stone walls. In 1772 this is suggested may be used for a dwelling house.
3. In 1717 (see n.1), this is described as being new covered with slate.

NORTH BRADLEY vicarage

90   n. d. late 16th cent. (D1/24/24/1)
The parsonage belongs to Winchester college. To the house appointed as the parsonage house 4a. in a field called [. . .] adjoining the land of William Pryor. 5a. of pasture ground.

By me George York; John Guley, churchwardens. Richard Cowche [X] Richard Crynyll, William Pryor, Henry Chappell, sidesmen.

91   21 Aug 1608 (D1/24/24/2)
The vicarage house containing 6 fields of building. The old house containing 2 fields. The garden lying toward the church the orchard by it all containing 1yd. 2 little parrocks of meadow, 1¼a., lying between the vicarage house and the W. end of the church bordering on the common. A small garden plot on the S. side of the house between the kitchen and the common.

Leonard Cox, vicar, William Iles, William Willis, churchwardens, Henry Longe, Thomas Ducye, John Drue W. Druse, John Smalwill, Edward Greenhil, William Byssey, William Rundell, John Baylye, John Pryer, Edward Jones, Thomas Barterton, Robert Wheller, John Weste, John ?Pryor.

92   9 Jan 1705 (D1/24/24/3)
A large tiled strong dwelling house with stable with room enough to contain 2 or 3 horses. A close adjoining c. 2a. The parsonage being at this time divided from the vicarage, the vicar receives neither tithe corn, hay, wool nor lambs. But by the order of the warden and fellows of Winchester college, his patrons, has £10 p. a. paid out of the parsonage. Oblations and offerings are paid to him at Easter each year. Also the tithes of young calves and milk of cows. Privy tithes as apples pears and the like. 1d. for eggs of hens and gardens. Tithe of underwood

from Acre field when the several owners have cut their share. From other copses in near Faggs hill, 3 in Brokers wood, once in 14 yrs. and part of one in Yarnbrook. The customary payment of 4s. p. a. for a corn mill from Grace Greenhill wid. From Langdam 8s. p. a. for a corn and tucking mill. Nathanial Emmel for old Mr. Crabbs land is to pay according to old payment 2s. 6d. every Easter. William Willis senior is to pay every Ladyday [25 Mar] for a ground he bought of Joseph Combes near Rode 1s. Henry Ball 6d. p. a. for a ground near Mr. Edward Webb. Abel Wiltshire or his son Thomas is to pay 3d. every Easter according to custom for Hilly ground above Orft mead in Rode [*Somerset*]. Mr. James Davis of Devizes according to ancient composition is to pay to the minister for his land near Studley 3s. 3d. p. a. The present incumbent formerly received mortuaries from many persons by custom; but for few years past some opposition has been made that therents from the Parsonage have been set against the payment to him.

Daniel Philips, vicar, Edward Webb, Moses Ashton, churchwardens Anthony Silverthorne, John Hurne.

92A   30 Jul 1783 (D1/24/24/4)

A large substantial stone built dwelling house consisting of a dining room, drawing room, study, kitchen, back kitchen, butler's pantry, dairy, scullery, and cellars on the ground floor; with 6 good bed chambers on the first storey, together with store room and lumber room; 3 good garrets above; all in compleat repair; the rooms above papered, those below stuccoed and papered. The house is covered with strong stone tile. Adjoining to the house, on E. side, is a piece of ground designed for a pleasure ground, planted with shrubs, mostly enclosed within a wall bounded E. by the churchyard, S. the common road and N. by the glebe land. On the W. side of the house is a kitchen garden walled around on all sides with stone and brick walls bounded S. and W. by the common. Adjoining to the kitchen garden is the stable yard, having a stable for 4 horses and 2 coach horses, surrounded for the most part with a stone wall and bounded by the common. On N. side of the vicarage is a close of glebe land, c. 2a. The parsonage being at this time divided from the vicarage, the vicar receives neither tithe corn, hay, wool nor lambs; but by order and appointment of the warden and fellows of Winchester college, his patrons, has £10 yearly paid unto him out of the parsonage.

Oblations and Easter offerings are paid unto the vicar at Easter yearly. Also the tithe of young calves and the milk of cows. In short all privy tithe apple, pears and the like, gardens, eggs, geese and suchlike, pigs, colts and suchlike. So likewise tithe of under wood growing in the several coppices, when the several owners therof cut; as namely from Acrefield, from coppices near Fags hill, from those in Brokers wood and from part of one in Yarnbrook. The payment of 10s. 6d. customarily from a corn mill every year now occupied by William Francis as tenant; from Langdon mill 8s. p. a.

Charles Daubeny L. L. B., vicar, Joseph Francis, John Doel, churchwardens, Joseph Greenhill.

BREMHILL vicarage

93   10 May 1588 (D1/24/25/1)
A little plot called the Coniger, *c.* 5a.; Suttons mead, *c.* 3a.; 1a. by itself; a plot of ground called the Furlong, *c.* 9a.; a little plot of meadow, *c.* 5a.; a leaze called Broade mead, *c.* 24a. The tithes of a little plot of ground called the Shrubs and a little plot once held by John Wisdome, *c.* 7a. Total *c.* 54a.

John Ollyfe, John Jaffrey, churchwardens, John Baynton, Roger Cooke, William Taylor, Robert Trymnell, Robert Edmunds.

Memorandum: totals of baptisms marriages and burials 1585 to 3 May 1588 43 baptised, 20 married 38 buried.

94   4 Nov 1628 (D1/24/25/2)
A little plot called the Conigar, 5a.; the way to it is through Mr. Colliar's backside. Suttons mead, *c.* 3a.: the way to it is down the lane by the parsonage. 1 several a. by itself; the way to it is the same as the way to Sutton mead. 1 plot of ground called the Furlong, *c.* 9a., at the upper corner of W. side of Mr. Colliars house. 1 little plot of meadow, *c.* 5a. in which the hay belongs to Whitly; the way to it is through Robt Jenkin's ground. 1 leaze called Broad mead, *c.* 24a.; the way to it is under the hanging of the hill called ?Speknells. The tithes of 1 little plot of ground called Shrubs and 1 little plot of [. . .] occupied by John Wisdome, *c.* 7a. Memo. the way that leads to Robert Jenkin's ground called Eastere mead lies down the lane by the vicarage and through the vicar's ground. Total 44a.

William Tayler, Andrew Shepprd, Robert Jenkens, Richard Davis [X], John Heath.

95   16 Dec 1677 (D1/24/25/3)
A dwelling house and orchard, barn and stable. Another barn and yard. A ground called Cunniger, 6a. A ground called the Furlong, 9a. A ground adjoining the Furlong, 4a. A ground which borders on Whitly Brook, 5a. A ground called Broad mead, 30a. At the E. end of the churchyard a plot, *c.* 7 lugs.

Edward Sadler William Willcox churchwardens.

96   10 Oct 1704 (D1/24/25/4)
The house outhouses and garden. A little close called the Ox Barken, *c.* ½a. A close called Conyger, *c.* 6a. A ground called the Furlong, *c.* 8a. An adjoining ground called the Four acres. A ground called the Five acres. A ground called Broad mead, c 26a. The splot of land joining the churchyard, *c.* 6 lugs.

John Wilson, vicar, Robert Essington, churchwarden, Edward Sadler, John King, Adam Tuck, George Leavis, Oliver King.

BREMHILL: Highway vicarage

97   1 Oct 1622 (D1/24/25/5)
Parsonage house with barn and backside. A several close 1a. A churchyard in the Town mead 2a. In a common called the Marsh 2 beast leazes to feed with the

lord's tenants. In the common called the Streat 1 horse leaze to feed with the
lord's tenants. 30 sheep leazes in the same common between St. Thomas's day
[21 Dec] and St. Mathias's day [24 Feb]. 21a. of arable land no longer as the lords
tenants and 30 sheep leazes in the common fields of Highway and to feed as the
sheep of the lords tenants. This we do present to be as much as we know by our
oaths that we have taken the whole tithe of the parish in kind.

William Stevens, John Reverstone, churchwardens, John Barns, John Whole,
sidesmen *Names in the same hand.*

98   23 Nov 1677 (D1/24/25/6)
20a. above hill in equal parts in two fields. 30 sheep leazes above and below hill.
1a. of meadow adjoining the church beside the churchyard. 1a. between Alphonsus
Priest and Richard Potter. 5 beast leazes in the lower common 1 horse leaze in
the upper common. 1 house and barn with the feeding of the backside and the
churchyard.

James Stockwell, curate, William White, churchwarden.

BREMILHAM rectory

99   Dec 1704 (D1/24/26/1)
The churchyard. Tithes in kind. John Harris, rector, Thomas Ritchens,
churchwarden.

100   25 Jul 1786 (D1/24/26/2)
An exact account of the lands that pay tithes to the rector of Cowage [Cowitch]
or Bremilham as I had from a worthy friend at the Malmesbury visitation.

Cowage farm yearly £20 5s. Mr. Lyne of the Light 20s. Mr. Pyke of
Brokenborough for Crabtree farm 16s. Mr. Brooks for Butts and Twindas 3s. 6d.
Thomas White for 3 x ½a. 1/6. Mr. York for Little Tining and Mays Orchard 9d.
William Pryor for the Rose and Crown 1s. Thomas Pit for Pools Mead 6s. wid.
Pit for Bockbridge Closes 8s. Mr. Garlick for Spurmead 3s. 9d. Mr. Mincher 6s.
Osborns leaze 4s. Mr. Hill for Cooks leaze 13s. Sam Pit of Bishoper 5s. John Pit
for Hankerton corner 3s. 6d.

Daniel Freer, rector.

BRINKWORTH rectory

101   16 Dec 1671 (D1/24/27/1)
The parsonage house, gardens, orchard and backside, barn and stable, and a close
adjoining, c. 1a. 2 closes called the Home Breaches, c. 12a. A lammas plot in
Pewken meadow in the tithing of Grittenham, c. 1a. A meadow or pasture
ground called New leaze, c. 8a. 1a. called Wilhiers acre. A meadow called Wyvorne
Heale, c. 2a. A tenement called Wilhiers and a ground adjoining, c. 2a. A plot of
meadow in the Windmill fields, c. ½a. A tenement adjoining the churchyard
with a close adjoining, c. 1a. A meadow or pasture ground called Pendertons, c.

3a. 1a. called Pendertons acre. A tenement called Boudlyes with 2 grounds adjoining, *c.* 6a. A ground called E. Breach with 2 little meadow grounds adjoining, *c.* 12a. A tenement called Dovis with a barn, garden and backside of *c.* 1a.; Dovis meadow belonging to it, *c.* 14a. The Purlieu in the forest of Braydon, *c.* 14a.

John Fry, Thomas Church, churchwardens.

102   6 Jan 1705 (D1/24/27/2)
A messuage called the Parsonage house consisting of 12 bays. A stable of 2 bays. A cow house. A little court before the house. An outward yard a garden and orchard, 2a.

The glebe lands consist of enclosed grounds, meadows and pasture.

A close of meadow or pasture called Breach or Home close, 11a. A plot in Pewkin whereof the grass to be mowed and carried off yearly by 1st Aug, 1a. 2r. The Little Breach, 6a. Ovens house consisting of 2 bays. A close belonging to it, 3a.[1] A house on S. side of the churchyard consisting of 2 bays. A close belonging to it, 3r.[2] A close adjoining a meadow called Louse Bridge, 3r. A close of meadow or pasture called New Lease, 11a. A close commonly called Wiltshire's acre, 1a. 2r. A ground called Wivurn[3] Heal, 2a. 2r. A close called the Purlieu, 27a. A messuage called Dove House with stable adjoining consisting of 4 bays occpied by Richard Hammond[4] A little outhouse, A paddock near the house. A pasture ground called Home close with meadow adjoining, 20a. A messuage called Pinnells consisting of 3 bays occupied by Richard Hammond aforesaid.

Several grounds of meadow and pasture: Pendertons Mead, 3a.; Pinnells mead, 2a. 2r.; Bowdleys mead, 3a. 2r.; Pendertons acre, 3r.; E. Breach with a plot of meadow next the river, 13a. 2r.; Bay mead, 1a. 2r.; New enclosure, 2a.

Offerings at Easter of 2d. a piece ought to be paid by all above 16. Tithes are due in kind, except the minister and any of the parishioners who come to a temporary agreement for them. The commons of Little Somerford within the precincts of Brinkworth pay tithes to the rector. He has usually allowed 8 leazes for the tithe of 72 beast leazes till Michaelmas [29 Sep], after Michaelmas 3 sheep leazes for each beast leaze. The commons of Milbourne within the precincts of Brinkworth pay tithe to the rector either in kind or as they can agree. Several grounds of arable and pasture part of a Bargain called the Farm in the tithing of Brinkworth are pretended to be tithe free by the earl of Suffolk and Berkshire. Several closes of meadow and pasture together with Great wood, 140a., in the tithing of Grittenham are pretended to be exempted from the payment of tithe.

Francis Henry Cary, rector, John Ponting, John Simpkins, churchwardens, Richard Hamond, Edward Cripps.

1. Ovensis lease 3a. in **103** in which terrier Ovens house is omitted.
2. Called Hundred acres in **103**.
3. Wivions Heal in **103**.
4. Jas. Nicholls in **103**.
5. Omitted in **103**.

103   24 Jul 1783 (D1/24/27/3)

The parsonage house consisting of 12 bays of building, the sidewalls made partly of stone, brick and wood, the tile covered with slates and in part slabbed to the pin. The lower apartments; the entrance on N. side a passage paved with stone *c.* 20ft long by 4ft 9in. broad. Out of the above entrance on the right another passage 10ft long by 4ft 4in. broad leading to the western apartments. On the right side of this entrance to N. a very ordinary cellar *c.* 12ft square. On the left towards S. a coal hole 7ft long by 4ft broad. At the extremity of this passage towards S. W. a parlour wainscotted, floored and ceiled 16ft long by 15ft. 6in. broad. On N. W. side a small parlour, wainscotted and ceiled, a brick floor, a lumber room, and passage leading thereto all put together of the same dimensions as that to the S. W. On the left of the first entrance a kitchen paved with stone 18t 6 in. long by 15ft broad. To N. within the kitchen a small pantry 10ft. long by 9eet broad. To E. adjoining the kitchen a brewhouse 19ft. long by 9ft. broad. A lumber room to N. E. 13ft. long by 10ft. broad.

The staircase leading to the apartments above is from the second passage leading to the parlour to S. W. On the range of the first floor there are 7 rooms. The room over the parlour to S. W. of the same dimensions with the room below, the floor and ceiling very irregular and uneven. A chamber to N. over the small parlour and lumber room and part of the passage 20ft by 1 ft badly floored ceiled and uneven.

On N. side leading to the eastern appartments 2 small rooms, one 9ft. 9in. by 7ft., the other 14ft. 10in. by 10ft. A closet facing S. 8ft. by 5ft. Beyond this over the kitchen a room 18ft. by 15ft. 6in., within this a study a lumber room and passage in the whole altogether 35ft. by 24ft. Over the whole of these appartments a very long range of garrets fit only for scaffolding to repair the roof.

Outbuildings; a barn built with timber of 3 bays of building besides the porch covered with straw and at present altogether useless. A stable of 2 bays of building the walls partly brick and partly timber, covered with straw. A hovel or cowhouse supported to the S. by 5 posts to N. by a brick wall 31ft. long by 12ft. wide, covered with straw. A small green court facing the parsonage house N, the walk paved with stone encompassed with a brick wall and coped with freestone, with gates at its entrance *c.* 3p. square. The garden to S. surrounded by a quickset hedge, 1r. 37p. The house garden and green court measure 2r. 34p. The outward court without buildings, pond, and orchard, 1a. 1r. 6p.

There are no trees on the premises that will properly come under the denomination of timber being all either pollards or of young growth. *Glebe lands, tithes and offerings as **102** with amendments in footnotes.*

The church and churchyard fence is repaired by the parish and everything contained therein, such as the bells, the clock, the pulpit cloth the communion cloth with the surplices. The chancel and the seats are repaired by the rector. The communion plate; the flagon the gift of Sir George Ayliffe 1737, the chalice 1631 and the salver given by the parish, in all *c.* 24 ounces.

J[*ohn*] Penton rector, William Stratton, Francis Hart, churchwardens, John Mapson, James Smith.

BRITFORD rectory (impropriate) and vicarage

104   16 Oct 1615 (D24/4/1)
Terrier made by the churchwardens and sidesmen and with the approbation
and information of the ancientest men of the parish of Birtford alias Britford
given at a visitation of the communer of the dean and chapter of Salisbury.

Tithe corn and grain in Britford and E. Harnham belongs to the parson
saving 1a. at W. end gate and ½a. in the Ryalls which together with all manner
of tithes there belong to the vicar. Tithe hay of 2 common meads in Britford
appertain to the parson saving 2½a. in the Great mead which belong to the
vicar. Tithe hay of E. Harnham common mead belongs to the parson. There
belongs to the parson for the hay of 10a. in the Great common meadow upon
the cow pasture on the S. side only the right to cut and go: The hay also of 5a. of
meadow in the Great common mead by themselves shooting upon the last 10a.,
Goodman Love lying on N. side. 5a. in the said common meadow and bounds
upon the river at Stakeham end and Mr. Blacker lying on N. side, wherein it has
no common nor feeding but only the share or the hay to cut, make and carry
away. The parson has the glebe of 1 meadow, 5a., lying eastward from the parsonage
house and bounding upon the river. The parson has Ferne Close, c. 2a., joining
to the said close of 5a. He has a pasture or ground called Church close, c. 3a.,
lying on the S. side of the church. He has a close, c. 2a., abutting on the W. side
of the vicarage house and orchard. He has a close, c. 2a., lying W. from the last
close, with only a lane going between them. He has a little ground lying alongside
the E. side of Langford ground, a ground of Sir John Portman lying between.

All tithe of all the hams lying below Harnham bridge between the river and
the Cow lane belong to the parson saving that there is a meadow now in the
possession of William Gillo senior lying between the river and some of those
hams, the tithe whereof belongs to the vicar.

Tithe of winter grain, viz. wheat, rye, and winter vetches within the manor
of Landford [Langford] belong to the parson, saving the tithe of 16a. of Sir John
Portman's land now in the possession of Mr. John Brent which belong to the
vicarage and also the tithe of 3a. of which 1½ belongs to Sir Edward Gorges the
other 1½ to Mr. William Holmes, which bound upon the W. end of a ground
called Dines [or ? Dives] which belong to the vicar and also the tithe of Smocke
acre and the tithe of 3 x ½a. bounding upon the S. end of Smocke acre which
belong to the vicar whether it be wheat, barley or any other grain or hay
whatsoever.

Tithe of a close called Nutbeames, c. 12a., and High orchard and the higher
part of the dry close without High orchard belong to the parson.

Tithe wool and lamb and privy or small tithes, cow white, calves, pigs, geese
and swans, and the tithe of all the spear[1] or hay in the hams or islands growing in
the manor of Britford and E. Harnham belong to the vicar and every fisherman
that has recourse to and fro on the water with a boat pays 6d. p. a. for the tithe
of his boat.

All tithe hay within all the ingrounds of Britford belong to the vicar saving
a croft [craft] of Matthew Poor and a little close by the lane which goes into the
common marsh and a croft of Cofferer Hughes[2] joining to the common fields

the tithe corn or hay whereof belongs to the parson. All tithe of the inground lying between W. and E. Harnham belong to the vicar. All privy or small tithes, pig, goose, wool and lamb without controversy were paid out of the parsonage to the vicar by old Mr. Wroteslye's[3] days.

All tithe within the manor of Landford, viz. privy or small tithes, cow white, calves, pigs, and geese, tithe wool of chilver sheep[4] and lambs belong to the vicar. Tithe hay of Marie close, Woor, Wet Gaston, Dry Gaston, Conyer, 2 Privieshott marshes, manor barn close otherwise called the lower port of High orchard, Callie ham, all the grounds between the mill and Kingswell belong to the vicar. For the close next to the mill and for a little ham between the 2 bridges and for the mill the miller pays tithe yearly to the vicar.

Nathaniel Poore, Arthur Poore, churchwardens, John Hayter, Anthony Willshire, sidesmen.

1. Spear grass probably couch grass.
2. Coffer Hughs in the parish register.
3. Henry Wriothesley was granted a lease on the rectory in 1537. A lease was granted to William Blacker in 1565. (WSRO CC/chapter 88/3)
4. Ewe lambs.

BROMHAM rectory

105   2 Sep 1608 (D1/24/28/1)
A parsonage house of 9 fields from beam to beam. Several rooms viz. 1 hall and within the hall a [. . .] 2 other little rooms. Over the buttery 1 chamber, [. . .] the Chamber another chamber over them. 1 study [. . .] hall and loft on W. side of the hall an entry with a porch. A white house and a larder house. Over the porch a little chamber over the entry a little loft. Over the white house a chamber over the larder house another loft. 1 barn of 5 fields and a cut end [coot end] thereunto adjoining for a stable. A pigeon house. A garden, orchard, backside and a hop yard. 1 ground by the house called the Moor, 9a. 1 ground called the Balls, 3a. 1 ground called Reddlands, 9a. 1 ground called Pillory close, 9a. 1 ground called Hawkstree leaze with a cottage, 5a. 1 ground called the Ham, 1½a. 1 little ground with a cottage, 3yd. 1 plot of ground with a cottage occupied by John Fryer and George Ballard, 1yd. Arable land in a common field, called the Yard, 10a. Meadow ground in a common mead called Broad mead and 1 plot called the Thorny piecee adjoining the plots of Sir Henry Baynton, Mr. Andrew Smith and John Withers, 40a. A little plot called Sheephills and 1a. adjoining by the plots of Thomas Webb Andrew Smith and Robert Seagar containing, less the plot, 3a. Another plot of called Thachmeade lying by the plots of Sir Henry Baynton, Mr. Andrew White and John Slade 7a. 1a. there lying by the plot of John Slade. Arable in a common field called the Clay next Heddington; 3 x ½a. lying between Paul Knight and Andrew Overton, 1a. there between the land of Joseph Ansty and James Tyse, 1 other a. there between the land of Andrew White and Paul Knight.

In the further Clay 1a. in Caswell furlong and 1a. in the bottom of that field adjoining to Broad mead. Common of pasture as the tenants there have for beasts in all the fields of Bromham in the Marsh and in the Stroud and Broad mead. Commons of pasture for sheep in the said fields and in the Marsh. 6d. a year for Burbrooke mead and for a plot in Broad mead adjoining the Moors occupied by Mr. Thomas Eyre. Customary dues; marriage 6d.; at thanksgiving of women 4d.; of every communicant at Easter 2d. except at his first receiving then but ½d. Cow white the summer 2d. For a calf sold the tenth penny, if killed for provision of a man's house, a shoulder; if weaned ½d. For the fall of every lamb under 7½d. For the fall of a calf 1d. All other things titheable in kind.

Robert Richard, Andrew White, Thomas Eyre, Paul Knight, Andrew Pountrie, William Lynes, Jeremy Scott.

106   31 Oct 1671 (D1/24/28/2)
The parsonage house with a barn, a stable and other outhousing and a garden and orchard, c. 1a. A ground called Pigeon close, c. 2a. A little coppice in the moor and another ground adjoining, c. 4a. Balls mead, c. 3a. A ground called Redlands, c. 8a. A ground called Pillory close, c. 9a. 3 grounds called the Yards, c. 22a. A ground called the Parsons Ham, c. 1a. A ground in the Clayes called Broadmead, c. 9a, A house and ground occupied by Francis Baily, c. 6a.[1] A little ground occupied by Edward Ladd, c. 1a.[2] A cottage and little garden ground occupied by Samuel Hobbs.[3] A cottage occupied by Thomas Friar.[4] A cottage occupied by Dorothy Watts.[5] 6 beast leazes in the Commons.

Thomas Wyatt, rector, Eleazar Webb, Richard Hiscocke, churchwardens.

1. Daniel Hicks and his sister in **107**.
2. wid. Ladd in **107**.
3. James Wootton in **107**.
4. wid. Alexander in **107**.
5. Edgar Fey in **107**.

107   8 Mar 1705 (D1/24/28/3)
*As **106** with amendments in footnotes.* Thomas Wyatt, rector, Robert Paridice, John Trowe, churchwardens, William Webb, Samuel Hicks, Abraham Webb, William Webb, Henry Tucker, John Gaby.

BROUGHTON GIFFORD rectory

108   n. d. early 17th cent.[1] (D1/24/29/1)
1 dwelling house, garden, woodyard and stable within the compass of the churchyard, 1 barn, ox house and hay house standing in a pasture of 8a, part of the glebe, the highway N., the running brook S. 1a. the common field called Bradley: a piece of arable of c. 16a., Monkton[Mowncton] farm S. John B[lan]chard N.; ½a., Monkton farm N., Harry Barrett S., a piece of 2a. [...] the highway W.; [...] a. the mill land [N.], John Blawnchard S.; [...], Michael Cuff N., [...]ton S.; total in this field 20a.

Southfield: 1 [...] in Shepherds Corner the mill land S., Nicholas [...] N.; [...] ½a. the same Nicholas S., Robert Nash N.; [½]a. Robert Nash S., Nicholas

Prior N.; [. . .]owte Nash bush 1a. Nicholas Prior S., Mr. Maye N.; ½a. Arthur
Chard N., John Gerysh S.; ½a. under the hill Nicholas Gore S., William Gore
N.; ½a. on Barforlonge Nicholas Gore S., William Gore N.; 1a. Monkton farm
S. the mill land N.; 1yd. the lord's mead S., John Tooker N. 3yd. on Anorlonge
John Gerysh W, John Bull E; 1yd. in Wellmead Nicholas Moxam W.; 1a. meadow
in Mitchell mead John Redman S., the Lott ground N.; 1a. meadow called Lott
acre; a little plot of meadow called the Hoode John Redman N., Harry Barrett
S.; total in this field 8a. arable 2½a. meadow.

    In the common field called Anfield: ½a. in Stevens piece, Mowncton farm S.,
Mr. Maye N.; 1a., Mowncton farm E., John Gerysh W. 1a., the footway S., John
Redman N.; ½a., Mr. Horton S., Michael Cuff N.; ½a., Harry Barrett N., Robert
Bull S.; ½a. John Prior E., wid. Edmondes on the W.; 1yd., Nicholas Prior W., wid.
Edmondes E.; 1yd., John Bull N., Agnes Redman wid. S.; total in this field 4½a.

    In the common field called Chessell field: 1yd., Mr. May S., Thomas Gerysh
N.; 1yd., William Gore N. and S.; a headland of ½a., William Gore N.; ½a.,
Nicholas Moxam S., John Gerysh N.; ½a., William Prior N., John Prior S.; total
in this field 2a. ½a. in Woodforlonge field, Mr. Horton S., John Gerysh N.; 1a. in
Hales field, John Bull S., William Gore N.; total in these 2 fields 1½a. Total 36a.
arable, 8a. pasture, 2a. meadow.

    John Bold rector, Michael Cuffe, Nicholas Gore, churchmen.

1.   John Bold was rector 1600-1621.

109   Oct 1671 (D1/24/29/2)
A house, stable and garden, ½a. adjoining the churchyard. Parsonage barn and
oxhouse. 1 pasture ground called Parsonage leaze, 2 little meadows lying near to
Monkton Farleigh, 11a.,[1] let at the price of £16 p. a. In a field one part called
Brodly[2] and the other part Stanly, 20a.[3] of arable ground viz., 1 piece of 16a. in
Bradly adjoining Monkton Grounds, ½a. in the same field, 1 piece of 2a. in
Stanly called the Butts shooting against Bradly lane, ½a. shooting upon the
Butts, 1a. at the yonder side of Stanly towards Monkton. In Southfield 10a. viz.
8a. of arable, 2a. of meadow ground. 1 whole a. in Mochell mead near Monkton
Gate and the other acre called Lott acre lying on both sides of the water some in
Mochell mead[4] some in Broadmead in several places with 2 hoods[5] that belong
to the a. in the same field. 3½a. of arable at Sheppards corner, 1½a. in Naishe
Bush furlong ½a. going down the hill 1½a. and a plot of lain in Barefurlong 3yd.
lying towards Monkton near to an enclosure of Thomas Horton esq., containing
7a. In Awfield 4a.[8] of arable, ½a. of laine:[9] 2a. in a furlong called Stephens piece;
1a. lying under the hedge of an enclosure of Richard Phelpes, the field away
going down by it; ½a in an enclosure of William Pryer[10] some part in the field;
1½a. in Town furlong; 2yd. lying in the upper end of the field; 1a. in Brodfurlong[11]
and the other shooting upon that containing 3a. In a field called Wood furlong
½a.[12] in an enclosure of Wm. Pryer containing 60 lugs. In a field called Halle 1a.
of arable lying under the hedge of wid. Harding's enclosure of 120 lugs.[13] In a
field by name of Cheselle 1a. and 3yd.;[14] ½a. in a furlong that shoots down upon
a mead called Challemead has been enclosed by Joseph Hutton; 1yd. more in
that furlong at the head ½a. of that furlong; 1yd. enclosed by Joseph Hutten;[15]

1yd. enclosed by William Hickes containing *c.* 1a. and 1yd.[16] The sum of the glebe in the fields is 37a. 3yd.[17] valued at £30 p. a. The tithes are valued at £60 so glebe and tithes amount to £90 p. a. taxes and payments discharged.

Nicholas Gore, Henry Harding churchwardens, Francis Sewe, John Hutton sidesmen.

1. 10a. in **110** and **111**.
2. Bradly in **110** to **111**.
3. Described as 20a. so usually accounted, but by measure *c.* 14a. in **110** and **111**.
4. Michell mead in **110** and **111**.
5. The meaning of hoods is unclear but presumably they are small plots.
6. Described as near an enclosure called Frying Pan in **111**.
7. Omitted in **110** and **111**.
8. Described as 3a. by measure in **110** and **111**.
9. ½a. of arable ground in **110** and **111**.
10. Nich. Pryor in **111**.
11. Broad Furrowe in **110**.
12. Of laine in **110**.
13. Omitted in **110** and **111**.
14. 1½a. by measure in **110** and **111**.
15. 1½a. head a. at the upper end of that furlong added in **110** and **111**.
16. 1 piece of pasture ground in Barfurlong *c.* 10 lugs included in **110** and **111**. Described as 1yd. in Wellmead by the Slough in **111**.
17. 37a. *c.* 3yd. in **110** and **111**.

110   11 Dec 1677 (D1/24/29/3)
A true and just terrier of both pasture and arable and what substance it contains by measure in the ordinary account and what by strict measure. *As **109** with amendments in footnotes.*

Edmond Proby, parson, Francis Lewis, Richard Gardiner, churchwardens.

111   n. d. [1704x1705].[1] (D1/24/29/4)
*As **109** with amendments in footnotes.* William Hickes rector William Sarten, churchwarden, Charles Iels sidesman, Edward Lewis overseer.

1.   The churchwarden was recorded in the bishop's vistitation book, Oct 1704 (WSRO D1/50/6)

112   28 Jul 1783 (D1/24/29/5)
Terrier of the glebe lands which were measured and a plan taken of them by Rev. Mr. Hickes the present incumbent in 1780. From which the following account is taken:

Parsonage house stable and garden, 26p. Church and churchyard, 1r. 34p. Baileys Great ground, 4a. 1r. 25p., pasture. Shepherds Corner 5a. 2r. 26p., pasture. Hundred Acres 2 r. 13p., pasture. Barn ground (a barn therein), 5a. 19p., meadow. Little Barn ground, 2a. 2r. 1p., meadow. Little Well Mead, 1a. 24p., pasture. Triangles 5a. 34p., meadow. Further Bradley Mead, 1a. 1r. 37p., meadow. Total 34a. 2r. 12p.

About 20 years ago on making a turnpike road from Melksham to Holt, Bradford, etc., rather more than 1½a. was taken from the glebe through part of which the road passes. The turnpike commissioners valued the land at £50 gave a bond to Mr. Hickes the incumbent and agreed to pay the interest of this sum, viz. 50s. p. a. to Mr. Hickes and his successors forever. This 1½a. added to the land now remaining brings it nearly to the same quantity of land which is specified in the old terriers extant in the office of the bishop at Sarum, viz. 36a Robert Adams Hickes, rector, John Hayward, Stephen Darke junior, churchwardens.

BULFORD rectory

113 n. d. late 17th cent.[1] (D1/24/30/1)
An enquiry made at the instruction of bishop Seth. The parsonage is impropriate. The curate receives from the lay impropriator only such yearly stipend as is agreed. A little house adjoining the church which with the churchyard usually belonged to the curate.
Thomas Webb, curate.

1. Thomas Webb signed bishop's transcripts for 1669 and 1679.

BURBAGE vicarage and prebend

114 22 Jan 1615 (D5/10/1/6)
According to the 87th canon set forth by Convocation held at London in 1603 we the parishioners of Burbage certify that the prebend of Burbage is endowed time out of mind with the tithe corn, hay and wool only, except the tithe corn and hay growing on all the enclosed grounds, several grounds, pasture grounds and crofts lying in several in the E. and easterly parts of the town or village of Burbage from Long mead adjoining to S. grove to Grigglands belonging to the farm of Burbage inclusively which belong to the portion of the vicar. Except all tithe great and small of S. grove and the meads and pasture grounds belonging thereunto all manner of tithes of the demesnes of the earl of Hertford, that is to say Earls heath, the Hile, Ridge lands, Lady well, Bowden, Netherfrithhays and Motsons coppice belong to the vicar.
The glebe of the prebend is 1 yardland, a dwelling house containing 3 rooms, a great barn containing 5 rooms, a little barn containing 3 rooms, a stable and another out house. All other tithes belong to the vicar.
George Commyn, vicar, John North [X], Thomas Sommerset [X], churchwardens, 1613, Richard Raynold [X], Francis Noyes, sidesmen, John Stagg, John Upton, churchwardens, 1614, John Scarlet [X].

115 22 Jan 1615 (D5/10/1/6)
According to the 87th canon set forth by the convocation held at London in 1603, we the parishioners of Burbage certify that the vicarage has a dwelling house under one roof containing 3 rooms, a barn containing 3 rooms with a

stable at the N. end of the barn, a little garden upon the N. side of the vicarage house another garden and orchard lying on the N. side of the vicarage house, all containing *c.* ½a. The feedings or profits of the churchyard with 4a. of arable land called the Fox acres lying 1 piece together between S. grove on S. and the bottom ham and the Great ham on N.; also common pasturing and feeding for 1 mare or gelding in the commons or common fields of Burbage. *The document is badly torn and lacking several lines of text. These and the rest of the document, which is clear, appear to cover tithes due to the vicarage and only give more detail of the varieties of small tithes than in the previous terrier. Thus the rest of the document has been heavily calendared.* Tithe wood herbage, pasturage and all great and small tithes on S. grove and the meadow and pasture grounds adjoining. Tithe wood and fuel on Motsfonts al. Motsons coppice, Goff's coppice, Harmers Counte, Ladywell and throughout the whole parish. Tithe parsnips, carrots, turnips, onions, garlick, leeks, apples, woad, flax and hemp throughout the parish.

Witnesses as **114**.

116   1672 (1678/2)[1]
Parsonage: 1 dwelling, 2 barns, 1 stable, 2 gardens, a backside, 1a. of ground worth 20s. p. a.; 4a. of arable called Preslands [at] the N. end of the town bounded on Tarrants land, worth 40s. p. a.; 3½a. of turnip ground called Preslands at the S. end of the town, bounded on the common, worth £2 6s. 8d. p. a.; 16a. of arable land called E. clay shooting N. and S. bounding upon Netherfreethay, worth £4 p. a.; 3a. of arable land called S. clay shooting N. and S. bounding upon Collingbourne field, worth 15s. p. a.; 4a. in the same field shooting N. and S. bounding upon a furlong called Pensley worth £1 p. a.; 1a. in the same field called Head acre shooting N. and S. bounding upon the last 4a. worth 5s. p. a.; 6 beast leazes in the common worth £3 p. a.

Vicarage: 1 dwelling house, 1 barn, 1 stable, 1 garden and backside, 100 lugs worth £1 6s. 8d. p. a. The churchyard worth 10s. p. a. 3 beast leazes in the common worth £1 10s. p. a. 4a. of arable land called Fox acres shooting E. and W. bounding on a coppice called Sowgrove worth £1 p. a. Tithe lambs to be taken on St. Mark's day [25 Apr] each year. Tithe gardens or old enclosures of parsnips, turnips, carrots, onions and other roots and plants. 14lb. of wool of the parsonage. The custom upon calves weaned and killed within the parish, viz. for every calf weaned ½d. and for every calf killed the best shoulder.

Richard Cherry, vicar, John Ragburne, William Morrants, churchwardens, William Baynten, Edward Sweeper, John Gawen. *Names except the vicar in the same hand.*

1.   Copy in parish register.

117   1705 (D5/10/1/6)
Vicarage: A dwelling house, barn, stable, garden and backside containing 100 lugs of land valued at £1 6s. 8d. p. a. The churchyard valued at 10s. p. a. 3 beast leazes in the commons, valued at £1 10s. 4a. of land called Fox acres shooting E. and W. bounding in a coppice called S. grove valued £1 p. a. Tithe lamb valued

£4 p. a.; tithe of the old enclosures and gardens for parsnips, turnips, carrots, plants, onions valued £20 p. a.; tithe wood valued £10 p. a.; tithe of the glebe land of the parsonage valued £4 p. a.; tithe cow white, calf, pigs and orchards valued at £6 p. a.; tithe of part of Wolfhall farm[1] valued at £10 p. a. Total £58 6s. 8d.

Thomas Andrews, vicar, Augustine Batt, Arthur Gammon, churchwardens, Henry New, John Andrewes, William Browne.

1.   In Great Bedwyn.

BURCOMBE (South Burcomb) vicarage

118   12 Jan 1705 (D1/24/31/l)
A composition for tithe wool, lambs, apples, cow white, calves, honey, pigeons, pigs, now paid at 10s. a yardland as follows: the farm belonging to Squire Clerk, 11 yardlands, £5; William Sellwood's living, 2½ yardlands, £1 5s.; Thomas London's 2 yardlands, £1; the mill, 10s.; Mr. Chalk's living, 1 yardland, 10s.; William Hibberd's living, 1½ yardlands, 14s.; Jasper Strong's living, 1 yardland, 10s. Elias Down's living, 1 yardland, 10s.; Richard Hoskins's living, 1 yardland, 3s.; Eleanor Hibberd's living, ½ yardland, 5s.; Henry Elliot's living 2½ yardlands, 5s.; Robert Walker's living, 2 yardlands, 5s.; wid. Joan Hibberd's living, 2½ yardlands, 5s.; total £11 2s. No house or the least ground to build a house on.

Benjamin Hope vicar, Thomas London churchwarden, Richard Hiskins, William Selwood, overseers, William Hibbeard, Robert Walker.

BUTTERMERE rectory

119   1671 (D1/24/32/1)
A dwelling house, barn and backside with a plot of ground adjoining, c. ½a. 1a. in the W. field with Mr. Curl's field on all sides, 1a. in the Church field, the N. end of the butt bordered on Mr. Curl's hedge.

Joseph Nixon rector, Thomas Waller, William Letts, churchwardens.

120   8 Jan 1705 (D1/24/32/2)
Arable land; 2a., 1 lying in Lay Bridge field, the other in Ivy's field. Garden and backside, c. 1½a.; churchyard, 40 lugs. 1 house 1 barn, 2 stables, 1 small outshouse.

Edward Eliot, rector, Thomas Elton and Walter Curle, churchwardens.

121   28 Jul 1783 (D1/24/32/3)
Terrier exhibited at the primary visitation of bishop Shute at Marlborough. The parsonage house built with brick and covered with tile, 2 rooms on the ground floor with a brewhouse and 3 rooms above with a garden c. ¼a. with a barn. 1a. of arable land on White farm in Lower Ivy's field and 1a. of arable in Lawbridge field on the Home Farm. All tithes within the parish paid to the rector.

There belongs to the church: 1 chalice with cover, 1 linen cloth and napkin for the communion table, 1 surplice, 2 bells with the frames. Churchyard repaired by the parish by a rate.

Thomas Baker, rector, John Batt, churchwarden, Joseph Barns, chief inhabitant.

CALNE rectory (impropriate)

122   n. d. c. 1700[1] (D5/10/1/7)

A capital messuage or parsonage house, stable, barnes, outhouses, garden, orchards, backsides, court yard and close, 5a. A close of pasture called Pound close, 7a., lying near the parsonage house on the backside of the barn and orchard. A close of meadow called Old orchard, 14a., having old orchard grounds and being part of the premises, on S. E., land of Mr. Gifford called Long close S., land of Mr. Wastfield called Hill croft W., land of Sir George Hungerford called the Rudges N.

2 closes of pasture lying E. side of the last meadow, 30a., the old orchard mead W., Cow lane S., land of Sir John Button now occupied by Walter Dolman N., land being part of the prebend of Calne E.; 3 closes of meadow and pasture called Newcrofts, 40a., having the N. field of Calne W., a common called the Marsh E., a common meadow called Hony Garston S., lands of Mr. Duckett and Sir George Hungerford called Roundhills and Rudgemead N.; certain closes of arable and pasture called Lukhill, 65a. and 15a., sometimes in coppice but grubbed up and destroyed many years since abutting on a river N.W., and having the N. field of Calne S. E., lands late of William Jordan esq., called Lower Withy N., land of Israel Noyes W. and a lane from Calne to Whitley E.; 2 closes of meadow and pasture and the moiety of a close all abutting on N. field W. and a ground called Bestbrook N.; 10a. being part of and adjoining to Lickhill; 2a. of arable land abutting on the Armitage in the N. field of Calne called Headlands; 16a. of arable called the Parsonage piece abutting on the town of Calne SE., and the lands formerly of John Oath.

5 closes of meadow, pasture and arable land called Penn, 3a., abutting upon Compton; a close of meadow and pasture, 8a., abutting on Cherrill Pen E.; 2 closes of pasture, 20a., abutting on the lands of Mr. Black, which premises, occupied by William Romyn, are called Penn Bargain; a close of Lammas ground called Beavensbrook or Beaversbrook encompassed with the lands of Mr. Touchett, 5a., in the tenure of Romyn; a close of pasture called Taylors close, 7a., abutting on highway S., a brook N. and bounded with the lands of the said Mr. Black and Mr. Touchett; a close of meadow and pasture called Woodbreach or Woodbreath, 3a., abutting on Calne marsh lying next to Taylers close both in the tenure of William Romyn; a close of meadow and pasture, 1a., abutting on Calne marsh, lying near Pen coppice; a parcel of arable land lying in N field in the tithing of Quemerford and another piece of arable land in the S. field of Quemerford tithing both abutting on the way from Yatesbury [Gatesbury] to Calne containing 20a., lying near Snapp; 2a. more by Snapp and 5a. lying on Boredown now in the tenure of Robert Banister; 12a. in Cherrill field in the occupation of [. . .]; a parcel of arable lying in a place called Westmington in the tithing of Stock, 2a.,

bounded N. land of Mr. Snadden, S. land of Mr. Duckett, lying near the quarry; a messuage in the tithing of Barwick with a barn, parcel of ground near adjoining, 1a., called the Parsonage house and close; 21a. of arable in the N. field of Barwick abutting on a furlong called the Ore; a parcel of meadow, 5a., lying in Abbord mead abutting on a ground called the Gore on S. E.; 1a. in the same mead lying under the Lower hedge all in the tenure of Arthur Robbins; 2a. in the same mead called the Abbord abutting on a common called the Lowe; 2a. of meadow in the same mead abutting on the lands of Mr. Hungerford on E. end; a messuage and shop in Calne Green in the tenure of Henry Fildowne, blacksmith, purchased by John Gent of Mr. Davenant, rent 10s.; a cottage in Quemerford called Chinnocks, in the tenure of Roger Pountney; a cottage in Frog lane called Nash in the tenure of George Tibold; 19a. of arable land in Cherrill field in the tenure of Thomas Low; 2 pieces thereof contain 12a. bounded with an a. of John Pountney S. and 5a. in the possession of Peirce N.; 2 x ½a. shooting down to a river called Riversbrook, 1a. of John Browne shooting along by it; 2a. more headed with the said Robert Peirce's land; 2a. more shooting with the way leading to the common, 1a. of William Cadwell N.; 2a. on Boredown and 5a. of meadow in Abbord in the tenure of Kew, 4 of which shoot upon the Gore and the other against the Low gate. Tithe corn, hay, lamb and wool of Calne except part of Calne park pretended to be extra parochial and claimed by the cathedral of Salisbury by grant of Charles II. George Long.

The rest of the document is a schedule of copyhold estates of the manor of Calne and quitrents with the rights of the manor, a similar amended document is attached to a lease of the rectory in 1761, WSRO CC Treasureship 7.

1.   The document is written in a late 17th century hand and includes reference to Sir George Hungerford who died in 1714 having succeeded his father who died in 1667.

CALSTONE rectory

123   29 Jul 1783 (D1/24/33/1)

A mansion house built with white stone rough cast and tiles, consisting of a large kitchen, parlour, hall, passage, outer and inner pantry with cellars under the parlour and passage. Parlour, oak floor and papered; kitchen, hall, passage etc., stone floored and ceiled; the hall ceiled, papered, and wainscotted chair high with oak; upstairs over the kitchen a large dining room, elm floored, an imitation wainscot chair high, papered and ceilinged; 3 bed chambers, elm floored, 1 papered; a small lobby; a ceiled garret, plastered and floored with elm, and a lumber garret near.

A garden and orchard of c. ¾a., a barton, stable and barn adjoining. The long close E. of the barn of c. 3a. The church close with the church yard of c. 1¼a. The ground in the Slades near Abbord common, 2½a.; 2½a in the W. Homm and 4a. in the E. Homm, both in Abbord. In the S. Field 22a. 3yd. as follows: 5a, in Church furlong; 1a. in Vaccum; 1¼a. in Wadwyn; 1a. in Horse combe; 1½a. in Broadwell; 1½a. in Blackland field near the Devizes way; 1½a. in Short Broad lands in Black furlong; 1a. in Lower furlong; 1½a. in Mart lands; 3yd. in Pease furlong; 1yd. in Horse combe. In the N. field 14a. as follows: 1½a. in Goddin's Head; 1a. in Woodroffs combe; 3½a. in Hockley; 3a. in Stridge furlong; 3a. in Blackland field; 1a. in Racks furlong. The tithes of Mr. Mitchell's farm, now the earl of Shelburne's. The above common field lands viz. 36a. 3yd. with the great and small tithes of the earl of Shelburne's farm are now let to the earl or tenant for £37 p. a. £1 5s. p. a. composition for a ground called Zeimons in Stockley payable by John Bishop of Calne at Michaelmas [29 Sep]. £1 composition for grass lands now occupied by farmer Hill, formerly by Mr. Ernly. £2 p. a. composition for 13½a. of the lands formerly Mr. Ernly's, now occupied by Farmer Jenner. 10s. p. a. for Mr. Bayly's mill. The tithes of Mr. Oriell's 6a. in Stockley; c. 11a. in Abbord formerly part of Mitchell's farm, now belonging to Robert Rawling. A piece of arable, c. 9a., on the N. of Blackland Common called Parsonage lease, rented by William Bewly at £12 p. a. Right of common in Calstone and query if not on the Downs too.

The discharged living was augmented by Queen Anne's Bounty during the incumbency of Mr. Millar;[1] the present incumbent, knows neither when this was nor who are the trustees, but supposes it was c. 50 years ago as he remembers Mr. Millar. The estate of c. 22a. lies in Box, the greatest part pasture with no building, and is well known there as Calstone church land, now rented by William Wiltshire who pays £26 p. a. clear rent.

Thomas Heath rector, instituted 3 Nov. 1758, Robert Crook churchwarden, Robert Bailey.

1. Recte Millard. George Millard was rector, 1701-1740. This augmentation took place after the establishment of the Queen Anne's Bounty in 1705.

[A copy (WSRO 727/3/16) of an account of the lands and tithes of Calstone rectory let to James Smith, rector of Blackland, in 1720 includes the land as in **123** with the following tithes.

Hay: Take the tenth cock of all hay whether English, French or clover and the seed of it. Colts: for every colt fallen within the parish 3s. 4d.; Cows: for every cow milked within the parish 8d. due at Lammas tide [1 Aug]; calves: for every calf fallen within the parish 4d. due at Lammas tide; for every calf weaned ½d., and if sold before they come to be milked or yoked the tenth of the money. Sheep: the tenth weight or tenth lb. of all wool and the tenth of the locks. But if the sheep be sold before shear time ¼d. per month for every sheep and the same for every lamb sold after St. Mark's day and ¼d. per month for every sheep and the same for every lamb sold after St. Mark's day [25 Apr] and 1s. 4d. per month for all sheep taken in as agistments. Lambs: the tenth (or if no more the seventh) of all lambs fallen within the parish to be paid on St. Mark's day if less then the 3d. for each lamb or to carry them to the next year. Unprofitable cattle: to pay the tenth penny rent of their feeding. N. B. Unprofitable cattle are horses taken in from any one being out of the parish or in it; sheep bought in to be fatted just after they are shorn and sold again fat; all cows, oxen or young beasts that are put to fattening and sold. Fruit: tithe apples, pears and all other fruit. Pigs: the tenth, if no more the seventh of all pigs, if less then 3d. for each pig. Customary dues: every communicant pays at Easter 2d., every hen ½d. every cock 1d. at Easter.]

ALL CANNINGS rectory

124   14 Oct 1608 (D1/24/34/1)

A parsonage house with gardens and backsides, *c.* 2a.; a stable of 3 fields; 2 barns of 11 fields, 1 cut[1] and 2 porches;[2] all this W. of a close of the demesnes called Bery garden, S. to the street, E. to Priest lane, N. to Moor brook.[3] Another house[4] in the middle of the village with a garden and backside, *c.* 3yd. lying S. of John Hiscocks,[5] Joan Masling wid.[6] N. A little plot called Prebend close with a little house lying S. and W. to William Peerse,[7] N. to Richard Philp,[8] E. to Richard Masling.[9] A close called the Parson's ham with a meadow adjoining, both, *c.* 6a., lying between East hams and Whitepitt mead. A plot of meadow called Nithes and a little dole in Stantons mead, *c.* 1 yd. A plot of meadow called the Parson's gore between Great Oxemoor and Allington mead, *c.* ½a.; the hay of 1a. meadow in Great Oxemoor adjoining the same gore; the hay of a plot of meadow in Little Oxmoore commonly called the Parson's plot.

24a. of arable, 4a. of which lie in Little Westbrook; ½a. in the N side at Sheepbridge;[10] 2a. in Short Haslett; 1a. at Brandiron; ½a. in Chestels; ½a. in Rugfurlong; ½a. adjoining Blackland; 2½a. in Canningsmarsh furlong; 1a. on the top of Woodway; 3 x ½a. in Whetton ditch; 3 x ½a. on Stibbe; ½a. in the Crosse furlong shooting on Hare Path way; ½a. in Short Hytchings; ½a. in the further Coombe; 3 x ½a. in the Panne; 2 x ½a. on top of Foxhill; ½a. shooting up to Marlborough W.; ½a. at Leyne; ½a. at Ashmeade; ½a. at Nithes. 1a. in the S. field under the Windmill ball; 1yd. in Upper Wednsfurlong;[11] 3yd. At Drove Elm;[12] ½a. shooting on Stewards mead.[13]

Feeding for 42 sheep, 3 rother beasts on the E. down; feeding for 30 sheep in the common fields; 1 beasts leaze and 3 sheep leaze in Farrell; 4 kine leaze in the farm ground called Hillground and the meadows adjoining, either into Great Oxmoore or into Old [Owld] mead, to be kept from the Invention of the Cross [3 May] until St. Martin's day [10 Nov]. [. . .] We have heard that the parson ought to have 8 oxen to go and to feed with the farmer's oxen, but we never knew them to, only 4 marks to have been paid.[14]

Jeffrey Pottenger, William Burden, John Hiskox, churchwardens, Ricard Redell, William Hiskox.

1. Cut end in **125 – 127**.
2. A coach house added in **125 –127**.
3. Churchyard of 1yd. added in **125 – 127**.
4. A little close in **125 – 127**.
5. Copyhold lands anciently of William Fowler in **125 – 127**.
6. Robert Maslen in **125 – 127**.
7. William Aston in **125 – 127**.
8. Thomas Stevens in **125 – 127**.
9. Daniel Maslen in **125 – 127**.
10. N. field in **125 – 127**.
11. Upper Whettons furlong in **126** and **127**.
12. Drove Elm way in **125**.

13. Stits mead in **125**.
14. Which the farmer did usually pay to the parson added in **126** and **127**.

125   16 Nov 1680 (D1/24/34/2)
*As **124** with amendments in footnotes.* William Baldwin, rector, John Hurford, John Beake, Edward Want [X], churchwardens. William Masken John Goodman, Thomas Simes, sidesmen.

126   22 Dec 1704 (D1/24/34/3)
*As **124** with amendments in footnotes.* George Stoodley, rector, William Fowle senior, Thomas Ashton, Stephen Barrett, Thomas Neat, churchwardens. John Beake, William Holloway, Jeffery Neal, sidesmen.

127   30 Jul 1783 (D1/24/34/4)
*As **124** with amendments in footnotes.* John Fullerton rector, Thomas Andrews, William Maslen, churchwardens, William Gale, Thomas Maslen, Thomas Maslen, William Miell.

ALL CANNINGS: Etchilhampton chapelry

128   n. d. early 17th cent. (D1/24/34/5)
A dwelling house now made a barn and a close adjoining, c. ½a. A meadow by Shortlands adjoining Woodroses meadow of Coate, *c.* 3½a., which is to be hained at Candlemas [2 Feb], cut and rid by Lammas [1 Aug], afterwards it belongs to the inhabitants. 1 ridge in Shortlands field.
      William Pinel [X], William Jankins, churchwardens, John Woodhouse, William Lawrence, questmen.

GREAT CHALFIELD rectory

129   1671 (D1/24/35/1)
No house or outhouse, only a chamber in the manor house called the minister's chamber, but ancient men have heard there was a parsonage house in Parsonage close alias Pen close near the manor house. On the report of men long since dead there have been glebe lands but we never heard that any of this incumbent's predecessors possessed them, nor is any terrier to be found although diligent search has been made in the courts at London and elsewhere. We have heard that Mr. Bradshaw,[1] parson before the present incumbent, had his diet, the keeping of a horse, and £16 p. a. of the owners of the manor in lieu of tithes for 40 years. The present incumbent has had for 40 years a composition of £32 p. a. paid by the owners of the manor in lieu of tithes and the keeping of a horse, and discharge from all taxes and payments except tenths payable to the king and procurations to the bishop. The tithes of Moxhams farm worth £5 p. a., and tithes of a ground called Bowood worth 10s. p. a. 40s. p. a. from the owners of W. Chalfield who usually come to his church.

John Wilton rector, Christopher Moxham.

1.   Robert Bradshaw was rector 1603-1629.

130   21 May 1705. (D1/24/35/2)
John Sartain, tenant of John Hall esq., pays £32 p. a. Christopher Moxham pays
£4 p. a.
          John Deacon, rector Christopher Moxham., churchwarden.

131   14 Jul 1783. (D1/24/35/3)
There is no house, outhouses or glebe. A composition of £50 p. a. is paid to the
incumbent in lieu of tithes due from the manor of Great Chalfield exempt from
all taxes except land tax and procurations to the bishop. The incumbent is paid
£3 10s. p. a. in lieu of great and small tithes due on lands in the parish belonging
to John Blagden of Gray's Inn, London esq., occupied by farmer John Reynolds.
The present incumbent has tithe hay, wool and lambs on lands in the parish
belonging to James Moxham, London, sugar refiner, but the agistment tithe due
for depasturing barren cattle on the same estate is not yet settled. The incumbent
is paid 19s. in lieu of tithe of a field called Bowood.
          The rectory has been augmented with £400, £200 of which was from the
governors of the Queen Anne bounty, the other is the benefaction of late Robert
Neale, Corsham esq., The annual interest is £8.
          For every wedding by banns 2s. 6d., by licence 5s.; the minister and
parishioners pay to the clerk and sexton the usual Easter dues and fees at weddings
and funerals. The church has a communion table and linen cloth, 1 silver chalice
with a cover, 1 silver patten, with the inscription 'Deo et Ecclesiae'. 1 pulpit and
reading desk. 1 pulpit cushion covered with blue cloth. 1 large bible of the last
translation, 1 large common prayer book, 2 bells, a chest, a surplice, 2 register
books. The chancel has been repaired by the rector, the aisle by the owners of
the manor and the body of the church by the parish.
          Clement Glynn, rector James Fricker, churchwarden, William Pain.

GREAT CHALFIELD: Imber chapelry

132   14 Apr 1678 (D1/24/35/4)
Nothing belonging to our minister but only what salary Thomas Thynne esq., is
pleased to allow him. Gregory Tinker, William Harwood, churchwardens.

BOWER CHALKE vicarage

133   n. d. late 16th cent. (D1/24/36/l)
Tithes of 24½a. arable land, 24a. meadow. Tithe wool, lambs, calves, pigs, geese
and all other privy tithes within the liberty of Bower Chalke. The parson has
nothing but tithe corn and hay.

134   1671 (D1/24/36/2)

The vicar's tithing. Woodminton: Jn. Shergold[1] pays tithe on his Layes Barn close, c. 3a. Thos. Penny[2] pays tithe on Hobbs at S. end from Barns to the Bank by an ash tree on one side and the other side contains ½a.; for Rookehayes in Quidham Street he pays tithe to the vicar from S.W. end to Robert Shorts close end,[3] 1yd. of ground. Roger Brittaine[4] pays tithe for an orchard. Thomas Clarke[5] pays tithe on Cow close behind his dwelling house, c. 3a.; for Payne mead at S. end from the bars to the bank athwart the ground, c. 1yd.; for Church close at S. end to the Watercross 1yd. of ground. Richard Burrough pays tithe on W. meadow at the S. end to the willow tree, c. ½a. of ground; for E. meadow at the S. end of the willow tree c. ½a. John Penny[6] pays tithe on his Home close at S. end to the Walnut tree, c. 10 lugs of ground and the tithe of ½a. of arable ground. W wid. Gold[7] pays tithe on W. Close at W. end, c. lyd. of ground. Alexander Lawes[8] pays tithe on W. Meadow at S. end, c. 1yd. of ground.

Quidham Street: Richard Burrough[9] pays tithe on the meadow called W. orchard lying by the Pounds c. l0 lugs of ground. For N. end of the meadow lying against Henry Morgan for Rookehayes from the Street to the 2 small ashes c. 20 lugs of ground. Henry Morgan[10] pays tithe on W. end of his meadow called Rookhayes to the plum tree in the middle of the ground, c. 1yd. AlexanderLawes[11] pays tithe for c. 20 lugs of ground. Snooke[12] pays tithe for an orchard. William Randoll[13] pays tithe on W. end of his meadow called Rookehayes to the Bank, c. 10 lugs of ground. Robert Short[14] pays tithe on W. end of his little meadow, c. 25 lugs of ground. For all of his[15] meadow called Rookehayes, c. 10 lugs of ground. Wid. Lawes[16] pays tithe on E. end of her meadow adjoining the orchard c. 10 lugs of ground; for her[17] meadow called W. Hoskins, c. lyd. of ground. Henry Morgan[18] pays tithe for c. 10 lugs of ground. John Norris[19] pays tithe on his meadow called Greenhayes, c. ½a. and for 6a. of arable ground.

The Lower Street: Henry Good[20] pays tithe for his meadow called Cemis orchard, c. 30 lugs of ground; for his[20] ham lying against Knole, c. 20 lugs of ground; for his Barneclose, 3x ½a. W. wid. Hutchins[21] pays tithe for c. l yd. of ground. Robert Button[22] pays tithe for c. la. and 1yd. of ground. Robert Fry[23] pays tithe for c. la. of ground. Thomas Burden[24] pays tithe for an orchard and he[25] pays tithe for c. l yd. ground. Edmund Pitman[26] pays tithe for an orchard. William Gold[27] pays tithe for his little meadow, c. ½a. of ground. John Gold[28] pays tithe for his W. meadow except a little in the over corner from the willow tree athwart the ground to the way. John Shergold[29] pays tithe for c. 60 lugs of ground. Andrew Harris[30] pays tithe for an orchard.[31] Wid. Penny[32] pays tithe for an orchard. wid. Heysome[33] pays tithe for c. 20 lugs of ground. wid. Shergold[34] pays tithe for an orchard. Edward Hardiman[35] pays tithe corn for 18½a. of arable. John Randoll[36] pays tithe for an orchard. Thomas Penny[37] pays tithe for c. ½a. of ground. John Best[38] pays tithe for an orchard.[39] John Ellery[40] tithe for c. la. of ground. Dorothy Holmes[41] pays tithe for 1yd. of ground.[42] John Gold alias Hawkins[43] pays tithe for c. l yd. of ground.

Moreover the vicar has all the tithe wool and 1½d. cow white for calves; if the inhabitants sell them he has the tenth penny if we kill them he has ½d. For the fall or if we weane them he has ½d. for every calf weaned. He has a vicarage house (he had a barn but now there is none), a garden a churchyard belonging to our vicar and now in his own possession. All the aforesaid parties do and ought to pay the vicar tithe wool and lamb and all privy tithes whatsoever (only except according to our custom the tithe of our sons and daughters and servants) wool and lambs everyone his parcel by himself. Also every tenant of the earl of Pembroke that dies possessed of his tenement and pays a heriot to the house of Wilton is to pay a mortuary to our vicar and the Easter book belongs to our vicar.

John Sloper, vicar, Robert Short, Thomas Penny, churchwardens.

1. Henry Good in **136**.
2. Sarah Penny wid. in **136**. John Good in 1718 (see **136**).
3. Deborah Short's close end in 1718 (see **136**).
4. John Fulford in **135**. Thomas Bond in **136**.
5. John Clarke in **135**. John Clark in **136**. Chas. Clark in 1718 (see **136**).
6. Henry Good in **136**. Thomas Penruddock esq. in 1718 (see **136**).
7. John Gould in **136**.
8. William Coster in **136**. Thomas Day in 1718 (see **136**).
9. Thomas Burrough in **136**.
10. John Gould in **136**. Robert Gould in 1718 (see **136**).
11. William Foyle in 1718 (see **136**).
12. William Ferguson in **136**. Thomas Foyle in 1718 (see **136**).
13. Henry Randall in **136**. Edward Hardyman in 1718 (see **136**).
14. Deborah Short in **136**. Nicholas Good in 1718(see **136**).
15. Deborah Short in **136**.
16. Richard Lawes in **135**. Wid. Lawes in **136**. Richard Bristow in 1718 (see **136**).
17. Richard Lawes in **135**. Wid. Lawes in **136**.
18. Mary Morgan in 1718 (see **136**).
19. Henry Good in **136**.
20. Roger Good in **136**. Henry Good in 1718 (see **136**).
21. Roger Good in **136**.
22. Deborah Short in **136** Robert Short in 1718 (see **136**).
23. Wid. Savage in **136**. Wid. Herrington in 1718 (see **136**).
24. William Coster in **136**.
25. Wid. Savadge in **136**.
26. Thomas Gould in **136**. John Gould in 1718 9 (see **136**).
27. John Gould in **135**. Wid. Gould in 1718 (see **136**).
28. John Gould in **135** and **136**.
29. Henry Good in **136**.
30. Henry Toomer in **136**.
31. William Harris pays tithe corn for 6a. of arable in **135**. Henry Toomer in **136**.
32. Thomas Gould in **136**.
33. Henry Good in 1718 (see **136**).
34. With John Shergold in **135** and alone in **136**. Edward Hardyman in 1718 (see **136**).
35. James Hardyman in **136**. John Witt in 1718 (see **136**).
36. Francis Morgan in **136**.
37. Avice Penny in **135**. Thomas Penny in **136**. Mary Penny in 1718 (see **136**).
38. William Norris in 1718 (see **136**).

39. John Winterbourne for an orchard added in **135**.
40. Mary Ellery in **135**. John Best in **136**. Elizabeth Best in 1718 (see **136**).
41. Thomas Sansum in **135**. Henry Best in **136**. Elizabeth Best in 1718 (see **136**).
42. Edward Hardyman for 1 yard added in **136**. David Hardyman in 1718 (see **136**).
43. Nicholas Gould alias Hakins in **136**. Nicholas Goold in **136**.

135   13 Dec 1677 (D1/24/36/3)
As **132** with amendments in footnotes. John Sloper, vicar, Alexander Lawse, John Clarke, churchwardens.

136   1704 (D1/24/36/4)
*As **134** with amendments in footnotes.* This is a copy made in 1718 of a terrier of 1704 held by Mr. Roger Good. *The names ascribed to the year 1718 in the footnotes to **134** are added in another hand in this copy.*

BROAD CHALKE vicarage

137   1609 (D1/24/37/l)
The vicar has tithe corn of 24½a. of which 18a. belong to a copyhold called ?Whitmarsh occupied by Edward Hardeman, 6a. occ. Rowland Morrice and ½a. occupied by Henry Peny. He has the tithe of 24a. of meadow ground. Tithe wool, lambs and calves in the liberty of Broad Chalke with pigs, geese and all privy tithes. The parson has tithe corn of all except the above excepted.

Thomas Sheregall, Nicholas Penny, churchwardens. John Shargall, Rafe Curtis, sidesmen, John Archer, minister. *Names in the same hand.*

138   1671 (D1/24/37/2)
A vicarage house consisting of 4 bays of building, a brewhouse and stable with a garden and backside, *c.* lyd. of ground. The herbage of the churchyard. Tithe corn of 40½a. of college[1] ground occupied by John Folliat and Anthony Archer.[2] Tithe wool, hay, calves, cow white and small tithes in Broad Chalke except on the farm and except the tithe hay of a little plot of ground of wid. Dwe[3] and 2 parcels of ground called Marchmead and Greatcroate occupied by Henry Randoll except also a little plot in Mr. Watkinson's[4] living and a little ground called Little Cozens and Wett Mead occupied by Ralph Good and a little mead in the river about a half of ground occupied by Thosmas New.[5] Tithe hay on the orchard and penning upon the down and a small parcel of ground[6] adjoining in W. Gurston [Gerarsdon], together with tithe calves, cow white and all small tithes and 2 parts of 3 of tithe wool there. The parson's third in E. Gurston belongs to the vicar, and a third of tithe wool except John Lodge's living. The parson has 2 parts, the vicar has tithe of a little plot in E. Gurston occupied by Mr. Thynne. The vicar also has tithe wool, calves and cow white there. The vicar has tithe wool of Knighton farm, the tithe hay of part of a ground called Barn close, *c.* 1½a.; 1 other ground called Barge close; another ground called the Picked croft and a little plot over the river called the Paddocks. Tithe calves, cow white and tithe hay in Knighton.

Stoke Farthing: The vicar has tithe wool, calves, cow white and hay on tenements there except on 3 plots of ground on S. side of the river belonging to the farmer. He also has tithe calves and cow white and other small tithes on the farm of Stoke Farthing. The vicar has a salary of £16 5s. p. a. paid by the parsonage of Broad Chalke.[7]

John Sloper vicar, Henry Randol, Ralph Good, William Lawes, George Lawes, John Penny churchwardens.

1. King's College, Cambridge.
2. John Folliate and Anthony Archer in **139**.
3. Dewe in **139**.
4. Mr. Henry Watkinson in **139**.
5. Anthony Penny in **139**.
6. Called the close under the hill in **139**. A little plot called Church Hays added in **139**.
7. Paid by Mr. George Penruddocke out his rents due to the college in **139**.

139   19 Feb 1678 (D1/24/37/3)
As **138** with amendments in footnotes and additions as follows: Tithe hay of Rookehyes part of the farm of E. Gurston [Gerrardston]. Tithe hay of a ground belonging to Timothy Lodge's tenement on W. side of Philip Bennett's house and orchard and on Philip Bennett's orchard all in E. Gurston. Tithe hay of a ground belonging to William Whitmarsh's tenement next to his house in W. Gurston. Tithe wool of Thomas Thorne's freehold in Knighton. Easter offerings of all communicants.

John Sloper, vicar, William Smith, Henry Goody churchwardens.

140   28 May 1705 (D1/24/37/4)
A vicarage house in very good repair, consisting of 5 rooms in a floor, a stable, an outhouse, a court and garden adjoining, c. 60 perches. The churchyard and all tithe hay except on Chalke farm, on a little plot of wid. Dewe, Marsh meadow and Great croft belonging to Henry Randoll, little plot occupied by Henry Wattkason, Little Cozens and W. meadow occupied by Ralph Good and a little meadow by the water belonging to Anthony Penny. In W. Gurston [Gerrerdstone] tithe hay of orchard and small parcel of ground adjoining and the penning upon the down, and tithe calves cow white and 2 parts in 3 of tithe wool there. In E. Gurston 1 part in 3 of tithe wool, except John Lodges living where the vicar has none. The vicar has all tithe wool of Knighton part of tithe hay of Barn close and Burges close and the tithe of Picked croft and the Parrock. Tithe hay, calves, cow white of all tenants of Stoke Farthing [Stoke Verdon] except 3 small meadows on S. side of the river. He has tithe calves, cow white, garden and orchard of the farm of Stoke Farthing. All tithe wool except of Stoke farm and before excepted. Tithe corn of college copyhold[1] occupied by Walter Folliatt and Ant. Penny. 5s. p. a. from the parsonage in lieu of privy tithes. In all worth £32 p. a.

Henry Austen vicar, Thomas Read, Thomas Lewes, churchwardens, Phillip Witt, David Smith, Thomas Lodge.

1. see **138** note 1.

141 n. d. mid 18th cent.[1] (D1/24/37/5)

Glebe: E. field on S. side. At Berry Hill 10a. W. end against a head a. of wid. Odbur, S. side against a small piece of Down and N side lying by 3 x ½a. of land belonging to the rectory. 3 x ½a., E. end abutting against Knighton hedge W. end abutting against the foresaid head a. of wid. Odbur, S. side lying against the foresaid 10a., N. side by 3a. of the same. 3a., E. end abutting against Knighton hedge, W. end abutting against the foresaid head a. of wid. Odbur, S. side lying by the 3 x ½a., at N. E. corner a short green linch. 8a., S. end abutting against the foresaid 3a., N. end abutting against the highway, E. side lying against Knighton hedge, W. side lying by a linch. 12a., S. end abutting against the highway, N. end abutting against a hedge, E. side lying by Knighton hedge, W. side bounded by a linch. 2a., W. end abutting against the way, E. end abutting against a ½a. of Phil. Witt, S. side headland to a furlong belonging to several persons, N. side bounded by 1a. belonging to Bulls living. 2a. at the field end, S. end abutting against the Down, N. end abutting against an a. of Robert Gold, E. and W. sides bounded by 2 linches.

The Middle field on S. side: 4a., E. end abutting against an a. of John Foliat, W. end abutting against an a. of Henry Randol, N. side bounded by a linch, S. side bounded by an a. of Henry Randol. 10a., the upper piece called Pisshill, S. end abutting against an a. of Bull, N. end abutting against the highway, bounded on both sides by linches. 10a. in the same furlong, S. end abutting upon Welcomb hill, N. end abutting upon an a. of Bulls bounded on both sides by linches.

The W. field on S. side: Broken Bridge piece, 5a., S. end abutting upon an a. of wid. White, N. end abutting upon an a. of Phillip Witt, bounded with highway W., linch E. Pound Piece, 7a., N. end abutting upon an a. of Phillip Witt, S end abutting upon ½a. of Phillip Witt, bounded with 2 linches. 4a., E. end abutting upon 5a. of Robert Gold, W. end abutting upon Richard Lushe, N. side with ½a. of William Dean, S. side. 1a. of John Foliot. 3a. in Hay furlong, W. end abutting upon Mr. Combe, E. end upon Middle field, bounded on both sides with 2 linches. 10a., E. end abutting on an a. of William Bennet, W. end abutting upon the Down, bounded with the Down S. side, a linch upon N. side.

The E. field on N. side: 2a., E. end abutting upon Henry Penny, W. end upon a piece of the rectory, bounded on N. side with wid. Odbur, highway S. side.

The Middle field on N. side: 4a., E. end abutting on 2a. of the rectory, and 2a. of wid. Odbur, W. end upon Mr. Good and Henry Penny, bounded S. side with the highway, N. side with a linch. 6a., E. end abutting upon Mr. Good and Henry Penny, W. end abutting upon ½a. of the rectory, bounded both sides with linches. ½a., being headland to the said 6a., W. end abutting against the highway, S. and N. ends against an a. of Mr. Watkinson, W. side bounded with an a. of Mr. Watkinson. 4a., E. end abutting upon 20 ridges W. end upon an a. of wid. Odbur, bounded on both sides with linches.

The W. field in N. side: 3a. N. end abutting upon an a. of Henry Penny, S. end against a linch, with linches on both sides. 2½a., N. end abutting upon the last piece, S. end abutting upon an a. of Henry Penny and bounded with a linch on E. side and Anthony Penny on W. side. 240 sheep leaze on S. side, of which 40 have been abated. 10 sheep leaze on N. side with 19 cow leaze on the Downs and stubble fields.

1a. out of the earl of Pembroke's wood in Cranborne Chase, to take his choice of 1 corner, 40 perches in length; the tithe of 4 coppices called Shewsbury Coppices and the tithe of Knighton coppice belonging to Knighton farm. 1 parcel of wood called Parsonage Goar bounded Knighton Down E. side, the Clear Down N. side, Stockeys and Crays W. side, Marten, S. end.

Tithe: Lamb: The whole parish except Chalke farm, Stone farm, Bulls Living belonging to the rectory and Anthony Penny. Wool: A third part of W. Gurston [Gerardston] farm, 2 third parts at E. Gurston farm. Hay: At W. Gurston farm tithe of Pigeon close, Collins close, part of the hanging belonging to the meadow. At E. Gurston farm, except part of a close called Brookman and the paddock belonging to William Whitmarsh lying against the water. At Chalk farm: Hengor penning, Longmead, Marsh mead [. . .] Mill mead, Great Cozens, Great Horsemead, Piggs close, Little Horsemead, Backside acres, Bury orchard. At Knighton farm, Long mead, the Ham lying at Hatch field stile, part of Barn close lying next to the house, Wiseman's close, French Grass close, Square croft, Hangmills, the upper part of Bright Pool mead, the Grass Penning. Due from Mr. Good in N. Side: The Little mead against Staple Ash, Little Cozens, the Mead lying in Long Bridge furlong. Little mead belonging to Anthony Penny; a Little mead belonging to Mr. Combs. The Cleave belonging to wid. Dean. The mead belonging to Mr. Watkinson. A close by the field belonging to Mr. Cray a mead lying by the water and tithe hay that shall come or increase of the seeds sown in the corn fields. 3 pit ridges due from Fifield farm[1], 1 ridge yearly for which we receive £1 18s. p. a. 4 pit ridges due from Stoke farm, 1 ridge for which we receive £1 p. a. Wheat from Chalke farm 6 ridges each ridge containing 3 perches in breadth and 35 perches in length to be cut and brought home to the parsonage in good husbandlike manner. Corn: The whole parish except Chalk farm, Bulls Living, a living belonging to Anthony Penny and Chalk farm for which we receive the ridges mentioned before. N. B. This is a copy of a terrier in the hands of Mr. Barns, Mr. Penruddock's tenant.

Aaron Thompson.[2]

1.   Fifield Bavant.
2.   Aaron Thompson was rector 1724-1752.

CHARLTON (near Pewsey) vicarage

142   1609 (D1/24/38/1)
A dwelling house and barn adjoining, a dove house, a several ground belonging to it, c. 1a., in which there is an orchard and a garden. Tithes of 36 yardlands and privy tithes of 7 yardlands.

John Amer, John Mundy, churchwardens.

143   5 May 1705 (D1/24/38/2)
A dwelling house, barn, stable, dovehouse, garden, orchard and backside, c. ⅓a. The feeding and agistment of the herbage in the churchyard adjoining.

All small and privy tithes. Great tithes on 11 yardlands are appropriated to the vicarage.

Thomas Twining, vicar, Robert Mundy, Thomas Earle churchwardens, Thomas Fowle, William Miles [X] William Amor [X] Robert Pinckney.

144 8 Jul 1735 (D1/24/38/3)

A dwelling house, pigeon house, a barn, backside garden and orchard c. la. The whole tithes, arable and pasture of 11 yardlands in the parish viz. a farm owned by Esq. Drax occupied by John Lavington, 5 yardlands; Mr. Mundy 's estate occ. by himself 3 yardlands; John Coopers 1 yardland occupied by Robert Michel; 1 yardland farm, owned by Ann Smith now Robert Michel occupied by by himself; 1 yardland farm, Costards, now Mr. Fowle.

All small dues for offerings, calves, cow white, apples, eggs, and gardens. The tithe of Still's orchard with the tithe of Farm close above it as far as the Croft hedge and footpath but no more than the width of Still's orchard.

As for the mudwall bounding the vicarage close next to the highway to the W., the owner of the Great farm or is tenant is to keep it in repair from the great stone towards the upper end of it down to the vicar's buildings. The vicar is only responsible for the repair of the gate within the wall. The vicar has the right to a small portion of tithe on John Simper's estate when the close is cut. An annuity of £10 has been lately given by the will of Rev. Dr. Robert Smith late canon of Christchurch Oxford for ever payable out of certain lands. The dean and canons are overseers and trustees.

Thomas Twining, vicar, John Fowle, John Lavington, churchwardens, Thomas Fowle, John Mundy, Robert Medl, inhabitants of Charlton.

GREAT CHEVERELL rectory

145 3 Dec 1677 (D1/24/39/l)

The parsonage house with 2 barns, a stable, bartons, orchard, gardens, and the Home close adjoining, c. 3a. A ground called Merricks, c. 3yd. Meadow grounds: in the common mead 2a. 1yd.; in the N. mead 3yd. Arable land in the W. field next to Erlestoke: in Witcombe, 3 yd.; in the Sand[1] 2½a., a thirdingdeale, and a butt; in the Clay,[2] 2a. 1yd.; on the Hill 6a. 3yd. Arable land in the E. field next to Little Cheverell: on the Hill 4a. 1yd.; in the Clay,[3] 3 x½a., a butt, and a stitch; in the Sand,[4] 5½a. All tithe[5] corn, wool, hay, cow white, calves, lands, and whatever else is tithable; all tithes of gardens, orchards, home closes and the mill. Feeding for 2 horses and 4 rother beasts in the commons and fields[6] and common of pasture for 24 sheep in the tenantry flock as it is now stinted by the yardland. 2 plots of ollett or fern in the common, c. 2a.

Henry Wright, rector, William Gibbs, John Hampton, churchwardens, William Somner.

1. Sand field in **146**.
2. W. Clay field in **146**.
3. E. Clay in **146**.

4. E. Sand in **146**.
5. The following note in the parish register by the rector in 1711 explains the tithe customs: When I took possession first of this rectory, in 1680, I found the privy tithes rated in my predecessors book in the following manner: Offerings 2d., the farm lambs 3d. each, the tenantry lambs 2d. each. Cow white 3d. per cow. Each calf killed or sold 4d. Each weaned -½d. Eggs, apples and wool paid in kind. None of the last sort paid for lambs. My immediate predecessor, Mr. [*Thomas*] Jekyll, compounded with his parishioners for 8 groats per acre, one with another in lieu of his tithe corn, which composition I have all along continued to 1711 except for that part of the common lately enclosed and other new broken up grounds and except Mr. Bruges' farm for the whereof of all kinds I received annually £20 and £19 for Mr. Townsend's farm exclusive of that part of it which Mr. Townsend holds in his own hands. Mr. Somner has paid yearly for some time past for all tithes £19 10s. Since my allotment in the commons the tenant for the glebe has paid yearly £13 10s. reserving out of it Merricks close (valued at 19s. p. a.) and my home close. Since the enclosure of the common [*in 1700 see VCH vol. 10, p. 46*] I have allowed me 2 leazes in the mead for 2 beasts at Michaelmas [29 Sep] but what I have done is no precedent to my successor for he may act otherwise if he pleases. However this short account may be of some use to him. Nathaniel Shute. (WSRO 207/2)
6. Replaced by New enclosed ground 10a. out of the common in lieu of 7 beast leaze in **146**.

146   15 Dec 1704 (D1/24/39/2)
*As **145** with amendments in footnotes.* Nathanial Shute, rector, J. Townsend, Henry Somner, Henry Bruges, An Mattocks, Thomas Harris Bruges.

147   27 Oct 1780 (D1/24/39/4)
The parsonage house with barn, stable, barton, orchard garden and home close adjoining containing in the whole 4a. 24p. Churchyard, 2r. 8p. 1 close of pasture called Merricke, by estimation 3r., by statute 2r. 11p. N. B. on part of this stands part of the blacksmith Thomas Purnell's house and part of his workshop, and outshop. These stand upon 8p. of land whereof 5p. are glebe land and 3p. wasteland. 2a. 1r. of meadow by estimation in the common mead, by statute 2a. 3r. 38p. 3yd. of meadow ground in N. Mead, by statute 2r. 10p. 3yd. of meadow ground in Witcombe, by statute 2r. 10p. 2½a., a thirdindale and butt of arable land, wood waste land by estimation in W. Sand field, by statute 2a. 2 r. 20 p. 2a. 1yd. of arable land, by estimation, in W. Clay field, by statute 1a. 2r. 34p. 6a. 3yd. of arable land, by estimation, upon W. hill, by statute 5a. 3r. 4a. 1yd. of arable land, by estimation, upon E. hill, by statute 3a. 1r. 28p. 3 x ½a., 1 butt, 1 stitch of arable land, by estimation, in E. Clay, by statute 1a. 2r. 11p. 1 new enclosed ground, 10a., lately enclosed out of the common in lieu of 7 beast leaze. Commons of pasture for 24 sheep, as it is now stinted by the yardlands, in the Tenants' flock on the hills and in the common fields of Great Cheverel and 2 beast leaze in the common mead. *Tithes as **145**.*

James Stonhouse M. D., rector, William Bartlett, John Butcher, churchwardens, John Alexander, Richard Staples, overseers, Thomas Purnell, Daniel Newman, William Chandler, Mathew Somner.

148 1783 (D1/24/39/5)

Dr. Stonhouse, rector of Great and Little Cheverel finding that no terrier had been made in either of his parishes since the year 1704 delivered into the Registry of Salisbury an accurate terrier made at some expense in measuring lands etc., date 27 Oct. 1780, and in answer to such questions as your lordship has been pleased to ask and were not there answered has added as follows. Timber on the glebe: In Henning 30 maiden oak trees at 7s. per tree In Home Close 25 maiden elm trees at 9s. per tree, 21 maiden ash trees at 7s. per tree. Round the churchyard 8 maiden elm trees at 7s. per tree. In the rickyard 8 maiden elm trees at 9s. per tree with many saplings and pollards. The rector planted 50 elm trees last autumn and a considerable number the previous autumn. Measurements of the outhouses: Stable 23ft. by 17ft. Coach house 17ft. by 12ft. 9 in. Large barn 93ft. by 19ft. 6 in. Small barn 26ft. by 17ft., Little stable 12ft. by 6ft. Stable with a loft over 14ft. by 8ft.

The parsonage house: Parlour 18ft. 8ins. by 12ft. 4ins. floor oak or elm, ceiled no wainscot. Hall 23ft. by 14ft. 8in., floor grist, ceiled. Kitchen 19ft. 3ins. by 14ft. 3in., floor grist, ceiled. Brewhouse 15ft. by 15ft., floor brick, ceiled. Parlour chamber 20ft. by 15ft., floor deal, ceiled. Back chamber 15ft. by 10ft. 4in., floor elm or oak ceiled. Second chamber 15ft. by 14ft. 3in. floor elm or oak, ceiled. Third Chamber 15ft. 6in. by 9ft., floor oak or elm ceiled. Chamber over the servants hall 23ft. by 12ft. 2in. floor elm, ceiled and hung with tapestry. The parsonage house was built at 3 different times. Part of it is rough stone part lath and plaster and part brick and timber. Covered partly with tile partly with stone slates.

No tithes due to the minister from any other townships. No bequests except from Mr. Townsend whose will[1] was enclosed [with the terrier]. 5 bells, a clock, a large silver flagon, a chalice, a patten, no mark of weight on it. No land or money in stock for repair of the church. The parishioners repair the church and the minister the chancel. 1third of the churchyard is fenced by the parish, 1 third by Mr. Warriner, 1 third by Mr. Wadman.

The same person who is clerk is sexton. His salary is small chiefly arising from marriages and burials and some trifling matter from the owners of the pews in payment of which the inhabitants are too often deficient.

James Stonhouse rector.

1. A printed extract of the will of James Townsend, proved 1730, is with the terriers (D24/39/3).

LITTLE CHEVERELL rectory

149 n. d. late 16th – early 17th cent. (D1/24/40/1)

The parsonage house containing 7 fields built in the form of a half quadrangle; a barn adjoining N. containing 6 fields and a porch; a stable, cowhouse and carthouse built together containing 5 fields and a cut; a rick barton adjoining the barn; a barton to feed cattle in the winter adjoining the barn and stable; a court adjoining the dwelling house; an orchard and hop garden N. of the house of *c.* 1a.; a garden adjoining the dwelling house reaching from the rick barton to the street; a meadow ground called Deakons below the town of 1a. and more.

Arable land in the S. W. field: beyond the farmer's forehill 7a. in the bottom of the Tenantry field of which 1a., called the Picked acre, lies between 2 linchets [lincherds] at the foot of Catehill; 1a. heads Longfryday furlong; 1a. on the highest knap of the field heads lands of Nicholas Smithe, Philip Doale and William Planke; 1a. shoots E. on the farm land between 1a. of Philip Doale, and 1a. of Nicholas Smithe; in the S. middle bottom towards Great Cheverell field 2 x ½a. on either side of 1a. of Nicholas Smithe; ½a. heads the last 2 x ½a. and other lands of the tenants; 1a. in the same furlong having S. E. 1a. of William Bower, N. E. ½a. of William Web; in the furlong that the farmer's way to Oatehill begins on ½a. between ½a. of John Hollowaye and ½a. of Thomas Forde.

Arable land on the fore side of the hill towards the town in the furlong called Hopes Nine acres: ½a. on the S. W. of the Forecliffe heading Great Cheverell field; 1a. bounded on one side by ½a. of William Bower and a linch end and the other side 1a. of William Planke; ½a. shoots towards Great Cheverell field at the end of the hollow way heading a picked a. of William Bower on one side, and ½a. of Philip Cumlyn on the other side; 2a. bounded on one side with ½a. of Nicholas Smithe, and ½a. of William Planke on the other side, shooting S. W. on Great Cheverell field; a piece of 5a. in the same furlong bounded S. E. with ½a. of William Bower and N. W. with 1a. of William Bower, one end shooting on Great Cheverell field. The last 8½a. shoots on a linchet parting the farmer's Cley and Hopes furlong, the herbage of which, as far as the land buts on it, is the parsons either to mow or eat with cattle from sowing till Lammas [1 Aug].

Arable land in the Hitche Cley: towards the higher end of the Cley 3 x ½a., one end shooting on Great Cheverell field and the other end on the farmer's Cley hedge, between 2 x ½a., one of Alice Ward, the other of Thomas Hayward; lower towards the town, about the middle of same furlong 1a. shooting from the farm hedge towards Great Cheverell field, between 1a. of Philip Doale, and 1a. of Thomas Hayward; at the end of the last a. and Thomas Hayward's a. are 3 x ½a. more belonging to the parson shooting towards Great Cheverell field, between ½a. of Nicholas Smithe, a mere, and part of ½a. of Philip Cumlyn; lower towards Stoakeway in the same furlong 2 x ½a. more. ½a. of Joan Tanner between them, on the other sides 2 x ½a. of William Bower; lower in Ham furlong ½a. more, one end shooting on Great Cheverell field, the other on a head a. of John Stille, bounded with 2 x ½a. of Thomas Hayward; at the N. end of the Hitche Cley mere to the corner of the farmer's hedge, a piece of 4a. between 2 linchets partly N. and partly S.

Arable land in the Crosse furlong: 1a. bounded S. with a yd. of William Bower, on the other side with 1a. of Philip Doale, and shooting on the farmer's close called Court close; ½a. bounded with William Bower and Nicholas Smithe, shooting as the last.

Arable land called Stoakeway: ½a. shooting W. on Great Cheverell field, bounded with a linchet, and ½a. of Nicholas Smithe which reaches only to the way; ½a. abounded with ½a. of Nicholas Smithe and 1a. of Nicholas Smithe, shooting as above; ½a. bounded with ½a. of Philip Doale, and 1a. of Nicholas Smithe, shooting as above.

Shubwell furlong: all the meadow and laine ground from the gutter dividing Great Cheverell field to a yd. of Thomas Hayward; 1yd. shooting N. and S. bounded with a yd. of Thomas Hayward, and ½a. of William Bower; ½a. shooting as the last bounded with ½a. of William Bower and ½a. of wid. Warde; ½a. more shooting as the last, bounded with ½a. of Nicholas Smithe and a yd. of wid. Warde.

Arable land in the Picked furlong: ½a. shooting E. and W. bounded with ½a. of Nicholas Smithe on either side; ½a. shooting as the last, bounded with ½a. of Thomas Hayward and 1a. of John Stille; 1a. shooting as the last bounded with 1a. of Philip Doale, and 1a. of wid. Bowlter; 1a. shooting E. on the farmer's yeate and W. on Shubwell, bounded by ½a. of Nicholas Smithe and ½a. of Henry Coaltstone; 3 x 12a. shooting N. and S. bounded with ½a. of William Bower, and the other side below the row of trees with 1a. of Philip Doale; a row of trees called Shilrowes belonging to the last 3 x ½a.; 1a. shooting as the last bounded on the lower side with a butt of Nicholas Smithe and a row of trees, and on the other side with lands end of the tenantry field; 1a. shooting W. on Shrilrowes and E. on Washingsteed, bounded with ½a. of William Bower, and ½a. of Nicholas Smithe; 2a. lying above Deakones shooting S. E. on the farmer's orchard and N. W. on 2a. of Mr Parson bounded with 1a. of Nicholas Smithe and a row of trees belonging to the parson. N. B. the parson is to have the herbage of every lands end and linchet lying next to his arable to eat or to mow before Lammas.

Arable land beyond the hill lying next to Littleton field: 2a. land shooting E. and W. bounded with the farmer's field and ½a. of wid. Tanner; 1a. more shooting as the last bounded with the hill, and ½a. of William Planke; 1yd. shooting N. and S. bounded with 1yd. of Henry Coaltstone, and 1yd. of William Bower; 1a. shooting E. on Littleton field bounded with Littleton field and ½a. of Thomas Hayward.

Arable land on the Forehill: ½a. shooting N. and S. bounded with ½a. of William Bower, and ½a. of Nicholas Smithe; 1a. more shooting as the last bounded with the farmer's field and ½a. of William Bower; ½a. more shooting as the last, bounded with ½a. of William Planke, and Littleton field.

Arable land in the Somerfield Cley: 1a. shooting E. and W. bounded with the hill and ½a. of wid. Warde; 1yd. shooting as the last bounded with 1a. of Philip Doale, and 2 butts, one of Thomas Haywarde, the other of Thomas Forde; 1a. more shooting as the last, a bounded with 1a. of John Hollewaye and ½a. of wid. Tanner; 2 x ½a. bounding ½a. of wid. Tanner, shooting W. on the farmer's Cley hedge and E. on Littleton field; 2 x ½a. more bounding ½a. of William Bower and shooting as above.

Arable land in the Hitche Cley: ½a. shooting S. W. on the farmer's Cley hedge and N. E. on Littleton field, bounded with ½a. of wid. Warde, and ½a. of Philip Cumlyn; ½a. more shooting as the last, bounded with ½a. of Philip Cumlyn, and ½a. of William Planke; ½a. more shooting as above bounded with ½a. of John Stille, and 1a. of Nicholas Smithe; 1yd. shooting N. and S. bounded with 1yd. of William Bowers and the Tenantry field; ½a. more shooting on Park hedge, bounded with 1a. of Nicholas Smithe and 1½a. of William Bower; 1a. more shooting on Park hedge bounded with ½a. of wid. Warde, and ½a. of Philip Doale.

Arable land in Wettlands furlong: ½a. shooting S. E. on Littleton field, bounded with ½a. of Philip Cumlyn, and 1yd. of William Bower.

Arable land in Uptables furlong: 1a. shooting E. on Littleton field, bounded with ½a. of Thomas Hayward and Littleton field; ½a. shooting as the last, bounded with ½a. of Thomas Haywarde and ½a. of wid. Tanner.

Arable land in the furlong by Doales Oakes: 1yd. shooting S. E. and N. W., bounded with 1yd of wid. Tanner, and ½a. of William Bower; 2 thorow a. shooting as the last lying by the barn door; 2a. of the butts at the lane end, shooting as the last, bounded with ½a. of Thomas Hayward, and ½a. of William Bower; a butt at the lane end bounded with the Chauntry close, and ½a. of Thomas Haywarde; 3yd. by the butts shooting as the last, bounded with 3yd. of Thomas Forde and 1yd of William Bower and the parson's butts; 2a. more shooting as the last, bounded with ½a. of William Bower, and a butt of Philip Doale; ½a. more shooting E. and W., bounded with Littleton field, and the highway.

Arable land in Broadlands furlong: 2 x ½a. shooting N. and S. and bounding ½a. of Nicholas Smith; ½a. more in the same furlong bounded with ½a. of Henry Coltstone, and ½a. of wid. Tanner. ½a. in Katheryne Crosse furlong shooting E. and W., bounded with ½a. Thomas Haywarde, and a piece of Philip Doale.

Arable land in the Slade furlong: 1a. called the Slade acre shooting E. and W. bounded with ½a. of Philip Cumlyn, and ½a. of William Planke; the row of trees lying on the S. W. side half along the Slade acre; a head ½a. more shooting as the last, bounded with ½a. of William Planke, and a furlong in the N. field.

Arable land in the furlong shooting on Borden stile: 1a. shooting on Borden stile, bounded with 1a. of Philip Doale, and 1a. of William Bower: 2a. together in the same furlong bounded with ½a. of Thomas Haywarde, and ½a. of William Smithe.

Arable land in Fursacre furlong: a head ½a. bounded with ½a. of William Bower, and the furlong of the N. field.

Arable land in Cleve hedge furlong: ½a. shooting on Cleeve hedge, bounded with 1a. of Thomas Haywarde and ½a. of William Planke; ½a. more shooting as the last, bounded with ½a. of William Planke, and 1yd. of wid. Tanner; 1yd. shooting as the last bounded with 1a. of Thomas Hayward and 1yd. of wid. Tanner.

Marslong Sherde furlong: ½a. shooting on Marslong Sherde between 2 x ½a. of Thomas Hayward: ½a. more shooting on Little Foxditche bounded with ½a. of Henry Coaltstone, and 3a. of Nicholas Smithe.

Churchland furlong: ½a. shooting E. and W. bounded with ½a. of John Stille, and 1a. of William Webbe; ½a. more shooting as the last bounded with ½a. of Nicholas Smithe and 1a. of William Webbe; ½a. more between 2 x ½a. of Nicholas Smithe shooting as the last; a head ½a. in Queedsarse shooting N. and S. bounded with ½a. of John Holloway and the N. field furlong.

Arable land in the N. field: 2a. together shooting towards Littleton hedge, bounded with ½a. of John Stille, and 1a. of John Hollowaye; ½a. in the same furlong bounded with ½a. of Philip Cumlyn and 1a. of Nicholas Smithe; in the same furlong 3 x ½a. together bounded with 1a. of Henry Coaltstone and ½a. of Philip Doale; 2a. more together shooting as the last, bounded on one side with

1a. of Henry Coaltstone, and ½a. of wid. Warde; 1a. more shooting on Becketts hedge, bounded with ½a. of Thomas Forde, and ½a. of Henry Coaltstone; 3 x ½a. together shooting on Becketts hedge, bounded with ½a. of William Bower, and ½a. of Henry Coaltstone.

4 rother beasts or 2 horses, and a bull feeding in the common called the Marsh from The Invention of the Cross [3 May] or 10 May until the breach of the barley field, then into the barley, wheat and rye fields as long as they will hold, then into the Marsh again until St. Thomas's day [21 Dec]. 14 rother beasts feeding in Longleaze from Whitsun eve formerly, now 1 June, until the breach of the fields; which beasts used to feed also over the other part of the common now called Sheephouse leaze and Oxen leaze which was then one common for the 14 beasts, the farmer's oxen and other cattle, and certain of the tenants' cattle; this is the common fame and speech of ancient men and women inhabiting the village and places near adjoining. The inclosure was procured by William Warde, then farmer of Little Cheverell, not consented to by the parson and the tenants with cattle feeding these, and the bounds made by William Cumlyn, father of Philip Cumlyn, and the gate [yeate] in the bounds thrown open some years after by William Hayward and John Doale, when the pasture grew short in the Longleaze, and the beasts turned in to feed as before in other parts of the commons enclosed by the farmer. Trees and fern with the under frith in Longleaze bounded with Sheephouse leaze hedge and certain mere stones. 2a. meadow in the Lord's mead with all the trees and underwood growing there, and the parsons always made the bound between the farmer's coppice S. and next to Mr. Richard Titharly N. A plot of furzes in the Marsh shooting from the Craftes towards Littleton hedge, and the parson makes a plot of the hedge, and has the trees and frith growing there. Any furzes and fern in the lower Cliffe and Foxditche at all times Feeding for 80 sheep with the tenants in the fields, downs, commons and Foxditch, and by a recent composition between the parson and the tenants, feeding for 100 (sheep) in the same commons, except Foxditch, in the winter. Feeding for 50 sheep with the farmer's flock the whole year. Longleaze has been surcharged by the late farmer, William Warde, with 3 other beasts, and at the breach of the fields the above 14 beasts are to feed with the other beasts of the Marsh in the fields, and after the ending of the fields in the tenants' lower common with their rother beasts and horses. Where any of the parson's land shoots on any hedge he makes the bound and has the trees and frith growing there. In various places linchets next to his arable land, and all the trees or bushes growing there are the parson's.

Hugh Goughe, parson, Philip Comlin [X], Philip Doale [X], William Planke [X], John Still. Endorsement: South Wiltes Terriers 1588-1610.

150   1671 (D1/24/40/2)
4 yardlands of glebe (80a. and 3yds.) of arable lying dispersedly in the fields of the parish with 100 sheep leaze in the field with 4 beast leaze in the common. Tithe corn, wool, hay, cow white, calves, lambs, gardens, orchards and home closes of the farm and throughout the parish. The summering of 14 rother beasts in Long Leaze belonging to the farm. Tithe of the coppices belonging to the farm. Tithe of the mill. 1 dwelling house 1 barn of 6 bays, 1 stable of 2 bays, 1 cart house, 2 gardens, 1 orchard, 1 enclosure called Deacons c. 2a.

2 little patches of pasture *c.* ½a. at a place called Shubwell and a little butt of pasture at the end of Boulters lane.

Richard Broadhead, rector, Stephen Flower (X), Thomas Smith (X) churchwardens.

151   9 Jan 1705 (D1/24/40/3)
Parsonage house or tenement with barn stables, backside, orchard, and gardens, *c.* 2a. Arable land in W. field next Great Cheverell. Beyond the Fore Hill, 7a.: In the Hop furlong, 2a.: In the Clay, 10a.: In the Upper Sand, 6a. 3yd.: In the Lower Sand, 6a. 2yd. Arable land in E. field next to Littleton: Beyond the Fore hill, 4a. 1yd.: In the Fore hill, 1a. 2yd.: In the Summer field under the hill, 4a. 1yd.: In the Clay. 3a. 3yd. In the Upper Sand. 13a. 2yd.: In the lower Sand, 12a. 1yd. Land in the Common of late years enclosed 1 plot, *c.* 3a. Meadow and pasture ground: In the Custom mead called Lords mead, *c.* 2a.: A ground called Deacons, 1a. 2yd.

The depasturing and feeding of 14 rother [rudder] beasts in Long Lease and common of pasture for 80 sheep in the Tenantry flock and likewise 1 plot of ollet or ferne in Long Leaze, *c.* 1a. Tithe corn, wool, hay (except of Lord's mead), calves, cow white, lambs, orchards gardens and of the mill.

Jacob Meredith rector, William Cumlyn, Brian Hayward, churchwardens.

152   27 Oct 1780 (D1/24/40/4)
Parsonage house with barn, stable, backside, orchard, garden, grass platt, 1a. 2r. 27p. The churchyard, 1r. 8p. Arable Land: N. field, 58a. 1r. 19p., whereof 4a. 1r. 7p. are enclosed bounded Littleton enclosures and Catherine Cross N. E., turnpike road and Littleton enclosures S. E., Philip's and Glasses grounds and Axfords new enclosure now laid open, N., fore common and the parish ? boundary S. E. Catherine Cross, 2a. 1r. 29p. formerly part of N. field but now enclosed. The common enclosure, 3a 1r. 18p.

Meadow and pasture ground: Deacons, 1a. 1r. 31p. The fore common 7a. 19p. Common mead called Lords mead, the mowth[1] of 2a. 2r. 1p. formerly laid out by tradition, in lieu of tithe for the said mead. The depasturing and feeding of 14 rother beasts in Long Leaze, 1 plot of ollet or fern in Long leaze, *c.* 1a. Tithe corn, wool, hay, except the tithe of Lords mead (for which see above), cow white, calves, lambs, gardens, home, closes and the mill and whatsoever else is tithable in the parish.

James Stonhouse M. D. rector, William Butcher John Cumlyn Axford, churchwardens, William Butcher junior, Thomas Etwell, overseer, James Coleman, William Crouch. N. B. The difference of this between this terrier and that of 1705 is owing to an exchange of land belonging to the rectory, with the bishop's consent, made by the earl of Radnor and Dr. Stonhouse 31 Dec 1767.

1.   Mowing, see **502–3, 598.**

153   30 Jul 1783 (D1/24/40/5)
Dr. Stonhouse rector of Great and Little Cheverell finding that there had been no terrier made in either of his parishes since the year 1704 (old style) delivered

into the registry of Salisbury an accurate terrier made at some expense in measuring lands etc. dated 27 Oct 1780 and in answer to such questions as your lordship has been pleased to ask and were not there answered. He has added as follows:

Timber on the parsonage glebe: In the Common ground 13 maiden elms trees at 9s. per tree. 1 maiden oak tree 7s. On Fury hill 9 maiden elm trees at 7s. per tree. In the Dean 13 maiden elm trees at 8s. per tree. In the orchard 10 maiden elm trees at 10s. per tree. In Deacons 31 maiden elm trees at 8s. In the enclosure 8 maiden elm trees at 8s. per tree.

1 large barn, with 2 threshing floors, 84ft. by 23ft., boarded floor, brick and stone foundation to the external building, the rest board and thatched, skilling to it 24ft. by 9ft. Stable 44ft. by 17ft. built with brick and thatched, stalls for 8 horses. Court house 49ft. by 11ft. supported by oak posts and thatched. There was no granary when I came to the rectory there is one on the premises but it belongs to the tenant. Parsonage house: last year there were 4 rooms added to the parsonage, the plan of it before the alteration and after is in your lord's registry together with the dimensions of the rooms, materials and every other circumstance. This spring I have rebuilt the middle part of the house, the inside of which will be finished in about a month. The dimensions of the bed chamber are 19ft. 7in. by 15ft. 2in. floored with deal. Under that is a passage and laundry, paved with square paving brick, and servants' pantry, floored with elm. The house is built of brick with freestone quoins, freestone window frames etc. There is a part of the building standing at the end of rough stone plastered over and drawn in lines so as to resemble brick, consisting of offices and servants' rooms. The house is covered with brick tiles.

There are no tithes due to the minister from any other township. There are no bequests in the parish. There are only 2 bells, a clock a silver cup and paten (no flagon) no weight on it. No lands or money for repairing the church. Parishioners repair the church, the minister the chancel. The bounds around the churchyard are repaired one part by lord Radnor the other part by the parish.

The same person who is Clerk is sexton. His salary is small chiefly arising from marriages and burials, and some trifling matter from the owners of pews.

James Stonhouse.

CHICKLADE rectory

154   n. d. late 16th cent. (D1/24/41/1)
30a. arable in 3 fields: 11a. in the E. field; 11a. in the W. field; 8a. in the Middle field. Pasturing of 75 sheep and pasturing of 7 beasts on the downs and commons. ⅓a. enclosure adjoining the parsonage house. Tithe of 200a. of all kinds of corn; tithe wool of 1,600 sheep; the value of a load of hay p. a. or very near.

155   17 Dec 1677 (D1/24/41/2)
30a. arable land in the several fields viz. 11a. in E. field, 8½a. in Middle field, W. field 10½a. 1 paddock garden and backside, c. 1a. 1 barn stable and 2 outhousings or hovels. Commons of pasture for 8 cows, 80 sheep leaze in the common fields and downs. Luke Sympson, rector, Elias Lucas, Geoffrey Moody, churchwardens.

156   8 Jan 1705 (D1/24/41/3)

Glebe land: In the Middle field ½a. lying E. and W. under Coronel hedge between Berwick St. Leonard and the town of Hindon. ½a. lying N. W. and S. W. by Wyley-way and Mullen's lane at Hindon. 1a. lying E. and W. shooting against the Hollow way under the hedge going from Chicklade to Hindon called Court mead acre. 3a. lying N. and S. shooting against 2a. occupied by Mary Shergold, wid. N., bounded E. 2a., W. 1a. belonging to Henry Dowle's living. 1½a. under Hoken Down hedge lying N. and S. sbooting against London road on N., against 2a. belonging to wid. Shergold on S. end, 2a. belonging to Mr. Hewes' Bull living E. 1a. lying N. and S. shooting against London road. 1 head a. lying E. and W. bounded E. 1a. belonging to Dominick farm E., 1a. of Henry Burnet's living and 1½a. of Mr. Hewes' Bull living W., N. 1a. belonging to Dominick farm. In E. field: 1a. lying N. and S. being cut with the path on Lungevas lane going to Hindon, bounded London Road S., 2a. belonging to Henry Dowle's estate, N. 3a. called Hanging piece lying E. and W. bounded a hedge belonging to an enclosure of Chicklade W., the highway going out to the E. from Chicklade N. 1a. lying E. and W. bounded Berwick down E., Mr. Hewes' land S., 1a. belonging to the rectory W., 1a. belonging to Thomas and Elias Lucas N. 1½a. lying E. and W. bounded 3 x ½a. belonging to Henry Dowles' living N., 1a. belonging to Henry Dowle E., 1a. of Henry Dowle's estate W., 2a. of Henry Burnet S. 1a. lying N. and S. bounded with a pasture called Layes N., 3 x ½a. of Henry Dowle S., 1a. wid. Moody W. 3x ½a. lying N. and S., 1a. belonging to Henry Burnet's living S., 3a. belonging to Dominick farm W., part of 3a. belonging to the Well living N., 3a. belonging to Dominick farm E. with 3 x ½a. of Mr. Hewe's land. 1a. lying N. and S. called Hanging acre, the N. end shooting against the Cow down bounded 1a. of the rectory and 5a. of Mary Shergold wid. E., 3a. belonging to Dominick farm W. 1a. lying E. and W. bounded the last mentioned acre W., Cow Down N., the pasture called Lays E., 5a. of wid. Shergold S. In W. field 1a. lying E. and W. bounded 1a. of Henry Burnet E., 1a. on each side belonging to Henry Dowle's estate N. and S., a piece of 4a. of Mr. Hewe's lands W. 3a. lying N. and S. bounded with farm down W., a piece of 2½a. of George Dyer N., W. Knoyle way S., 2a. Henry Burnet E. 1a. lying N. and S. bounded Bockerley Way N., acres of Mr. Hewes' lands E., 2a. of Dominick farm 5., 3 x ½a. of Mr. Hewe's lands W. 3 halves or 1½a. lying N. and S. bounded Bockerly way S., 1a. belonging to wid. Moodye's living W., 2a. of Mr. Hewe's land N., 2a. of Henry Dowle's estate E. 1a. lying E. and W. bounded 1a. of wid. Moody N., 3 x ½a. belonging to Well living E., 1a. of Henry Dowle's land S., 2a. of the half yard lands belonging to Mr. Sympson W., 3a. lying N. and S. bounded with Bockerly Way N., 1a. belonging to Well living E., 2a. belonging to Henry Dowle S., ½a. belonging to Henry Burnet W.

A parsonage house, barn, stable, cow house, carthouse, backside, garden, 17p. 1 little meadow, 61¼ p. Feeding and pasturage for 80 sheep yearly and for 8 cows or horses on the commonable downs and fields belonging to Chicklade. Also we confess and acknowledge a right and privilege of cutting down and carrying away of wood and ollet to the rector for his own use on and of the downs and commonable places or commons of Chicklade proportionable to what the other inhabitant usually cut down and carry away. Tithes and tenths of everything growing and increasing in Chicklade may be taken and received by our minister at the usual times of our having and taking the increase of our substances as corn, hay, wool, lambs, pigs, calves, honey, apples and all other tithes both great and small may be taken in kind. Offerings to be due and that according to the accustomed manner and times they ought to be received by our minister all which we esteem and value at £30 p. a.

Luke Sympson, rector, Henry Burnett, John Helbert, churchwardens, Elias Lucas [X]

157   4 Aug 1783 (D1/24/41/4)
A parsonage house built of stone and thatched with straw *c.* 47ft. by 18ft., 2 small rooms and 2 pantries on the ground floor. 1 room at the N. end floored partly with board partly with stone only, the other at S. end floored with stone only, and the pantries with earth 3 chambers with elm floors, ceiled but not wainscotted. 1 barn 18ft. by 58ft. with a small living *c.* 20ft. long. A stable joining to the barn at N. end both under 1 roof and covered with thatch. 1 farm yard 1 meadow and garden 3r. and fenced with dead hedge.

The parish being lately divided by Act of Parliament the arable glebe land is in one entire piece, 32a. 2r. 32p., at the W. end of the parish on the left hand of the turnpike road leading from Chicklade to Mere, bounded the turnpike road N. old London road S., road leading from Chicklade to Hindon E. lands of Harry Edgell esq., and Elias Lucas W.

All tithes on every thing growing and increasing in the parish may be taken by the minister at the usual times and in kind. Offerings are also due to the minister.

The furniture of the church: 2 bells a font in the church In the chancel a communion table with 2 small linen cloths a small chalice and a small plate of silver. The plate with the inscription 'John Hibbert and Elias Lucas Chicklade Anno Domini 1705'. 1 pewter flagon, 1 oak chest, a small box annexed to the communion table containing the [*enclosure*] plan and award of the parish. The church is maintained by the parishioners and the chancel by the minister. The churchyard fence on W. side is maintained by the inhabitants, N. side by Mr. Richard Randall; S. and E. sides by the minister. The clerk and sexton's wages are paid by the parish and appointed by the minister.

Benjamin Blatch, rector, William Blake, Richard Randall, churchwarden, Nathanial Wright, inhabitant.

CHILMARK rectory

158   1588 (D1/24/42/1)
Terrier taken by 'the churchwardens and ancientmen there abydynge or dwellynge'.

Long close, *c.* 14a., arable shooting on the down, the farm field W.; another close of arable, *c.* 2½a., shooting on the highway to Salisbury, part of the farm field W., a close of John Snowe E.; Culver close, *c.* 8a., arable adjoining the parsonage barton; another close called Trynleyes, *c.* 10a., arable, the common called Pittes S., a close belonging to the farm N. A close of pasture, *c.* 6a., towards Ridge [Rudge], William Bowles having a close W., William Furnell E.; Bentes close, *c.* 1½a., pasture, William Moore W., Edward Sparye E. A house in which the curate lodged with a backside and a little close. All tithes except the tithes wool of 300 sheep belonging to the farm or manor.

159   n. d. early 17th cent. (D1/24/42/2)
1 dwelling house with a barn and other outhouses and barton. 1 pigeon house orchards and garden. 1 vicarage house and garden plot. 1 close called Trenly, 9a., by lug. Long close of the same measure. Little close, 2a., by lug. Culver close, 5a. Rudge close, 4a. Kents close, 2a.
    Richard Prist, James Tabor churchwardens.

160   19 May 1705 (D1/24/42/3)
1 close adjoining the house with orchard and garden, 6a. Long close adjoining the Down, 3a. Trenly close, 9a. Kence close, 1½a. Rudge close, 4½a. Vicarage house with garden, 30p. A house, part on the vicarage garden, part on the highway, 10p. No modus nor any exemption of tithes claimed in Chilmark or Ridge [Rudge] by any one except Mr. William Jesse now in possession of the farm which accepts 300 stock sheep and Hodney mead, his orchard and partly his backside not allowed tithe by the present incumbent. The sum of pasture, meadow and field 32a. 40p.
    Richard Roots, rector, William Privett, John Moore churchwardens in 1704, Robert Moore, churchwarden in 1705, Edward Fricker.

CHILTON FOLIAT rectory

161   12 Sep 1608 (D1/24/43/1)
The parsonage dwelling house, another house called the kitchen, a barn with a stable adjoining, a hovel standing in the middle of the barton, an orchard and garden. 2 parcels or quillets of ground, f *c.* ½a. *c.* 4a. pasture commonly called the Hams. 1½a. arable in the common fields southward. 1½a. arable inclosed and in a several called The Butts. *c.* 1a. of meadow bounded out in Soley mead.
    By me Robert Collard, rector; John Plaisted, Richard Palington [X], William May [X].

162   n. d. [1704 x 1705].¹ (D1/24/43/2)
The parsonage house stables gardens orchard, barns and outlet. 3a. of glebe of which 1½a. lies against the backgate of Lovelace Bigg esq. 1½a. lies next to Gold hill. 1 water meadow called Parsons ham *c.* 5a. 1 lot in Soley lot mead now and formerly bounded with merestones. Tithe corn, grain, hay, wood, wool, lambs and all other titheable things.
    Timothy Topping rector, John Gregory, John Tyler [X] churchwardens.

1.   The churchwardens were recorded in the bishop's visitation book, Oct 1704 (WSRO D1/50/6).

CHIPPENHAM vicarage

163   29 Aug 1608(D1/24/44/l)
A dwelling house at Chippenham with an orchard, garden, and the herbage of the churchyard. A dwelling house at Tytherton Lucas with a barn, garden, brewhouse or stable, and bakehouse. 12a. arable in 3 closes or leasues at Tytherton Lucas: the New leasue, 3½a.; the Mill field divided by a quick hedge into 2, the lower lying to the river Marden, *c.* 7½a. together; the Home close in which the barn stands, 1a. The herbage of the chapel yard at Tytherton Lucas. Commons with other inhabitants of Tytherton Lucas for 2 kine one year and 3 kine another year. ½a. of meadow there in Bull mead. Tithe corn and grain, hay, and all other tithes in Tytherton Lucas. The Easter book and Easter reckoning throughout the whole parish; tithe hay in Chippenham W. mead and certain other grounds with the dues for marriages and churchings, and tithes of eggs throughout the parish at Easter.

William Proudlove, vicar, John Hindes, Robert Hawkyns, churchwardens, by me John Scotte, Edward Stafford, Thomas Beryman.

164   1 Nov. 1671 (D1/24/44/2)
A terrier[1] of the lands, etc., belonging in the parish church of Chippenham according to the several gifts and grants thereof.

1.   A tenement called Codes Place in the High St. in Chippenham. A tenement called Wases in Chippenham between the tenements late of Robert Tabeler on both sides with a way lying without the S. door. Trendlowes mead (in the possession of Mr. William Bailiffe) lying near the river Avon and a close of the prior of Farley called Elmhey. 1 close in Cockleborough with appurtenances near the kings highway and a close of William Payne with pasture for 1 cow in the common of Cockleborough. 1a. of arable of which ½a. called Odecroft in Cockleborough field near the land late of John Holbrooke and ½a. in Ballswell furlong in Chippenham field near lands late of Thomas Gay.

2.   [By the gift of] Robert Trendlowes and Maud his wife, daughter and heir of Isabell 12 Dec. 1 Henry 5 [1413]. A tenement in High St. near the land of William Love and a tenement of the abbey of Stanley; 3½a., of which ½a. lies in Hambreach, 1a. in W. field in Poltingham furlong, 1a. at Ellford and 2 x ½a. in Theggs furlong. 1 parcel of meadow in Homefield and Ballismead. ½a. in Lolledown furlong.

3.   By the gift of Thomas Fenice dated St. David's day 33 Henry 6 [1455] a tenement in High St. near the tenement of Ralph Palmer. 4a. 3 farndells of arable land in the fields of Chippenham, Cockleborough and Langley Burrell of which ½a. is the headland in Lolledowne furlong, ½a. lies at a place called the Cleeve, ½a. lies under Henden, ½a. lies in the same field and extends itself upon the head of Rolnesdene, ½a. in a furlong called the Fleete, 1a. extends itself upon Ringway near land late of Robert Mandevill and 3 farndells lie in Odecrofte towards Mouncton.

4.   2½a. and 1 farndell lie in the fields of Langley Burrell and Cockleborough of which 1½a. lies in Hendon extending upon the heath of Langley, ½a. in Cockleborough in a close called Sanderditch near the path there and 3 farndells in Odecroft.

5.   1a. of arable land in Cockleborough lying under the Cleve. ½a. of arable land in Langley Burrell in Bramelattland furlong. 1½a. of arable in Chippenham and Cockleborough of which 1a. lies in Midsummer furlong. ½a. in Bramelattland. 1a. of arable in Cockleborrough in Morfurlong. 1a. in Nethercliffe furlong. 1 farndell of arable near the way towards Mouncton. 1a. and 2 farndells of meadow in E. field of Langley Burrell lying 'dispersely', the said acre lying in a meadow called ? Westbroke the head thereof extends upon the bank of the Avon and 1 farndell in the same meadow, one head thereof extending on the same bank, 1 farndell lies in the Marsh one head thereof extends upon Marbrooke, a third part of 1 ham of meadow in Langley field near Felditch one head thereof extends upon the bank of the Avon and ½a. of meadow under the Clyve.

These lands [ie. 3, 4, 5 above] were sometimes Enford's which were conveyed to John Steere who by his deed dated 21 Nov. 11 Henry 4 [1409] gave the same lands and all other his lands in the town and fields of Chippenham, Langley Burrell, Cockleborough and Hardenhuish or elsewhere within the hundred of Chippenham to William Newman, then vicar of Chippenham and others.

1 messuage called Sewey in Notton was granted by William Sewy alias Stouford to William Newman and John Salway, John Peis, Thomas Godwyn, clerk, and others by deed of 13 May 19 Edward 4 [1479]. A close called Meggiscroft in Notton in Laycock which was granted to the said William Sewy alias Stouford by Robert Somerset and his wife Agnes 13 May 19 Edward 4 [1479] which said messuage the said Thomas Godwyn granted to John Tru, clerk, vicar of Chippenham and to Henry Perry and others by his deed dated 1 Nov. 8 Henry 8 [1516] which said messuage Henry Perry and others granted (by name of that messuage called Maggatts croft in Notton in Lacock) unto Thomas Weld[2], clerk, vicar of Chippenham, Henry Farnell alias Goldney senior and others by deed dated 1 Nov. 13 Eliz. [1571].

½a. lying in Breach furlong in Chippenham abutting upon a pasture called Rowdens Down, lands of the parish church lying on the N. part granted to John Panter of Chippenham by his deed dated 22 Feb 1 & 2 Philip & Mary [1555].

Jonathan Giare, vicar, William Lord, John Flower, churchwardens.

Glebe and privileges belonging to Tytherton Lucas rectory in the parish of Chippenham 2 tilled grounds, 9a. New leaze, 4a. Homeclose, ½a. ½a. in Butmeade, 3 beast leaze in W. ham, 1 year, 2 another. 10 sheep leaze in W. ham.

Jonathan Giare.

1.   This document is published in *Wilts Endowed Charities (1908) Northern Division*, pp. 230-231. The church lands provided income for the upkeep of the church and thus it is only the details about Tytherton Lucas which constitute a true glebe terrirer.
2.   Recte Wild.

165   1704 (D1/24/44/3)

The vicarage house and garden walled in adjoining to the churchyard. Another house and garden at Tytherton. The parson's close joing to it which with the churchyard is 1½a. 2 grounds, 8½a. and 6 lugs, joining to Mr. Gouldney's estate on one side and Mr. George Townsend's on the other. 1 ground, *c.* 4a., joining to Mr. Andrews on one side and Thomas Beavis at the end and John Watts on the other side. 1 piece, *c.* ½a., in Bull mead. 1 piece of ground called the Parsons patch, *c.* 40 lugs, lying on the other side of the lane over against the Four acres.

3 beast leaze in Westham one year and 2 the next year. 10 sheep leaze from All Saints [1 Nov] to St. David's day [1 Mar] every year. The whole tithe of Tytherton. The tithe hay of all the freehold in Westmead, Lord's Hamme and several other pieces of land in Chippenham.

R[*obert*] Cock, vicar, Charles Pickering, William Stevens, churchwardens.

CHIRTON vicarage

166 3 May 1609 (D1/24/45/l)
A house, barn, backside, orchard, garden, and the herbage of the churchyard. 6a. land called the Vicar's piece at Elcrofts hedge. 1a. in Suthmead furlong next to Bondies. ½a. shooting N. and S. 2a. land above Elcroftes hedge next to Bartlets head ½a. shooting E. and W. 3yds. between ways next to a yd. of Thomas Lonnes shooting N. and S. ½a. in Sandslad next to ½a. of wid. Hatter shooting N. and S. 2a. land in Acredicke furlong next to ½a. of Taskees shooting E. and W. Feeding in the common fields and downs and other places for 40 sheep, 4 rother beasts, 2 horses, as other tenants have for a yardland. Tithe corn of 3 yardlands held by Robert Bartlet commonly called the Tenantry land containing 3 score a. [*60a.*] and of a yardland held by Roger Phillips; and of 1½ yardlands held by John Hatter. Tithe hay, wool and lambs, with all other privy tithes, and at Easter 10 eggs for every yardland.

By me Richard Stockton vicar; William Gilbert, Thomas Polton, churchwardens. *Names in the hand of the rector.*

167 11 Dec 1677 (D1/24/45/2)
A dwelling house of 3 bays of building and a small bay at the W. end. A barn of 4 bays of building and a stable at the W. end. A backside, orchard and 2 gardens adjoining to the house. 1a. with tithe in S. Mead furlong, Robert Earle W. Richard Amor E. Elcrofts piece, 6a., with tithe, Robert Hayward E., Robert Gilbert S., Francis Smith N, the way W. ½a. with tithe in E. and W. furlong Clackes, John Heyward N., Richard Amor S. 3yds with tithe in a furlong called Between Ways, John Wells E., John Farr W. ½a. with tithe in Sandslade furlong, Thomas Byge E., Michall Burgis senior W. ½a. with tithe in Acreditch furlong, John Hayward S., Michael Burgis senior N. The tithe of 2 yardlands, in the possession of John Heyward, parson, 1 yardland in the possession of Robert Heyward, 1 yardland in the possession of Richard Amor, 1½ yardland in the possession of Thomas Bygge. The tithe of ½a. in the possession of Robert Earle in the furlong called E. and W. Clackes, John Farr N., the said Robert Earle S. The tithe of 2 butts or short ridges in the possession of Michael Burgis senior in Clackes furlong, Thomas Bygge and John Hayward N. end John Hayward S. end. The tithe of ½a. in possession of George Hatter in Acreditch furlong, John Hayward N. and S. The tithe of ½a. in the possession of William Morrant in Short Meere furlong, Robert Heyward N., John Farr S. The tithe of ½a. in the possession of William Morrant in a furlong called Between ways, Richard Amor E. Thomas Bygge W.

The tithe hay throughout the parish except a meadow in the possession of Thomas Shergold called the Freehold meadow in the tithing of Conock and 1 meadow in the possession of Richard Cryppes on W. side of the said freehold meadow, 1 meadow lately in the possession of William Bewley on S. side of the said freehold meadow. Tithe of wool and lambs. Composition for Edward Gidding's mill, 3s. 4d., formerly made by Mr. [John] White vicar. For offerings 2d. for every person of age within the parish. 10 eggs or 2d. for every yardland. 1d. for every garden. Tithe apple of every orchard. 1d. for cow white. 2 horses, 2 cows and 40 sheep to feed and depasture in common and common fields according to the custom of the tennants. 1 seat in S. E. corner of the church 5ft x 2½ft. 1 seat in the S. W. end of the chancel 5ft. x 3½ft. A burial place in the E. end of the chancel within the rails for the vicar and his family.

Nathanial Cooper, vicar, William Giden, Michael Burgges, churchwardens.

168   14 Feb 1705 (D1/24/45/3)

A dwelling house, barn, stable, garden, orchard and churchyard, c. 1a. 8 small arable a. lying disperseded in the common fields worth 4s.

Tithe corn of 2 yardlands in the possession of John Heyward, of 1 yardland in the possession of Walter Earle esq., of 1 yardland of Richard Amor of 1½ yardlands in the possession of Thomas Bigge when sown, worth 7s. Tithe of ½a. of Eliz Earle wid. of William Earle, of ½a. of John Hatter, of 2 x ½a. of Mary Morant wid. and of 2 butts of Anne Burgis when sown worth 8s. Tithe wool and lambs worth 9s. 6d. Tithe grass and hay except the freehold meadows of Gifford Yerbury esq., 1 meadow of Isaac Warriner gent. and 1 meadow of John Ruminge usually taken up by John Hayward, impropriator (excepting the tithe of a swathe lying on the upper W. side near halfway of the said meadow and of some 4 lugs within the gate of the meadow of the said Isaac Warriner belongs to the vicar) worth 7s. 10d.

All Easter dues as offerings, tithe gardens, orchards, pigs, calves, cow white, and mill. Feeding and depasturing of 2 horse beasts, 2 cows and 40 sheep according to the customs of the tenants and the tithe of all other tithable things, except the tithe corn which belongs to John Hayward, and Gifford Yerbury, impropriators, worth 2s.

Nathanial Cooper vicar, Richard Amor, churchwarden, Michael Manning, Richard Stratton, Thomas Bigge.

169   25 Jul 1783 (D1/24/45/4)

1 dwelling house, barn, stable, cowhouse, garden, orchard, and churchyard, c. 1a. The dwelling house, oak-framed brick panes part of the front cased with brick, covered with straw, 50ft. by 16½ft., containing 4 rooms on the first floor, 2 elm board bottomed rooms, 1 brick, 1 earth. The parlour wainscotted with old oak panels, 3 ceiled rooms, the kitchen unceiled. In the second or upper floor, 2 elm, 2 oak bottomed rooms, all ceiled. Outhouses 1 barn 47ft. by 20ft. A stable adjoining 11ft. by 20ft., cowhouse 6ft. by 10ft., 7ft. in the stem all built with oak elm and mud wall covered with straw.

Glebe land: 8a. 1qtr., customary or small a. in the common field: The Parson's piece enclosed with a lawn on 3 sides and a hedge on the other. 5 customary a.,

1a. at Reeves close end, ½a. jetting on the mere; ½a. in Sandslade; 3yd. in Tweenways; ½a. in E. and W. furlong. A right to depasturing and feeding 2 horses, 2 cows, 40 sheep, according to the custom of the Tenants. Adjoining the dwellinghouse, a small garden and orchard on N. side, c. 1/4a., fenced off by a mud wall, a thorn and an elder hedge. Churchyard, c. ½a. on E. adjoining the vicarage house. Garden and orchards fenced by the same rails and the neighbours' gardens. On S. side of the vicarage house, a small garden and yard, fenced by a mud wall.

Timber: In the orchard 12 small elm pollards, 4 maiden sticks (elms). In the churchyard 1 yew tree, 1 pollard elm.

Tithe corn of 2 yardlands in the possession of wid. Holloway, occupied by Gifford Bruges; of 1 yardland in the possession of Philip Hayward occupied by Gifford Bruges; of 1 yardland in the possession of Mr. Powell occupied by wid. Burges; of 1½ yardlands in the possession of William Hazleland occupied by Gifford Bruges; of ½a. in the possession of Mr. Powell occupied by wid. Burges; of 2 x ½a. in the possession of Mr. Seymour Pierce occupied by Jonathan Parry; of 2 butts in the possession of Mr. Warriner occupied by wid. Burges.

Tithe wool and lamb and feeding for the time being. Tithe grass and hay except freehold meadow of Gifford Yerbury esq., 1 meadow of Isaac Warrener gent., 1 meadow of John Rumminge usually taken up by John Hayward, impropriator, excepting tithe of a swathe in the upper W. side near half way, the said meadow belongs to the vicar and the tithe of a few lugs within the gate of the meadow of Isaac Warrener gent. belongs to the vicar.

All Easter dues. The tithe of all gardens, orchards, pigs, calves, cow white and mill. Tithe of all titheable things excepting the corn belonging to John Hayward, and Gifford Yerbury esq., impropriators. £2 p. a. payable to the vicar from the trustees of a little charity farm in Chirton for inspecting the buildings of the farm.

1 pew. in S. part of the chancel and another in S. E. part of the church belonging to the vicar.

Furniture of the church: a communion table, linen cloth, and napkin, silver chalice, measure about 2 pint, a patten inscribed 'Ex Dono Joannis White olim Ecclesiae de Churton Vicarici', weight together c. 10oz. and an old pewter flagon. A surplice, a pulpit cloth, and cushion, a large font, and 5 bells. Books, only those for the use of Divine Service. The church is repaired by the parishioners, the chancel by the said impropriators. The churchyard fence is supported by the parish. The Clerk's wage, by custom, is 40s. p. a. payable by the parish. The Clerk is appointed by the vicar.

Samuel Clarke, vicar, William Gidding, John Burges, churchwardens, Gifford Warriner, John Powell, Samuel Pinchin, John Barnes.

CHISELDON vicarage

170   22 Aug 1608 (D1/24/46/1)
½a. in the Long furlong shooting E. and W., John Kinge S., Thomas Carter N.; 1a. in Forse hill shooting E. and W., John Kinge S., James Goddard N.; ½a.

shooting E. and W. in the same furlong, James Goddard N., Robert Combe S., 1yd. in the same place shooting E. and W. James Goddard S., Robert Combe N.; ½a. shooting N. and S. in Smythway furlong, John Kynge E., Robert Moleyn W.; ½a. shooting E. and W. in High Street furlong, Robert Mollyn N., Thomas Smith alias Miller S.; ½a. in the same furlong, Robert Combe N., James Goddarde S.; a butt in the Nether Hitchins shooting E. and W., the parson N. and Thomas Carter S.; ½a. in the Upper Hitchins shooting E. and W. John King S., the parson N.; ½a. in the Townsend furlong shooting N. and S., John Kinge W., the parson E.; ½a. shooting N. and S. on Harpers way, John King E., the parson W.; ½a. in Upper Hitchins shooting E. and W., John King on both sides; ½a. in Nether Hitchins shooting E. and W. Robert Mollyn N., Thomas Smyth alias Miller [S]; 3yds. in the same furlong shooting E. and W., the parson N., Robert Combe S.; 1a. in Rudding Ditch shooting N. and S., John King E., Robert Combe W.; ½a. shooting on Parsons Hedge N. and S., Thomas Carter E., Robert Combe W.; 1a. in Forse Bush furlong shooting E. and W., Robert Mollyn N., John Kyng S.; ½a. in the same furlong, Robert Mollyn N., Robert Combe S.; ½a. shooting E. and W. over the Bourne, James Goddard S., the parson N., 1a. in Witch Hills furlong, shooting N. and S., John King W., the parson E.; 1a. in Catesbryne furlong shooting E. and W., the parson S, Robert Molyn N. ½a. shooting N. and S. on Parsons Down way, John Kyng E., Robert Combe W.; a piece of c. 3a. by itself behind Parsons down shooting E. and W.; 1a. in Crowe Bush furlong shooting E. and W., Thomas Miller alias Smyth on both sides; 1yd. shooting N. and S. on Wakelin's pit, Robert Combe W., John King E.; 1yd. shooting on Thomas Buckeridge's gate E. and W., John Kinge on both sides; ½a. in the Born furlong shooting E. and W., the parson N., Robert Mollyn S.; 1yd. shooting E. and W., Robert Mollyn N., John King S.; ½a. shooting E. and W. on High sher furlong, John Kyng N., the parson S.; ½a. in the same place, John King S., the parson N.; ½a. in the same furlong, shooting E. and W. Richard Webbe S., John ?King N.; ½a. in the same place shooting E. and W., Robert Mollyn S., Robert Combe N.

John Hollymore, vicar, Thomas Buckeridge, one of the churchwardens, John Kyng, Robert Combe, Robert Molyn and others.

171   1705 (D1/24/46/2)

1a. shooting upon Devizes way [Fiseway], Mr. Keeping on E. 1 three yd. in Short Urchings, wid. Cook on N. ½a. in the same, Anthony Allin on S.; ½a. in Long Urchins Mr. Hering on N. ½a. on S. side of Born ditch, the parson on N.; 1a. in Wichall Pit furlong [furland], the parson on N.; 1yd. in Catsbrain, the parson on S.; 1 three a. at Vicarage corner, Mr. Twitti on N.; ½a. shooting upon Aborn way, Mr. Hering on W. ½a. shooting upon Morsis stones, Mr. Twitti on N.; ½a. lying near Histreet way, wid. Miles on E. ½a. lying in the Narow, the parson on E.; ½a. shooting upon the Pound, the parson on E.; ½a. in Long furlong, Mr. Hering on S.; 1a. in Forsball, the parson on S.; 1yd. in the same furlong, wid. Cripes on N. ½a. in the same furlong William Carpenter on S.; ½a. shooting upon Histreet way, Henry Lovlock on S.; ½a. in Smithway furlong, Mr. Twitti on W.; ½a. in the bottom of the field, the parson on N.; ½a. shooting in Midell way Ambrose Wilshear on N. 1a. in the breach, William Lord on S.; 1yd.

at the heath gate [geat], Mr. Twitti on N. ½a. shooting upon Ackerman field, William Pontin on W. 1yd. shooting upon Weaklandes pit Mr. Hering on W.; 1yd. shooting Mr. Hering's piece, Mr. Twitti on N.; ½a. on Histreet furland, Mr. Dean on N.; ½a. in the same furlong, Mr. Hering on N.; 1a. in the same furlong, Mr. Hering has ½a. between. ½a. in the bottom of the field the parson on N.

All manner of tithes except tithe corn, hay, wool and lambs belong to the vicarage. A composition of £3 6s. 8d. p. a. by the impropriator for the tithes of his glebe land to be in equal portions on Ladyday [25 Mar] and at Michaelmas [29 Sep]. 1a. of meadow, Thomas Ring on S. Mr. Hering on N. 1 pasture ground, 2a., Mr. Hering on W., Henry Lovelock E. The vicarage house containing 3 bays. 1 barn containing c. 4 bays. 1 stable. The garden and little paddock, c. ½a.

Thomas Twittee, vicar, Richard Little, John Salsburry [X], churchwardens. Francis Berry, William Combe, William Crook.

172   22 Jul 1786 (D1/24/46/3)
Under the Chiseldon enclosure Act 1779 all tithes except corn, hay, wool and lambs were exonerated. As compensation the vicarage was granted in lieu of tithes 38a. 28p. in lieu of glebe 14a. 1r. 2p. and in exchange for a small close 1a. 1r. 16p. These 3 articles were laid together in 1 piece measuring 53a. 3r. 6p. bounded the lands allotted to Thomas Brown Calley esq., and Mr. William Dyke S., Mr. William Dyke and Mr. Richard Webb W., road to Devizes N. and N.W. land of Mr. John Brown E. 1 old enclosure of meadow called Long closes ?[bounded W. land] belonging to Mr. Thomas Herring, E. a meadow property of Mr. John Brown. Composition £3 6s. 8d. p. a. to be paid by the impropriator for the tithe of his glebe in equal portions on Ladyday [25 Mar] and at Michaelmas [29 Sep].

The vicarage of 3 bays, a barn of c. 4 bays and a stable. The garden and orchard, c. ½a. and the churchyard. An estate in Stratton St. Margaret purchased by the governors of Queen Anne's bounty for £3 2s. 5d., part of a sum of £400 granted by the governors for the perpetual augmentation of the vicarage. The £75 over and above the purchase price is held by the governors who allow interest at the rate of 2%.

W[illiam] R[ichard] Stock, vicar, Richard Webb, William Hilliar, churchwardens, Jonathan Brown, Thomas Hilliar, overseers, J. Phelps, William Brown, Thomas Herring, John Baldwin.

CHITTERNE ALL SAINTS vicarage

173   17 May 1588 (D1/24/47/l)
By Thomas Flower and Edward Furnell. In the Home field above the church, 4a.; at Mother Stubins gate, 1a.; by the garde–waye, 1a.; in Angels gore shooting up the hill, 2a.; in Connyger dean in the bottom, 2a.; on Dickes knoll, 5a.; in the same furlong a headland a.; in the furlong shooting on the greenway, 1a.; joining together at the far end of the same furlong, 3a.; on the top of the hill towards the meadow, 2a.; on the hill at the Bushe, 3a.; shooting on Nimme down, 1a.; shooting

on the greenway up the hill, 1a.; shooting on Ellingtons bushes, 1a.; above
Ellingtons bushes on the hill, 3a.; in the bourne beyond the bushes, 1½a.; shooting
on the bourn by the Devizes [Vize] way, 1a.; on the hill above Hell, 1a.; a piece
of laine, c. 1a.; in Shorden shooting towards the mead, 2a. The tithes of N. mead;
the tithe wool of Mr. Flower's flock; the tithe of Combedowne. The whole
Easter book with other privy tithes. In the W. flock among the tenants, 152
sheep leaze. A mansion house, barn, kitchen, barton, a backside, with a mud wall,
a garden plot in the side of the churchyard, with the herbage and trees growing
in the churchyard.

174   21 Sep 1609 (D1/24/47/2)
As 176 with amendments in footnotes. The last three lines are illegible. Hugh
Hinde, vicar, John Gye, Humphry Compton, Thomas Flower, John Imber [X]
John Compton [X] William Pyrnell [X].

175   1671 (D1/24/47/3)
A dwelling house, barton, stable, barn, churchyard and gardens. A few ajoining
apple trees in the garden. A few trees in the churchyard. 1 horse leaze, 152 sheep
leaze to feed in the W. tenants flock. The tithe of the W. farm flock and tenants
flock. The tithe of Comedown flock. The tithe lamb belonging to those 3 flocks.
Tithe lamb of Cromdown flock. Privy tithes.

2a. of land butting against N. mead, Mrs. Gyles her 4a. on each side. 2a. of
picked land adjoining to Christopher Slade his 1a. and Thomas Pryor his 2a. on
either side. 1a. between Mrs. Gyles a. and Thomas Pryor butting against Elintons
hedge. 3a. joining to Christopher Slade his a. and heading Mrs. Gyles her 2a.
and John Gye his 5a. 4a. adjoining to Mrs. Eyles her 3 x ½a. on 1 side and ½a. on
the other butting against the greenway. 1a. joining to 2a. of Mr. Michell and 1a.
of Thomas Pryor. 1a. joining to Christopher Slade his 3a. and butting against the
down. 1a. above Padams pool joining to Mr. Michell his 4a. 2 outland a. joining
3a. of Mr. Michell and butting against Imber way. 5a. butting against Mr. Michell
his 8a. 1 head a. joining to Mrs. Gyles her 4a. on Dicks knoll. 4a. joining to John
Gye his 4a. upon Dicks knoll. The White acre lying under the green way 1a.
joining to Christopher Slade his 9a. 1a. joining to 1a. of Thomas Pryor above
the hedge. 3a. joining to wid. Huntley her 2a. 1 head a. at Clerckenlane joining
to Mr. Michell his 3a.

Gervase Bland, vicar, Tristram Compton, John Smith, churchwardens.

176   18 Dec 1677 (D1/24/47/4)
Commons of pasture for 152 sheep in the W. flock. 3a.[1] in 1 piece abutting upon
the head a. of Mr. Charles Mitchell[2] S., 2a. belonging to John Gey[3] N. 1 head a.
butting upon the way by the farm field in the field above the church. 1a. at
Thomas Pryor's[4] gate butting upon his garden hedge. 1a. at Gardway called
Gardway acre. 1a. shooting up at the hill a little from Gardway. 1a. called White
acre on the top of the hill. 1a. butting upon the greenway above Thomas Pryor[4]
in the middle of the field. 1 short a. between 2 linchets [lanchards] at the end of
the last acre. 2a. at the end of the last short acre upon Dick knowle. 1 head a. in
the top of the hill above Dicks knoll at the end of the greenway. 5a. in 1 piece in

the side of the hill below the said head a. abutting upon 8a. N. E., upon 5a. S.W., both of Mr. Charles Michell. 2a. of outland in the bottom butting upon Imber way. 1a. butting upon Nonnye down above Gregories hedge. 2a. upon Nonny down at the top of the hill. 4a. in 1 piece lying on the top of the hill by Priory head ½a. and butting upon the green way S.W. and the part which is called Hell N. E. 1a. above London way between 2 linchets. 1a. by the pool beyond Padham Cross near 5a. occupied by Joan Slade wid.[5] 1 long a. on the top of the hill above Hell bounded with a lanchard on each side. 3a. upon the top of the 5 hill above Ellingtons meadow, 8a. of Mr. Charles Michell[6] S.W., head a. of Thomas Pryor[7] N. E. 1 long a. by the said head a. butting upon Ellingtons bushes. 2a. in a piece of outland butting up the bourne by Ellingtons bushes some part being picked at the lower end butting upon Thomas Pryor's[8] 2a. of outland. 2a. of outland upon the hill above N. meadow butting towards S. side of the meadow adjoining an a. of the Priory above the said 2a. and 5a. of the Priory below the said 2a. next to the pathway.

Commons for 1 horse in W. field. A mansion house, barn, stable, barton and a garden plot behind the church butting on Symes his close at one end and the stile going to Imber at the other end. Tithe wool of Milborn farm flock occupied by Edward Jones. Tithe of W. flock fully [i. e. lamb and wool], tithe of Comdown[9]. Tithe hay of the whole parish. Tithe lambs of all flocks except Francis Paulet's esq.[10] The Easter book, privy tithes oblations and profits.

Anthony Delacourt, vicar, Christopher Hews, Jordan Slade, Thomas Smith [X].

1. Described as in the field above the church in **174**.
2. Formerly of old John Coppe in **174**.
3. Edward Comlelore in **174** Charles Michell esq., in **177**.
4. Stabbins in **174**, Frances Pryor wid. in **177**.
5. Mr. Thomas Flower in **174**.
6. Edward Farrell in **174**, Charles Michell esq., in **177**.
7. Edward Marshall in **174**.
8. Frances Pryor wid. in **174**, Edward Marshall in 177.
9. Described as the flock Mr. John Flower now in the use of Mr. Philip Browne in **174**.
10. No exception in **174**, Norton Paulet esq., in **177**.

177 18 May 1705 (D1/24/47/5)
*As **175** with amendments in footnotes.* John Dowland, vicar, Thomas Shephard, John Compton, James Kinge.

CHITTERNE ST. MARY vicarage

178 n. d. [1588][1] (D1/24/48/1)
The vicarage house with a barn and a small garden plot, and a close of ½a. between the farm and the tenement called the Smithes. A meadow of 1a. between Spurgins and Jures close, and 140 sheep leaze, and 12 in the W. side. The tithe of Tunne mead, Broade mead and Parkers mead. In the Greeneway field: in the

Gassen furlong 1a. between 1a. of John Ember, the farmer, and 2a. of Erasmus Chamberlayne; 2a. shooting along by the Gasson hedge; 1a. shooting on the Gasson hedge between 1a. of John Ember, the farmer, and 1a. of Thomas Pottowe; 1a. more in the same furlong; 1a. in the Oute furlong; 1a. more in the same furlong; In the Upper Oute furlong 3a. between 1a. of Erasmus Chamberlayne and the farmer's 19a.; 2. between the 19a. of John Ember, the farmer, and the Bath way.

In Cross ball field: In Flexlande furlong, 3a.; in Cross ball furlong 1a.; in Longland furlong 1a.; 1a. between 2 linchets on the upper side of John Ember's short furlong; 2a. between John Ember's piece and 1a. of Erasmus Chamberlayne.

In Tadd Hill field 2a. between the farmer's piece called the Hanginges and ½a. of the farmer; in Woe Hill furlong 1a. between 1a. of Thomas Pottowe and 1a. of John Ember; 1 head a. in the same furlong; 1a. between the linchets shooting on Codford Down above Parkers mead; an outland a. shooting along by Codford Down, headland to the farmer's outland piece; in Pitt acre furlong 2a. between ? Chilpnam path and 3a. of Thomas Pottowe; 1a. more in the same furlong between 1a. and 4a. of Erasmus Chamberlayne. In total 28½a. arable land. Tithe wool of the farm flock and of the tenants, sheep in the W. field, also of 200 sheep there belonging to a tenement of William Tinburie. Tithes of wool of the Wormesie flock.

1.   Written in the same hand as **173**.

179   1609 (D1/24/48/2)
The vicarage house covered with tile with 2 bartons and 2 garden plots on N. and S. sides of the house. A barn with 2 fields of building and a midsty and a stable with 2 fields. In the vicarage 3 rooms below a hall with a chimney, a kitchen and a buttery with 3 chambers above.

Glebeland: 12a. of land on N. side and 8a. of land on S. side of Bath way. 8½a. of land on S. side of Warminster way. A close between the farm house and the farmer's tenement called Smithes house.

Meadow ground: A meadow by Spurgins that lies several to the vicarage from Sunday after the feast of the Purification of the B. V. M. [2 Feb] until Lammas [1 Aug.] for hay and the aftergrass. 3 lots of meadow < Eve at noone> on Tunmead for the tithe of the meadow that his several to the vicarage for hay and aftergrass as the freeholder and tenants. As from the Sunday after the feast of the Purification of the B. V. M. until Lammas. Tithe hay <Eve at noone> of Broadmead, Parkers mead and the tithe of all other plots and closes of the farmer freeholders and tenants; Mr. Codford his meadow only excepted, the tithe whereof belongs to Codford St. Mary.

Sheep leaze: For 152 sheep to have their pasturing and feeding in all places and fields with the farm flock 'horn by horne as they commonly tearme it, that is to say, to goe as farre for them in theire pasture and lease as the farmor freeholder and tenants maye without lett or contradiction'.

Tithe wool growing in the W. flock in the Farm field and in the Warminster side [Wormestide] tithe lamb and all privy tithes, oblations and dues except pulse and corn belonging to the rectory. Part of an enclosure named Gasson occupied by Thomas Flower gent., belonging to Chitterne St. Mary; Thomas lives in Chitterne All Saints. The tithe whereof paid these 30 years past time to time demanded by the incumbent viz. the tithe of Windmill down belongs to the vicarage, Sir William Jordan and Thomas Flower gent., 'inter comminers' there who dwell in Chitterne All Saints.

By me Anthony Lynne, vicar; John Atwoode [X], William Huntley [X], churchwardens.

180   27 Dec 1671 (D1/24/48/3)
1a. of arable land in Gascen Corner, 1a. of Thomas Mills[1] S., 1a. of Thomas Hopkins[2] N.; 1a. in the same field, Thomas Mills[1] N., Christopher Hughse[3] S.; 2a., the Gasson E., the farm land W.; 1a. in the same field, John Gye[4] N., Christopher Hughse S.; 2a. in the same field, Bath way S., The farm land N.; 3a. in the same field, wid. Sanders[5] S, the farm land N.; 1a. in the same field, wid. Sanders[5] S., Christopher Hughse[3] N.; 1a. in the same field Thomas Mills[1] N., Thomas Hopkins[2] S.; 3a. called Flaxland on S. side of Bath way, Jordan Sanders[6] N., John Atwood[7] S.; 1 picked acre butting on the E. end of Crose Ball,[8] Thomas Hopkins N., Mrs. Davis[9] S.; 1a.[10] in the same field, Mrs. Davis[9] N., the farm land S.; 1a. in the same field, Christopher Hughse[3] E., Thomas Mills[1] W.; 2a. of outland in the same field, the farm land N. W., Mrs. Davis[9] S. E.[11]

1a. in Woehill field, Mrs. Davis E., Thomas Mills[1] W.; 1head a. in the same field, wid. Sanders[5] N., the furlong, which at its S. end, abuts on Codford down S.; 1a. in the same furlong, Christopher Hughse[3] N., Thomas Mills[1] S.; 3x ½a. in the same field, Christopher Hughse N., the way leading to W. Codford S. 2a. in the Farm field, Thomas Mills[1] S., the farmland N.; 1a. of outland in the same field Codford Down W., the farm land E.

Commons for 152 sheep in the farm flock. 1 enclosed pasture ground between the farm orchard and the garden and orchard of Thomas Mills.[1] 1 plot of Lammas meadow ground Jewes[12] called the Vicarage meadow the watercourse E. close W. 1 plot of Lammas meadow called the Vicars. 3 lots in Sun meadow, 3 lots of John Attwood S., 3 lots of Mrs. Davis N.

A dwelling house, barn, backside, cow house, 2 gardens, on the N. and S. sides of the house. The tithe of Windmill Down for the summer time. 2s. p. a. for the winter feeding the Priory in Chitterne All Saints (by composition we suppose) paid to the vicar of Chitterne St. Mary. Mr. Michell pays to the vicar for the tithe of a corner of his Gasson 6d. p. a. All other tithes except tithe corn and the tithe of Sun meadow which belongs to the vicarage.

John Redman, vicar John Attwood, Thomas Wells, churchwardens.

1. wid. Mills in **182**.
2. Jonathan Flowers in **182**.
3. wid. Hughse in **182**.
4. Edward Gye in **182**.
5. Jordan Sanders in **182**.
6. wid. Deane Sanders in **181**.
7. Mr. Charles Flower in **182**.

8. Described as at the Townsend in **182**.
9. James Davis in **182**.
10. Described as between Bath way and Warminster way in **181** and **182**.
11. Arable land below this apart from **3** x ½a. omitted in **182**.
12. Dewes Close in **182**.

181   10 Oct 1677 (D1/24/48/4)
*As **180** with amendment in footnotes.* John Redman vicar, John Gie, John Sanders churchwardens.

182   8 Jun 1705 (D1/24/48/5)
*As **180** with amendments in footnotes.* That part of a barn built against the parsonage barn on N. side of vicarage garden occupied by Mr. James Slade held at pleasure from the vicar. The Easter book with the rest of the small tithes and oblations and profits.
      John Dowland vicar, John Sanders [X], Jonathan Flower, churchwardens.

CHOLDERTON rectory

183   18 Dec 1677 (D1/24/49/1)
The dwelling house at the N. end of the parish in good repair with 2 gardens before and behind, a barn, stable, and other outhouses, all in good repair. 1a. pasture behind the barn. 12a. land in the 3 town fields i. e. in the N. field 4a.: 1a. in the Upper furlong not far from Long hedge; ½a. a little below not far from Long hedge; 1a. in the same furlong called Broad acre; 1½a. in the Middle furlong not far from Long hedge. In the Middle field 3½a.: 1a. in the Upper furlong, 1½a. in the same furlong below the other, and 1a. in the Middle furlong called the Little acre. In the S. field 4½a.: 1a. in the Upper furlong; 1½a. in the same furlong, the lower end adjoining the 1½a. in the Middle field; 1a. more on Churchill, the end adjoining London way; 1a. more called the Picked acre, the end adjoining the London Way. Common of pasture for 2 cows and a bull in the Cow down and stubble field, also commons for a boar and other hogs and pigs in the stubble field. Common of pasture for 30 sheep in the lower farm. The full and entire tithes nothing at all excepted.
      Samuel Heskins rector, Thomas Wheeler [X], Richard Noyes, Henry Desmore [X], Edward Noyes [X].

CHRISTIAN MALFORD rectory

184   1608 (D1/24/50/1)
Glebe land, *c.* 120a. The tenements with orchards and gardens: Cuthbert White, 23a., orchard and garden; Thomas Higgins, 8a., orchard and garden; Richard Hull, 8a., orchard and garden; David Butten, 12a., orchard and garden; wid. Weaste, 9a., orchard and garden. 4 cottages: [*occupied by*] John Collman, Thomas Russ, wid. Hament, wid. Pullmer.

Simon York, curate, George Cox, William Keane churchwardens, Thomas Butten, William Selman, sidesmen, Thomas English, John Butten, David Butten, Cuthbert White. *All signed with a mark except the curate.*

185 4 Jan 1672 (D1/24/50/2)

A dwelling house, orchard, garden, barn and backside, outhouse, oxhouse and stable, *c.* 2a. The churchyard and the grounds of arable land, pasture and meadow adjoining the dwelling house, *c.* 80a. 1 ground of pasture called Lewes his leaze, *c.* 15a., lying between the grounds of John Ferris and Philip Cogswell.

2 houses and land occupied by John Ferris. 1 house and land occupied by Philip Cogswell. 2 houses and land occupied by Francis Hatherill. 1 house and land occupied by Robert Collman. 1 house and land occupied by Richard Madits. 1 house and land occupied by John Scott. 5 cottages occupied by William Hull, William Harding, William Smart, John Warden, wid. Aliffe.

William Pierce, rector, William Pullin, John Rich, churchwardens, John Bendry, Anthony Keene, sidesmen. *Names in the same hand.*

186 14 Mar 1677 (D1/24/50/3)

A dwelling house, orchard, garden, backside, barn, stable, pigeon house, *c.* 1a. Enclosed grounds; Hunts, adjoining the backside, 1½a.; pasture called Church leaze, 8a. adjoining the churchyard; 2 meadows called the Avens, 5a., near the river; arable called Mead close, 8a., adjoining the last meadow; 2 arable grounds called the Avens, 15a., adjoining Mead close; arable called the Ox leaze, 12a., adjoining meadows called Avens; arable called the Dry leaze, 13a. adjoining Church leaze; arable called Lews his leaze, 10a. adjoining Strattons leazes S., a ground of John Ferris N.

Copyhold tenements: one occupied by John Scott, 6 lugs or poles, adjoining the churchyard; one occupied by Richard Smith and Alice Madits, 6 lugs, adjoining ground called Hunts; two occupied by John Ferris gent, 12a., whereof 2a. adjoin the house of one tenement and 5a. the other, 3a. of meadow, 2a. of arable in one ground lying against the way to Hairstreet; one occupied by Francis Ratherill, 7a., of arable enclosed in 2 grounds called Strattons leaze and Gullys; one occupied by Isaac Belisheare, 7a., in 2 enclosed grounds called Home close and Harestreet; one occupied by Philip Cogswell, 6a., in 2 grounds one adjoining Harestreet the other adjoining Lewis his leaze; one occupied by Robert Collman, 2a., whereof 1½a. adjoins the house and ½a. adjoins Narrow Harestreet.

All great and small tithes as corn, hay, wool, lambs, cows, calves, pigs, geese and oblations, excepting the tithes of lands called Greenes and Canheddens formerly belonging to Bradenstoke abbey.

William Pierce, rector, Richard Palmer [X], George Leah [X], churchwardens.

187 21 Dec 1704 (D1/24/50/4)

The parsonage house, stable, barn, dovehouse, garden, orchard and plough barton, the Paddock, Hunt's, Doglease, Barneclose, Churchclose, 2 meadows, Drymead, Broad Haven, 2 Long Havens, Oxenlease, Lewces 2 grounds, the feeding of the church yard and little Hear Street, *c.* 110a.

A tenement of Thomas Ody; a house, garden, orchard, an orchard called Wardens, the Home Close, Coalmans Acre, Southfield lease, Westfield lease and W. acre in Kingsmead, *c.* 16a. A tenement of James Hatherill, a house called the Ancray, Gulleys lease, Strettons 2 grounds, a garden and an orchard, *c.* 12a. A tenement of Isaac Belcher; a house, garden, orchard, barn, stable, Home close, and a Field close, *c.* 8a. A tenement of William Trimnell; a house, garden, orchard, barn, stable and 2 Home closes, *c.* 3½a. A tenement of John Ferris; a house, barn, garden, orchard, 2 Home closes, Pusscrat, 2 Field grounds, and a piece of ground in Kingsmead, *c.* 22a. A tenement of George Coulman; a house, garden, orchard, Home close, *c.* 2a. A cottage of John Scott, a house and garden. 2 cottages of Richard Madits alias Smith, 2 houses, a garden and orchard. 2 cottages, one of Samuel Ashley and the other of Elizabeth Stanford, now in dispute. All the parish pays tithe except on 2 pieces of pasture called Greens and Canheadons.

'These are to certify that I Henry Margetts, rector, have diligently lookt over this terrier and that I approve of it in all things ?[except] what is said there to be to the cottages of Ashley and Stanford in dispute which I will not alow to be I having enjoyed them ever since I was Rector as also did my predecessor. '

Henry Margetts, rector, John Skues, Thomas Trimnell, churchwardens, Isaac Belcher, Thomas Ody, John Bendry, John Sellman, William Trimnell, Thomas Peacocke junior, George Jaques.

CLYFFE PYPARD vicarage

188   28 Oct 1671 (D1/24/51/1)
A vicarage house with a little court, backside, garden and orchard adjoining, *c.* ½a. Tithe wool, lambs, cow white, calves and all privy tithes, also tithes of hay from the lower end of of Cleeves Wood corner adjoining Mounkton Laines corner, along the lane by Copped Hall alias Weekehouse, along Marlborough way by the row of bushes above the hill to Ricardson field, and from there over all the N. and E. parts of the parish. The vicar has also all tithes of and from the parson i. e. corn, hay, cow white, calves, wool, lambs, and all privy tithes, also the rent of 5s. for the Vicarage close.

William Stampe, vicar, Ambrose Spackman, William Young, churchwardens, Thomas Spicer [X], Thomas Greenaway, sidesmen.

Endorsement: Exhibited at Marlborough 10 June 1817 in the case in Chancery between Edward Goddard clerk comp. and Thomas Ayliffe, Peter Dove and Edmund Maskelyne def.

189   16 Dec 1704 (D1/24/51/2)
A little garden and orchard adjoining the vicarage house.[1] Tithe wool, lambs, cow white, calves and all privy tithes.[2] Tithe hay from the lower end of Cleeves Wood corner adjoining to Mounckton Laines corner, along the lane by Copped Hall alias Weeke house along Marlborough way by the row of bushes above the hill to Ricarston field and from thence over all N. and E. parts of the parish. The vicar takes all the said tithes from the parson and the rent of 5s. for Vicarage Close.

Thomas Foster, vicar, William Garlick, Ambrose Spackman, churchwardens, William Chrrch,[3] Joseph Parsons, Roger Spackman, William Wheeler, John Hopkins, Nicholas Greenaway.
Endorsement as **188**.

1. An estimate of dilapidations of the vicarage house in 1769 lists all the rooms including a schoolroom (WSRO 1064/43).
2. An assessment of tithes in 1742 indicates that they had by then been commuted to money payments (WSRO 1064/30).
3. Probably Church. A William Church was buried in 1728.

190   21 Jul 1783 (D1/24/51/3)
Survey delivered to the apparitor by the churchwardens, 31 Jul 1783. A little garden and orchard adjoining the vicarage house.[1] Tithe wool, lambs, cow white, calves and all privy tithes. Tithe hay from the lower end of Cleeves Wood Corner to Mounckton Lains corner and along the lane by Copped Hall alias Weeke house, along Marlborough way by the row of bushes above Hill to Richartson alias Snap field and from there over all N. and E. parts of the parish. All these tithes also payable by the parson to the vicar and rent of 5s. for vicarage close.

16 pollards and sapling trees in the churchyard. 5 bells in the tower. 1 plain communion cup and lid. 1 plate marked: 'Gul. Stamp 1683'. An old velvet pulpit cloth. Communion cloth and linen. Sexton appointed by the vicar, wages 40s. p. a. paid by the parish.

Edward Goddard, vicar, John Gale, churchwarden, Isaac Woodward, Edward Goddard, Broome Pinniger, James Archer.
Endorsement as **188**.

1. See **186** note 1.

CODFORD ST. MARY rectory

191   12 Jun 1609 (D1/24/52/l)
The parsonage house, gardens and orchard, *c.* 1a.; a tenement with garden and close, *c.* 1½a. 2a. meadow abutting N. and S., 1a. of Philip Ingram one side, the common water the other; 2a. more near Maton's weir abutting E. and W. 1a. of Maton one side, the common water the other. Home field: 1a. arable, land of Richard Smith E., Dorothy Wort wid. W. the ends abutting N. and S.; 2a. abutting N. and S. between lands of Christopher Eyre and Richard Smith; 3a. abutting N. and S. between lands of Christopher Eyre and Dorothy Wort wid.; ½a. abutting E. and W. between the common meadow and the way. 3 x ½a. in Snape bottom abutting N. and S. between lands of Dorothy Wort wid.; 1a. abutting N. and S. between the lands of Richard Smith and Dorothy Wort; 3a. abutting E. and W. between the land of Dorothy Wort N and the highway S.; another 3 x ½a. near Foxholes bushes abutting E. and W., the farm land N.; 1yd. in Snape bottom abutting E. and W. between land of Richard Smith S. and Christopher Eyre N. Middle field: 1a. on Snape hill abutting E. and W., land of Dorothy Wort S., the

common downe N.; ½a. abutting E. and W., the highway N., land of Richard Smith S.; 3 x ½a. abutting E. and W., lands of Richard Smith both sides; ½a. abutting E. and W. between the highway and lands of Dorothy Wort; another ½a. abutting E. and W. between the lands of Richard Smith and Christopher Eyre; 3 x ½a. on S. Kingshill abutting N. and S., land of Dorothy Wort both sides; 3a. in Kingscombe bottom abutting E. and W. between lands of Richard Smith and Dorothy Wort; 1a. abutting E. and W. lands of Richard Smith both sides. N. field: 1 picked a. abutting E. and W. between the land of Richard Smith and Dorothy Wort; 7a. in Kingscombe bottom abutting N. and S. head furlong on one side, land of Richard Smith on the other; 3a. on N. Kingshill abutting E. and W. between lands of Richard Smith and Dorothy Wort; 2a. in Longdeane bottom abutting E. and W. land of Richard Smith N. and the common down S.; ½a. in Sandhills abutting E. and W., land of Richard Smith both sides; 1yd. in Sandhills abutting E. and W., Richard Smith N., the common down S.

The old stint of sheep 200 but now according to a proportionate abatement of the rest of the freeholders 160, of horses and rother beasts it cannot be agreed. The parsonage barn of 6 fields of building, the stable of 1 field, the dwelling house of 1 field.

Gilbert Hyeuet[1] [rector], John? Slack, William Tuckey, Christopher Smyth, John Withers, clerk.

1.   Huet in record of his institution in 1572 (WSRO D1/1/17).

192   8 Jan 1672 (D1/24/52/2)
A mansion house, barn, stable, pigeon house, with a yard, backside, an orchard and garden, c. 1a. 36a. 1yd. of arable land lying dispersed in the freehold fields with commons of pasture for 180 sheep in the fields according to the custom of the manor of Codford St. Mary. 1 meadow ground, c. 3a., in E. meadow lying between a meadow of John Ingram W., and wid. Sedenham E. A little house and garden occupied by Jerome With with a close of meadow adjoing, c. 1a. All tithes great and small, the tithe of 1½a. in Chitterne mead adjoining Codford mead for which the occupant pays by custom 12 chickens or 2s. p. a. for tithes. Tithe of c. ½a. in Bapton mead near the parsonage mead for which the occupant pays by custom 1d. or ½d. p. a.

Thomas Edwards, rector, Augustine Tuggy, Thomas Wort, churchwardens.
Names in the same hand.

193   17 May 1705 (D1/24/52/3)
A parsonage house, barn, backside, stable and outhouses. 1 close c. 1a. 3½a. meadow. 14½a. of arable in the Home field. 8½a. of arable in the Middle field. 12a. 3yds. of arable in the Further field. Tithe corn, hay, wool, lamb, gardens, cow white, calves, Easter offerings, apples, pears, wax, honey, after grass. Sheepleaze for 133.

Samuel Blundell, rector, Giles Ingram, John Ingram churchwardens.

194   28 Jul 1783 (D1/24/52/4)
Terrier of glebe, tithes, and other rights of Rev. Dr. [*Thomas*] Smith, rector, made according 'to the old evidences of knowledge of the ancient inhabitants'

delivered at the visitation held at Salisbury, 4 Aug. 1783.

The parsonage house is built with stone and wood and tile containing a large hall with oak floor wainscotted chair-high and papered, a small parlour, floored with deal and wainscotted, a kitchen bricked and plastered, a small flagged scullery, 4 bedchambers floored with deal, 2 of them papered, with 4 garrets. A large barn made with boards and thatched with straw; a stone walled stable thatched.

c. 25a. in the Common field with c. 3½a. of enclosed meadow. An orchard, garden and rickyard, 1½a. The garden and yard enclosed by a mud wall and the orchard by a hedge fence. Right of commons for 140 sheep. The minister received a tenth of everything titheable as customary. There are no pensions payable out of the living nor any chapel established in the parish.

The furniture of the church and chancel; 3 bells, a communion table covered with green cloth, a chest, a bible and prayer book and a green velvet cloth for the desk and pulpit. A font and 1 surplice. 1 linen cloth and napkin for the communion table, 1 large soft metal cup and 1 small silver cup, a small silver plate for the bread. No lands nor money left towards the repairs of the church. The church and churchyard fence to be repaired by the parishioners, the chancell by the rector. The clerk is appointed by the minister and is paid the sum of 1s. for every yardland in the parish. The parishioners appoint and pay the sexton's wages.

Henry Williams, minister, John Ingram, John Hayter, churchwarden.

CODFORD ST. PETER [West Codford] rectory

195   1588 (D1/24/53/1)
Tithe corn, hay, wool, lamb, etc. 15a. of glebe land: 1a. by 1a. of Mr. Christopher Eyre lying N. and S.; 1a. by the greenway by 1a. of Walter Ratford lying N. and S.; 2a. by the greenway at Brokewaie lying N. and S.; 2a. shooting on Stardwaie W. from Thomas Snelgar's a.; 1a. on Ronehil between 2 linchets lying N. and S.; 1a. in Echer furlong between 2 linchets E. and W.; 1a. by Medowaie, headland to Hake furlong by W. of 1a. of John Hibbert, lying N. and S.; 1a. in Sidehill linchet with 1a. of Thomas Snelgar, shooting E. and W.; 1a. in Longfullonge between ½a. of Thomas Snelgar and 2a. of Mr. Eyre, a linchet between N. and S.; ½a. in Ashtons N. field, ½a. of Tristram Crouche E.; 1a. in the W. hill between Robert Morren and John Randall W. and S.; 1a. in Woland between Walter Ratford and wid. Pearce E. and W.; 1a. in the W. Bottom between Robert Morren and George Pashion lying N. and S.; ½a. overthwart Dot path by Christopher Combes on one side, headland the other. Total 15a. Pasture and feeding for 1 gelding etc.

Antony Atkings, John Randall churchwardens; Christopher Combes, Thomas Snelgar, John Hibberte, sidesmen. *Names in the same hand.*

196   1608 (D1/24/53/2)
Terrier of glebelands belonging to the parsonage now in the possession of Mr. William Boorme bachelor of divinity and fellow of Trinity College Cambridge.

In the Low field, 2a., the N. end butting on Stardway, S. end on 1a. of John Atkins, 4a. of John Prior and ½a. of John Cucke, on E. side 1a. of Thomas Snelgar, on W. side the greenway to Chitterne. 2a. in the Low field one shooting upon the other, the greenway on W. side, the N. end of one butting on 3 x ½a. of Thomas Snelgar, S. end of the other on part of 1a. of Philip Bennet and part of 1a. of Mr. Eyre, having on E. side 1a. of John Bright and 1a. of Agnes Coward.

In the Home field 2a., one next the mead shooting N. and S., N. on 1a. of Thomas Snelgar called Cotford, S. on ½a. of Mr. Eyre, W. 1a. of Mr. Eyre and a head a.; the other next the said greenway on W., 1a. of William Ratford E., shooting S. on ½a. of John Atkins, N. 1a. of Agnes Coward.

On Roane hill 1a. shooting S. on 1a. of John Atkins, N. on Ashton N. field, W. 1a. of Tristram Crouch, E. ½a. of John Bright.

1a. in Hakefield shooting W. on 1a. of John Atkins that lies on Roane hill, E. ½a. of Philip Bennet, N. 2a. John Hibhard, S. ½a. of Thomas Snelgar. In Hakefield 1 head a. to a furlong in Long Hake shooting N. on 3a. of Mr. Eyre, S. 1a. of wid. Cocke, E. 3x ½a. of John Hibbard. In Hakefield 1 head a. shooting E. on **½a.** of John Prior, W. 1a. of John Rendall, S. headland to a furlong on side hill, N. 1a. of Thomas Snelgar. In Long furlong 1a. shooting on Smeathway, S. 1a. of Thomas Hide, E. 2a. of Mr. Eyre, W. ½a. of Thomas Snelgar.

In Ashton Gifford field; in the N. field ½a. shooting N. on 1a. of William Pierce, S. on ½a. wid. Stevens, W. a quarter linch, E. ½a. Philip Bennet. On W. hill 1a. shooting N. on the down, S. 3x ½a., E. Alexander Turner and 1a. Michael Munday, W. 1a. of William Goddard. In W. bottom 1a. shooting N. on 3 x ½a. of William Ratford, S. the way to Warminster, W. 3x ½a. John Pashen, E. 1a. William Goddard.

In the Lower W. field ½a. lying athwart Dodpath, E. a headland to 3a. of Alexander Turner and ½a. of John Pashen and 3 x ½a. William Goddard, W. ½a. Alexander Turner, butting S. on 4a. Alexander Turner. In Woeland 1a. shooting N. W, on 1a. Alexander, N. E. on 1a. of Tristram Crouch, S. E. ½a. William Ratford, S. W. ½a. William Pierce.

A dwelling house, part now in building, the other old and ruinous, a barton, *c.* 1 yd., 2 sufficient barns, no garden nor orchard, no meadow, pasture, nor in ground, no sheep leaze no feeding for other cattle in the commons, only to have 1 nag in the field at harvest time. The parson is to keep at his charge to our use a bull and a boar.

Thomas Crockford, curate, Philip Bennett, William Ratford, churchwardens, John Bright, Nicholas Monday, sidesmen. *Signature of the curate; other names in the same hand.*

197   2 Nov 1671 (D1/24/53/3)
A mansion house with a backside, 2 barns, a stable, 15a. in the several fields; 1a. in Long furlong field lying by Shepards linch [Lench]; 1a. on Mownsham field lying below the greenway; 1a. in the same field next the meadow; 2a. in the Lowfield[1] abutting one upon the other and lying below the greenway; 2a. in the same field lying below the greenway and butting upon Stardway; 1a. upon Ronehill bounded with ½a. of Mrs. Bright E., 1a. wid. Crouch W.; 1a lying

upon Roan linch butting upon Braiden path; 1 head a. to Hakefield; 1 head a. in Sidehill field; ½a. in Ashton Gifford field, called W. field, lying athwart the footpath to Upton Lovell; 1a. in the W. Bottom field abutting on the highway; 1a. in Woland bounded ½a. of Henry Thringe N., ½a. wid. Davies S.; ½a. in N. field bounded 1a. of Christopher Turner W., ½a. wid. Hinton E.; 1a. in W Hill field bounded 1a. of Mr. Robert Steavens W., 1a. Philip Hinton E. ¼a.[2] of meadow lately enclosed out of the common marsh in Codford shooting athwart the footpath to Sherrington mill. Tithe wheat, barley, peas, oats vetches, lentils [tills] and all other grains. 1 horseleaze in the fields. Tithe of hay and yeargrass [yeagrasse]. Tithe lamb, wool and pig, Easter offerings; for cow white 1d., for a calf sold a tenth of a penny, for a calf killed the best shoulder, for a calf weaned ½d. Tithe pears, apples and all other fruit, wax and honey.

John Swayne, rector.

1. Described as in the same field i. e. Mownsham field in **198**.
2. This land omitted in 198.

198 1677 (D1/24/53/4)
*As **197** with amendments in footnotes.* John Swayne, Philip Ingram, Richard Withers, churchwardens.

199 1 Jan 1705 (D1/24/53/5)
*Tithes, parsonage house and outhouses as **197**.* A bull plot and 15a. of arable: 1a. in W. bottom butting on the highway and bounded by 1a. of Mr. Madox E. ½a. in W. field running cross the footpath, part of it a headland. 1a. in W. field bounded by 1a. of Emmes E., 1a. of Madox W. 1a. in Ashton N. field butting on Hake bounded by a large linch W. 1a. on the Brow running cross the way to the down butting on the Swarth bounded ½a. John Gilbert S. E. 1a. in N. furlong butting on Smith way bounded by Shepherd's linch E. 1a. in Mounson butting on Meadway field bounded by the greenway. 1a. in Mounson butting on Meadway field bounded by the mead. 2a. in Lowfield butting one upon each other, part bounded by the headland to Hake and part bounded by the greenway. 2a. in Lowfield butting on Stardway and bounded by the greenway. 1a. headland to Sidehill. 1a. headland to Hake. 1a. lying upon Roan linch butting on Braiden path. 1a. on Roanhill butting on Ashton N. field and bounded with ½a. of Henry Flower E. John Crouch his a. W.

Charles Wroughton, rector, Richard Withers, Branker Thring [X] churchwardens, John Bennet overseer, Henry Flower, John Crouch.

COLERNE vicarage

200 n. d. early 17th cent. (D1/24/54/l)
A dwelling house, a dove house, 2 gardens and the churchyard adjoining, *c.* 1a.

William Sallmon, Henry Woodruff [X], churchwardens; John Tyley [X], John Smith [X], sidesmen.

201   12 Dec 1677 (D1/24/54/2)

The vicarage house of 5 bays with outlets and gardens, a dovehouse, churchyard with a little garden adjoining to the same occupied by Robert Ford.[1]

For cow white, 3d. paid at Lammas [1 Aug] for every cow fed in the parish. For calves born [fallen], 6d. at Lammas; if they are weaned ½d.; if sold before they come to be milked or yoked a tenth of the price. The tenth weight or pound of all locks of sheep and 1d. for each sheep sold. Tenth or seventh lamb to be paid at St. Mark's day [25 Apr]. Tenth or seventh pigs. For every hen, 2 eggs for the cock, 3 eggs. Tithe apples, pears and all other fruit. The tenth a. of coppice wood. The tenth of the money of hedgerow that are sold. Easter offerings of every communicant 2d. for every garden 1d. 2 mills, one in the possession of wid. Sumption[2] pays 10s. p. a., the other of John Chap[3] pays 2s. 6d. p. a. £3 paid by composition at midsummer from Euridge [Uridge] farm by the appointment of Mr. William Blanchard, owner of the farm.[4] Mortuary payment for if the person had any considerable estate or money.

Francis Gallimore, rector, John Smith, James Trelay, churchwardens.

1. John Aust in **202.**
2. John Nichols in **202.**
3. John Edwards in **202.**
4. No owner mentioned in **202.**

202   3 Dec 1704 (D1/24/54/3)

As **201** *with amendments in footnotes.* Benjamin Griffin, vicar, Richard Melsam, George Green [X], churchwardens, Mary Houghton.

202A   [1783][1] (D1/24/54/4)

Answer to question 13. I have no terrier. I have applied by letter to the officers at Salisbury several times for a copy of any terrier which might be found in the bishop's registry. But I know not for what reason my applications have been totally disregarded. There is no land belonging to the vicarage and the tithes, as at present, are of very small value and very ill paid. A terrier made according to the present payments and without the guidance and authority of any old one may possibly be prejuidicial to some future incumbent. It is intended to bring a bill into parliament during the next session for an enclosure,[2] when it is proposed to commute the tithes for a corn rent. But the plan is not yet settled. An old terrier might serve to direct the commissioners in that business. It is humbly conceived that it will be better to defer the making of a terrier until the enclosure is completed or at the idea of one entirely dropped.

Answer to question 14. William Harris D. D., schoolmaster at Winchester college by will dated 6 Nov. 1700 bequested the sum of £300 to be laid out in land for the use of such poor housekeepers of the parish of Colerne, where he was born, as receive no alms of the parish, the income thereof to be distributed at Easter and Christmas yearly, at the discretion of the vicar, churchwardens and overseers of the poor. Charles Savage esq. of Westwood, one of Dr. Harris' executors, did by his deed, 30 nov. 1702, which deed is now in the possession of the churchwardens, settle a rent charge of £12 p. a. free of all taxes and payments whatsoever to be paid out of a certain estate in Keevil in lieu of the said sum of £300. Which rent charge is regularly received and distributed according to Dr. Harris' directions.

The hon. Mrs. Elizabeth Forrester, who died in 1777, left by will the sum of £300 to be disposed of in every particular according to Dr. Harris' directions. This bequest was void by Act 9G2 ch. 36 [1735-6],[3] but her excutor, John Morris esq. of Box, willing to fulfill the intentions of the testatrix, has vested the money in the funds for the present, until an opportunity offers of making a suitable purchase. The stock purchased is £552 18s. 4d., half a year's interest of which viz. £8 5s. 10d. was distributed according to Dr. Harris' directions at Easter last.

N[athanial] Bliss [vicar].

1. This document comprises detailed responses to questions 13 and 14 of the Returns of Visitation Queries, 1783 (D1/56/1; published in WRS vol. 27). Clearly Bliss needed more space than that allocated in the printed format. This sheet was placed with the glebe terriers.
2. An act was passed in 1784-5 and the award completed in 1787 (WSRO. EA 30 and WRS. vol. 25).
3. A general act about Charitable Uses.

COLLINGBOURNE DUCIS rectory

203   3 Oct 1608 (D1/24/55/1)
E. of the town: at Hill hedge 3½a. by the wayside; at Slatfurlong ½a. between Thomas Hearne and John Passion; at Bricklinch 4½a in one piece; at Spitlefurlong 1a. between Hungerford way and John Marshall's ½a.; at Crosle 1a. between Edward Blackmore and John Marshall; at Hanger 1a. with a linch on the lower side, John Marshall's ½a. on the upper; at Myrke hill 2a. in a piece, a linch on the lower and upper sides; at Stonecraft 2½a. in a piece by Mr. Richard Dowse's wick; at Weeke path 1a. shooting towards Coopers plants the other side of the way; at Gartridg a long a. between John and Edward Blackmore's land; ½a. which goes from Gartridge on W. side by Richard Bat's 2a.; ½a. and at the end of it a stony a. shooting on the way above Edward Blackmore's ½a.; a little a. shooting on the way to Heaven corner; 1a. in the bottom under little down side. 1a. shooting upon little down by 1a. Thomas Hearne on the lower side. Colt acre shooting on Portland gate by a piece of Sir Francis Dowse. Shim coppice, 1a. shooting on the plants. 1a. shooting athwart Largs path and on Suddon Hungerford way by Thomas Caloway's land. On Knowle a little a. in the side shooting along by Mr. Vincent's ½a. and Edward Black's. 1 long a. between Mr. Dowse and Edward Blackmore. 2 picked a. on the top of Knowle between Edward Blackmore and Richard Kent. At Limepits 2a. one shooting down upon the pits the other shooting on Poples acre. A little head a. shooting on Popely land. The sum on the E. side 33a.

W. of the town: at Church land 1a. between Edward Blackmore's ½a. and Mr. Dowse's a.; at Red land 1a. between Thomas Hearne and William Diper; 7a.

between William Woram and Edward Blackmore; above Isleborow ½a. between Richard Batt and William Fidler; at Isleborow 1a. next to Sunton field; at Woland 1a. between Edmund Raumsie and Mr. Dowse; at Mixton 1a. between John Passion and John Palmer; 8a. crossing the way to Smith's cross between 2 lands of Thomas Hearne; 1a. at the W. end of Eight acres between Edward Blackmore and Mr. Vincent; on Smiths cross 1a. between John Marshall and Edward Blackmore; 1a. shooting along the green way to Horsedown within 2a. of the way between William Woram and John Passion; 1a. at the end of the green way shooting down to Stoniples by ½a. of Edward Blackmore; in Over Coopland 1a. shooting on Horsedown way between Mr. Dowse and Edward Blackmore; at Harpath 1a. between Thomas Hearne and John Passion's ½a.; another ½a. between Edward Blackmore and John Passion; at Lamsgoare 1a. between 2 linches by 1a. of Mr. Dowse; 1a. more shooting to Lickford Way by Mr. Dowse's piece; at Lickford 1a. between Mr. Dowse and Thomas Brunsden; at Wodway 1a. between Edward Blackmore and William Diper; at Stonyples 5a. and in the bottom 1 stony a. between 2 pieces of sir Francis Dowse; at Long Linch 1a. above ½a. of John Passion; beneath Long Linch 1a. between Edward Blackmore's a.; 1a. shooting on Netheravon [Natherhaven] way called Snayle Down acre between Richard Batt's land. Sum of arable land in the W. side 27½a.

In the common meadow for hay a piece called the Parsons' ropes, 1a., of land and ? more [better] between Sir Francis Dowse's land and Edward Blackmore's ropes. The dwelling house of 6 bays, 3 barns, 2 stables, a gatehouse, garden and orchard all, ½a.; a meadow adjoining the orchard, c. 1½a.

George Hunt, rector, Thomas Brunsden [X], John Passion [X], churchwardens, Edward Blackmore, sidesman.

204 30 Oct 1671 (D1/24/55/2)
Arable land on the W. side 26a.: Isleborrow acre shooting N. and S.; Isleborrow half acre E. and W.; churchland E. and W.; Rudland[1] acre E. and W.; Seven acre N. and S.; Woeland acre N. and S.; Eight acre N. and S.; 2 Smiths Cross acres N. and S.; Horse down acre E. and W.; Long Linch acre N. and S.; another Long linch acre N. and S.; the Long acre in the bottom E. and W.;, Stonaples piece shooting upon it c. 4½a.; Netley acre shooting N. and S., 1a. at Greenway end N. and S., Little acre N. and S., Hare path acre N. and S.; Woodway acre, N. and S.; Lickford acre, E. and W.; 1a. at the end of Lamsgood piece E. and W.; Little acre between the linchards N. and S. 26a. Pasture ground, the ropes and home closes.

Arable land on E. side 34½a.: Hell hedge[2] piece shooting E. and W.; a grot head[3] shooting N. and S.; Bucklinch piece[4] c. 4½a.; Hungerford way acre N. and S.; 1a. E. and W. upon Hungerford way; Hagar acre E. and W.; Oatridge acre E. and W.; 2a. N. and S. at Micoke hill; Stone croft piece, c. 3a.;[5] the a. of Plants or Weekway acre E. and W.; Oatridge acre E. and W.; ½a. shooting N. and S. upon it; Allars Dean, 1½a.[6] N. S.; Heaven corner acre N. and S.; Well acre E. and W.; Little Down acre E. and W.; Colt acre E. and W.; Head a. upon the Knowle E. and W.; Long acre upon the Knowle N. and S.; 2 picked a. upon the Knowle E. and W.; Pophley acre N. and S.; Lime pit acre E. and W.; Little acre narrow at one end shooting E. and W. upon Hungerford way; Shaw acre N. and S.; Bragganten acre N. and S.; ½a. shooting N. and S. upon farmer Knowle.

Arthur Charlett rector, John Vincent, William Fidler churchwardens.

1. Redland in **205**.
2. Hill Hedge Piece 2½a. in **205**.
3. 'a great acre at the head almost as big as the former' in **205**.
4. Bucklands Piece *c.* 4½a. in **205**.
5. 3½a. in **205**.
6. Allans Dean acre in **205**.

205   1704 (D1/24/55/3)
Tithes: all sorts of grain, underwood, all sorts of hay, horsemeat, orchards. A modus of 2d. for each lamb, the tenth penny for calves sold, the best shoulder for calves ?killed [spent] and 1½d. for calves weaned. Wool, pigs. A modus of 1d. for each garden, 2d. for eggs. A modus for milk. Tithes of hops, honey, geese and pigeons.
    Arable land as **204** with amendments in footnotes. Meadow land: 2 meadows near the parsonage house each 1a. 4 ropes in the common meadow, 1a. 2r. The churchyard. 140 sheep leazes, 8 horse leazes, 8 cow leazes.
    William Sherwin, rector, William Jennens, Thomas Edny [X], churchwardens, Thomas Akerman, John Batt, William Blanchard.

206   1783 (D1/24/55/4)
The glebe, 2 yardlands viz. the parsonage house, courtyards, and garden meadows adjoining, 3a. 1r. 29p. Meadow called the Ropes, 1a. 1r. 21p., bounded by the meadow of Mr. Daniel Blacks E., meadow of earl of Ailesbury W. 14a. of enclosed arable land bounded the Hile road N., a lot of Thomas Lewis[1] E., Mr. George Webb Poor's old inclosure S., a lot of Giles Shepherd now Thomas Marshment[2] W. Enclosed arable called Cow down, 5a. 2r., bounded by a lot of John Hutchins E., a lot of the earl of Ailesbury W. 1 open piece of arable land in W. Common field 9a. 30p., bounded by a lot of John Hutchens N., a lot of the earl of Ailesbury for late Avis Fay. 1 open piece of arable land in Middle Common field, 8a. 2r. 8p., bounded by a lot of Thomas Marshment N., a lot of John Hutchens S. 1 open piece of arable land in E. common field, 8a. 2r. 32p., bounded by a lot of Mathew Hutchens N., a lot of late Mary Black. 1 open piece of arable land in Out Common field, 6a. 3r. 14p., bounded by a lot of the earl of Ailesbury for late Avis Fay W., a lot of John Hutchins E. Right of common for 140 sheep in open common fields and common downs.
    Tithes as **205** *also with herbage and feed of agistment and unprofitable cattle.*
    The parsonage house: of timber lath and plaster, tiled, the front rough cast. Part of the offices brick and chalk, sash windows in front of the low rooms. A hall at entrance with a brick floor, butlers pantry within it. 2 wainscotted parlours, a good kitchen paved with brick. A laundry, 2 pantries, brewhouse with a draw well. 3 cellars, 7 rooms or chambers on the first floor upstairs, 2 large, with closets, the rest small. 2 garrets,, 2 other rooms over the offices all rooms ceiled and floored. A 3 stall stable, a 3 bale stable, a large bale stable for farm horses with lofts over them. A straw house, coal pen, woodhouse, garden or bottle house,

coach house, 1 large barn with 2 floors, 1 oat barn, a small carthouse, a cowhouse, all the outbuildings are covered with thatch the sides boarded and the barns partly board and partly wattle. The farm yard and barton enclosed with mudwalls except on the side to the parsonage meadow where there are posts and rails. The court in the front of the house separated from the street by open paling the fence of the garden partly mudwall, the greatest part dead hedge. The house and premises are all in good and sufficient repair.

The furniture of the church: A clock, 4 bells, a stone font, a large church bible, a folio common prayer book, a crimson pulpit cloth with fringe, a cushion, a communion table, and crimson cloth, a Quarto common prayer book, a silver chalice with cover, a pewter flagon, 2 pewter plates, an ordinary linen cloth for the table and napkin. A surplice. A parish chest. Pews in the church or sitting in the pews are private property and kept in repair by the owners. N. B. the church has been pewed within a very few years by agreement of the parishioners. There are 2 pews in the chancel which belong to the rector and 1 in the body of the church. The church is repaired by the churchwardens at the charge of the inhabitants. The chancel by the rector. The church and churchyard contains 2r. 8p. and is fenced partly by posts and rails partly by dead hedge where it is contiguous to other property. The part of the fence which is railed is repaired by particular farms. The rector was told on his arrival that the churchyard wicket and 1 perch of rails belong to him but on what authority he does not know but he has kept them in repair. There are some fine horse chestnut trees in the churchyard and a few young ash and other trees. There are some young elms in the parsonage meadow.

The same person serves as clerk and sexton, appointed by the rector, his pay by custom, 4d. for every yardland and so in proportion 4d. from every householder at Easter, 2s. 6d. for burials. Easter offerings: 2d. to the rector for all persons over 16 years. A pension or quit rent of £8 p. a. is paid to the crown.

William Tomlins, rector, Edmund Andrew, Robert Croome, churchwardens, John Hutchens, John Mortimer, Joseph Grace.

1.   Now John Reeves in **207**.
2.   Rev. Chas. Francis in **207**.

207   1792 (D1/24/55/5)
As **206** with amendments in footnotes. The rector has 1 harvest way for carriages, horses and servants to and from the 3 common fields leading from Small way across Key Croft field to the parsonage farm yard and barton.

Charles Francis, rector, William Blatch, William Bailey, churchwardens, Edmund Day, Robert Croome, William Lewis, John Hutchens.

COLLINGBOURNE KINGSTON vicarage

208   10 Dec 1677 (D1/24/56/1)
A dwelling house of 4 bays near the church, a barn of 3 bays, a stable, a backside between the barn and churchyard, 2 gardens E. and W. of the house. Tithe wool

except the 5 farms: Mr. Ayre's in Kingston, Mr. Vince 's and Mr. Andrews' in Brunton, Mr. Hide's in Sunton and Mr. Pile's in Aughton; only 14 lbs. tithe wool from Mr. Hide's farm and the fourth lb. from Mr. Pile's farm. Tithe lamb except the 5 farms; only half the tithe lambs of Mr, Pile's farm. Tithe cow white, calves, gardens, eggs, pigs, honey, apples, hops etc., except of the first 4 of the said farms. Easter offerings of all communicants and 6d. from every woman churched. Great and small tithes from the glebe lands belonging to the impropriate parsonage. £20 p. a. augmentation to be paid quarterly out of the appropriate parsonage by appointment of the dean and chapter of Winchester and now confirmed by Act of Parliament.

Henry Jacob, vicar; John Andrews, John Brunsden, churchwarens.

209 n. d. [1704x1705][1] (D1/24/56/2)
Rectorial glebe: John Smith esq., tenant to the dean and chapter of Winchester, impropriators. Arable land: 2 long lands, 28a.; 3 ridges, 2a.; 5 ridges, 3a.; Upper Pressland, 14a. and 40 lugs; Lower Pressland, 10½a.; the Cow Down, 15½a. Meadow land: Long Croft, 1a., Lower Mead, 1a., the orchard, 120 lugs and Common Croft, 3½a.

Stamford Wallace, vicar, Thomas Meere, Henry Norris, churchwardens.

1. The churchwardens were recorded in the bishop's visitation book, Oct 1704 (WSRO D1/50/6).

210 1783 (D1/24/56/3)
Rectorial Glebe land: Thomas Asheton Smith esq., tenant to the dean and chapter of Winchester, impropriator. Arable land: Longlands in S. field, 9a. 1r.; Five Ridges, 3a. 13p.; Two Ridges, 1a. 2r. 35p.; Longlands in Middle field, adjoining the said Longlands, 14a. 2r. 7p.; Upper Presland, 14a. 25p.; Lower Presland, 10a.; 1 enclosed piece called Cowdown, 15a. 24r.; c. 1a. enclosed piece of meadow called Long Croft; Lower mead, c. 1a.; 1 piece of enclosed meadow called Lower Croft, 3a. 2r.; The orchard, c. 3r.; 3a. of arable occupied by James New held by lease under Thomas Asheton Smith esq.

All great and small tithes received from the glebe lands belonging to the impropriate parsonage. Tithe wool for whole parish except 5 farms; Mr. Greviles in Kingston, Mr. Macham's and Mr. Thomas George Edward's in Brunton, Mrs. Earle's in Sunton and Mr. Gilbert's in Aughton. The vicar has 14 lbs. of tithe wool from Mrs. Earle's farm and the fourth lb. of tithe wool from Mr. Gilbert's farm. Tithe lambs for the whole parish except the said 5 farms the vicar only has ½ tithe of lands of Mr. Gilbert's farm. Tithe milk, calves, garden, eggs, pigs, honey, apples, hops, etc., of the whole parish, except of the first 4 mentioned farms. Easter offerings from all communicants through the parish except of the first 4 mentioned farms. 6d. from every woman churched. £20 p. a. received as an augmentation paid by even quarterly payments by the impropriate parsonage, confirmed by Act of Parliament.

Description of the vicarage house. Brick stone and timber built, tiled. Kitchen and parlour, each 14ft. square, a hall with staircase 11ft. square, board floors, the parlour wainscotted and a cellar, 3 chambers 14ft. square, ceiled and floored, a small skilling, brewhouse not ceiled, the floor earth. A small barn containing 3 bays, thatched, the sides partly mudwall partly boarded. A backside between the barn and the churchyard fenced with dead hedge. The garden separated from the churchyard and street by a mudwall.

The furniture of the church: A clock, 5 bells, a stone font, a large church bible, 2 folio common prayer books, a green pulpit cloth and cushion, a communion table and green cloth, a silver chalice, and cover, a pewter flagon and pewter plate, a linen cloth for the table and napkin, a surplice, a parish chest and vestry table, a black cloth for burials. The pews in the church are private property and kept in repair by the owners. The church is repaired by the churchwardens at the expence of the inhabitants and the chancel by the impropriator.

The church and churchyard, 3r., fenced partly with posts and rails against the street and partly with dead hedge against private property. The railed parts are repaired by particular farms. There are 13 small ash trees, value about 4s. each. 7 small chestnut trees value about 2s. each, 1 yew tree. Church acre in Sunton field, 1a. 24p., belongs to the church, value 15s. p. a. and ½a. in Aughton, 9s. p. a. under the directions of the churchwardens for the use of the church.

The same person serves the office of clerk and sexton, pay by custom 4d. for every yardland and in proportion 20s. from the churchwardens at Easter and 2s. 6d. for burials. N. B. There has been for many years houses built on the church land in Aughton which the several proprietors pay 9s. p. a. as a ground rent.

Nicholas Westcombe vicar, John Barnes, Robert Mackrell, churchwardens, Thomas Gilbert, Michael Ford, John Canning, Thomas Barnes, William Cook.

CASTLE COMBE rectory

211   1608 (D1/24/57/1)
Hill close, a garden and orchard adjoining the parsonage house, a backside bounded by the parson except a wall from the barn end to the orchard, and by the orchard to be made and kept by the tenement held by Christopher Stokes.

S. field: 3a. of arable in the furlong adjoining the Townese end at Over Coombe: 1a. adjoining the Townese end with a pool, 1a. belonging to the tenement of Agnes Harris S.; 1a. having ½a. belonging to the copyhold of Warborow Osborne N., 1a. belonging to the tenement of Elizabeth Bishop S.; 1a. a. having 1a. belonging to the tenement of Warborow Osborne N., 1a. belonging to the tenement of Elizabeth Bishop S.; ½a. in the furlong above the W. way, ½a. belonging to the tenement of Elizabeth Bishop N., a farndell belonging to the tenement of Ann Brewer S.; 1a. in Hooke furlong, ½a. belonging to the freehold of Christopher Stokes E., 1a. belonging to the tenement of Warborow Osborne W.; 3a. in the furlong on Steart, the lower end of 1a. heads 2a. belonging to the tenement of John Organ; another 1a., ½a. belonging to the tenement of William Tovy N., 1a. belonging to the tenement of Robert Smith S.; the third a. shooting on the way to Chippenham, ½a. occupied by William Allway N, and ½a. belonging to the freehold of Christopher Stokes S.; 1a. in the furlong shooting towards Stockbridge, a broad mere W.; 1a. in Chestell furlong, ½a. belonging to the tenement of Nicholas Smart E. and 1a. belonging to the tenement of Hugh Seargeant W.; ½a. in the same furlong, 1a. belonging to the tenement of Robert Daniell E., ½a. belonging to the tenement of John Daniell W.; 1a. in Bullmeade furlong, 2a. belonging to the tenement of John Organ S., 1a. belonging to the tenement of Edmund Smith, N.; ½a. in the same furlong, ½a. belonging to Edward Bristow S., 1a. belonging to the tenement of John Waterford N.; ½a. in Garston furlong, 1a. belonging to the tenement of John Waterford W., ½a. belonging to the tenement of John Daniell E.

N. field: 1a. of arable in the furlong adjoining a ground called Binnell, ½a. belonging to the tenement of Edward Bristow E., and 1a. belonging to Oriel College, Oxford, W.; ½a. in the same furlong, 2a. belonging to the tenement of Hugh Seargent W., ½a. belonging to the tenement of Edmund Smith E.; 1a. in the furlong shooting over the highway to Grittleton, 2a. belonging to the freehold of Christopher Stokes W., 1a. belonging to the tenement of Robert Smith E.; ½a. on Stonehill, 1a. belonging to the tenement of Robert Daniell N., ½a. belonging to the tenement of William Tovy S.; 1a. land which heads Stonehill, 3a. belonging to the tenement of Robert Daniell W.; 1a. in the furlong under Stonehill having ½a. belonging to the freehold of Oriel College E., 1a. belonging to the tenement of Henry Keynes W.; 1a. in the furlong called Woodborough, a farndell belonging to the tenement of John Daniell W., 1a. belonging to the tenement of Robert Daniell E.; 1a. more in the same furlong, 1a. belonging to the tenement of Jane Corre W., ½a. belonging to the tenement of Henry Keynes E.; 1a. in the furlong called the Burrowe, a piece of arable belonging to the Screap N., ½a. belonging to the tenement of John Daniel S.; 1a. on Gattcomb, ½a. belonging the tenement of John Daniel S., 1a. belonging to the tenement of Edward Bristow N.; 1a. in the furlong called Barrowe, 1a. belonging to the tenement of John Browning S., ½a. belonging to the tenement of Agnes Harris N.; 1a. in the furlong adjoining Thornegrove, 1a. belonging to the tenement of Henry Keynes S., 1a. belonging to the tenement of Richard Brewer N.; 1a. in the furlong shooting down from Thornegrove, 1a. belonging to the tenement of John Waterford S., the Foss [Force] way N.

A tenement adjoining the parsonage house. A house in the churchyard for poor folks. A lot of meadow of c. ½ farndell in the freehold meadow of Christopher Stokes adjoining his fulling mill at Longdeane at the N. E. end of the meadow. A lot of meadow of c. ½ farndell on the N. E. end of Woolfull mead. A lot of meadow adjoining a ground called Hatch S. E., the river N. W., at the lower end stands a witch hazel tree which divides it between Nettleton and Castle Combe. A lot at Hatchpoole lying over the river between the ground of Henry Keynes and bounded from Nettleton by the parsonage.

W[illiam] Forde, rector, Thomas Merecliffe, John Daniell, churchwardens, William Webbe, Thomas Byshop, sidesmen.

212   30 Oct 1671 (D1/24/57/2)

A dwelling house, 1 barn, 1 stable with a backside garden and mill adjoining, ¼a. 24a of arable, 12a. in N. field, 12a. in S. field.[1] 1 beast leaze in Shrub common. 2 small parcels of meadow ground, ¼a. in a meadow occupied by wid. Terrill[2] and ¼a. in a meadow occupied by Thomas Wild gent.[3] 2 small parcels of meadow ground, one near Hatch pool, the other a little distance from it.

John Hayes, rector, John Stokwell, Nicholas Elver, churchwardens.

1. 10½a. in N. field and 13½a. in S. field in **213**.
2. wid. Banks in **213**.
3. wid. Wild in **213**.

213   2 Dec 1704 (D1/24/57/3)
*As **212** with amendments in footnotes.* With tithes in kind. John Hayes rector, Francis Child, Thomas Mills junior, Walter Fisher, churchwardens, Thomas Bray, William Taylor, Thomas Elver.

214   25 Jul 1783 (D1/24/57/4)
The parsonage house is built of stone and covered with tile. It consists of a hall 17ft. by 12ft., 7ft. high, the floor earthen. A kitchen of the same dimensions, the floor earthen. A parlour 9½ft. by 9ft. with a boarden floor. 4 bedchambers over these with boarden floors and ceiled. No wainscotting or hangings to either of the rooms but only white walls. A brewhouse built with stone covered partly with tile and partly with thatch. A barn 60ft. by 20 ft. built with stone and covered with tile. A stable built with stone and covered with thatch, large enough for 6 horses. A granary built with stone and covered with tile. A garden containing *c.* ½a., an orchard and pasture adjoining called Parsonage Hill together 2a. The house and adjoining premises with rick barton and yard occupy 4a.

Glebeland: formerly in common fields new enclosed: Arable closes: 5½a. at Townsend formerly in S. field. Hook furlong, 5a. adjoining the last close at Townsend. Longlands, 3½a., adjoining the last close. Pennylands, 8a. adjoining Sargents Wall Tyning. Meadow: a small patch in Mathnages alias Margerys mead for which the lord of the manor pays the rector an ancient rent of 5s. p. a. A small patch in Brown's living for which a similar rent is paid. The end of a land, ¼a., at Townsend shooting against Bristows pool. 1 beast common in Shrub, in lieu of which since the enclosure, the lord of the manor pays the rector 11s.

Tithes of all things tithable of common right without any modus or any claim of exemption. The timber on the glebe does not exceed the value of £10. None has been cut by any incumbent in the memory of man. No pensions, augmentations, gifts or bequests.

The furniture of the church: a purple cloth cushion for the pulpit, with a cloth of the same apending. A covering of the same for the communion table, and a linen cloth for the same. Some napkins, a surplice, a folio bible and common prayer book for the use of the minister, a folio common prayer book for the use of the clerk. A large chest in the vestry in which the parish writings are preserved. A very old clock, a large tenor bell and a small bell.

Communion plate: 2 silver patens, a pair [fellows] in the form of modern waiters, each with this inscription 'The gift of Mrs. Frances Scrope to the Parish Church of Castle Combe Wilts, 1775'. No weight is marked on any of the pieces of plate. The rector repairs the chancel, parsonage house and premises. The fences of the churchyard are kept up by the parish.

There is no sexton. The clerk is appointed by the rector by ancient custom. His settled stipend, paid by the parish, is only £3 p. a. But the whole profits of his place from a voluntary contribution and from fees in addition to the stipend amount, on an average, to about £8 p. a.

Richard Scrope, rector, Samuel Martin, Thomas Jenkins, churchwardens, James Archard.

COMPTON BASSETT rectory

215   1671 (D1/24/58/1)
Terrier of the glebe of the rectory and vicarage. A dwelling house, 2 barns, a stable, a vicarage house with ½a. meadow belonging to it, a yard and garden adjoining the dwelling house, *c.* 1a.; an old enclosed meadow, 4a.; a ground called Berrymead, 6a.; a ground called the Marshe, 8a. Arable lands in the common [coming] South field: 4a. in White ditch furlong; 1a. in Overne ways furlong; 3 x ½a. in Sheep lands furlong; 1a. in Wasbreach; a butt in Isbreach furlong; 3a. in Wadlingstras furlong; a butt under Hiching furlong hedge; 2a. adjoining a piece of 6a. of Sir John Welde. Arable lands in a common field called N. Down: ½a. in Eaneing land furlong; ½a. in Blackfurlong; ½a. in Rouache furlong; ½a. in Tadburye furlong; ½a. in Upper Tadburie furlong; 1r. in Sharplands furlong; 2 x ½a. in Higheway furlong; 1r. and 1 butt in Trindlegrove furlong. Arable lands in a common field called the Middle field: 2a. in a furlong under Hicheing furlong hedge; 4a. in a piece called Cockleberie; 1a. in Hollie Riges furlong; 2a. in Wettlands furlong; 1a. in Shortlands furlong; 1a. in Lower Ridlands furlong; ½a. in Upper Ridlands furlong; ½a. 1r. in Moaltlands furlong, 2 x ½a. in Longefurlonge; ½a., 1/3a., 1r. in Low Widle furlong; ½a. in High Widle furlong; ½a. in Stat furlong; ½a. in the Lower Barune furlong; ½a. in the Upper Boarune furlong.

Thomas Skinner, curate, Richard Hill, churchwarden.

216   22 Jan 1705 (D1/24/58/2)
The house, a barn 5 bays long, a stable 2 bays long, with garden, orchard and backside the, ground on which these stand containing 1a. 2 willow beds. Home close, 4a. Berry mead, 6a. Bursiters, ¾a. The Marsh, 8¼a.

Land in the common fields. S. field: At White ditch, 4a. At Overn ways, 1a. In Sheep lands, 1a. and ½a. In W. Breach, 1a. A but in E. Breach 1/8a. At Oat Land cross, 3a. 2a. in the Coombs. 1 but under Hitching Furlong hedge.

N. field: In Highway furlong, 2 x ½a. In Eaning land, ½a. In Cadbury furlong, ½a. In Black furlong, ½a. Upon Roach, ½a. In Sharp lands, 2 x ½a. In Ringle Grove, ¼a. Upon Water combe, ⅓a.

In Middle field: ½a. in the Upper Bourn. In the hither Bourn, ½a. In Slatt furlong, ½a. In high Widle, ¼a. In Horsehead hedge furlong, ¼a. In Low Widle, ⅓a. and ½a. In Wet lands, 2a. In Morres land, 2 x ½a. In Long furlong 2 x ½a. In farther Redlands 1a. In hither Redlands ½a. In Short lands, 1a. Upon Hitching furlong, 2a. At Oat Lands cross, 1a. Upon side way, 4a. 60 sheep leazes.

Michael Geddes, rector, Robert Maundrell, Robert Burchall, churchwardens, Thomas Sharpe, Thomas White.

COMPTON CHAMBERLAYNE vicarage

217   n. d. early 17th cent.[1] (D1/24/59/1)
A dwelling house of 4 rooms, a barn of 6 rooms, a house for hay and stable of 4 rooms, a backside with garden and orchard adjoining, c. 1a. Another house of 2 rooms, newly built on a close of pasture in Eastbrooke, c. ½a. 3 pasture grounds newly enclosed out of the common, c. 12a., and a dole in Broadmead; a parcel of meadow in Little Courtmead, c. 1a.; another close of pasture enclosed out of the fields called New close, c. 3a.; in the common fields of arable, c. 24½a.

James Elliott, Thomas Watts, churchwardens. *Names in the same hand.*

Endorsement: Of these houses the vicar is to have, by composition made long since, a high chamber, a low chamber on the S. side of the hall with use, together with the parson, of the hall, kitchen, and well, also all the offerings in the church, a garden on the E. side and another on the W. of the hall. The parson is to pay 12 marks p. a. at the Quarterdays.

John Dugmore, James Elliot, Thomas Watts. (*Elliot and Watts in the same hand*)

1. John Dugmore was vicar between 1594–1634.

218   26 Oct 1672 (D1/24/59/2)
A dwelling house, a little building adjoining and a small garden plot. The parrock now in the use of the present incumbent is part of the glebe belonging to the impropriate parsonage.

An annual salary of £20 payable from the impropriate parsonage held by Thomas Penruddocke esq., by virtue by a composition made at the bishops palace between bishop John Davenant and John Penruddocke senior, in the presence of Richard Berry[1] churchwarden in 1672. By this composition the vicar and his successors are freed of all fees, charges of induction, first fruits, all rates taxes, etc. There belongs to the parish church a rent charge of £30 p. a., the free gift of Alexander Thistlethwaite, Winterslow esq. decd. in a deed 23 Jan. 1621, chargeable on land called W. Barnes in Witham Friary, Somerset, upon consideration of certain sermons to be preached in Compton Chamberlayne church. Whereas the annuity is forfeitable upon certain causes mentioned in the deed by his deed 20 Oct. 1669 Col. Thomas Penruddock provided a like sum out of the parsonage in the event of the former being forfeit.

2a. of arable land called Church land in the common fields late occupied by Thomas Watts.

1 silver chalice, a paten of silver, a pewter flagon for the administering of the holy sacrament.

John Martin, vicar and prebendary[2] of the cathedral, John Porter, Richard Berry, churchwardens.

1. Deceased by 1705 see **219**.
2. Of Yatesbury.

219   10 May 1705(D1/24/59/3)
As *218* with amendment in footnote. Nathanial Hancock, vicar, Robert Foard [X] Thomas Berry, [X], churchwardens.

CORSHAM vicarage

220   6 Dec 1671(D1/24/60/l)
The churchyard and an orchard with 2 little gardens taken from it for the use of the vicarage house, *c.* 3a.

Edward Wells vicar, Robert Sparrow, Thomas Steevens, churchwardens.

221   28 Feb 1705(D1/24/60/2)
Vicarage house with brewhouse, barn, and stables adjoining with garden, orchard and backside, 1½a. The churchyard. The great tithes of glebe land of the rectory of Corsham occupied by Thomas Smith and Jonathan Deek, gent. viz. tithe corn grain and hay. All privy tithes of wool, lambs, calves, colts, pigs, pigeons, geese are due to the vicar. 10s. was anciently paid out of the rectory to the vicar in lieu of cow white. [Great] tithes as above due to the vicar of the bottom or broad meadows. Tithe coppices, hedgerows, woods and wood grounds, gardens, ancient garden grounds and old and new orchards. All such tithes of all decayed tenements being ancient head holds commonly called Rough lease things and tithes of curtilages belonging to such head holds. Tithes of land lying out of the parish; some in Weaver meadow, some in Biddestone St. Peter and some in Chippenham. Privy tithes of the whole parish, excepting lambs, are due to the vicar viz. wool, feeding of sheep, fat oxen, calves, colts, pigs, geese, pigeons, turkeys, eggs, hens, ducks, honey and wax. Tithes of fruit trees growing in gardens and orchards. Tithe hops. 2d. for every person over 16 years in the parish due to the vicar for offerings, 1d. for every garden. Great tithes of the 2 parks.

Francis Greene, vicar, William Guy, Robert Gibbs, churchwardens, Thomas Hulbert, William Handcock.

CORSLEY rectory

222   14 Oct 1608 (D1/24/61/l)
A little dwelling house for the minister, a barn, orchard, garden, backside and little barton empaled at the front of the house, 1a. in all; adjoining the W. end of the barn a close of meadow called the Parson's mead, *c.* 5a. A close of pasture above the orchard called the Lowest Browme close, *c.* 2a.; the W. Brome close of pasture adjoining, *c.* 2½a.; The Broad close of pasture adjoining both on the N., *c.* 8a.; a close of meadow and pasture W. of the Parson's coppice, *c.* 2a.; a close of meadow S. of the lane, *c.* 1½a.; a coppice of underwood, hazel, withy, alder, and oak adjoining, *c.* ½a., called the Parson's little coppice; the Parson's coppice of underwood, hazel, oak and ash between 2 of the closes, *c.* 2a. and 1a. meadow in Bristowe mead shooting E. and W. by the land of Thomas Browne N. and land of the farm where Christopher Eyer lately dwelt S.

In Chedlands: 1a. of which ½a. lies athwart Bristowe way; ½a. in the Middle furlong shooting on the E. end of the first ½a.; ½a. in Willowshad furlong. In Bickenham field 4a.; ½a. in the Blacklands; ½a. shooting on Trappes hedge; ½a. between land of Mr. Bowton and Mr. Gifford; ½a. shooting across the highway that stretches accross Bickenham; ½a. shooting down Kingmead; ½a. in the same furlong also shooting on Kingsmead; 2 x ½a. in the Sands bounding E. and W.

Richard Slade, John Greene, churchwardens, Robert Fitzhugh, Edward Rawlyns, sidesmen.

223   7 Feb 1705(D1/24/61/2)
Glebe lands with orchard and garden belonging to the house of the rector valued at £20 p. a. Tithes of wool lambs and cow white valued at £8 p. a.

Thomas Ailesbury, rector, John Holway, Richard Knight [X], churchwardens.

224 15 Apr 1784 (D1/24/61/3)
The parsonage house is built of stone and covered with slate[1] tile. The front measures 31ft. The front has 2 rooms of equal dimensions; a parlour hung with flock paper, board floor; a hall with a grist or dirt floor, bare walls into which the door opens. Behind the parlour is a narrow staircase and a small kitchen with an oven. Behind the hall is a small pantry. The passage from the hall to the kitchen being in the middle accounts for the back rooms being of less dimension than the front. There are 2 chambers over the front rooms of equal size with those below, the one over the parlour is hung with paper. 2 small chambers behind and 2 low garrets. All the rooms are ceiled. A cellar under the parlour. A narrow shed covered with pantile and boarded round shelters the kitchen door from the N. wind. The stable is built of stone; it contains 4 bales or stalls, and is thatched. Behind the stable runs one continued building, thatched, divided into 3 parts; a small brewhouse, a barn and a pig sty. This building is 30ft. long. The walls of the brewhouse are stone, the other two are boarded. Glebe: old glebe around the parsonage house, 29a. 35p. of arable and pasture. The other part of the glebe is allotted land under an Act in lieu of tithe 27 March 1784 and lodged in the parish church of Warminster. This land is 66a. 1r. 21p. is within a ring fence in and near Bickenham field.

In consequence of the award tithes were exonorated in return for a portion of land except for tithes due from several small estates in all *c.* 25a. which are still subject to an annual composition for tithes to the impropriator and rector. These sums are collected together the rector's portion amounts to £28 8s. 6¾d. The right to Easter dues or surplice fees were not set aside by the Act. Corsley was formerly dependant on Warminster, the rector pays an annual stipend of £1 6s. 8d. to the vicar of Warminster by way of acknowledgement of his 'vassalage'.

An augmentation of £28 p. a. is paid to the rector by Viscount Weymouth.

A crimson coloured cloth fringed with 2 cushions of the same cloth, 2 office books belonging to the Communion table. Between the table and the rails is a Scotch carpet. In the pulpit a crimson velvet cushion, silk fringe and tassels with a cloth of garnet colour, fringe and tassels. A cloth of same colour with fringe and tassels in the reading desk. A large bible and prayer book. A black bier cloth for the use of the poor. 6 bells. Communion plate: 1 flagon 3 pints, the gift of John Minty, 1 small chalice no mark, 1 modern salver for the consecrated bread, marked 'John Barton William Down'. 1 very small plate silver gilt for collecting the oblations but not large enough for that purpose. The whole weight of the silver 3lbs. Church acre let for 12s. 6d. p. a. The repair of church churchyard and gates falls upon the parish. The impropriator, Viscount Weymouth, repairs the chancel. The fences are kept up by the rector. The clerk is appointed by the rector and receives £1 5s. stipend p. a.

Thomas Huntingford, rector, George Marven, John Knight, churchwardens, John Silcox, James Smith, overseers, James Smith, Ebenezer Coombs.

1. Stone tile in **225**.

225   6 Jul. 1808 (D1/24/61/4)
*As **224** with amendment in footnote.* At present there is a sexton. The clerk wishing not to take on himself to execute the whole business of his office the sexton received the £1 5s. and also a further sum of £2 10s. from the parish.

George Isaac Gloucester, rector, Nathanial Barton, Ebenezer Coombs, churchwardens, James Knight, Joseph Jones, overseers, Joseph Singer, Thomas Vine, William Gane, James Collyns, inhabitants

EAST COULSTON rectory

226   n. d. early 17th cent.[1] (D1/24/62/1)
2 meadow grounds, 10a. next to the Long meadow. 3a. arable in a close, William Belson one side, John Edmonds the other. 2a. of wood shooting on the Conygere gate. In the Sands 1 whole a., ½a. and 2 butts adjoining next to Stoke field. In the Great Clayes 3 x ½a. next to Mr. John Langebe on every side. In the Little Clayes ½a., 1yd. next to Edington field. 8a. arable on the Hill, Mr. Lambe on either side. 10 sheep lease going with the farm flock.

Henry Moore, rector, Bartholomew Cromal [X], Robert Ailow [X], churchwardens.

1. Henry Moore was rector 1602-1626.

227   3 Apr 1672 (D1/24/62/2)
Parsonage house with barn, orchard and garden, c. 1a. 16a. of pasture lying near Mr. Norbornes 20a. 9½a. of arable lying upon the hill in several parcels. ½a. of coppice lying next to Sir Giles Hungerford's. 1a. of arable in W. Clay, ½a. being ?[now] sainfoin [Cingrefoy] in E. clay. 1½a. in E. clay. 1½a. in the Sand. 1½a. of land upon the Knoll being now furzes. Tithe corn, wood, wool, hay, cow white, calves, lambs and whatsoever is tithable, tithe gardens and orchards. Depasturing and feeding of 30 sheep in Mr. Bennet's flock.

Samuel Bat, rector, Edward Purchase, Thomas Ellexander, Peter Townsend, Thomas Toghill.

228   n. d. [1704x1705][1] (D1/24/62/3)
House, outhouses, barn, stable, backside, garden and orchard, 1a. 9½a. of arable
lying in several parcells in the field upon the hill. ½a. of arable land in W. Clay.
½a. of underwood at the lowermost side of a parrock adjoining W. Clay. ½a. of
arable land in the enclosure [inclosier] adjoining W. Clay. 3 x ½a. in Long furlong
shooting against the hill in E. Clay. 1 little piece of arable called a butt in the
same field shooting upon a ground called Great Lains. 1a. and a butt at the end
lying in the field adjoining a pasture ground called Hope Wood and 1 arable
ground called Little Lains. 1 little piece of ground lying in an inclosed ground
called the Knoll. 3 pasture grounds, 19a. Tithe of all corn and grain, and also hay,
wool lambs, calves, cow white, according to the custom of the parish. Tithe of
underwood and fruit.
        James Meredith, rector, Edward Toghill, churchwarden, Richard Whiting.

1.   The churchwardens were recorded in the bishop's visitation, Oct 1704 (WSRO
     D1/50/6).

229   31 Jul 1783 (D1/24/62/4)
A parsonage house 38ft. by 30ft., the walls built of brick and stone covered with
stone and brick tiles, consisting of a parlour and kitchen with board floors,
plastered walls and ceiled; a milkhouse with stone floor, plastered walls and
ceiled; a brewhouse and pantry with grist floors and rough walls; 5 chambers
with plastered walls and ceiled; 3 garretts, one of which is ceiled. A barn 42ft. by
22ft. and a stable *c.* 22ft. by 16ft., both built with timber and covered with straw.
A yard bounded with walls, postrail and hedge. A garden bounded with walls
and hedge and orchard or close bounded by hedge the whole *c.* 1a.
        2 pieces of enclosed meadow or pasture land bounded by hedges, *c.* 10a. 2
pieces of enclosed arable land bounded with hedges, *c.* 8a. A road or drove of
enclosed pasture land leading to the above fields bounded with hedges, *c.* 1a.
with 2 timber trees growing thereon value 20s. A piece of arable in Erlestoke
field bounded all round by the lands of Joshua and Drummond Smith esqs., *c.*
¾a. 2 pieces of arable land in the common field belonging to Coulston severally
bounded all round by the lands of the same gentlemen, ½a. and 1¼a. A piece of
arable lying in the enclosure in Coulston field bounded by the land of the same
gentlemen, ½a. A piece of arable in W. Clay in the said field bounded by the
lands of the same gentlemen ½a. A wood or coppice lying against Hornets Nut
wood bounded by the hedge or lands of the same gentlemen, ¼a. 7 pieces of
arable lying in different lots on the top of the hill within the lands of [. . .]
Norris and bounded by the lands formerly called Lambs farm, 5 x 1a., c. ¾a., c.
¼a. total *c.* 6a.
        Great and small tithes belong to the rector. The furniture of the church: 2
bells, a silver cup, stand with cover with the inscription 'This cup and cover is
the gift of Mrs. Rebecca Bennet, wid. to the church of Coulston', weight *c.* 2lbs.
A silver salver weight *c.* 1lb. 2oz. A bible and common prayer book. The church
repaired by the parish, the chancel by the rector. The N. aisle by Joshua and
Drummond Smith esqs. The churchyard fence repaired by the same gentlemen,
executors of the late William Godolphin esq., the gates repaired by the rector.

The clerk is paid by the parish 1 guinea p. a. and appointed by the minister. N. B. the above lands give an unlimited right of stocking in Steeple Ashton common.

John Montague, rector, George Tayler, churchwarden, William Sainsbury, Richard Perrett, John Hall.

CRICKLADE ST. MARY rectory

230   1608 (D1/24/63/1)
A parsonage house with hall, upper chamber and garden with a close on which the house and garden stand of c. ½a.; another house that Robert Crosse dwells in, William Burge S., wid. Trindar N. A ham in N. mead, c. 1a., the brook and highway E., the close of Salisburie W. 1a. in Calcutt [Calkot] mead with the Parsons close, Ball close one side, Pike close, the other.

Ralph Butlar, parson, Henry Dennis, Giles Keeble, churchwardens.

231   11 Sep 1677 (D1/24/63/2)
Terrier presented at the bishop's vistation at Marlborough. The churchyard. A mansion house with outhouse, a garden, 1 close of meadow, c. ½a. 1 house in High St., Cricklade, with a garden on S. side of the George Inn. 1 close of meadow or pasture called Long close, c. 3a., part in Cricklade St. Sampson, part in Cricklade St. Mary. 1 close of meadow or pasture. c. ½a. in Dudgemore furlong in Chelworth field in Cricklade St. Sampsons. Commons of pasture for 1 rother beast in the Lammas mead of Cricklade St. Sampson alias Rushey mead. 1 ham in N. mead in St. Sampsons, c. 1a. 1a. in Calcott mead in St. Sampsons adjoining the furlong called the Lights. All great and small tithes and garden pence of the whole parish paid by ancient custom (the Priory and 2 Priory closes and Priors ham excepted).

John Flood, curate, Thomas Miller, John Lane, churchwardens, Henry Dennis.

232   10 Jan 1705 (D1/24/63/3)
Terrier according to order made at the bishops visitation at Marlborough 6 Oct. 1704. *As 231*.

Edward Cuthbert, rector, William Saunders, Thomas Habgood, churchwardens.

CRICKLADE ST. SAMPSON rectory and vicarage

233   1588 (D1/24/64/1)
Parsonage: a mansion house, 2 gardens, backside and orchard, a ground taken out of Whome close in which are 2 pools, a barn, stable and ox house. 4 grounds called Hyll close, Pytt close, Colverhey and Whome close. 1 yardland in the fields with common for 30 sheep in the fields of Chelworth; also 12 beasts pasture with a bull in Dudsmore or wherever the tenants' cattle go in the manor of Chelworth; all other common at the breach of the fields as any man has. 27 tithe a. of meadow in Kingsmarshe alias Southmeade with all tithe corn, hay, flax, hemp, and all other tithes that the vicar does not have by composition or prescription.

Vicarage: a mansion house, garden, a backside adjoining, *c.* 3r. The churchyard. The tithes of a yardland belonging to the parsonage in the fields of Chelworth; the tenth penny of an ancient rent of the ingrounds of the parsonage except it be mown, then the tithes of hay abating a quarter of the rent according to ancient custom. 2a. meadow in the moors in Calcutt [Colcate] mead shooting on the Gose acre; 2 hams in the same meadow, *c.* 5a. on the W. of the Ray [Rea]. Oblations and the tenth penny of the ancient rents of ingrounds according to ancient custom. Cattle going in the common. Tithe wool, lamb, calves, pigs, geese, eggs, flax and hemp growing in gardens or orchards and backsides where no tenth penny of rent is paid, onions, garlic, apples, and garden penny; lammas tithes of cattle going in common according to ancient custom; 2 gallons of ale to be paid by every tavern; tithe calves and cow white where no tenth penny of rent is paid, the cow white to be paid as by ancient custom; 2d. for every corpse [corse] buried in St. Mary's church or churchyard. The whole tithe of the tithing of Wydyll, greater or less, with all emoluments and oblations. 1a. meadow in Kembles mead, Kembles land S., Mr. Bridges' land N.; 1a. meadow in Vernyse mead, land of Mr. Bridges S., of Mr. Verny N.; 2a. land in the marsh at Wydyll, Kembles hedge S. and W., land of Mr. Verney N. and E.

William Pollen, Daniel Browne, churchwardens, Jenevere Lyndoe, Robert Waterhouse, Thomas Townsend, Richard Trynder, sidesmen, Richard Patashall, Thomas Denys, Henry Barnard, John Elerdew, bailiffs, John Bushe William [. . .], Richard Dennys, Chas. Tayn?[*ter*], Thomas Morris, William Burge, [. . .], Jenever Teynter, William [. .]. *Names of the officers in the same hand.*

234   1608 (D1/24/64/2)
Vicarage house; a hall, parlour, buttery, kitchen and chambers over, stable backside garden, orchard and the churchyard. 2a. in Calcutt mead; 2 hams in the same mead *c.* 5a. called Vicars acres and Vicars hams. By an inquisition taken 23 Sep 1605 upon the oaths of William Holcroft gent., William Garratt gent., and others by virtue of a commission of the court of Exchequer to Sir Henry Bainton and Sir Henry Poole we find that the jurors presented that the glebelands in Widhill viz. 6a. of land, 2a. of arable, 2a. of pasture and 2a. of meadow[1] with the Chapel close, *c.* ½a. have always been enjoyed by the vicar; likewise the tithes of Widhill.

Andrew Lenn clerk, William Messenger, John Taynter churchwardens.

1. In Kembles mead and Isles his mead in **235**.

235   1611 (D1/24/64/3)
As **234** *with amendment in footnote.* Andrew Lenn vicar, William Walton, John House [X] churchwardens, Thomas Pullen, questman, John Burge, John Lindoe [X].

236   31 Oct 1671 (D1/24/64/4)
Terrier made in accordance with an order at the bishop's visitation at Marlborough 15 Sep 1671. *As* **237** *with amendments in footnotes.* John Flood, vicar, William Champnowne, Richard Byrt, churchwardens.

237   10 Jan 1705 (D1/24/64/5)

Terrier exhibited according to an order of the bishop made at his visitation at Marlborough, 6 Oct 1704. A mansion house, garden and backside. The churchyard. The tithe of 1 yardland belonging to the parsonage in the fields of Chelworth. Tenth penny of the ancient rent of the Ingrounds pertaining to the parsonage except it be mown and then the vicar is to have tithe hay abating a quarter of the rent. 2a. of meadow in the moors in Calcutt [Chalcot] mead. 1 ham, *c.* 5a., in the same mead. Oblations and tenth penny of the ancient rent of the Ingrounds according to ancient custom by composition. Of cattle going into the common tithe wool, lamb, calf, pig, goose and eggs as by composition. Tithe flax or hemp growing in gardens or orchards or backsides when no tenth penny of rent is paid. Onions, garlick and garden pence as by composition. Lammas tithe of cattle going in the common according to ancient custom. 2 gallons of ale to be paid by every tavern to the vicar brewed in the parish. Cow white in all places where no tenth penny of rent is paid according to ancient custom. 2d. for every corpse[1] [coast] buried in St. Mary's church or churchyard. 7½d. as a quit rent for the house that was formerly John Hazell[2] now occupied by Henry Williams or his tenant. £40 to be paid yearly by her Majesty's farmers of the disforested forest of Braydon in lieu of all tithes as more fully appears by a decree of the Exchequer. Chapel[3] and yard and the whole tithe of the tithing of Widhill together with all amoluments and oblations there. 1a in Kemble mead, 1a. in Iles' mead. And as we have heard there also belongs to the vicarage out of the tithing of Widhill some other lands but of the certain number of acres or places where they lie we are not as yet sufficiently informed. For all other tithes we refer to compositions.

Edward Cuthbert vicar, Henry Dennis, Robert Bristow, churchwardens.

1. Coast means a side of a body, in this context a corpse.
2. John Miflin in **236**.
3. Described as a Chapel of ease in **236**.

CRUDWELL rectory

238   n. d. early 17th cent.[1] (D1/24/65/l)

The Okes; [. . .] [ara]ble; [. . .] 'hall; [. . .] upon 10a.; [. . .] Gibbes several; [. . .]usemoore' arable; [. . .] upon Stadborough; [. . .] furlong; [. . .]ntesway, the short furlong; [. . .]glande;. . . Short furlong upon the Fosse [forse]; on Barly hill. The further N. field: [. . .] of arable in Brandyron piece; [. . .] a. shooting on Fox quare; 1a. in Longthowge; 1a. at Quare hill; 1a. at Cockerdowne; 1a. at Elfurlonge; 1a. in Longblakeland; 2a. in Bechester; 2a. in Cokcoweslande; 1a. on Quare hill; 2a. on Bechester; 2a. in Longblakelands. In the Home fields: 1a. in Foxholes; 2a. on Goldhill; 1a. on Goldmore; ½a. at the Steepstones; 1a. at Ranwell; 2a. shooting at Smithe's headens; 1a. under the Hayhedge in Pisse furlong; 1a. behind Nowells on the hill. Hunyham alias Morecotes field: 1a. arable at Drysine well 2½a. shooting on Morcates way; 2a. shooting on Hankertons field; 1a. at Ronwell gate; 1a. shooting up by Malmsbury highway; 1a. lying between William Clarke and Richard Yongue in the same field; 2½a. more in that field; 1a. in Morcootes field to bear grass. Chelworth home field: 6a. arable. Chelworth further field: 4a. arable; 1a. at Quelfurlong hedge; 1a. at the Lype; 1a. at Golthill; 2a. at Rigeway; 1a. in the Farm piece; [...] 1 farndel of meadow [...] Sinderam; 2 lots in Chelam headends.

The parson's yardland in Hankerton: the Home field; 2 lands on Butterwell between a headland of Mr. Warneford and a land of John Curtisse; 2 lands on the further side of Oaksey [Oatsei] hill S. of Henry Yerringtonne; 2 lands on the Garsconne by a land of John Dicke; 2 lands in Avers ham furlong shooting down to Avers ham mead; 2 lands in Morcells Great furlong between John Dicke and Walter Rundle; 1 land in the same furlong next to John Looker; 2 lands in the Quare furlong, 1 next to John Dicke, the other by John Gagge; 1 land on the further side of Mercell by a headland of John Looker. In the Middle field: 4 lands shooting on Morcootes wall between Henry Mylles and Edmund Hibberd; a little land on the W. of Tynknell by a land of Margery Peryen and a butt not a yard [eared] also by Margery Perin; 2 little lands in Dunge Pattes furlong shooting on a headland; 1 land on the top of Midden hill between 2 lands of Edmund Hibberd; 1 land by Roger Curryer next to the highway to Malmsbury; 1 headland to the farmer's piece on Midden hill; 1 land in Great Shortlands by Henry Yerrington; 1 land in Little Shortlands by Mr. Warneford; 1 enclosed ground in the W. fields, 3a.; a parcell of meadow in the Lot mead. Common in the fields and moor of Hankerton for 8 beasts, 20 sheep, 2 horses.

John Bradshawe, rector, Thomas Avery, George White, churchwardens, Thomas Hardinge, John Haywarde, John Dicke, Giles Clarke, Henry Pierce, William Gingell, William Clarke, Roger Clarke, Thomas Earle, John Archar alias Hayes.

1.   John Bradshawe was instituted in 1599 and signed bishops transcripts to 1635.

239   30 Oct 1671 (D1/24/65/2)
The dwelling house, barn, stable, dovehouse, garden, orchard with 1 little tenement adjoining. 1 ground of arable called the Parsonage piece, 6a., lying against the orchard on W. and the highway parting them. 2 small cottages together in Crudwell adjoining the common street with a small close of pasture, c. 1a. Closes of pasture: c. 4a. adjoining Frog lane pool; Lype leys, c. 8a.; c. 1a. at the end of Lype furlong; c. 1a. on W. side of Honniham field. 3a. and 3 x 1/7a., called Seven Parts acre, in Upper Crudmore common meadow; 1a. of meadow in Lower Crudmore common meadow. 7 beast pastures in the Lammas [Lamach] or later feeding of the said Lower Crudmore. 1a. of meadow in Chellome Straddens. In Eastcote churchfield 1a. of Scralle.

Arable land in common fields: Honniham field; 2a. shooting on Head leys; 2a. shooting on Hankerton ditch; 1a. shooting on Mucote way; 1a. shooting on Balls leyes; 1a. shooting on John White's leyes; 1a. lying on Malmesbury way; 1a. shooting on Youngs Withers. Golthill field: 1a. shooting on Rommell; 2½a. shooting on Ridgeway; 1a. on Pisse furlong; 1a. in Lype furlong; 1a. on Golthill. In Homeward lower field: 3a. shooting on Ridgeway; 1a. shooting on Henry Common's close; 1a. shooting on Tetbury way. Homeward N. field: 4a. in a piece at the home hill; 5a. in Brimsmoore furlong; 1½a. in long furlong, 2½a. on Stadborough; 7a. in the furlong shooting on Nuts way; 2a. in E. Longlands; 1a. in Hooke furlong; 1a. shooting on the Fosse way; 3a. in Middle furlong; 1a. in

Sandy furlong at Parsonage bush; 1a. shooting on Whites head a. on N.; 1a. shooting E. and W. lying by White's head a.; 1a. in Barly hill. Upper N. field: 4a. lying on Bichester; 3a. in long Black lands; 4a. in a piece shooting on Tetbury way; 1a. lying between the ways; 2a. shooting overthwart the Middle way; 2a. in the bottom shooting on Kemble way; 1a. in Long Thong; 1a. on quarre hill lying along the Middle way; 1a. on quarre hill shooting on middle way; 1a. in a furlong that shoots N. and S. by the Foss way; 1a. shooting on Cookedown. Chelworth far field: 3a. in Foxholes; 1a. shooting on Portway hedge; 1a. on Muscle hill; 1a. on Sower lands. Chelworth home field: 3a. shooting on Hoglane end; 1a. in Crowmore; 1½a. in Crowmore in one piece; ½a. in Horse Croft.

In the parish of Hankerton lands belonging to the rectory of Crudwell: 1 close of pasture called Hankerton Leyes, 6a. 1yd. of lot mead; 1 small plot of mead ground lying in Westerley moor, ¼a.; 12 ridges in the field adjoining Murcote, 2½a.; 10 ridges of arable in Merrfell field, 2½a.; 4 ridges in the Home field, arable, 1a.

Tithes: in the hamlet of Chedglow tithe corn and other matters belong to the rectory. In the rest of the parish the whole tithes belong to the rectory except those of corn which are appropriated.

As far as almshouses, hospitals and free schools there are none in the parish. A house which ancient people have reported to have been the Church house but it has time out of mind been leased out to tenants by the lord of the manor.

Norreys Jameson, rector, Giles Clarke, John Archard churchwardens.

240　　20 Dec 1677 (D1/24/65/3)
Glebe land: In Crudwell: In Upper N. field in Bitchester 4a.; at Short hedge end in 1 piece 4a.; between the ways, 1a.; in the Bottom, 2a.; in Long Thonge furlong, 1a.; at the quarry, 1a.; at Quarry hill next to John Hillar's and a head a., 1a.; at Cockerdown, 2a.; at Blacklands furlong, 3a.; overthwart the ways, 2a. Total 21a.

In Lower N. field: Parsonage piece, 4a.; a piece at Brimsmoore, 4a.; in the middle of Brimsmoore, 1a.; on Stadborough shooting on Brimsmoore, ½a.; on Long Stadborough on Ashly churchway, 1a.; Behind Stadborough on Risdown, 1a.; shooting on Nutsway between Ashly churchway and Ten Acres Corner, 4a.; In Long furlong, 1½a.; in E. Longlands, 2a. in Hooke furlong, 1a.; on the Fossway at Ashly mead end, 1a.; In the Middle furlong between the Fossway and Crowfurlong, 3a.; at Parsonage Bush, 1a.; 1a. shooting N. and S. within a little of Ansdowne way; On Gibbs several 2a.; 1a. shooting on Ten Acres; 1a. on Barlyhill shooting on Brownings headacre; 1a. on N. side of wid. White's headacre. Total 31a.

In the S. fields: In Honiham field 1a. shooting against Balls lane end; 1a. lying by Hurcott way side; 1a. shooting against Ramwell Gate; 1a. shooting against Bails leaze; 1½a. against Heads leaze; 1a. in the middle of the field lying against Sandy furlong. Total 8½a.

In the second field: 3a. in the Little field next to Crudwell shooting on the Ridgeway; 1a. shooting against Cummings close; 1a. on the hill shooting against Tetbury way. Total 5a.

In the third field called Goldmoore field: 3a. on Gold hill; 1a. in Lipe furlong; 2½a. betwixt Ridgeway and Goldmore; 1a. betwixt Ridgeway and Ramwell; 1a. on Pisse furlong. Total 8½a.

In Chelworth field: 4a. in the Home field by the quarries; 1½a. in Crow more; ½a. in Horse Croft. Total 6a. In Chelworth N. field: 1a. in Foxalls; 1a. on Musle hill; 1a. shooting on Porters hedge; 1½a. on Sower lands; 1a. in Eastcott churchfield. Total 7a.

Meadow ground: 1 parcel of ground called Chelmheadens, 1a.; 1a. called the Parson's headacre in Lotmead called Crudmoore betwixt Ashlies Lotmead and Chedgloes Lotmead and the Twelve acres; 1a. in Long dole; 1a., 1 farndell and ½ farndell in Short dole, 1a. ¼a., ½?yd. Total 4¼a., ½?yd.

Pasture ground: A close called Long hay, 3a.; A close called Parsonage piece, 6a.; a close called Lipe leaze, 5a.; 1 tenement rented by William Canter with garden and close adjoining, 1a.; a piece let to William Canter called the Lipe leaze, ¾a.; a close called the Hay leaze, 1½a.; a small tenement and garden rented by Richard Webb; a small tenement and garden rented by the parish for the use of Henry Curtis. The parsonage house, gardens, close adjoining and churchyard containing in whole 2a.; W. close, 2½a.

In Hankerton parish: in W. grounds 2 closes, 4a. Arable in Home field; 2 ridges on Butter hill; 2 ridges lying in the furlong against Oversham. In Middle field: 2 ridges on Gassen furlong; 2 ridges lying on Oversham; 1 ridge lying on Merse hill; 2 ridges in the same furlong; 1 ridge in the furlong against Tucks leaze; 2 single ridges lying on Barrell furlong. In W. field: 1 ridge on Lower Tingle hill; 4 ridges against Muscott wall; 1 ridge lying on Middle hill; 1 headridge on Middle hill; 1 ridge on Ruffridge furlong; 1 ridge on Greene meadow; 2 ridges shooting on the Crooked meadow over against Muscott; 1 ridge on the other side against them. The whole being 26 ridges of arable land containing 9½a.

Pasture and meadow ground: 1 little patch of meadow ground ½ farndell lying near the Crooked meadow, 1 portion of Lotmead where it shall happen after the custom of a yardland commonly of the value of 6s. p. a. Privileges of common: In the Lower commons pasture for 2 horses or 4 other beasts. In Braydon common pasture to the value of 4s. p. a.

Daniel Harford, rector, William Archard [X], Charles Wording, churchwardens, William Canter.

241   1704 (D1/24/65/4)
Closes of pasture and meadow are rented by John Reeve and his mother, wid. Reeve. Arable land rented by Giles Archard alias Hay. Corn tithe of the manor of Chedglow. The rector has not of late years been possessed of the corn tithe of lands in the manor of Crudwell.

Thomas Shewring rector, Thomas Ludlow, Richard Stockwell churchwardens, George Farewell, John Parker, Richard Alexander.

DAMERHAM vicarage

242   20 May 1588 (D1/24/66/1)
The most ancient and substantial persons affirm. . . the portions and allotments of tithes and profits of the vicarage. [. . .] that all the [. . .]age is but ¼a. Tithe corn and hay in the tithing of Nothington belong to the parsonage, the vicarage

land excepted viz. 37½a. in E. field; 36a. in W. field, and the tithe [tithing] of 1a. in
W. field held by Thomas Powell. Tithes of hay of 2 plots called Little Mill belong
to the vicar, also a grist mill and the Mores, c. 11a. The vicarage house and pigeon
house are greatly in decay and part of the rooms fallen down, with 8a. arable
adjoining, and 1a. in Southend field. 2 plots, c. ½a. in Stonie lane and at Brownes
land. Common for 160 sheep on the downs, and 8 beast leaze at the breach of the
field. All privy tithe wool and lambs in Damerham and Martin; tithe corn from
the land once called Peverel's land now in the use of Mr. Bartholomew Jorsey;
tithe wood of all coppices of Mr. Bartholomew and Mr. Mullines, with Wollande
copse. 20s. p. a. due to the vicar for the tithe of Boulsbury [Bolsborowe].

George Kenwen, vicar, John Thomas, John Yealfe, churchwardens, John Forde,
?William Brether, Henry Shorte, Arthur Hunte, sidesmen. *Names in the same
hand.*

243   20 Dec 1680 (D1/24/66/2)
c. 6a. of watered meadow. c. 8a. of pasture called Vicarage Mowres and Sedgebuts,
these lie together and are bounded by the water current running between them
and Dammerham common S. Arable land consists of plats enclosed and plats in
the common field: The enclosed plats are Heyward close, c. 8a., Great Sowre
land and Little Sowre land, c. 10a. 1a. in Little field. ½a. in Stony lane. 2 plots, c.
20 lugs and the Home grounds, c. 6½a. adjoining the vicarage house, barn,
stable and outhouses. Part of these are the vicar's garden and orchard plot and
some other part is converted to gardens which Michael Downton and John
May rent at present of the vicar. There is enclosed arable land between Knole
field and Rockbourne land, Great White Style close, c. 8a. and Little and Middle
White Style closes, 9½a. The [*unenclosed*] arable lands are all in Knole field viz.
Slack Bottom piece, 7a., Butts piece, c. 2a. and Cheselton piece, 2 ½a.

The vicar may keep 110 sheep on the common sheep down. Tithe corn, hay,
copse wood and all other things titheable in South End tithing. The tithes of
Owland coppice as often as it goes out [*i. e. is cut*] and tithe hay made in that
part of Dears meadow[1] that lies next to Green close.

All manner of privy tithes throughout the parish except those of Court
farm, Boulsbury [Balsbury] farm, and the copses belonging to lord Holles, Owland
copse alone only excepted, and the mill and the meadow plot[2] near the mill
which plead exemption because they never paid in the memory of any now
living in the parish. Herbage of the churchyard and liberty to turn whatever
cattle he sees convenient into Damerham common.

Thomas Derby, vicar, Joseph Gould, Thomas Smith, churchwardens.

1. Mrs. Richmands meadow in **244**, described as a piece of land belonging to John
    Randall in **245**.
2. Formerly belonging to the earl of Salisbury [recte Shaftesbury] in **244**, now Sir Eyre
    Coote in **245**.

244   1704 (D1/24/66/3)
12a. of watered meadow; *c.* 3a. of meadow not watered commonly fed on by
cows; 3a. of 'cawsd' meadow called Sedgbutts, these lie altogether. Enclosed

arable land: Home grounds adjoining the vicarage house and gardens, c. 5a.; Great Sowreland, 7a. 80 goads; Little Sowreland, 3a. 80 goads; Heyward ground 7a.; Great White style, 16a.; Middle White Style, 6a., Little White Style, 3a.

Arable land in the common fields. Slade Bottom piece, 7a.; Chesleton piece, 3a.; Butts piece, 3a.; 1a. in Little field; 1 plot in Stony Lane called Half an acre and 2 plots in Lenicks Cross.

110 sheep leaze in the common down. *Tithes as in* **245** *with amendments in footnotes.* 3 garden plots occupied by Michael Downton, John May, and John Gray. The whole has been let for £76 p. a.

Henry Pincke, vicar, Richard King, John Clarke, churchwardens.

245   Aug. 1783 (D1/24/66/4)
The vicarage house, brick and tile, consists of 5 rooms on the ground floor, 1 wainscotted, the others plastered. 2 cellars, 6 chambers on the first floor, 2 papered the others plastered. 3 rooms in the attic all plastered. A barn, carthouse and stable all timber and thatch. Adjoining to the house a garden, orchard, farmyard and rickyard. Enclosed arable land: Home closes adjoining the orchard 5a.; Great Sowerland, c. 7½a.; Little Sowerland, c. 3½a.; Hayward, c. 7a.; Great White Style, c. 16a.; The Six acres at White Style, c. 6a.; Little White Style, c. 3a.; Stony Lane, c. ½a.; 2 plots at Linicks Cross each c. 20 poles.

Arable not enclosed: In a common field called Slade Bottom 1 piece, 6¼a.: In Nole field 1 piece in Cheselton bottom, 3a.; 1 piece near the field gap, 2a.: In Little field, belonging to the earl of Shaftesbury, 1a.

c. 13a. of mead land, part which is watered. Adjoining the meadow are 2 alder beds, c. 3a., and c. 1a. and a small osier bed, c. ¼a. *Sheep leaze and tithes as in* **243** *with amendments in footnotes.* 3 garden and orchards occupied by Edward Reade, John Rogers and Joseph Hannaway.

The several enclosed lands are enclosed by hedges. Timber on the glebe consists of a few small elms. Furniture of the church: 5 bells, a pulpit cloth, cushion and communion cloth. The plate: a salver, flagon and pint cup. The fence around the churchyard is repaired by the parishioners. The clerk is usually chosen by the minister and parishioners. N. B. 2 meadows belonging to Court farm called Marsh meadows pay privy tithes to the vicar.

C[*harles*]M[*ein*] Haynes, vicar, Robert Budden junior, George Tiller, churchwardens.

246   Jul 1808 (D1/24/66/5)
Vicarage house, garden, orchard, Home close occupied by Anthony Davidson, the present curate, c. 6a. 1r. A large barn stable and yard, 1r., occupied by G. R. Tiller gent. Arable: Hayward close, 8a. 3r. 11p.; Great Sowerland, 7a. 1r. 37p.; Little Sowerland, 3a. 2r. 4p.; 2 plots at Eleven Cross, 2r. 23p.; Hither White Stile close, 6a. 11p.; Great White Stile close, 14a. 2r. 12p.; Little White Stile close, 3a. 1r. 15p.; a piece of land in Slade Bottom common field, by estimation 7a. 6a. 25p.; 2 ½a. in Middle furlong in Knowl field, by estimation, 2a. 2r. 32p.; 3a. in Blackful furlong in Knowl field by estimation 1a. 3r. 22p. Common of pasture for 110 sheep in the Tenantry downs and fields.

In the occupation of George Budden gent.: The Vicarage mead, 7a.; Woody ground in ditto, 1a.; The Vicarage moor adjoining, pasture, *c.* 4a.

In the occupation of Charles Miles: Arable; 1a. in Little field in Damerham Parva farm, by estimation 3r. 15p.; Stony lane plot open to lands belonging to the same farm, 2r. 20p. Total 75a. 27p.

C[*harles*] M[*ein*] Haynes, vicar.

DAMERHAM: Martin vicarage

247 18 Oct. 1608 (D1/24/66/6)
A dwelling house and garden adjoining on W. side Mrs. Clefton's farm. 1 cottage in Church lane end with backside. 1 cottage with garden adjoining the churchyard. Church close on E. of the church. 1 close of meadow called Anggers Lane, c. 2a. Closes of pasture ground: Haskell, c. 10a.; Heath close, ground c. 3a. Closes of arable ground: Six Acres furlong, c. 10a.; Crooked hedge, c. 4a.; 1 close of arable or pasture adjoining the last close; 2½a. of arable ground in E. field of Tulse farm 'but and bounde' upon the earl of Pembroke's land. Commons of pasture for 60 sheep on the sheep downs of W. Martin.

John Humphrey, vicar, William Lannam, Thomas Grove, churchwardens, Peter Storke, Barnard Blanford, sidesmen, George Read, Jeffery Lannam, Richard Compton. *Names in the same hand apart from the vicar*

248 1631 (D1/24/66/7)
Belonging to the vicarage of Damerham S.: 2 dwelling houses, a barn and hayhouse. 31½a. glebe; 3a. in the fields of Sir William Uvedale [Uvidoell]; 10a. called Haskall by the way from Blandford to Salisbury; 9a. adjoining Townesend lane; 4a. called Crooked hedge; 2½a. at Heath; a meadow called the Grange joining a meadow of Sir William Uvidale; 2½a. at the E. end of the churchyard [*which is*] ½a. All tithe wool and lambs, calves and pigs; composition according to custom for the milk of cows, for every cow 1d., and ½d. for a heifer; Easter duties; tithe bees, apples and all privy tithes except certain parcels of hay. For tithe of the meadow of Sir William Uvidale, 2s. p. a. We have heard that a little parcel adjoining the vicarage barn and hayhouse of c. ½a. held by Richard Compton, but when it came into his possession we have not heard; formerly belonged to the vicarage.

John Bishop, clerk, Walter Follett, George Reade, churchwardens.

249 23 Oct 1671 (D1/24/66/8)
The vicarage house with a barn, backside and garden. 1 small cottage and garden. The churchyard and a plat joining to it, c. 30 lugs, 1 garden joining to the churchyard. 2a. of cow pasture 16½a. of arable. 1½a. of meadow. 1 heath [hearthe] close, c. 2a.

Timothy Harris, churchwarden, Henry Parker, Francis Streete, Richard Compton.

250 1 Jan 1705 (D1/24/66/9)
2 houses, 3 gardens, 1 barn, 1 backside, 1 mead plot, 1½a., lying against Angese lane. 1 plot of ground lying against the churchyard called Parecke. 1 field called

Haskel, 9a., lying against the road. 1 ground lying against the drove, 4½a. 1 field in Tomsen lane, 9½a. 3a. in Mr. John Grove's field in E. Martin. 1 copse, 3a., lying against High Colbery. 60 sheep leaze upon the common down.

Henry Pincke, vicar, John Rogers, George Compton, churchwardens.

251   Aug 1783 (D1/24/66/10)
The vicarage house is built with brick covered with thatch. 2 lower rooms and 2 chambers, neither wainscotted nor ceiled, but floored. A barn thatched and boarded, a fuelhouse walled and thatched. Glebe: enclosed fields; Townsend lane, 9a. 3qtrs. 20p.; Haskle field, 9a. 30p.; Drove close, 4a. 18p.; the field adjoining Lord Shaftesbury's rick close, 4a. 18p.; the field adjoining Lord Shaftesbury's rick yard, 1qtr.; the ground on which the house and barn stand, 22p.; the garden next the churchyard, 17p.; a paddock next the churchyard, 1qtr. 20p.; a meadow adjoining to Anges lane, 2a. 1qtr. 20p.; the coppice on Martin heath, 2a. 3qtr. 36p., borders on Thomas Sweetapple 's ground N., John William's S., Damerham down E. Unenclosed land in Bustard farm, now Mr. Bryant's, contains a portion of land in a field called Forty Acres, 3a.; a piece in a field called Hill Top, 2a. Right of commoning 60 sheep on the common down. Tithe wood and all the privy tithes are due to the vicar. Furniture of the church: A bible a prayer book a communion cloth pulpit cloth and cushion, a silver salver, silver plate a pewter flagon, 3 bells and a clock. The churchyard fence is repaired by the parishioners. The clerk is paid by the parish and appointed to his office by the minister and parishioners.

C[harles] M[ein] Haynes, vicar, William Waters, J. Sweetapple, churchwardens.

252   Jul 1808 (D1/24/66/5)
A small dwelling house with a small barn and yard, 26p. A garden adjoining the churchyard, 20p.; the churchyard, 3r. 12p.; a plot of pasture adjoining the churchyard, 1r. 20p.; Angers lane mead in E. Martin, 2a. 1r. 32p.; Haskells ground, arable, 9a. 3r. 12p.; Heath close, wood, c. 3a. Townsend lane ground or 6 acres furlong, arable, 10a. 1r. 28p.; Drove close or, Crooked Hedge ground, arable, 4a. 2r. 9p.; A piece of arable in Bustard farm, E. Martin in an enclosure called Hill Top field, arable, 2r. 27p.; A piece in the same farm in a field called the Lower four acres, arable, 3a. 24p. Commons of pasture for 60 sheep on W. Martin down. Total 35a. 3r. 11p. The above now in the occupation of John Williams.

C[harles] M[ein] Haynes, vicar.

DAUNTSEY rectory

253   1671 (D1/24/67/1)
Formerly the Parson's lease belonged to the parsonage, and a piece of land, c. 30a. in the New field. The glebe now is 4 enclosed grounds, 3 of which are arable, the other pasture, the whole containing c. 40a., with a garden and backside, c. ½a.

Thomas Power, clerk, Ralph Bendry, Richard Harford, churchwardens.

254 1698 (D1/24/67/2)

Terrier presented at the triennial visitation of bishop Gilbert. The parsonage house, a large barn and stable at the end of it, a carthouse, 2 gardens at the front and back of the house, with a small paddock called the Slip, c. ½a. These premises are bounded by the highway leading from the Highgate to Mr. Allen's house N. E., by a moat and the river on the other sides.

Glebe:[1] 1 ground of pasture called the Brick field, 8a. Another ground of pasture called Oxlease, 7½a. A ground of arable, 7a., another, 8a., these lie together and are separated from the parsonage house by a ground of Mr. Allen called Cheshires. The 4 grounds are bounded the highway to Christian Malford N. and E., by grounds of Mr. Allen, Mr. Watts and one of Mr. Butcher called the W. fields S., the river S. W.

There is a little patch of ground in S. mead belonging to the parish of [*Great*] Somerford[2] called Dockham, to cut and to go not to feed, it amounts but to a small cock of hay of a ¼ tun.

All manner of tithes throughout the parish it being a rectory, but the demesnes have been tithe free time out of mind. (Query): Note, the tithes[3] of a farm in Wilsford were given by the earl of Danby to Dauntsey and the present incumbent receives £16 p. a. of Mr. Lavington, present occupier[4] of the farm.

William Clement, rector, Robert Panting.

1. Total acreage 40a. in **255**.
2. See **256**.
3. Tithes valued at £105 p. a. in **255** according to ancient composition.
4. Occupier not mentioned in **255**.

255 15 Dec 1704 (D1/24/67/3)

*As **254** with amendments in footnotes.* John Stump, curate, Simon Alline, John Morse, churchwardens.

256 24 Jul 1783 (D1/24/67/4)

The parsonage house containing a small parlour, wainscotted and floored, a hall with earthen floor, a large closet, a kitchen stone floored and ceiled, with a pantry, 5 bed chambers, a garret, an ancient building covered with tile. A large barn and stable at the end of it. A court house with a large barton, a garden surrounding the house with a small paddock called the Slip, ½a.; all these premises are bounded by the highway leading from the High bridge to a field formerly called Cheshires now Waytes-patch on N. E. and by a moat and the river on the other side.

The glebe: A ground of arable called Brickfield, 11a., Oxlease, 10a., the Further corn ground, 6a., the Near corn ground, 13a., an ash plantation, 1a.; all these lie together and separated from the parsonage house by the Wayts patch which runs between the glebe and the parsonage garden. Those 4 grounds are bounded N. and E. by the highway leading to Christian Malford, S. by the 3 W. fields in the possession of Mr. John Osborn, S. W. by the river. There is a little patch of ground lying in the S. mead belonging to the parish of Great Somerford called Dock ham to cut and go and not to feed, it amounts but to a small cock of hay not a ¼ tun.

All manner of tithes of the whole parish ought to be paid it being a rectory. Though the demesnes are claimed to be tithe free let at about £600 p. a. - query by what right [quere quo jure]. The Park farm let at about £200 p. a. pays no tithe or acknowledgement although disparked for many years. The common of Dauntsey, enclosed about 20 years, has paid no tithe yet; the rest of the parish claim a composition rent in lieu of tithes at the rate of about 1s. in the £ amounting to £100 p. a. The tithes of a farm in Wilsford were given by the earl of Danby to the parsonage of Dauntsey and the present incumbent receives £20 p. a. of Mr. Hayward in whose possession the farm now is.

There is belonging to the chancel an oak chest containing a surplice, 2 silver cups, 1 gilt on the inside, 2 silver plates,[1] 1 damask table cloth for the communion, 1 napkin to cover the bread and wine, 1 black cloth to cover the corpse, 1 green cloth to cover the chancel table, the church bible and common prayer book, a prayer book for the clerk, 1 marriage register, 1 pewter basin for baptisms, a bier, 6 mats for the use of the church. The church pewed with oak, in the tower 5 bells and a clock. The churchyard bounds and edifices repaired at the expense of the parish. The clerk's wages is according to custom 40s. p. a. paid by the parish and appointed by the rector.

Francis Marias West, rector, John Tanner, Robert Hooper, churchwardens, John Osborn.

1.   This plate was stolen in 1823, letter to Mary Pike, I Jun 1823 (WSRO 3047/6).

WEST DEAN and EAST GRIMSTEAD rectory

257   n. d. late 16th cent. (D1/24/68/1)
[...] of a certain tenement [...], 10d. rent p. a. A tenement in Dean now in the parsons own use which has been let for 14s. rent p. a., 2½a. arable and 3½a. of meadow in several. 1 cottage [cote] with garden plot occupied by Thomas Blancharde. 20a. of pasture or arable in several lying about the parsonage. 1 ground of pasture in severall called the Chowe, 8a. 1 coppice at Grimstead called Lyver coppice, 6a. 1yd. 1 meadow in common in Grimstead called Lyver Mead, 4a. Pasture in common in Grimstead called Lyver close, 1a. 3yd. 2 plots of meadow in Dean, ½a. 31a. of arable in the common fields. 50 sheep leaze in the common fields.

258   5 Dec 1677 (D1/24/68/2)[1]
House, barns, stables and other outhouses with backside courts, garden and orchard, 2a. 2 meadow grounds called Lussells and Culverscroft, 8½a. Arable land: Croked close, 3a; The Six acres; Old orchard, 5a.; Pitt Close, 6a.; Cunnigere, 6a.; The Common, 20a. Pasture land: Ashen close, 3a.; The Five acre; Bushey Lease, 10a.;. A piece of ground called The Seven acres. Sinke Coppice with hedgerows, 8½a. Lyvers Coppice in East Grimstead, 10a. Meadow adjoining called Livers, 6½a. Pasture adjoining called Lyvers, 3a. 2 cottages and gardens in West Deane. All the tithes of West Dean and East Grimstead being nothing in the parish tithe free.

Gabriel Thistlethwayte, rector, Edward Waterman, Richard Harroway, churchwardens.

1. A valuation of the glebe in 1810 refers to the rectory house and 97½a. of glebe in W. Dean and 28a. of glebe with a barn in E. Grimstead with 2 vicarage houses (WSRO 120/1).

BRIXTON DEVERILL rectory

259   [1588][1] (D1/24/69/1)
60a. and 3 x ½a. i. e. 19a. in Woodcomb field;[2] 8a. against Nershill; 8a. in Billinge field;[3] 6½a. in Ichiscombe; 18½a. in Orcomes field, 2a. of which lies in a tithing of Whitecliffe [Whitley] parish to the manor of Brixton Deverill.[4] 3a. in several.[5] It is customary to keep in the common rother beasts, 6 oxen and a bull; a cow or a breeder and 6 horses; 120 sheep.

1. An 18th. cent. copy in the parish register is dated 1588 (WSRO 1180/2).
2. Home field in **261**.
3. Middle field in **261**.
4. The meaning is unclear; Whitecliffe was a separate tithing and manor.
5. Described as 3a. of pasture with a house barn stable and outhouses on it and the churchyard in **261**.

260   24 [. . .] 1608 (D1/24/69/2)
'The in ground or in closure'. Home close behind the orchard; 1a. meadow called The Together close over against Richard Humphryes house, 1½a. 1 orchard and 1 penning lying behind the dwellinghouse, ½a.

Arable land: In Wodcome called Woole furlong, 6a. In Wodcombe called Long furlong, 2a. 4a. in Wodcome in the furlong shooting upon the way leading to Leegrove. 7½a. in the Over furlong next the down side at Whitway end. In the homefield called Cockwals field, in the Lower furlong 3a. In the middle furlong called Cockwals field 3a. In the over furlong called Cockswals field, 2a. 1a. without Mother Watsones gate [yeat] called the Ore. 2a. above Bils Linch called Bils Linch field. 2a. in Bils Linch field shooting upon Meeth hill. 2a. of short land shooting upon Meeth hill. 1a. at Apple Dore way. 3½a. in the Long furlong at Erchiscoume. 1a. in Erchiscoume shooting upon Munton side. 9½a. above Orcome. 1a. in Orcome. 3a. shooting down upon Orcome. 2a. upon Bils Linch. 1a. at Bils Linch end. 2a. without Hunnykots in the Ore. 1a. in Whitlye field called Bushisdoune. 1a. and 1a. in Whitlye field shooting upon the new close.

Common for 6 oxen, 1 bull, a cow and 1 runner and 2 horses in the fields and downs and for 120 sheep.

Philip Lodge [X], William Strett [X], churchwardens, Robert Boswell, William Slad [X] Edward Cooper, Richard Humfrey [X][1]

1. The names of Peter Stile, [. . .] elder, Michael Sargent, Thomas Kerley and Edward Cooper are included as witnesses in the first line of the document.

260A   n. d. prob. 1670 or 1671[1] (D1/24/69/3)
As **259**. Christopher Kerly, Noel Kerly, churchwardens.

1.   These churchwardens signed the bishop's transcript for 1670.

261   8 May 1705 (D1/24/69/4)
As **259** *copy with amendments in footnotes.* Walter White, rector, Hugh George, churchwarden, John Gerresh, Richard Humfry, Robert Cooppar, William Buckler, tenant for the farm.

KINGSTON DEVERILL rectory

262   n. d. early 17th cent.[1] (D1/24/70/1)
2a. in the S. field called Kings hill; 3a. in the field called Above town; 1a. without W. lipgate [leape yeate]: 3a. in the S. W. field called Pesecoome; 1a. in Kildon field; 1a. at Weeland on N. side of the Brookes; 1½a. in Hiscoomefield; 4½a. in the W. field called Cuckenell; 1a. in the field called Longslade; 1a. of arable in the field of Sir Edmund Ludlow in Hill Deverill and 1 parrock of wood ground adjoining the park of Sir Edmund Ludlow called Bitcoome.

Guy Clynton, rector, Thomas Barnard, Jerome Cox, churchwardens, William Curtis, Peter Batt, overseers.

1.   The rector signed the bishop transcript for 1608 but was dead by 1616.

263   3 Feb 1705 (D1/24/70/2)
A dwelling house, with hall kitchen and brewbouse, 2 butteries, 1 milkhouse, 6 chambers, 1 malt loft and 3 garrets, 1 porch with a little room over it with garden adjoining on S. of the hall, and a little strip of land on S. of the house, a little garden plot at E. end of the brewhouse. A barn of 13 bays of building, A wagon house, A stable with a barton adjoining.

Arable land in the common fields: 3a. in the Churchfield abutting upon Mere way bounded lands of hon. Henry Thynn esq., E. and W. 2a. at Kingshill 1 lying E. and W. abutting on the way to Monkton Cow down bounded 1a. of William Kiddel N., ½a of William Kiddel S.; 1a. in the same field lying N. and S. bounded 1a. of Bodinghams farm by the way side that leads to Monkton cow down E., 1a. of Blackhall W. 3a. in a field called Piscom lying E. and W. bounded ½a. of William Phillips N., ½a. of Mary Curtice S. 1a. at Townsend lying N. and S. bounded 1a. of Thomas Ryal E., ½a of William Phillips W. 1 little cottage adjoining bounded a garden of Richard Gerrat E., a garden of Peter Trimby W. and abutting against Blackhall close. 1a. under Cilden lying N. and S. abutting on Townsend way bounded with an a. of Blackhall E. and with 2a. of Bodinghams farm W. 1a. above Rowlench lying N. and S. abutting on the Broches bounded with an a. of Blackhall on E. and ½a. of Michael Humphry W. 1a. in Longslade lying N. and S. abutting on the Broches bounded with an a. of Blackhall W. and an a. of Blackhall E. 4½a. in a field called Cocknell whereof 2a. lies N. and S. bounded with an a. of Mary Curtice E. and 2a. of Chas. Blake W. 1a. on the top of Cocknell lying N. and S. abutting on the way from [Maiden] Bradley to Kingston [Deverill] bounded with an a. of Deborah Leversedge E. 1 head ½a. lying E. and W. bounded with an a. of Blackhall N. and the lands of Margery Hurle and Roger Curtice S. 1½a. in a field called Hiscomb, the ½a. lying E. and W. bounded with ½a. of Brune Berjew on N. and the footpath that leads to Markham on S. 1a. in Hiscomb field lying E. and W. abutting up against Hiscomb paddock bounded with an a. of Brune Berjew S. and with ½a. of Thomas Ryall W.

1 little plot of coppice on the top of Bitcomb hill in Hill Deverill bounded with the sheep down of Mr. Ephraim Westly E. and with the sheepdown of Little Horningsham farm W.

Edmund Ludlow Coker, rector, Brune Berjew, William Liddill, church-wardens.

264   29 Jul 1783 (D1/24/70/3)
The parsonage is built of stone and tiled. It contains a cellar, 6 rooms on the first floor, all of which are ceiled except one; 5 rooms on the second floor all ceiled. 2 dark garrets not ceiled. The walls are mostly plastered and white washed. A small brewhouse, a stable for 7 horses, a large barn containing 2 threshing floors, 1 for wheat, the other for spring corn. A carthouse and pigsty.

The glebe is undefinable at present. An Act of Parliament past last year by virtue of which the estates in this parish are to be exonerated from tithes by an allotment of glebe land. The award is not yet made, when it is made and a plan annexed, there will be a perfect terrier of the glebe. The tithes will be extinct. There are no pensions to or from the minister. There is no church impropriate in this parish.

There is a pulpit cloth and cushion, 6 bells, a silver cup for the communion containing a pint, 2 small silver dishes. or plates, the one with the inscription 'Ex dono Rachel Berjew 1711', the other 'Mary Curtis wid. 1704' and a pewter chalice containing 3 pints.

There are no lands or money in stock for repairs of the Church or writings concerning the same. The parishioners repair the church the rector repairs the chancel. The parishioners repair 3 sides of the churchyard fence viz. E. S. and W. sides and the owner of land on N. has usually repaired the N. fence. Whether the land on the N. will be charged with the fence will depend upon the commissioners' award.

The clerk is sexton. His wages are 40s. p. a. paid by the churchwardens besides Easter offerings. He is paid likewise for graves and knells. He is appointed by the minister.

M[illington]Massey, rector, William Slade, John Knight, churchwardens.

LONGBRIDGE DEVERILL vicarage

265   n. d. [1663x1682][1] (D1/24/71/1)
William Crafts now in possession of the vicarage house with garden, orchard, barn, stable, and another outhouse adjoining the stable. c. 1a. meadow on the W. of the house; 2½a. arable by the same hedge in the W. field; 2½a. more in the

same furlong, 2a. of Mr. Robert White N.; ½a. in Lords corner, a footpath S., ½a. of the wid. Starr N.; *c.* 2a. of meadow E. of the street by the water side; 3yds. of arable in Sand field, 3a. of wid. Long N., 3yds. of Mr. John Langle S. If Blakes ground, *c.* 20a., is mowed, tithes in kind of as much as is yearly mowed. Tithes of *c.* 3a. of Thomas Kerly's meadow, and 2a. of meadow called Thatchers held by Thomas Carraway. Lammas tithes at Crockerton, and tithe wool and lambs from the tenants of Deverill and Crockerton. 4d. a cow, tithes of pigs, and for offerings, gardens and eggs payable from tenants and cottagers. Tithes of Great Broome close and Little Broome close. For saying prayers Mon. Tues. and Thurs. mornings to 8 alms folk £8 p. a. paid quarterly left by Sir James Thynne decd.

William Durneford, John Easton, churchwardens, Adam Leaver, Henry Baker, sidesmen.

1.   William Crofts was vicar between these dates.

265A   1705 (D1/24/71/2)

The vicarage house consisting of a hall, kitchen and chambers. A garden, orchard and glebe ground, *c.* 8a. Easter offerings, cow white, gardens, and fowls according to the custom of the parish. Tithe fruit in kind as apples, pears etc. Tithe wool, lambs and pigs in kind. A certain rate on Lammas day [1 Aug] in lieu of grass of certain according to the custom of the parish. Tithe grass of certain grounds paid in kind. Those grounds that pay Lammas tithes to the vicar, if the property be altered to pay in kind. All tithes great and small of Rodmister and Crockerton excepting what is by custom reduced to a rate paid at Lammas to be paid in kind. The ancient demesnes only of the farm and of the priory of Longleat are tithe free. The full value of all the profits amount yearly to *c.* £30 for which they have of late been let for divers years past. For the confirmation of the particulars recourse may be had to the first endowment of the vicarage yet in the registrar's [register's] office.

William Carroway [X], Richard Hiscock, churchwardens. This terrier is approved by me John Foster, vicar.

265B   n. d. [1783]¹ (D1/24/71/3)

The vicarage house is built with stone, the old part covered in thatch and the new part with brick-tile. In the new part are: 4 cellars floored with brick and ceiled; a passage floored with oak; a parlour floored with oak, wainscotted chair high between base and surbase, stuccoed and ceiled; an oak staircase leading to a withdrawing room floored with deal, wainscotted chair high, hung with paper and ceiled; a bed chamber floored with deal, plastered between base and surbase, hung with paper and ceiled; 2 garrets floored with ash and ceiled.

The old part of the house contains: a kitchen floored with stone and ceiled; a pantry floored with brick and ceiled; a servants' hall with grist floor and ceiled; 3 pantries with grist floors and ceiled.

Outhouses: A stable, 38ft. by 19ft. and a coach house, 18ft. by 16ft., both built with stone and covered with thatch; a saddle house, 8ft. by 6ft., built with timber and brick and covered with thatch; a brewhouse, 18ft. by 13ft., built with stone and covered with tile; a greenhouse, 14ft. by 7ft., built with stone and, at the back of it, a bottle rack both covered with brick tile.

Glebe: Enclosed; a meadow called the Moor, 2a., bounded E. by the river, W. the turnpike road, S. an enclosure belonging to Mr. Wickham, N. an orchard belonging to William Skrane; a field, 2r., pasture, bounded E. by the vicarage garden, W. a field belonging to the vicarage, S. an orchard belonging to John Gilbert, N. an orchard belonging to Revd. Dobson; a field, 2a., pasture, bounded E. by the last field, W. the common fields, S. an enclosure belonging to Mrs. Hawkswell and part of the common fields, N. an enclosure belonging to Revd. Dobson.

Glebe: In the common fields; in W. field a piece, arable, 1a., bounded E. by an orchard belonging to Edward Ducey, W. a piece of ground belonging to Mr. Barter, S. an enclosure belonging to Revd. Dobson, N. by 3 pieces of ground belonging to Mr. Starr, Mary Ford and Edmund Adlam. In Sand field; a piece, arable, 3r., bounded E. by a piece of ground belonging to Mrs. Bedbury, W. and S. 2 pieces of ground belonging to Revd. Dobson, N. the road leading to Sutton [*Veny*].

Unlimited rights of commoning horses and beasts and of feeding on the Cow down in summer as many cows as I keep in winter. The garden, *c.* 1a., divided into 4 parts and fenced with walls, quickset and hornbeam hedges. Stable yard fenced with with stone walls; the outlets; 2 enclosed grass fields. No timber on any part of the glebe.

Tithes: Hay of the meadows and pastures of the whole parish, except an estate called Lord's farm which belongs to the impropriator and is tithe free. Great Broom closes, Little Broom closes, Blakes ground, Wherrit's ground, King's ground, grounds occupied by lord Weymouth, Manswood farm, great and small tithes, in all 217a. 2r. Cricket coppice, Broom close coppice and Godscroft coppice. Tithe lamb, wool, cows, pigs, eggs, gardens and orchards.

Augmentations: An estate at Keinton Mandeville and another at E. Lydford both in Somerset. I have the title deeds but they are too long to send copies of them. A yearly stipend of £30 paid by lord Weymouth. A yearly stipend of £8 paid by lord Weymouth for reading prayers to the poor of the almshouse.

No pension payable out of the living; nor stipend to any chapel.

Furniture of the church and chancel; 5 bells, a crimson velvet pulpit and cushion cloth; a silver plate; a silver cup; a pewter flagon; a woollen cloth and a linen cloth for the communion table; a pewter plate. 8a. of land given for the repair of the church.

Parishioners charged with the repair of the edifice and churchyard fence. Clerk appointed by the vicar and paid £2 p. a. by the parishioners. Sexton appointed and paid £2 p. a. by the parishioners.

John Dobson, vicar, Thomas Heall, Joseph Sturgis, churchwardens, John Sturgis, overseer.

---

1. The churchwardens were recorded in the bishop's visitation book, Jul 1783 (WSRO D1/50/30).

MONKTON DEVERILL vicarage

266   1609 (D1/24/72/1)
A house, garden and orchard, with a backside, and the herbage of the churchyard, with middle tithes, which are wool and lambs, the Easter book with all other privy tithes.
    Mark Searchfield, reader, John Hooper, Thomas Marshman, churchwardens.

267   9 Jan 1705 (D1/24/72/2)
1 little plot of ground called the vicarage garden, *c.* 20 lugs, adjoining the churchyard on one side and Cloves orchard on the other. All the small tithes except Kersly farm and the parsonage. The churchyard. Value £12 p. a.
    John Foster, vicar, Benjamin Beach, John Batt, churchwarden.

268   n. d. [1783]¹ (D1/24/72/3)
No house or buildings of any kind. A garden, 5p. Year composition for the tithes of several farms, £11 12s. 5d. Part of the estate mentioned in the terrier of Longbridge Deverill was given to augment the chapelry of Monkton Deverill. No pension paid out of the chapelry.
    Furniture of the church and chancel: 2 bells, crimson velvet cushion cloth. Plate: a cup marked D. M. 2 plates 1 marked 'Ex dono M. B. 1681'. The other marked 'Ex dono Rachel Berjew 1711'. The weight not marked. A pewter flagon. 1 woollen 1 linen cloth for the communion table. Parishioners charged with repair of the edifice and churchyard fence. Clerk appointed by the vicar and paid £1 p. a. by the parishioners. Sexton appointed by the parishioners without salary.
    Henry Follhett, churchwarden, John Whiting, overseer and churchwarden

1.   The churchwarden was recorded in the bishop's visitation book, see **265B**, n. 1.

DEVIZES ST. JOHN rectory

269   1704 (D1/24/73/1)
A tenement and garden let to John Allen at 30s. p. a. 9 little gardens held by Mr. Richard Walter, Peter Clarke, Richard Gaisford, Walter Seager, Henry Paradice, Richard Smith, Robert Paine, John Smith and John Jorden now let at 48s. p. a. in the whole, on part of which the parsonage house formerly stood, and which were formerly occupied by the rector. Tithes of an orchard called W. Croft Hill, *c.* 2a., held by Mr. Matthew Figgins, now let to Mr. Figgins at 10s. p. a. The feeding of the churchyard let at 20s. p. a., and 4d. as an offering for every woman churched. Total: £5 8s.
    Robert Townsend, rector, James Davis, Thomas Massey. churchwardens.

270   1783 (D1/24/73/2)
Terrier given in at the primary visitation of bishop Shute.
    The parsonage house purchased *c.* 7 yrs. ago by Queen Anne's Bounty the writing in the Governors' hands, is built of brick and tile. Rooms on a floor:

Parlour 10ft. high plain ceiling, 1 venetian sashed window, floor with deal, wainscotted chair high and papered above, 15ft. by 20ft. Another parlour 10ft. high, plain ceiling, c. 16ft. square, wainscotted throughout with an oak floor. Another room 7ft. 4in. high, 13ft. by 11ft., plain ceiling, sashed and papered, with an oak floor. An entrance 10ft. high between the 2 last rooms, papered, with an oak floor, 13ft. by 7ft., plain ceiling, with a staircase in it. A kitchen, plain ceiling, 7ft. high, the floor partly oak and partly paving stone, plain white walls, 15ft. by 10ft., 2 closets besides and 2 good cellars under the house. A washhouse behind the house, brick and tile, open to the tiles, 18ft. by 9ft. and a small stable adjoining 9ft. by 9ft. and tile with a plot of ground 31½p., behind the house with a brick wall on each side and at the bottom, wall and pales.

The house facing the street to E., back to W., S. and N. sides of the house butting on a house and garden of Mr. Walter Grubbe leased for 3 lives now occupied by William Adlam, gardener, N. side butting on a house and garden belonging to Mrs. Bevan occupied by Mr. Richard Fenner, presbyterian teacher. Beside this there is a small thatched cottage 100yd. from the parsonage house facing the street to E. abutting to S. on a house and garden belonging to Mr. Francis Baily occupied by John Sayer, below that a garden and house belonging to Mr. Samuel Tayler, part of the garden occupied by Mr. Tayler, the house occupied by Mrs. Wells and Mr. Dyer, below that to W. by a house called the Ark occupied by the parish poor and by a high bank, N. by the churchyard. In the said garden is another thatched stable. The cottage outhouses and garden contain c. 1r. 3p. and the garden is let out into small plots. A small plot bounded the churchyard E., the stone steps leading out of the churchyard S., land occupied by Benjamin Miel W., land, c. 19p., occupied by William Bishop N., let for a garden to Mr. George Gibbs, surgeon.

£8 p. a. settled on a house at the bottom of the Brittox in St. John's parish, occupied by Mr. William Swan, whitesmith, the writings in the hands of Peter Delme esq., trustee, enrolled in Chancery 11 Jul. 1765 by Humphrey Hackshaw.

Church plate: Flagon, the gift of Sir Edward Ernly weight 63oz. 15dwt.; 1 cup 9oz. 7dwt.; 1 cup, the gift of Elizabeth Imber, 9oz.; 1 salver marked 'John Sawer sen. and John Powell', 10oz. 7dwt.; 1 salver 5oz. 13dwt.

Church furniture: 2 surplices, 1 great bible and testament, 1 crimson velvet cushion and pulpit cloth, 2 sacrament books, 1 communion table and cloth and napkins, 1 book for the clerk, 1 font, 8 bells, 2 chests for register books and parish writings and 1 sentry [centry] box for funerals.

Clerk's wages £4 p. a. paid by the churchwardens and appointed by the minister. Sexton appointed by the parish and paid by Christmas gifts.

Edward Innes, rector, James Gent, Stephen Powell, churchwardens, Matthew Figgins Samuel Tayler, George Gibbes.

DEVIZES ST. MARY rectory

271   4 Oct 1704 (D1/24/74/1)
A garden let to Mr. John Horton at 20s. p. a. A little strip of garden next to Mr. Horton's garden let to Mr. Joseph Wright at 4s. p. a. The feeding of the church-

yard let at 16s. p. a., and 4d. as an offering for every woman churched. Total:
£2.
    Robert Townsend, rector, Roger Shaul, John Gamble [X], churchwardens.

272   1783 (D1/24/74/2)
Terrier given in at the primary visitation of bishop Shute.
    A small plot of ground, 30 1/2p., walled on each side and bounded by lands of
Mr. Horton E., lands of James Sutton esq. S., lands of Mr. James Maynard W., lands
of Mr. Samuel Filks, N., now occupied by Mr. Francis Bayly and let for a garden.
    Church plate: 1 silver cup, 1 salver, 1 flagon, total weight 36oz. 12dwt.;
inscriptions round the cup 'Mr. Henry Johnson, minister. This Cupp and Plate
belongeth to St. Marys Church in the Devizes Bought by Phillip Strong and
Ambrose Zeley June 1654.' On the middle of the salver: 'Robert Townsend,
Rector of St. Mary's Devizes, John Hill, Richard Paradice churchwardens Anno
1716.' On the flagon as on the salver with the date 1718.
    Church furniture: 1 stone font, 1 pewter basin, pulpit, velvet crimson cloth,
velvet crimson cushion, reading desk, velvet crimson cloth clerks ditto [?reading
desk], bible and prayer book, clerk's prayer book, communion table, cloth old
crimson silk, linen cloth, napkins and cloth for the bread, 2 handsome folio
prayer books for the clerk, 2 suplices all in very good condition, 6 bells, 1 clock
and chimes.
    Clerk's wages £4 p. a. paid by the churchwardens appointed by the minister.
Sexton appointed by the parish and paid by Christmas gifts.
    Edward Innes, rector, Thomas Whitfield, Thomas Lacy, churchwardens,
Richard Read, George Sloper, Robert Hale.

DINTON vicarage

273   26 Sep 1608 (D1/24/75/1)
A dwelling house containing a hall, buttery, and a chamber; a stable and a hayhouse.
2 gardens belonging to it of 6 lugs each, an orchard of 50 lugs, and a barton of
10 lugs. A close of meadow adjoining the orchard of 140 lugs. [...] The churchyard,
1a. by lug and more.
    William Phillips [X], Roger Coales senior [X], churchwardens.

274   n. d. mid 17th cent. (D1/24/75/2)
The Rectory: The common grounds, 12a.; About the house orchard garden and
1 close, 3a.; 3 grounds on the hill, 7a.; a little coppice near the house, 1a.; 47
sheep leaze in common. The vicarage; about the house, 2a.; at Four Corners 120
lugs. The churchyard with the 'shrouds' there.
    Philip Pynckney, clerk, Robert Ames, Ralph Elmes, churchwardens. *Names
in the same hand*

275   n. d. [1704x1705][1] (D1/24/75/3)
A house containing 4 rooms above and 4 below, a stable, woodhouse all in good
repair, orchard and garden, 1a. 1 ground lying by a place called Four Corners,

1a.The whole tithe of a farm[2] in the possession of Mr. Nicholas Daniel and Far' Lanham. Tithe grass of all the stock meadows, tithe wool, lamb, gardens and orchards, some coppices held by custom, pig and cow white. Leaze of the churchyard.

Edward Polhill, vicar, Thomas Dawks, John Jesse, churchwardens.

1.   The churchwardens were recorded in the bishop's visitation book, Oct 1704 (WSRO D1/50/6).

2.   Probably the capital messuage of Dinton which the Daniels family held of the earls of Pembroke. (VCH vol. 8, p. 27)

276   11 May 1786 (D1/24/75/4)

Terrier of the parsonage and vicarage. A house of freestone and covered with tile containing 4 rooms on a floor with ceiled garrets. A hall, 2 parlours floored and wainscoted chair high. A stone kitchen and small room adjoining. The outhouses are a brewhouse, coachhouse, wood and coal houses all lately built.[1] A barn, 2 stables, carthouse, pigeon house and granary tiled. There is a cottage in the farmyard.

The glebe land according to measurement taken not long since is as follows: Pasture common Grounds: meadow: The Portion ground with a small cottage and garden adjoining, 5a. Arable enclosed lands, 9a.; Arable common fields, 15a. 21p.; Meadow ground in the front of the house, 3r. 2p., Ash close, [meadow], 2a. 3r. 14p.; orchard, 1a. 3r. 22p., Vicarage orchard and garden adjoining the barn, 1a. 16p., Four Corner ground, 3r. 25p. 1 coppice called Hydes, 5a. 1r. 2p. 48 sheep leaze. A large churchyard, 1a. Tithes great and small.

6 bells and a clock. Communion plate; 1 large chalice 44oz. 1dwt. the gift of Mrs. Martha Harris with the inscription 'In Honorem Dei Opt. Max. Patris Filli & Spiritus Sancti et In Usum Ecclesiae Parochialis De Dinton in Com. Wilts. A. D. 1730/1'; 1 small cup and cover no weight, marks and without any inscription. Pulpit and communion table. The fence to the churchyard is repaired by Dinton and Teffont [*Magna*], the W. side by the latter. The clerk and sexton offices united. The clerk is chosen by the vicar. Salary £40 p. a. for Dinton 18s. p. a. for Teffont paid by the parish.

William Deane, vicar, William Wyndham, Richard Andrews, churchwardens.

1.   A letter from Magdalen College, Oxford, patron, refers to the vicarage being in a ruinous condition and anewly built house has been appropriated to the vicars' use, with an adjoining house for a farmer, 1780 (WSRO D1/14/1/18).

DINTON: Teffont Magna vicarage

277   18 May 1705 (D1/24/75/5)

All the small tithes of wool, lambs, cow white, fruit and hay. No house nor glebe.

Edward Polhill, vicar; Robert Martin, chapelwarden.

DITTERIDGE rectory

278   1677 (D1/24/76/1)

Housing: Part of the parsonage house, 2 bays, not tenantable having been let fall in the time of the last incumbent's ejectment, with the outlets and garden[1] belonging to it; the parsonage barn; the churchyard, the bounds and hatch to be kept by the parish.

Glebe lands: The Parsonage mead, 3a., and the Parsonage orchard, *c*. 2a.; Arable lands 2a. in W. field and 6½a. in E. field. Common: 50 sheep in the fields.

Tithes: The tenth cock of hay and French grass or the tenth bushell of feed; the tenth cock of barley; the tenth of oats, peas, and vetches [fitches]; tithing of wheat or the corner sheaf; for the cow white of every cow fed in the parish 3d.[2] at Lammas [1 Aug]; for all calves falling 9d., if any are killed by the owner 1 shoulder, if the owner weans them ½d.; the tenth weight on the tenth pound of the wool of all sheep, and the tenth of the 'locks' if the sheep are sold before shearing, ¼d. for each sheep for every month they have been kept in the parish; the tenth or seventh of all lambs paid on St. Mark's day[25 Apr]; the tenth or seventh of all pigs; for every hen, 1 egg, and for a cock 2 eggs;[3] tithe apples, pears, and other fruit; and the tenth a. or tenth p. of all coppice wood, the tenth of the money of hedgerows that are sold, and the tenth of hedgerows reserved by the owner to his own use if they are above a perch.

Offerings: For every communicant 2d.; and for a garden 1d. Customary dues: for the mill called Cuttings mill 2s. 6d. paid at Easter.

Charles Bridges, rector, and Anthony Wilshire, churchwarden [X].

1.   20 lugs in **279**.
2.   4d. in **279**.
3.   3 eggs for every hen 3 eggs for every cock in **279**.

279   23 Dec 1704 (D1/24/76/2)

*As **278** with amendments in footnotes.* Tithes from the commons in the parish. The tenth quart or tenth lb. of honey when taken. The tenth of all Yermoth or aftergrass.

James Butter, rector, Edward Lewis, William Clement, John Bolwell.

DONHEAD ST. ANDREW rectory

280   1608 (D1/24/77/1)

A meadow called Church meadow, 4a., the grounds of William Stryde N. and a little close of Thomas Butler W. 2 meadows behind the barns, 5a., the grounds of William Stryde on one side and the highway on the other; and 2 meadows near the Parsonage house, 3a., a ground of Mr. John Grove called Berry Wood S. and W.

An arable ground called Somerleaze, 3½a., the same grounds of Mr. John Grove S. and a little close of Thomas Butler W.; a ground called the Parson's Wood close, 12a., grounds of Alexander Wykes N., of Robert Barnes W., and a little close of Jane Lownes, wid. S.; 3 closes called Parson's Sand in the field, 30a., grounds of Bartholomew Colwell, tenant to Mr. Richard Worsley, N., William Stryde W., Mrs. Thomasine Grove, wid., E.; a close under White Sheet, 12a., grounds of Thomas Butler S. and the highway on the other sides; a down at White Sheet, 60a., a down of Mrs. Thomasine Grove, wid., and a down of the tenants of Berwick St. John S. E. and a down of Bartholomew Colwell N.; a sack of rye paid yearly on St. Andrew's day [30 Nov] out of the tenement of Thomas Butler which has been long in the possession of Richard Hayma and his predecessors who always paid it; and an old rate of 20s. paid yearly by Thomas, lord Arundell at his audit for the tithes of Wardour in the same parish, but for inclosed grounds called the Frythe, taken into the park about 30 years ago no tithes or rates have been paid.

A note of all those grounds which lie out of the parish and yet the tithes belong to the parson of Donhead St. Andrew. A close of Mr. Grove lying near Ashmere Sheet, a close of Francis Mayne S., a ground of wid. Mounckes of Berwick St John W., and the residue bordering the highway; a close of wid. Mounckes near the same ground, a close of Edmund Wykes W. and the rest bordering the highway; 2 closes of Alice Cooke, daughter of Edmund Cooke, at Brookhill, a ground of Andrew Barrett E., a ground of Lawrence Burden S., and the rest bordering the highway; 3 grounds of Richard Scamell about Ludwell bordering the highway; a little parcel of Thomas Mullins of Donhead St. Mary, 2a., bounded with a little old ditch from another ground there belonging to the parson of Donhead St. Mary although it lies in that parish; 2 grounds of Mr. Grove lying at Red Cross and 2 grounds of Thomas Butler lying hard by them; a ground of Thomas Bunter of Donhead St. Mary sometime part of the tenement of Richard Scamell, a ground of Mr. Bower, 2 closes of Thomas Rose, and 2 closes of William Stryde lying at Rushmore; and a parcel of John Parham called Whete Hills in the parish of Donhead St. Mary, 10a. in the whole, from which half the tithes of 5a. belong to the parson.

A note of all the tithes [?glebes] of the tenements belonging to the parsonage of Donhead St. Andrew: The tenement which Edmund Butler sometime possessed: 2 meadows behind the house, 2½a., a ground of the parson N., a ground of Joan Lownes, wid., W., and the rest bordering the highway; a little meadow called the Grove, 1a., ground of Edward Scamell S. W., a meadow of David Brooke N., and another meadow of David Brooke E.; 4 little closes of sand ground in the field, 4a., grounds of the parson N. and E. and the rest bordering the highway; a common close, 4a., a ground of Christopher Hellyer W. and S. and the rest bordering the highway.

A tenement now in the possession of John Compton and Edmund Budgen, 2 closes near the house, 3a., a ground of Alice Cooke S. and a river running near it W.; a ground called New Hayes, 2½a., grounds of John Compton called Bremble Coombes N. and W., a ground of William Stryde S., and a ground of Mrs. Thomasine Grove, wid., at the E. end; a little close called Nownes, 1½a., a ground of Mr. John Groves N. and E., a ground of David Brooke S., and a ground of Bartholomew Colwell, tenant of Mr. Richard Worsley at the W. end; and a little close called St. Mary's croft, 14a., a ground of Mr. Grove S. W., a ground of Richard Speering E., and a ground of Alexander Pearman at the N. end.

A little tenement now in the possession of Richard Bugden: a close in the field called Mayden Ashe close, 2½a., a ground of the parson at the N. end and a ground of Thomas Rose W.; 5 parcells of arable in Eston fields, 6a., in the farm field easily known, now in the tenure of Richard Bugden; and 1 little a. of arable in Minchington field in the parish of Hanley [*Sixpenny Handley*], Dorset, easily known, now in the tenure of Richard Bugden.

A tenement in the possession of Roger Burden: a close behind the house, 2a., a ground of Andrew Barrett N. and E. and the rest bordering the highway; a little close by Brookhill, 1½a., a ground of John Black N. and E. and the rest bordering the highway; and a common close, 3a., a ground of Mr. Grove S. and a close of Christopher Hellyer W.

John Britton, rector, Andrew Barrett and Alexander Pearman, churchwardens, and John Stride [X], Thomas ?Fainndr [X], and John ?Compton.

281   5 Nov 1677 (D1/24/77/2)
*As **282** with amendments in footnotes.* Robert Frampton, rector, W. Newmean, Robert Fooke, churchwardens, William Knight, Richard Fezard, Alexander Mercer, Roger Garend.

282   20 Dec 1704 (D1/24/77/3)
The parsonage house covered with tile, in it a brewhouse, hall, kitchen, 2 parlours, buttery, cellar, milk house and other small rooms and chambers over them all. On S. E. a garden and orchard on W. a backside containing a stable, woodhouse, carthouse, and pigsty all covered with thatch. Adjoining the backside Kitching meadow, 3a., Pond meadow, 2a. and Green close, 4a.

N. of the parsonage house a backside containing 2 thatched barns adjoining the backside; Langteries meadow, 3a.; behind the great barn an orchard, ½a.; Barn meadow, 2½a.; Church meadow, 5a., of which the shear yearly of almost 1a. belongs to the mill living[1] being now a leasehold estate in the possession of Richard Fezard and which said a. is on the lower side of the meadow, and is to be cut and carried away before St. James's Day [25 Jul]. On the other side of the river a ground called Fewells, 6a. 1 old house with garden and close of pasture adjoining called Sturmey, 3a. on S. of Pigstrough lane. 1 house with wood house adjoining, a garden, meadow called Butlers, 2a., 2 closes called Wood closes, c. 7a., adjoining the last meadow and between them 2 coppices, c. 6a., on N. of Pigstrough lane. 1 arable close called New Hayes, 4a., lying near Bramble corner. 1 close of common ground called Flitmore, 6a., lying near John Bridle's house. 1 meadow close called Grove, 3a., lying near a house lately belonging to John Fowell gent.[2] 1 arable close called Nowers, 2a., adjoining Lyes court farm grounds. 5 closes of arable called the Sands, c. 37a., with a barn in them, Clay field, 15a., and a sheep down, c. 6a., adjoining, all of which are near the highway called Whitesheet. 1 arable close called St. Mary Craft, 8a., lying W. of Ferne farm.[3] 1 arable close called Legg Two acres adjoining Rowborough lane. 1 house, woodhouse and garden[4] near the river with ½a. of a piece of arable in Minchenton field, Dorset.[5] In Easton Bassett[6] field 4 pieces of arable viz. In E. field 2 pieces, 1½a., 1 against the Down the other linchet land to that bounded with linchets [lanchotts], butting against an a. belonging to the rectory of Berwick St. John; In

W. field 1 piece, *c.* 2a., lying under the Down, bounded with a linchett, butting E. and W.; ½a. bounded with a linchet, butting against a meadow called Hook Hills belonging to Easton Bassett farm.[6]

Certain grounds belonging both to Donhead St. Andrew and Donhead St. Mary, the tithes belonging to the rectory of Donhead St. Andrew are as follows: Berry court farm; half the tithe of the fields and sheep down and of the closes and part closes as follows: Picked close, the Two Oxe leases, all near adjoining to the said fields, 1 close called Eighteen acres, E. close, Quarr close, Long meadow, Dry meadows, 1 close called Ten acres, Raynhay and Gilbert moor, of grounds called Madgrove and Shiled Stones and 3 coppices called High wood Short wood and Sumerfold. 3 closes called Nowers, Privit coppice, 1 close called Upper Bubbery and the upper parts of Outer Bubbery and Lower Bubbery viz above the footpath from late Dennis Sturgeis' house to Berry Court farm house. 1 arable close called Red Cross, 2 arable closes called Whethills belonging to a tenement of George Knype gent., lying in Donhead St. Mary whereof the whole tithe of Red Cross and two thirds of the tithe of Whethills belongs to the rector of Donhead St. Andrew.

The whole tithe of *c.* 1a. of a ground of Richard Frickers called Lower Donhead close, bounded by a ditch S. and W. from the other part of the ground. The whole tithe of 1 close of common ground called Flitmore S. of Flitmore lane, and belongs to a tenement late Henry Tripat.

Mathew Bowles, rector, John Gould, John Swaine, churchwardens, Henry Foot, John Comage, overseers.

1. Copyhold tenure belonging to William Grove gent. In **281**.
2. Foyle in **281**.
3. Described as Fern farm of Robert Grove esq., in **281**.
4. Described as 20p. and the house being near the church in **281**.
5. In Sixpenny Handley see **280**.
6. A detached part of the parish now in Berwick St. John.

283   1 Aug 1783 (D1/24/77/4)

A parsonage house partly modern partly old, the new part consisting of 2 parlours floored oak and wainscotted and ceiled with cellar under, 2 bed chambers over floored with deal, wainscotted chair high, papered and ceiled, 2 garrets over floored with elm plastered and ceiled. The old part a hall floored with stone plastered and ceiled, a chamber over floored with various sorts of wood, plastered and ceiled, an old parlour floored with oak wainscotted and ceiled, a garreted bed over with 2 closets floored with various sorts of timber partly wainscotted chair high and ceiled, a pantry, milkhouse, kitchen and brewhouse floored with flag pavements and ceiled, over a store room floored various and ceiled, a nursery floored with oak, plastered and ceiled; a garret over floored various plastered and ceiled. The new part built with stone and covered with brick tile, the old chiefly stone with stone and brick tile.

The garden, *c.* ½a., fenced partly with stone wall and part a quick set hedge. In the yard adjoining to the house are 2 stables under a roof covered with thatch, some chicken houses and a granary made of wood covered with brick tile. On

N. of the house is a farm and yard with wood or fuel house covered with thatch. A barn or stable covered with thatch. A cottage house covered with thatch with a garden by the river. Another cottage in Barkers Street covered with thatch with a garden adjoining. On W. of the parsonage garden: Kitchen mead, Pond close and the 2 Green closes being thrown together, 7a. Church meadow, N. of the church 7a., but the mill has the shear of 1a. p. a. On E. of the church 1 meadow called Fewels, 6a. W. of the farm yard 1 meadow called Langteries, 2a. Lower Wood with Butlers Mead thrown to it N. of Pigstrow lane, 6a. 1 meadow called New Hayes N. of Pigstrow lane, 4a. 2 coppices adjoining Pigstrow lane, *c.* 5a. In the coppices and meadows *c.* 40 oak trees, but their real number and value unknown. In the grounds 4 elm trees value unknown. N. of the coppices 1 pasture called Higher Wood, 4a. The above are statute measure. Near Park Gate Grove mead, 3a. Near Semley common, *c.* 5a. of furze or common ground. S. of Pigstrow lane 1 piece of arable called Sturmies Close, 2a. At Sandies N. of Whitesheet hill is a barn. 1 barn on staddle stones, 1 stable, 2 carthouses, 1 small house containing only 1 room. N. of the barns 1 piece of arable called Barn close, 8a. Budgen close next to the above 3a. [?Grove mead]. 1 close called Long Sands, 14a. A close adjoining called The Twelve acres, 12a. W. of White Street 1 piece of arable called Clay field, 10a. 1 adjoining close called Peaks, 4a. N. of Fern wood 1 piece of arrable called Mary Craft, 8a. E. of Rowberry lane 1 close called Rowberry, 2a. 1 close W. of Nower coppice called Nowers, 3a. All the said lands enclosed with quickset hedges. The sheep down on White Sheet computed at 60a. Land in Easton Bassett[1] fields as 28½a. of arable in Minchington field, [2] Dorset.

All tithes, a modus is claimed for Wardour park. The churchyard wall is repaired by the parish likewise the church, but the chancel by the rector and the aisle by lord Arundell. 4 bells, 1 bible and common prayer book. 1 silver salver marked on the reverse side ★ on the other with the inscription 'Tributum Gratiarum Deo Opt. Max. Hanc patinam offert Matheus Bowles Rect. Ecclesiae Parochialis de Donhend Sti Andreae Anno Dni 1701'. 1 cup and cover. The clerk is appointed by the rector, his wages, exclusive of some small dues, £3 p. a. paid by the parish. The above terrier will be found to vary much from any former terrier as the house and buildings have been much altered and the small grounds in many parts have been thrown together to make one large one.

John Benet, LL. D., rector, John Bunter, Hugh Barratt, churchwardens.

1. See **280** note 6.
2. In Sixpenny Handley see **280**.
★   The mark is a triangle of 3 letters; H at the top, I bottom left, A bottom right.

DONHEAD ST. MARY rectory

284   21 Sep 1608 (D1/24/78/1)
The [par]sonage with [. . .] [do]vehouse under [. . .] [gar]den lying within [. . .] [co]whouse [. . .] [gar]den between the parsonage house and the barn.

A close of pasture adjoining the backside or barton called Pond close, 4a.; a coppice or wood adjoining that close, [. . .] a.; 2 closes lying [. . .] house, 9a.; a copse adjoining those closes, 3a.; a close of pasture adjoining that coppice called Brache, 3½a.

2 closes of arable on the E. part of the field called Wildens Dean, 11a.; a close of arable on the W. part of the fields called Black furlong, 7a.; a close of arable over against the same close called Biddle Dean, 10a.; and a close of arable near Whitsoncross called Marlen Pitts 6½a.

Tithes:[1] Of a close, 2½a., belonging to the farm of Lyes Court in the parish of Donhead St. Andrew lying near Whiteshoote; a close, 6a., in that parish belonging to the tenement lately in the tenure of Edmund Cooke, decd.; a close, 4a., adjoining the last close, both called Nyvers, belonging to Mr. Thomas Bower's tenement; a close, 3a. at Nowers belonging to one of the parsonage tenements of Donhead St. Andrew now in the tenure of John Compton; a close, 3a., adjoining it, belonging to Lyes Court farm; the full tithe of a parcel of a meadow, ½a., belonging to William Stryde's tenement in Donhead St. Andrew adjoining his ground called Hare; 2 closes, 9a., lying together in Donhead St. Andrew called Cleyes belonging to Thomas Bower's tenement and bordering on Ferne field; a sand close, 5a., of Thomas Bower near Whitson Cross adjoining Mrs Grove's close; a meadow, 2a., of Thomas Bower called Butbrooks near his mill; half of the tithe of 3 grounds called Nowers, 50a., in Donhead St. Andrew belonging to Berrycourt farm; and the tithe of a close called Bramble Combes, 12a., belonging to Alexander Weekes's land in Donhead St. Mary but lying in Donhead St. Andrew.

Noted by the view of, and witnessed by, George Pope, rector, Roger Burden, William Wyatt, churchwardens, John Lush, Robert Knight, sidesmen, Edward Elliott, Warnard Gourd, Thomas Bunter senior, and John Bugden, parishioners. *Signature of rector only*

1.   Land all in Donhead St. Andrew see **285.**

285   1 Oct 1677 (D1/24/78/2)
Terrier exhibited 17 Nov 1677. A parsonage, tiled, in it a kitchen hall, parlour, buttery, milkhouse, with other small rooms and chambers over all and a long table board in hall that was given by Mr. George Pope, a former rector, to remain in the parsonage house. A little old tiled house adjoining S. of the tower of the church. E. of the parsonage house a garden on E. of the garden a great barn thatched. On S. of the garden an old woodhouse. W. of the parsonage house a brewhouse and stable, 1 side of the roof tiled, the other thatched with a little orchard adjoining it and an old dovehouse, tiled.

1 pasture ground called Pond close; a little meadow, 2½a. adjoining on S. E. of parsonage house; a coppice, *c.* 4a.

Broadmead and pasture ground, 10½a., called Copped mead on N. of the parsonage house, and a coppice, *c.* 6a. Pasture ground called Breach, *c.* 15a., adjoining part of the coppice. 2 arable grounds, *c.* 15a., one sand, the other clay, lying S. from Five Ways. 3 arable grounds, *c.* 17a., 1 called Marnell[1] Pit the other 2 called Wildersdeanes[2] lying near Whitsuncross.[3]

Certain grounds in Donhead St. Andrew which the tithes and half tithes belonging to the parson of Donhead St. Mary. Whole tithes: a close called Amor mead, *c.* 6a., 1 sandy close lying N. W. adjoining John Goulds ground near Whitsun Cross, 1a. of meadow of Mr. William Grove.[4] Half tithes: Mr. Foyle's at Nowers, 4½a. At Lyes court farm, a ground called Copped Nowers half, ½a.; Clay close, *c.* 2½a.; a close, 4a., at Hengrove heretofore Bowles'; 1 close of Richard Kerlies called Nivers, *c.* 7a.; 1 close of Robert Collins[5] called Nivers, *c.* 3a.

Richard Osgood, rector, John Fricker, John Brockway, churchwardens, Renaldo Weekes, Luke Weekes, Richard Lush, William Lush.

1. Called Marling pit, *c.* 5a., from a marl pit in it in **286**.
2. Wildersdean alias Nivers, *c.* 12a., in **286**.
3. A field barn near Fiveways added in **286**.
4. Farmer Fezard in **286**.
5. Heretobefore Robert Collyns in **286**.

286   6 Dec 1704 (D1/24/78/3)
As **285** *with amendments in footnotes.* Great and small tithes. Some tithes divided between the rectors of Donhead St. Andrew and Donhead St. Mary. All the lands of Berry Court farm except that part of Lower and Outer Bubberys that lies beneath a footpath (towards Ludwell way) from Berry court house to Dennis alias Sturgis cottage, the whole tithes of which belong to the rector of Donhead St. Mary. Whole tithes of the horsehills, breaches, farm closes in Donhead St. Mary. *Tithes as* **282**.

Rice Adams, rector, John Bower, Luke Wake, churchwardens, David Speering, James King, John Brockway, John Lush, Jacob Lush senior, Richard Lush, Robert Mullens, James Brockway, Richard Fricker, John Gurd, John Goddard, James Goddard.

Endorsement: Note of the production of the terrier in 2 Chancery cases between Richard Jackson, DD., v. Andrew Barratt and others. Shown to Matthew Bowles gent., Silas Marchant, Mary Williams, Nicholas Lilly, Thomas Frome gent. 1 Apr 1752 and to William Brockway and John Lush 15 Apr 1752.

DOWNTON vicarage

287   1671 (D1/24/79/1)
A dwelling house with hayhouse, stable, and woodhouse adjoining. A garden, *c.* ½a., bounded E. with the highway or lane, S. with a little lane called the Church lane, W. with the churchyard and parsonage court, N. with land of Gilbert Rawleigh esq. All tithe hay and copse wood, calves and cow white, pigs and bees, hops, apples, pears, and all other orchard fruits; 1d. in lieu of garden fruits; 1d. for the cock in lieu of tithes of eggs.

John Leight, William Michell, churchwardens.

288   1677 (D1/24/79/2)
A dwelling house and garden and plot of ground adjoining, *c.* 1a. Tithe cow white, coppice wood, hay, garden and orchards to be paid in kind. The tithing of

Charlton in lieu of tithe hay 4d. p. a. for every yardland. Bodenham and Nunton pay the same tithe in kind except in lieu of tithe hay they pay 4d. an a. and 2d.[1] a ham p. a.

William Gale, vicar, John Brewer, Richard Whitier, churchwardens.

1.   Omitted in 1705.

289   1705 (D1/24/79/3)
*As **288** with amendment in footnote.* William Gale, vicar, John Bampton, Robert Allbright, churchwardens.

BODENHAM and NUNTON vicarage

290   n. d. early 17th cent. (D1/24/79/4)
1 vicarage house with garden and orchard adjoining, *c.* 40 lugs. The value of vicarage dues £5 p. a. The annual pension from Winchester College, £2 10. 0.

Charles Farner, John Chubb, churchwardens, John Barham, sidesman. *Names in the same hand.*

DRAYCOT CERNE rectory

291   n. d. early 17th cent. (D1/24/80/1)
Arable land: 16a. called [*name omitted*]; 6a. near it called Deans; and 7a. of arable and meadow called Broklands. Pasture: 4¼a. called Upper Knowle; 4¼a. of arable and pasture called S. field; 4a. called the Clay; and 5a. called Lower or Home Knowle. Another pasture, 1a., adjoining the parsonage house called Coulver close and now made a garden.

Nicholas Fawconer, rector, Richard Thorne [X], Henry Wharton [X].

292   21 May 1632 (D1/24/80/2-3)[1]
1 meadow ground called the Clay *c.* 4a. 1 pasture ground called the Home Knowle, *c.* 7a. 1 arable ground called the Further Knowle, *c.* 5a. 1 ground called Bucklands, *c.* 6a. A ground enclosed called the Parsons Six acres. 1 ground adjoining unto Bucklands called Perryhill *c.* 5a. 1 arable ground called the Parsons Sixteen acres.

John Rand, rector, Walter Long, <Richard Godwyen *struck through* >, John Warton, churchwardens, Thomas Taylor, Samuel Rudman, Thomas Tayler, churchwardens, George Bishop [X].

1.   D1/24/80/2 is the original signed terrier on paper. D1/24/80/3 is a final version on parchment without any signatures.

293   15 Mar 1678 (D1/24/80/4)
1 dwelling house, barn and stable with garden and orchard. 1 farndell. The home ground of arable called the Knowle, 5a., adjoining the orchard. 1 enclosed

ground of meadow called the Cley, 3½a. 1 enclosed ground of arable or pasture called the Upper Knowle, 4a., lands of Walter Long W., the ground of wid. Bailey E. 1 enclosed ground called the Sixteen acres, being so much by estimation, land of Sir James Long E., land of Thomas Taylor W. 1 enclosed ground of arable called the Quar, 6a., adjoining the Sixteen acres on S. 1 enclosed ground of arable or meadow called Brooklands, 5a., adjoining the Sixteen acres. 1 enclosed ground of arable called Perry Hill, 3a., adjoining the Sixteen acres.

A composition for the tithes due from Sir James Long of Draycott, £20 p. a. All the tithes of Sir James Long's tenants in Draycot, great and small as corn, hay, cows, calves, wool, lambs, orchard, fruit and oblations.

James Nichell, rector, Robert Joanes, Lawrence Chalner, churchwardens.

GREAT DURNFORD rectory and vicarage

294   1622 (D5/10/1/9)
Parsonage: The hall parlour and kitchen and 2 barns. 2 closes adjoining to the barns, c. 3a.; 1 orchard and garden; 1 parrock lying next unto the vicarage barn; 4a. of meadow ground lying in Long mead; 1a. of meadow called the Pecked acre. 4 yardlands lying in diverse places in the N. fields of Durnford out of which yardlands the vicar has tithe corn, hay, wool and lamb.

Vicarage: The hall, parlour and kitchen and barn; an orchard and garden plot lying near unto the vicarage houses; the churchyard. All the tithes of half of the farm in Little Durnford in the tenure of Mrs Younge. Tithe corn of 8a. called the Mill lands belonging unto the farm of Mr. Erington in Salterton within Durnford. Tithe hay of a meadow, ½a. in the tenure of Thomas Batchelor in Newtown; of a meadow, 1yd., in the tenure of Simon Grace in Newtown; of a meadow, ½a., in the tenure of John Biggs; of a meadow, 1a., in the tenure of Henry Pettie. Tithe hay of all dry ground which is cut and the odds of wool and lambs from the parsonage throughout the whole parish and all the privy tithes. The vicar is to have 40s. p. a. from the prebend of Durnford.

Richard Cunditt [X], John Stovin [X], churchwardens, Edward Godfrie [X], Thomas Cundit [X], sidesmen, Henry Sigings.

295   1631 (D5/10/1/9)
28a. in the S. field. 28a. in the Middle field. 41a. in the N. field. 4a. in the common meadow only cut and be gone upon Lammas day [1 Aug]. 1a. of a several meadow called Picked mead, ½a. of dry ground lying by the street. A cow down lay at Ladyday [25 Mar] for 11 cows and a bull to be broken on Whitsunday. 220 sheep leazes to feed with the farmer. We present the vicarage house to be in default both in timber work and tiling. We do certify the presentment at our visitation as books, bell ropes, glass windows are provided and done.

Timothy Copper, Thomas Hayward [X], Thomas Williams, Richard Pile [X], Edward Rattue, Thomas Dawkens [X], Mathew Collier [X], Robert Mundie, George Jarvis, John Stoven. This was made by the churchwardens as a presentment at a visitation by the dean.

296 1634 (D5/10/1/9)
Terrier presented at the metropolitan visitation.[1] The parsonage has 4 yardlands
containing *c.* 115a., viz. 31a. in the S. field, 33a. in the Middle field, 46a. in the
N. field, 4a. of meadow in the middle of the common meadow against Colemans
Mirsh. Of several, a meadow called Picked meadow, 1a., at the lower end of
Coleman's Mirsh; ½a. of dry ground by the vicarage. The parson has tithe corn,
hay, wool and lamb over the whole parish except certain places which hereafter
follow which belong to the vicarage.

Common for 6 kine and a bull to feed and depasture on Woodberry and in
the farm fields of Great Durnford from Whitsonday until St. Martin's day [11
Nov] Feeding for 232 sheep to depasture and feed upon the downs and fields of
the farm of Great Durnford.

The vicarage has the tithe of the 4 yardlands of parsonage glebe and tithe
wool and lamb on the same; half of the tithe of Little Durnford farm, *c.* 8
yardlands; the tithes of *c.* 12 ridges or a. in Salterton fields near the pennings;
tithe of Hawkins mead near the bridge at Newtown; all other small tithes in
the parish.

John Waters, Zacheus Collier, churchwardens, John Swaine, Nicholas Williams.

1. The visitation of the archbishop of Canterbury.

297 26 Feb 1640 (D5/10/1/9)
Parsonage: In S. field: the Long Breach 8a.; the Short Breach, 10a. In N. End
field: 8 ridges, 6a., 2a., 5a. in the Ham. In Middlefield: 7a. in Oakberrie furlong;
8a. in the Midfurlong; 4a. in Pettic Dean; 4a. in Woollie Lane; Peeked a. in
Middlefield; 4a. in Lightberrie; the Stony acre and 2a. in the bottom; 2a. at
Conie Holes and 1½a. In N. field: Pigeon hill, 12a.; 1a. shooting upon Umsberrie
down; 15a. lying by a place called Ten acres; 2 picked a. by the wayside; 13a.
shooting upon the Broad furlong; 2a. shooting up the same furlong; 3a. shooting
upon Broken Berrie; 4a. lying upon Broken Berrie; 1a. in the bottom called
Pepler acre; 1a. called St. Andrew's acre; ½a. upon Broken Berrie.

Meadow: 4a. in the common mead called Long mead; Picked mead, *c.* 3 x
½a.; a little close by the vicarage barn.

Common with Mr. Hungerford's farmer: 233 sheep to feed side by side
with Mr. Hungerford's farmer; 11 kine and a bull to go upon Oakberry and the
fields from Whitsonday until Martinsday [11 Nov.] to be hained by 25 Mar.
Feeding in the marsh with Mr. Hungerford from Lammas [1 Aug] until the 25
Mar. 2 little grounds and an orchard, 3a., lie about the parsonage house.

Thomas Williams [X], churchwarden, Richard Cundett [X], John Batchler
[X], Robert Mundie [X], Thomas Borwne [X].

DURRINGTON rectory

298 26 Sep 1608 (D1/24/81/1)
Terrier of the parsonage, being an impropriation in the occupation of Mr.
?Thomas Waldorne gent. of Albourne which he holds of the dean and chapter

ofWinchester. 4a. of meadow. 120a. of arable. Pasture for 300 sheep.The parsonage house and a tenement.

William White, minister, Matthew Bendole [X], Henry Batchelor [X], churchwardens.

299   18 Oct 1677 (D1/24/81/2)
Terrier of the 'Curateshippe'. Belonging to the curate for officiating in the parish church a house[1] containing 5 rooms, viz. a hall, 2 butteries, 2 lofts, 1 small garden, 7 or 8 lugs[2] adjoining the house.

£40 p. a. to be paid quarterly in equal amounts. 1 sack of wheat and 1 sack of malt to be paid each year on St.Thomas's Day [21 Dec].[3] The offerings of all the parishioners payable at Easter.All offerings for the churching of women and all marriage money.[4] The £40 and sack of grain is paid out of the impropriate parsonage of Durrington.

Leonard Maton, curate, Edward Poore, John Allen, churchwardens.

1. Rooms not specified in **300**.
2. *c.* 10 lugs in **300**.
3. Described as 4 bushells of good sweet clean and well winnowed wheat and 4 bushells of good sweet clean and well dried malt in **300**.
4. Also fees for christenings and burials in **300**.

300   8 Jan 1705 (D1/24/81/3)
As **299** *with amendments in footnotes.* Robert Forster, minister, Roger Pinckney, William Binder, churchwardens.

EASTON donative curacy

301   1 Jun 1705 (D1/24/82/1)
No glebe lands or tithes belong to the minister. What is given to him that officiates is by the charity of lord Bruce, lord of the manor, and the hon Edward Seymour esq.

Joseph Wall, minister, Thomas Stagg [X] and Edward Foach, old church-wardens, John Batt and Henry Frewin, new churchwardens, and Edward Seymour, William Visc, John Clark, Benjamin Kinton, Thomas Morrant, and George Goodall.

EASTON GREY rectory

302   n. d. late 16th cent. (D1/24/83/1)
House, pigeon-house, stable, barn, garden, and home close, 1a. A leaze called the Breach abutting the highway to Hampton W., adjoining N. a ground of Mr. Parry and a ground of Robert Lurges called Breach, and S. on a ground called Broad leaze, 24a. In William Ader's Grove leaze 2 beast pastures and 6 sheep pastures for winter. In Town Grove 1 beast's pasture and pasture for 3 sheep in winter.

303   1608 (D1/24/83/2)

A mansion house with kitchen, stable, dove house and barn with garden, backside and barton all conjoined together.

2 beast pastures for ever in Grove leaze belonging to William Adye junior of Easton Grey with 6 sheep pastures in wintertime. 1 beast pasture in Town grove belonging to Thomas Hedges gent., patron of the rectory, with 3 sheep pastures in wintertime. 1 lease of 22a. of arable in a field called Breach Lease as it is now enclosed, occupied by Peter Wyere clothier, bounded by 2 leases called the Breach, occupied by William Weston of Easton Grey N., by 2 leases called N. meads, one occupied by Thomas Goodcheape alias Cowley and the other by Peter Wyere clothier at E. end., and partly the highway, and a lease occupied by Edward Goodcheape alias Cowley on W. and by the same lease on N. which has been enclosed.

By me John Symes, rector; Robert Waters [X], William Weston [X], churchwardens, William Adye senior, [X] Lancelot Walleys, [X] sidesmen.

304   16 Dec 1671 (D1/24/83/3)

1 enclosed ground, c. 14a., called the Breache butting a ground of Mr. William Parry gent of Easton Grey called Broad Leasour S., grounds of Thomas Hodges of Shipton Moyne called the Breaches N., a ground of the said William Parry called N. meads on E. end, partly by the highway from Easton Grey to Westonbirt and partly by the Breaches belonging to the said William Parry on W. end. A dwelling of 5 bays, a barn, a stable of 1 bay with a court garden and a little close, c. 4a., lying on S. of the garden.

Pasture for 1 rother beast be it a cow or a yearling in the ground that belongs to Mr. Thomas Hodges called Town Grove onto which the beast is to be put from 3 May until All Saints [1 Nov] and then to be taken thence. Every second year a horse to be put into the grounds there to abide until the feast of St. Andrew the Apostle [30 Nov] when the horse is to be taken out and 2 sheep are to be put there each year to abide until Ladyday [25 Mar] at which time all cattle are to be taken from the ground which is to remain void until the 3 May then next ensuing. Pasture for 2 rother beast be they cows or yearlings or other beasts in N. ground of Mr. Joseph Adye of Easton Grey called Mr. Adye's grove, arrangements as for animals in Town grove except a single horse is put on the ground every year and is replaced by 4 sheep.

Tithe of a water mill with water wheel belonging to Thomas Hodges esq., occupied by Isaac Waters, 1s. 8d. paid each Easter. Tithe of a water mill belonging to William Parry gent. occupied by Isaac Punter, the sum of 3s. 4d. usually paid each year on the feast of St. Bartholomew [24 Aug].

Samuel Hieron, rector, Arthur Adye, Nathanial Wallas, churchwardens.

305   Dec 1704 (D1/24/83/4)

The mansion house of 5 bays, a brewhouse of 1 bay, stable, dovehouse of 1 bay, a barn of 3 bays, with the garden, close, backside and barton adjoining.

2 beast pastures for ever in Grove leaze in the possession of John Ady junior, gent. The inheritance of the leaze belongs with the Ady family. 6 sheep pastures in the same grove for ever. Pasture for 1 beast for ever in Town Grove the

inheritance of the grove being in William Hodges clerk; 3 sheep leazes in the said grove for ever in winter time.

1 leaze of pasture ground called Breach leaze, lately divided, according to ancient estimation 22a., S. with Broad leaze, E. 2 leazes called N. meads, all of which 3 leazes are freehold and the inheritance of William Parry gent., N. 2 leazes called Breach leazes, the inheritance is now of the said William Hodges clerk, W. the highway and a ground called the Breach, the freehold of the said William Parry, gent. The churchyard.

John Harris, rector, Henry Curtis, Robert Jefferis, churchwardens.

306   1786 (D1/24/83/5)

The parsonage house, stone built and tiled, consists of a room with freestone floor, and ceiled, a kitchen, rough stone floor, a pantry and cellar, earth floor, partitions lathe and plaster. The rooms over board floors, 2 of them only ceiled. A dairy and wood house adjoining stone built and tiled. Likewise a small barn and stable, both thatched. The land surrounding the house c. 1¼a., divided into a paddock, garden, yard and court. Fences stone. 2 enclosures of pasture at a distance, c. 7a. and 9a. 2 beast pastures in Mr. Ady's grove. 1 beast and 3 sheep pastures in Mrs. Powell's grove.

3 bells in the tower. Communion plate: a silver basin, tin paten, silver flagon. Folio bible, prayer book and a large octavo prayer book.

John Savage, rector.

307   28 May 1808 (D1/24/83/6)

The parsonage house built of stone and elm timber covered with stone tile. An underground cellar ceiled and the walls plastered. The principal storey contains 4 rooms: 2 parlours floored with deal boards, a kitchen floored with stone pavement the walls plastered and ceiled, a pantry floored with rough stone pavement the walls plastered and part of it ceiled. A brewhouse detached from the house floored with rough stone and the roof plastered to the pin. The chamber storey contains 3 rooms, 1 floored with elm boards, 1 with ash boards and the other with deal boards. The attic storey contains 2 garrets, one of which is floored with ash boards the other with elm boards, ceiled and the walls plastered. A stable built of stone and elm timbers covered with stone tile ceiled and the walls plastered. A skilling built of stone and elm timbers, the roof plastered to the pin. A carthouse or skilling built of stone and elm timber covered with stone tile. A farm yard adjoining the stable fenced with stone walls. A garden adjoining the house with stone walls abutting a freehold piece of land belongong to revd. John Harman Howes E., the Sherston road W., the farm yard N., the road from the manor house to the village S. The above premises constitute the homestead containing 1r. 28p.

The glebe consists of 16a. 3r. 18p. called the Breach leases bounded S. Broad lease belonging to Thomas Smith esq., N. 2 leases called Breach leases also belonging to Thomas Smith esq., E. end 2 leases called N. meads also belonging to Thomas Smith esq., W. end the highway and the lease belonging to Thomas Smith. It is enclosed. A small piece of glebe, 3a. 1r. 33p., was sold to Walter Hodges esq., for the redemption of part of the land tax charged on the living.

This land lies partly in the road and partly in the pleasure ground, the property of Thomas Smith esq. abutting the S. side of the rectory garden.

Pasture of 2 beasts for ever in Grove lease, the property of Mrs. Joan Bennett of Easton Grey and 6 sheep pastures for ever in wintertime. The pasture of 1 beast for ever in Town grove the property of Thomas Smith esq., with 3 sheep pastures in wintertime for ever.

Timber growing on the glebe is not sufficient to keep the premises in repair. The rectorial and other tithes are due to the minister.

Church furniture: 3 bells, 1 bible, a common prayer book, a purple velvet pulpit cloth, 2 chests a linen cloth and napkin. Communion plate. 1 silver cup, 1 silver salver, I pewter salver. The rector is charged with repairs of the edifices. The clerk is appointed by the rector, his salary is paid by the parish.

John Harman Howes, rector, Isaac Bennett, churchwarden, Henry Jefferis Vizor, clerk, Richard Washbourn, John Rogers, principal inhabitants.

CASTLE EATON rectory

308 n. d mid 17th cent.[1] (D1/24/84/1)
W. furlong, 10a.; Long furlong, 12a.; the cow pasture, 16a.; Long Leonard, 16a.; the Little pasture, 4a.; these grounds are together and are bounded N. with the highway to Hannington Wick, S. by the highway to Highworth, E. by the grounds of Mr. Hayles and John Skinner, W. with a ground called the Forty acres. The Parsonage down, 21¼a. lying between a ground of Mr. Goddard called the Farm downs, and a ground of Mr. Parker called the Ningard. 9 small a. in the common meadow called Parsonage meadow. A little close adjoining the dwelling house, 1½a. A dwelling house, barn, stable, cow house, malthouse, garden and orchard.

Thomas Staniford, rector, John Tipping, Humphrey Blackwell, David Richins, churchwardens.

1. Thomas Staniford was rector in this period.

309 1664 (D1/24/84/2)
1 close of pasture, 2a., between the house and river.[1] 3 closes called Long furlong, West furlong, Long furlong, 33a.,[2] of tillage with 2 closes called Cowpasture and in the Little close, 20a. of pasture which 5 closes are bounded[3] by the lane leading to Highworth and the lane leading to Hannington Wick, W., N. and S. 1 ground called Parsonage downs,[4] 21a. 3yd. 9a. in the common mead bounded mostly with farm meadows and distinguished by merestones.[5]

1 dwelling house, 1 barn containing 7 bays, 1 stable or cowhouse containing 2 bays, 1 malthouse, 1 brewbouse or bakehouse[6] and 1 dovehouse.[7]

John Skinner, Edmund Morse, churchwardens. *Names in the same hand.*

1. Thames in **310** and **311**.
2. Long Lenerd in **310** and **311**.
3. Bounded by the highway to Hannington Wick only in **310** and **311**.
4. Described as bounded lands of Walter Parker esq. E., in **310** and **311**, and lands of

Mrs. Goddard wid. W. in **310**, Mr. Burgess in **311**, lands of Mr. Henry Goddard N. in **310**, no bounds in **311**, lands of Humphrey Blackwell, S., in **310** and **311**.

5. Meade stones in **310** and **311**.
6. Described as bounded by the street of Castle Eaton S. the river Thames N., lands of John Tippen E. in **310**, Shailer in **311**, lands of John Cooper W. in **310**, the daughter of John Hales deceased in **311**.
7. Omitted in **310**, but tithes of hay and privy tithes included in **310** with corn added in **311**.

310　　1 Oct 1671 (D1/24/84/3)
*As **309** with amendments in footnotes.* Richard Goddard, parson, John Skinner, Henry Curtis, churchwardens. *Endorsement as **311**.*

311　　22 Jan 1705 (D1/24/84/4)
*As **309** with amendments in footnotes.* Thomas Goddard, rector, William Goddard, William Keble, churchwardens.
　　Endorsement: Presented at a commission at Cricklade St. Sampson in the cases Thomas Goddard clerk querent v. Walter Parker defendant, Thomas Goddard querent v. Thomas Keeble defendant, 11 Oct 1721.

312　　1783 (D1/24/84/5)
The parsonage house consists of 1 parlour 22ft. square, near 10ft. high, deal floor, wainscotted and ceiled. 1 large hall, larder, kitchen, floor oak. 5 bedrooms 1 garret 1 stable, fuel house and wash house built with stone covered with slate.
　　1 large barn 82ft. by 17½ft. built with stone covered with slate. 1 barn thatched and a stable under the same roof 66ft. by 17ft. 4in.
　　The glebe lands according to an account from Edward Goddard esq., patron, consists of 83a. and upwards; Downs, 14a., arable; Downs mead, 7a., meadow; W. furlong, 8a., arable; Long furlong 12a., arable; Cow pasture, 14a., arable and pasture, Long Leonards, 12a., arable and pasture; Little mead, 7a., arable and pasture; in Town mead, 9a,. meadow.
　　Right of common in Town mead for 6 beasts. All the rectorial tithes. A carthouse in the close. A garden and orchard behind the house, the garden, 146ft. by 66ft., the width of the orchard 86ft., quick fence. A farm yard 156ft. by 60ft. A court behind the house 62ft. by 66ft. A garden with quick fence before the house 72ft. by 60ft. No timber on the glebe.
　　6 bells, with a small one to call the parishioners to church. Communion cup and plate. The clerk's wages 34s. p. a. a collection made at Easter by custom.
　　Lancelot Kerby, rector, Robert Green, Richard Bennett, churchwardens, David Archer.

EBBESBOURNE WAKE rectory

313　　n. d. late 16th cent. (D1/24/85/1)
1a. called Drove acre; 1a. shooting on the N. side of Green way; 2a. shooting on (?)Green way [...] being on the side of the land of Mr. Thomas [...]; 1r. shooting

on Chilmark in the [. . .] side of 1r. of Mrs. Gawen; [. . .]a. in Bainting furlong in the W. side of 7a. of Mr. Henry Bodman; and ½a. lying on Chilmark in the S. side of Green way.

Meadow: 1 plot in the common mead, 3r.; a plot in Little Krellyes rented at 6d. a year; and a plot in Bounds close adjoining the churchyard at the rent of 6d. a yd. p. a. Half of tithe corn throughout the parish; and tithe hay except arable grounds where the parson has only half the tithe hay. Common for 3 horses, 2 oxen, 3 kine, a bull, 3 bullocks, a boar, and 200 sheep. All other tithes as wool, lambs, Lammas tithes, and privy tithes belong to the parsonage.

[*Added later*] Also in the common woods of Ebbesbourne there is a plot of coppice wood, 5a., that belongs to the parsonage; and a plot in Forloren coppice, 1a., belongs to the parsonage.

314 1608 (D1/24/85/2)
Half tithe corn, all privy tithes with the glebe lands. 15a. of arable in S. field; 6a. of arable in W. field; 6a. of arable in E. field. 12a. in Bitcombe field. 200 sheep leazes in the common fields and downs. 6 beast and 3 horse leazes.

John Reace, Simon Younge, churchwardens.

315 n. d. [1704x1705][1] (D1/24/85/3)
The particulars of the parsonage house and barn and a meadow joining, 2a. 6a. in little N. field and E. field. In Great N. field and Bitcom, 12a. A piece of ground called the Passing Gut in W. field. 6½a. In S. field 15[finthen]a. A coppice, 4a. Leaze for 3 horses, 3 beasts, sleight for 200 sheep.

Half tithe corn, all tithe wool lambs and other small tithes. Tithe hay except Priory mead and Greencleft mead and the rides [wrides] in W. field and 2a. in Bennets mend which pays half tithe. The whole value £80 p. a.

Giles Cookman, churchwarden.

1. The churchwarden is recorded as churchwarden in the bishop's visitation book, Oct 1704 (WSRO D1/50/6).

EDINGTON rectory

316 n. d. [1704x1705][1] (D1/24/86/1)
Account of the dues pertaining to the bishop of Salisbury. The parsonage and all tithes and profits belong to the duke of Bolton who gives a salary to have the cure served. 6s. 8d. a year is paid to the bishop, 3s. 4d. as we think to the archdeacon, and 3s. 4d. to the dean and chapter.

Presented by David Thomas, clerk, Ralph Hooper and Robert Ford, churchwardens, and Thomas Read [the writer].

1. The churchwardens were recorded in the bishop's visitation book, Oct 1704 (WSRO D1/50/6).

EISEY vicarage

317   12 May 1588 (D1/24/87/1)

The vicarage house, barn, and stables. The churchyard and a garden adjoining it. 2 closes of pasture and 2 hams of enclosed meadow, 6a. in all. No glebe land, nor pasture for any cattle without the vicarage gate

All manner of tithes of Eisey, tithe corn, hay, wool, lamb, calf, pig, goose, hemp and flax, apples and eggs, Lammas tithes and Easter book offerings, and all other duties belonging to the church except 2 plots of meadow, one called the ?W. meadow lying at Cowneck now in the occupation of Mr Anthony Hungerford esq., and the other called Alinton meadow lying under Water Eaton, of which two it cannot be proved by any parishioner now living that any tithe was ever paid

As for Water Eaton, a chapel annexed to Eisey, we know not what is due to the vicar.

Found and witnessed by Nicholas Blackwell and Edmund Barrett, churchwardens. *Names in the same hand*

318   7 Jan 1705 (D1/24/87/2)

Vicarage house barn and stables. The churchyard and garden adjoining. 2 closes of pasture and 2 hams of meadow ground enclosed containing together *c.* 6a. No other glebe or land pertains to the vicar nor any pasture feeding or common for any cattle without the vicarage gate.

Tithe corn and hay throughout the parish except Middle leaze ocupied by Elizabeth Clarke wid., Picked leaze belonging to the said Elizabeth Clarke, Shipton Bridge ground belonging to Mr. Felix Coward and occupied by Christopher Poulton, 1 ground belonging to John Hedges alias Parsons called his Shipton Bridge ground, Mr. Blackwell's upper leaze, Mr Dennis's upper ground, John Bennett's, formerly Hayne's, 2 upper grounds pen, orchards above the house, Allick's and Mrs. Barrett's 2 farm closes; these are all tithe free save only the 2 grounds belonging to the said Mrs. Barrett called Bennett which are titheable and except Mrs. Lawrence's ground called Webbhay which is tithe free and part of Eisey meadow at Cowneck. Mr. Calvard's meadow, 35 ¼a., and Mr. Henry Barrett's 10a., John Barrett's 6a., Edward Ware's 6a., Thomas Hinton's 4a., Sir Richard Anslowe's and esq. Thomas Master's 17a. and Mrs. Lawrence's 2 upper leazes all tithe free.

Tithe wool, lamb, calf, pig, goose, hemp, flax, apples, pears, eggs and Lammas, Easter book offerings and all other duties belonging to the church.

Water Eaton, a chapel annexed to Eisey, pays to the vicar 10s. p. a. for the chapel yard, Easter book offerings from the inhabitants of Water Eaton. The vicar has the right to 1 cow pasture p. a. in Town leaze from May day to Michaelmas [29 Sep].

Memo. Middle leaze belonging to wid. Clarke is questionable whether all tithe free or not.

Edward Head, vicar, Edmund Clarke, churchwarden, Edward Laurence, John Hedges, Hungerford Barrett, Nicholas Eacot [X].

ENFORD vicarage

319   1588 (D1/24/88/1)

The certificate or presentment of elders, the church officers, and parishioners of Enford on a precept or commandment delivered to the churchwardens, Thomas Hardyng and William Bawdwyn.

Sir Alexander Culpepper is lord and patron of the manor of Enford and Fyfield and the parsonage is impropriate; there is a chantry house in Enford in the tenure of Thomas Maton as tenant to Sir Alexander.

John Powell, minister, is vicar: there belongs to the vicarage a garden and an adjoining orchard; a meadow adjoining the farm meadow, 1a.; 2a. of arable in the common fields of Enford; 6a. of arable together in the common field of Longstreet; 2 yardlands in the common fields of Compton with common for 100 sheep; a little several close of pasture in Compton, ½a.; and 2 plots of meadow in the common meadow of Compton, 5yd., in which common meadow he ought to crop and go without any further common as his predecessors used it 'sithens as the memory of man by report of most parishioners'.

Edward ? Falker, Richard Hunt, Simon Hunt, Matthew Grove, ?Christopher Hunt [X], Thomas Harding [X], William Baw[. . .][1] [X].

1.   Probably the churchwarden named at the start of the document.

320   n. d. [early 17th. cent.][1] (D1/24/88/2)

In the tithing of Compton 2 yardlands, 44a. of arable. In the 4 Summerfields [Sommerfields], 21a. (as they were divided at the writing hereof). In the Summerfield next unto the farm field[2] 1½a. butting upon the long ditch[3] at the end thereof 4 picked a. Below that 1 head a. In the second Summerfield 1½a. In the outside of the field, *c.* 4a. in 1 piece;[4] 1a. below that;[5] 1a. lying a little below the path leading to the down. In the third Summerfield 2a. lying above a great lawn E. In the fourth Summerfield 3 picked a. upon the top of the hill in a piece together; 2a. below that next adjoining unto the highway towards Lavington.

In the 2 Homefields: In the Homefield called the Dean next unto Chisenbury field, ½a.;[6] 2a. together at the end thereof;[7] 1a. below these called the Broad a. then 1½a. in a piece;[8] 2 several a. a little above the village; 3 x ½a. in the drove above;[9] 2a. together butting upon the highway that leads to Devizes.[10] In the Homefield where the great barrow is 4 several a. above; 4a. in a piece a little above the barrow. 4 several a. below;[11] 1 picked ½yd. by the village butting upon the pits.

As part of the 2 yardlands [*in Compton*] 1 close of pasture, 1a., lying between a close belonging to Richard Guyne and a close of Simon Rolfe.[12] In Compton mead 1a. of meadow shooting towards the river; ½a. of dry ground under the quick frith hedge

Appertaining to the same 2 yardlands the vicarage has 100 sheep to be fed and depastured on the downs, fields and commons as any freeholder or tenant has in the tithing, and horses and rother beasts to be kept in as large and ample manner without stint or limitation as any other inhabitants of the tithing of Compton.

2a. of arable in the tithing of Enford. 1a. lying above Salisbury way[13] the other shooting along by the drove down to the town. 1 plot of meadow enclosed *c.* 1½a.,[14] both for hay and the after leaze without any intercommoning whatsoever.

5a. of arable land lying together in a piece in the fields of the tithing of Longstreet yearly to be sown.

Thomas Jeaye, vicar, William Bawden [X], Thomas Frie, churchwardens.

1. Thomas Jeaye was vicar between 1592-1623.
2. Described as belonging to Enford in **321**.
3. And adjoining Enford farm field in **321**.
4. At the upper end of Cuckoo bush linch in **321** on N. side in **322**.
5. In the middle of the field in **321**. Between 1a. of John Brumham S. and 1a. of John Gurne N. in **322**.
6. Lying nigh Dean Way in the second furlong of the field in **321**.
7. In the next furlong towards the village in **321**.
8. In the next furlong nearer the village in **321**.
9. In the third furlong nearer the village in **321**.
10. These lands included in a separate Homefield in **321** described as lying on each side of the village. The lands are described as follows: In N. side: 2a. in sheep drove, abutting the highway to Devizes In the second furlong from the highway 2 several a. In S side: 1a. in the furlong part shooting against the E. of the great barrow. 2 several a. in the next furlong E. In the next furlong which shoots N. and S. 1a abutting Enford farm field.
11. Described in **321** as 1a. abutting Enford farm field in the next furlong W., 1a. near the middle of the field in the same furlong 1a. lying an acre's breadth above Cuckoo Bush linch. In the next furlong W. is 1a. adjoining S. side of the said linch. At the town's end a picked 1a. adjoining the pits.
12. Described in **321** as between closes belonging to John Bromham W., Dorothy Rolfe, wid. E., Christopher Rutt N., the water from the Dean S.
13. In the Homefield in **321**.
14. Described in **321** as adjoining the great meadow belonging to Enford farm, called Broad mead.

321   11 Feb 1678 (D1/24/88/3)
1 dwelling house in the tithing of Enford, adjoining to it 1 wood house, 1 stable, and 1 barn, extending and reaching from within *c.* 4ft. of the wall of the kitchen chimney S. unto the highway leading to Enford street. A garden on E. of the house adjoining churchyard N., churchway E. 1 barton or backside on S., the ground belonging to it extends beyond the fence enclosing it as far as S. E. end of the barn. On N. of the vicarage house is a little court called the Mount adjoining the churchyard with a little piece belonging to the manor of Enford on W. The vicarage house is partly bounded on W. by the Mount and partly a garden and orchard of Edward Bear. Beyond the wall on S. of the garden the vicarage land reaches unto the willow trees planted along the highway. *Other land as* **320** *with amendments in footnotes.*

Tithe wool and lamb throughout the whole parish except that the prebend of Chisenbury pretends a right to these tithes on the little farm of Chisenbury but not from the 5 yardlands which formerly were small tenements but are now annexed to the farm nor from any other tenements belonging to his prebendary. The vicarage has tithe colts, calves, geese, pigeons, eggs, honey, wax, and milk. Tithe of mills, gardens, apples, pears, beans, hops, hemp, and flax, throughout the parish and all other tithes except tithe corn and hay which belong to the impropriate parsonage.

Easter offerings; 2d. for everyone above 16 years, 4d. for every woman churched, 2s. at least for every couple married in the church, 1s. for any person being an inhabitant of the parish, and married out of the parish, either by lawful licence or banns published in Enford church. Mr. Thomas Jay, sometimes a vicar of the parish, bequeathed by his will £10 the interest of which 6s. 8d. is yearly allowed for a sermon to be preached on Easter Monday in the church.

Thomas Jacob, vicar, Thomas Slatter, John Brumham, churchwardens.

322   4 May 1705 (D1/24/88/4)
A large vicarage house of [...] bays, 1 barn, 1 stable, 1 wood house of 6 bays, all in good repair with a little court, garden and backside adjoining to be fenced all round by the vicar bounded by churchyard N, land of George Clerk esq., called the Mount, and, the garden of Edward Biffen W., the highway S. and E. The bounds of the garden and backside on S. and E. reach beyond the walls of the garden and pales of the backside as far as the withy trees planted by the vicar. The feeding of the churchyard.

2 yardlands of arable land, 44a., in the tithing of Compton. In the first Summerfield adjoining Enford farm field 1½a. butting upon the long ditch. At the end thereof 4 picked a. together, lawned in on both sides. Below that 1 head a. butting on Enford farm field, lawned in on E. side and part of W. side. In the second Summerfield 1½a. shooting E. and W. and lawned in on both sides. In the outside of the field 4a. in one piece lying E. and W. on N. side of Cuckoo Bush lawn. 1a. below that between 1a. of John Brumham on S. and land of John Guine on N. 1a. a little above the well between the land of farmer Rolfe on N. and 1a. of James Franklin on S., all lawned in. In the third Summerfield 2a. bounded by the great lawn on N. and a piece of farmer Rolfe on S. 3 picked a. on the top of the hill in a piece together, Michael Clarke's land on N. and farmer Rolfe's on S., all lawned in. 2a. below that next adjoining to N. side of the highway that leads to Lavington

In the first Homefield, called the Dean field, next unto Chisenbury fields: 1a. lying an acre's breadth from the highway. At the E. end thereof 2a. in a piece. In the next furlong homewards, 1a. called the Broad acre, farmer Rolfe's land on S.; 1½a. in a piece, William Dickman's land on S., James Franklin's on N; 3 x ½a. in the Drove above, 2 acres' breadth from Chisenbury field. All this field lawned in.

In the Homefield in which the great barrow [burrough] [lies] 2a. a little above the village, lawned in, Mr. Straight having 1a. between them; 2a. together in the drove butting upon the way that leads to Devizes; 4 several a. upon the Hill viz. 1a. in the cleve shooting towards the barrow, having 1a. of Mr. Straight on N. and 2a. of Michael Clarke on S., 1a. between 3a. of James Franklin's on N. and 1a. of Michael Clarke on S.; 1a. shooting upon the last a. of Michael Clarke;

1a. shooting upon Enford farm field, Michael Clarke on W. and Mr. Straight on E., all lawned in.

In the Homefield above the barrow 4a. in a piece a little above the barrow, the drove on N., a piece of farmer Rolfe on S; 4 several a. viz. 1a. butting on Enford farm field, an a. of Michael Clarke on W., a piece of farmer Rolfe on E., 1a. lying 2 acres' breadth from the N. side of the drove, with Mr. Straight's land on S. and James Franklin on N., a picked a. lying by Cuckoo Bush lawn on S., 1a. a furlong nearer home an acre's breath from the lawn. All lawned in. A picked a. adjoining the pits.

As part of these 2 yardlands the vicarage has the following: 1 close of pasture, 1a., lying between a close of Michael Clarke E. and a close of John Brumham W. In the common meadow of Compton 1a. of meadow shooting towards the river and 1a. of dry ground under the quick frith hedge. 100 sheep to be fed or depastured on the downs, fields and commons as far as any freeholder or tenant has in the tithing of Compton.

2a. of arable in the fields of the tithing of Enford. one lying by Salisbury way, land of Thomas Adams on W., the other shooting along by the drove called Wheaten ditch down to the town, with land of Thomas Rolfe on N. 1 enclosed plot of meadow, 1½a., adjoining Broadmead, both for hay and after leaze without any intercommoning whatsoever. 5a. of arable lying together in a piece within the fields of the tithing of Longstreet, yearly to be sown, bounded with a lawn of E. and part of W. sides.

All the tithes, great and small, of the glebe land the tenth weight of wool according to the proposition for any other quantity to be paid in kind; for sheep sold out of the parish and agistments [justments] not shorn in the parish ¼d. for each sheep for each month that they have been kept in the parish.

Tithe of lambs bred in the parish to be paid in kind and due proportion to be paid for lambs brought into the parish or whose dams have been wintered in any other parish. St. Mark's day [25 Apr] and the following 3 days have been the usual days for tithing the lambs. For every new milk cow 2d., for every thorough milk cow 1½d. to be paid yearly at Easter. For every calf 4d. except the cows bred on Enford farm for which the vicar customarily has received 6d. at Easter. Tithe pigs, geese, pigeons to be paid in kind.

Tithe of honey in kind and the tenth penny for what is sold and not tithed in kind.[1] For tithe of eggs of the several inhabitants 1d. except the vicars have received customarily 6d. for the tithe eggs of Enford farm, now belonging to Mrs. Hester Clerk[2] 4d. a piece of Mr Charles Gresly's farm in Littlecott and of the 2 farms in Longstreet[3] and of Combes[4] farm and 3d. of Mr. Thomas Hunt's farm in Littlecott.[5]

Time out of mind the vicars have received 6s. 8d. for the tithes of Enford mill and the same for Combe mill. All other tithes not mentioned which are or may arise within the parish are due to the vicar in kind, except the tithe corn, grain and hay arising from the estates of the parishioners. The tenants of the hospital of St. Catherine in London[6] prescribe to all tithes arising from the demesne lands of St. Catherine's farm in Chisenbury priory and pay the vicar at Easter each year vicarage tithes of the farm and tithes of Chisenbury mill, the sum of £1 6s. 8d., but on what grounds it is not known. The prebendary of

Chute and Chisenbury prescribes for all tithes on the demesne lands of Prebend farm, but pays nothing in lieu, on what grounds it is not known.

The vicars have received for about 60 years past, composition for the tithes of certain copyholds belonging to the Prebendary annexed to his demesne containing 5 yardlands, 26 lbs. of wool each year at shear time and for the tithes of cow white, calves and eggs 3s. 4d. each year at Easter.

Easter offerings 2d. for every inhabitant over 16 years. For every woman who is churched at least 4d. For the marriage of parishioners 2s. at least. For funeral sermon 10s.[7] at least. Mr. Thomas Jay, sometime vicar bequeathed to the parish by his will £10. Out of the interest 6s. 8d. to be paid yearly by the churchwardens and overseers for a sermon to be preached in the church on Easter Monday.

Thomas Jacob, vicar, John Baden, George Munday, churchwardens, Thomas Slater, Thomas Addams, Edward Tarrant.

1. Tithe of garden 1d., hops to be paid in kind in **323**.
2. Owner not stated in **323**.
3. Owners Mr. John Poore and Mr. Robert Baden in **323**.
4. John Poore owner in **323**.
5. Tithes of all fruit in **323**.
6. The hospital of St Katharine's by the Tower.
7. 5s. at least in **323**.

323 1783 (D1/24/88/5)
1 large vicarage house, I barn, 1 stable, 1 wood house, with a court, garden and backside adjoining to be fenced all round by the vicar, bounded churchyard N., land of Thomas Benet esq. W., the bounds of garden and backside reaching without the wall of the garden, and the pales of the withy trees planted by the vicar, S. and E. The vicarage house and outbuildings are in a very ruinous state and must be immediately rebuilt. The walls around the garden are of mud. The trees in the churchyard number 22, chiefly pollards of little value. The churchyard and feeding thereof belong to the vicar.

Compton tithing: The vicarage has an allotment of arable land containing by statute measure including roads, 59a. 1r. 35p., bounded land Thomas Benet esq., S., part of the allotment set out for Mary Atwood wid. W. and another part of her allotment and that of William Hussey esq. N., part of the land allotted to William Hussey esq., late part of Compton common mead, the allotment made to Robert Baden and river Avon E. 1 little close of pasture, 1a. between 2 closes of William Hussey esq., on E. and W. sides.

Enford tithing: 2a. of arable, 1a. lying in Salisbury way, with lands of William Rook, W. the other a. shooting across the drove called Wheaten ditch down to the town, 1 plot of enclosed meadow, 1½a., for hay and after leaze without any intercommoning.

Longstreet tithing: 5a. of arable lying in a piece yearly to be sown, bounded with a lawn on E. and part W. side.
Tithes, exceptions and offerings as 322 with amendments in footnotes.

Furniture of the church: 1 clock, 1 sundial, 5 bells, 1 pewter flagon, 1 silver chalice, 2 silver plates, one inscribed 'Given to the church of Enford by Thomas

Jacob A. M. and vicar of that church Anno Domini 1716', the other inscribed 'The gift of William Scratchly to the parish of Enford 1753'. The weight of the plate is not marked thereon.

The mud walls on W. N. and E. sides of the churchyard were built by the lord of the manor. Part of the E. wall has been repaired by the parish, in a case of emergency but by no obligation. The S. wall is built and repaired by the vicar. The sexton is appointed by the parish and is paid £1 13s. 6d. by the parish.

James Boyer, vicar, Richard Rickword junior, William Baden, churchwardens, J. Poore, Thomas Hunt, William Barnes, Richard White, Richard Rickword, overseer, John Bell overseer.

EVERLEIGH rectory

324   1 Oct 1662[1] (D1/24/89/1)

1yd. or a. of arable in W. Field butting upon William Monke's yard in Drove field. ½a. of arable in W. Field in the furlong called Short breach. 6a. of arable in Coopathe field 1 siding with Anthony Kinton, 1 with wid. Reynolds, 1 called Stone acre sides with Mr. George Reynolds another sides with wid. Reynolds and has a lawn on the other side, 1 more sides with wid. Reynolds and another with Mr. George Reynolds.

6½a. of arable in Middle E. Field, whereof 2a. side with Anthony Kinton in the Gatten, 1a. shoots down the highway and sides with wid. Reynolds, ½a. heads the same furlong and runs on N. side of Collingborne paths, ½a. butts against Bottom Croft, another ½a. butts upon Collingborne way another ½a. in the furlong called Shorthitchings siding with Anthony Kinton, another ½a. which is headland called Broad Half butting on Collingborn field, 1a. sides with William Prater.

5½a. in N. E. field whereof 1a. butts upon the park and sides with Anthony Kinton, ½a. sides with wid. Reynolds, 1a. sides with William Prater butting on Hartford way, 1a. in the same furlong sides with wid. Reynolds, 1a. that shoots out upon Goare Down and sides with wid. Reynolds, 1a. butting upon the stone, sides with Francis Fisher. Total 18a. 3yd. 1 orchard, 1 small garden, 1 little parcel of meadow, ½a. on S. side of the house.

Thomas Ernle, rector, Francis Fisher, churchwarden, Edward Gale, Richard Monk, sidesmen.

1. A note in the parish register by John Barnstone, rector, 9 Sep 1610, records the 'custom that the parson should cut the tithe corn that grows on the ancient arable land of the farm (being as they said 8 or 9 yardlands). Which custome I also consented unto and though the present farmer to the king hath cut it some years yet I paid for the same' (WSRO 651/1).

325   28 Oct 1671 (D1/24/89/2)

Terrier given in after the 2nd visitation of bishop Seth. 6a. of arable in Coopath field. 6a. of arable in Middle E field. 5½a. of arable in N. Field. ¼a. of arable in W. Everleigh field bordering upon Drove field. ½a. of arable in W. Everleigh in the furlong called Shortbroach. Total 18a.

1 parcel of ground, ⅓a., on S. side of the house used for a rick barton. 1 small garden in the orchard bordering on the great farm. The keeping of 2 kine upon the down and warren according to the custom of the parish. The summering of 1 horse upon the down according to the custom and the keeping of a bull there likewise.

Thomas Ernle, rector, Thomas Gale, Edward Shadwell, churchwardens.

326   Nov 1705 (D1/24/89/3)

3yd. in W. Town field. In E. Town field 5½a. in N. Division, 4a., 4 x ½a. and 3yd. in Middle Division and 6a. in South Division, in all 19a.

The tenth part of all things that are titheable and that yield an increase as all sorts of grains roots, grass, apples, pears, plums.

2d. each year from everyone that is at age for Communicating, paid about Easter. As also are 1d. for every garden. The tithe eggs although no great exactness in tithing them is used. For calves sold the tenth penny; if reared ½d; if killed a shoulder; cow white 1d. a year each cow.

Exceptions: The tithe of coneys for which there has been no more paid by the year for this 15 years than 20 couple a year or 20s. in their stead at the choice of the parson. Nor can he learn for certain that more has ever been paid. The real value of the tithe is worth twice as much. It is said that 30s. nay 40s. has been paid. The present incumbent has never had tithe of honey and when he demanded it he was answered with it never has been paid.[1] The farm pays no tithe of wood for what is spent on the farm only for what is spent other which is sold. The farm is allowed for cutting the tenth ridge in the old arable in the farm field (not for what is cut any where else upon the Parks, etc.[2] which comes to about 40s. a year; sometimes less but often more).

Walter Garrett, rector, Thomas Knightman, churchwarden, the renter of the farm, Robert Mathews [X], churchwarden, the warrener.

1. The fall of each lamb is 2d. Added here but this is clearly not an exception and should be included with the tithes due.
2. An illegible note refers to the word(s) struck out between Parks and etc.

327   1783 (D1/89/4)

The parsonage house, courtyards and garden, 1a. 1r. An open piece of arable land, 19a. 2p. bounded by droveways N. and W., an enclosure called Pig Leaze S., land of John Summersby E. There is no modus or prescription everything pays tithe in kind.

The parsonage house is of timber and lath, tiled. The front rough cast, sash windows in front of the low rooms. A hall at entrance with a brick floor, a glass closet within it. A study papered, a common sitting parlour partly wainscotted and partly papered. A best parlour partly wainscotted and partly stuccoed. A butler's pantry; a china closet. 3 cellars, 4 bed chambers, a large garret over the hall, all the rooms ceiled papered and floored. A kitchen detached from the house and communicating thereto by a passage. Thatched brewhouse adjoining. A lumber room over the same. A large pantry, 2 bed chambers over the kitchen ceiled and floored. 3 stall stables brick and timber built. 1 other stable for farm horses. 1 wheat barn, 1 barley barn, 1 oat barn, a large carthouse. All the out-buildings are covered with thatch. The sides of the barns boarded. A small court in front of the house. Separated from the farm yard by a brick wall. The farm yard separated from the rick barton by the barns and open paling. The rick barton separated from the street by a dead hedge. The garden is fenced partly with mud-wall partly a brick wall. The whole in good and sufficient repair.

The furniture of the church: 3 bells, a stone font, a large church bible, a folio common prayer book, a crimson velvet pulpit cloth and cushion of the same. A communion table and green cloth and cushion, a folio common prayer book for the same. A silver flagon weight 36oz. inscription 'The gift of Mr. William Sweatman the 15th of July 1754'. A silver cup and cover 14oz. A silver plate 18oz. 7 dwt. 12 grains. A linnen cloth and napkin for the table, a surplice, a parish chest, a black cloth for burials. The church and churchyard contains *c.* ½a. and is fenced with posts and rails which are maintained by the lord of the manor. The church is repaired by the parishioners, the chancel by the rector. There are 3 pews in the chancel which belong to the rector. The same person serves the office of clerk and sexton appointed by the rector, his pay is by custom 8d. for every yardland at Easter and 3s. for burials and 2s. for marriages. Easter offerings: 2d. a head from all persons upwards of 16 years of age to the rector. There is payable out of the living a pension of £2 p. a. to his Majesty on 10th October[1] and a freehold quit rent of 4d. payable to the lord of the manor yearly.

Taken by Basil Cane, rector, witnessed by Samuel Starky D. D., curate, James Gibbs, John Chandler, churchwardens, F. D. Ashley, John Carr, Thomas Palmer, principal inhabitants.

1.   Everleigh was an estate of the duchy of Lancaster until the mid 17th. cent. and was thus associated with the crown. The significance of the date is not clear.

MONKTON FARLEIGH rectory

328   n. d. late 16th. cent. (D1/24/90/1)
14a. arable land in the fields; 8a. in several of pasture; 2 orchards, a garden, and a backside of *c.* ½a.; the church hay, ½a.; the parsonage house with the barn.

329   1608 (D1/24/90/2)
1 mansion house with 3 fields, 1 barn with a stable, 1 orchard with the churchyard. 8a. of pasture. 8a. of arable in S. field. 6a. of arable in W. field.

Lewis Jones, rector, George Grant, Richard Gaile, churchwardens, George Bakar, John Woodard with others. *Names all written by the rector.*

330   2 Jun 1625 (D1/24/90/3)
Terrier according to the 12th article concerning the church enquired of at the visitation of bishop John at Devizes on the said date.

1 mansion house containing 8 several rooms, 1 barn, 1 stable, 1 orchard, 2 gardens, 1 hopyard with 9a. of pasture ground adjacent called Inoxe.

In the Upper field, 3a. in W. part of the field. 1a. 1yd. in the same field abutting on 3yd. of Mr. William King at a place called Ashwell furlong. 2 x ½a. abutting on the Parsons Inoxe. 3yd. abutting on 1a. of Overlands in the possession of Walter Graunt, 1a. abutting upon Inoxe.

In the Lower field ½a. shooting towards W. field. 1a. abutting on a pasture ground of Den Meades 1a. 1yd. abutting upon Green mead. ½a. abutting on a meadow of Roger Baker. 2a. abutting on the same meadow. 1a. lying on the lowest part of the said field. 1a. abutting on a furlong of Mr. William King. ½a. shooting upon Rough lease.

1 coppice and the borders belonging to the rectory, c. 5a., abutting on the Haies and upon the ground of John Woodward called Little field. The tithes of Pound close and Paddoxe and of the land in the tenure of wid. Druce and her son Anthony Druce belong of right to the parsonage. The tithe of Rogers, Chandlers grove and Pitmans belong of right to the rectory.

George Grante, William Baker [X], churchwardens, Roger Baker, John Woodard [X], Anthony Baker [X], John Butler.

331   18 Feb 16[. . .][1] (D1/24/90/4)
1 mansion house of 4 fields of building, a stable of 1 field adjoining. The churchyard, 3yds. The orchard gardens and bartons, ½a. 2 pasture grounds called the Innox adjoining the rectory, 8½a. In the common field called Overfield, 6a. In the common field called Netherfield, 8½a. 1 coppice of underwood, 4a.

By me Lewis Jones, rector; William Kinge, John Wodward [X], churchwardens.

1.   Lewis Jones was rector 1606-1639.

332   4 Dec 1671 (D1/24/90/5)
1 parsonage house, 1 stable, 1 barn containing about 2 bays of building with earthen thrashing floor, 1 small cow house adjoining to it. 1 garden on E. of the dwelling house, adjoining the churchyard. 1 backside and churchyard bounded with a stone wall. 1 enclosed ground called Innoxe or Inoss, c. 8a., on S. side of the churchyard and parsonage backside.

1 wood grove or coppice [cops], c. 5a., bounded with a ground called Hays on N. and E., John Grant's land on W.; c. 3a. of arable land in the Upper field towards the down part of which lie under Mr. King's conygar stone wall and goes in length E. and W. At the W. end of it there is a small parcel of glebe that goes N. and S. Another part goes E. and W. in the same furlong under Mr. Kings wall; only 3 x ½a. of wid. Baker's lying between them. The rest of the arable glebe lies in the upper side of this field bounded by John Grant's land N., which is partly arable and partly not, being ancient tilepit [tilepite], bounded by land of John Grant, W. and some land of Nathanial Harris on S. Non arable land in the same field, being ancient tilepit, c. 1a., having on N. side the ground called Downestille part of wid. Baker's living.

In the Lower field c. 8 x or 9 x ½a., 3 of which lie by the footpath called Green meare and go in length N. and S., bounded at N. end by wid. Denmeade's enclosed ground called the Grippe and by Nathanial Harris' field land on W., another 3 of which butt on the same way lying lower in the field, ½a. butting that way, between both of these lie 1a. of wid. Walter's field land, both of these are bounded on N. end by James Bassat's meadow called Tinning mead. 1 tenant a. in the lowest part of Lower field bounded by John Grant's enclosed land E. and S. and by some of this field land on W.; ½a. butting N. and S. having Bath road and Mr. Watson's cowlease on N. end and William Cottle's field land on W. and Nathanial Harris on E. 1a. butting E, W. and every 2nd year the way to the parson's coppice and several other grounds lie along, bounded on W. side with the footpath of green meare.

John Hinly, James Butler, churchwardens, Thomas Coppe.

333   30 May 1705 (D1/24/90/6)
A parsonage house, barn, stable, and other outhouses. An orchard, a garden and a backside adjoining. Innex, c. 8a. 5½a. in the Upper field and the feeding of 16 sheep when the field lies fallow. 10a. in the Lower field and the feeding of 30 sheep when the field lies fallow. A coppice of 6a. which the inhabitants say given in lieu of tithe wood for which they pay no tithe wood. The greatest part being the bishop's land none of the demesnes pay any sort of tithe to the rector only an annual rent to the bishop.

Copyholds and leaseholds pay all sorts of tithes to the rector, as hay, corn, small tithes as fruit, calves, lambs, wool, cow white, pigs, bees and colts, also offerings, oblations mortuaries and all other tithes except tithe wood. Note of the grant of an augmentation to the rectory of £10 p. a. by bishop Gilbert with extract from the lease, but giving no details.[1]

Thomas Sartain, rector, Henry Stallard, churchwarden, Thomas Sartain, collector of the tithes [*not the rector*].

1.   The earliest extant lease of the manor by bp. Gilbert Burnet, 29 Sept. 1697, mentions the payment of this sum to augment the benefice (WSRO 866/1).

FIGHELDEAN rectory and vicarage

334   10 Jul 1634 (D26/4/1)
Rectory: In Knighton: In the S. field 2a. lying E. and W. between a piece of 2a. of Mr. Linche on one side and the long ½a. of Mr. Linche on the other.

In the Middle field 9a. (in 3 pieces; 3a. in a piece); the lower 3 between a piece of 4a. of Mr. Linche on E. and a piece of 3a. on W. The next piece between a piece of 5a. of Mr. Linche on the one side and a piece of Mr. Poore on the other side, and the other 3a. in the same furlong lying between a piece of 4a. of Mr. Linche on the upper side and a piece of 3a. on the lower.

In the N. field 4a. in 2 several pieces; the lower 2a. lying between a piece of 3a. of Summerfield of Mr. Linche on one side and a piece of 2a. of Mr. Poore on the other side; the other 2a. lie on the side of the last 2a. of Mr. Poore and have 1a. of Mr. Poore on the other side: In the Ham in several 6a. And a little close of pasture lying next Mr. Linches Mup[...] on E. side and a close of Mr. Poore on the other side, on the S. side Durrington field and on N. side the lane. 66 sheep leazes and all other tithes (except the offerings).

In Figheldean: A barn and backside, *c.* ½a.; a meadow running from the backside to the river, 1a.; a little meadow called the Marsh lying by the great bridge and a plot of meadow on the N. side of Newton and the river on the N. side of it.

In the fields of arable: The N. field, 7a., by estimation 3 several a., in Nordean Bottom ending one upon another, the Nordean linchet on N. side; ½a. at the Cleeve end; 3 x ½a. at the end of him, 1a. of Goodman Pollerne on the one side and the wid. Moggridge on the other side; a picked a. lying between 1a. of John Joel on N. E. and James Lawrence on the other end; 1a. lying between 1a. of the wid. Smart on N. and 1a. of Nicholas Subdean S.

In the Middle field, 29a., the upper 2a. lying between 1a. of the wid. Moggridge on E. and 1a. of Richard Pollerne on W.; 2a. the other side of Richard Pollerne's a. westward and 1a. of Richard Pollerne on E.; 1a. lying between 1a. of Richard Jackman on E. and Richard Pollerne on W.; 1a. Richard Pollerne's 2a. on one side and wid. Smart on the other; 1a. lying between 1a. of Richard Jackman on N. and the wid. Moggridge on S.; ½a. lying between 1a. of the wid. Moggridge on S. and 1a. of the wid. Holmes and Peter Story on the other side; 1a. lying between 2a. of farmland on N. and a piece of Rumbol's on S.; 3a. lying between 1a. of the wid. Smart on N. and a piece of Rumbol's on S.; 1a. lying between 2a. of John Muggridge on N. and 1a. of Nicholas Subdean S.; ½a. between John Joell N. and Richard Jackman S.; 2a. between 2a. of Richard Jackman S. and Richard Pollerne on N.; 1a. between 1a. of farm land on N. and the wid. Holmes on S.; 1a. between 1a. of Richard Jackman on each side of it; 1a. lying on N. side of the Shard way and ½a. of the wid. Holmes on N.; 3a. lying athwart the church path Pollernes way being on S. and the wid. Moggridge's 2a. on N.; a ham of 8a. lying by the vicarage orchard and shooting upon Pollernes Crafts.

In the S. field, 9a.; 4a. lying between 1a. of the wid. Smart on N. and 1a. of the wid. Moggeridge on S.; 1a. in Benfield between Richard Pollerne on W. and Richard Jackman on E.; 1a. ?across [Cross] Ludgershall way Richard Jackman W.; ½a. on Sherborough, 1a. of Richard Jackman S. the wid. Smart on N.; 2a. between 2a. of the same land on N. and 1a. of Richard Jackman on S.

100 sheep leazes in the town flock and all tithe corn and hay of Choulston [Cholson] and tithe hay in the N. meadow; tithe of all the corn of Figheldean and tithe of Ivy [*mead*] lying on N. side of the river and 2d. per a. for Norton meads and all tithe corn in Ablington tithes of Mr. Longe's Lewe and tithe of Edmund Cooper's croft and Mr. Longe's ham when they are cut and tithe of the Pyer mead and common mead. All tithe corn on Syrencott [Sissencot] and the tithe of Syrencot mead.

Vicarage: The dwelling house, a barn, a stable, and a little orchard and the churchyard. Tithe wool and lamb of Choulston, Figheldean, Ablington and Syrencott. Tithe of all dry ground and the parsonage marsh and tithe hay of all meadows between Figheldean and Ablington and tithe of the court mead and the court close belonging to Mr. Gifford Longe. Easter offerings.

All small tithes of Choulston, Figheldean and Syrencott and 40s. p. a. from the King for Alton and the Easter offerings and the tithes of gardens, cow white and calves of both Altons and the offerings of Knighton and a groat for each yardland at Easter of Figheldean, Ablington and Syrencott.

John Lee, rector, George Pitt, vicar, Richard Jackman, John Cooper, churchwardens, Anthony Shiflin, George Holmes, sidesmen, Thomas Sheappard, tenant to the parsonage, Edmund Coopar, John Joell [X], William Holmes [X], Jaspar Remboll [X].

FIFIELD BAVANT rectory

334A   29 Jul 1608 (D1/24/91/1)
The backside, ½a., about the house and barn. 20a. of arrable land in the field; 6a. in E. field, 8a. in Middle field, 5a. in W. field. Pasture for 60 sheep with the farm flock upon the downs and fields of Fifield. Common of pasture for 6 rother beasts with the herd in the fields and downs according to their custom. All tithes.
    Thomas Ingram, churchwarden, Thomas Coles, rector. *Names in the same hand.*

FISHERTON ANGER rectory

335   20 May 1588 (D1/24/92/1)
8a. in the hands of Thomas Pratt. 4 beast leazes in the common according to the custom. 3 x ½a. of meadow. A several mead of pasture in the hands of Thomas Pratt valued at 40s. p. a. 1 little dwelling house valued at 6s. 8d. p. a.

336   25 May 1638 (D1/24/92/2)
The dwelling house, barn, stable, orchard, garden and backside, *c.* 1a.; Rackeclose, 2a. 8a. of arable in the common fields: 3a. in Lower field upon Wilton way; upon the N., 1a.; in the furlong next the church 3a. from Church acre exchanged with Thomas Sadler esq., for a certain time yet to come; 1a. in Lower field next the drove hedge; 1a. shooting down upon Wilton way upon S. end; 2a. in N. field, the one butting on the plashetts, the other against 1a. of the said Mr. Sadler near a place called Cole Harbour; 3 x ½a. of meadow or pasture at Cole Harbour near the Plashetts. 2a. of pasture taken out of the common marsh together with 2a. belonging to Dades hold. 6 beast leazes in the common fields.
    Philip Laversuch [X], Thomas Biggs, churchwardens.

FISHERTON DELAMERE vicarage

337   n. d. late 16th cent. (D1/24/93/1)[1]
29a. called a yardland of arable land in the common fields. 1a. of meadow ground in the common mead. 1a. of meadow called Paradise lying in several. ½a. of tithing hay in the common mead of Fisherton in the common mead of Bapton and in Banmeade in the parish of Norton [*Bavant*]. All the tithe [tithing] hay of the hamlets below the street that goes through Fisherton. The tithe of orchards and garden plots. Tithe hay in Bapton of all the hamlets between the moor and

Bapton Street which is 3 hams. The closes, hamlets and orchards on W. side of the way to Hindon except 2 closes of Henry Eyles. All the orchards and gardens of Fisherton and Bapton.

The middle plot in Brymel close. Tithe wool, lambs, calves, pigs, geese, eggs, apples, 1d. for every garden, cow white, 12 bushells of tithe corn from the mill viz. 1 bushell of wheat and 1 bushell of malt to be paid quarterly. Tithe corn of 1½yd. lying above the town in Bapton. 24 tithe pigeons out of the farm pigeon house.

3 horse leazes and for 3 beasts and a breeder. Offerings throughout the whole year at Easter. Half the tithe hay in Pill mead. 60 sheep leaze at winter, 60[2] in the common mead and 20 in the common called the Moor.

John Heky, Rynalde Eyles, Thomas Rebuke, Richard Inguoram, John Wanbery, Harry Snelgar, John Andrew, William Easson, Thomas Foster, with other men.

1. Written on the back of a section of the court roll of the common court of Salisbury, 1531-2.
2. ?Recte 40. The number is written vi[ti] in the text and is probably a mistake for iv[ti] (40).

338   n. d. late 16th cent.[1] (D1/24/93/2)
As **339** with amendments in footnotes. The vicar or deputy saying a prayer or gospel on Tuesday in Procession week in the mills at or by the wheat bin is to have to his own use one cake and a penny for his labour, as some have said the cake is certainly known.

Joel Doughty, vicar and writer; William Eyles alias Hix, Henry Rebuke, churchwardens, with a few rather than many [*Cum alliis quare plurimis*].

1. Joel Doughty was vicar 1595-1613.

339   10 Jul 1605 (D1/24/93/3)
A mansion or dwelling house, a barn, a stable,[1] a cowhouse,[2] an old pigeon house, 1a. of ground called Paradise; 1a. in the town mead;[3] 2a. of ground taken out of the marsh next to Bapton fields; 30a. of arable land in Fisherton fields with the tenants. Commons for 60 sheep in the fields and downs, for 3 horses, 3 kine, and a rearer[4] at the breach of the fields. Half of the tithe of the tithing hay with the impropriate parsonage in 4 places viz. in Fisherton town and mead, in Bapton town mead[5] and in Pilmead[6] belonging to Fisherton farm. Half of the tithe [tithing] hay of 10a. in Banne mead with the impropriate parsonage lying between Heytesbury [Hatchbury] and Norton Bavant. Tithe hay of the overlands and hams adjoining the river in Fisherton and in Bapton. Tithe hay in the marsh. 12 bushels of toll [towle] corn at Fisherton mill, viz. 6 bushells of wheat and 6 bushells of malt, each paid in 1 bushell amounts every Quarter. Tithe corn of 5yd. of ground in Bapton fields near to the smith's house[7] if it is sown. Tithe wool and lambs in the parish of Fisherton and Bapton. Oblations, purifyings and weddings. Cow white and calves; tithe swans if any fall within the lordship, bees, apples, pears [wardens] and all small tithes whatsoever as geese and pigs with suchlike.[8]

Joel Doughtie, clerk and vicar, John Ingram, William Passion junior, churchwardens, John Slade, William Eyles alias Hix, Samuel Forster, George Hodder with others. *Names in the vicar's hand.*

1. A little house by the stable door included in **338**.
2. Described as a new cow house erected on S. end of the old pigeon house by Joel Doughty vicar in **338**.
3. Common mead in **338**.
4. Or a weaned calf or bullock and common throughout Fisherton for 1 yardland as for other tenants added in **338**.
5. Bapton common mead in **338**.
6. Omitted in **338**.
7. House of Edward James in **338**.
8. Tithes hops, honey, wax, pigeons and marriage money added in **338**.

340   4 Nov 1671 (D1/24/93/4)
31a.[1] of arable called a yardland in the common fields. 1a. of mead called Paradise lying in several. 1a. in the common mead of Fisherton. Half of the tithe [tithing] hay in the common meads of Fisherton and of Bapton, of Bannmead belonging to Fisherton farm and lying in Norton Bavant and of Pilmead. Whole tithe hay of the hamlets, orchards and garden plots[2] beneath the street that goes through Fisherton and of the hams and grounds called the Home closes and orchards on N and W sides of the street in Bapton.

All the tithes of orchards and gardens in Fisherton and Bapton. The whole tithe of the meadow called Brimble close[3] in Bapton. Tithe wool, lamb, calves, pigs and all other private tithes. 12 bushells of tithing corn out of the mill viz. 1½ bushells of wheat and 1½ bushells of malt to be paid quarterly. Tithe corn of half of 5yd. of arable belonging to Robert Haytor[4] lying against the leap gate in Bapton. Commons of pasture for 60 sheep on the fields and downs in Fisherton and for 6 sheep in the common mead at winter. Commons of pasture for 3 horses, 3 beats, and 1 breader in all commonable places with the tenants in Fisherton.

2a. of pasture in the Marshes being in several against Bapton fields. A dwelling house barn and stable.[5] 24 tithe pigeons out of the farm pigeon house in Fisherton.

Robert Wansbury, John Rebeck [X], churchwardens, Henry Pearson, John Ingram, Edward Green.

1. 30a. in **342**.
2. Described as the Home closes in **341**.
3. Belonging to farmer Davis in **341** and to Bapton farm in **342**.
4. Belonging to Haytor's tenement in **342**.
5. With garden and backside in **341**.

341   10 Sep 1680 (D1/24/93/5)
Terrier taken by Richard Ingram and Richard Wansbury, churchwardens. *As **340** with amendments in footnotes but omitting all references to commons of pastures for animals.*

342 15 Jan 1705 (D1/24/93/6)

As *340* with amendments in footnotes. Commons of pasture for all manner of cattle according to the number, usage and custom of 1 yardland. The impropriate parsonage has no right to any of the tithes on the land or meadow belonging to the vicarage.

William Wansbrough, John Eyles [X], Francis Turvile junior, overseer, Fras. Turvile, vicar, writer of the terrier, by whom the vicarage has been let for £30 p. a.

FITTLETON with Haxton [Hackleston] rectory

343 1629 (D1/24/94/1)

A house containing hall, parlour, kitchen, brew house, bakehouse, pantry, 2 cellars, wool house, and 11 upper rooms and chambers. Without doors: 3 barns, 2 stables, 2 cow-houses, a hog sty, well house, and a hovel for wood; an orchard with a little house adjoining the end of it, garden, backside, and meadow, 2a. in all. Edward Pyle S., Leonard Stapelhorne N. A dry close of ground, ½a., between Thomas Bushell W. and Edmund Rumsey E.

Arable in the Summer field: a furlong at the Mile Ball abutting Haxton field, 7a.; 4½a. near Greenway in the Summerfield and 16a. in the field called Warrborough by Coombe side.

In the Home field: 6a. in the field called Blissemore; 5a. in a furlong called Hitching; 2a. on Norridge; 3a. in Redland shooting on Haxton field; 1a. at Sparrow bush; 2yd. by the waterside. Common of pasture for 80 sheep, 6 rother beasts, and 4 houses belonging to that 2 yardlands of glebe.

Tithe corn, grain, and hay in Haxton and Fittleton and all other tithes as wool, lambs, and all privy tithes; from 12 yardlands of the farm of Haxton only a third of the tithe wool and lambs, all other tithes, but no tithe corn of any grain except a rudge of barley and a rudge of oats out of the farm.

William Jeaye, rector, Robert Rolfe, John Soop junior [X], Thomas Boshell [X], Thomas Clark, Robert Hart, Thomas Rolfe [X], Jacob Bromham [X], Thomas Diper, Robert Butler.

344 22 Apr 1676 (2094/1)

Terrier taken by Dr. Henry Edes from John Carter and Thomas Biffen, inhabitants. Copied into the parish register by Roger Kay, 15 Jan 1694. As *345* with amendments in footnotes.

345 6 Mar 1705 (D1/24/94/2)

A large parsonage house consisting of a hall, 2 parlours, a kitchen, a pantry, a buttery, 2 cellars, 8 chambers besides closets and garrets. A brewhouse, woodhouse and a summerhouse in the garden, all in good repair.

A meadow, 1a. 1r., adjoining the garden and backside. A little close of pasture, c. 20 lugs, near Benjamin Hart's[1] house, Thomas Carter E., Hart[1] W.

2 yardlands in the common fields, formerly with 40 sheep leaze to a yardland, but since the breaking up of the down, reduced, with all the tenants, to 32 to a

yardland. Commons for 2 cows and a bullock to each yardland. A particular of the land in the common fields: In Sparrow Bush field; 1a., Mr.[2] Edes land belonging to Piper's living W., late Hart[3] now Mr.[2] Edes E.; in Redland furlong, 1a., Mr. Beach W., Mr. Edes late Bushell[4] E.; 1½a., John Bromham W., Robert Sopp[5] E.; 1a., Sopp[5] E., Mr.[2] Edes late Piper W.; a head a shooting E. and W. that is headland to Redland furlong.

In Milehall field; 2a. in the lower part of the field, John Bromham W., Mr. Edes late Hart[3] E.; ½a. that shoots on Mileball; ½a. next to Haxton field, except ½a. of Mr.[2] Edes; 1a. above Mileball, John Bromham W., Mr.[2] Edes E.; 1a. that crosses the way, the S. end being a headland; 1a. across the way, Mr. Beach on S. W.; 1a. Mr. Beach on S. W., John Bromham on N. E.

In Greenway field; the lower 2a., Mr. Edes late Piper[6] W., Edmund Hulbert[7] E.; 2½a. in the same furlong, the lower end is headland to E. and Mr. Beach on W.; ½a. by Greenway side. In Norridge furlong; 1a., Jeffrey Lovegrove W., Edmund Hulbert[7] E.; 1a., John Bromham on W., Benjaman Hart[1] E.; in Scales furlong; 1a., Sopp[5] on both sides. In Hitching furlong,; 1a., Mr. Edes late Hart[3] W., John Ivy[8] E.; 2a., Richard Sopp[9] W., Mr.[2] Edes late Piper E.; 1a., John Bromham W., Sopp[5] E.; ½a., Mr. Beach W., Mr.[2] Edes E.; ½a., Mr. Edes on both sides[10]; ½a. that shoots E. and W., Benjaman Hart[1] on both sides. In Broadland furlong; ½a. picked, Sopp[5] S., Mr. Edes[6] N.; 1a., Mr. Edes late Piper[6] W. and Mr. Carter[11] E.; ½a. Mr. Beach N., Mr. Edes late Piper[6] S. In Blissmore Bottom 1a. Mr. Edes[12] on both sides; 1a.[13] Robert Sopp[5] S., Mr. Edes late wid. Hart[3] N.; 1a., half of it headland, Mr. Edes[14] S., Mr. Beach on N.; ½a. between the linches that shoot upon the Summerfield, Mr. Edes on both sides.[12]

In Ashball furlong; ½a. John Bromham S., Robert Sopp N.; 2a. Mr. Edes late Piper[2] S., John Ivy N. In Ashball bottom; ½a. Mr. Beach W., Mr. Edes[3] E.; 1a. Mr. Edes E. and W. The Butt half, Robert Sopp[5] S., John Bromham N. In Twelve acre furlong; 1a. Richard Sopp[15] S., Mr. Edes[14] N. In Tenantry furlong; 1a. Mr. Edes[16] N. and S.; 1a. that shoots upon Everley way, Edmund Hulbert[17] W., Mr. Beach E.; a head a. Mr. Beach N.

In Cowpath; 2a. John Bromham on both sides; ½a. that shoots on Cowpath, Mr. Edes[2] N. and S. *This land is included in Walborough field in* **344.**

In Walborough field; 2a. that shoot on crooked land[18], John Bromham N., Mr.[2] Edes S.; ½a. John Bromham S., Edmund Hulbert[7] N.; 1a. that shoots upon Combfield, Mr. Beach E., John Bromham W.; ½a. John Bromham E., Edmund Hulbert[7] W., ½a. near Sopps Croft, Comb footpath W., Sopp[5] E. Total 46a.

All sorts of great and small tithes in the parish of Fittleton and Haxton except a portion of tithes impropriated out of Mr. Clerk's farm in Haxton.

The rectory is endowed with the tithe of 57a. of land part of Mr. Clark's farm aforesaid, commonly called Odd land, lying dispersed in the common fields of Haxton, not more than 2a. in any one place. Namely in the Little Gaston, 3a., in the furlong next to Fittleton, 3a., in the Summerfield next to Fittleton, 5a., in the Great Gaston, 1a., in the Bottom furlong, 6a., in the same bottom in the Summerfield 6a., in the furlong against Staple Crosshill, 4a., in Shortland furlong, head and crooked land, 14a., in the Summerfield 2a. These lands are attested by Robert Rolfe who was farmer of the Farm.

At Easter 2d. for offerings from every person over 16 years. 6d. due from every woman that is churched. 2s. 6d. for every marriage without licence. The herbage of the churchyard. Tithe lambs,[19] pigs, pigeons, apples and honey in kind. 6d. for every cow and calf. 2d. for every thorough white cow. 1d. for eggs. 1d. for every garden of herbs. Tithe hay growing upon Mr. Clerk's farm in Haxton except Millmead and Airesmead, a third part of wool and lamb, the other two parts are claimed by the impropriator but by what right we know not.

R oger Kay, rector, Robert Rolfe, John Tackle [X], churchwardens, Wiliam Beach, Leonard Mundy.

1. Bushell in **344**.
2. Dr. Edes late Piper in **344**.
3. Wid. Hart in **344**.
4. Wid, Bushell in **344**.
5. John Sopp in **344**.
6. Piper in **344**.
7. John Hulbert in **344**.
8. William Barton in **344**.
9. William Barton late Rumsey in **344**.
10. Piper W., wid. Hart E. in **344**.
11. John Carter in **344**.
12. John Hulbert N., wid. Hart S. in **344**.
13. Described as in another furlong in **344**.
14. Dr. Edes late Bushell in **344**.
15. Rumsey in **344**.
16. Wid. Hart S., Dr. Edes N. in **344**.
17. Described as 1a. in Sheephouse furlong, John Hulbert W., Mr. Beach E. in **344**.
18. Crooked land furlong in **344**.
19. A note by Stephen Kay, rector, in the parish register records that he agreed to accept 2½d. a lamb or 2s. 1d. for the tenth lamb 'if I had taken them up in kind they had been worth more, my successor may do as he pleases', 25 Apr. 1662. The same was agreed by John Buckenham, rector, 25 Apr. 1692 (WSRO 2094/1).

346   4 Dec 1718 (D1/24/94/3)[1]

Since the terrier [**345**] was lodged in the bishop's registry in 1705 part of it has become useless because the owners of the capital farm of Haxton for which the tithe corn is impropriate have at several times since then purchased land in Haxton for which the tithe corn belongs to the rectory. These lands called Oddlands are no part of the farm and should be distinct. In 1711 an exchange was made of a furlong which was impropriate with one which was not. This new terrier is necessary to prevent any dispute between the rector and impropriator.

All tithe hay with a third of the tithe wool and lamb on the capital farm of Haxton now in the possession of Abraham Gapper esq., belong to the rectory together with all other small tithes. All tithe corn and two thirds of tithe wool and lamb of the said farm are impropriate and belong to Henry Edes esq. These were the endowment of a free chapel of Haxton and are called the Portionary.

The farm land whose tithe is impropriate can be easily known from land which is not because it lines in great pieces of many a. in the common fields of Haxton and is bounded with linches. The land which is not impropriate, which belongs to the owner of the farm and is occupied by the same tenant, lies dispersed in several furlongs in the tenantry common fields. Some a. are joined to the farm land and are only separated by a linch. These linches should not be plowed up by the tenant but should remain as perpetual boundaries to distinguish the farm land from that which is not.

Lands belonging to the owner of the capital farm in Haxton of which the tithe belongs to the rectory: The Cleeve piece, separated from the farm land by a linch, 3a.; the side of Cleev hill, 2a.; headland to Cleev hill furlong, 2a.; in Oland furlong, 2a., ½a., 1½a.; the Peeks, ½a.; in Great Linch furlong, 1½a., ½a.; ? in Shortland furlong, 2a., a linched a. (1a.), 2a., 2a., 2a.; in Half furlong, 1a., 1a.; in Picked land furlong, 1a., ½a.; in the Great Gasson, separated from the E. side by a small linch, 1½a.; in Larden, 1a., a headland, 1a.; under Red linch; ½a.; Little ?Barton, 1½a., 2a. 1a.; in the Little Gasson, 2a.; in the furlong that shoots upon Fittleton Bullen, 1a., 2a., ½a.; in Cutlinch furlong, 1½a.; under Cutted linch, 1a.; Stanch hill 2a., 1½a., separated from the farmland on the E. side of a linch; next Fittleton Greenway, 1a.; in the Upper Bottom, 2a.; in Carret land, 1a.; in Goos land, 2a.; Hardenhill, 1a., 1a., separated from the farm land on the W. side by a linch; at Breach, 1a., 3a., bought by Mr. Clerk of Robert Petty, 1a., that was Samson's; in the Upper Berry the Portionary half a. of which the rector always had the tithe, 1a., bought of Mr. Beach by Mr. Gapper. Total 62½a. 1yd.

In 1711 Mr. Hen. Clerke, late owner of the capital farm in Haxton, exchanged with Sir Richard How and his tenants in Haxton a furlong of farm land called Broadland and other lands for a furlong of tenantry land called Whiteditch. Despite the exchange the tithes remain unchanged. The bounds of Whiteditch shoot upon the highway on N., separated from the farm lands by linches on E. W and S. Broadland is bounded on E. by a linch having 2a. belonging to Mr. Joseph Barton on E., and 1a. of his on W., which a. is the furthest a. of the farmland in Broadland to the E. On W. it is bounded with a linch, next to which is an a. belonging to Nathanial Manning, which is the hithermost farmland in Broadland to the W. so that the tithe corn of Mr. Barton's a. to E. and of the ½a. of Nathanial Manning to W. and of all the furlongs between, belong to the Portionary or impropriators, although in the hands of the tenant.

Broadland is not as extensive as Whiteditch but to make it equal Mr. Clark parted with some of his Oddlands with the tenants, Mr. Barton, Robert Rolfe, Richard Piper, Thomas Lawes etc., which Oddlands always paid tithe to the rector and are none of the abovementioned lands. Mr. Clerk had 2a. in Whiteditch of his own before the exchange, 1a. bought of Robert Petty the other of Thomas Adams.

In order that the bounds are better known and may not be extended beyond, the rector has caused 2 great stones to be placed in the ground next to the highway against the E. and W. sides of Broadland. Both the furlongs have been exactly measured by Henry Reeves. Whiteditch contains 15a. 27p. 6ft., Broadland 10a. 2p. The rector has been careful both as to the Oddlands and to the exchange. He knows through long experience that most of the details are true and for the rest he has taken the best information from the most ancient inhabitants of Haxton.

Roger Kay, rector, William Piper, Soloman Ranger, churchwardens, Thomas Lawes, Thomas Rolfe, John Truckle [X], John Ivy senior, Richard Piper. 3 Feb 1719 this terrier was exhibited in the bishop's registry.

1. This terrier is stitched to **345**.

347 n. d. [1783][1] (D1/24/94/4)
1. Brick built parsonage house covered with brick and tile. The house has 11 rooms, all floored with elm except 2 floored with brick. They are ceiled with lath and plaster. The parlour is wainscotted with walnut. The outhouses are a back kitchen, 3 large barns built with boards and covered with strawthatch, 60ft. long, 50ft. long and 30ft. long, a large stable for 6 hourses and a stalled stable for 1 horse.
    2. 34a. of arable, bounded by land of Michael Beach esq. 1a. of pasture bounded by a dead hedge separating it from land of Michael Beach esq. Commons of pasture for 66 sheep and 4 cows. A kitchen garden c. 20 lugs, bounded by a mud wall. A large barken and rick yard fenced with a mud wall, An ancient yew tree in the churchyard and c. 4 pollarded withies in the 1a. of pasture glebe.
    3. Great and small tithes on all the lands in the parish except the farm of Robert Crapper esq. in Haxton which owes a third of the tithe hay, sheep, lamb and wool.
    4. The only gift to the church is the benefaction of the late Henry Clarke esq., of 10s. and 6s. 8d. for the preaching of 2 sermons upon 19 Dec. and St. Stephen's day [26 Dec or 3 Aug] by the minister for the time being.
    5. Nothing relates to the rectory.
    6 Church furniture; 1 communion table and cloth, 1 surplice, 1 bible, 1 large prayer book, 5 bells. Communion plate; a flagon with the inscription 'Deo & Ecclesiae de Fittleton Rogerus Kay A. M. Rector dedicavit An. Dom. 1720'. 18 oz. 10 dwt, 1 large chalice with the same dedication as above, 12 oz. 10 dwt, 1 small chalice without any inscription, 1 gilt cup with the inscription 'The gifte of Mr. Robert Johnson sometymes Parson of Fittleton in the county of Wilts'.
    7. There are no lands for the repairs of the church. The landholders are charged with repairs of the church and churchyard fence.
    8. The clerk is paid 4d. from every yardland.
    John Yeomans, curate, William Sutton, Thomas Harris, churchwardens.

1. The churchwardens were recorded in the bishop's visitation book, Jul 1783 (WSRO D1/50/30).

FONTHILL GIFFORD rectory

348 23 May 1670 (D1/24/95/1)
A dwelling house orchard and garden in Stop, a bigger barn and skilling on W. of the house, a little house used as a barn on E. of the house, a little stable on S. and a little meadow, formerly an orchard, all of which contains 2a.

A close called New field, 14a.; a little close called Midwinters coppice, 1½a.; Grove close, 1½a.; a close called Parsons croft, 3a.; an enclosed ground with a little coppice adjoining called Hatch lane close and coppice, 8a.; a close of pasture or meadow bordering in Berwick St. Leonard called Parson's close, 1½a.; a close of pasture or meadow also called Parsons Close, 2a., on which about 40 years ago 2 small cottages were erected which have ever since been leased by the parson.

The parson has commons of estover in 7a. in Hodways Coppice for which the lord of the manor, by an old composition, pays each Christmas 8 loads of wood[1] upon demand of the parson or £4 whichever the lord chooses. All things tithable within the perambulation of the parish except that for every cow 3d. and for every heifer or thorough milk cow 2d. is paid.

Robert Haysome, rector, Richard Andrews [X], Robert Waterman[X], churchwardens, Henry Clement, William Bisse [X], overseers, Anthony Sumner [X], old man and ancient inhabitant.

1.   Billet wood in **349** and **350**.

349   28 Sep 1671 (D1/24/95/2)
Terrier presented at the bishop's visitation. *As **349** with amendment in footnote.* Richard Andrews [X], Henry Clement, churchwardens.

350   14 Sept 1680 (D1/24/95/3)
Terrier presented at the visitation of bishop Seth. *As **348** with amendment in footnote.* Robert Haysome, rector, John Canteloe [X], Randolph Gartrill [X], churchwardens, Richard Andrew [X], Francis Barter [X], Richard Vowles [X], Henry Clement.

351   1704 (D1/24/95/4)
A close of meadow or pasture called New field, *c.* 20a., on S. side of the parsonage house. 1 close of meadow or pasture called Crate, 3a., on N. side of the parsonage house. 2 little closes of meadow or pasture, each 1½a., near Berwick Street. 1 close of meadow or pasture called Hatch lane, *c.* 6½a., adjoining Hatch lane. All these closes are valued at £20 p. a. All great and small tithes valued at £60 p. a.

Robert Olden, rector, Richard Gatrel, Thomas Powell, churchwardens. *Names in the same hand.*

FOVANT rectory

352   25 May 1588 (D1/24/96/1)
An inquisition and survey of the glebe lands and duties together with christenings weddings and funerals[1] which have been since Michaelmas 1585 unto this [*bishop's*] visitation presented by Thomas Vinsent and Thomas Caundle, church-wardens.

We present 34a. of glebe. 1a. in the common meadow. A mead adjoining the house with the close and orchard, 2a. 20a. of pasture grounds enclosed out of the common. A coppice in the Ivers, ½a. A cowshed [neate] with a garden. 68 sheep leaze to be kept in the common fields and downs of Fovant.

1. Not with the terrier or in the series of bishop's transcripts.

353 n. d. early 17th cent.[1] (D1/24/96/2)
A close adjoining the house with the orchard, c. 1½a.; 1a. of ground in Broad mead; a ground called the Haise, 12a.; a ground called the E. Close, c. 6a.
    In the fields of Fovant: 2½a. at a place called the Gate, William Candell E.;[2] 3a. adjoining the highway[3] in the furlong beneath; 1a. at a place called Ashen hedge; 1a. on Shrovehill; 2a. below that on the W. of Edward Feltham,[4] 2a. in Longland on the W. of Mr. Staples;[5] ½a. in that furlong on the W. of Nicholas Law;[6] 1a. on Church hill bounding on the farm land; 1a. below Barters Oak, William Dune[7] S.; 1a. in Stony dean, Mr. Staples[5] N.; 1a. on the W. of it, William Lucas[8] N.; 1 head a. of clay ground bounding on the farm land; ½a. bounding on the same land; 5½a. on Verne hill, 1a. in the Clay field bounding on the W. of Mr. Staples;[5] 1a. in that field bounding on the S. of Mr. Staples;[10] 1a. in the same field, William Dunn[10] S.; 2a. on Horrage; 1a. next to Long Hedge; 1a. in Mare furlong in the next field bounding on the W. of Richard Chapell,[11] ½a. shooting on Whyteridge mead; 2a. shooting on the farm land; 1 head a. to the farm field, William Candell[12] N.; and 1a. in the middle of the field, Ambrose Baker[13] W. Total of pasture mead and field 55a.
    Robert Moody, parson, and William Stronge [X] and Robert Marten [X], churchwardens.

1. Robert Moody was parson between 1554–1613 but the terrier is probably later than **352**.
2. 2a. at the end of the Slea Drove bounded Mathew Martin on E. in **354**.
3. The highway called Limber way in **354**.
4. 2a. below Shaftesbury way bounded on W. by Osmond Martin in 1705.
5. Mr. Waistfield in **354**.
6. Edward Nightingale in **354**.
7. Between wid. Elizabeth Down in **354**.
8. Edward Nightingale in **354**.
9. 5a. in **354**.
10. Elizabeth Donn in **354**.
11. George chapell in **354**.
12. Mathew Martin in **354**.
13. William Macy in **354**.

354 27 Jan 1705 (D1/24/96/3)
The parsonage house containing a kitchen, parlour, milk house, 2 butteries and abovestairs, 5 chambers. near the house 2 barns, 2 stables, a close with orchard and gardens, 3 x ½a. 1a. in Broad mead and E. close, c. 6a. *Land in the fields of Fovant as* **353** *with amendments in footnotes.*
    A small vicarage house next to wid. Ann Chappel. Ivar close, c. 1a. The mill pays 5s. to the rector. Total of pasture meadow and field 55a. ½a. of ground

called Broad mead drove. A large silver bowl to give sacramental wine given by Mr. William Wastfield and Aled, his wife. A less silver chalice or covered bowl with a large pewter flagon bason and plate. 3 bells.

Robert Cary, rector, John Dier, James Mould, churchwardens, David Feltham, Thomas Carpenter.

FOXLEY rectory

355   13 Oct 1608 (D1/24/97/1)
S. Field; Blackwell furlong, 15a., each a. worth 3s. p. a. Lassyndon mead, 5a., each a. worth 3s. p. a. An arable ground called Rutchill, 16a., each a. worth 3s. p. a. A ground of meadow and pasture called Wanslade, 6a., each a. worth 10s. p. a. ½a. near Foxley heath.

N. Field: A ground of meadow and pasture called Kingslade, 4a., each a. worth 10s. p. a.

The Croft adjoining the parsonage house, 3½a,. each a. worth 3s. Total 50a.

Commons of pasture in Foxley heath for 8 beasts and 2 horses in the summer and 50 sheep in the winter, worth 20s.

Edmund Hart, churchwarden, John Bennytt, sidesman. *Names in the same hand.*

356   18 Oct 1698, taken a second time 5 Dec 1704 (D1/24/97/2)
A parsonage house, barn and stable, garden plot and a little close. Lands or enclosures called Broad lease, Long meadow the Lane, Little meadow, Trench meadow, Middle hill, Three acres, Kingsleet, The Patch at Kingsheath gate. Total *c.* 54a. All great and small tithes except small tithes on a ground called Old Mills claimed by the vicar of Westport.

John Stump, rector, Robert Gingel, Robert Player, churchwardens.

357   21 Jul 1783 (D1/24/97/3)
The parsonage house adjoins the churchyard and is built of stone and oak and covered with stone tile. The principal storey: A kitchen floored with rough stone pavement the walls plastered but is not ceiled. A pantry not floored or ceiled. A hall floored with plaster, ceiled and wainscotted a chair high A parlour floored with oak board, ceiled and the walls plastered A pantry floored with plaster, ceiled and the walls plastered. A cellar paved and arched with stone. A brewhouse. The chamber story: 6 rooms floored with oak board, ceiled and the walls plastered. The attic story: 3 garrets all floored with oak board and the roof plastered to the pin.

A stable adjoining the house, built of stone and oak timber covered with stone tile, 46ft. by 38ft. A farmyard adjoining 2 closes of arable called Pressmeads, 13a. 2r., abutting to N. on the highway from Foxley to Norton, to S. and W. on a meadow to Edward Gould esq., and on E. on Frys close. 2 closes of arable, 10a., with a meadow called Goodenough's closes one abutting on Fry's close to W., the lane leading from Foxley to Norton on N., the highway to Malmesbury common on E., a meadow on Edward Gould esq. on S. The other to the highway from Norton to Malmesbury on S., late Player's land on N., the highway from Foxley to Malmesbury common on W., a meadow of Edward Gould esq., on E.

A close of meadow called Twatmead, 6a., abutting on W. to the road from Foxley to Malmesbury common, on S. to Malmesbury common, on E. to Jeffery's meadow, on N. to late Player's meadow. A close of arable called Starveall, 6a., abutting to S. N. and E. on Cowage farm and to W. on a close of pasture of Edward Gould esq. Total of new glebe 35a. 2r.

The barn, fenced with stone walls. A garden adjoining the house fenced with stone walls, abutting to E. the churchyard wall, S. the road from Foxley to Malmesbury, N. and W. other parts of the premises. A garden adjoining the farm yard, fenced with quickset hedges and stone walls, abutting on N. and E. late Player's lands, now Lord Holland's, S. on the churchyard wall and the road from Foxley to Malmesbury, W. on Lord Holland's lands. The above premises constitute the homestead and contain 4a. 11p.

Old glebe: Kingston mead, 4a. 2r. 20p., abutting N. and W. Lord Holland's lands, S. and E. late Player's lands and lands belonging to Peter Holford esq. Trench mead (meadow or pasture), 7a. 14p., abutting N. E. and W. Lord Holland's lands, S. other parts of these premises. A close of arable called Middle Hill (divided in 2), 16a. 3r. 8p. abutting E. and W. Lord Holland's lands, N. and S. other parts of these premises. 2 closes of meadow called Long mead and the Parsons Hole, 7a. 12p. abutting E. and W. Lord Holland's lands, N. and S. other parts of the premises. 2 closes of arable called Broad Leaze (previously 1 close), 18a. 2r. 28p. abutting E. W. and S. Lord Holland's lands, N. other parts of the premises. Total 54a. 1r. 2p.

New glebe: This is an augmentation to the living, valued £20 p. a., granted by Judith Ayliffe in 1728, on receiving Queen Ann's Bounty. The deeds are not at Foxley.

Common right: unlimited common rights in Foxley Green and a limited rights of common in part of Malmesbury common for depasturing sheep in daytime, from sunrise to sunset, but no other kind of cattle. A right to cut furze for the rector's own use but not for sale.

6 pollarded ashes in the churchyard of little value. The timber growing on the glebe is sufficient only for repairs to the premises. Rectorial and other tithes are due to the minister. Church furniture. 1 bell, 1 bible, 2 common prayer books, crimson velvet, pulpit cloth, cushion and cloth to cover the communion table all laced with gold. A linen cloth and napkin.

Communion plate: 1 small silver cup, 1 small silver salver, with the inscription 'Jefery Penel of Foxles Parysh 1606'. 1 silver flagon gilt with gold with the inscription 'The Gift of Mrs. Judith Ayliffe to the Parish of Foxley 1727'. 1 silver cup gilt with gold with the same inscription. 1 large silver salver gilt with gold with the same inscription. The Ayliffe arms are on the 3 last articles.

The rector is charged with repairs of the edifices and churchyard fences on N. and W. sides; the S. and E. sides are repaired by the parish. The clerk is appointed by the rector and paid £15 p. a. by the parish.

Seth Thompson, rector, Neville Carter, churchwarden, Thomas Carter principal inhabitant, Joseph Vizor, parish clerk. Signed by them 28 Jul 1783.

FROXFIELD vicarage

358   1609 (D1/24/98/1)
c. 23a. in E. field, *c.* 10a. in W. Field. A close of several called Pencions, 3½a., on
E. side of the parsonage house. A close of several, *c.* 4a., on W. side of the parsonage
house. A close of several on N. side of the parsonage house with backside orchard
and garden adjoining, *c.* 2a.
   John Kimber, vicar, John Green [X], Thomas Chiker [X], churchwardens.

359   23 Feb 1678 (D1/24/98/2)
Terrier of the glebe of the vicarage; the parsonage belongs to the church of
Windsor, being an impropriation. A vicarage house. A small garden plot, *c.* 1r. A
churchyard, *c.* 1r. A yearly stipend of £28 paid to the vicar by the impropriator.
   Thomas Foster, vicar, Edward Platt, John Pike, churchwardens, Robert Smith,
John Quarrington senior.

360   1678 (D1/24/98/3)
Land as **358**. Thomas Foster, vicar, Edward Plat, John Pyke, churchwardens,
William Platt, Robert Smith.

361   18 Dec 1704 (D1/24/98/4)
Nothing is found witheld from the vicarage. 15s. 8d. paid by the vicar for Tenths
to the Queen which it is humbly desired may be let off according to her majesty's
grace. A stipend of £28 paid to the vicar by the dean and canons of Windsor
made up of several augmentations.
   John Snead, vicar, Thomas Pyke, Alexander Platt, churchwarden, Edward
Savage.

362   1783 (D1/24/98/5)
Terrier made at the primary visitation of bishop Shute.
   1. Vicarage house built of brick and timber and covered with tiles. On the
ground floor a boarded parlour 13ft. by 13ft., a study with a brick floor 10ft. by
8ft., a kitchen with brick floor 13ft. by 13ft. all properly ceiled with lath and
morter, a wash and brew house 19ft. by 8ft., a cellar 13ft. by 8ft. On the middle
stairs, a room 13ft. by 8ft. and a small closet. On the first floor 2 rooms each 13ft.
by 13ft. ceiled with lath and morter, 2 garrets each 12½ ft. by 8ft. ceiled with lath
and morter. A stable adjoining the house 14ft. by 14ft., and a garden, *c.* ¼a.
   2. No glebe or tithes. A small stipend of £28 paid quarterly by the
impropriator with £8 Queen Anne's Bounty money.
   3. 2 small bells in a small wooden tower, no clock. A pulpit cushion made of
cloth fringed with worsted. The reading desk and communion table covered
with the same. A decent white linen cloth and napkin for use of the sacrament.
A small silver chalice washed on the outside and part of the inside with gold,
with the following letters TS RD IQ, 1619. No mark to ascertain its weight. 2
volumes in folio of Dr. Henry Moore's Theological and Philosophical Works
with the first volume of Dupin's Church History in octavo make up the whole
of the vicarage library.

4. The repairs of the church belong to the parish; of the chancel to the impropriator. The churchyard fence is kept up by the impropriator and part by the occupier of the several estates in the parish.

5. The clerk is chosen by the minister, the sexton by the parish. The two offices are now united in one person. He receives 4d., a house and the fees from marriages and burials.

George Jenkins, curate, Ananias Goodall, Richard Smith, churchwardens, W. C. Noyes, Robert Noyes, Nathanial Ball, Alexander Newman, Charles Cooke.

FUGGLESTONE AND BEMERTON rectory

363   13 Aug 1616 (D1/24/99/1)

A parsonage house with a barn and other edifices and houses built in a quadrant with a garden plot, and a barton with a backside, all joining together, 1a. in all, which is all the glebe.

The tithes of the following land: In the earl of Pembroke's park adjoining the common marsh of Quidhampton in the hands of William Phillips, 1½a., John Smith, 1½a., John Feltham, 1½a., John Hilman, 1½a. and William Feltham, nearly ½a. In the hands of Mrs. Young of Little Durnford Porters mead, 17a., together with 2 closes, 5½a., together with the tithe of any cattle feeding. In the hands of William Davis of Avon, 12a. of arable in the common field with 2 closes, 5a. by lug, and a meadow, 6a. by lug, of which the tithe, with 7lbs. of fleece wool, belongs to the parson of Fugglestone and Bemerton. In the hands of Mr. John Shuter of the Close of the cathedral church of Salisbury a close adjoining the common field of Bemerton called Nordean near Kings bridge, 2a. All the rest of the tithes lie within the ancient precincts of our perambulation in Rogation week and are well known to all the parish.

William Lewis, parson, John Feltham and Steven Hayes, churchwardens of Fugglestone, John Hillman and William Scammell, questmen of Fugglestone, Philip Stevans and John Best, churchwardens of Bemerton, and Edward Barrow and Edward Warde, questmen of Bemerton.

FUGGLESTONE and BEMERTON: Quidhampton rectory

364   28 May 1705 (D1/24/99/2)

A dwelling house, orchard or garden, 1a., a barn stable, backside and other outhouses.

All great and small tithes in Bemerton and Quidhampton except tithe hay from Kings mead and W. mead for which a piece of ground in Kings mead called Seven acres belongs to the rectory in lieu of tithes. All great and small tithes in Fugglestone except a mead, *c.* 6a., belonging to Mr. John Thorpe's farm now occupied by farmer Brine, which is tithe free.

Tithes of 10a. of arable in Avon [Awen] fields called Chicke Bottom; of 18a. upon Chicke hill; of 2 crofts [crates], *c.* 5a., now in the possession of Mr. Townsend; of Mr. Townsend's other mead near Little Durnford; of 60 sheep in the Avon

[Awen] flock; of 3 meads, *c.* 19a., in Little Durnford on S. side of the river; of 2 crofts of arable, *c.* 9a., now in the possession of farmer Baryet; of Parkers mead, *c.* 2a. in Stratford [*sub Castle*] now in the possession of Michael Dawes.

John Norris, rector, Edward Scamell, Robert Goodhind, churchwardens, John Spelt, John Chamberlen, John Eastman.

GARSDON rectory

365   13 Jul 1608 (D1/24/100/1)
1 close of several, 3a., adjoining the parsonage house. A several close of pasture, 7a., called Poulshill between the ground of Katherine Broade on E. and Isabel Brook on W. The vicarage of Lea belongs to the parsonage, with the vicarage house standing in a close of several ground, *c.* 1a., 4 several enclosed grounds, 35 or 36a., called the Parsons leases, 3 of which lie together with Maudet park on S., ground of Thomas Erle on N. E. The other close lies next to Jeffery Wheller on E., Richard Thorner on S.

Richard Woodroffe, Elias Hayward, Robert Biggs, Edmund Hayward [X], Nicholas Munden [X].

366   16 Dec 1671 (D1/24/100/2)
The parsonage house, barn, stable, gardens, backside and a little close adjoining, ½a. 2 pasture grounds called Rowsells, 7a., 2 arable grounds called Courte Hill leazes, 11a.

Abraham Griffin, rector, John Cullurne, Edward Gyles, churchwardens.

With Lea and Cleverton vicarage

367   25 Jul 1783 (D1/24/100/3)
Terrier taken and renewed according to the old evidences and knowledge of ancient inhabitants and exhibited in the primary visitation of bishop Shute at Chippenham.

Garsdon rectory· A house built of stone covered with stone slates. A thatched barn and stable under the same roof built with stone. 2 gardens walled in an orchard adjoining with a hedge fence. A church 69ft. long, 17ft. 9in. wide with a chancel 19ft. 10in. long and the same width as the church. A communion table with linen cloth. A large flagon, 2 large cups, 1 small cup with a cover, 1 plate for bread, all of silver, all given by lady Pargiter with the inscription 'To Garsdon Church'. She was formerly the wife of Lawrence Washington esq. They both lie buried in the church. A pulpit cloth and cushion A table and 2 common prayer books, 5 bells. The churchyard is 9 lugs long 7 lugs wide, with 22 elm trees growing round. The rails and gates are made and repaired by the parish. 8a. in 2 fields called Rowsles two fields, 5a. and 3a., called Parsons glebe.

Joseph Simpson, rector, William Freeth [X], churchwarden, Joseph Orum, Morris Simpson, John Ovens, William Sampson.

Lea vicarage: Brown Willis in his edition of Ecton's *Liber Valorum*[1] stated of Lea and Cleverton that there had never been in the memory of man a chapel at

Claverton. Lea was consolidated with Garston, and is called a vicarage. There is no house, glebe land; Vicarage close, 1a., Great Goss, 16a., Goss mead, 4a., Picked leazes, 6a., Long Goss, 8a. Right of common.

Chapel furniture, a communion table with white linen cloth, a bread plate, a small pewter cup with the inscription 'Henry Miller and Robert Croom churchwardens'. A bible, a common prayer book, 5 bells.

Joseph Simpson vicar, Richard Reeve, George Tanner, John Millard, Daniel Whit.

1. *Liber Valorum et Decimarum, being an account of the Valuations and Yearly Tenths of... Ecclesiastical benefices in England and Wales* By John Ecton, 1711. An edition by Brown Willis was published in 1754 under the title *Thesaurus rerum Ecclesiasticarum.*

368   20 Jul 1808 (D1/24/100/4)
The parsonage house, barn, stable garden and orchard with the churchyard, 1a. 2 arable pieces, 10a., 2 pasture fields called Glebe lands, 8a. 1 enclosure near the church at Lea called the Vicarage close, 1½a. 1 enclosure called the Allotment, 1½a. 4 arable fields at Cleverton called the Glebe, *c.* 39a.

William Lewis, rector, John Plummer, William Hart, churchwardens of Garsdon, John Stockham, churchwarden of Lea and Cleverton.

WEST GRIMSTEAD rectory

369   1671 (D1/24/101/1)
In N. Field in 2 parcels one called Four acres, by measure 2a. 54 lugs, the other called One acre, by measure ½a. 5 lugs. 3a. in S. field by measure 2a. 20 lugs. In W. field in 2 parcels, *c.* 1a. The ground behind the barn, 136 lugs. The rest of the enclosed ground with the garden and orchard, 1a. A barn, a stable, a cowhouse, a woodhouse and a pigsty.

John Barrow, Edward Hayter, churchwardens.

370   n. d. late 17th cent. (D1/24/101/2)
Pasture, meadow, an orchard and garden all 4a. near the house. In W. field adjoining a piece of ground called Whole Half, 2a. In E. field, 5a. Right of Common is those fields for 20 sheep. Tithe hay in those fields and tithe wood of all coppices, except on 30a. in W. field that belong to Whaddon. For some years Madam Hungerford has taken the profits of a piece of ground called Forewood, 13a., between W. Grimstead and Whiteparish, whether rightfully is under dispute.

William Hilary, curate, John Pilgrim, Christopher Dew, churchwardens, John Thomas, sidesman. *Names in the same hand*

371   9 Jan 1705 (D1/24/101/3)
A house containing 5 rooms on the lower floor. A garden, orchard and backside adjoining the barn. Stable and carthouse of 7 bays, another outhouse. 2 closes, *c.*

3a., about the house. In the field behind Hayes, 2a., in 2 places. In Bugdean field, 3a. in 1 piece. In Canny Pit field, 5a. in 2 places. Common of pasture in the fields for 25 sheep and other commons at large. Tithe in kind of corn, all kinds of grass, wood, cow white, the custom of which is 2d. per cow, calves, the custom of which is 6d. per calf, wool, lambs, hops, honey, geese and customary eggs. Pot furlong, 40a., in W. Grimstead pays great tithes to Whaddon farm by what right it is not known. Value of the whole £60.

John Foote, rector, Charles Foote, churchwarden.

372   1783 (D1/24/101/4)
A dwelling house, tiled, part brick wall and part brick panes; a parlour with boarded floor, part wainscotted, part plastered, and ceiled; a kitchen with a brick floor, sides of plaster and ceiled, joining a buttery 10ft. by 12ft.; above these chambers up one pair of stairs, plastered and ceiled. A barn, stable and carthouse. A garden and orchard surrounded by a hedge, c. 3r. A ground by the barn with hedge fence, 1a. 3r. 35p. A hop ground in the hedge fence near the garden, 3r. 10p. In these 2 grounds and in the churchyard are standing 18 elm trees and 1 ash.

In E. field Lineys piece, 2a. 1r. 21p., adjoining Mr. Cooper. In Redlinch field 1 piece called Romsey, 2a. 1r. 32p., joining Mr. Blake on E. and Mr. Long on W. A piece in the same field joining Mr. Bungey's called the Piece between linchets, 2r. 17p. In Kitchill field 2 pieces, 1a. 1r. 27p., one on S. the other on N. of Mr. Blake. In W. field a piece 3r. 7p. Mr. Earnol on S., Mr. Blake on N. A ground called Parsonage common with hedge fence near the Salisbury road, 7a. 2r. The tithes of the whole parish except c. 30a. taken by the tenant of Whaddon farm whose right is much doubted and must be enquired into.

The wardenship of the Farley hospital built by Sir Stephen Fox in 1681 and annexed to the rectory in 1711. Church utensils: a pulpit cloth and cushion, 2 bells. Communion plate: a pewter flagon inscribed with the name of George Flower esq., a small silver cup and stand weighing about 6oz.

The churchyard fence is repaired by the parish except the wicket on W. entrance which is repaired by the rector. The clerk is appointed by the rector and the parish, his wages are 30s. p. a. paid by the parish.

Neville Wells, rector, William Read, Aaron Harison, churchwardens.

GRITTLETON rectory

373   early 17th cent.[1] (D1/24/102/1)
Parsons close, c. 6a., farm land on N. and W., the Parsons tenant land on E. and abutting on [the parson's] orchard. An orchard and backside called the Greenehaye, c. 2a., adjoining the parsonage house.

Henry Oateridge, Isaac Bristow, churchwardens, Roger Kelburyt, John Jones, sidesmen. *Names in the same hand.*

Endorsement: the terrier was exhibited in an Exchequer case. Thomas Pollock, clerk, plt. v. Daniel Sargent, Joseph May, Lawrence Chandler, dfts. and shown to Charles Millett at his examination, 2 Sept 1771.

1. This is probably the terrier described as given in 1610 in **374A**.

374   1671 (D1/24/102/2)

A dwelling house of 8 bays. A barn, stable and 2 necessary houses. 2 gardens, an orchard, a close of pasture adjoining called Green Hay, 1a. No more glebe is known. Value £5 p. a.

Tithes are all paid in kind and were worth £100 p. a. but are not so much worth now.

Nicholas Pewarden, curate, Joseph Beames, Isaac Bristow, churchwardens.
Endorsement as 373.

374A   1675 [1620/11][1]

Tithe of all things due: 1d. A garden p. a. For a cow 3d., a calf 6d., a colt [. . .] Bees the seventh swarm due in kind. For lambs and pigs the seventh in kind or if you can agree; if the number be under 7 you may either drive (that is make it up the next year and the remainder to run for another seventh) or have for each lamb 3d., for so Mr. White always pays but I think that it should be but 2½d. For mortuaries as expressed in the statute. Til one Earth's[2] time some 4 score a. of glebe belonged to the rectory but now the terrier runs thus: *Land as 374.* 9½a. lying in Clapcot fields (which yet goes not now for glebe) part of the 80a. questionable: in Little Clapcot fields 5a.; 1a. shooting upon Berry Croft; 1a. adjoining to the lower end of the leaze [lees] now in the possession of Thomas Bristow; ½a. shooting on the way to Clapcot; 1a. near Samuel Seils house shooting on the way to Clapcot. In the further field shooting towards Surrendell, 4½a.: 1a. in Port furlong; 1½a. near the quarry; ½a. on Tinkers hill; 1a. near W. Bullocks leaze called Lippyats. In Small mead 2 arable lands of about a farndel and 2 lots of meadow. The terrier was given in without these these a. in the field in 1610. The rector also has 10 sheep going in the fields. Every other year a horse or 2 beasts going in Small mead excepting always even fifth years which belong to John Jaques.

1. Terrier recorded by Thomas Tully, rector, in his tithe account book. This book and a successor volume both have the same endorsement as **373**.
2. William Earth, rector 1597–1619.

375   n. d. [1704x1705][1] (D1/24/102/3)

A house with a garden and orchard on N., of a fair extent and well walled. A little close behind the barn called the Green Hay. A close of 5a. above the orchard. A lot in Small mead, one in Hill mead and one in Ashmore, the last two received in dry hay. Tithes in kind.

Thomas Tattersall, rector, Thomas Brokenbrow, John Freem, churchwardens, W. White.
Endorsement as 373.

1. The churchwardens were recorded in the bishop's visitation book, Oct 1704 (WSRO D1/50/6).

HAM rectory

376   Dec 1677 (D1/24/103/1)

The parsonage house, barns, stables, orchard, garden, backside, etc.; ¼a. of meadow ground in Boare mead bounded with Mr. Gunter S. and Matthew Hunt N.; a meadow ground called the Parsonage Several, 2a.; and 5a. of inclosed ground in Astly having the drove S. and Farmer Hunt N.

E. field: 1a. shooting up to Ten Acres stile Mr. Gunter S. and N.; 1a. in the middle of the field called Shipway acre, Mr. Gunter W., Farmer Hunt E.; 1a. in Short mead furlong shooting up to a head a. of Mr. Gunter W., John Hedges S. and N.; 1a. in the Ridge furlong next to Pill's field W., Lawrence Hunt E.; 1a. in the Ridge furlong John Hedges E., George Webb W.; 1a. in Houndsill furlong John Harrold E. and W.

Pill's field: 1½a. adjoining Hockly hedge N., Mr. Gunter S. Up field: 2a. shooting up towards the hill Mr. Gunter E., wid. Smale W. Little field: 1a. in Broadways furlong John Hedges E., John Harrold W.

W. field: 1 head a. in the furlong next to the farm bounded John Harrold E., Mr. Gunter on each end; 1a. in Judas furlong Robert Bright S., Richard Dyer N.; 1 head a. in the furlong called the Dean, William Simms W., the end shooting towards Shawbourne field N.; 1½a. in the Deane furlong John Cooper N., Robert Bright S.; 1a. toward the river John Hedges S. farmer Hunt N.; 1a. shooting towards the W. hill George Webb E., farmer Hunt W.; ½a. in Allridd furlong William Simms E. and W.

John Newbin, curate, John Harould, John Cooper [X], churchwardens.

377   16 Oct 1684 (D1/24/103/2)

A dwelling house, barn, stable, dovehouse (all in to one) and other outhouses. The rick yard behind the barn, an orchard, a garden in all *c.* 1a.

A parcel of land called the Parsons Several, *c.* 2a., between the severals of Robert Bright and wid. Smales. A parcel of land in a place called Spray, *c.* ½a., between the severals of John Hedges on E. and of Robert Bright on W. A several at Ashly, *c.* 4a. 3yd., William Benet E., John Hunt W.

Pill's field: 1½a., Thomas Gunter esq. S., Mr. John Hunt N. E. field: ½a. between Mr. Alexander Goddard W., Laurence Hunt E.; 1a. between Robert Bright E. and Andrew Web W.; 1a. John Hedges both sides; 1a. between the lands of Robert Harold; 1a. between the lands of Thomas Gunter esq.; 1a. Thomas Gunter esq. W., Mr. John Hunt E.

W. field: 1a. Mr. John Hunt W., George Web E.; 1a. Mr. John Hunt N., John Hedges S.; 1½a. John Cooper N. and Andrew Web S.; 1a. Richard Dyer N., Robert Brighton S.; 1a. Robert Harold E., Thomas Gunter esq., Mr. Alexander Goddard, Mr. John Hunt, John Hedges, etc. W. Upfield: 2a. between lands of Thomas Gunter esq.

Ambrose Meredith, curate, William Bennet [X], John Cooper [X], churchwardens, John Hunt, John Hedges [X].

378   9 Jan 1705[1] (D1/24/103/3)

A fair and convenient dwelling house, a pigeon house, barn, 2 stables and some other outhouses. A rick yard, small orchard, 2 gardens and a backside, c. 1½a. 2 meadows called the Parsonage severals, c. 2a. 1 several called the New Enclosure or Iname ground, c. 5a. 1 several on the hill at Ashley, c. 5a. 1 several at Spray, c. ½a. W. field: 7a. of arable. E. field: 3a. of arable. Upfield: 2a. of arable. Churchyard, c. 30 lugs.

Richard Gillingham, rector, John Rumball, John Habgood, churchwardens, Lawrance Hunt, John Hunt.

1. The terrier was sent in to the registry on this date.

HANKERTON vicarage

379   9 Oct 1608 (D1/24/104/1)
A mansion or dwelling-house with a barn and other buildings, two gardens, an orchard, a ground adjoining it, 2½a., on the W. of a ground called Broadheis and on the E. of the dwelling house of William Necke, the churchyard.

All tithes in kind within the parish (except corn) with the commons, commodities, fruits, profits, and advantages belonging to the vicarage.

A ground called Eame ham which the incumbent holds by composition in lieu and consideration of tithe hay of all the Lot meadow except the part belonging to the farm.

Made and taken by William Beale, vicar, John Brown and John Panter junior, churchwardens, Robert Woodward, William Necke, Henry Yearington, Edmund Browne, and John Dike. *All marks except the vicar and John Brown.*

380   12 Dec 1671 (D1/24/104/2)
Terrier made according to an order we received at the visitation of the bishop held at Devizes concerning the vicarage: Mr. Norris Jemson, rector of Crudwell, is the present patron. Mr. John Hopkins, our present vicar. Glebe: Home close, c. 3a. of pasture, valued £3 10s. A close of pasture called the Hinham c. 3a., held by the ministers of Hankerton time out of mind in lieu of the tithes of the Lot meadow, valued £2 p. a. Total value of the vicarage between £50 – £60 p. a.

No hospitals almshouses or free schools. A church house with stable, 1 garden and 1r. of land called Church paddock. This was given for the relief of the poor and the reparation of the highways in the parish and for any other good use according as the greatest number of the inhabitants should think fit by Thomas Wallton of Crudwell and Margaret Wallton, his wife, by deed of feoffment 10 Jun 1554. Feoffees in trust John Warneford esq., Thomas Strange, Robert Wye, Mary Browne, John Head, William Dicke, William Hibberd, John Hillier, John Hibberd, Robert Woodman and Thomas Curtis, their heirs and assigns, who have the power of letting leases. Annual rent is £2.

Joseph Tomson Salter, a very sufficient man, is the present tenant of the church house by a 21 year lease dated 21 Mar 1662 granted by on the present feoffees in trust with the consent of the inhabitants or the major part of them, according to the meaning of the ancient deeds which are safely kept in a great chest in our church having 3 good locks and keys The tenant is to keep and leave the houses and bounds in good and sufficient repair. The annual rent of £2 which is employed according to the true intent meaning and purport of the deeds.

Margaret Warneford; John Norgrove [X], Robert Tomson [X], churchwardens, Thomas Andrews, William Beale, sidesmen, Richard Gagg, Thomas Loodlo, John Tucker, Mary Overberry wid., John Curtis, Edward Brain, Giles Hay, Samuel Sanders. *All the names after the sidesmen seem to be in the same hand.*

380A   16 Dec 1704 (D1/24/104/3)
A vicarage house and barn A home close and garden, 3a A close called Hymham which the incumbent holds by a grant in lieu and consideration of the tithe hay of all the Lot meadow except the Lot meadow belonging to the Farm. A churchyard, *c.* 2a. All tithes in kind as hay, lamb, etc., excepting corn only. Commons in Braydon [*Forest*] according to the proportion of a 1/2 yardland. Right of commons in the home commons.

Thomas Shewring, vicar, Giles White, John Dolman, churchwardens, Richard Gagge, Thomas Ludlow, Richard Harris.

HANNINGTON vicarage

381   n. d. [late 16th – early 17th cent.][1] (D1/24/105/1)
The answer for the vicarage and parsonage by the churchwardens and sidesmen. The vicarage has ½yd. of glebe. He is parson and vicar [*for tithes*] of all the houses and commodities that come of them below the lake commonly called and known by the name of Ninger lake [2] according to the old custom. The parson and vicar of all the free lands in the manor of Hannington, viz: 2 yardlands [3] of Robert Savarie; 1 yardland of Walter Parker gent.; ½ yardland of John Lowde; 2 closes, a padhay whereon stand a house, 3a. of mead in the Hitchmans land, 3 x ½a. of arable land and 1a. of mead in the tenure of Richard Plummer; 3 x ½a. of arable lying unto a plot whereon stands the house lying unto the parsonage close on E. of the vicarage. He is parson and vicar of a tenement and ½ yardland called Bide mill except 2s. which [as] the parson has. He is also parson and vicar of the 2 yardlands of glebe lying unto the parsonage.

All privy tithes in the manor except for the parson all money for tithe white where the vicar is not parson. Tithe ?swine [swinte], it is not know not whether the vicar or parson to have it. Tithe of 3 x ½a. occupied by William Weston, now of late the parson has carried it away who has the right it is not known. The vicar has 1 cock of a plot of meadow lying unto the parsonage called Ten acres and 1 cock of corn of 1a. lying unto the body of the church. Tithe of 1a. of arable land and ½a. of stean [steine] meadow lying to the ?bury [burge] of Hannington. Tithe of ½a. of arable called the Parsons ham. The parsonage has a barn with backside or pen behind 2 yardland of glebe, 2 closes, 2 x ½a. of arable, a new built house upon one of the closes. Tithe corn, wool, and lamb, [*cow*] white excepted and reserved to the vicarage save only from lands and lays called the Lords lands. There is a tithe called Horrell tithe[4] for which [*the vicarage*] has 2 cocks and the parsonage 1. The parsonage has 2s. a year from Bide mill and 2s. a year from a house of Richard Plummer at a place called Knill but wherefore he has these sums we know not.

The Horrell tithe has a house at Bide mill called Horrell house. But there is neither parson or vicar that has any tithe of a stean meadow of any of the Queen's customary tenants save only the vicar on a quarterne of land now occupied by Joan Sheppard wid. Also the parson has the tithe of a plot of meadow called Nithe occupied by William Berriman and also ½a. of meadow in the same mead now occupied by Catherine Batson wid.

John Sherman, Thomas Savery, churchwardens, Richard Marsh, John Batson, sidesmen, William Harperer. Written by Henry Marche.

1. The churchwardens were in office in 1600 but may have served together for several other years. (WSRO 1819/2)
2. The enclosure agreement of 1632 includes reference to Ningram and parcells of land within it (WSRO 1033/42). Ningram is identified as a common field in C.B. Fry, *Hannington: the records of a Wiltshire Parish* (1935).
3. A yardland is stated as being 30a. in a custom of the manor. Fry *op. cit.* p. 104.
4. Horrell tithes formerly belonging to Wherwell abbey. In 1533 it held the tithes of the S. field, the E. field and Breche field. Fry, *op. cit.* p. 29.

382   1671 (D1/24/105/2)
A vicarage house, gardens, orchard and close adjoining the old enclosure and churchyard, 2a.[1] 48a. of new enclosures let for £49 10s.[2]

The tithe of Stert farm both parts [*of the farm*] by composition £11 p. a.[3] The tithe of Rauf Freke by composition £2 14s. p. a. The tithes of wid. Mathew, Thomas Mathew, wid. Boulton, William Sanders and small tithes and offerings, the value which is all unknown, but are conceived to be £3 p. a.

Edward Pinnell, James Clarke, churchwardens. *Names in the same hand.*

1. Valued at £2 in **383**.
2. Valued at £48 in **383**.
3. Valued at £11 in **383**.

383   1677 (D1/24/105/3-4)
*As **382** with amendments in footnotes.* John Freke, vicar, Richard Clarke, William Weston, churchwardens.

384   n. d. [1704x1705][1] (D1/24/105/5)
A dwelling house with little outhouse, stable and backside, containing an orchard and garden, *c.* ½a. Colman Acre, *c.* 10a., on N. of the backside, bounded by a ground of William Weston on N., Parsonage corner on left hand, and a ground of William York on right hand.

3 grounds called Wateridge, *c.* 47a., bounded by a lane on S. and W., by Brockfurlong and Greenfurlong on E., by Longmead on N. and by a 3 cornered mead on N. W.

Benjamin Young, vicar, Henry Curtis, Richard Deverall, churchwardens, William Yorke, Charles York, William Weston.

1. The churchwardens were recorded in the bishop's visitation book, Oct 1704 (WSRO D1/50/6).

HARDENHUISH rectory

385   21 Dec 1704 (D1/24/106/1)
A parsonage house with a barn adjoining the orchard and paddock, ½a. A ground called the Home lease, 3a.; a ground called West close, 2a.; a ground called Buckwell lease, 2a.; and a ground called North Field lease, 4a. 1a. in Little field near the common gate, Mr. Henry Hawkins E. and Mr. Read, minister of Langley [*Burrell*] W.; 1a. of arable in the middle of Mrs. Eleanor Pinchin's lease in N. field near 4a. of glebe belonging to Langley [*Burrell*] below Black Hedge copse; 1a. of meadow in the middle of the Home ground belonging to an estate called the Barrow; ½a. of pasture in the middle of a ground called Smalden formerly in the possession of Robert Brewer; 1a. in the middle of a ground belonging to Matthew Smith adjoining a ground of Samuel Ash esq., called Six acre pit, arable; 1a. of meadow or pasture in a ground called Pew hills belonging to William Bedford of Chippenham; and 1a. of meadow or pasture in the E. side of a ground of Edward Baker abutting on the highway near Kelloways [Calways] bridge.

Thomas Keat, rector, Robert Hawkins, churchwarden.

HEDDINGTON rectory

386   n. d. late 16th cent. (D1/24/107/1)
For his tillage, 6a. in a field for one year and as many for another year to be sown; 6a. of meadow, 'and, to be playne in few wordes, and truthe he hath putt it out before tyme' for £30 a year paying a curate out of that £10 a year besides all other charges to the Queen or to any other to whom duties do belong whatsoever.

387   9 Apr 1611 (D1/24/107/2)
A dwelling house consisting of a hall, kitchen and 2 lesser underooms with 3 upper rooms, chambers and a cock loft; a barn of 3 fields on the S. side with a stable and swine sty adjoining, a garden and orchard together, within one bound, ½a., on the E. side, a little plot on N. side and a backside on S. side. A cottage on the further side of a little lane at E. end of the dwelling house called Dilayten, ½yd. A pasture ground called Little Hook, 1a., on S. side of the lane at the end of the said barn. 2 other grounds, each 4a., called the Bigger and the Lesser Crofts one opposite to the other upon Crockerne Lane. The E. end of the

Bigger shooting upon a common mead called Broadlay, the other ground bounding upon the N. side of Sandy lane. 2 grounds, one bounding on the W. side the other on the E. side both belong to the holding now in the tenure of John Townsende.

Meadow: 2 lots whereof one belongs to the parsonage the other to the hold now in the tenure of John Longe parcel now of the land of Sir Henry Bayntun, chargeable each year lying at the S. W. end of the common meadow called Rowmead [and] at the N. end of the ground called the Wood. 1½yd. in the middle of the common mead called Broadmead and another [plot] of the same quantity there on the W. side belonging to the said hold of John Longe, the N. end of both bounding upon Broadlease. 1yd. on E. side of the common mead called Weeke mead at N. end of the ground called Goldstones.

Arable: In the S. field; ½a. at the lower end of Bagden hedge; 1a. at the tween ways next to Bagden bridge; 1a. heading the N. end of one of the pieces called Wetlands; ½a. heading the upper part of Cusners piece at the W. end; 1a. on the Knap called Vinsuns Bale; 1½yd. shooting on S. side of ? Marlborough way at the upper end of the water gripe called the Whitch; 1a. in the middle of the field called Sherrenddown, the S. end shooting upon Canning's way.

In the N. field; 1a. lying ?[in] the hook called the Parson's hook, the W. end shooting upon Whittit lane, John Longe having another of the same on S. side thereof; 1a. heading part of the upper end of Fold furlong ?adjoining in that part of the field called Blagden hill, John Longe having ½a. on N. side; 1a. in the part of the field called Whiteshrippe [. . .] of the said way, John Longe having ½a. on W. side; [. . .] in upper end of Cusine Combe, John Longe [. . .] another of the same lying on E. side; 1a. in the furlong [. . .] of Marlborough way, William Dyer having another on S. side; 1yd. [. . .] the field called Sherrendown, John Longe having [. . .] on S. side; 1a. not far from the said [. . .] 1a. belonging to the hold in the tenure of Robert P[. . .].

Of tithes issuing out of or growing in the parish [. . .] whereof are now in the tenure of Henry Rogers pays [. . .] parson 2s.; with the offerings of all communicants there dwelling. [. . .] occupation of [. . .] Townsend pay also yearly at Easter 18d. [. . .] of all communicants there or upon any part of either of the F[. . .]ds dwelling.

Robert Rogers, rector, Andrew Townsend [X], Robert Frayling, churchwardens, John Pearce [X], John Townsend, sidesmen, Robert Scott [X], John Frayling [X], ? William Dyer, inhabitants.

388   8 Dec 1671 (D1/24/107/3)
Terrier taken by the commandment of the bishop. A mansion house with garden orchard backside, c. 1a. 2 grounds of pasture and arable called Two Hooks lying near the house, c. 2a. 3 grounds of meadow and pasture called the Crafts, c. 7a. A pasture ground called Sandy Leaze, c. 3a.

Field land: In N. field; 1a. at White Shrippe; 1a. at Blaggen hill; 1a. at the upper end of Boltupright; 1yd. upon Stert; 3yd. at Shirnedown; 1yd. in the Middle furlong above hill; 3yd. in the Middle furlong near Marleborough. In S. field; 1a. shooting upon Shirnedown; 1yd. of headland shooting upon Marlborough way; 1a. upon the Ball on N. side of the hollow way; 1a. at Beacon bridge; ½a. shooting upon against Fishbury. A churchouse well in repair. Henry Rogers, rector, William Scott, John Scott, churchwardens.

389   17 Mar 1681 (D1/24/107/4)
1 mansion house with gardens, orchards and backside. A barn of 5 fields of building with stable adjoining and other outhouses. 3 meadow grounds called the Three Crafts joining together, 7a. 4a. of arable sandy ground enclosed by the highway side of Sandy Lane. 3a. of pasture and arable ground by the field side near the dwelling house. 3a. of arable land in the N. field; 4a. 1yd. upon the hill in the S. field; ½a. in the Hanging hill on S. side, called Kings Plays; 1a. below the hill by Beacon bridge.

Henry Rogers, minister, Thomas Child, William Lanfire, churchwardens.

390   1783 (D1/24/107/5)
Belonging to the church: 5 bells, a font, pulpit, cloth and cushion, a surplice, a communion table, green cloth, holland cloth, a silver cup and cover weight not marked, but dated 1578, flagon, a plate, both pewter. Rails around the communion table, 2 oaken pews in the chancel, a vestry room, a bier, reading desk, a large English bible and Common prayer book, the body of the church fully pewed and a gallery for singing.

A dwelling house built with timber and paned [pan'd], covered with tile and thatch enclosed by a brick wall and part of stone, a parlour, wainscotted and ceiled, with a boarded floor: a hall ceiled and plastered with a stone floor: a brewhouse thatched with an earthen floor: a dairy ceiled with a stone floor. 1 story above stairs, best room half wainscotted the other part plastered, ceiled, with a boarded floor: the other 2 rooms, no ceiling, plastered with boarded floors: a study ceiled and plastered with a boarded floor; 3 garrets, 1 ceiled plastered and boarded floor, the other 2 no ceiling with a boarded floor; a cellar, ceiled with a stone floor; a pantry boarded with a stone floor.

2 gardens, 1 enclosed with a brick and stone wall, the other fenced with a dead hedge and ditch, 1 orchard fenced part with a dead hedge and part with thorn. A barn and stable, built with timber and board and covered with thatch. A rick yard, enclosed partly with a stone wall and partly with thorn. A pig sty, a poultry roost built with stone and covered with thatch, a stone floor; a yard at the front of the house enclosed partly with pales partly with the dwelling house and barn and a stone wall at one end. Lands and ground: Arable: 2 ¼a. in the field enclosed by the parish. 4a. called Sandy lease enclosed with hazel timber 12 pollard ash. Pasture: 3 grounds called the Crafts: Upper Craft, c. 3a., 22 sapling elms, 11 pollard elms, 13 pollard ashes, 3 maiden oaks, 13 pollard oaks and 2 maiden oaks enclosed with thorn; Lower Craft, c. 4a., 7 pollard oaks, 2 maiden oaks, 18 pollard elms, 9 pollard ashes, 3 timber elms, 17 sapling elms enclosed with thorn; Lower Craft, c. 1½a., a maiden ash, 6 pollard ashes, 9 sapling elms, 4 pollard elms, 1 maiden oakes, 6 pollard oaks enclosed with thorn; Hooke ground; c. 2a.; 2 maiden ashes, 18 pollard ashes, 7 sapling elms, 5 pollard elms, 2 timber elms enclosed with thorn.

Church yard containing 3 timber elms and 3 sapling elms enclosed by the parish. £1 10s. paid yearly to the second poor out a house called Bonds. Clerk and Sexton's wages 40s. paid each year by the churchwardens out of the church rate.

Francis Rogers, rector, Thomas Crook, David Hill, churchwardens, James Humphreys, Walter Crook, overseers, John Pearse, James Pound, Robert Child, John Rogers, John Snook.

HIGHWORTH vicarage

391   n. d. [1671][1] (D5/10/1/13)
Terrier of the customary tithes to the parish of Highworth, Eastrop, Westrop, Hampton, Fresden, Sevenhampton, Prior Farley, S. Marston, Broad Blunsdon and Berry Blunsdon.

A vicarage house with garden plot and backside with a little tenement in Eastrop being part of the vicarage with a little garden plot, 1yd., worth *c.* 13s. 4d. p. a. and the feeding of the churchyard.

Customary tithes: For the fall of a calf 4d. or drive and then he is titheable at 5 weeks and 1½ days old. The tithes for milch kine at 2d. a piece at Lammas [1 Aug] for a thorough milk cow ½d. If a calf is weened be he male or female there is no tithe to be paid for the first year. If it is sold before it comes to plough or pail [*i. e. a draught or a dairy animal*] it shall be valued what it is worth if it were sold, the tenth penny is the tithe, that it is sold for the first year being deducted; if kept to plough nothing; if kept to pail the fall of the calf or drive: As beforesaid for the sale of a colt 1d. after that, if bred to service no tithe, if sold after 1 year old at the year's end he shall be valued what the colt is worth and that being deducted the tenth penny is the tithe that it is sold for or compounded. If any have 10 mares with colt then the vicar may have the tenth colt and nothing for the fall of any of the 9. The colt is titheable at 5 weeks and 1½ day old. For an ox or horse or mare that is bought either draught or burthen or saddle no tithe to be paid. For a cow that has given milk until Lammas [1Aug] and then sold nothing but for her milk 3d. and no more. For a cow and calf that is bought and does not prove good for milk if turned for beef it is not counted grazing nor yet titheable. For a cow and calf that is bought after Lammas the vicar has no tithe if it is milked except she has a calf before Lammas next ensuing if then for the sale of the calf, 4d., for the milk at Lammas after, 2d. For a cow that is killed in a house no due to the vicar. For a bull that is killed in the house or sold no due to the vicar for his tithe is paid in gendering or bulling.

For a sow that has pigs, if 7 pigs the vicar may have 1 but the pig shall be valued what it is worth, if 20d. then the vicar shall pay the owner for so many as it did want to make up his tithe which is 6d.: And if the pig is worth 30d. then he shall pay the owner 9d. and the next year the vicar shall not have a pig out of 10 but shall have 1 out of 13 and then the pig shall be valued as before and then the vicar shall receive for every pig that was above 10 that is for the 3 pigs, 6d. if it were valued at 20d., if at 30d. then to pay the vicar 9d. and the vicar to have the pigs: And it is titheable at 3 weeks old.

For sheep if sold before Lady day [25 Mar] ½d. if after Ladyday until Midsummer that shearing time is past, 1d. If sheep be shorn the tenth lb. of wool, if for a year: And no tithe for sheep keeping under 30 days for wool or else for sheep if sold after sheartime nothing until after Michaelmas [29 Sep]: For putting the rams to the ewes everyone is to use his discretion. For the fall of a lamb, 2d. or drive and then titheable on St. Mark's day [25 Apr.] after this manner; to let them run or the owner to take up what 3 lambs he will and then the vicar 1 and then the owner to make up his 9 and then the owner to draw out 9 more after and the vicar 1. If a man has 10 lambs or more fallen after Markstide he shall not keep the 10th lamb until Markstide next but shall take his lamb at the age of a calf or compound colt as above said.

For eggs for the cock [male], 3, for the hen [female] 2 on Good Friday. For bees the tenth penny if sold but if taken then the tenth pint [of honey]. For a cow sold before Lammas having had a calf before nothing for the vicar, he had his tithe in the fall of the calf. All grazing ground is to be compounded and the vicar is to even his tithes once a year with his portions.

For marrying a couple the vicar or curate is to have 10d. and the clerk 4d. For churching a woman the vicar or curate is to have 4d. and the clerk 1d. For offerings at Easter every one that receives the sacrament is to pay 2d. For a garden 1d., except he sells his garden stuff, for apples and fruits the tenth bushell or compound except windfalls being not titheable. For hemp the tenth handfull or compound while the seed is in it and the like for flax.

For the keeping of sheep 4d. a month a score if caught without of the same parish, except the man with whom they are kept has compounded for his tithe then nothing; for an ?agistment [silement] beast 6d. except if he be a parishioner. For a calf killed in the house and the vicar not paid for his fall nor yet drove forward the tenth then the vicar or curate shall have the left shoulder.

The mark for tolling the passing bell, 4d.; if rung out, 1s. For digging a grave in the churchyard 4d. in the church 1s. The tithe hay and corn belongs to the prebendary of Highworth and is tithcable as soon as the hay is cocked and so to be set out by the owners of the hay or corn. The corn before any is carried being sheaf or cocked. Except certain plots of ground in the tithings of Prior Farley and in S. Marston whose crop of tithe hay and corn belongs to the parson of Stanton Fitzwarren which we believe that parson has presented. That parson is to pay 1 load of hay out of E. mead each year to the vicar. In the tithings of Prior Farley and S. Marston there is no glebe land. We have a donative and a house there with garden plot and a close given to the inhabitants of those tithings for ever for the better maintenance of the curate there. The donor is unknown to us. The house and garden plot is bounded on S. E. by a ground of John Briante, on S. W. by the brook and with a donative next adjoining given to both tithings for the same purposes as above. That land is bounded on S. E. with land of John Briant, on S. W. with a tenement of Thomas Mondy, on N. W. with the common pound, on N. by the said brook. A tenement of John Steevens bounds the curate's [glebe] on E. c. 4p. in length.

The ground belonging to the curate's donative besides the house and garden plot lies near c. 3 furlongs from the house full E. and is bounded at the end with its own mound next the lane, on N. E. by its own mound and ditch and a ground of John Briant, and on the other end by a mound and ground of John Gleed being E., on S. W. it is mounded with the mound and ground lately of Mr.

Thomas Goddard now occuppied by Charles Garrard gent., of Lambourne Woodlands, Berks. The curate has always enjoyed this which is worth £3 10s. p. a.

The clerk of Prior Farley and S. Marston has a cow leaze in a ground called Coate Year leaze and his equal part of wintering and summering what the ground will keep: It is worth c. £2 10s. p. a. with the homestall and is part of the said donative he enjoys it. The partners in the leaze are Thomas Pearce gent., William Morse gent., William Rogers; the cottagers and clerk maintain the end mounds. There was also a cow [leaze] given for the better maintenance of the clerk of the two tithings but it was sold away which is not made good to the clerk and his successors.

The churchyard is bounded N. E. by a sufficient wall and at both ends of the church, on S. by posts and rails on N. it is mounded by the tenants of John Steevens.

Broad Blunsdon and Berry Blunsdon: No glebe land [i. e. of the vicarage]. A house and garden being part of a donative to the tithings for the better maintenance of the curate for ever with a ground mounded on N. by a ground and mound of Sir Stephen Fox called Water Eaton lying over against Widhill house and mounded on that side next the road with his own mound and on S. as on N. side. It is mounded by the parishioners of Broad Blunsdon. 6½a. dispersed up and down the common field in almost every furlong in 1a., ½a. and 1yd. [plots], worth c. £3 p. a. The churchyard is mounded about by both tithings. There is another donative of a house, a close and 1yd. in the common fields of Broad Blunsdon for the better maintenance of a clerk for ever.

Sevenhampton: No glebe land [i. e. of the vicarage]. The chapel yard is bounded N. E. by Edmund Warneford esq., with stone wall except 1 little plot of several belonging to the tithing at the upper end eastwards and the other part belonged to the farm which is now in the possession of Edmund Warneford esq., the rest of the mound is made up by the tithing, viz. from the chapel stile next the lower end of Beards close to a gate or door at the upper end of that close. There is another gate adjoining to this little door eastward that was set up by Mrs Margaret Warneford for her coach that they do maintain still.

Thomas Derham, vicar, Richard Stephens, John Fisher, John Cullerne, William Winninge, John Diper, John Archard, John Humpris, Joseph Sheppard, John Arden, Richard Humphris, Thomas Cullerne, Richard Tanner, churchwardens and sidesmen.

Endorsements: In the Exchequer between William Jones, clerk, complainant and John Large, William Pinegar, defendants. This was produced by Joseph Warden gent., a witness, 14 Oct 1801. Memorandum that it is our custom to have our clerks chose in no places but within our tithings of S. Marston and Prior Farley.

1. The churchwardens accounts for this year include a payment for the making of this terrier. (WSRO 1184/19). Thomas Derham was vicar at this time.

HILMARTON vicarage

392   8 May 1588 (D1/24/108/1)
The inquisition touching all the glebe lands, rights, duties, customs, tithes, profits, and ecclesiastical emoluments belonging and appertaining to the vicarage of

Hilmarton, and by what portions it is divided from the 'proprietaire' of the parsonage made by the churchwardens, sidesmen, and the other eldest and substantial men of every village of the parish uprightly and truly according to the furthest of their knowledge. All kinds of tithes of the village, manor, and farm of Clevancy [Cliffe Auncie] and of all grounds belonging thereto, with all offerings and other eccliastical duties.

In Great Beversbrook [Bestbrook] the pasturing of 6 oxen, called the Six Oxen leaze, from 3 May until Michaelmas [29 Sep] to be put in at the gate next to Penn and to feed 'thorous' the whole Goulds to Burfurlong.

Out of Little Beversbrook no other tithes but 10s. p. a. and for 'Arterrells'[1] 3s. 4d. p. a.

Out of Mr. Button's little cot for the tithes 14s. 4d. and out of the earl of Hertford's little cot 10s. p. a., but we have heard say that the ancient due of those little cots was the summer leaze for 4 kine p. a. For a close called Tarrants Troughe 12d. p. a. Nothing out of Corton farm but the offerings: what is further due out of that farm we cannot certainly affirm. Out of all other villages, farms, yardlands, tenements, commons, pastures, and grounds all offerings and ecclesiastical duties and all other kind of tithes, except tithe hay and the tithe of all kind of corn and grain which belong to the rectory.

The glebe: 3a. of meadow in Wittcome mead to be cut before Lammas [1 Aug] without any common after Lammas; 2a. of arable in the furlong under Penn; 2a. of arable in Eastlake; and ½a. in Hook furlong and ½a. in the N. field of Hilmarton in Grase furlong to be used according to the custom, that is 2 years tilled and the 3rd year to rest without common.

There belongs to the mansion house a barn, stable, forecourt, as it is now bounded, and the kitchen and garden in the N. side, with that plot of ground from the kitchen and garden down to the brook; but the bounds on the E. and W. of that plot could not at this time be certainly found out and therefore it is deferred until the lord of the manor of Hilmarton holds his next court there.

William Horte and Thomas Helliar, churchwardens, Thomas Saveacre, William Heyward, and John Robins, sidesmen, and Robert Jeffery and John Arnold of Clevancy, Thomas King and William Helliar of Penn, Edmund Packer and William Rimell of Catcomb [Catcome], William Bailie of Goatacre, John Tiler of ?Hil[marton], and William Coole of Beversbrooke.

Memorandum: that William Nicholas of Calne affirms that when he held Little Beversbrook he paid for the tithes of it to Sir John Babthrop, the vicar's farmer, 13s. 4d. p. a. and a further consideration.

1. In Lyneham see **394**.

393   1671 (D1/24/108/2)
Terrier taken by the commandment of the bishop. A mansion house, a forecourt and a plot of ground from the backside of the house down to the brook.

In Witcombe mead 3a. to be cut before Lammas [1 Aug] without any common after Lammas. 2a. of arable in the furlong under Penn to be used according to custom; 2 years to be sowed, 1 year to lie still without any common. A pasture ground called Prists lease. All kinds of tithe of the manor and farm of Clevancy and offerings and other ecclesiastical duties. All the other villages, farms, yardlands, tenements, commons, pastures and grounds all offerings, ecclesiastical duties and tithes except tithes hay and corn which belong to the rectory.

In Great Beversbrook [Bestbrooke] the pasturing of 6 oxen from 3rd May until Michaelmas [29 Sep]to be put in at the gate next unto Penn and to feed through the whole grounds unto Burfurlong.

Custom tithes: From Sir Robert Button's Littlecott [Littlecoates] 14s. 4d. p. a.; from Mr. John Rummin's Littlecott 10s.; from Tarrant's Trough 1s.; from Mr. Robert Forman's Beversbrook 10s.; from Arterils 3s. 4d.: It is not known what is due from Corton farm more than the offerings.

John Scott, curate, Thomas Norborne, Humphrey Bernard, churchwardens.

394   17 Jan 1705 (D1/24/108/3)

A mansion house of 3 bays of building and something more with a barn and stable in a piece of ground, c. ¾a.

A close of pasture called Priestleaze in the hamlet of Pen, c. 3a., with a house at the further end built by Adam Wiltshire, labourer, by the allowance of Mr. Rouswell,[1] vicar, which has been ever since allowed by the sufferance of succeeding vicars to be the property of the said Wiltshire and his descendants, they paying rent for the standing thereof and for the garden plot. 2a. of arable of large measure in Penn field lying together and bounded with meers on both sides. 3a. of grass in Witcomb Mead lying 1a. by itself and 2a. together, each parcel bounded with merestones, to be hained by the farmer at Candlemas [2 Feb] and to be carried by the vicar at Lammas [1 Aug].

The churchyard, ½a., to be mounded partly by the manor, partly by the parish and parsonage, except 1 gate to be maintained by the vicar.

A custom upon Beversbrook [Beaversbrook] farm held by John Tomson yeo. and John Angel yeo., of feeding 6 oxen through the full range of all the summer grounds.

A custom upon Hither Beversbrook farm held by John Tomson yeo. and Yonder Beversbrook held by John Angel yeo., of feeding 6 oxen through the full range of all the summer grounds namely the Home close, the Middle marsh, the Cours marsh, the Upper leaze and Brewers leaze in the former farm and the Little marsh, the Great marsh, the lane to be put in at Mortimers Gate and to feed to Burfurlong corner from 3 May to Michaelmas [29 Sep], in the latter farm all lying behither Burfurlong corner.

Tithe moduses: 14s. 4d. paid at Lammas from lady Britton's farm in Littlecott held by Thomas Bathe yeo.; 1s. from a close called Atherills or Trowmead in Lyneham but which adjoins the last farm; 10s. from a bargain in Littlecott held by John Bernard yeo.; 10s. from a bargain of Mr. Forman's of Calne called the Lower Beversbrook held by Thomas James yeo.; 3s. 4d. from Cowage farm held by Richard Broom yeo.; 1s. at Easter from Corton farm held by John Parsons alias Seegar.

All great and small tithes on the hamlet of Clevancy. Small tithes at the following rates: cow white 4d., calf 6d., fat beast 9d., sheep 3d. from the whole year unless the wool is tithed in kind otherwise 1s. 4d. a month, lamb 3d. If the lambs and calves are of sufficient number they may be tithed in kind. The sheep lambs and calves are due at St. Markstide [25 Aug], the cow white and fattening cattle at Lammas, when the lambs that are kept begin to pay as sheep; persons' [*i. e. communicants'*] offerings 2d., 1d. a house for eggs where poultry are kept and 1d. for a garden. The parson receives great tithes on the vicar's glebe but pays no small tithe on his own glebe to the vicar.

Thomas Smith, vicar, Edward Tugwell, John White, churchwardens, James Ruming, George Lawrence, sidesmen, Roger James.

1.   No record of the institution of this vicar has been found.

HILPERTON rectory

395   12 Jun 1605 (D1/24/109/1)
As *396* with amendments in footnotes. William Buckle, rector, John Slade, John Hiscocks[X], churchwardens, John Selfe [X], John Fenill [X], sidesmen, John Fryer [X], John Stevens, Luke Smyth, 'the ancientest of the parishe'.

396   1 Sep *c.* 1615[1] (D1/24/109/2)
A dwelling house containing 4 fields of building whereof the parlour and hall contain 2 fields and the kitchen across at the end of the hall contain the other 2. 1 little field of building for a study adjoining the house towards the garden. A barn containing 5 fields of building, a stable containing 1 field, a hayhouse and cowhouse containing 3 fields [*with a cut at W. end in* **395**]. A pigeon house, an outward barton and one inward barton with the situation of all the houses containing ½a., and an orchard and garden containing ½a.

A close of meadow and pasture of 3a. in Kidcroft. ½a. in Haven[2] mead lands of Edward Smith W., Thomas Smith on E. 1a.[3] of meadow in the E. field at Shorthedge lands of John Self[4] W., Anthony Stevens E.

32½a. [*recte 33½a. as in* **395**] of arable in the common fields: 11½a. [*recte 9½a. as in* **395**] in the W. field namely 1a under the hill[5] land of wid. Fenill[6] E., wid. Hisocks[7] on W.; 3a. on Steepe land of Anthony Stevens on W. and William Selfe[8] on E.; 2a. above the down land of John Slade N. and wid. Longe on S.; 1 little a. in Middle furlong land of Edward Longe esq., S[1], John Weale[9] N.; 2a. in the last furlong land of John Stevens junior S,.[10] William Selfe[11] N.; ½a. by the way side behind the church land of John Sarten W., the way to the marsh E.

In a field called Whaddons marsh[12] 1a. by Dockers bush land of the rectory of Whaddon W., wid. Smith E.[13] In the former W. field 2a. abutting on the Home close of wid. Grant land of wid. Longe E., Thomas Hunt on W. In the E. field 11a.; 2a. upon the Hill land of John Selfe senior S., land of Whaddon rectory on N[14]; 2a. at Marlin pit[15] across the highway land of Edward Longe esq., E. and W.; 1 head a. at Mannocks moor both ends abutting on the highways; 2a. by Henton lane, land of wid. Grant S.[16], wid. Hiscocks[7] N. E.; 2 single acres[17] in Lower Moonelight, having 1a. of George Smithe between them; 1a. at Lyppyat land of Thomas Longe E., wid. Smith W.; 1a. at Short hedge with a plot of meadow at the end land of Henry Fryer E., John Slade W. In a field[18] called Hirside 5a.; 3a. with a plot of mead land of Richard Gravenar N., wid. Fenill

S.[19]; 2a. in the same furlong on the ditch S. Anthony Stevens N.[20] In the S. field 4a.[21]; 3a. at Stony stile land of Edward Longe esq., N., William Derington[22] S.; 1a. at Hilpeswell land of John Slade N., John Weale S.

From Balls gate to Monckwood in Whaddon Lower field the tithe on all the meadow in Avon mead that appertains to the manor of Hilperton [Hilprington]. From Allmarsh along the highway to the gate[23] then going to Whaddon, then along Courtleaze hedge and Dollmead hedge[24].

The tithes of the fields called Horside[25] and Whaddons Marsh and all leazes, ingrounds, arable and pasture all of the land belonging to Whaddon and to Hilperton within except 1a. of wid. Bruncker[26] in Dollmead.[27]

Tithe of E. field both the land belonging to the manors of Whaddon and Hilperton except the tithe of the glebe land of the parsonage of Whaddon in the field and of 1a. of meadow at the head of the pit called a thirdendeale. The tithes of the new enclosure at Woodberry as well of the land[28] of Henry Fryer of Paxcroft [pascroft] in Whaddon as lessee of George Smith of Hilperton and also of the lands[29] of the said Henry Fryer and John Weale of Paxcroft in any of the common fields of Hilperton.

The tithe of all the lands of the town of Trowbridge that lie within the perambulation of Hilperton.

In Whaddon Lower field at the upperside of a furlong called Mervilland under the Breach hedge[30] the tithe of ½a. of laine belonging to the tenement of wid. Fenill[6] of 1yd. of laine belonging to the farm of Edward Longe esq.[31] and of 1yd. of laine belonging to the capital messuage of Thomas Smith of Hilperton.

In a common pasture[32] called the Down 5 beast leazes; 4 kine and 1 bull from Whitson eve until Michaelmas [29 Sep].

William Buckle, rector, John Slad, John Stevens, churchwardens, Edward Smith, Anthony Stevens[X], George Smith, William Self, John Serten, Richard Gravenar [X], John Selfe [X], Thomas Smith [X], 'The ancientest and chiefest of the parish.'

1. The year is omitted from the document but Luke Smith, John Hiscocks and John Fenill who are mentioned in 1605 are replaced in this terrier by widows of the same name; their wills were proved 27 June 1610 (Arch. Sarum), 8 Apr 1611 (Cons. Sarum), and 21 Oct 1613 (Arch. Sarum) respectively. William Buckle witnessed **395** and was suceeded as rector in 1626.
2. Avon in **395**, **395**, and **399**.
3. Omitted in **395** which has instead 1a. of laine in Whaddon lower field in a furlong called Bittom, William Self S., John Fenill N.
4. No landholder on W. in **398**.
5. In the furlong under the hill in **395**.
6. John Fenill in **395**.
7. John Hiscocks in **395**, formerly wid. Hiscocks alienated by James Gibbs and enclosed in **398**.
8. Thomas Smith in **395**.
9. Selfe crossed out in **398**.
10. Richard Gravener in **395**. No landholder mentioned in **398**.
11. Thomas Sarten in **395**.

12. Described as the little field near to Whaddon town end in **395**.
13. No bounds in **398** but described as having the footpath to Whaddon along it. Luke Smith on E. in **395**.
14. No bounds on N. in **398**.
15. Marlin pool in **398**.
16. William Feltham in **395**.
17. Described as in a furlong called Lower moonlight by Henton lane in **395**.
18. In the N. field called Hirside in **395**.
19. John Smith in **395**.
20. No landholder on N. in **395** described as having a ditch at the lower end.
21. 6a. in **395** with the addition of 2a. in a furlong called Frythes, George Smith W., Edward Smith E.
22. John Derington in **395**.
23. Red gate in **399**.
24. Pottmead hedge in **398**.
25. Horse lease in **399**.
26. No landholder in **398**.
27. Dollmead corner in **398** and **399**. The tithe of the rectory of Whaddon added in **398** and **399**.
28. This land in Whaddon omitted in **395**.
29. Described as two tenements in Paxcroft in **395**.
30. Shordach hedge in **398**.
31. Sir Walter Longe in **399**.
32. Common of pasture omitted in **395**.

397   26 Sep 1631 (D1/24/109/3)

1a. adjoining the dwelling house in orchard, garden and backside. A dwelling house 60ft. by 27ft. A barn and stable adjoining 64ft. by 21ft. An hayhouse and oxstall adjoining 40ft. by 19ft. A dovehouse and other small buildings for necessary offices.

A close of pasture, 3a., called the Parsons Kitcroft.; ½a. in common Chestland, John Golledge N., William Derington S.; 1a. in Halfacres, William Bartlett E., Christopher Smith W.; ½a. in the same Halfacres William Bartlett E. and W.; 1a. 2p. in a new enclosure behind Pound mead, William Slade S., John Golledge N.; 1r. of meadow in Avon mead, 60p., called the Parsons Half.

Arable in the E. field: 2a. upon the hill shooting westwards no lower than the a. belonging to the rectory of Whaddon adjoining it on N. and William Slade S.; 1a. in Hooreside, rector of Whaddon W., a footpath E.; a little a. at Shorthedge, John Slade W., butting on N. upon the highway from Hilperton to Whaddon. 1a. at Flexland, John Slade E., Henry Frier W.; 2a. at Lower Moonlight, Henry Grant S., Luke Hiscox N.; 1a. at Lower Moonlight, Christopher Smith N., John Selfe S.; 1a. near adjoining, John Selfe N., John Graunt S.; 2a. above Shorthedge butting N. on John Stevens, S. on William Derington. A head a. to Dead Mens lands, John Weale E.; 1a. at Lypyate butting southward on the highway from Trowbridge to Devizes.

Arable in the S. field: 3a., Christopher Smith, N. William Derington S.; 1a., John Slade N., John Weale S.

Arable in the W. field: 2a. above the Grove, George Smith E. and W.; 3a. upon Stibbs, William Selfe E., John Grant W.; 1½a. above the Down John Slade N., William Derington S.; 2a. in the Little furlong, George Smith E., John Slade W.; ½a. joining to the hedge of Christopher Meriwether E. Haniel Brown W.; 1½a. above Stichens, William Derington E., John Selfe W.; 1a. above the Hill, John Fenill E., Luke Hiscox W.

Pasture and feeding in the Down for 4 beasts and a bull from Whitsun eve til 29 Sep.

Henry Hulbert, rector, Christopher Smith, John Smith, churchwardens, John Fenell, Anthony Steephens, Christopher Merewether.

398   27 Mar 1672 (D1/24/109/4)
A fair new built dwelling house containing 4 fields or bays of building with 1 croft bay of field of building for buttries and out houses with lodging rooms over, 1 barn of 1 bay a stable of 1 bay 1 out barton and 1 in barton with the situation of the houses 1 garden and orchard, 1a. Land, tithes and commons as **395** with amendments in footnotes.

Archibald Buckeridge, rector, Richard Gayton, William Steevens, church-wardens. *Names in the same hand.*

399   20 Apr 1678 (D1/24/109/4)
A dwelling house of 3 bays, 1 barn of 5 bays, 1 stable of 1 bay, 1 pigeon house, 1 garden of ½a. in front of the house and 1 little court.

A close of meadow in Kidcroft, 3a. ½a. in Avon mead Edward Smith W., Thomas Smith 3. 1a. of meadow in the E. field at short hedge, John Selfe W., Anthony Stevens E.

A close of meadow or pasture called Church lands, 5a., having 1a. in enclosure of James Slade N. side. In the W. field 6a. 10p. viz.: 1a. adjoining the highway lands of John Selfe on both sides; 2 pieces on Steepe, lands of Mr. Thomas Beach W., lands of Obadiah Moxon on E., with land of William Hullett between the two pieces; 1 piece land of Richard Smith N. and land of William Slade junior S.; 2 pieces one bounded by lands of James Slade N. and Henry Wallis on S. the other by lands of Richard Smith on S. and William Slade on S.

In S. field 2½a. 12p. bounded land of Thomas Welland on S. and James Slade on N.

In E. field 6½a.; 2 pieces at Lipyeat one lying with the land of Sir Walter Long on W., the other with the land of Sir Walter Long on E.; 2 pieces in Moonlight, one with lands of Francis Hiscocks on N. and Richard Deverell on S., the other with land of Francis Hiscocks on S. and Mr. Shipman on N.; 2 pieces at Pitts hedge, one bounded by the hedge on N. and land of William Slade junior on S., the other being a head a. bounded with the glebe of the parsonage of Whaddon on E.; a piece at Short hedge lands of William Slade senior on W. and William Shergall E.; 1 piece adjoining to Ten acres lying with the land of John Browne on N. land of Gifford Gerish on S.; 2 pieces at Marlin pit, one bounded with land of James Slade on E. and Richard Smith on W., the other with land of Richard Smith on E. and Nathanial Smith on W.; a piece in the middle of the field with land of Anthony Stevens on N. In a field called the Hill 2a. with land of William Slade junior on S. and Mr. Iles on N.

Tithes and commons of pasture as **395** with amendments in footnotes.

James Garth, rector, James Slade, Gifford Gerrish, churchwardens, William Slade senior, 'ancientest and chiefest of the inhabitants'.

400   31 Jul 1783 (D1/24/109/6)

A parsonage house *c.* 156 ft. x 27 ft. with stonewalls covered with stone tiles consisting of a small parlour with board floor plastered walls and ceiled. A kitchen, brewhouse and pantry with stone floors and plastered walls, only the brewhouse ceiled. 5 chambers with plastered walls and ceiled. A barn *c.* 64ft. by 19½ft. built with stone walls and covered with stone tiles. A stable *c.* 30ft. by 24ft. built with stone and covered with straw.

A yard bounded with walls. A garden bounded with wall and hedge and an orchard bounded with hedges all adjoining the parsonage house, containing in all *c.* 1a.

A piece of pasture land called Sleep craft, *c.* 2½a., on E. of Hilperton's marsh, bounded with hedges, lands of Edward Eyles esq., on E., S. and W., lands of Philip James Gibbs esq., on N. A piece of pasture land called Chestling, *c.* 5½a., on E. of Hilperton's marsh, bounded with hedges, having the lands of the said Edward Eyles all around it, with the lane or drove that leads to it lying between the closes of the said Edward Eyles. A piece of pasture land called Coming Hill, *c.* 2a., on N. of the lane or road leading from Hilperton to Whaddon, bounded with hedges, lands of the said Edward Eyles on N. and E., lands of John Rickman on W., lands of Mr. Tubb on S.

A piece of arable land called S. field, *c.* 5a., bounded with hedges, S. side lying against the turnpike road from Hilperton to Semington and lands of the said Edward Eyles on N. W. and E. A piece of arable land called Little Buckland, *c.* 1¾a., bounded with hedges, S. side lying against the said turnpike road, N. part against the lands of John Hicks gent., W. part against the lands of Thomas Cottle, N. part against the lands of Edward Eyles esq.

A piece of arable land called Moon Light, *c.* 6a., on N. of the said turnpike road bounded with hedges, lands of Edward Eyles esq., on E. N. and S., lands of the rector of Whaddon on part of the W. end. A piece of arable land in Hilperton field, *c.* ¼a., lands of Edward Eyles esq., on W. and N., lands of John Hicks on S. A piece of arable land called Step, *c.* 6½a., lying between the lanes or roads leading from Hilperton to Trowbridge, lands of Edward Eyles esq., on E., lands of Mr. Henry Slade on S., lands of Mr. Houlton on W. and the lane or road on N. N. B. with an unlimited right of stocking Hilperton marsh.

The great and small tithes.

Church Furniture: 4 bells, a silver cup *c.* 8ozs., a pewter flagon and pewter plate. A bible and 2 common prayer books with 2 registers of marriage, etc.

The Church is repaired by the parish, the chancel by the rector, and the churchyard fence by the parish.

The clerk has what he can collect at Easter and is appointed by the minister.

John Montagu, rector, Gabriel Still, churchwarden, James Rudman, Robert Lay, Adam Martin.

BROAD HINTON vicarage

401 18 Oct 1671 (D1/24/110/1)

A dwelling house with barn, stable, garden and backside adjoining. The benefit of the churchyard. A meadow on N. side of the house, ¾a. 1a. of meadow in Town mead under the W. hedge next to Maskelins Town mead. 3 x ½a. of arable in the W. field; ½a. next to the Vicarage hedge on E. and a ½a. of Richard Banckes on W.; ½a. abutting on Pooles between John Greenoway on E. and lately Henry White W.; ½a. abutting on the land lately George Hedge's called Lindalls Yard on E. and lying between William Glanville esq., on N. and John Greenoway on S. 1a. of arable in the E. field shooting towards Juggins Bourne, lying between John Brown on N. and Giles Wheeler on S. 1 head a. of arable in Uffcott field abutting on the end of William Spicer's headland next to the way which parts Uffcott and Hinton fields. A little head a. called Small tithes in Uffcott N. field next to John Cleeter junior[1] on S.

Tithe corn, hay and all other tithes on parsonage glebe belonging to the vicar. All the tithe hay from N. Breach, Cobham, Heyden and the meadows beyond Heyden Millway and Hammpond fields. All tithe hay about the town in any of the grounds which were at any time arable and of all meadows of 1a. and under. Tithe hay of Broad Town, Hamm, and Thornhill in Broad Hinton. Tithe hay of Little Town grounds, Cottmarsh, part of Bincknoll and Chaddington in Broad Hinton. Tithe wool and lamb, calves, cow white and all other tithes except corn, with offerings at Easter.

A tithe composition of 5s. paid 1 Aug p. a. out of grounds called Barnehill, Stafford and the meadows belonging to the same. A tithe composition of 13s. paid 1 Aug p. a. out of grounds called Goldsboroughs.

Henry Dudley, vicar, Matthew Pounde [X], Obadiah Crooke, churchwardens, John Grenoway junior of Uffcott [X], Christopher Pike, sidesmen.

1. Anthony Cleeter in 1705.

402 16 May 1705 (D1/24/110/2)

As 401 with amendment in footnote. 1a. in Bincknoll field shooting upon the Dipe. Tithe of meadow and pasture belonging to Mrs. Stone's farm in the occupation of Roger Spackman belong to the vicar unless the impropriator can make it appear that any belongs to him. This according to the best information I can have at present is a true terrier.

Basil Davenport, vicar, Edmund Taylor, John King, churchwardens, Thomas Norborn.

1. At the start of his tithe account book begun in 1766 Algernon Clavering, vicar, noted that there were no moduses except the 2 Lammas (1 Aug) dues mentioned in **401**. The other tithes were paid in cash according to a composition for a fixed term. He had a right to put 2 cows in Broad lease, and also in the fields taken out of Broad lease. Offerings at Easter 1d. from all over 16; 1d. for tithe gardens from every housekeeper unless the house belonged to farms which pay composition tithes. A new farm called Andrews always pays yearly 24 pigeons because its pigeon house was built since the composition of £4 10s. was agreed (WSRO 829/3).

403   30 Jul 1783 (1505/15)[1]

1. A dwelling house for the vicar with barn, stable, garden and backside adjoining and the benefit of the church yard. It is built of stone thatched on W. and tiled on E. side, containing a small stone passage, on the right, a parlour 12ft. square, ceiled and papered with a deal floor, on the left a stone hall 17ft. by 15ft., ceiled and plastered within the hall to the S., a stone kitchen not ceiled 17ft. by 12ft. A cellar under the parlour, 5 bedrooms all small ceiled and floored some with deal and some with ash. Outhouses: a stable *c.* 12ft. square, brewhouse 10ft. square, a barn 26ft. by 12ft. all built of stone and thatched.

2. Lands: The church yard, ½a.; a garden, *c.* 20p.; on W. side of the house 2 meadows, *c.* ½a. and *c.* ¼a.; on S. a meadow, *c.* ¾a.; on N. a meadow, *c.* 2a., bounded S. and W. by the land, N. by Churches (given in exchange for 2½a. in the common field which formerly belonged to the vicarage). A meadow called Poole's, *c.* 1a., bounded Taylor's on N., Churches on S., the street through the parish on E. A head a. of arable land in Uffcot field abutting upon the end of William Spicer's headland next the way which parts Uffcot and Hinton fields. A little head a. called Small Tithes lying in Uffcot N. field next to the land of the Charterhouse on S. side.

3. Tithes: All tithes corn, hay, and all other of the parsonage glebe lands. All tithe of hay growing upon Northbreach, Cobham, Heyden and the Meadow beyond Hayden, Millway and Hamm pond fields. Tithe hay about the town in any of the grounds which were at any time arable and likewise of all the meadows which are but an a. and under. Tithe hay of Broadtown, Hamm and Thornhill. Tithe hay of Little Town grounds, Cotmarsh, parts of Binknoll and Chaddington. Tithe wool and lamb with calves, cow white and all other tithes, except corn, offerings at Easter. A composition of tithe of 5s. p. a. out of Barnehill, Stafford and the Meadows belonging to the same is and of 13s. p. a. out of Goldsborough all due to be paid on 1 Aug.

4. No augmentations: 6. Furniture etc.: A crimson pulpit cloth and cushion, 5 bells. 2 very large flagons, a large plate with this inscription 'Given by the Worshipful and religious William Glanville, Esqr. to the parish Church of Broad Hinton'. A cup inscribed 'Belonging to the Parish Church of Broad Hinton'. A small plate with no inscription. All of silver.

7. No lands etc., for the repairs of the church.

8. The churchyard is repaired on E. and S. side by the rector, the rest by the parish.

9. The clerk appointed by the vicar, the sexton by the parish.

1.   An unsigned copy with the parish records.

LITTLE HINTON rectory (405–7) and vicarage (404)

404   15 Nov 1671 (D1/24/111/1)

A vicarage house, barn, stable, hovel, backside, garden, and 2a. of meadow called Dr. Hungerford's ground.

Thomas Pekins and John Green, churchwardens.

405   18 Dec 1677 (D1/24/111/2)

Terrier according to the 87th canon. The churchyard, *c.* 12p. A dwelling house of 3 bays of building, a brewhouse of 2 bays adjoining at the W. end. A barn of 6 bays, a stable and a malthouse adjoining, each consisting of 1 bay. A hovel and a house of office.

A garden on S. of the dwelling house, a brewhouse equal in length and *c.* 1 lug in breadth. *c.* ½ lug on the E. was enclosed out of the common and is charged 2d. rent p. a. at 29 Sep to the lord of the manor. A backside of *c.* 4 lugs enclosed with the said houses and churchyard on W. end. On N. of the barn ground for the settling of a ladder, *c.* 5ft. in breadth.

All manner of tenths and tithes, great and small. The farmer has the tithe of his hay in Long mead in consideration of a portion of meadow called Parsons Two acres which the rector only mows and carries off by Lammas [1 Aug]; afterwards the feeding belongs to the farm until Ladyday [15 Mar]. 1a. in Longmead called Inmead acre belonging to the farm was liable to pay tithe to the rector but by an agreement 28 Jan 1660 between Mr. Francis Cross, rector of Little Hinton, and the inhabitants and a decree in Chancery to confirm an enclosure of commons, by which the rector and his successors receive a rent in lieu of tithes rated as follows: <one estate only paying in kind>: Francis Hungerford esq. £30 1s. 9d.; William Glanville esq. £6 19s. 3d.; Henry Hedges £3 2s. 7d.; Edward Jinner £5 4s. 9d.; Thomas Lord £5 9s. 8d.; William Morley gent., £5 13s. 1d.; Robert and John Whipp gent. £5 17s. 2d.; Joan Lowday, wid., £2 11s. 4d.; William Harding 4s. 11d.; William Heath £5 15s. 7d.; Thomas Pekins £5 0s. 9d.; Henry Hunt gent. £5 10s. 9d.; Robert Harris senior and junior £9 8s. 3d.; William Berry £2 19s. 3d.; John Walrond gent. £9 8s. 3d.; Daniel Heath £3 5s. 11d.; Robert Heath 17s. 8d.; Thomas Lowday £6 5s. 9d.; Daniel Wells 16s. 4d. These rents to be paid on Quarterdays. The miller pays 6s. 8d. at Easter for the tithe of his mill and the rector enjoys 2a. of Lammas mead by the decree.

John Stubbs, rector, Robert Harris, John Berry, churchwardens, Thomas Lord, William Loveday.

406   1705 (D1/24/111/3)

The churchyard, dwelling house and adjoining brewhouse as **405**. 2 stables and a woodhouse all under 1 roof, being 4 bays of building. 1 house of office in the backyard. A garden on S. side of the dwelling house and brewhouse equal in length to them and 26ft. in breadth enlarged by the present to 56ft. by virtue of a copy of the court roll held by the rector and his successors. *Tithes and details of the enclosure agreement as* **405** *omitting the rate.*

Thomas Coker, rector, Francis Atkinson, Thomas Edwards, churchwardens.

407   27 Jul 1783 (D1/24/111/4)

The parsonage house is thatched and contains 13 rooms. The building, partly Flemish, partly stone, the rooms all have boarded floors except the kitchen which has an earth floor; the best parlour is wainscotted 'quite up' and ceiled. The common parlour is wainscotted half way and ceiled. The outhouses are a stable of stone and thatched and a barn weather boarded and thatched. A garden before the house fenced with pales, *c.* 8 or 9p., a garden behind the house *c.* 20 or 25p., fenced with a stone wall. The glebe is 2a. in the common meadow, abutted on N. by Sansums Lower meadow and S. by the Upper meadow called Town meadow.

The churchyard is fenced with stone, partly by the parish, partly by the rector and partly by the farm. The chancel is repaired by the rector, the church by the parish. There are no trees on the glebe or churchyard. A payment in lieu of tithes was settled by a decree in Chancery. A pension of 40s. is paid out of the rectory to Winchester cathedral.

4 bells, 3 large and 1 saint bell. No clock. Communion plate; 1 large silver flagon weight 40oz. 18dwt., 2 silver salvers 16oz. 14 dwt., 1 cup and cover 11oz. with the inscription 'Ecclesiae de Hinton Parva com. Wilts Thomae Coker Rectoris Donum An. Do. 1719'.

The clerk's wages are £1 1s. p. a. lately raised to £2 2s. p. a. paid by the parish. He is appointed by the rector.

Caleb Colton, officiating minister, N. Wilson, George Lea, churchwardens, John Edwards, John Brunsden, overseers, Ralph Withers, Manuell Batt.

HORNINGSHAM prebend (rectory)

408   1634 (D5/10/1/14)

A parcel of ground or field called Brimgo, 12a., which lies between the highway from Maiden Bradley to Longbridge Deverill on S. side and the highway called Brimgo lane on N. side, a ground called Kingslade occupied by William Style on W. side and a ground called Anste, occupied by Osmund Hunt on E. side.

A field called Parsonage land, 19a., with a meadow of 2a., lying at the S. W. of the same field, on S. side lies the way from Horningsham to Deverill, on W. end is bounded some part with a parrock of Joan Northen called Whites and the other part with Hitcombe lane, the N. side is bounded with grounds of William Bosse called Hitcombe, one of Robert Hill called Parkers, another field called Hitcombe, the E. side is bounded with the Great field occupied by one of the tenants.

The Parsonage acre, 1a., lying in the S. E. corner of a field called Udborough bounded with Charlock hill hedge on S. side, is now occupied by Mr. William Arundel esq., lord of the manor. For which a., when there was an enclosure made by Mr. Stanter, then lord, the prebend was allowed 2a. in exchange for that a. which 2a. lay in the common field called Hitcombe bounded S. with a parcel of land of Roger Foster, N. with 1a. of Margery Styles; the other a. is enclosed and bounded N. with a ground occupied by Christopher Young, S. with a ground occupied by William Roe.

Benjamin Walter, curate, Edward Style, Roger Exton [X], churchwardens, William Marsh [X], Roger Foster [X], sidesmen, Robert Adlam, Martin Card, Robert Hill.

HUISH rectory

409 n. d. early 17th. cent.[1] (D1/24/112/1)
A dwelling house and a barn each containing 3 fields. 3 closes in several, 3a. 8a. 3yd. in the E. field. 9a. 3yd. in the W. field. 2 several a. in the E. field of Oare [Woar]. 100 sheep leaze. The keeping of 4 oxen and 2 houses.
John Cooley, parson, George Stagge.

1. John Cooley signed the bishop's transcript for 1605. He was dead by 1628 when Andrew Cooley was instituted although Andrew signed the bishop's transcript from 1619.

410 6 Nov 1671 (D1/24/112/2)
A parsonage house, garden and orchard, barn, backside and outhousing with a little close, 1a. A little meadow called Cote, *c.* ½a. An enclosed ground of arable called Lysbourne, *c.* 6a., on S. side of the W. field.
In the W. field 2a. of arable land. In the E. field lying in several places, 8½a. In Oare E. field 2a. of arable.
Tithe rates from the living in Oare of George Bengar 6s. 8d. p. a.; a third of the tithe of the living of Mrs. Barbara Skilling wid.; a third of the tithe of the living of Roger Gale, both in Oare.
1 enclosed ground of pasture or arable at E. end of Cow common, 6a. Right of common of pasture with the farm and tenants for 100 dry sheep. All other great and small tithes are taken up in kind.
Geofrey Thistlethwayte [*rector*], George Stagge, Thomas Chandler, churchwardens, Charles Head, James Stagge [X], farmers and inhabitants there. *Names of the inhabitants in the same hand.*

411 1677 (D1/24/112/3)
As **410***.* Geoffrey Thistlethwayte, rector, George Stagg junior, churchwarden, Charles Head, George Stagg, James Stagg, Thomas Chaundeler, inhabitants. *Names of the inhabitants in the same hand.*

412 25 Sep 1705 (D1/24 112/4)[1]
The chancel adjoining to the church, the feeding of the churchyard, a dwelling house of 3 rooms on a floor, a barn, a stable, a cart house with some necessary buildings there, a backside a garden with some few apple trees. A close called Coat, ½a.; an enclosed ground called Lisborn, 6a.; an enclosed ground in the Hill, 7a.; 4a. in the W. field of Huish [Hewish] and 5a. in the E. field; 3½a. in the Middle field with common of pasture for 70 dry sheep. Tithe corn, hay, coppice wood, and small tithes. Tithe corn, hay and small tithes of the estate of Margaret and Richard Edmonds in Oare except the little mead lying next to Mrs Cheyney's backside and ½a. lying in a ground called Ashes, ¾a. in the same ground and ½a. more in the E. field of Oare between the lands of Mrs. Spencer; 1½a. and 27r. lying shooting on the way to Ramscombe between the lands of Mrs. Cheyney and John Benger. A third of tithe corn, hay and wool of the estate of Roger and John Gale of Oare in Wilcot except 1½a. and 27r. in the field next to Ramscombe

shooting N. and S. and the land of Margaret and Richard Edmonds on W. and a furlong shooting thereon on E. Two thirds of tithe corn, hay and wool of the estate of Susanna and Michael Pontyn of Oare in Wilcot except 1a. shooting on the way to Ramscombe between the land of John Chandler and Henry Jackson. 6s. 8d. from the estate of John Benger of Oare payable each year at Michaelmas [29 Sep].

Richard Edmonds, Thomas Chandler, churchwardens, Charles Head, George Stagg, Thomas Stagg.

1.   A copy made 26 Jul 1783 witnessed by Charles Mayo [*rector*], John Tarrant, John Reeves, churchwardens.

HULLAVINGTON vicarage

413   18 May 1605 (D1/24/113/1)

The parsonage is an impropriation of the possession of Eton College and holds the tithe corn and hay of all the parish, viz. of Hullavington, Surrendell [Surrinden], and Bradfield, and all manner of tithes of the demesnes.

The vicarage is endowed with a dwelling house on the S. side of the churchyard with a barn, a stable, a garden, an orchard, and a close adjoining together, and 2 yardlands of meadow, pasture, and arable land in the fields and territories of Hullavington, which premises are held of the manor of Hullavington for 5s. free rent to be paid yearly to the lord and suit of court.

Arable in W. field: 1a. in Townsend furlong between 3 farndells of John Punter N. and 1 farndell of Thomas Layne S.; ½a. there between ½a. of Alice Hathewaie N. and ½a. of Robert Watts S.; ½a. there between John Bleke's ½a. N. and Agnes Power's ½a. S.; ½a. in the Weell between Joan Sergiant's ½a. E. and Edmund Broke's farndell W.; ½a. in the Lower Blake between Edmund Broke's ½a. E. and Robert Barnard's ½a. W.; ½a. in the Upper Blake between James Punter's ½a. E. and Wolfran Gingill's 1a. W.; ½a. on Hillridge between William Coleman's ½a. E. and James Punter's ½a. W.; ½a. in Hilslade between Maud Jake's ½a. N. and Robert Barnard's ½a. S.; ½a. in the ? Healsditch [or Headsditch] between ½a. of Maud Jake N. and Edmund Broke's ½a. S.; ½a. in Dew furlong between John Bleke's ½a. N. and Wolfran Gingil's 1a. S.; ½a. there between James Punter's ½a. N. and Robert Barnard's ½a. S.; ½a. by Bath way between Maud Jake's ½a. E. and Bath way W.; ½a. in Long furlong between ½a. of Richard Punter of the Stone E. and John Bleke's ½a. W.; ½a. there between John Bleke's ½a. E. and ½a. of Richard Punter the eldest W.; ½a. there at Maroe's gate between John Bleke's ½a. W. and William Colman's 1a. E.; 1 farndell at Owlands between Agnes Power's ½a. N. and John Bleke's farndell S.; ½a. with the hedge in Nethecotts between the Clapcotts field S. and James Punter's ½a. N.; 1 farndell in Broadmore between George Balie's ½a. S. and Richard Punter the eldest's farndell N.; ½a. there between Robert Watts' ½a. on S. and Edmond Broke's ½a. on N.; ½a. in Six acres between Maud Jake's ½a. on N. and Alice Hathawaye's ½a. on S.; a farndell at the Slowe between George Balye's farndell on S. and Edmond Broke's ½a. on N.; a farndell in Long Hunnar between James Punter's

farndell on S. and Short Nattockes on N.; ½a. at the gate between Richard
Punter the eldest's ½a. on W. and Maud Jake's ½a. on E.; ½a. in Short Nattockes
between John Bleeke's ½a. on W. and Joan Sergiant's ½a. on E.; ½a. in Long
Nattockes between Agnes Power's ½a. on W. and John Bleke's ½a. on E.; ½a. at
Lingcrofte between James Punter's ½a. on S. and Robert Watts' ½a. on N.; ½a. in
Long Orredge between Maud Jake's ½a. on E. and Agnes Power's farndell on W.;
½a. in Short Orredge between John Stevens' ½a. on E. and John Bleke's ½a. on
W.; a farndell in Waynesbinch between James Punter's farndell on S. and the
Down on N.; a farndell in Lower Midnill shooting upon the Dean between
Giles Bullock's a. on W. and Richard Punter's ½a. on E.; ½a. there between
Thomas Cosen's ½a. on W and Joan Sergiant's ½a. on E.; ½a. there between Joan
Sergiant's ½a. on W. and Maud Jake's ½a. on E.; ½a. there at Broken bridge
between Alice Hathewaye's ½a. on W. and John Bleke's ½a. on E.; 1a. in Upper
Midnill between Thomas Laine's ½a. on W. and James Punter's farndell on E.; ?
2a. there between Maud Jake's ½a. on S. and Edmund Broke's ½a. on N.; ½a. in
the Uppershill between James Punter's ½a. on S. and William Genkings' a. on
N.; ½a. at Sandpitts which is a headland; ½a. at Long Sands between James
Punter's ½a. on E. and Robert Watts' a. on W.; a butt at Aylesdown between
Agnes Power's butt on W. and John Bleke's butt on E.; a farndell in the marsh
between Robert Watts' ½a. on S. and Edmund Perton's farndell on N.; ½a. in
Great acres between Joan Sergiant's ½a. on W. and Maud Jake's ½a. on E.; a stitch
at Little mead between a farndell of John Bleke and a stitch of Edmund Perton.

Arable land in the E. field: just in the Innocks; ½a. in Milfurlong between
the way on E. and Agnes Power's ½a. on W.; ½a. in Dead lands between the way
on W. and Agnes Power's ½a. on W.; ½a. on Rushill between Edmund Perton's
½a. on N. and Alice Hathywae's ½a. on S.; ½a. there between John Punter's ½a.
on N. and Wolfran Gingil's ½a. on S.; ½a. in Hilpitt between John Sergiant's ½a.
on N. and Edmund Perton's ½a. on S.; a ½a butt in the Cleve between William
Colman's farndell on S. and Wolfran Gingil's ½a. on N.; ½a. there between
William Genkin's ½a. on S. and James Punter's ½a. on N.; ½a. of land mead
between Catchdoll on W. and John Punter's ½a. of land mead on E.; ½a. in
Burridge furlong between Edmund Broke's ½a. on S. and Edmund Perton's ½a.
on N.; ½a. in Hardnill between Robert Watt's ½a. on S. and Edmund Perton's
½a. on N.; a farndell in Hardnillslade between Thomas Layne's farndell on S.
and Edmund Perton's farndell on N.; 1a. on Fulbroke between Richard Punter
the eldest's ½a. on W. and John Sergiant's ½a. on E.; ½a. there between George
Balye's ½a. on W. and William Colman's ½a. on E.; ½a. there between Alice
Hatheway's a. on W. Thomas Cosen's ½a. on E.

In Broad field: A farndell at Lyetmore between Alice Hathewaye's a. on W.
and John Davies' ½a. on E.; ½a. behind Hayes between Wolfran Gingil's farndell
on W. and Edmund Perton's ½a. on E.; ½a. in Garson between Wolfran Gingill's
½a. on S. and Richard Punter the younger's ½a. on N.; ½a. there between the
said Richard Punter's ½a. on S. and Agnes Power's ½a. on N.; ½a. in Topshill
between Agnes Power's farndell on E. and Robert Barnard's ½a. on W.; ½a. in
Oathill between John Punter's ½a. on S. and Agnes Power's ½a. on N.; ½a. in
Nypnill between John Punter's ½a. on N. and Robert Hathewaye's ½a. on S.;
½a. there between John Punter's ½a. on N. and James Punter's ½a. on S.; 1a. in

the Scoole between William Colman's farndell on W. and Agnes Power's ½a. on E.; ½a. in Shapland between Richard Punter's ½a. on W. and Edmund Perton's ½a. on E.; a butt lying along Smithes mead on W. and a butt of Robert Barnard's on E.; ½a. on Gawnhill between John Sergiant's a. on S. and Edmund Perton's ½a. on N.; ½a. there between George Balye's ½a. on S. and Agnes Power's ½a. on N.; ½a. in Dunfurlong between John Sergiant's ½a. on S. and Edmund Perton's ½a. on N.; ½a. there between John Sergiant's ½a. on S. and John Punter's ½a. on N.; ½a. in Hayfurlong between James Punter's ½a. on W. and Richard Punter's ½a. on E.; ½a. in Longfurlong between Agnes Power's ½a. on N. and Alice Hathewaye's ½a. on S.; ½a. there between Thomas Cosen's ½a. on N. and Maud Jake's ½a. on S.; ½a. in Kingsway furlong between Thomas Cosen's ½a. on N. and Maud Jake's ½a. on S.; ½a. in Grasden furlong between James Punter's ½a. on N. and John Bleke's ½a. on S.; ½a. in Chollwell between Robert Watt's ½a. on N. and Richard Punter's ½a. on S.; ½a. in Oldland furlong between Robert Watt's ½a. on N. and Edmund Perton's ½a. on S.; ½a. there between Agnes Power's farndell on N. and John Stevens' ½a. on S.; ½a. there between Edmund Perton's ½a. on N. and Greenway on S.; ½a. in Broadlands between Edmund Perton's ½a. on E. and Joan Sergiant's ½a. on W.; ½a. in Pease land between Agnes Power's ½a. on E. and John Stevens' ½a. on W.; ½a. in the Upper Barrow between John Punter's ½a. on N. and Robert Watt's ½a. on S.

2 lugs of meadow mead in Broad mead lying in the ninth lot with John Bleeke, with a whole part and meadow belonging to 2 yardlands through all the lott meads of Hullavington always lying in the said ninth lot with the said John Bleke and 3 house lots in Bidfield.

The whole pasture and portion of pasture ground and feeding belonging to 2 yardlands in the town leaze and in the downs.

John More, vicar.

414   12 Dec 1671 (D1/24/113/2)

A dwelling house, garden orchard, backside and a close of pasture or arable adjoining all containing 2a. 1 ground of arable or pasture called Fulbrook lately enclosed out of the E. field, 18a. 1 close of pasture or arable lately enclosed out of the Common, 10a. 1 close of pasture or arable called the Sands lately enclosed out of the W. field, 5½a. 4 lugs of meadow in Broadmead, 2a. A parcel of meadow in Catchdole lately taken out of the E. field, ½a. 17a. and 3 farndells of arable land in the W. field. 11a. and 3 farndells of arable in the E. field Six acres. A close of pasture in Surrendell [Surrenden], called the Vicar's close, 1a.

John Diston, vicar, Henry Hulbert, Anthony Blike, churchwardens. *The names of the churchwardens in the same hand.*

415   23 Jul 1783 (D1/24/113/3)

Taken by the direction of the bishop at his primary visitation at Chippenham.

A vicarage house built with common stone covered with stone tiles, containing 4 rooms on the ground floor, kitchen, hall, parlour, pantry and cellar, all ceiled except the kitchen. The kitchen floor is a composition of lime and sand. The floor of the hall is stone and pavement and the parlour is floored and wainscotted with deal. In the second floor there are 4 chambers or lodging rooms, and a little room called the study, all ceiled beside a lumber room over the kitchen which is not ceiled. Adjoining the vicarage house is a brewhouse and over it a small lumber room not ceiled. A barn and stable built of stone and stone tiles under the same roof, 44ft. long, 20ft. wide. The churchyard surrounded by a wall, 2 small gardens one of them surrounded by a wall the other partly by a wall and partly by a gooseberry hedge, and an orchard partly fenced by a wall, partly by a quickset hedge. A close fenced with a quickset hedge, c. 2½a. All these are close to the vicarage house and are contiguous to each other.

3 pieces of ground lying together at some distance from the vicarage house called Fullbrooks, one of them arable, c. 10a., 2 of them meadows, 5½a. and 3a. 3 pieces of pasture land, 2 large, 1 small, called Town Leases, c. 20a. A piece of pasture called the Tining, c. 10a. 3 small pieces of arable, c. 1a. each, 2 in a common field called the Lower and the other in the Upper field. c. ½a. of meadow ground bounded with stone land marks, lying in a meadow belonging to Henry Stephens esq., called Catsdole. The above is an account of the old glebe amounting to 50a.

The following is an account of the augmentation or new glebe. This lies in Kington St Michael and is called part of Upper Marsh, c. 30a., and known by the particular names of Innocks, Great mead, Five acres, Wheat Ground, Quarry Lease. All the writing relating to this augmentation are not here and are assumed to be in the hands of the trustees of Queen Anne's Bounty.

There is no timber in the churchyard and very little on the glebe, hardly sufficient for the necessary repairs of the buildings and gates belonging to the vicarage.

Under the will of Ayliffe Green gent., a sum of £20 p. a. was left to the vicar for preaching a sermon yearly on St. Thomas's day [21 Dec]. Also a pension of 5s. p. a. from Eton College which has the right of presentation to the vicarage.

2 bells, a bible, 2 common prayer books, a pulpit cloth and cushion. The communion plate consists of a large silver cup with the following inscription: 'The Gift of Tho. Jacob Esq. 1729' with the arms of the family, and a silver salver without an inscription. 10s. p. a. is paid out of certain lands towards the repair of the church. The churchyard wall is repaired by those whose lands abutt against it. The gates are repaired by the parish. The clerk is appointed by the minister but paid 1guinea p. a. by the parish.

William Adlam, vicar, Francis Henly, John Sargent, churchwardens.

IDMISTON vicarage and rectory

416   n. d. late 16th cent. (D1/24/114/1)

The parsonage: 1½ yardlands with 4a. called Smyeth land. 2 plots of meadow in a Broad mead which belongs to Mr. Tut's farm to cut the hay and to cut the grass until Lammas [1 Aug] and a little meadow lying by the said 4a. called Picked mead. 4a. of meadow in Alderbury mead to cut the grass and no feeding. All the mortuaries, the tithe of all kinds of grain and hay with the tithe of a meadow in Forde belonging to Mr. Tut's farm except the tithe of a farm called Birdlime [Burdlymes] from which the parson has the 30th sheaf and the 30th cock except 1a. called Bedden acre and a plot of meadow called Frymead from which the parson has the whole tithe with 135 sheep and feeding for 8 kine and a runner.

The vicarage: All maner of tithes of a farm lying in the Red lane[1] in the use of Walter Bath. The tithe of a close by Red land in the use of Richard Great and all tithe wool and lamb' geese, pigs, apples bees, Easter book, calves, cow white except the farm of Birdlime from which the vicar has no right to tithes. The parson has a horse going in the marsh from Whitsontide to St. Martin's day [11 Nov].

John Bynder, Henry Stapell, churchwardens, John Brownejohn senior, John Brownejohn junior, sidesmen, Henry Wheler alias Carpenter. *Names all in the same hand.*

1. A detached part of Idmiston lay in Winterslow although it is described as being in Winterslow in **417**.

417   11 Jan 1671 (D1/24/114/2)
All the tithes of a farm in Winterslow by Red lane occupied by [. . .] Baugh senior[1] and of a close by Red lane occupied by Ambrose White.[2] Tithes of wool, lamb, oblations, geese turkeys, pigeons, pigs, beer, apples and all other fruit. Easter book, calves and cow white.[3] A noble paid each year out of the farm of Birdlime [Burdlimes], occupied by Robert Reade.[4] The tithe of a mill in Gomeldon [Gumbleton] the composition of which is 20s. p. a. Previously the composition for mill and orchard was 24s.

Robert Sharpe, vicar, Edward Bendar [X], Anthony Batt, churchwardens.

1. John Baugh in **418**, Edward Cooper in **419**.
2. John Cooper in **418**. Described in **418** as lying by John Baugh's farm and in **419** as part of Edward Cooper's farm occupied by Edward Cooper, suggesting that it had been added to the farm by Red lane.
3. Described in **418** and **419** as throughout the tithings of Idmiston, Porton and Gomeldon [Gumbleton] in **418** and **419**.
4. This payment is not mentioned in **419** or **420**.

418   9 Jan 1705 (D1/24/114/3)
*As **417** with amendments in footnotes.* Tithes of a living in Winterslow called Shripples occupied by John Cooper.[1] Thomas Clemens, vicar, Richard Lywood, Nicholas Reeves, churchwardens.

1. Edward Cooper in 1783.

419   5 Aug 1783 (D1/24/114/4)
The vicarage of Idmiston: A dwelling house with flint walls covered with tiles, consisting of 2 small parlours with oak floors and ceiled, the least of which, by the brewhouse, is wainscotted with deal 2ft. 10in. from the floor; a kitchen paved with brick and ceiled; 2 pantries separated from the kitchen by a partition of oak, not floored or paved; a cellar, a brewhouse, both paved with brick; 6 bed chambers with deal floors and ceiled; 2 closets.

1 outhouse 48ft. by 14ft., mud walls covered with thatch divided into 2; one part 20 ft. long is used as a wood house, the other as a stable.

A kitchen garden bounded by the dwelling house, outhouse and 30ft. of mud wall on E.; an irregular mud wall on N.; by a hedge on S. and W. The buildings and garden occupy 1½r.

Idmiston church has 4 bells, a stone font with a cover, a folio bible and folio common prayer book, a linen surplice for the use of the minister. A folio common prayer book for the use of the clerk. In the chancel there is a decent communion table to which belong 2 linen cloths, 1 pewter flagon marked Idmiston 1737, 1 silver cup, the original weight not marked, the present weight of which is 10oz. 3dwt. 13qtr., a patten of silver marked 'Jhs', the present weight of which is 2oz. 2dwts. 12qtr.

30 small pollards in the churchyard, viz. 24 ash, 4 sycamore, 3 lime, valued at £3. The churchyard is bounded on E. by a barn and mud wall belonging to a farm yard the other sides are fenced with rails. Church and yard occupy c. ½a.

Porton Chapel: 2 bells, a font of stone with a cover, a folio bible, folio common prayer book and linen surplice for the use of the minister and a folio common prayer book for the use of the clerk. In the chancel there is a decent communion table to which belong 2 linen cloths, 1 pewter flagon, 1 pewter plate marked 'Porton Chapel 1733', 1 silver cup marked 'R. D. 1671', the present weight of which is 9oz. 3dwt. 5qtr.; a silver patten engraved in the centre with a head crowned with thorns, the present weight of which is 1oz. 15dwt. 12 qtr. The parishioners are charged with the repairs of the church and churchyard fence of Idmiston and the chapel of Porton. The clerk, who is also sexton, and is appointed by the vicar is paid by the parishioners, a voluntary gift of 20s. p. a. and Easter offerings.

Tithes as in **417** *with amendments in footnotes and* **418**. Edward Moore, vicar, John Massey, churchwarden, Peter Percy, chapelwarden, Thomas Barnes, Jonathan Barnes.

INGLESHAM vicarage

420   30 Sep 1671 (D1/24/115/1)
4 grounds called the New leazes, bounded Richard Stirte yeoman S., John Loader esq., N., the River Thames W., and the highway E. The vicarage house, a close, and a meadow called the Ham together, Reginald Bray esq., S., W., and E. and John Howe esq., N. All tithes of hay and privy tithes.

Bernard Babb, vicar, and John Crooke and John Matthew [X], churchwardens.

421   12 Dec 1704 (D1/24/115/2)
2 grounds joining together, part of New Leases, one 26a. the other 8a., both bounded with lands formerly of Richard Stirte, yeo., now John Rundle of Latton, yeo. S., lands of Jane Bray wid. N., River Thames W., highway E.

The vicarage house garden orchard and outhouses, 1 close and 1 meadow called the Hamm joined together, bounded land of Jane Bray wid. S. W. and E., land formerly of John How esq., now Edmund Smith gent. N.

2a. in N. mead, one of which lies in the lots, the other bounded with the lands of John Rundle W., [. . .] Cleave on E. and S., and the river Thames N.

All tithe hay, wool, lamb, hemp, flax and all other small tithes, except the tithes of a meadow called Blecham and the tithes of mills and fishery. Right of common of pasture for 14 rother beasts in the Marsh and N. mead (the whole number to stock the Marsh which is a cow common being 64) in lieu of commons for as many cattle and sheep pertaining to 4 yardlands. With the tithe of Dish Clout Ham in captain Lovedon's Size mead in Buscott [*Berkshire*] and with the tithe of a little ham in Powells mead and of a staft in Kempslord mead, and which to be a certain yearly pension of corn namely 2qtr. of wheat 2qtr. of barley and 2qtr. of oats to be paid to the vicar before the octave of St. Martin[1] out of the rectory of Inglesham; two thirds of which is paid at present by Charles Loder esq., one third by Jane Bray wid. according to a decree in Chancery, 1611x1612, a copy extant under the broad seal in the custody of the vicar.

John Berrow, vicar, Samuel Sadbery junior., William Butler, churchwardens.

1. St. Martin's day falls on 11 Nov.

422   n. d. [1783][1] (D1/24/115/3)
The vicarage house is built with stone the front faced with brick and slated. 4 rooms on the ground floor; the kitchen brewhouse and dairy floored with stone and the parlour with deal. Up 1 pair of stairs are 3 bed chambers and 3 large closets all floored with deal ceiled with lath or reed and plaster. 2 garrets, 1 floored the other not, neither of them ceiled. A small stable, *c.* 15ft. long almost the same breadth. An outhouse at the end of it rather less than the stable, both covered with thatch.

The vicarage house, home stall, orchard and gardens, 1a. 3r. 10p. A mead bounded by the homestall and the farm orchard on S., the river Thames [Isis] on W., a running water called Mortlake ditch N. and the Little marsh on E., 3a. 3r. 5p.; 2a. in N. mead, called Dock acre and Lot acre, 1a. 2r.; 2 grounds called Wharf ground, 6a. and Woad ground, 28a. or 30a., both these grounds lie together bounded by the river Thames and a piece called Picked ham on W., the highway from Lower Inglesham to Highworth on E., a farm occupied by William Cooper, S., a ground called Millfield N.

30 ash and elm trees, most dotterels or lopped trees, in the churchyard and glebe and a similar number of willows in the meadow.

14 cow commons in the Marsh and N. mead with a yearly pension of corn namely 2qtr. of wheat, 2qtr. of barley and 2qtr. of oats, payable by the impropriators, before the octaves of St. Martin.[2]

Tithe lamb, wool, hay and all other tithes except of corn and hay from a meadow called Bleacham, 15a. The grounds are all of them several (meadow and pasture) are enclosed with hedges and ditches.

Stanhope Bruce, vicar, Thomas Chisley, churchwarden.

1. The churchwarden was recorded in the bishop's visitation book, Jul 1783. (WSRO D1/50/30)
2. See footnote to **421**.

KEEVIL vicarage

423   5 Apr 1678 (D1/24/116/1)

A dwelling-house containing 3 bays, a stable and woodhouse and 2 bays, a garden, an orchard, and the churchyard, ¾a. in all.

All privy tithe calves, cow-white, wool, lambs, pigs, geese, pigeons, bees, apples, eggs, and fattening of all beasts and sheep; all pasturages and feeding lands belonging to Keevil, Keevil Wick [Week], Wick Leaze, and Bulkington [Buckington] from the river belonging or running to Baldham [Balnham] mill which bounds it N., with the grounds of Steeple Ashton W., the grounds of Edington S., and the grounds of Poulshot E.; all the commons to the parish of Keevil and the other said tithings and places, viz. Oxen lease and a common at the upper end of Keevil called West Wood; and all Easter dues, offerings, and oblations.

James Garth, vicar, and William Marriott [X], and Robert Planke, [X], the 'ancientest and chiefest' inhabitants.

424   10 Jan 1705 (D1/24/116/2)

Terrier drawn by the vicar and aproved by the churchwardens and other inhabitants.

The vicarage house with garden and orchard, c. 1/2a. The feeding of the churchyard. All privy tithes and customary offerings. A noble or thorough paid yearly to the vicar from the mills in Keevil. A endowment of £25 p. a. paid by the dean and chapter of Winchester quarterly on the feat of St. Thomas [21 Dec], Ladyday [25 Mar], the feast of St. John the Baptist [24 Jun] and the feast of St. Michael the Archangel [29 Sep].

Nathaniel Brewer, vicar, James Nash, Samuel Harris, churchwardens, Richard Norris, Thomas Purchell, Thomas Sealls, William Hill, Matthew Hancocke.

425   11 Jul 1783 (D1/24/116/3)

A dwelling house containing 3 bays, built with brick in a frame of wood, the front part tiles, the back thatched (except the brewhouse which is tiled). On the ground floor 2 parlours, 1 pantry, 1 kitchen, and 1 brewhouse; above stairs 4 chambers and a closet over the porch. The eastern parlour is wainscotted with deal, floored with deal and ceiled; the western parlour is papered, floored with deal and ceiled; the passage between floored with lime and ashes; the pantry floored with deal and ceiled; kitchen and elm dresser belonging to it, floored with brick and white washed; in the brewhouse an earthen floor; the chamber over the eastern parlour papered floored with oak as is the closet adjoining; the chamber opposite floored with oak plastered and ceiled with 2 deal closets for cloths; the other chamber floored with oak plastered and ceiled. 1 woodhouse built with brick containing 1 bay, tiled, a cellar under arched with brick.

A garden with a draw well, 2 orchards with a quickset fence and the churchyard all containing c. 1a. A new necessary of elm, thatched.

*All privy tithes as **423**. Endowment as **424**.* The feeding of the churchyard. The churchyard fence is railing except for 30yd. of wall. 30yd. of railing between the wall and the large elm tree belong to the vicar; 13yd. incl. the gate, belong to the parishioners; 10yd. to Mr. Beach and the rest to Miss Eleanor Blagdon. The repair of the chancel belongs to the rectory, 2 parts to the tithing of Keevil, 1 part to the tithing of Bulkington. Church furniture: 5 bells, 2 surplices, 1 bible and common prayer book, a small book of offices, a pulpit cloth and cushion, and cloth for the communion table, 1 large pewter flagon, 1 small silver cup, 1 pewter patten, 2 linnen cloths for the Communion, 2 large chests. The clerk is appointed by the minister, his wages by custom are £1 8s., the rest by contribution. The sexton is appointed by the parishioners, his wages by contribution.

L[ancelot]Docker, vicar, J[ames] Fothergill, curate, Robert Jefferies, William Bartlett [X], churchwardens, George Gilbert, James Bartlett, C. Matthews.

KELLAWAYS rectory

426   1704 (D1/24/117/1)
As much arable now in the hands of Nicholas Pontin as pays £3 p. a. So much in the hands of Chapman Uncles as pays £1 p. a. From pasture and meadow grounds: Sir James Long for Griffins £3 10s., that in the hands of Nicholas Pontin £4, Chapman Uncles' own in Barnsbridge £1 10s., George Knight's 7s. 6d., Hilmead in the hands of Chapman Uncles 7s. 6d., and Mr. Charles Bayly for Newman's in Lady mead 1s. All small tithes, oblations, obventions, and offerings as are customarily due in other places.

Thomas Thompson, rector, George Knight, churchwarden.

KEMBLE vicarage

427   14 May 1588 (D1/24/118/1)
A parsonage impropriate to which belongs the tithe corn and hay, impropriate to Oliver Pledell gent.

To the vicarage pertains the wool and lamb with all other inferior tithes; tithe corn and hay of Ewen [Yewen], part of the parish of Kemble, and the wool and lambs with all other inferior tithes; 24a. of arable in both field in Ewen and a close called the Chapel close, 1½a., sometime belonged to the vicarage but for 20 years past has been detained from the vicarage under the name of concealed land, by what right or equity we know not.

William Courtis, William Pitt, churchwardens, Robert Timbrell, John Brown, sidesmen. *Names in the same hand*

428   1608 (D1/24/118/2)
A vicarage house and barn situated on W. side of the village of Kemble, standing in a plot [platte] of ground, ½a. In Ewen a ruinous chapel standing in a plot of meadow, 1a. 1 farndell meadow in the Ham. Pasture for 2 rother beasts in Poole moor. 12a. and 3 farndell of arable ground in Park field that is to say; 1a. below Ewen green; 1 farndell in a furlong butting on Peesones hedge; 3½a. in Great furlong; ½a. at the end of Great furlong; ½a. in Lower Wamstone furlong; 1½a. in Boorne hill furlong; 1½a. in a furlong on the top of Smerehill; 1a. and 1 farndell

in a furlong below Smerehill; 1a. in Breche hill furlong; 1 farndell in a furlong butting upon the Fosse [Forse]; 1a. in Whorestone furlong; 1a. in Wilkenes Hatchets furlong.

11a. and 1 farndell in Hill field; that is to say; 1a. in Emplediche furlong; 1a. in Cote Thornes furlong; 1a. in Smeerehill Foot furlong; 1a. in Middle furlong; 1a. in Water Slade furlong; 1a. in Peerestone furlong; 1a. in Lidwell furlong; 1a. in a furlong below Peerestone; 1a. in a furlong shooting on Truesburie gate [Yeate]; 1a. in Forse furlong; 1a. in the Hill furlong; 1 farnedell in Deanes Lands furlong.

Pasture for 2 rother beasts at the breach (i. e. breaking) of the fields. Sheep pasture according to the custom of the place.

John Hawkins, vicar, Henry Smith, George Townesende, churchwardens. *Names all in the same hand*

429   1 Oct 1622 (D1/24/118/3)
Terrier taken by the view of the churchwardens, sidesmen and other credible and honest persons old and ancient inhabitants.

A vicarage house with a barn, backside and garden. An old decayed chapel in Ewen a tithing in the parish rents which there his a glebe counted for ½ yardland. The particulars of which are these: 1 close of pasture called Chapel Close, *c*. 1a. 1 farndell of mead in the Ham between an a. of Robert Curtis and 3 farndells of wid. Timbrell.

The common of Poole moor which is now enclosed by Sir Nevil Poole for 2 beast leases. 1 enclosed ground called Park Lease.

In the Park field of Ewen; 1a. of arable shooting upon Chapel close along by the ground allotted the vicar by agreement for his part of common in the green; 1 farndell of arable land between a piece of the farm and ½a. of John Smith; ½a. between a head a. and ½a. of Mr. Hardcastle; ½a. in Lower Wamstoone next to the wayside; 1a. of arrable upon Bornehill between an a. of John Smith on S. and 2a. off Robert Timbrell on N.; 1a. of arable shooting upon Chesterton field between ½a. which the tithingman of Ewen always has on S., and 1a. of Rowland Freman on N.; 1a. at Whorestone between 2a. of wid. Timbrell and a piece of Robert Curtis; 1a. being butts in Hockumslad between land of Robert Timbrell and the farm; ½a. upon Ghosthill, Robert Timbrell's land on both sides of it; 1a. at Smirrillhill Pitts, the pitts on W. and land of Robert Timbrell on E.; 1a. in the Thongs next to the highway. A farndell in the same field at the Forsfurlong between a piece of Mr. Hardcastle and Robert Timbrell.

In the Hill field 1a. in Short Waterslad between 1a. of Robert Timbrell and ½a. of wid. Timbrell; 1a. in Emdleditche between 1a. of farmland and ½a.; 1a. in Short furlong below Bornehill, 1a. of the farmland on S. and 1a. of wid. Timbrell on N.; 1a. in Middle furlong between ½a. of Mr. Hardcastle and 2a. of farm land; 2a. upon Peerstoone one lying between 1a of the farm and 3 x ½a. of Robert Timbrell, the other lying between 1a. of Rowland Freeman and ½a. of Mr. Hardcastle; 1a. in Lidwell furlong between a piece of the farm and ½a. of wid. Timbrell; 1a. in Hungerslad next to the fallow field; a farndell in Denings land between 1a. of John Smithe and ½a. of Mr. Hardcastle; 1a. by the Hull] [*sic*] a piece of Robert Curtis on S. and 1a. of wid. Timbrell on N.; 1a. upon Truwsberie gate [Eate] lying by the wayside; 1a. in the Forsfurlong a little above Trewsburie corner, a piece of Rowland Freeman on W. and 1a. of Robert Timbrell on E.

Tithe wool and lamb and all other kinds except corn and hay which the impropriator has. All tithes from Ewen tithing are paid to the vicar. All manner of cattle that Ewen has despastured in Poole moor 'ever tyme oute of mynd' have had their tithes paid to the vicar.

Although Sir Nevil Poole has lately enclosed, by agreement, that part of Poole moor which he has in lieu of that common we know no reason but the tithes should be still paid to the vicar.

Henry Pitt [X], John Morrell [X], churchwardens, Henry Hayward [X], Robert Tymbrell, sidesmen, Robert Tymbrell, miller, Robert Curtis [X], John Smithe [X], wid. Constable [X[, Robert Constable, wid. Smithe [X], wid. Timbrell [X].

430 1 Nov 1672 (D1/24/118/4)
1 house. barn, stable and garden. Tithe wool and lamb in Kemble and all other tithes and dues saving corn and hay, part of which the impropriator receives, part is swallowed up by being abbey lands. In Ewen tithing tithe corn, hay, wool and lamb.

½ yardland of glebe, viz: Chapel close, c. 1½a., in which are the ruins of an old chapel. A farndell of pasture in Ham between Robert Tymbril and Mr. King.[1,2] In the Park field, of arable, a ground called Park lease, c. 3½a.; 1a. in Ewen Green called Chapel acre, ½a. running along by the wayside against Park lease; ½a.[3] by the Broad mere between a head a. and ½a. of Mr. Master; 1a. on Boorn hill; 1a. shooting on Chesterton field hedge, the tithingman's ½a. on S.; 1a. in Whoreston running over Cirencester way; ½a. on Smirrilhill, Mr King[1] on both sides; 1a. in the same hill by the Pits; ½a. in the Thongs lying by the wayside to Cirencester. 1 farndell in the same furlong; 3 farndells in Hokumslad called the Butts; 1 farndell shooting on the Fosse way between Richard Stevens and Henry Hayward.

In the Hill field: 3 x ½a. shooting on Embleton bush; 3a. shooting on Boornway; 1a. in Hungerslad next the fallow field; 1a. shooting on the several hedge at the corner; 1a. in Peerston furlong between Thomas Freman and Walter Stevens; 1a. in Lidwell furlong; 1 farndell on N. of Coats way between Henry Stevens and Henry Hayward; 1a. by the Hull between the wid. Tymbrel and Mr. King; 1a. running along by Coatsway and shooting on Trewsbury gate; 1a. in the same furlong shooting on the Fosse way against Trewsbury hedge corner.

The vicar had 2 beast leaze in Poole moor and tithe of all Ewen cattle depastured in Poole moor which being now enclosed by consent the vicar has by composition 1 mark[4] yearly of the parson of Poole [*Keynes*].

John Stevens [X], Henry Stevens, churchwarden, Richard Stevens, sidesman.

1. Walter King in **431**.
2. Between the highway and chapel close lie some lugs allotted to the vicar for his part of common in Ewen Green where now is the house of wid. Symons added in **431**.
3. No bounds stated in **431**.
4. Expressed as 13s. 4d. in **431** and **432**.

431   22 Oct 1677 (D1/24/118/5)

As **430** with amendments in footnotes. Thomas Holloway, vicar, Henry Pitt, Henry Stevens, churchwardens, William Hall, John Smith, sidesmen, Richard Stevens churchwardens and other ancient inhabitants. Additional note, 27 Apr 1681: The composition of 13s. 4d. is denied by the rector of Pool Keynes and affirmed to be but 10s. p. a.

Thomas Myles, rector of Poole Keynes.

432   4 Dec 1704 (D1/24/118/6)

Vicarage house and buildings, etc., tithes and composition as **430**.

½ yardland of glebe, viz.: Chapel close, 1½a. in which are the ruins of a chapel. A farndell of pasture in the Ham between Robert Timbrell's hams. Park lease, c. 3½a., in the Park field.[1] 1a. called Chapel acre by the Green and some lugs mentioned in the old terrier cannot be found and 'neither have we heard of any minister ever possessed it'. 1½a. in Lower Wamstone lying by the wayside in the Park field. ½a. lying by the Green mere between Mr. John Pitt's lands. 1a. on Boorn hill shooting upon the way between Henry Steven's lands. ½a. on Smerhill Robert Timbrell's lands on both sides. 1 farndell in the same furlong by the Green hill Robert Timbrell on E. 3 farndell butts in Hooke Ham Slad[2] Henry Steven's lands on both sides. 1 farndell shooting on the Fosse [Force] Henry Stevens on E., Richard Plummer on W. 1a. at Whorstone, Robert Timbrell's lands on both sides. 1a. shooting against Chesterton field, Tithingmans ½a. on E., Thomas Freeman on W.

In the Hill field: 3 x ½a. shooting one end upon Boorn way the other upon Coates way, Henry Stevens on S., Mr. John Pitts on N.; 3a. in the same furlong Robert Timbrell's lands on both sides.; 1a. shooting upon the several hedge Mr. John Pitt on S., Robert Timbrell on N.; 1a. in Peastone Thomas Freeman on S., Edward Stevens on N.; 1a. in Lidwell Robert Timbrell on E., Henry Stevens on W.; 1a. near Smerhill Quarr Robert Timbrell on S.; 1 farndell on the brow of the hill shooting upon Coates way, Henry Stevens on S., Richard Plummer on N.; 1a. near the hill Robert Timbrell's lands on both sides; 1a. shooting upon the Fosse [Force] near Truesberry corner having Thomas Freeman on S., Henry Stevens on N.; 1a. lying by Coates way shooting against Truesberry gate, Thomas Freeman on E.

Thomas Holloway, vicar, William Hall, Michael Ferribee, churchwardens, Robert Timbrell, William Poulton, Thomas Stevens, Richard Plummer, Henry Stevens senior.

1.   See **430** n. 2.
2.   Hokum Slad in **431**.

KINGTON ST. MICHAEL vicarage

433   n. d. late 16th cent. (D1/24/119/1)

A dwelling house with orchard, garden, backside and Home Close. 4a. of arable land adjoining the close. 9a. of arable land in the E. field. 6a. of arable land in the

Ham. All offerings, marriages and churching of women. Tithe wool, lamb, kine white, calves, pigs, geese, colts and honey. Tithe hay of Langley[1] and Peckingell[2]. The parson has all the rest.

William Gale, John Salter, Richard Tanner, William Coller, John Tanner, William Hadnam, Thomas Barrett. *Names all in the same hand*

1. Probably Kington Langley.
2. In Langley Burell.

434   1608 (D1/24/119/2)
The house with the orchard garden and [...] closes of pasture adjoining, *c.* 7a. 1 close of pasture in the Ham between the land of Sir Thomas Snell and butting on the land of Francis Whit, *c.* 5a. 1½a. of arable land on the Quare hill between the lands of Sir Thomas Snell. 3 farndells upon Henly between the lands of Sir Thomas Snell. 5a. upon Swenshill between the lands of Sir Thomas Snell. Tithe hay of Langley and of 2 tenements in Peckingell[1] [Pegengell]. All the predial tithes of Kingston Langley and Pecckingell.

Nicholas Fawconer, vicar, Thomas Wayett [X], Edward Bell [X], churchwardens, John Gale, Richard Tanner [X], questmen.

1. In Langley Burrell.

435   7 Nov 1671 (D1/24/119/3)
The house with orchard and garden and 3 closes of pasture adjoining, *c.* 7a. A close of pasture in the Ham between the land of Mr. James Gastrill and butting upon the lands formerly of Mr. Francis White, *c.* 5a. 1 close of pasture upon Swenshill between the land of Mr. James Gastrill and Mr. John Stokes, *c.* 6a. 3 farndells upon Henly between lands of Mr. John Stokes and Mr. James Gastrill. 1 farndell upon Midfurlong between the land of Mr. James Gastrill and Mr. John Stokes. *Tithes as **434**.*

John Ferris, vicar, Jeffery Deeke, churchwarden, David Tanner, John Browne, sidesmen. *Names in the same hand*

436   1704 (D1/24/119/4)
A dwelling house, penthouse, barn, stable and pigsty. A garden backside orchard and rickbarton. 3 adjoining closes, *c.* 7a. 1 close of land called Swinsell, 6a. 1 close of land called the Vicarage ham, 5a. 2 x ½a. of land lying in an enclosure of Mr. Thomas Stokes near Malmesbury highway. *Tithes as **434**.*

Richard Humphreys, vicar, Richard Hildown, Robert Hewett, churchwarden. *Churchwardens' names in the same hand*

WEST KINGTON rectory

437   1678 (D1/24/120/1)
Inclosures: the home close, an orchard, adjoining Hardings orchard, and a little garden for flowers inclosed out of the barton; the Upper close, 3a.; Doles close,

counted *c*. 1 small a.; a small tenement and a little garden that the clerk pay a couple of capons for yearly; Doles ham; a small tenement in Hollow way rented by wid. Harding and a very little patch of land for which she pays 10s. rent p. a.; 1a. as it is counted at Sharwell; and a close at Harkum with a small patch of meadow in the Bottom counted about 1a.

6 beasts' leaze summering on the Cow down and 3 beasts' leaze allowed for the tithe of Stert that was payable and after laid as pasture to the Cow down; the wintering of 48 sheep from St. Catherine's tide [25 Nov] to the Sunday after Candlemas[1] proportionable to the 6 beasts' leaze and the 3 for the tithes of Stert.

In the S. field: ½a. in Bargasin; ½a. in Holdcroft; 1a. shooting on Nowels leaze, that heads Weeke furlong; 1a. shooting on Ishmeers way; 1a. on Boyhill shooting on the same way; 1a. that heads the Gores; 1a. in Long down; a piece of 3a. behind Ivy grove; a piece of 2a. at the end of that shooting on the way to N. Wraxall; ½a. in Bragdowns Bottom shooting athwart Marshfield [Mars fields] way; 1a. beyond the bottom shooting on Marshfields hedge; 1a. by Lilburies bush; 1long ½a. not far thence; 3 farndells by 3 farndells of Leonard Bishop; 1a. called Darbie acre in Darbie furlong; 1a. by Marshfield hedge by 1a. of the farmer; 3 farndells by Paneridge hill; 1a. above High grove; 1a. above Paneridge way; 1a. below the way over against it; 1a. called Quarre acre; 1a. by the Lanes end; 1a. shooting on Marshfields way above Ham Staff. Memo. there was 1a. in Moor down belonging to the rectory but, that down being sold by Mr. Horton and inclosed in the troublesome times, there was laid out instead 3 farndells at the head of Bear furlong and a farndell that joined to 3 farndells which are said above to be by Paneridge hill (so that there is 1 whole a. now together by Paneridge hill whereas there were formerly but 3 farndells), and it is that which shoots on Thomas Norman's new tining, and which it has ever since been possessed of.

In the N. field sowed the same year with the S. field: 1a. in the lower end of Woodhurne; 2a. (very small ones) at the Hurne gate; 1a. at Step stile; 1a. shooting on the way to Nettleton's gate; 1a. called Tayle acre shooting from Nettleton's hedge toward the frith; 1 little a. towards the sheep house; ½a. in the Weaks; ½a. by Hollow Ways end. In all in S. and N. fields 32a. of arable land.

Ebbdown [Abdowne]: 1a. shooting on Ebbdown wood; ½a. in the Burrie; 3a. shooting on Radcliffe wall.

Stert: 1a. on Chawne hill; 1a. in Lower Stert shooting on the way; 1a. in Upper Stert almost by the Little down gate; ½a. in upper Stert by Sharewell gate.

In W. field: 1a. by the Even path; 1a. by Touldown hedge, 1a. at the Ruckle, 1 farndell in Grumble slade; 1a. above Hazel grove shooting on the Green way; 1a. at the upper end of Lock's ½a.; 1a. shooting on Lock's ½a. above Piked stone; 2 single a. above Wool Groves bush; 1a. below Wool grove; 1a. that heads Harvords furlong; 1a. in Harvords furlong; ½a. shooting on the broad way near Woolgrove; ½a. by Blacklands shooting on the same; ½a. by Doles ham; 1a. called Russels acre; 1 little a. shooting on the further end of Russels acre; 1 head a. at the hither end of Russels acre; 1 square a. above the Broad way; 1a. at Penns quarry shooting along the hillside; 1a. on Sheepland hill; 1a. shooting down Driffle down; the 'millpownd' acre. The sum is 29a. wanting a farndell but it is to be noted that the abovementioned 3½a. in Stert were laid to pasture and added to the Cow down with so much proportionably of everyones in the parish, to wit: ½a. to every beast leaze. Because the Cow down before was not sufficient to maintain the beasts allowed for it neither was there without it any conveniency for water. So 3a. were laid in for the 6 beast leazes before mentioned. And for the ½a. the minister is to have ½a. instead in W. field from Richard Terrill.

James Butter, curate, Daniel Woolands [X], Ferdinando Bishop [X], churchwardens, Thomas Laurance, Robert Southerd, sidesmen.

1. Candlemas falls on 2 Feb.

438　　8 Nov 1704 ((D1/24/120/2)
Inclosure: The home close, orchard and kitchen garden adjoining to Sir Richard Howe's mead and a little garden for flowers enclosed out of the barton.

c. 3a. in the Upper close. Doles close, a small a. A small tenement and a little garden which the clerk pays a couple of capons as yearly rent. Doles ham. A small tenement in Hollow way, 10s. as yearly rent. 1a. at Sherwell. A barn at Harkem, c. 1a., with a small patch of meadow in the Bottom. 6 beast leaze summering on the Cow down and 3 more beast leaze allowed for the tithe of Stert that was arable and after laid for pasture to the cow down. The wintering of 48 sheep be it more or less according as its it ordered by the jury and the rector for the good of the parish.

Formerly there was 8a. in the N. field but that was exchanged by Sir Richard Howe and Dr. Ralph Bohun and 8a. laid out in the S. field as follows: 1a. at Baldwin gate between the land of Roger Baldwin and Richard Marsh; 6a. by the wall of Baldwin's Lye. 1a. shooting upon Comb way.

[*Other land in the S. field*] In Bargarsen ½a.; in Hold croft ½a. shooting upon Edwards leaze; 1a. that heads Week furlong; 1a. in Longdown; 1a. shooting upon Ishmeads way; 1a. upon Boy hill shooting upon the same way; 1a. that heads the Gores; 1a. shooting upon Marshfields way above Hamstaffe; a piece of 5a. behind Ivy grove shooting upon the way to N. Wraxall; ½a. in Bragdown bottom shooting athwart Marshfields way; 1a. beyond the bottom shooting upon Marshfields hedge; 1a. by Lilburies Bush; a long ½a. not far from there; 3 farndells by 3 farndells of Ferdinando Bishop; 3 farndells at the head of Bear furlong; 1a. called Darbie acre in Darbie furlong; 1a. at the upper end of Normans tyning shooting towards Marshfields hedge; 1a. more in the same furlong; 1a. above High grove hill; 1a. above Panchridge way; 1a. below the way over against the other; 1a. called Quarry acre; 1a. at the Lane's end. Total of arable land in the S. field 32a.

There was formerly 4½a. upon Ebbdown [Abdowne] but that was exchanged by Sir Richard Howe and Dr. Ralph Bohun so that 4½a. was laid out in the W. field as follows: 1a. near Stert gate by ½a. of Nathaniel Bennett; ½a. shooting against Greenways corner lying between 1a. of Terrill and ½a. of John Ford; ½a. shooting on the Down hedge lying between ½a. of Gabriel Russell and ½a. of Thomas Davis; ½a. at the upper end of Grumbles Slade by ½a. of Nathaniel Bennett; 1 farndell in Grumbles Slade by a farndell belonging to the rectory; 3 farndells against the Down gate lying between Terrill land and ½a. of Daniel

Wolan. 2 x ½a. shooting almost to the Down way by ½a. of Thomas Davis lying between them.

[*Other land in the W. field*]: ½a. near Stert gate; 1a. in Longden near the Ruckel; 1a. by Teldwice hedge; 1a. at the Ruckel; 1 farndell in Grumble Slade; 1a. above Hazel Grove hill shooting upon the greenway; 1½a. at the upper end of Lock's ½a. above Picked stone; the single a. above Woolgrove bush; 1a. that heads Harvards furlong; 1a. in Harford furlong; ½a. shooting upon the Broad way near Wool grove; ½a. by Blackland shooting upon the same way; 1a. called Russells acre; a little a. shooting upon the farther end of Russells acre; a head a. at the little end of Russells a.; a square a. above the Broad way; 1a. at Pens quarry shooting along the hillside; 1a. upon Sheep Drift down; the millpound acre. Total of arable land in the W. field 25a. 3 farnedells.

William Craig, rector, Nathaniel Bennett, churchwarden, Thomas Beaker, John Lawrence.

439   26 Jun 1786 (D1/24/120/3)
House, stone and tiled: Hall 22ft. by 18ft., mortar floor; on the right hand a parlour 15ft. by 12ft., elm floor; from the parlour a staircase to 3 small chambers; from the hall near the parlour door a small cellar; left hand of the hall 2 little rooms, the largest 9ft. by 7ft.; a kitchen and washhouse; a small cellar and coal hole; a staircase to 3 bedchambers above all elm and mortar floors and white walls. In the yard a large barn, stable and chain house.

Land in the W. field: The millpound acre, 1a.; 1a. shooting up and down Drifdown hill, land of Sarah Terril on W.; 1a. shooting upon Sheep Lan hill, 1a. of Edward Tyler on E.; 1a. near Pen's quarry shooting in the side of the hill, land of John Baldwin on S.; Russels acre (a headland), 1a., with ½a. of Richard Bennet on N.; 1a. shooting on the farther end of Russel's acre, land of Edward Tyler on E.; 1a. heads the home end of Russels a., 1a. of Richard Bennet on E.; 1a. above Broad way, 1a. of Sarah Terril on E.; ½a. beyond Blackland Bush shooting on the Broad way, land of S. Terril on W.; ½a. shooting upon the Broadway near Richard Bennet's tyning; 1a. headland on E. of Richard Bennets tyning; 1a. in Harford's Furlong shooting upon the last headland; 1a. homeward of Woolgrove bush, 1a. of Richard Bennet on W.; 1a. above the last a., 2a. of Edward Tyler on W.; 1a. in Picked Stone furlong, 1a. of John Baldwin on E.; 1½a. at the Farther end of Lock's ½a., ½a. of John Baldwin on S.; 2 x ½a. shooting near the Down way, a land of Nathaniel Hill between them; ¾a. shooting to the Down gate, land of Sarah Terril on W.; ½a. in Grumble Slade, ½a. of John Baldwin on S.; 1a. near the Down beyond Grumble Slade between 2 lands of Sarah Terril; ½a. in the same furlong, ½a. of Richard Bennet on N.; 1a. in the same furlong, 1a. of Henry Nowell on S.; 1a. in the same furlong, 1a. of Richard Bennet on N.; 1a. in the furlong above the last furlong, a piece of Sarah Terril on N.; ½a. shooting by Henry Nowell's tyning near Stert gate; 1a. near the last ½a., a land of Richard Bennet between them; 1a. shooting upon the Broad way near Haslegrove hill, an a. of S. Terril on E. Total 25 computed a.

In the S. field: 2a. in Longdown furlong, ½a. of Richard Bennet on S.; ¾a. in the same furlong, ½a. of John Baldwin on S.; 1a. on Boy hill, 1a. of Harry Nowell on N.; 1a. that heads Wick furlong, 1a. of John Baldwin on N.; 1a.

shooting upon John Colman's tyning at Marshfield way; 1a. shooting upon N. Wraxall road near Magg's grave, land of John Baldwin on S.; ½a. in Bragdown bottom, ½a. of John Baldwin on N.; 1a. shooting upon Marshfield hedge, 1a. of Harry Nowell on N.; 1a. near Lilbury bush, ½a. of Edward Tyler on W.; ½a. called the Long acre, ½a. of Richard Bennet on E.; ¾a. in Inward Lilbury, ¾a. of John Baldwin on S.; 1a. called Darby acre in Darby furlong 1a. of Sarah Terril on W.; 1a. shooting to the upper end of Stephen King's tyning, 1a. of Sarah Terril on S.; 1¼a. more in the same furlong, ½a. of John Baldwin on S.; 1a. upon Highgrove hill, a land of John Baldwin on S.; 1a. shooting above Paneridge way, 1a. of Richard Bennet on W.; 1a. shooting below Paneridge way against the other a.; 1a. near the Ivy lane end, 2a. of Sarah Terril on N.; ¾a., a headland in Bear furlong, ½a. of John Baldwin on S.; Total 20½ computed a.

Enclosures: Home close and walks, c. 2a.; gardens and courts about the house, ¾a.; Upper close, c. 2½a.; Doles' close, c. ¼a.; Holloway close or garden, ¼a.; Doles' ham, c. ¼a.; Sherwell mead, c. ¾a.; Grove at Harcomb, c. 1¼a.; the Tyning at Lye corner, c. 6a.; the Tyning near Magg's grave, c. 3½a.; Churchyard, c. ½a.; cottage at Holloway; cottage at the end of the bridge. Total 18 statute a.

6 beast leazes in the Cow down. 3 beast leazes more allowed for the tithe of Stert which was arable and after laid for pasture to the Cow down. The wintering of 48 sheep be it more or less according as it is ordered by the jury and the rector for the good of the parish.

Nathanial Hume, rector, John Baldwin, churchwarden, Richard Bennett.

KNOOK rectory

440   29 Oct 1605 (D5/10/1/15)

A tenement in Knook in which Thomas Yonge dwells. E, mead, 1a., lying next unto Heytesbury mead adjoining on S. a close called the Crest occupied by Henry Clifton. A close of pasture called the Parsonage close, c. ½a., lying next unto a tenement occupied by John Vaughan alias Cantle on N.W. and 4a. of arable in the N. field belonging to the parsonage of Knook on S. 2a. of arable land in the N. field between land occupied by Roger Moondaye on E. and land occupied by Richard Lambert W. and butting on a furlong called Waterhole. 1a. of arable in the same furlong between land now occupied by Henry Clifton on W. and Moses Coles on E. 1a. of arable in a furlong called Nether Shortland between land occupied by William Leowes on E. and John Pryor on W. and butting on the highway. 1a. of arable lying by Chitterne way between land occupied by Richard Lambert on N.W. and Richard Button S. E. 2a. of arable land on Storm hill between land occupied by William Frampton esq., on both sides. 2a. of arable lying on W. hill between land occupied by William Leowes on S. E. and 2a. of arable occupied by Henry Clyfton on N.W. 1a. of arable lying on W. hill with land occupied by William Frampton esq., on both sides.

4 rother beast leazes and 60 sheep leazes to be fed and depastured on the common downs, meadows and pastures of Knook in such sort as the other tenants of the manor.

The churchwardens and sidesmen certify that the pavement of the church is amended.

Richard Button [X], John Pryor [X], churchwardens. John Cantle, Philip Hulett, sidesmen.

EAST KNOYLE rectory

441 1671 (D1/24/121/1)

E field: a piece lying for 3a. on Way furlong abutting 1a. of Mr. Hewes[1] W., 2a. 2p. 1li.; 1a. abutting 1a. of wid. Brown, 2a. 6p. 5li.; a piece lying for 2a. abutting a. of Mr. Hewes, 1a. 24p., a piece for 2a. abutting as the former, 1a. 35p.; 1a. abutting 1a. of James Dominick,[2] 2r. 18p. 6li., all upon Way furlong; and 1a. at the end of the field lying S. E. to 1a. of William Obourne, 3r. 38p.; 2 x 3yds., 1 lying across Hindon Horse way, 2r. 13p., the other abutting it, 2r. 14p. 2li.; 2 head a., 1 next to Hindon way abutting a. of Nicholas Williams, 2r. 31p. 4li., and 1 on Hindon way, 2r. 28p. 3li.; a piece for 2a. in the middle of the field between 1a. and ½a. of Mr. Dominick, 1a. 3r. 39p. 8li., a little a. in the middle of the field abutting the rector's a. E., 2r. 9p.; 1a. abutting 1 head a. of Mr. Rootes[1] W., 1a. 16li.; 1a. on Portway lying E. of wid. Brown's 1a., 1a. 1p.; 1a. abutting a piece of James Dominick,[2] 2r. 34p.; a piece for 2a. E. of a meadow ground of James Dominick, [2] 1a. 2r. 36p. 4li.; a piece for 2a. at Dewes Bush abutting Warminster way, 1a. 1r. 17p. 3li.; and a stitch of headland in 'Broakeland'[3] bottom.

W. field: 1a. at Milton townsend abutting Hindon, 1a. 1r. 14p.; ½a. abutting as the former, 3r. 30p.; 2 single hookland a. both abutting 1a. of Robert Farnell,[4] the lower 2r. 6p. 5li., the upper 3r. 5p. 7li.; 1yd. near Marshmans hedge abutting on 1a. of Sir George Howe[5], 21p. 2li.; 1 great a. there abutting 1½a. of Christopher Williams W., 1a. 1r. 11p.; a piece of 3a. abutting 1 headland yd. of William Davis S., 2a. 1r. 6p.; the Redland Acre abutting a piece of 4a. of William Obourne N., 3r. 13p.; a piece for 2a. abutting West Knoyle way, 1a. 2r. 16p. 1li.; 1a. abutting as the former, 3r. 34p. 3li.; 1a. at Reades Cross abutting 2a. of James Dominick[2] E., 1a. 4p. 3li.; 1a. in Little Holden bottom abutting the farmer's piece called Downlands, 1a. 17p. 2li.; 1a. abutting Warminster way E., 3r. 20p. 16li.; 2 single a. across Holden bottom both abutting 1 head a. of Ingrams N., 2r. 6p. 2li. and 2r. 3p. 4li.; 1a. on the Butts abutting West Knoyle way S., 2r. 15p.; a piece for 2a. in Summergold abutting 1 head a. of James Dominick[2] N., 1a. 3r. 6p.; a piece of 3a. across West Knoyle way abutting a headland of Ingrams S., 2a. 1r. 7p. 2li.; 1 single a. across the same way abutting 1a. of Mr. Goddard[6] N., 2r. 1p.; a piece for 2a. across Holden bottom abutting a piece of 2a. of Robert Farnell[4] S., 1a. 1r. 28p.; 1 head a. abutting 1a. of Mr. Rootes[1] W., 2r. 20p.; 1a. in the middle of the field abutting 1a. of Sir George Howe[5] S., 3r. 5p.; ½a. in Touchorne furlong abutting a piece of 2a. of Edward Strong S., 1r. 28p. 4li.; 1a. in Sudden abutting 1a. of Thomas Bennett N., 1a. 11p.; and 1a. under Bowles's hedge abutting 1 head yd. of William Davis N., 20p. 6li.

Middle field: 1a. upon Way furlong E. to 1a. of Anthony Burbadge, 2r. 18p. 3li.; 2 x ½a. there, one W. of 1a. of William Obourne, 2r. 4p., the other E. of it, 2r. 14p. 10li.; 1 long a. abutting the farmer's penning, 1a. 2r. 6p.; a piece for 2a.

abutting on that a., 1a. 3r. 9p. 4li.; 1a. in the Bottom abutting 1a. of Ingrams W., 2r. 24p.; ½a. abutting a piece of the farmer called Brach E., 1r. 12p.; 1a. below the Drove, 2r. 7p., and 1a. upon the Drove, 2r. 6p., both on the N. of 2a. of William Obourne; 1 headland stitch by Hindon way having 3a. of Mr. Coker,[7] 3a. of Mr. Hughes, and 1a. of Thomas Bennett abutting it; in Eltrot furlong, 1a. abutting Hindon way, 3r. 6p.; 1a. abutting ½a. of James Dominick, 2r. 26p.; 1a. abutting as the former, 3r. 4p. 3li.; 1a. upon Barnes abutting 1 head a. of James Dominick, 2r. 5p.; 1a. there abutting 1a. of William Davis, 3r. 3p. 2li.; 1a. across Small Dean bottom abutting 1a. of James Dominick, 2r. 27p. 5li.; a piece of 1½a. abutting Portway, 1a. 1p.; 1 little a. in the Butts abutting a piece of Mr. Coker[7] E., 1r. 22p.; 1a. across Portway abutting a stitch of William Obourne W., 3r. 5p.; ½a. ground abutting Mr. William Burleton of Slade, 1 part belonging to Mr. Burleton and the other to the rectory. A peculiar down and feeding in Milton field 240 sheep, the down being bounded by a part of down belonging to the farm[8] E. and a part of William Obourne's[9] W.

Pasture: a ground called Hemhey by common estimation 2a.; a ground called the Grove, by common estimation 6a.; an allotment in the common by measure 13a.; and 10 cows and a bull's leaze in a ground called Summer leaze from 3 May to St. Andrew's day [30 Nov].[10]

The parsonage house with a garden and orchard by common estimation ½a., and an outhouse called the old kitchen, a pigeon-house, 2 barns, a stable, and a coach-house.

A custom a. of grass in a meadow of William Obourne of Lye. Tenements: (1) a tenement in the tenure and occupation of Mary Fryer wid., with a garden adjoining it and an allotment in the common of Knoyle, by measure, 3a.; (2) a tenement in the tenure of Francis Turvill with an outhouse, with a stable adjoining it, a garden, and an orchard, and with an adjoining paddock, ½a., a close of 1a., and 3a. of allotment in the common, part of which is in the tenure of Edward Rockle with a house on it, 4a. 2r.; (3) a tenement in the tenure of Richard Hascoll with a garden adjoining it and 1a. of allotment in the common, 1a.;[10] (4) a tenement in the tenure of William Edmonds with a garden and orchard adjoining it and 3a. of allotment in the common, 3a.; (5) a tenement in the tenure of John Sheane with a garden adjoining it and 20p. in a garden of Mr. Philip Rootes[11] and 3a. of allotment in the said common belonging to Mr. Rootes,[11] 3a.; (6) a tenement in the tenure of John Kemp;[12] (7) a tenement in the tenure of Nicholas Frowde with a garden adjoining it and 3a. of allotment in the common, 3a.; (8) a tenement in the tenure of Thomas Perman[13] with a garden adjoining it and 4a. of allotment in the common lane, 4a.; (9) a tenement in the tenure of Virtue Marchant wid.,[14] with a garden adjoining it; (10) a tenement of William Obourne now in the tenure of William Bleek with a garden and orchard adjoining it and 3a. of allotment in the common, 3a.; (11) a tenement in the tenure of Anthony Burbadge alias Brindly,[15] with a garden and paddock adjoining it and 3a. of allotment in the common, 3a.; (12) a tenement in the tenure of Anthony Taylor with a garden and orchard adjoining it and 3a. of allotment in the common, 3a.; (13) a tenement in the tenure of Susan Perman[16] wid., with a garden and orchard adjoining it and 3a. of allotment in the common, 3a.; (14) a tenement of Edward Hicks lately in the tenure of John Salisbury with a garden and orchard adjoining it and 3a. of allotment in the common, 3a.; (15) another tenement of Edward Hicks lately in the tenure of John Salisbury with a garden and paddock, ½a., adjoining it and 2a. of allotment in the common, 2a. 2r.; (16) a third tenement in the tenure of Edward Hicks with a garden and orchard adjoining it and 3a. of allotment in the common, 3a.; (17) a tenement in the tenure of Philip Fennell with a garden and orchard adjoining it and 3a. of allotment in the common, 3a.; (18) a tenement in the tenure of Edward Strong[17] with a garden and orchard adjoining it and a paddock, 1yd. of pasture, and 3a. of allotment in the common, 3a.; (19) a tenement of Gillian Goldesborough,[18] widow, now in the tenure of Robert Getly with a garden, an orchard, and a paddock of 1a. adjoining it and 3a. of allotment in the common, 4a.; and 3a. of allotment in the common now in the occupation of James Dominick, 3a.

Richard Hill, rector, and Edward Hicks and Robert Farnell, churchwardens.

Endorsement: In the exchequer, between the Revd. Charles Wake, LL. D., and Edward Sheppard, complainants, and John Russ, clerk, defendant, 17 Jan 1792 this parchment writing shown to William Boucher gent., and by him deposed unto in his answer to the second interrogatory on the part of the said complainants. Signatories: Henry Stephens and Richard Messiter, Charles Bowles.

1. Mr. Hughs in **442**.
2. Mr. Dominick in **442**.
3. In Brookeland bottom measuring 14p. in **442**.
4. Wid. Farnell in **442**.
5. Lady Howe in **442**.
6. Mrs. Goddard in **442**.
7. Mr. Still in **442**.
8. And also part of James Dominick in **442**.
9. Philip Ingram on W. in **442**.
10. The allotment in the occupation of Edward Sharp in **442**.
11. Mr. Robert Compton in **442**.
12. Widow Kemp in **442**.
13. Widow Perman in **442**.
14. Mary Loofman in **442**.
15. John Sangar in **442**.
16. Mary Perman in **442**.
17. Edward Strong senior in **442**.
18. In the sole tenure of Edward Strong junior in **442**.

442   10 Dec 1677 (D1/24/121/2)
*As **441** with amendments in footnotes.* Richard Hill, rector, William Sangar, Edward Trowbridge, churchwardens, Robert Compton, William Oborn, Robert Burleton, Robert Loveland, John Helliar. *Endorsement as **441**.*

443   19 May 1705 (D1/24/121/3)
A parsonage house, an [? outhouse] called the old kitchen 2 barns a stable a coach house, a pigeon house a carthouse with a garden orchard and ground called the Grove, 5a. A ground called Himph[ey] 1a., a ground called the Allotment 16a.

In the E. field 23a. 1yd. by computation. In the Middle field 1a. 1yd., in the W. field 30a. 1yd. A piece of down, 30a. upwards with a drove leading to it through the tenantry down and Mr. Hewes down and sheep leaze for 240 sheep in Milton field. A drove leading to Milton field by estimation 1a., half of it belonging to Mr. Robert Burleton and the other half to the rectory. The foreshare of 120 lugs of ground in a meadow of [. . .] Oborne called Bottom mead. 10 cows and a bull leaze in summer leaze from 3 May until the feast St. Andrew the apostle [30 Nov].

A small manor of cottages and lands leased out: John Wigmore, cottage, garden, orchard and 3a. of ground; John Marchant, cottage, garden and orchard; Thomas Hix, 2 cottages, 2 gardens, 2 orchards with 6a. of ground; Elizabeth, wife of [sic] George George, cottage, garden, orchard and 3a. of ground; John Sanger, cottage, garden, orchard and 3a. of ground; John Scamel cottage, garden and 3a. of ground. George Wigmore, orchard. Rebecca Rockell wid., cottage, garden, orchard and 2a. of ground; Mr. Turvey, cottage, garden orchard and 1a. of ground. Grace, wife of Philip Fennell, cottage, garden, orchard and 3a. of ground, the ground now in the possession of Mr. Court or his undertenant; John Edmence, cottage, garden, orchard and 3a. of ground; John Scamell, cottage, garden, orchard and 3a. of ground, the ground now in the possession of Mr. Biggs; Edward Troubridge, cottage; Nicholas Frowde, cottage, garden and 3a. of ground; Peter Perman, cottage, garden and 3a. of ground; Edward Stronge, 2 cottages, 2 gardens, 2 orchards and 8a.; George Wigmore, cottage and garden; Edward Sharpe, 1a.; Mr. Biggs, garden c. 5 lugs of ground.

Tithes: the tenth sheaf and tenth pook or cock of corn. The tenth cock of grass, tenth fleece of wool, tenth lamb, tenth calf, tenth pig. Tenth day's cheese for 20 weeks. Tenth apple. Tenth lug of wood in the coppices [if sold]. Tithe of eggs paid on Good Friday. The churching of women, 4d. Marriage, 10d. Offerings at Easter, 2d. The tenth day's skim cheese for 20 weeks, the first to begin 20 days after Hollyrood day [14 Sep].

Charles Tippet, rector, Edward Wigmore, William Oborne, churchwardens. *Endorsement as **441**.*

WEST KNOYLE chapelry

444   19 May 1705 (D1/24/122/1)
Terrier of W. Knoyle chapelry and appertaining to North Newnton vicarage.[1]

A little dwelling-house with a skilling joined to the N. end, a little garden at the S. end, and behind the house a little meadow, c. 1a., on the N.W. part of the house; and a church yard.

£2 a year paid by the churchwardens by equal shares and proportions at Easter and St. Luke's tide [13 Oct] for preaching a sermon in memory of, and keeping the accounts of Christopher Willoughby esq., deceased.[2] £10 given as an augmentation to the chapelry by Philip, earl of Pembroke, deceased.

The right of feeding and pasturing as many cows, bullocks or heifers, horses, sheep, and geese, etc., in the common and commonable places of West Knoyle, New Common only excepted, at the usual times and in the manner, and according to the proportion, as the inhabitants. Yearly offerings and all tithes, small and great (except corn and hay), payable yearly in kind or by composition as the vicar or his successors shall think fit.

Luke Sympson, vicar and Thomas Gibbons and William Bannister, churchwardens. *Churchwardens' names in the same hand*

1. West Knoyle was a chapelry annexed to North Newnton parish until 1841. Both were formerly held by Wilton abbey.
2. A parish charity established in 1678.

LACOCK vicarage

445   12 Jul 1688 (D1/24/123/1)
The vicarage house with garden, orchard, and backside, 1 farndell of land. 1 close of arable, 8a., the way leading to a ground called Ellrigg on S., a ground in the tenure of Richard Grist on N.

Richard Rocke, vicar, Christopher Tiderleigh, John Ashley, churchwardens, William Bewsion, John Quarrell, sidesmen.

446   9 Dec 1671 (D1/24/123/2)
The vicarage house with orchard, garden and 6a. of arable ground. Tithe wool, lamb and calf and Easter dues.

John Barnes, vicar, Nicholas Barret, William Arnoll, churchwardens.

447   28 Jul 1783 (D1/24/123/3)
The vicarage house, built of brick containing 2 rooms, one wainscotted, the other stuccoed, a kitchen, scullery and cellar on the ground floor. 3 bedchambers, 2 closets and 2 garrets on the first and second floors. Outhouses, brewhouse, bakehouse, etc., 3 small gardens, a paddock, c. 1a., stable for 3 horses, and a chaise house. c. 6a. of enclosed arable land in the way leading to a ground called Eldrige with all vicarial and Easter dues.

Edward Popham, DD., vicar, Robert Tayler, churchwarden, Henry Tayler, parish clerk.

LANDFORD rectory

448   n. d. [1588][1] (D1/24/124/1)
Right reverend father in God these surely notify unto your lordship that we whose names under here subscribed have made surveyance according to your honourable precept unto us in this directed of all and singular lands as are and do apertain to the rectory or parsonage of the parish of Landford do represent the same here to your reverance to be (as forth as we can guess) by our estimation so many acres as here that may appear together in so with the names of all such persons as have been either christened married or buried within the term of 2 years in your honour's precept prescribed.[1] But as for such lands, limits,

emoluments, tithes, duties, such other like things as thereunto be accidents (for that it is only a simple parsonage without any vicarage thereunto belonging we have not in this our presentation specified because it seems to us not much necessary to this purpose.)

Arable land: 1 close called the Parsons acre, 2a.; a little parrock, 1a.; ½a. in John Mershmans close. Meadow land: ½a. Pasture land: 1 close called Newlands, 10a.; 1 close called Stockerclose of wood and pasture, 10a.; 1 heathy close of furze, 2a.; 1 close called Broomye close 1a. Coppice; 1 close lying within Henry Hussies ground, 2a.; 1 close called the Codlelyes, 2a.

Surveyed by Henry Hussie, Henry Whytyour churchwardens, Richard Emmerye, John Presye, yeoman.

1.   Parish register transcript for 1585-1587 appended.

449   n. d. [1608][1] (D1/24/124/2)
A close of arable called Newlands, 12a., bounded by the highway on one side and land of Sir Christopher Compton on the other. A close, half coppice, half arable, called Stockclose, 12a., bounded by Stockclose lane on one side and land of Sir John Dantesye on the other side. A coppice called Colelies, 1½a., bounded on one side by land of William Stockman esq., and by land of Sir John Dantesie on the other side. A little close of arable, ½a., bounded at one end by the highway and by land of Mr. Lovell gent., at the other end. A coppice, ½a., bounded on one side by land of Sir John Dantesy and by land of William Stockman esq. The Little meadow, c. ½a., bounded on both sides by land of Mr. Lovel gent. A close of barren heathy ground called Heathie close, 3a., bounded by land of Henry Clifford esq., on one side and by the common on the other. A close of barren heathy inground, 3a., adjoining Partriche hill at one end and land of George Coomes at the other end. A close of arable land, ½a., called the Brome close enclosed with the land of John Stantor gent. A little close called the Parrock adjoining the parsonage house with a garden and an orchard, ½a. A freedom in a close called Colelyes for the feeding of cattle. Where that freedom is not known then the parson pays 4d. p. a. at the King's lawday at Whiteparish. Customary freedom of common with freeholders and tenants and as yet never denied.

William Heathe, parson, Thomas Hartwell, John Lushe, churchwardens, Robert Immery, John Stoks, sidesmen. *Names in the same hand*

1.   The incumbent and churchwardens signed the bishops transcript for this year.

450   n. d. early 17th. cent. (D1/24/124/3)
The dwelling house of the parsonage, 3 rooms and a stable, a barn and 2 cut [coot] ends, ½a. 20a. of arable. 19a. of coppice and row ground. 6a. of waste ground. A little orchard and a garden.

William Heath, parson, Henry Whiteere, William Winter, churchwardens.

451   1671 (D1/24/124/4)
A dwelling house in good and sufficient repair with a convenient barn, a stable, and at each end of the barn a skilling for fuel. A Brome close adjoining the

dwelling house, 2a. A ground called the Acre, 3a. A little mead, 1a. ½a. of meadow adjoining Great Beryfield. 3 grounds called Stock close, 15a. Newlands, c. 14a. A ground called Partridge hill, c. 4a. Heath close, 5a. 3a. in White house park.

Charles Luke, rector, Andrew Kellow, John Rice, churchwardens.

452   24 Sept 1677 (D1/24/124/5)
The parsonage house, well and decently repaired, containing a cellar, 3 low rooms, 3 upper rooms, a study and a porch, 1 well house. A barn containing 3 rooms, a stable and 2 skillings. A little coppice near the Earldoms. An orchard and a garden. One Brome close near the dwelling house. The Acre, a little meadow in the lane. One arable ground at the lane end and another called Partridge hill and a Brome close in the park. An arable ground called Newlands, and 3 other arable and meadow grounds called Stock close. All of which lands contain c. 48a. and except the 3 home grounds are let at £19 1s. p. a. All the rest of the tithes of the parsonage are demised and valued at £31 13s. p. a.

Charles Luke, rector, Ralph Copdeane, Henry Osmond, churchwardens, Anthony Kellow, Thomas Dening.

453   2 Jan 1705 (D1/24/124/6)
Buildings as **451** and **452**. A garden an orchard, one Brome close, one ground called the Acre, one called the Land end one called Patredg hill, a little ground lying by the Stock land, a little piece in the park under the Earldoms [Arldoms], an arable ground called New lands, 3 grounds called Stock closes, all amounting to 'by guest' 48a. now let for £20 [p. a.]. The tithes are let for £40 [p. a.].

Joseph Thorpe, rector, John Munday, Thomas Barns, churchwardens. *Names of the churchwardens in the same hand*

454   1 Aug 1783 (D1/24/124/7)
The parsonage house built of brick covered with tiles, containing 1 porch, an entrance hall, a parlour, a study, 5 bedchambers, 2 other small rooms and 3 garrets. All floored with board, all partly papers, partly wainscotted and ceiled, except the garrets which are whitewashed. A kitchen, stone floor, a wash house brick floor, a laundry ceiled and floored with brick. Standing in a court adjoining to an orchard and a garden. Fenced all round, partly with pailing partly with a hedge containing in the whole c. 1a. A barn built of wood now used as a rough stable. 2 skillings one now used as a coach house the other stable all under one roof; 50ft. by 17ft. A woodhouse built of wood covered with straw, 18ft. by 12ft.

A ground called Lane end ground, 5a., with 18 small oak and ash trees, supposed 70ft. of timber, bounded on E. by the Heath common. Partridge hill ground, 4a., with 6 small oak trees, supposed 30ft. of timber, bounded on S. by the Heath common. Little meadow, 1a., with six small elm trees, supposed 30ft. of timber, bounded to the N. by the high road called Goulding's lane.

A ground called the Acre, through which is now made the Sarum and Ealing turnpike for which a compensation in money was made to the rector which was expended on the premises belonging to the parsonage; the ground contains at present 2¾a., ½a. being destroyed by the turnpike, contains 10 small trees, supposed 45ft. of timber. One ground called the Half, ½a., 10 oak trees supposed

45ft. of timber, bounded to the S. by Great Berry field. 3 fields called the 3 stock closes, all lying together, 14a., with 50 oak and ash trees. Supposed 220ft. of timber, bounded to W. by a high wood called Stock lane.

A piece of rough ground lying in S. W. corner of White House park, 3a., 4 small trees, supposed 20ft. of timber. A piece of ground called Parson's coppice now arrable, 2a., with 6 small oak trees, supposed 18ft. of timber, bounded on E. by Stock lane. A ground called Newlands, 14a., with 14 oak and ash trees, supposed 58ft. of timber, bounded on N. by Landford wood. One Home close adjoining to the garden, 1a. with 4 trees, supposed 24ft. of timber. In the garden 2 elm trees, supposed 30ft. of timber.

In the orchard and court 6 trees, supposed 70ft. of timber. The number of trees standing on the whole premises is nearly 118 supposed to contain c. 674ft. The Total is nearly 48½a. All tithes are due to the rector.

Belonging to the church: 2 bells; a large pulpit cloth and cushion of crimson velvet, bordered with deep gold fringe with tassles; a green cloth to cover the communion table when not in use; 2 silver plates with a silver flagon and chalice with the inscription on each 'For the use of the Parish of Landford A. D. 1759'. The clerk's wage is £2 p. a. with the addition of 3s. for washing and mending the surplice and communion linen according to custom; appointed by the rector and paid by the parish. The parish is chargeable with the repairs of the church and churchyard fences excepting the chancel which is repaired by the rector. The rector has unlimited right of common for all kinds of cattle.

Henry Eyre, rector, Thomas Hicks, John Tucker, William Heathcote, J. Eyre, J. M. Eyre, inhabitants.

LITTLE LANGFORD rectory

455   9 Jan 1705 (D1/24/125/1)
A dwelling house, 1 barn, 1 stable, 6a. of arable land, 3a. of meadow, 1a. of pasture, and the tithes of 2 farms, the whole worth £65 p. a.

William Powell, rector, John Burrow, churchwarden.

456   Aug 4 1783 (D1/24/125/2)
Parsonage house built of stone and thatched, contains 3 rooms below, with carthen floors, not wainscotted or papercd; 2 rooms above in very bad condition. A barn and stable.

6a. of arable lying in 4 parcels in the Upper farm, 1a. of water meadow lying in Broad mead and about 1a. of pasture adjoining the Parsonage house. A very small garden, not more than 5p., with a hedged fence.

All great and small tithes of Upper and Lower farms except the tithes of Little mead, Noad mead, Lower mead and Putnam in lieu of which is allotted 2a. in the middle of Broad mead belonging to Lower farm.

Furniture of the church; a bell, a silver chalice, no mark, or weight or inscription.

Clerk's wages £1 paid in proportion to the values of the estates.

Samuel Weller, curate, John Davis, churchwarden.

STEEPLE LANGFORD rectory

457 n. d. late 16th cent.[1] (D1/24/126/1)

We find by general inquisition and survey the glebe land: Arable land: 7a. in Whome field; 3a. in a field called Cleffat; 7½a. in the Middle field; 7a. in Little Down field; 12a. in E. field; 2 rudges in the Middle field called the Farm field at the W. gate; 2 rudges in the farm field called the E. field; and a yard called the ? W[or]pp yard. That the parson has no further to do in the Farm field as than to cut and go, the parson has to keep in the tenantry flock 80 dry sheep and 4 rams and no more, finding the shepherd after his portion rate like with his neighbours and allotting 8 hurdles to the 4 corners of the field. The parson has to keep on his glebe 6 oxen and a couple of hauliers [hallyers], 1 bull, 1 boar and [...] any other kind of cattle.

8a. in the common meadows; 1a. at the mead gate called Half furlong; 1a. in the Middle field [...] mead in the Long furlong by Chantry bridge. Memo: That the parson ought not to have any tithe hay of the tenants and freeholders of Steeple Langford except tithe of 3 x ½a. at the mead bridge with 3 x ½a. belonging to a living called Tucking mill. Tithe hay of the Farm mead[...], an a. called Haske acre and of a. called Haywards ham and another piece of ground called ? Poole half at the old weir that was in the lower end of the mead. Memo; That there is another piece of ground in Prestnam mead a picked ½a. belonging to the parson out of which there is a custom that the parishioners shall have yearly Whitsun Friday eve and Midsummer sufficient grass or cuttings to cover [frows] the floor of their church. There is ½a. of meadow ground in Prestnam belonging to the farm of Steeple Langford in the possession of Mr. Nicholas Mussell of which tithes ought to be paid by ancient custom. The Parsons croft. A close adjoining the parsonage house a garden and orchard.

Tithe of all grain; of wheat the tenth sheaf, of barley the tenth pook, of peas and vetches the tenth pook, of oats and lentils the tenth pook, otherwise there has never been paid or demanded any tithe of green peascod or raking of our fields. Memo. there is an ancient custom from time out of mind that the parson is to have of Mr. Nicholas Mussell or his assigns for all tithes, duties and demands arising out of his mills in Steeple Langford 3s. 4d. payable yearly at Easter. There is likewise an ancient custom time out of mind that the parson is to have of Mr. Nicholas Mussell or his asigns for tithe, duties or demands of fishing out of the waters of the said mills and all other waters and streams in Steeple Langford 5s. 3d. yearly at Easter. From the mills of Bathampton [Battington] now in the possession of Mrs. Mompesson or her assigns yearly at Easter 3s. for tithe; out of the mill of Hanging Langford occupied by Walter Dewe or his assigns yearly at Easter 16d. for all tithes.

The tenth lb. of wool. Tithing of lambs by custom: if any parishioner has 10 lambs on St. Marks day [25 Apr] the parson is to have 1, the owner to choose 2 the parson to choose the third and so forward in excess of number and he is to take [rydd] the lambs away the same day. There is a custom in tithing that if a man has but 9 lambs or 8 or 7 the parson is to have 1 lamb paying the parties ½d. for every lamb that [...] for the tithe. If 6 the parson is to have 3d. but no lamb; if 5, half a lamb; if 4, 2d.; if 3, 1d.; if 2, 1d.; if 1, ½d. There is a general custom in paying privy tithes to pay at Easter yearly for every cow 1d, for heifers nothing in the first year. The parson is to have the tenth calf and so of 9, 8 or 7 and if it be 7 the parson is to pay [awnswere back] the party 1½d.; if 8, 1d.; if 9½d.: of 5 calves the parson is to have the half; of 6, 3d.; of a calf, killed the shoulder; of any sold the tenth penny: The fair calves so due to the parson to be taken [rydd] away from the rest [saving] at 3 weeks' end. For gardens 1d. yearly at Easter; of apples the tenth bushell. For all privy tithes of everyone that ?dwells here 2d. at Easter; of pigs and geese as before for calves and lambs.

1.   The terrier is written on the back of a court roll for the city of Salisbury, 1550.

458   1608 (D1/24/126/2)
Arable land in the W. field of the manor of Steeple Langford. In the furlong [. . .] way [. . .] John Maye W [. . .]; 1a. in the furlong [. . .] of John May W.; In the furlong called Picked [. . .]; in Lower Stan furlong [—]; in Over Stan furlong 1a. of Richard Foote, E., 1a. of the farm called Tucking mills W.; in the furlong called Cliffe 2a., ½a. Richard Foote E., ½a. John Maye W.; in the same furlong 1 picked a., ½a. Richard Wstely W., ½a. Thomas Rowden E.; in the same furlong 1a., ½a. Richard Potecary N., ½a. Richard Foote S.; in the furlong called Lower Mill way 1a., 1yd. Dennis North E., ½a. John Mate W.; in the furlong called Over Mill Way 1a., a tenement of the Farm called Tucking mills E., 1a. Richard Foote W.; in the furlong next [. . .] ½a., the Down N., 1a. John Willis S.

17a. of arable land in the Middle field of the manor of Steeple Langford: in the furlong [. . .] 1a., 1a. of Guy Everlie E., [. . .] belonging to the Tucking mills W.; in the same furlong 1a., 3yd. of John Maye E., [. . .] John May W.; in the same furlong 1a., 1yd. Richard [. . .] E., ½a. William Lawes W., in the furlong above the way called Slade ½a., John Maye E. and W.; on the hill above Horsnam 1a., 1a. William Lawes W., 1a. John Thringe E.; [. . .] Presnam 1a., ½a. Guy Everlye E., ½a. Robert Davis W.; in the bottom above and beneath the way 1a., ½a. Edmund Ednie E., ½a. Guy Everlie W.; in Long Short furlong ½a., ½a. John May S., ½a. Robert Davis N.; [. . .] furlong 1a., 1a. Robert Davis N., ½a. John Maye S.; in Russe furlong 1a., ½a. John Maye E., 2a. John Maye W.; in the bottom next little down ½a., ½ yd. Guy Everlie E., 1a. Robert Davis W.; in the furlong called Stubbles 1a., [. . .] Thomas Rowden E., 1a. Richard Poticary W.; in the Long furlong 1a., ½a. John Waterman E., 1a. John Waterman W.; in the furlong called Clannam 3 x ½a., 1yd. Richard Poticary N., 3yd. Thomas Rowden S.; in the furlong called Shoverland 1a., 1a. Robert Davis E., a headland to the furlong called White land W.; in the furlong called Whitland 1a., 1a. Guy Everlye N., 1a. Robert Davis S.; in the same furlong 1a. Richard Foote N., Robert Davis S.; a. of headland on W. side of Whitland; in Drove furlong 1a. 1a. Richard Foote N., 1yd. Richard Whale S.; in the furlong called Upright land, 1a., ½a. Waterman E., 1a. John Maye W.

[. . .]a. of arable land in the E. field of the manor of Steeple Langford; in the furlong [. . .] E. hill 1a., a linch on W. and ½a. Richard Poticary E.; in the furlong called Breach [Brache] 1a., 1a. John Maye N., a linch S.; in the same furlong ½a., ½a. Robert Davis N., ½a. Richard Whale S.; the Gentle Woman acre, linches E. and W.; in the furlong called Long Buttocks 1a., ½a. John Willis E., 1yd. John

Thring W.; in the same furlong 1a., ½a. Guy Everlie E., 3a. occupied by Richard Potticary pertaining to the farm called Tucking mills W.; in the furlong called Broad Buttocks ½a., 2 x ½a. Robert Davis E., ½a. belonging to the farm called Tucking mills W.; in the same furlong ½a., ½a. Richard Whale E., ½a. John Maye W.; in the long furlong against the hill along the way ½a., ½a. Robert Davis E., 1a. John Maye W.; in the same furlong 1a., a linch E., 1a. Thomas Rowden W.; in the bottom at Dead Man 1a., a linch E., ½a. Thomas Rowden W.; in the furlong that lies athwart Salisbury way 1 picked yd., ½a. Edmund Ednie E. a ground of land of Thomas Rowden W.; in the same furlong ½a., ½a. Richard Foote E., ½a. Robert Davis W.; ½a., ½a. William Lawes E., ½a. Guy Everlie W.; in the furlong over the breach upon Kytam 1yd., ½a. John Thring N [...]; in the furlong that lies upon ? Kytam [Bytam] ½a., ½a. Guy Everlie N., 1a. John Maye S.; in the same furlong ½a., 1yd. John Waterman N., 1yd. Richard [...] S.; [...] furlong 3yd., 1yd. Richard Whale N., [...] Robert Davis S.; on W. side of the same furlong 1yd. [...] Robert Davis; in the furlong against the hill upon Kytam 1a., 1a. belonging to the farm called Tucking mills E., 1a. Guy Everlyc E.

[...] Nicholas Mussell gent., c. 2½a. lying under the cliff beneath B[...] way [...] a rudge of Dorothy Paishan wid. 3a. of arable land [...] lying in the Middle field of Nicholas Mussell, gent. without W. gate [...] in or near the highway.

3½a. of mead ground [...] lying in Sundry places as follows: In the common mead of Steeple Langford 1a. called F[...] acre [...] a certain mead of Nicholas Mussell gent. and divided also with mere stones; in the same mead 1a., 1yd of mead of Guy Everlye W.; 1a., 1a. of the farm called Tucking mill N., 1a. [—] S., divided on both sides with merestones; In the mead called Presnam ½a. being a headland on N. [...] ½a. of mead of Nicholas Mussell gent. divided with a mere stone on W. end. c. 1a. of pasture called Earthpit close.

The parsonage house with a stable and barn adjoining a garden ground [...]; the old orchard on E. side of the house; a plot [...] S. side of the barn; a barton lying between the houses. [...]4 sheep to be pastured in the commons as the other tenants; [...]6 rother beasts [...] pasture for 3 hauliers [halliers] being horses as other tenants do.

James Collier, rector, Thomas Meriotte, Robert Hickes [X], churchwardens, ? John Gyrdler, sidesman, Nicholas Mussell, John Maye, Nicholas Perdwold, Richard Foote, Robert Davis [X], Thomas Foote [X], John Waterman [X], Denis North [X].

459　4 Jul 1698 (529/218)
Terrier taken by Robert Daniell, and witnessed by John Furnell, Robert Nicollis, John Watterman, inhabitants.

The field next the town;[1] against the hill ½a., ½a. of John May on W. side, and 1yd. of John May on E. side; at Slopeway ½a., 3 x ½a. of John May E., ½a. of Thomas Baker W.; in Great Pale land 1a., 1a. of John May E., ½a. of John Watterman W.; in Stand furlong 1a., 3 x ½a. of John May N., ½a. of Thomas Baker S.; Graces acre, 1a. of Robert Nicollis N., 1a. of farmer Rolfe S.; upon Clifford 1 great a., ½a. of Robert Nicollis N., ½a. of John Watterman and ½a. of John May S.; 1 picked a., ½a. of Thomas Rolfe E., Mrs. Mussel's Cheeke acre W.; 1a., 2a. of John May N., ½a. of Robert Nicollis S.; 1a. laying by the Down and shooting against Barwick way, 1a. of John May S.; in Upper Mellow way 1a., 1a. of Rolfe E., ½a. of Robert Nicollis W.; in Lower Mellow way 1a., 1a. of John Watterman W., 1yd. of Elizabeth Spier E., Total 10a.

In the Middle field; in the Water land, 1a. at the mead bridge being headland to the Tucking Mill piece, 1a. of John May E.; 1a., 1yd. of Thomas Baker E., ½yd. of John May W.; ½a.,[2] ½a. Sellwood W., 1yd. of Thomas Potecarye E.; ½a., 1a. of John May W., ½a. of Lawes E.; in the Hill furlong, ½a. shooting on the bank beyond the box hedge between 2 x ½a. of John May; 1a., 2a. of Thomas Baker W., 1a. of Sellwood E.; 1a., 1a. of farmer Rolfe W., ½a. of Thomas Baker E.; 1a. in Stubbles, 1a. of Rolfe W., 1a. of Mrs. Mussell E.; in Long Short land, ½a., ½a. of Henry Mussell S., 1a. of John May N.; 1a., ½a. of John Watterman S., 1a. of Rolfe N.; ½a. in the bottom, 1a. of Rolfe W., a linch E.; in Lanke furlong, 1a., 1a. of John Watterman W., ½a. of John Watterman E.; in Clannames, 3 x ½a., 1yd. of Mrs. Mussell S., 1yd. of John May and 1yd. of Thomas Potecarey N.; in Rush furlong 1a., ½a. of John May E., ½a. of John Watterman W.; in the Upright land ½a., ½a. of John Watterman E., 1a. of John May W.; in Drove furlong 1a. shooting against Upper Catlinch, 1yd. of Rolfe S., 1a. of Robert Nicolis N.; 1a. called Shoule acre being headland to E. end of Whiteland, 1a. of Rolfe E.; in Whiteland, 1a. 1a. of Rolfe S., 1a. of John May N.; 1a., ½a. of Robert Nicollis N., ½a. of Christopher Mussell S.; ½a. of headland to a furlong in the Home field (ie the field next the town) called Whiteland. 1yd. of John May W.: 1 piece in Farm field, 2 /12a.[3] Total 16a. beside the piece in Farm field. [*ie the field next the town*]

In the field next Stapleford down: in Hill furlong, ½a., Sellwood's piece W., ½a. of Rolfe E.; ½a., ½a. of Rolfe E., 1a. of John Watterman W.; 1a., 1a. of Mrs. Mussell W., a linch E.; in Broad Buttocks, ½a., ½a. of John May W., 1 ½a. of Rolfe E., ½a., ½a. of Rolfe W., ½a. of Rolfe E.; in Long Buttocks 1a., 3a. of Rolfe W., ½a. of John May E., 1a., ½a. of Thomas Baker E., 1a. of John May W.; in Gentlewoman 1a. with a linch on both sides, 1a. of Rolfe W., ½a. of Thomas Pottecary E.; in Middle Hills 1a., ½a. of wid. Spier W., ½a. of Thomas Baker E.; in Breach [Brach] ½a., ½a. of Christopher Mussell N., ½a. of Rolfe S.; 1a., ½a. of John May S., 1a. of John May N.; against Kittom hill 1a., 1a. of John May W., 1a. of Rolfe E.; athwart the hill 3yd., 3yd. of Henry Mussell S., 3yd. of Rolfe N.; 1head yd., 1yd. of Henry Mussell W.; ½a. athwart Kittome, ½a. of Thomas Potecary S., ½a. of John Watterman N.; ½a. there, 1a. of John May S., ½a. of Mrs. Mussell N.; 1yd. < ½a. > at the upper end of Kittome, 1yd. of the wid. Spier S. E., ½a. of Thomas Baker N.W.; ½a. athwart Salisbury way, ½a. of Sellwood E., ½a. of John May W.; ½a. there, ½a. of Robert Nicollis E., ½a. of Rolfe W.; 1yd. there, ½a. of wid. Lawes E., 1yd. of Mrs. Mussell W. Total 14a. 1 piece in the Farm field lying below the malm [maame] pitt which is 2½a.

An account of the meadow ground: In the Great Meadow at the gate in the Marsh furlong is 1a. with 1a. of Rolfe N. and ½a. of John May S.; in the Middle furlong is 1a. with 3yd. of John May W. and 1yd. of Selwood E.; In the Long furlong be 2a. together one end shooting against Chantry bridge and quite athwart the mead to the N. river with the farm 12a. on E. and a. of Henry Mussell on W.: In Pressonham is ½a. with ½a. belonging to the farm on S. and the lands end on N.; a marsh ground of 2a.; 1 close by the name of Earth pit close.

1. Note added 23 Nov 1708 by Thomas Selwood [rector] as a result of a survey by his tenant Francis Thistlethwayte and his servant Thomas Yates: In this Home field are by common reputation 10a. and by measure 10a. 3yd. 38 lugs.
2. As n. 1. This appears in the original in The field next the town a mistake noted in 1708.
3. As n. 1. Belonging to this field are 4 large a. lying in the field called New field. The Farm field piece belongs to Home field.

460   4 Aug 1783 (D1/24/126/3)

New close 4a. 1yd. 30 p. In the field next the parish; the half a. against the hill, 1yd. 16p., the a. in Great Park lands, 3yd. 1p.; the a. in Stand furlong, 2yd. 6p.; Graces's acre, 2yd. 34p.; the picked a. on Clifford, 2yd. 30p.; another a. in Clifford, 2yd. 28p.; the great a. in Clifford, 1a. 2yd. 4p.; the great a. at the Down, 3yd. 9p.; 1a. in Upper Milloway, 2yd. 18p.; an a. in Lower Milloway, 3yd. 20p.; an outside half in lower Milloway, 2yd. 25p.; a picked half at Slope way, 1yd. 17p. Total 8a. 2yd. 8p.

Middle field: The half by the Box hedge, 1yd. 23p.; 1a. in Length furlong, 3yd. 22p.; 1a. in Stubbles, 2yd. 26p.; the first a. in White land, 2yd. 6p.; the second in ditto, 2yd. 18p.; Showl acre, 3yd. 24p.; ½a. in the Upright furlong, 1yd. 13p.; 1a. in Drove furlong, 2yd. 32p.; Middle acre in New field, 1a. 32p.; Upper acre in New field, 1a. 22p.; the first a. against the hill, 1yd. 31p.; 3 x ½a. in Clannims, 1a. 1yd. 8p.; 1a. in Rush furlong 2yd 39p.; Lower acre in New field, 1a. 1yd. 30p.; another a. in Newfield, 1a. 23p.; one half in Long Short land in the Bottom, 28p.; another half in Long Short land, 1yd. 29p.; 1a. in the same land, 3yd. 25p.; the second a. against the hill, 1yd. 20p.; ½a. over against Prestenham, 1yd. 27p.; 1a. in the water land against the bridge, 1yd.; another a. near Prestenham 1yd. 15p.; another a. crossing the road, 1yd. 12p. Total 15a. 2yd. 25p.

Field next Stapleford down; first half against the hill, 1yd. 33p.; second half ditto, 1yd. 3p.; 1yd. against the hill, 2yd 17p.; 1yd. in the Bottom, 3yd. 2p.; Kite hill acre, 3yd. 35 p.; Kite hill yard, 1yd. 23p.; Lower half across the hill, 2yd. 1p.; 3yd. across the hill 3a. 8p.; Upper half across the hill, 2yd. 2p.; New broke yard, 1yd. 7p.; East half across Salisbury way, 1yd. 31p.; 1yd. at Salisbury way, 3p.; 1a. in Breach, 2yd. 29p.; half in Breach, 1yd. 11p.; Gentlewomans acre, 2yd. 19p.; the last a. in Long Buttocks, 2yd. 30p.; west a. in ditto 2yd. 32 p.; 1a. in Middle hills, 3yd. 19p.; west half in Short Buttocks, 1yd. 17p.; east half in ditto 1yd. 9p. Total 11a. 1yd.

Meadow ground: In the Great meadow at the gate in Marsh furlong 1a. with an a. of Dr. Wells on N. and ½a. of Mrs. Blagden on S. In the Middle furlong 1a with 3yd. of Mr. Blagden on W. 1yd. of William Thring on E. In the Long furlong 2a. together, 1 end abutting against Chantry bridge and quite across the mead to the N. river with the farm 12a. on E. and Mr. Swayne's ½a. on W. In Pretenham ½a. with ½a. of the farm on S. and the lands ends on N. A marsh ground on 2a. Earth Pit close.

Thomas Swayne, churchwarden.

The parsonage house is in very good repair and consists of a hall with 2 good parlours wainscotted, bedchambers and other rooms corresponding, brewhouse and pigeon cote, stables for 8 horses, a barn with 2 new floors, and 9 chambers, a coachhouse, a wagon house now building, with a good rick yard. Right of commons for cows and horses and feed for 100 sheep in summer and 60 in winter. All the tithes are due to the rector. Mrs. Susan Mompesson devised to the parish forever £1 6s. 8d., which is to be paid out of the rent of Little Bathampton farm and dispersed to the poor yearly at Michaelmas [29 Sep]. The communion plate consists of a silver plate for the offerings given by the Rev. John Ballard, DD., a quart silver cup given by the Rev. John Ford, late rector, a silver salver for the bread and a cup for the wine.

Samuel Wheller [*rector*].

LANGLEY BURRELL rectory

461   n. d. late 16th cent. (D1/24/127/1)
The presentment of the churchwardens and sidesmen. There is a tenement, 3 closes of pasture of 8a. and 2½a. arable land. Other glebe land as follows: a close of pasture called the Home close, 6a.; 1 little parrock, orchard, and garden, ½a.; a close called the Parrocke, 1a.; Sharppes close, 1a.; a close called Ruecrose, 3a.; a close called Chepham, 7a.; a close called Whits, 1a.; 25a. and 3 farndells of arable land in the Home field; 15a. of arable land in the Farre field; 7a. of arable land in the N. [field]; 21a. of arable in the E. field; 4a. meadow in the E. field; a coppice of underwood of 3a.; common of pasture for sheep and other cattle in all the premises.

John Mylham, Thomas Stockman, churchwardens, John Wasefylde, Henry Lande, sidesmen.

462   20 Sep 1608 (D1/24/127/2)
An orchard, garden, a little parrock with backside, 2a.; Home close, 6a., a parrock, 1a.; a close called Rie croft, 3a.; Sharpe close, 1a.; A close called Clerksomes, 5a.; an enclosure out of the N. field called Backwell, 3a.; a tenement with 2 closes, 8a. A tenement or cottage with 1a. of ground whereupon Edward Knappe now dwells. An enclosure out of the Home field, 4a. A new enclosure of the arable land in the E. field, 6a. An enclosure in the N. field, 1½a. 16a. of arable land in the Farm field. 19½a. of arable in the Home field. 23½a. of arable and meadow land in the E. field. A coppice, 3a. Common for sheep and other cattle in all the premises. There has been paid out of the farm of Langley Burrell, besides the tithes, the sum of 20s.

By me William Berie, rector, Thomas Wastfield [X], Henry Jones, churchwardens, Charles Aland, John Elye, sidesmen. *Names of all except the rector in the same hand*

463   13 Sep 1677 (D1/24/127/3)
Terrier exhibited at the triennial visitation of bishop Seth at Devizes made by the churchwardens and sidesmen with the consent and advice of the rector.

An orchard garden and little parrock with backside, 1a. A close of meadow or pasture called Home Close, 12a. A parrock, 2a. 2 grounds of meadow or pasture lying near Mr. House, 12a. A little ground of meadow or pasture called

Hill close, 4a. A little ground of meadow or pasture called Knaps Lease, 3a. 2 grounds of meadow or pasture called Sandfurlongs, wherein lies 1a. belonging to William Wastfield of this parish, 16a. 1 ground of meadow or pasture called Rye croft, 5a., 1 ground of meadow or pasture called Checksomes, 7a. 1 ground of arable or pasture called the N. field, 6a. 1 little ground of meadow or pasture called Buckwell, 3a. 1 little close of meadow or pasture called Sharpes close, 1a. 1 ground of meadow or pasture called the Copses, 6a. A little ground of meadow or pasture lately enclosed out of the Home field near Comelyes house, 4a. 1a. of meadow ground in Blackpoole which Thomas Sergant now rents. 4a. of meadow or pasture lying dispersedly in E. field which Richard Aland senior now rents. 4a. of arable land in Pipsmore field. 2a. of arrable in the Outward Raxehill. 5a. of arable land in Hardenhuish Little field. ½a. of arable land in an enclosure of Mr. Thomas Hawkins called Walfurlong. 15½a. of arable land in a furlong called Standbold and at the Crossway. ½a. of arable or pasture in an enclosure of Mr. Thomas Scott called Allington lease. ½a. of pasture in Marling pit in Chippenham field. Beside the tithes £1 is paid out of Langley Burrell.

Aylmer Lynch, rector, Anthony Jenkins, William Ladds [X], churchwarden, John Crooke [X], Daniel Powell [X], sidesmen.

[*All the measurements of land are described as by estimation i. e. not statute.*]

464   20 Dec 1704 (D1/24/127/4)
An orchard and garden adjoining to the parsonage house, *c.* ½a. The paddock behind the barn, 2yd. 2p. The Parsonage Home close adjoining to it, 10a. 9p.; the Paddock opposite to the parsonage house 1a. 3yd. 8p.; Sharps close, William Herbert on E., 2a. 11p.; the Piece, anciently a coppice, Birch marsh on E. and S., 5a. 2yd. 36p.; Ryecroft, Birch marsh on E., 6a.; Chexoms, Malmesbury way on W., 7a. 2yd. 36p.; a ground in the N. field near Mrs. Pinchen, Hardenhuish glebe on N., 4a. 1yd. 22p;. Bookwell, Mr. Henry Hawkins on S., 3a. 31p.; Nap's lease, Greenaway lane on S., 2a. 1yd. 7p.; Hill close, Langley common on N. E., 3a. 2yd. 21p.; a ground, wid. Baker on S.W., 1a. 31p.; another ground on N. E. of it both shooting on Langley common on N. W., 7a. 1yd. 28p.; Old Sand furlong, Samuel Ashe esq., on N., 8a. 2yd. 4p.; the new Sand furlong, parted from the other only by a hedge, Samuel Ashe esq., on N. W. both opening to Sutton lane, 7a. 1yd. 31p.

In Langley Home field: An a. enclosed in Matthew Smith's ground, Samuel Ashe esq., on N. 2a. in Stanbull furlong, Matthew Smith's aforesaid land on N. 5a., Edward Baker S.; 1½a., Hugh Wastfield on S.; 1a. more, Edward Lamfire N.; ½a., William Hulbert N.; 1a. shooting upon the Cross way Edward Baker W.; ½a. in Marlin pit, Joseph Wootten S.; 1a. shooting up Popes hill, Edward Baker S.; a ground shooting upon Rhodes house, Malmesbury way N. E.

In Hardenhuish Little field: ½a., wid. Farmer S.; 1½a., Madam Pleydell Ashe W.; ½a. lying between Mr. Henry Hawkins land.; 2a. Richard Lewis esq., S.; ½a. Henry Hawkins S.; ½a. in an enclosed ground of Mr. Robert Hawkins called Wall furlong. 1a. in an enclosed ground of Mr. Henry Hawkins called Bullcroft corner, Mrs. Lambert W. In Wraxwell corner: 2a. Martha Thorp, S.

In Pipsmore field: 1a., William Russell S.; 1½a., Mr. Robert Hawkins N.; ½a. Matthew Smith N.; 1½a., William Bedford tenant, N. In Black Pool: 1 trencher patch *c.* ½a., William Hulbert W.; another trencher patch *c.* ½a., Madam Ashe W.; 3x ½a., Mr. Noble Phelps his enclosure S.; 1a. lying between Madam Ashe her lands; 2a., William Wastfield N.; 1a., Eleanor Miles S.; 1 little farndell, Richard Selman N.

In Fleet mead: 1a., William Hulbert S.; ½ farndell, wid. Farmer N.; ½a. at Pack-Yatts, William Hulbert N.; an a. in the Lower marsh, William Wastfield E.

Right of commons of pasture for 10 rother beats in aforesaid meadows of Black-Pool Fleet mead and Lower marsh and for 1 horse and 4 rother beasts in Langley common according to an ancient stint.

Thomas Read, rector, James Deeke, Jonathan Deek, churchwardens.

465   n. d. [1783][1] (D1/24/127/5)

1. The parsonage house is a new[2] modern tiled stone building containing 12 rooms garrets, cellars. The rooms are in general papered; the parlours half wainscotted and floored with oak, the rest are floored with deal or elm, the outhouses are a barn and stable tiled. The house was lately built at the whole expense of the incumbent.

2. The glebe consists of the following grounds now Angells. N. field: adjoining N. field house, 7a. 1r. 30p.; Great Jackson, abutting to Malmesbury road and Birch marsh, 8a. 1r. 3p.; Rye close, having Birch marsh on N. and E., 6a. 2r. 6p.; Roses ground abutting to Greenway lane, 2a. 2r. 30p.; Seven acres, arable, having Cambridges land on W. and Greenway on E., 6a. 1r. 16p.; 3a., arable, land of Ashe esq. S. and abutting to Malmesbury road, 2a. 3r. 24p.; Rhodes ground, Ashe esq. W., Malmesbury road E. Coppice ground, Birch marsh S. and N., 5a. 1p.; Sharps close, Merrywell lane S., Stein brook N., 4a.; ground at W. end of the common, abutting to Langley common Ashe esq. S.; Monument ground, adjoining to the turnpike and Malmesbury road, 1a. 1r. 11p.; a garden adjoining to the parsonage house hedged in, 8p.; Home ground adjoining to the same, 10a. 5p.; orchard and Home stall adjoining to the same, 2a. 2r. 14p.; churchyard adjoining to the same, 1r. 24p.; a close on the other side of the lane, Ashe esq. S., Draycot road E., 1a. 3r. 26p.; Picked ground N. of Berritts hill lane, Tuck's land N. and W., Berritts Hill lane S., 7a. 3r. 2p.; Long ground S. of the same, Berritts Hill lane on N., 3a. 2a. 26p.; Upper Sand furlong, Branthwayte S., Ashe esq., W. and N., 8a. 1r. 35p.; Lower Sand furlong adjoining to same, Sutton lane S., 7a. 3r. 17p.; 2 grounds adjoining to same, 4a. 2r. 10p.; Ropes ditch, Sutton lane on N., Ashe esq., S. and E., 4a. 10p.; Pack gate, not enclosed, 27p.; Broad patch, not enclosed, 20p.; in Sutton marsh, Sir James Long W., Ashe esq., E., 2r. 17p.; Long mead bordering on Bleek mead and Black Pool meadow, 4a. 6p.; in Bleek mead Ashe esq. N., Branthwayte S., 1r. 5p.; in Black Pool, Eddolls land S., Ashe esq. N., 2r. 23p.; in same Ashe esq. N., Tuck S., 12r.; in same, Singers enclosed land S., Tuck N., 3r. 19p.; in same Ashe esq. N., Tuck S., 1r. 21p.; in same, late Selman N., Branthwayte S., 15p.; in same, Crook N., Tuck S., 1r. 13p.; in same, Eddoll S., Ashe esq. N., 3r. 36p.; in same, Crook N., Ashe esq. S., 22p.

3 leazes or rights of common for 6 heifers or 3 horses and sheep leazes in the winter season. The timber on the glebe chiefly consists of pollard trees which not having been numbered their value cannot be ascertained.

3. The tithes are worth *c.* £90 p. a. are now paid by a composition by

proprietors of land in Langley Burrell and Tytherton Lucas. There are 2 modus's one arising all out of the estates of Robert Ashe esq., amounting to £10., the other belonging to John Fast amounting 3s. 4d. p. a.

4. No bequests whatever

5. [*Blank*]

6. The furniture of the church are a pulpit cushion and cloth of green, surplice bible and 2 prayer books communion table and cloth a silver flagon cup and plate the gift of Thomas Stumpe rector 1703. 4 bells iron chest with 3 locks.

7. Church land, *c.* 2½a., is allotted for the repair of the church.

8. The parish is charged with the repair of edifices and churchyard fence.

9. The clerks wages are £2 10s. paid by the churchwardens and he is appointed by the minister.

Samuel Ashe, rector, Jeremiah Knight, Jacob Henly, churchwardens, Robert Ashe, John Eddolls, William Knight, inhabitants.

1. A copy of this terrier made in 1799 states that it was presented at the primary visitation of Bishop Shute in 1783 (WSRO 118/146/1).
2. It was built in 1776-1778 (WSRO 118/152).

LATTON vicarage

466   1 Jul 1608 (D1/24/128/1)

There belongs to the vicarage a house, a kitchen, a barn, an orchard, a garden, and a backside, with the herbage and feeding of the churchyard. There are also 5 arable lands, to be sown according to the custom, lying in a close called Abbotscroft. There are also 3 hams of meadow called Vicar's hams, 2 of which lie in a meadow called Wayemoor and the third in a meadow called Southam, also the tithe hay of certain acres of meadow called the Colterne[1] acres lying in Wayemoor. There belong also to the vicarage all the tithes of half growing in the parish except for Wayemoor, Southam, Malborough and Sydnall,[2] and the whole farm grounds, to whomsoever they, or any part, shall be let. Instead of which tithe hay, and of all other duties due to be paid to the vicar out of the farm (except offerings and for churching of women according to custom, which the vicar is to have out of the farm) he is to have only £4[3] yearly to be paid at Michaelmas [29 Sep], Lady day [25 Mar] and the depasturing of 3 kine on the farm ground called the Court closes, or else 4 kine in the cow lease, at the choice of the lord of the manor, from 3 May until 11 Nov. yearly.[4] Tithe corn of 2 yardlands held by John Trinder,[5] 1 yardland held by John Roberts,[6] 1 yardland held by Richard Newman,[7] 1½ yardlands held by Richard Matthew,[8] 1 yardland held by William Wayne,[9] 1½ yardlands held by Edward Ware,[10] 1 yardland held by Thomas Roberts,[11] 1 yardland held by John Ferriby,[12] 1 yardland held by Alan Harrys,[13] half the tithe of 2 yardlands held by Thomas Townsend, and of ½ yardland held by Thomas Lane.[14]

The vicar is to have tithe wool of all sheep which have been depastured in the parish, except the farm ground, for the time they have been depastured if they are shorn, but if they are sold then he is to take ½d. for every sheep, to be paid on Lammas day [1 Aug] yearly. The vicar is to have 3d. for every new milch cow, and for every thorough milch cow and heifer 1 ½d. to be paid on Lammas day yearly. The vicar is to have the tithe of lambs throughout the parish, except the farm grounds, and to take them up on St. Mark's day [29 Apr] yearly to tithe them. First the owner is to take 2, and the vicar the third, then he is to let the owner draw out of the fold [cub] 9 and the vicar is to draw the tenth until they come to the last then the owner is to have 7 and the vicar none. The vicar is to have the seventh or tenth calf, pig, and goose, provided that there are not less. Then the vicar is to have for every calf weaned ½d., for every calf sold the tenth penny, for every calf killed the left shoulder, for every pig and goose ¼d. and for every foal 1d.; he is to give back the like if there are but 7 and under 10.[15] If a calf is sold with the cow then the vicar is to have only ½d. for the fall, but if a cow and calf which have been depastured [before in the parish], except the farm grounds, are sold to any of the parish, then he is to have for the calf if it is sold the tenth penny, if it is weaned ½d. The vicar is to have from every inhabitant tithe apples, wardens,[16] pears, walnuts, and for his garden 1d., except for the farm grounds. The vicar is to have for the Upper mill 4s., also he is to have for the nether mills 4s. to be paid at Easter by the tenant of the mills. The vicar is to have the tithe of honey if the owner kills any stall or stalls of bees, and if he sells them the tenth penny as they are sold for.

The vicar is to have certain oblations and offerings, 2d. due to be paid at Easter by everyone that does, or ought to communicate, except for the first year for which he is to have only 1d. The vicar is to have tithe eggs for hens, turkeys, ducks, cocks, and drakes, to be paid at Easter, for every hen 2 for the cock 3, and so for turkeys, ducks and drakes. The vicar is to have an accustomed duty which women offer to give God thanks after childbirth, a crisom and 2d., and if the child dies 2d. only. The vicar is to have the tithe corn of the plot of ground called the Eight acres belonging to the parson of Latton, and tithe hemp and flax throughtout the parish, except the farm. If any man of our parish lets or sells pasture, except the farm grounds, the party or parties that take it are to agree with the vicar for the tithe, except if the grounds are mowed, or depastured with tithing cattle, provided always that they may keep working cattle and cattle for store without paying tithe. Strangers that take pasture are to agree with the vicar to pay him on Lammas day. If any sell sheep one to another of the parish the vicar is to have the whole tithe of him that doth buy them during the time that they have been depastured in the common.

Randall Ashtone, vicar, William Wayne [X], Walter Tomes [X], churchwardens, John Hinder, John Roberts [X], sidesmen, John Hungerford, Edward Ware [X], Anthony Tomes, Bartholomew Brayne [X], Thomas Roberts [X], Richard Hopgood [X], Edmund Roberts, William Beames, Fulke Johnson [X], Thomas Fane, John Lan, Richard Hayward [X], John Wayne, Marian Trinder [X], Margaret Roberts [X], Elizabeth Thompson [X], Christopher Hinton [X], William Stone, Thomas Porklett [X].

1. Cotterne acres in **468** and **469**.
2. Seednoll in **467**.
3. £9 in **468** and **469**.

4. According to ancient custom in **467**; omitted in **468** and **469**.
5. John and Richard Trinder in **467**.
6. George Roberts in **467**.
7. Amy Saunders in **467**.
8. John Mathew in **467**.
9. Henry and Mary Waine in **467**.
10. Thomas Ware in **467**.
11. William Roberts in **467**.
12. Simon Roberts and Jane Feribee in **467**.
13. Yardland called Harrises, no occupier stated in **467**.
14. John Lane in **467**.
15. The vicar is to have only for the sale as aforesaid ½d., this replaces part of the sentence in **467**, **468**, and **469**.
16. A type of pear.

467   28 Oct 1671 (D1/24/128/2)
*As **466** with amendments in footnotes* Simon Roberts, John Bayston, churchwardens, John Lane, William Mathew, sidesmen, Thomas Ware, Thomas Beames, Thomas Roberts, William Trinder, John Trinder, John Mathew, Richard Townesend, Thomas Townesend, Thomas Braine, Thomas Tomes, Samuel Dunn, Edward Hinder senior, John Coocke, John Davice, Richard Hayward, Anthony Houze. *Names in the same hand*

468   25 Feb 1678 (D1/24/128/3)
*As **466** with amendments in footnotes.* The arrangement of the yardlands on which tithe corn is due is as follows: 1¾ yardlands held by John Trinder, ¾ yardland Richard Trinder, ½ yardland Ann Laffer, wid., 1 yardland George Roberts, 1 yardland Amy Saunders, 1½ yardlands John Mathew, ¾ yardland Henry Waine, ¼ yardland William Waine, 1½ yardlands Thomas Ware, 1 yardland William Roberts, ¾ yardland Simon Roberts, ¼ yardland Philip Mathew, 1 yardland Thomas Roberts, 2 yardlands Thomas Townesend.

Joseph Godwin, vicar, William Johnson, clerk, Edward Hinder, Thomas Roberts, churchwardens, William Trinder, John Trinder, Thomas Habgood, George Roberts, John Mathew, Richard Townesend, Thomas Townsend, Thomas Ware, Thomas Beames, Thomas Roberts.

469   28 Nov 1704 (D1/24/128/4)
*As **466** with amendments in footnotes.* The arrangement of yardlands on which tithe corn due to the vicar is as follows: 1½ yardlands held by Edward Ware, 1 yardland Simon Roberts and Joan Mathews wid., 1 yardland Jacob Roberts, ½ yardland Robert Roberts, 2 yardlands Thomas Townsend, 1½ yardlands Thomas Mathews of Hartnell, 2 yardland Henry Hedges, William Trinder, Wheeler [sic], Edith Laffer wid., and Edward Ware, 1 yardland Edmund Roberts, 1 yardland Nicholas Hardham and 1 yardland Henry and William Wayne.

Concerning charitable gifts in the parish: John Jordan of Latton gave £5 to be set at interest and the interest to be given each Christmas to such poor indigent people of Latton who in the discretion of the minister and churchwardens and overseers should be thought fit and convenient. The £5 is in the hands of the parish at present and the interest to be paid by the parish til such time as we have the conveniency to place it otherwise.

Michael Bingley, vicar, John Humphris, Thomas Mathews, churchwardens, John Hayward, overseer, Edward Ware, Thomas Hinton, William Trinder, John Cooke, Thomas Townsend, Henry Barnett.

LAVERSTOCK vicarage

470   Jul 1616 (D1/24/129/1)
Terrier made by William Creed and John Light, churchwardens and George Acrigge and Edmund Graye, sidesmen.

In the N. field are 2a. of arable land lying E. and W., the lands of Sir John Webb, held by Henry Pearson on the N., and the lands held by George Acrigge on the S., and the highway from Laverstock to St. Thomas's Bridge on the W.; 1a. more lying E. and W., the lands of Sir John Webbe called the Farm field on the N. and held by Thomas Merivale [Merrifall] on the S.

In the E. field of Ford are 2a. in the lower corner of the field, lying E. and W., the London highway on the E., John Batt's land on the N., a headland of the bishop of Salisbury held by Robert Sooper on the W. and the common down of Ford on the S.; 1a. near the lane from St. Thomas's bridge to Ford, lying E. and W., the lands of Sir John Webb held by Thomas Merivale on the N. and the lands of St. John's Hospital [*Wilton*] held by Richard Huddock gent. on the S.; 1a. at the Crafts end above Ford mill, lying N. and S., the lands of the bishop of Salisbury held by Robert Sooper on the N. and Crafts on the W.; 1½a. lying E. and W. being headland on the N., shooting against the common down, and John Stalling's land lying on the N.; 1½a. shooting against the common down, lying E. and W., being headland to Broken Crosse furlong, the lands of Sir John Webb held by John Pearson on the S.; 4a. in Whitbey furlong, lying E. and W., the lands of St. John's Hospital held by Richard Huddock on the N. and the lands of John Stalling on the S.

In Ford field called Anburroughs field are 2a. in Cane Bush furlong, lying E. and W., the lands of Sir John Webb held by Joan Bennet wid., on the N., and John Stalling's land on the S.; 2a. in the furlong below Lakes Bush, lying E. and W., the lands of John Stalling on the S. and the lands of Charles Sweeting on the N.; 2a. in the uttermost furlong in the field next Winterbourne lying N. and S., the lands of the bishop of Salisbury held by Robert Sooper on the E., and the lands of Sir John Webb held by Anthony Noble on the W.; 1a. in Brook furlong, lying E. and W., the lands of the bishop of Salisbury held by Robert Sooper on the S., and the lands of Giles Batter of Hurdcott in the parish of Winterbourne [*Earls*] on the N.

In confirmation of the truth of the premisses we have subscribed our names, Nicholas Clunn, curate, William Creed [X], John Light, churchwardens, George Acrigge, Edmund Graye, sidesmen, Christopher Kill, Thomas Williams [X], Nicholas Willis [X], William Storie [X], Robert Soper, John Stalling.

471 20 Sep 1677 (D1/24/129/2)
Terrier exhibited at the bishops registry. 21a. in the common fields of Laverstock and Ford as follows: In the Middle field at Ford; a little enclosed ground, c. 1a., lying next to Hurdcott; 2a. in a piece, land of Mr. Oliver Shergold E. and John Dewe W. 2a. in a piece in Travell Hill furlong, lands of Mr. Charles Sweyn [Swevin] N., Thomas Ray S.; 2a. in a piece in Cave Bush furlong, lands of Mr. Thomas Ray N. and S.

In the E. fields at Ford: 4a. on Whitebee, land of Mr. Anthony Wilkinson S., Mr. Oliver Shergold N.; 3x ½a. in Robbin Hood Butts, land of Mr. Henry Donny S. < 3 x ½a. more which is a head land at S. end of the same furlong>; 2a. in a piece in Green Plot furlong, lands of Mr. Oliver Shergold N.; 1a. in the Hook landfield, lands of Mr. Thomas Williams S. and Mr. Thomas Hawles N.; 1a. at Counsell Stile bounded by the hedge W. and land of Mr. Oliver Shergold E.

In the field of Laverstock: 1a. bounded with the farm field on N. land of Mr. Thomas Williams S.; 2a. in a piece, land of Mr. Edward Dowland N. Mr. William Senior S.

The tithes of the whole parish are valued at £60 p.a.

Thomas Williams, tenant, William Senior, Thomas Marton, churchwardens, Samuel Jecocke, curate, Richard Freemantle [X], George Williams.

472 7 Jun 1705 (D1/24/129/3)
The dwelling house and orchard barn and stable and backside, adjoining. 20a. as follows: In Middle field at Ford: A little close, c. 1a.; 2a. in a piece, land late Mr. Shergold E. and land of John Downes W.; 2a. in a piece in Grandle hill furlong, land late Charles Swaine N. and Godfrye on S.; 2a. in Cave Bush furlong, land of Christopher Batt N., Swaine S.

In the E. field at Ford: 4a. on Whidby, land of late Willkanes S. and late Mr. Edmonds N.; 3 x ½a. in Robin Hood's [Whodes] Butts, lands late Dineye S.; 3 x ½a. headlong to the Green plot; 2a. in Green plot furlong, land of Mr. Shergold N.; 1a. in Hook, land late Thomas Williams S. and late Mr. Holliser N.; 1a. at Counsel stile bounded with the hedge W. and land late Swaine E.

3a. in Laverstock field.; 1a. bounded farm field N. and land late Thomas Williams S.; 2a. in a piece, land late Dolande N. and Senior S. To the value of £50.

William Hayter, Joseph Everad, John Alexander, churchwardens.

MARKET LAVINGTON vicarage

473 1671 (D1/24/130/1)
1 yardland consisting of 27a. 1yd. lying dispersedly in the fields of the parish with 110 sheep leaze in the field and 14 sheep leaze with 4 beast leaze one year, 5 beast leaze the other in the meadow called W. park. All the tithes of St. Joan a Gore farm viz.; corn, wool, lamb and whatever else is tithable.

A dwelling house, a house called the Dairy house, a barn, a stable a fodder house, a woodhouse, 3 gardens, 1 orchard, a close adjacent to the orchard, a cliff [cleft] lying on the other side of the river called the Grove abutting upon the common fields called the Sands. An enclosure, *c.* 2½a. 3a. in the meadow called W. Park and 1a. in More mead. Tithe from the parson of 2½a. of Chantry acre in the E. clay, 5 x ½a. in the W. Clay and tithe hay of *c.* 2½a. in the meadow called W. Park. Tithe of a parcel of a parcel of of ground in Wish mead called Gore acre. Tithe of the gardens, orchards, home closes and mills in the parish. Tithe of 3 coppices one called Lady wood, another adjacent to the Ham wood and another called the Trollys. Tithe of an enclosure called the Kings side with 2 other grounds called Twenty lands belonging to Easterton.

Thomas Tanner, vicar, Leonard Bishop, William Shuter, John Androse, churchwardens, John Samwell.

474   15 May 1705 (D1/24/130/2)
Terrier handed in by the churchwardens to the bishop's registry. A dwelling house, barn, stable, fodder house adjoining, a little outhouse, and a woodhouse adjoining, and gardens an orchard a close adjacent, a withy bed, a close on the other side of the river abutting on the common field called the Sands.

1 yardland of 27a. 1yd. lying dispersedly in the common fields which we will take care that they may be distinguished by some land marks from other mens'; 100 sheep leazes in the fields and on the downs to feed with the parsonage flock. An enclosure of *c.* 2a. out of the ancient commons. 3a. of meadow in W. Park, an enclosed a. in Moore mead with beast leaze and sheepleaze in the winter feeding of the said meadow proportionably with others.

All the tithes of the farm called Gore consisting of corn, hay, wool and lamb and whatsoever else is tithable. Tithes of a portion of ground in Wish mead called Gore acre. The tithe of 5 x ½a. in the W. Clay of 2 x ½a. in the E. Clay, and of Chantry acre all from the parsonage glebe. Tithe hay from the parson in W. Park of *c.* 2a. abutting on Moore mead. Tithes of all home crofts and closes, orchards, kitchens, gardens, mills, milk [*cows*], calves, pigs, colts, eggs, pigeons in the whole parish except the pigeons and orchards on the parsonage. Tithes of Trolly and 2 other coppices of the earl of Abingdon. Tithe of all other wood and fuel that is titheable in the whole parish. Small tithes in fields or gardens viz. carrots, turnips, plants, rape, onions and their seeds, withy or osiers planted in enclosures used for gardens. Tithe corn and hay and titheable wood from all the enclosures in Easterton on that side called the duchy of Lancaster and 2 grounds called Twenty lands belonging to Easterton.

Thomas Tanner, vicar, Andrew Still, Leonard Bishop, churchwardens.

475   23 Jul 1783 (D1/24/130/3)
The vicarage house is built with brick covered with stone tile. It contains a cellar floored with brick, not ceiled; a passage floored with oak and ceiled; a kitchen floored with stone and ceiled; a parlour floored with oak and ceiled; 2 bed chambers, a closet and 2 garretts all floored with elm and ceiled. Outhouses: a brewhouse built with brick and covered with stone tile, 14ft. by 7½ft., a grist floor not ceiled; 2 skilling [skeiling] carthouses, one 18ft. by 10ft., the other 18ft. by 9ft., covered with thatch; a barn 16ft. by 14ft. built with posts and boards and covered with thatch; a stable 20ft. by 15ft., built with timber and covered with thatch.

Glebe enclosed: a field, 3r., of arable and willow bed behind the house, bounded E. and N. by enclosures of Mr. William Sainsbury, W. by an enclosure of lord Radnor, S. by a field of Mr. Hopkins; a close and rick yard 3r. 21p.; a field, arable, 2a. 1r., below Lodge common, bounded E. by an enclosure of Mr. Richard Hill, W. the high road, S. by an enclosure of Mr. Vince, N. by an enclosure of lord Radnor; a field, 1a., in Moor mead, bounded E. and S. by enclosures of lord Radnor, W. by an enclosure of Mr. Slade, N. by an enclosure of Mr. John Sainsbury.

Glebe in the common fields: E field; a piece of arable, 25a. 2r., bounded by pieces of ground of Mrs. Crawley, W. and S. of lord Radnor, N. of Mr. William Sainsbury; a piece of pasture, 6a. 1r. 8p., in W. path bounded by pieces of ground, E. of ld. Radnor W. of Mr. Richard Legg, S. of Mr. Richard Kill, N. of Mr. Wadman.

No right of commoning of horses beasts or sheep. Garden and yard fenced with pailes, 1r. 8p.; c. 30 young elms on the glebe. No augmentation to the living: No stipend or pension payable out of it.

Tithes as **474** omitting tithe on lands in E. and W. Clay.

Furniture of the church and chancel: 6 bells; purple thickset velvet desk, pulpit and cushion cloth; a linen cloth and napkin for the communion table; a clock and chimes. Plate: a flagon inscribed 'To God and the church of Market Lavington, Samuel Sainsbury, Jun[r] gave this Anno. Dom. 1733 etat sue 41',[1] weight, 61oz.; a chalice inscribed 'Market Lavington 1728', 12oz.; a dish inscribed 'To God and the church of Market Lavington this was given by John Tanner vicar of Lowestoft in Suffolk A. D. 1741', 30oz.; 2 salvers inscribed 'Market Lavington 1728', 11oz. and 6oz.

No land left nor money given by will or otherwise for repair of the church. Edifice and churchyard repaired by the parishioners. Clerk appointed by the vicar and paid 14s. 6d. p. a. by the parishioners. Sexton appointed and paid £3 p. a. by the parishioners.

John Dobson, vicar, John Williams, curate, H. C. Vince, J. Dampier; John Lanham, John Gauntlett, William Grant, Benjamin Saunders, Richard Perrott, John Millington, churchwardens and overseers, Francis Smith clerk and sexton, James Bartlett, John Garratt, William Baldwyn, James Philpott, George Wilmer.

1. Aged 41.

WEST LAVINGTON vicarage

476   1609 (D1/24/131/1)

There is a dwelling house, a barn, and stable, with a garden, orchard[1] and barton, all of c. 1a., and the herbage and profit of the churchyard as in times past.[2] 4a. arable land[3] lie in the W. field, of which 2a. lie on the upper side of the Portway, shooting E. and W., the land of Wid. Bailey on the S., and the boreland on the N.; the other 2a. lie on the lower side of the Portway, shooting E. and W., the furlong butting on the N. and 2a. held by Richard Chilvester on the S. 1 butt of arable is in the Eastfield shooting on Crooked bridge and lying between the headland of Christopher Merryweather on the E. and a butt of Ambrose Webb on the W.[4]

There is the tithe of 120 sheep belonging to a tenement called Long-lands[5] in the E. field, and of 50 sheep belonging to a tenement called the Prebend held by John Bull[6] lying in the W. Field; the tithe of a little butt in the E. field shooting E. and W. and lying headland to Richard Shatter's Gaston;[7] the tithe of hay[8] of all closes in Lavington and Littleton hamlet, except those taken out of the arable fields, with the tithe hay of all grounds not called meadows, as by name Grove House, Bawlie leaze, and Lubberhaies;[9] the tithe of coppice in the Frithe, sometimes called Harris coppice,[10] held by Sir John Dauntsey. The vicars of Lavington formerly had the tithe of another coppice of c. 7a., adjoining the N. field in Littleton which being now rooted up and destroyed, we suppose the tithe of that ground, however it is employed, belongs to the vicarage.[11] There is the tithe pigs, kine, cow white, calves, pigeons, all fruits and gardens, with all other small and privy tithes. There belongs to the vicarage the tithe of Fiddington hamlet, i. e. tithe wool, lambs, hay, corn and grain, cow white and calves with all other tithes, and the tithe of a coppice in Fiddington called Parham[12] wood. There has been time out of mind pasture for 10 beasts in the common of Fiddington. The vicar supposes that the tithes of all mills belong to the vicarage.

For all other rights and duties, if there are any, we refer ourselves to the vicar's composition,[13] delivered to the bishop's registry by Mr. Robert Pike,[14] sometime vicar of Lavington, as Mr. William Bower senior, affirms that he has often heard Mr. Pike say.[15]

James Waters, vicar, Hugh Bartlet, Thomas Pearsone, churchwardens.

1. And a little pond in **477**.
2. An augmentation of £30 p. a. payable on 25 Mar and 29 Sep out of an estate in the parish of earl of Abington in the parish in **477**.
3. Described as tithe free in **477** but no bounds given.
4. 10a. of arable land in the Bower field lately annexed to the vicarage by Gilbert bp. of Salisbury in **477**.
5. Called Long Hayes, held by James Newman in **477**.
6. Held by Mr. Henry Jones in **477**.
7. Headlong to William Webb's gate in **477**.
8. And corn in **477**.
9. Fields not named in **477**.
10. Frith coppice in **477**. No tenant named in **477**.
11. This coppice not mentioned in **477**.
12. Perham in **477**.
13. Described in **477** as being made between bishop Roger and William of Lavington at Potterne 7 Oct 1324.
14. Vicar between 1552-1568.
15. Offerings and oblations of all persons inhabiting the parish added in **477**.

477   Dec 1704 (D1/24/131/2)
*As **476** with amendments in footnotes.* John Marten, vicar, James Newman, John Mattocke, churchwardens.

478   30 Jul 1783 (D1/24/131/3)

The vicarage house is built in front with brick and the other part with stone and covered with stone tile. It contains 2 cellars floored with brick and ceiled; A hall wainscotted chair high and papered upward floored with elm and ceiled: A parlour as the hall in all detail except floored with deal; A small room or closet adjoining the parlour floored and ceiled: A kitchen floored with free stone ceiled and covered with thatch: 3 bed chambers, 2 of which are floored with elm and papered the other floored with beech and instead of paper stuccoed with fine plastering: 2 garrets floored with elm and ceiled.

Outhouses: A brewhouse built with stone 18ft. by 15ft. floored with freestone covered with thatch and unceiled: A barn with floor and field 34½ft. by 20½ft. built with posts and boards and covered with thatch: A stable adjoining the barn with 2 stalls 19¾ft. by 19½ft. built and covered with the same materials as the barn: A coal and pumphouse adjoining the barn and stable 15½ft. by 6ft. built with posts and boards and covered with thatch: Another stable adjoining the vicarage house with 2 stalls, 21ft. by 15½ft. built with stone and plastered over ceiled with lath and plaster and covered with brick tile. A quadrangular necessary house in the garden 7½ft. square, built with brick ceiled and covered with brick tile on a freestone globular stone upon top.

Glebe enclosed: The garden, 3r. 30p., bounded E. by a rivulet and a piece of meadow of the duke of Marlborough, W. the highroad and churchyard, N. a mud wall adjoining the free school, S. a hedge and garden of the duke of Marlborough.

Glebe unenclosed in the common fields: Arable in Bower field, 9a.; 2a. by Twopenny half bounded E. a piece of arable of the duke of Marlborough, W. a road and piece of arable of Mr. Long, N. apiece of ground of the duke of Marlborough, S. a piece of arable of Mr. Long; 2a., now barley, bounded E. and S. arable of the duke of Marlborough, W. a piece of arable of Mr. Long, N. a linchet and a piece of arable of the duke of Marlborough; 2a. by Gorefield bounded E. by a road and Gorefield, W. a piece of arable of Mr. Hunt, N. a linchet and a piece of arable of Mr. Hunt, S. a linchet and a piece of arable of the duke of Marlborough; 2a. above Warminster way bounded E. and W. by pieces of arable of the duke of Marlborough, N. a piece of ground of Mr. Hunt, S. a linchet and a piece of arable of the duke of Marlborough; 1a., now wheat, bounded E. a piece of ground of Richard Webb, W. a piece of ground of Mr. Long, N. and S. pieces of ground of the duke of Marlborough.

Arable in W. field: 4a. by Cheverell road with the road in the middle, bounded E., W. and N. by pieces of arable of the duke of Marlborough, S. a piece of arable of Mr. Griffin.

Glebe in E. Clay: c ½a. occupied by John Nutland, tenant, bounded E. piece of arable of Mr. John Sainsbury senior, W. garden corner of the duke of Marlborough.

Tithes due from lord Radnor on Littleton farm from Norcleys, 10a. of arable; Gastons, 2 meadow grounds of 23a.; 2 of the lands called Three grounds, 13a.; of Court close, 9a., sown every year.

The tithes of all home crofts or closes, orchards, kitchen gardens, mills, milk, calves, pigs, colts, pigeons, eggs in the whole parish except orchards and pigeons belonging to the parsonage, of wood and all other titheable fuel. The small tithes in fields and gardens viz. carrots, turnips, plants, rape, onions and their seeds, willows, osiers planted in enclosures used for gardening. Tithe corn, hay, wool and lambs, and everything else titheable on Fiddington farm. A right of commons for 6 beasts on Fiddington common the summer half year. The duke of Marlborough's augmentation of the living of £30. The same for garden tithes, £16.

Furniture of the church and chancel: 5 bells, green desk and pulpit cloth and cushion of the same. 2 surplices, 1 woollen cloth for the common covering of the communion table; 1 linen cloth and napkin for the same at the celebration of the Lord's Supper. A clock and no chimes. Plate: 1 tankard, no inscription 58oz.; 1 salver, ditto, 9oz.; 1 salver. 5oz.; 1 cup inscribed 'Ex dono Gulielmi Bower armigeri', no date, 17oz.

No land left nor money given by will or otherwise for repair of the church. Edifice and churchyard fence repaired by the parishioners. Clerk appointed by the vicar but has no stated salary. Sexton appointed by the parishioners but has no stated yearly stipend or salary.

E[dward] Emily, vicar, J. Williams, curate, Thomas a' Beckett, John Sainsbury, William Weeks, churchwardens, John Sainsbury, senior, William Giles, overseers. John Harris, Thomas Newman, John Griffin.

LEA AND CLEVERTON vicarage [see also 367 and 368]

479   13 Jul 1608 (D1/24/132/1)
There are belonging to the vicarage a house, a garden, and a close adjoining, and also 4 other severall grounds of arable and pasture containing c. 37a.

John Higgins; Thomas Wrighte, Giles Baylie, churchwardens, Thomas Earle, Richard Oliver, sidesmen. *Signature only of John Higgins, others in the same hand*

480   5 Dec 1671 (D1/24/132/2)
A vicarage house situate near and opposite against the church on S. side with 2 rooms below and 2 above and a little stable at the W. end, and at the E. end a little plot of garden ground a little close adjoining, ¾a.; 4 grounds one called the Great ground, 15a., adjoining the common on S. side, the W. part adjoining the ground of Thomas Oliver called the Upper ground; another ground called the Meadow adjoining to the N. part of the Great ground, 3a., bounded with a ground on N. part of Nathanial Watts called the Upper ground; another ground called the Picked lease lying on the E. end of the Great ground, 5a., bounding on a ground called the Parklease on the N. side in the possession of William Lawrence, on the E. side on a land called the Parkland and on the S. side adjoining the common; another ground called the Farthest ground, 7a., adjoining to the common on the N. and W. and to 3 grounds called the Nurnills on S. and E. All the grounds by estimation 31½a.

Abraham Griffin, vicar, Robert Church, William Rutty, churchwardens.

LEIGH DELAMERE rectory

481   n. d. late 16th cent.[1] (D1/24/133/1)

A dwelling house, barn, stable yard and orchard. 3½a. of pasture called the ?Spinet lease by the house; 1 other square close of pasture 4a.; 5a. of pasture ground, W. and N. the Great Marsh, E. Hurdwiche occupied by Thomas Rimer. One other close of pasture called New lease, 11a. 3 farndells, on W. side of farm ground called ?Twenty acres and butting down on the Great Marsh; 6a. 1 farndell of arable land in the E. field; 1 plot of meadow in the Lot mead; 19a. 1 farndell of arable in the W. field; 3 farndells; 3 lots and 3 swaythes of meadow.

Commons in the fields for sheep at the rate of 2 sheep an acre as the parishioners have customarily stinted commons for other cattle at the rate of 6 beasts and 1 horse to a yardland.

Tithes: Of wheat, barley, oats beans, peas, pulse [poulse] and hay being equally divided in sheaves or cocks the tenth sheaf or cock is due to the parson. For every cow at Lammas [1 Aug] 3d. and for a heifer or thorough cow 2d. For calves and lambs the tenth is due or otherwise as by the laws of the realm is adjudged. Of wool the tenth pound is due and of less less and of more more after the rate. Of any underwood the tenth acre or after the acre for more or less ground is customarily due unto the parson whether it be felled and cut down. For all other small tithes the tenth of everything as payable according to the laws of this realm provided in that behalf.

Anthony Eglesfelde, rector, John Dench, Richard Woodman, churchwardens, Thomas Rimer, James Stancombe, sidesmen. *Names in the same hand*

1. Anthony Eglesfelde was instituted as rector in 1580 and must have left some time before 1609 when Robert Latimer replaced Nicholas Taverner as rector.

482   1671 (D1/24/133/2)

A dwelling house with 6 bays with a barn a stable and other necessary outhouses with 2 gardens and orchards with a close of pasture adjoining containing 6a.

A ground of arrable land, 9a., a little ground of 3a. adjoining to Leigh Post. A spot of ground called Wainscroft, c. 4a. An enclosed ground called Six acres. A large ground called Newlease, 12a. A spot of ground in the W. field, 4a. The yearly value of these was anciently before these unhappy times £15 but now little more worth than £12 or thereabout although improved by enclosure. The tithes are all to be paid in kind without exception and heretofore valued at 30s. but now they are not so much worth.

By me Philip Kingsman, rector, William Jaques, churchwarden.

483   1677 (D1/24/133/3)

A message or tenement called the Parsonage house with a backside, orchard and a garden adjoining. A barn with 3 bays, an oxhouse and stable. A close of meadow or pasture ground, 5a., adjoining the Parsonage house. One meadow ground, 5a., called Winecoate. A meadow ground called the Bottom mead, 2a. Arable grounds: Cowelease, 12a.; 6a. by the Bottom mead; 1 paddock [paduck], 2a., adjoining the New field; 4a. lying on Binell. The rector has all manner of tithes as well of the farm or mannor house as of other inhabitants of Leigh Delamere.

Henry Rogers, minister, Robert Hollaway, churchwarden.

484 1704 (D1/24/133/4)

The parsonage house, barn, stable and backside. One close, *c.* 4a., adjoining the house, one pasture ground called Newlease, *c.* 10a., abutting against ground of Henry Chevers esq., called the Tyning. Arable ground called Six acres, meadow ground called Six acres mead containing 3a. all of which lie against a highway called Marsh lane. A piece of arable or pasture ground called Benell, *c.* 4a., bounded W. and S. by ground of Joseph Jaques called the Forest in which ground there lies a certain piece of ground which belongs to Ryleys [Rylees] farm. One pasture ground called Winecrat, *c.* 4a., adjoining a ground of the wid. Jaques called Hurdich. One arable ground called Newfield, *c.* 7a., siding along a ground of Henry Chevers esq., called New field. Another arable ground by the same, *c.* 3a., the highway from Sevington [Seventon] to Stanton [*St. Quinton*] lies through it. The truth of this terrier is attested by us whose hands are hearunto subscribed.

James Browning, Richard Jaques, Abraham Rimell, Isaac Woodman, churchwarden.

LIDDINGTON vicarage and rectory

485 n. d. mid-late 17th cent.[1] (D1/24/134/1)

Vicarage: 1a. in Upper field, the land of Mary Herring being on the N. and S.; 1a. meadow in Little field, the land of William Webb being on the N. and the land of John Herring on the S.

Richard Smith, vicar, Robert Hatt, John Skegglethorpe, churchwardens.

1. Richard Smith was instituted to the vicarage in 1634 and signed bishops transcripts up to 1679.

486 1677 (D1/24/134/2)

Rectory: A dwelling house of 4 bays, a barn of 4 bays, a stable and other outhouses of 3 bays. A garden, ½a.; a meadow, 1a. 1yd.

Land in the Little field: ½a., land of Sir John Talbot N., land of William Gardiner S.; 1½a. in Liddington Breach, highway E., Henry Herring W.; ½a., wid. Alice Webb E., Henry Herring W.; a head a., William Morse W.; ½a., <1a.>, the wid. Alice Webb N., the wid. Jane Morse S.; ½a., William Mathewe N., Robert Harward S.

Land in the field next to Wanborough [Wanborow]; 1a. Thomas Warman N.; ½a., William Gardiner N., the Wid. Martha Herring S.; ½a., John Morse N., William Gardiner S.; 1a., Richard Smith N., Thomas Smart S.; ½a., Thomas Smart N., Jane Morse wid. S.

Land in the Middle Down field; ½a., Thomas Warman N., John Morse S.; ½a., Henry Herring N., William Hawkes S.; 1a., Robert Harward N., Thomas

Smart S.; 1yd., Henry Herringe N., the wid. Martha Herringe S.; 1a., the Wid. Jane Morse N., William Morcocke S. 1a., John Morse E., Henry Herringe S.

Land in Down field next unto Badbury; ½a., Richard Smith N., Thomas Smart S.; ½a., Thomas Smart N., William Morecocke S.; ½a., Thomas Warman N., Richard Smith S.; ½a., John Morse N., Thomas Warman S.; 1yd., Sir John Talbot N., William Gardiner S.; ½a., William Gardiner N., Sir John Talbot S.; ½a., Richard Smith E., the Wid. Jane Morse W.; ½a., Henry Herring E., the Wid. Martha Herring W.; 1yd., Richard Smith E., William Hawkes W.; ½a., the wid. Alice Webb E., the Wid. Jane Morse W.; ½a., the wid. Jane Morse E., Robert Harward W.; ½a., Richard Smith W.; ½a., the Wid. Martha Herring E., Michael Haucks W.; 1a. at S. Down, a common linch E., Richard Smith W.; 1a., Sir John Talbot N.

Land in the W. field: ½a., Richard Smith E., Badbury mere W.; ½a., William Hawks E., Thomas Warman W.

Land in the Middle field: 1yd., wid. Alice Webb N., Richard Smith S.; ½a., the Wid. Martha Herringe N.; ½a., Robert Harward N., William Gardiner S.; 1yd., the Wid. Martha Herring W., 1a., William Gardiner N., Sir John Talbot S., 2a., William Gardiner N.; ½a., William Hawks N.; ½a., Sir John Talbot N., Robert Harward S.; 1a., Sir John Talbot N., Robert Harward S.; 1a., Richard Smith N.; ½a., Sir John Talbot N., John [. . .] S.; ½a., Thomas Smart W., the wid. Margaret Hammon ? W.; ½a. next unto Costers; 1a., Sir John Talbot E., Thomas Smart W., ½a. between 2 common linches; ½a., Sir John Talbot W. and E.; 1a., Thomas Smart S., the wid. Alice Webb N.; 1a., William Gardiner N., Robert Harward S.

3a in the Farm field. A meadow, 5a. The feeding of 5 beasts in a ground called Vanstans from 3 May until 29 Sep. Tithe corn and hay within the parish except the tithe of Liddington meadows and of the glebe belonging to the vicarage.

Richard Smith, minister, Henry Flewell, William Garnar, William Mathew [X], Henry Herringe, John Edwards, John Hopkins.

487   1677 (D1/124/134/3)
Terrier of the vicarage taken by the view of the minister and other sufficient men of the same parish. A dwelling house of 4 bays, a barn and stable of 4 bays, gardens and a backside, ⅓a. The churchyard. The tithe of all the glebe belonging to the rectory. Tithe of hay growing upon 1a. in Weekebreach. 1a. in the field commonly called the S. side. ½a. in the Upper field, Henry Herring N., a common linch S.; ½a. in the same field, Mullards hill N., a common linch S. Tithe wool, lambs, calves, milk of kine, grazing cattle and all other minute tithes within the whole parish.

Richard Smith, minister, Robert Harward, John Edwards, churchwardens, John Hopkins, Henry Flewell, William Garnar, William Mathew [X], Henry Herringe.

488   Dec 1704 (D1/24/134/4)
Vicarage: Terrier taken by the chief inhabitants of the parish whose names are underwritten. The ground on which the house barn stable and woodhouse are built with the garden in all c. ½a. The churchyard, c. 1a. ½a. in the Upper field

divided at one end from William Nash's land by a mere stone bounded on the other end and at each side by linchets. ½a. butting at one end on the said ½a.; the other parts surrounded with linchets. 1a. of meadow in Little field, ½a. of Robert Webb on one side, 3yd. of Henry Herring on the other.

The tithe of 5½a. of meadow in the Breach and Little field being glebe belonging to the parsonage. Tithe corn of all the glebe of the parsonage in the common fields as they are sowed in their course being 27½a. and 1yd. by estimation. Tithe of the Parsonage close, 1a. when sowed or mowed. Tithe of the enclosure belonging to the parsonage in the Upper field being 2a. 30p., but before being enclosed, 3a. by computation. Tithe of 1a. when sowed or mowed in the Upper Breach it being ⅓a. from Mr. Morse's hedge. Tithe conies, pigeons, honey and all other small tithes. Memo.: There was a mere stone set at this time by the inhabitants at the corner of John Hatt's garden to prevent his encroachment on the way to the vicarage barn.

William Spencer, vicar, William Nash [X], churchwarden, Giles Combe, overseer of the poor, Henry Herring, Thomas Smart, Henry Flewell, Robert Webb [X], Stephen Whipp, Frances Vinars [X], John Flewell, Robert Smart [X].

489   22 Jul 1786 (D1/24/134/5)

Vicarage: Lands allotted under the enclosure act of 1776 to compensate the vicarage for the tithes on lands in the parish of Liddington and hamlet of Medbourne including tithes on the glebe of the parsonage exonerated under the award; 49a. in Lower E. field bounded London road S., land in the same field allotted to the duke of Marlborough W., a brook dividing Liddington from Wanborough N., land in the same field allotted to Mrs. Mary Seymour wid. E. A close called Bay Days, c. 3a., bounded cottage garden of the duke Marlborough and an old road passing between it and the parsonage on S.W., land of the duke of Marlborough N.W., several cottages N.E., lands of Lovelace Biggs esq., on S.W. Part of a close adjoining on N.W. side to that just now described and at present thrown into and making a part of it, c. 1a. This was intended to make good the deficiency in value of an enclosed piece of meadow ground c. 9a., part of a cow common purchased of the duke of Marlborough by the Governors of Queen Anne's Bounty for the perpetual augmentation of the vicarage of Liddington bounded by the London road S, the road to Highworth W., and by divers old enclosures N. and E. A coney warren called Stephens's Down.

Tithes except corn and hay on all lands not exonerated from payment under the said enclosure act. The ground, c. ¼a. on which the house, barn, stable and woodhouse are built. The churchyard, c. 1a.

W[illiam] R[ich] Stock, vicar, Jeremiah May, James Brind, Giles Tombs, John Hatt, John Crips, churchwardens and overseers of the poor.[1]

1. The arrangement of the signatures makes it difficult to distinguish the churchwardens and overseers of the poor. The parish account book records the appointments of Tombs and Crips as churchwardens and Brind and Tombs as overseers on 18 April 1786. Brind and May, outgoing churchwardens, settled their accounts August 1786. (WSRO 1123/98)

LITTLETON DREW rectory

490 1671 (D1/24/135/1)

A dwelling house situated in the middle of the parish with a barn, stable, and other outhouses belonging to it, a backside, garden, and orchard, *c.* 1a.

Here follows a note of the arable land in the E. field: 1a. shooting on the parsonage orchard wall, having 1a. of the farm ground on the S. and on the N. a farndell of Thomas and John Chapman; 3 farndells in Middlegrase furlong having on the E. 1 farndell of Thomas and John Chapman, on the W. 3 farndells of Thomas Barnard; 2a. shooting on the common meadow, having on the E. 1½a. and on the W. 1a. of Thomas Ernle; at Brown's Pitts a furlong so called and 3 farndells having on the E. 1a. of Thomas Chapman, on the W. 3a. of the farm land; ½a. there also having on the E. 1a. of Thomas Ernle and on the W. 1a. of Thomas Chapman; in the lower furlong of Chessles shooting on the common meadow ½a. having on the E. half way the land shooting by the farm, and the other half by Richard Goodenough land, and on the W. 3 farndells of Richard Goodenough, ½a. in Chessells having on the E. ½a. of the farm land and on the W. 2a. or more of Thomas Ernle; in the same furlong 1a. having on the E. 1a. of Thomas Chapman, and on the W. ½a. of Richard Goodenough; 1a. called the Butts, having on the E. 3 farndells and on the W. 1a. of Thomas Chapman; 1 head a. shooting on Ox leaze, and having on the E. ½a. of John Hayes; 1a. on Kimswell furlong having on the E. 1a. of John Hayes, and on the W. 1a. of Thomas Chapman; 2a. shooting on the Fosse Way, having on the E. 1a. of the marquis of Worcester and on the W. 1 farndell of Walter Tanner; ½a. shooting on Lains corner on the E. half way heading the 3 furlongs on the N. having ½a. of Thomas Messiter; ½a. more shooting down towards the Old lands and having on the E. 1a. of Walter Tanner and on the W. 1a. of Thomas Ernle; a head ½a. shooting on the Old lands, also heading on the E. and having on the W. 1a. of the marquis of Worcester; 2a. in Pease furlong having on the E. 2a. of Thomas Chapman by Combe Parth, and on the W. 1a. of John Chapman; ½a. shooting on a ground of Walter Tanner called Innocks having ½a. of Thomas Chapman E. and W.; ½a. more in Pease furlong having on the E. ½a. of Thomas Chapman and on the W. 1a. of the marquis of Worcester; ½a. on Little Hill furlong having on the E. 1 farndell of Thomas Messiter, and on the W. 1a. of Thomas Chapman; ½a. in Innocks furlong having on the E. 1a. of Thomas and John Chapman and W. 2a. of Thomas Chapman; 1a. in the same furlong having on the E. 1a. of Thomas and John Chapman and on the W. 1a. of Thomas Chapman; ½a. there, also having on the E. 1a. of Thomas Chapman, and on the W. 2a. of the farm lands; ½a. in Long lands having on the E. ½a. of the farm land, on the W. 1 farndell of John Chapman; 1 head ½a. heading the S. furlong having on the N. ½a. of Walter Tanner; ½a. shooting up against the wid. Goddenough close having on the E. ½a. of Thomas Chapman, on the W. 2a. of the farm land.

Arable land in the W. field: 1a. called Goose acre, having the highway on the N., and on the S. ½a. of John Chapman; Mash acre having on the E. 1a. of the marquis of Worcester and on the W. ½a. of Thomas Messiter; 1a. more in the same furlong having on the E. 1 farndell of Walter Tanner. and on the W. 1a. of John Chapman; 1 head ½a. having on the E. ½a. of Walter Tanner and on the W.

½a. of the wid. Goddenough; 1a. more in the same furlong having on the E. 2a. of the farm land, on the W. ½a. of Walter Tanner; 3a. above Aske's house having on the S. 1a. of John Chapman and on the N. 1a. of Thomas Ernlie; 1a. in Smoake furlong having on the E. 7a. of the farm land and on the W. 2a. of Thomas Chapman; 3 farndells on Horsedowne having on the E. 1a. of the marquis of Worcester, and on the W. 1 farndell of Roger Huggens; 1½a. in the same furlong having on the E. 2a. of the farm land; and on the W. 3 farndells of Roger Huggens; 1 head farndell heading on the E., and having 1a. of Thomas Chapman on the W.; 1½. in W. Furrows having on the S. 1½a. of Thomas and John Chapman and on the N. 1a. of Walter Tanner; 2a. more in the same furlong at Hitching gate having on the S. ½a. of John Hayes, and on the N. the way that goes round the parish; 1a. in Hod-burrow having on the E. 1 farndell of Richard Goodenough, and on the W. 4a. of Thomas Chapman; 1a. on Slapphills having on the E. ½a. of Thomas and John Chapman and on the W. ½a. of Thomas Chapman; 2a. shooting down on the Fosse Way, having on the S. 2a. of Walter Tanner and on the N. 2a. of Thomas and John Chapman; ½a. more shooting on the Fosse Way having ½a. of John Chapman on the S. and ½a. of Thomas and John Chapman on the N.; ½a. more on the Fosse Way having 1½a. of John Chapman on the S. and ½a. of Thomas Chapman on the N.; 3 farndells shooting on the last ½a. having on the N. 1 farndell of Thomas and John Chapman, and being a headland southwards; 1a. on the Barrow having on the E. 1a. of Thomas Chapman and on the W. ½a. of John Chapman; 1a. in Innockes furlong having on the E. ½a. of John Chapman, and on the W. 1a. of the farm land; 3 farndells in the same furlong having on the E. 3 farndells of Walter Tanner and on the W. ½a. of Walter Tanner; 1a. called Frogge acre in the same furlong having on the E. 1a. of Thomas Chapman, and on the W. ½a. of John Chapman.

Pasture and meadow ground: 1 close at the town's end of *c.* 1a.; 2a. lately enclosed lying under Burton hedge in the W. field; ½a. in Marsh meadow having 1½a. of the wid. Goodenough on the E. and ½a. of Thomas Ernlie on the W.; 1 farndell in the same meadow having on the E. ½a. of Thomas Messiter, and on the W. 1 farndell of John Chapman; 1 farndell more having on the E. ½a. of Thomas Barnard and on the W. 1 farndell of John Chapman; 1 headen[1] having on the E. another headen of the marquis of Worcester, and on the W. a headen of the wid. Goodenough. In the common meadow are: 2a. with the hedge and ditch belonging to it having on the E. 1a. of Thomas Chapman and on the W. 1a. of the farm land; 1 farndell having on the E. 1 farndell of the farm and on the W. 2a. of Richard Goodenough; 3 farndells having on the E. 1 farndell of John Chapman and on the W. ½a. of Thomas Chapman; 1a. having on the S. 1a. of Thomas Messiter and on the N. ½a. of the farm land; 1 chicke[2] having on the E. 1 chicke of Thomas Messiter, and on the W. another of the farm; ½a. having on the E. ½a. of Thomas Messiter and on the W. ½a. of John Chapman; ½a. having on the E. ½a. of Roger Huggens, and on the W. ½a. of Richard Goodenough; ½a. called the Butts, with the hedge and ditch belonging to it having on the E. and W. land of the Wid. Goodenough; ½a. having on the E. ½a. of Thomas Messiter and on the W. 1a. of John Hayes; 1a. having with the hedge and ditch, on the E. and W. land of Thomas Chapman. Of pasture there is: 2 grounds called

Dunley Hill, *c.* 16a., having on the E. 1 ground of Thomas Chapman, on the W. a ground of John Chapman, and N. bounding on Alderton Lordship; 1 little ground called the Chapel of Dunley, *c.* ½a.; 2 grounds called Innocks, 8a., having on the E. the Fosse Way, on the W. a ground of Thomas Ernlie.

Taken by Henry Gough, rector, John Chapman and Amos Power, churchwardens.

1. The meaning of this word is unclear. It may refer to a piece in a pasture called Headland see **491**.
2. This may be a varient of cheek meaning here a piece of land on the side of the field.

491   20 Oct 1704 (D1/24/135/2)
Terrier taken by John Chepman and John Baker, churchwardens. A parsonage house with the garden and orchard, a barn, stable and oxhouse and all in repair containing *c.* 1a. 31½a. of pasture ground: 2 grounds called Donlow, 20a.; a ground called the Chapel, ½a.; 2 grounds called Enochs, 8a.; a ground called Burton lease, 2a.; a ground called the close at the Towns end, 1a. 12½a. of meadow ground; In the Common mead at the mead stile, 2a. 1 farndell lying near to Hilmead hedge: 1 farndell near to the Folly and 3 farndells abutting upon a ground called Nine acres, the lands of Hester Chepman on E.; 1a. called the Withy bed; ½a. called the Chick; ½a. in the furlong called the Headlands, lands of Smart Goodenough on E. and W.; 1a. in the same furlong lands of wid. Chepman on W. and 1a. more in the same furlong, lands of Elizabeth Young on E. and W.; 1a. in the lower end of the mead; 1 farndell abutting on a ground of John Chepman called the Ox lease; 2 x ½a. in the same furlong; 2x½a. abutting against Bemhill hedge, land of Elizabeth Young on E.; ½a. abutting on Bemhill pool; ½a. in Marshmead land of Smart Goodenough on E. and Mary Kemyes on W.; 1 farndell in the same furlong lands of wid. Chepman on W.; 1 farndell in the same furlong; 1a. in the same furlong lands of Robert Walker E. and Henry Gleed W.

31½a. of arable in the E. field; 2a. abutting on the parsonage orchard wall; 3 farndells in a furlong called Middle Great, lands of Henry Gleed on E. and Mary Barnett W.; 2a. abutting upon the Mead stile and 3 farndells abutting on a ground called the Camp, lands of the farm W.; ½a. in the same furlong, wid. Young W. Thomas Curnock E.; 1a. in the same furlong, wid. Chepman E.; 1a. abutting on Lower mead Henry Gleed E. and W.; 1a. in the same furlong, wid. Chepman W.; 1a. in the same furlong, wid. Young E. and W.; ½a. athwart a pathway called the Turning path, farm land W.; 1a. in the same furlong, John Chepman E.; 1a. in a furlong called Oate lands, Thomas Curnock S. wid. Young N.; 1 head a. near Dowly gate, Thomas Young E.; 1a. in Brimshill furlong, wid. Chepman E. wid. Young W.; 2a. in the same furlong, Mary Kemyes W.; 1a. in the same furlong, wid. Young W. Thomas Young E.; 1a. in the same furlong, farm land E. Henry Gleed W.; 2a. abutting on the Fosse lane, wid. Tanner E.; ½a. abutting on Lains corner; ½a. abutting on a ground called Old Lands Thomas Curnock W.; ½a. against Old Lands, Daniel Parker W.; ½a. abutting on wid. Tanner called Enochs, wid. Young E. and W.; ½a. in Enochs furlong, wid. Young W.; 1a. in the same furlong adjoining to the land of wid. Young; 2a. in the same furlong adjoining to land of wid. Young; ½a. in the same furlong, farm land E.; ½a. in Long furlong, wid. Chepman W.; ½a. upon Little hill, wid. Young W.; 1a. in the same furlong, Thomas Young E. and W.; ½a. in Pease furlong, wid. Young E.; 2a. in the same furlong, wid. Young E. and W.

22½a. of arable in the S.W. field; The Tyning at the Towns end, 2a.; 1a. near the Towns end, wid. Young E. wid. Chcpman W.; 3 farndells in the same furlong, wid. Tanner E. and W.; 1a. in the same furlong, the farm land on W.; 1a. called the Barrow, wid. Young E. wid. Chepman ?W; 5 farndells in the N. Headland abutting on the Fosse way; ½a. and 2a. abutting on the Fosse way, the farm land N.; 1a. upon Straphill, wid. Young W.; 1a. in Dod furlong, wid. Young E. and W.; 1a. 3 farndells in Wet Furrows, wid. Chepman S. wid. Tanner N.; 1 farndell heading the same furlong; 2a. upon Horse down, the farm land E.; ½a. in the same furlong lying near the duke of Beaufort's wall; 1a. abutting on the Parsonage tithing; 1a. called Smoke acre lying near the Farm Tyning; 1a. in Short Hedge furlong, wid. Kemyes E.; 1a. in the same furlong, wid. Young E. John Chepman W.; 1a. in the same furlong, wid. Tanner E.; 1a. called Goose acre near the Marsh Mead gate; ½a. abutting on the Marsh, Robert Walker E. Henry Gleed W.

George Child, rector, John Chepman, John Beaker, churchwardens.

492   25 Jul 1783 (D1/24/135/3)

Terrier of the glebe lands tithes and other appurtenances as they lie in the several fields and meads in the order of surveying. Taken by command of Shute lord bishop of Sarum.

A parsonage house consisting of one passage, a dwelling room or kitchen 14ft. by 16ft. and 7ft. high, a pantry and cellar of the same dimensions, the whole paved with stone, 3 bed chambers or garrets over unceiled, covered with tile and in good repair. A small outhouse covered with thatch. A garden containing about 25sq. lugs fenced partly with dry wall part hedge. A barn 20yds. long and 7yds. wide covered with thatch. A stable 4yds by 5yds covered with thatch. The wagon house 3yds. by 6ds. covered with thatch. All in repair. A close of pasture near the parsonage house, 1½a.

Land in E. field: 2a. abutting on Parsonage close, R. Daniels[1] N.; 2a. abutting on Mead Stile, Wallis E.; 3 farndells, Gleed[1] E., Wallis[1] W.; 2a. in the first mead at Mead Stile; 1a. in ditto, near the Folly, duke of Beaufort W. Wallis E.; 3 farndells in E. field near the Camp, duke of Beaufort E. and W.; ½a. in E. field near the Camp, duke of Beaufort W. Wallis E.; 1a. called Camp acre, Gleed W. Wallis E.; 1a. in the third mead called Withy bed under Mead hedge; ½a. in the third mead called Chick, Daniel E. duke of Beaufort W.; 1a. in headland to Chick, duke of Beaufort W. Wallis E.; 1a. in the fourth (or Camp) mead, Wallis E. and W.; 1a. in ditto, Wallis W. duke of Beaufort E.; 1a. in ditto under Barnets hedge; ½a. in E. field abutting on Lower mead, Daniel E. and W.; ½a. in the fifth mead (opposite a field ½a.), Wallis W. duke of Beaufort E.; 2½a. in E. field lying contiguous, Wallis W. duke of Beaufort E.; 1 farndell in the fifth mead on Wallis[1] Ox lease, duke of Beaufort E. and W.; ½a. in Bemhill hedge, Wallis E. and W.; 1a. in ditto on the duke's Ox lease, duke of Beaufort E. and W.; 2a. in ditto lying under the Hedge, duke of Beaufort E. and W.; 1a. in E. field on the mead, duke of Beaufort E. and W.; 1a. in Outland furlong, duke of Beaufort N. and S.; 1 head a. near Dunly Gate, duke of Beaufort E.; 1a. opposite Dunly Stile, Wallis E. and W.; 1a. near Parsons Dunly, duke of Beaufort E. Daniel W.; 5a. called Brimshill Tyning; 20a., part called Upper and Lower Dunly; 2a. in E. field on Fosse lane, Wallis E. and W.; ½a. under Lains Hedge Daniel N.; ½a. on Old Lands Wallis E. and W.; ½a. on Old Lands, duke of Beaufort E. and W.; 2a. near Beggars Bush, duke of Beaufort E. Wallis W.; ½a. on Whites Enochs., Wallis E. duke of Beaufort W.; ½a. in Enoch's furlong, duke W. Wallis E.; 1a. in Long furlong [. . .] E. and W.; ½a. from road to the Tyning duke of Beaufort E. Wallis W.; 4a. called Blind Tyning.

Land in S.W. field: 1a. near Wallis' house, Wallis E. and W.; 1a. called Goose near Marsh Mead Gate; 1a. in Marsh mead, Daniel W. duke of Beaufort E.; ½a. in ditto on the Walks, duke of Beaufort E.; 1a. enclosed abbutting on Marsh mead; ½a. in S.W. field, Daniel W. Gleed E.; 1a. near Walks gate Wallis E. and W.; 1a. near the Path Wallis W. duke E.; 1a. called Short acre, duke of Beaufort W. Wallis E.; 1a. called Parsons along Park piece hedge; 1a. called Parsons acre under Park Piece hedge; ½a. under Wallis' hedges near Horse down, Daniel E. duke of Beaufort W.; 2a. on Horse down, duke of Beaufort E. and W.; 2a. in Wet Furrows, Wallis N. and S.; 2a. of pasture on the road, a triangular enclosure; 2a. of pasture called Dydover on the road near Towns end enclosure; 2a. in S. W. field called Towns End Piece, duke of Beaufort S. and N.; 1½a. in the Barrow, a headland, duke of Beaufort N. toward the road; 1a. in ditto called Dod furlong, duke of Beaufort E. and W.; ½a. in ditto running down to the turnpike road, duke of Beaufort, S. Wallis N.; ½a. in ditto duke of Beaufort S., Wallis N.; 1a. near Daniels hedge, duke of Beaufort N. and S. 8a. of arable called Enoch's Tyning. ½a. of pasture called the Chapel near the elm and ash on the Fosse.

Tithe corn, grain and hay and all other tithes arising out of the parish. 6 ash, 12 elm 8 oak but of small value; n. b. There are about 30a. of land in this parish lying towards Badminton called the Walks for which the duke of Beaufort claims an exemption from tithes.

There is also the following set up by way of modus in this parish viz. For a cow 3d., a calf 6d., a heifer 2d., a pig 2s., summering a sheep 1d., a lamb weaned in winter 3d. The right of either is unknown.

C[harles] Page, rector, John Coates, Samuel Chappel, churchwardens, William Latcham, John Tanner.

Memo. The land in this parish being very cold and poor the usual course of cultivation is every other year some admit of no cultivation. Furniture of the church defective. One old cushion no pulpit cloth no desk cloth. A green serge cloth for the communion table with white linen on the usual occasions. One pewter flagon and plate one silver chalice and cover weight about 7oz. 3 bells. Clerk appointed by the minister wages 50s. p. a. paid by the parish. Church and yard repaired by parish rate, chancel by the rector.

Charles Page rector, John Coates, Samuel Chappell, churchwardens.

1. Robert Daniels, George Wallis, Thomas Gleed in land tax assessment, 1783 (WSRO A1/345/264).

LUCKINGTON rectory

493   11 Oct 1608 (D1/24/136/1)

The mansion house of the rectory, with an orchard, a garden and 2 courts adjoining. A meadow or pasture ground lying on the N.W. of the house, *c.* 1½a. A little ground lying on the S.W. of the house called the Cunniger, *c.* ½a. There is a little portion of ground within the Cunniger lying on the W. end, not fully a farndell, given to good and necessary uses viz.; the repairing of the church and relief of the poor. All the rest of the glebe formerly lay in the common fields, but is now enclosed at a place called Grinden and divided into 7 leazowes of *c.* 24 lug acres in all lying N. of the rectory and bounded on the S. with the highway called Howsegreen; on the N. with the leazowes of John Halling of Luckington, Philip Franklin and Robert Pen of Sherston Magna; on the E. with leazowes of Peter Edmay alias Hooper, William Clark, and William Dowling of Luckington and John Elisander of Sherston Magna; on the W. with the leazowes of Francis Neale of Sherston Magna and Henry Nott of Luckington. Another enclosed ground which is arable, called Chessels, lying in the lordship of Alderton [Aldrington], of *c.* 6 lug acres. 3 farndells bounded on the S. with the highway from Alderton to the Fosse Way, on the N. with the leazowe of William Davis of Luckington, on the E. with the leazowe of Arthur Terrill of Alderton, on the W. with the leazowes of Laurence Snell of Luckington and Laurence Alden of Alderton. A double hedge, the water course going between the hedges, with many ashes, maples, and other trees, with frithe at a place called the Hollow Lane in the lordship of Alderton, and with a quarry at the W. end being part of the ancient glebe, but refused to the rectory at the enclosure of the fields of Alderton. A yearly pension issuing out of the rectory of Alderton of 33s. 4d. p. a. payable at Michaelmas [29 Sep] by the farmer of the rectory.

By me Richard Jones, rector, Laurence Snell [X], John Edmay [X], churchwardens, Francis Jones, Thomas Bennet [X], John Booy [X], William Pen [X], Thomas Robins.

494   21 Dec 1704 (D1/24/136/2)

A terrier of Luckington church lands. A ground called Huntington's garden, *c.* 4a., bounded N.W. by Down lane, S. E. by Mr. Henry Fitzherbert's ¾a. in the common field, 3a. in the possession of James Lewis on the one side of him and ½a. of Francis Boyc on the other side of him. 1½a. having 2a. belonging to Humphrey Fitzherbert esq., on each side of them. ¼a. having 1a. of Humphrey Fitzherbert on the one side of it and 1½a. of his on the other side of it. ½a. adjoining to Shipway Jones Down leases. ¼a. on Hetherland having 1a. of Humphrey Fitzherbert on the one side of it and 1a. of Mr. Andrew Fitzherbert on the other side. *c.* 1a. called the Nursery bounded by the Church lane one way and by the parsonage close and garden on the other.

Henry Fitzherbert, rector, William Bishop [X] [*churchwarden*],[1] John Hollow, Thomas Jones, Stephen Maberly, John Newman.

1.   With the terrier is a an extract from the churchwarden's accounts whereby Bishop paid Joseph Boys 1s. for making the terrier.

LUDGERSHALL rectory

495 3 Aug 1786 (D1/24/137)

Terrier taken and made according to the old evidences and knowledge of the ancient inhabitants by the appointment of bishop Shute at his primary visitation held at Salisbury 5 Aug 1783 and exhibited before the bishop at his second visitation held at Salisbury 4 Aug 1786.

The churchyard, 1a. 1r. 8p., adjoins a close called Bullocks mead held by Robert Horne, and the garden of John Venn on the N., St. James's Street on the E., the garden of Thomas, lord Sydney on the S. and part of the W., and a field called the W. Town field on the other part of the W. The rails, gate and fences on part of the W., the greater part of the N., the whole of the N. and part of the S. are made and kept in repair by the churchwardens at the expense of the parish, the remainder of the S. and W. by lord Sydney, and a small part of the N. by John Venn. In the churchyard there are 14 pollard elms, 1 pollard ash and 1 pollard sycamore, value c. £5. To the rectory also belongs every species of tithe, both great and small, payable in kind, and the usual manner of tithing is as follows:

Wheat; the owner sets it up ten sheaves in every shock out of which the parson or his agent chooses on from any part, taking the same sheaf from every shock set up in one field at one time, but he may change his sheaf every fresh setting out of tithe. If there are any odd sheaves the tenth part is to be taken out of them. Spring corn; barley, oats etc., are tithed by taking the tenth pook or cock beginning at whichever end of the ground the parson or his agent choose, and dividing the odd pooks or cocks.

Hay, clover, seeds etc. are tithed like the last. Agistment; the tenth of the value of the feed or pasturage of all cattle yielding no other tithe, whether the occupiers own or strangers are taken into agist, of which the farmer renders an account yearly and pays in money. Wood; under 20 years growth the tenth lug or measure after it is felled, and before it is moved from the ground. Fruit; apples, pears etc. the tenth measure after they are gathered and before they are moved from the ground where they grew. Roots; potatoes, turnips etc. are tithed like the last. Calves, colts, lambs, pigs etc.; the tenth of the young when the farmer weans his own. The owner chooses one, then the parson chooses one, and the owner has the remaining eight, and so on if there are more than 10, but if there are under 10, or any odd ones they are either carried on to the next tithing or the farmer pays the tenth of the value, at the option of the parson. Wool; the tenth weight before it is moved from the place where it is sheared, and so of lambs wool. Milk; the tenth of the morning and evening meal of milk, computed from the time of notice given by the parson. Fowl of all kinds; the tenth of the young when they are able to live without the old ones, if under 10 the tenth of the value. Bees; the tenth weight of honey and wax in the comb. Mills; the tenth toll dish, or if they grind for money the tenth of the clear profit on a composition at the option of the parson.

Every person in the parish of 16 years and upwards pays 2d. yearly at Easter. An oblation of 6d. is paid for every churching of women. 1s. is paid for every publication of banns, 5s. for every wedding by banns, 10s. for every wedding by licence, 5s. for every certificate of the publication of banns, or of marriage, 1s.

for every certificate of baptism, or of burial. 13s. 4d. is paid for every person buried in the church and £1 1s. for every person buried in the chancel, 6s. 8d. for burying any person who died out of the parish. 3s. 4d. is paid for erecting a head or footstone in the churchyard, 6s. 8d. for a head or footstone with a flat stone over the grave, 13s. 4d. for a raised tomb in the churchyard, £1 1s. for a monument in the church. 3s. 6d. is paid yearly by the churchwardens for writing out the transcript of the register.

To the rectory belongs the right of a vote for two burgesses to serve in parliament for the borough of Ludgershall, which right has uniformly been exercised. To the rectory belongs the right of a wagon or draught [draft] road from the turnpike road at the E. end of Winchester St. into Kings field for bringing away the tithe between the houses now occupied by Thomas Batt and John Lay, where there used to be a gate, stopped up for the convenience of the present occupier, but opened and used by the rector on 6 Sep 1780 without hindrance or molestation. There is payable out of the rectory a fee farm rent of £4 p. a. to James Whitchurch esq., subject to land tax which is always deducted. This is probably the £4 granted to the priory of Amesbury by King Henry VIII at the dissolution of the monasteries. It is customary for the parson to find a bull for the use of the parish from Whitsun to St. Thomas day [21 Dec] yearly, which bull is allowed to feed on the common called Sprayley and all other commons free of cost to the parson.

To the parish clerk and sexton, from time immemorial, united and appointed by the rector, there is due 4d. p. a. payable at Easter for every family; for the Manor or Castle farm 3s. and a piece of bacon of c. 3lbs.; for the farm at Biddesden 3s. and a piece of bacon of c. 3lbs.; for the farm called South Park and Kings field 1s. and a piece of bacon of c. 2lb.; for Crawlboys [the Croylboys] farm is paid 2s.; for every wedding by banns 1s.; by licence 2s. 6d.; for every funeral, including digging the grave and tolling the bell 2s. 6d., and for every person buried in the church 10s. 6d.; for taking care of the church clock 20s. p. a., and for tolling the bell at 8.00 in the evening from All Saints Day [1 Nov] to Candlemas [2 Feb] 10s. p. a. paid by the churchwardens at the expense of the parish. Belonging to the parish are the parish church, an ancient building of brick and stone, within which are a communion table with a covering of green cloth and a damask tablecloth 2yd. square, also another damask table cloth 2yd. by 3yd. and a coarse napkin; a silver chalice and patten weighing c. 24oz., a pewter plate, and 2 old oak chests in the chancel, seldom used on account of the damp; a pulpit and reading desk covered with green cloth, very old and decayed, a large folio bible also very old and torn, a folio common prayer book for the officiating minister, a quarto ditto for the clerk, a pewter basin for the font, the Ten Commandments on 2 tables, 5 bells with their frames. Upon the smallest is inscribed 'Mr. D. Daniell and Mr. R. Hutchins Churchwardens I Burrough[1] in Devizes Founder 1749', on the second bell is this inscription 'Mr. E. Daniell and Mr. R. Hutchins churchwardens[2] I Burrough[1] in Devizes Founder', on the third bell 'O prayse the Lord ID 1631', on the fourth bell 'Ano Domini 1638', on the fifth or largest bell 'Edward Keinton and Ambros Downam churchwardens Clemant Tosear cast mee 1686'. There are a bier, a hearse cloth, a surplice, and six register books, the first of parchment begins in 1609, the second, also parchment, begins in 1653, the third of paper begins in 1697, the fourth, of paper also for marriages only begins in 1754, the fifth of paper for births and burials begins in 1782. There is a gallery at the W. end of the church erected in 1727 the N. side of which is at present used by the Sunday school. There is a large clock fixed in the tower. The body of the church and the tower are kept in repair by the parish, and the chancel by the rector.

John Selwyn, rector, aged 33 years and upwards; Roger Geater churchwarden, aged 30; John Beale, senior, overseer of the poor, aged 60; John Beale junior, miller, aged 31; Robert Smith [X], freeholder, aged 69; Thomas Parsons, aged 50; John Coombs, parish clerk and sexton, aged 74; John Edwards [X], carpenter, aged 80; Daniel Dobbs [X] the eldest, aged 91; Daniel Dobbs the elder, aged 60; Daniel Dobbs junior, constable, aged 30.

With terrier is a scaled ground plan of the church and churchyard; adjoining properties named.

1. James Burrough
2. Edmund Daniell and Roger Hutchins were churchwardens at the bishop's visitation in 1750 (WSRO D1/50/19)

LYDIARD MILLICENT rectory

496   1672 (D1/24/138/1)
A parsonage house, 2 barns, a stable, an oxhouse, a garden, and a backside. A pasture ground adjoining the house called the Meadow close, *c.* 7a. A close of arable land near the house, *c.* 6a. Another ground adjoining commonly called the Church close, 8a. 16a. enclosed arable called Stonefield. 2 grounds of pasture commonly called Midfurlongs, *c.* 24a. All the tithes of the parish of hay, corn, etc. Common in Webb's wood and the other commons for as many beasts and horses in summer as will be kept on the parsonage in winter.

Robert Jenner, rector, Richard Smith, John Smith, churchwardens. *Names of the churchwardens in the same hand*

497   24 Dec 1677 (D1/24/138/2)
The parsonage house barn and stable and 3 grounds adjoining, *c.* 24a. 1 arable field called Stone field, *c.* 16a. 2 grounds called commonly the Mid furlongs, *c.* 22a. The whole tithe of the parish in general of corn hay and all other tithes great and small in their kind. Right of commons in woods commonly called Clintons and Baskevill woods and wood titheable in kind.

Robert Jenner, rector, Thomas Strange, Jeffrey King, churchwardens.

498   5 Jan 1705 (D1/24/138/3)
The parsonage house 2 barns 2 stables with the backside garden and orchard adjoining. 3 grounds adjoining to the house and barns called the Church close, Corn close and Meadow close, 18a. 1 ground of arable called Stone field, 15a. next to the way leading to Highworth. 2 grounds called the Mid Furlongs next to the way that leads to Swindon, 24a.

Tithe hay, corn and wood and all other great and small tithes are due to the rectory by custom. A right of common in Chatterton and Clinton woods.

Robert Jenner, rector, William Green, William Mundee, churchwardens, Charles Pearce, Francis Batson, Thomas Strange.

499   n. d. [1783][1] (D1/24/138/4)

The parsonage house stone built and slated. The parlour boarded floor 2 rooms earthen floor 2 rooms stone floor. 5 rooms the second floor all ceiled and 3 garrets. A garden with post and railed fence. In the yard one stone built stable a barn and carthouse all thatched. 2 closes adjoining, 3a. *c.* 30 young trees on the premises. Glebe lands by estimation 59½a. The furniture of the church; 5 bells, *c.* 11oz. of plate. The church and church yard are kept by the parishioners except the chancel and that by the minister. The clerk appointed by the minister and his wages paid by the parishioners.

Robert Tuckey, Benjamin Bewley, churchwardens.

1.   The churchwardens were recorded in the bishop's visitation book, Jul 1783. (WSRO D1/50/30)

LYDIARD TREGOZE rectory

500   1608 (D1/24/139/1)

We the churchwardens and sidesmen, by virtue of our oath taken at the last visitation at Marlborough by Henry, bishop of Salisbury, do present that there belongs to the rectory a mansion house, a barn, a garden, an orchard, and a barton adjoining, a close of pasture, and a meadow adjoining, *c.* 30a. Also a close of meadow or arable commonly called Blacklands, *c.* 8a., and a pleck of pasture or arable adjoining called Prinnells, *c.* 5a. Also a piece of pasture ground commonly called Cleypiece, *c.* 5a., adjoining a ground called New ?Dike and Green down. Also the ?first crop of grass in a meadow ground lying in High meadow called the Parsons ham, 5a. and another ham of meadow ground lying in the same meadow containing *c.* 3a.

John Petty, clerk, parson, Gabriel Church, Ralph Wollford, churchwardens, Richard Jefferyes, William Cruse, sidesmen. *Names in the same hand*

501   1677 (D1/24/139/2)

A parsonage house and other outhouses, a barn and stable. A garden, walled partly with brick and partly with stone, adjoining S. end of the house. An orchard adjoining the N. end of the house.

A little ground called the Pleck, 1a. A ground called the Parsonage close, adjoining the said orchard, 30a. A meadow ground adjoining the Parsonage close called the Ham, 14a. A parcel of meadow ground lying in the ground of Mr. Thomas Hardyman, ½a. A ground called Prinnells, 12a. A ground called Claypeece, 6a. A ground called Blacklands, 12a. A ham lying in High mead alias Tenants mead, 4a. A parcel of meadow adjoining to ?Caw–illan bridge brook,[1] 8a. A horse leaze in the park of Lydiard Tregoze.

Compositions of £5 quarterly issuing and of the ancient demesnes of Lydiard Tregoze; of 16s. p. a. issuing out of Mannington [Meyington]; of 16s. p. a. issuing out of Toot Hill; of 8s. p. a. issuing out of Whitehill. One horse leaze, or a leaze for a mare and colt, one year in Mannington [Meighington] the other year in Toot Hill. An ancient composition issuing out of the manor of Midgehall for which the rector receive of John Pleydall esq., 50s. p. a., all the copyholds belonging to the manor are involved in the composition. Ancient compositions of 4 nobles p. a. issuing out of Studley farm and of 5 nobles p. a. issuing out of Can Court farm. The rest of the parish pay tithes in kind.

Timothy Dewell, rector, Toby Richman, Thomas Wheeler, churchwardens.
Endorsement: This for Mr. Byes the lord Bishops register with a shilling.

1. A map of the manor of Lydiard Tregoze, *c.* 1760s, shows Camel lane a short lane leading to the river Ray midway between Shaw and Mannington (WSRO 305/11/1). There was no glebe there in 1841 according to the tithe apportionment but the adjoining fields are called the Upper and Lower Bridge mead.

502   7 Dec 1704 (D1/24/139/3)
The Parsonage close and Great Ham lying together, 42a. 3r. 38p., both adjoining the N. side of the parsonage house and orchard.

1r. of ground in the possession of Mr. Thomas Hardyman which is separated from the Parsonage close by a little brook of water. The house orchard and garden containing 1a. 2r.; 3 closes called Prinnils, Blacklands and Claypiece lying together eastward and near to the parsonage, 25a. 8r. 18p. A close called High mead or Cut and Go mead because the parson is excluded from the later mowth [mouth] [1], 6a. 20p. lying on the left hand of the way to Swindon about 1 mile from the parsonage. A close called Parsonage mead or Cut and Go upon the same account as the former, 4a. 2r. 35p. lying on the right hand of the way to Swindon also about 1 mile from the parsonage.

Stephen Charman, rector, John Neate, Thomas Pyke, churchwardens, William Franklin, Charles Wilett, William Yorke.

1. The following or second mowing of grass; see **598**.

503   26 Jul 1783 (D1/24/139/4)
The buildings: A stone built parsonage house covered with slate. 4 rooms below one wainscotted the others not. A brewhouse covered with slate; a washhouse and woodhouse thatched; a barn without a floor and stable adjoining thatched. The buildings yard garden and lane stand on 1a. 2r. 12p. of ground.

Glebe lands: The Parsonage close and Great Ham, 42a. 3r. 33p.; both adjoin the N. side of the parsonage house and garden, meadow and pasture; The Shoulder of Mutton piece adjoining late Hardyman's, 1r. 16p. Garden grounds, 3 fields called Prinnels, Blacklands and Clay Pits lying together eastward and near to the parsonage house, 30a., meadow and pasture. A close called High mead or Brook mead, or Cut and Go mead because the parson is excluded from the later mowth [mouth] [1], 6a. 20p. [*location as* **502**]. A close called Parsonage mead or Cut and Go mead upon the same account as the former, 4a. 2r. 35p. [*location as* **502**].

Churchyard, 2r. 10p. In the churchyard 1 yew tree: on the glebe lands 2 or 3 elm trees and a few very old elm pollards.

Tithes: Tithing of Lydiard and Hook: The three estates of the governors of the Charterhouse are claimed to be exempt from the payment of tithes by the following payments: For Mannington £4 7s. one year then 17s. the following year and so on alternately: For Toot Hill the same payments. Whitehill the yearly payment of 8s. 6d. But some doubts have arisen over with the present rector respecting the validity of these claims during 1783, he gave those estates notice to pay him tithes in kind which they refusing to do no account has been settled with them since. The remaining part of the tithing is subject to the payment of tithes in kind. But the several tenants and occupiers of land (except the woods which are taken in kind) are in lieu thereof at present under a composition with the rector of 2s. in the pound according to the rack rent, with the further addition of 3s. for every a. of wheat and 2s. 6d. for every a. of lent corn. An abatement is made by the rector for the fallows according to the value of the land.

Midgehall tithing: The tithing is supposed to have been formerly lands of Stanley abbey some of the proprietors of these estates pay the rector nothing; others claim an exemption from the payment of tithe in kind by the following yearly payments; earl of Clarendon for his estates 8s. p. a.; Mrs. Maskelyne for her estate 7s. 4d. p. a.; Mr. Iles for his estate 9s. 3d. p. a.; Mr. Southby for his estate 9s. p. a.; Mr. William Bradford for Caen Court £1 13s. 4d. p. a.

Chaddington tithing: The whole of the tithing is subject to the payment of tithes in kind by several tenants and occupiers of land or in lieu thereof at present under the same composition as that applied in the tithing of Lydiard and Hook.

The chancel and church: The communion plate consists of 2 large silver flagons, a silver chalice and cover and a silver plate. On top of one of the flagons 'The Gift of Deborah Culme Daughter of Sir Charles Pleydell of Midghall'; in the middle a coat of arms 'This belongs to the Parish Church of Lidyeard Traygus in Wilts Sheire'; at the bottom 'D. C: 1670. ' On the top of the other flagon 'The Gift of the Lady Eliz. Newcomen Daughter to Sir Charles Pleydell of Midghall'; in the middle a coat of arms 'For the church of Lidyeard Trigoose'. On the chalice and cover a coat of arms each. On the plate 'This belongs to the Parish Church of Lidyeard Traygus in Wilts Sheire' on the bottom 'D. C.: 1670'. In the tower are 5 bells and a clock. The parish repair the church and churchyard fences; the rector the chancel.

The clerk is chosen by the rector. His salary £5 p. a. paid by the churchwardens.

R[ichard] Miles, rector, Simon Crook, John Matthews, churchwardens.

1.   See footnote to **502**.

LYNEHAM curacy

504   6 Dec 1671 (D1/24/140/1)

A return of the churchwardens in answer to an order that we received by Dr. Edward Lowe, chancellor of the diocese of Salisbury for sending in a terrier of the glebe lands.

We hereby certify that formerly Mr. Edmund Long of Lyneham Court always provided a minister to serve the cure and paid him out of the parsonage, and since his decease the minister was always maintained by Mr. Humphrey Long who now lives in our parish and enjoys part of the parsonage, until this six or seven years past in which we have had no minister settled. As concerning glebe lands, we know of none, only a churchyard, c. 1a.

Richard Jacob, Thomas Barnes, churchwardens, Humphrey Goodmane, sidesman.

505   16 Jan 1705 (D1/24/140/2)
The present rights of this church are founded in a decree of chancery passed in the behalf of Mr. Daniel Salway towards the latter end of the reign of King Charles II[1] by virtue whereof this church is at present possessed of the several profits following: A mansion house of 2 bays standing upon a piece of ground which with a little paddock annexed is c. ½a. The churchyard, c. 2½a. to be entirely mounded at the charge of the parish. A salary of £13 p. a. to be paid at Michaelmas by the several possessors of the several parts of the impropriation in the proportions following: Lady Button £1 3s. 8d., Mr. Pleydall £5 17s. 4d., Mr. Tuck £3 10s. 6d., Mrs. Danvers £1 3s. 8d., Mr. Baker 13s.; Mr. Salder 11s. 10d. The Easter offerings of the parish being 3s. a person and the garden penny being 1d. a house.

Thomas Smith, minister, Thomas Burchall, Thomas Skull, churchwardens, Robert Tuck, James Baker, William Mapson, William Burchall, John Broome, Thomas Bathe, John Bennett, Richard Huntley [X], John Hunt [X].

1.   1678. P. R. O. C78/1940 Entry 3, see *VCH Wilts*, Vol. 9, p. 101.

MALMESBURY vicarage

506   16 Dec 1671 (D1/24/141/1)
A parcel of land, c. 1½a., called Vicar's ham lying near a place called Coldharber. 2a. of arable land lying in a ground called Kenborow field. 1a. land held by Robert Bailey lying near a place called Staynes bridge. The church house. A little cottage lying near the churchyard.

John Clarke, vicar, Henry Frape, William Lockyer, churchwardens.

507   16 Dec 1704 (D1/24/14½)
A vicarage house of 1 bay. Land called Vicarage Ham, 1½a. 1a. of land in Cambray field. 1a. of land, by report near Strange bridge. Small tithes.

Christopher Hanley, vicar, Robert Huckings, Thomas Kaynes, churchwardens.

MANNINGFORD ABBOTS rectory

508   13 May 1588 (D1/24/142/1)
A true presentment or certificate of the glebe lands and rights of the rectory made before bishop John at his ordinary visitation for the archdeaconry of Wiltshire at Marlborough by John Swaine, churchwarden, Richard Hiller, John

Smith and Mathew Benger, sidesmen, concerning matters of reformation presentable in the said visitation.

A mansion house, barn, orchard, garden, backside or court with a close adjoining by common estimation *c*. ½a. In meadow and pasture 1½a. viz. a meadow of ½a. called the Parsons mead or the Parsons Wet mead abutting the water on one end and on the Nether Rye field on the other end, and a close of 1a. in the Upper Rye field. 1 meadow called Manmoor, *c*. 3yd. of ground which is in lieu of tithe of hay and grass of two several meadows belonging to the manor of Pewsey called Berry or Birry mead and Lotmead. Commons of pasture for a bull a horse or beast and a cow.

In arable land in the common fields 13a. 1yd.; viz. 7a. 3yd. in the N. field and W. field above Upavon path and 5½a. in the N. field, the W. field and Middle field below Upavon path. The third tenth weight of wool of the sheep belonging to the manor or farm of Pewsey kept on the commons and downs of Pewsey and Manningford Abbots called the Herd flock and the Manningford flock; the parson of Pewsey having the first two tenth weights. The sheep kept in Manningford may be pastured on the downs in the parish of Pewsey 'as tyme owt of mynde they have had and at this tyme have and not els.'

509   1608 (D1/24/142/2)
A parsonage house with barn garden and orchard, 13a. 1yd. of arable. A close of meadow called Barre Close, 3r. A little ground of pasture, c ½a. 3a. of pasture ground newly enclosed out of the common called the Marsh by the present rector.

By me Thomas Bromley, rector; Richard Hiller, Roger Blinckerne, church-wardens.

510   24 Oct 1671 (D1/24/142/3)
A terrier of the Sanctuary grounds and glebelands grounds called The Butlease, 3a. and The Wetmead, ½a. The pasture ground shutting upon the common, 1a. In the E. field above the hill 3½a. 1r.; below the hill, 1a. In the W. field above the hill, 3a.; below the hill, 1a. In the Middle field below the hill, 4a. In total 13a. 1r. The dwelling house, a garden a backside, a barn, a stable a backside to hold corn and hay with a little close, 1 r., on E. side of the stable, with the churchyard fenced on S. side by the parson E. side, by Robert Wells, N. side, and the parish on W. side. 15 sheep leaze in the common field.

John Hiller, Maurice Helliar, churchwardens.

511   1677 (D1/24/142/4)
A dwelling house, barn, stable, 2 gardens, *c*. 6r., with a little close at home, 30r., and a rick barton. A meadow called Bridge meadow, 100r., one end abutting the river, William Banks' little meadow on E., Robert Smith's meadow on W. A pasture ground called Butlease, 3a., John Hiller's ground N. E. and the other side lying next to John Godman's drove. An arable ground, 120r., one end abutting to the common, John Hiller's ground W., William Bankes' ground on E. In the E. field 1a. lying in the furlong called Longlands, Henry Heyward having 1a. on E. and John Smith's ½a. on W.

In the Middle field ½a. in the Lower furlong lying next to the side of the way, John Smith having ½a. on W.; in the furlong next above the way 1a., John Smith having 1a. lying E. and 1a. on W.; 1a. in the next furlong at the end of the said a. Robert Smith having 1a. on E. and John Hiller having 1a. on W.; 1a. in the furlong above the Sheep Drove, Robert Wells having 1a. on W. and John Hiller having 1a. on E.; ½a. in the next furlong upwards, John Hiller having 1a. on W. and John Smith having 1a. on E.; ½a. in Hill furlong lying next to the way Robert Smith having ½a. on W.

In the S. field ½a. in the furlong above Broadway, Robert Wels having 1a. on W. and ½a. on E.; ½a. in the furlong abutting Halebush piece John Hiller having ½a. on S. and Steven Phelps having ½a. on N.

In the Upper fields eastwards ½a. at the hill top, Robert Wels having 1a. on E. and John Hiller having 1a. on W.; in the next furlong upwards ½a., John Hiller having ½a. on E. and Henry Heyward having ½a. on W.; ½a. in the Cross furlong, Henry Heyward having 3yd. on N. and John Hiller having 1yd. on S.; 1a. in the middle of the E. field, Henry Heyward on S. and ½a. on N.; ½a. heading Members Down furlong; ½a. in Members Down furlong, John Hiller having 1a. on S. and Robert Smith having 3yd. on N.; 1 single yd. in Members Down furlong, John Smith having 3yd. on S. and Henry Heyward having 3yd. on N.

In the S. field 1a. lying between 2 mere lawns on Members Down; 1a. in the same furlong, Robert Smith having 1½a. on S. and Robert Wels having ½a. on N. 1 head a. in the same furlong, John Smith having 1a. on S.; ½a. on E. side of the S. field, John Smith having 3x½a. on W.

Thomas Clerke, rector, William Bankes, John Tarrant, churchwardens

512   Dec 1704 (D1/24/142/5)
A parsonage house, 3 little gardens, a backside, a barn, a stable and out houses, a rick yard, and a little close of meadow ground all fenced on S.W. and N. by the rector and all adjoining S. side of the churchyard (the property of which is alsothe rector's), the whole, including the churchyard, c. 1/2a.

Wet mead, c. 1a., on the N. side of the river fenced on N. end by the rector, bounded on W. side by a ground of Robert Smith, through which is the common church way over the river. A meadow, c. 3a., called Butt close, fenced on S. and W. by the rector and having on E. and N. grounds belonging to Sharcott and opening on S. to the highway. An enclosed ground of arable, 1a., abutting and opening on W. end to the common and fenced on E., S. and W. by the rector, having a ground of Timothy Hiller on S. and one of William Broadfield on N.

In the common field, arable land: In the furlong called Long Lands, 1a., being the seventh a. towards Pewsey from the parish drove and shooting at N. end upon a headland occupied by Peter Smith of Sharcott. In the Middle field one outside ½a. abutting on S. end to the road called Broadway having on E. the highway between the 2 corners. 1a. on the other side of Broadway being the outside a. westward of the Middlefield and abutting on N. end to the said road. ½a. shooting on to S. end of the E. half of the last a., running up into the next furlong and usually ploughed at length with the said ½a. to which it is joined. 1a. in the Drove furlong shooting down at N. end to the sheep drove having on

E. an a. of Timothy Hiller and on W. an a. of Edward Fowle. ½a. in the next furlong upwards, having 1a. of Timothy Hiller on W., ½a. of Richard Smith on E. In the Hill furlong one outside ½a. having that part of the parish drove called the Green way on E. and ½a. of Robert Smith on W.

½a. in the Outside field lying next to Manningford Bruce land, shooting at N. end on Broadway and having on W. 1a. and on E. ½a. both of Edward Foule. ½a. in Dock furlong being the fourth ½a. homewards from the headland and shooting at W. end upon a piece of ground of Timothy Hiller called Hare Bush piece.

Above hill on the side next to Pewsey field ½a. shooting on that green piece of the drove that lies across Upavon way having 1a. of Edward Foules on E. and 1a. of Timothy Hiller on W. ½a. in the next furlong having ½a. of Timothy Hiller on E. and 1a. of Henry Hayward on W. ½a. in the next furlong called Short furlong, shooting E. and W., having 1yd. of Timothy Hiller on S. and 3yd. of Henry Hayward on the home side. 1a. in the next furlong having 1a. on W. and ½a. on E., both belonging to Henry Hayward. ½a. being the homeward headland to Members Down furlong. ½a. in Members Down furlong having 1a. of Timothy Hiller on W. and 3yd. of Robert Smith on E. 1yd. in the same furlong having 3yd. of Richard Smith on W. and 3yd. of Henry Hayward on E.

In that part of the field lying next to Manningford Bruce field 1a. standing by itself bounded between 2 shelving deep lawns one on the home side and the other on the side towards Hocomb Bottom belonging to Robert Smith and ½a. on the home side belonging to Edward Foule. 1a. in the same furlong lying 3 x ½a. distant homewards from the last a., having on the home side 1½a. of Robert Smith remarkably shorter than the adjacent lands. An outside ½a. in another furlong above a furlong's distance from the last a., having a short head land on E. and 3 x ½a. on W. all of Richard Smith. Enclosed ground: 6½a. with the 13a. 1yd. in the common fields in all 19a. 3yd.

All great and small tithes throughout the whole parish except with tithes specie the parishioners pay by ancient custom the following compositions; for every calf 8d., for the fall of a colt 12d.; tithe of milk, usually called cow white, 1d. for every cow, for eggs 1d. by the yardland; for a garden 1d. There is due to the rector every year at Easter offerings of 2d. for every person liable to pay the same.

The rector has a sheep leaze for 15 sheep in the common field. The miller pays for his mill only the yearly rate tithe of 6s. 8d. For the churching of women 4d.

Robert Reeks, rector, Robert Smith, Timothy Hiller,[1] churchwardens, Timothy Hiller,[1] Bryan Phelps, overseers, Henry Hayward, Bartholomew Frye, Richard Smith, Edward Foule, William Bradfield.

1.   The same person signing twice for each of his offices.

513   23 Jul 1783 (D1/24/142/6)
Terrier by the appointment of Shute, bishop of Salisbury, and delivered at his visitation at Marlborough 28 Jul 1783.

A slated dwelling house 42ft. 9in. by 19ft. 6in. in the N. end built with brick, the other side with timber and rough cast contains a parlour 16ft. by 15ft. and 8ft. 2in. high, ceiled and wainscotted with oak; an oak floor very old; a bed chamber over the parlour of nearly the same dimensions, wainscotted chair high and papered, is ceiled and has a deal floor and small closet adjoining. A garret over the chamber with a boarded floor and partitions floored with mortar, ceiled and whitewashed. Another parlour 19ft. 6in. by 16ft., 8ft. high ceiled, wainscotted chair high and stuccoed, has a deal floor and vestibule adjoining; a bed chamber over the last, about the same dimensions, ceiled and papered, has a deal floor and dark closet adjoining: a garret over the last with a boarded floor, ceiled and partitions lathed and plastered. The whole built or repaired with the last 10 years.

An old building adjoining 14ft. by 17ft. 6in. the W. end built with brick the other sides with timber, plastered, the roof thatched, contains a passage and staircase, pantry, cellar, and kitchen 16ft. 6in. by 11ft. and a brewhouse 16ft. 6in. by 6ft. 4in. 3 chambers over of nearly the same dimensions, ceiled and boarded floors very old and decayed in some places.

Outhouses contiguous to the last and extended under the same roof 83ft. partly built with brick or mudwalls or with timber and boarded: the roof covered with thatch, contain a well-house and larder, 25ft. 2in. by 13ft.; a woodhouse and stable 29ft. by 15ft., another stable 16ft. 9in. by 15ft., a house for poultry, etc. Floors over the stables laid with elm boards.

A barn adjoining 84ft. by 33ft., another court 43ft. 3in. by 20ft. 11in. A garden including the dwelling house in front 117ft. by 105ft. having a brick wall on W. and N. sides, a quickset hedge and a pale fence on E. and a mudwall on S. A dove house brick and tiled in the N.W. angle. A small garden adjoining 42ft. 9in. by 36ft. with a mudwall fence thatched. A paddock 76ft. 3in. mean breadth by 107ft. 3in. A road at the top of the garden and leading to it 125ft. 9in. by 24ft. 9in. mean breadth. A rick barton 86ft. by 74ft. 3in. mean breadth.

A churchyard measuring on S. side 156ft. 9in. by 99ft. mean breadth now growing on the same 8 elm, 2 ash, 1 yew and of little value.

A church measuring on the outside 36ft. 6in. by 21ft.; the chancel 19ft. 6in. by 14ft. on the outside. The roof of the former covered in lead, the latter with slate. The belfry slated and contains 2 small bells. Within and belonging to the church are 1 communion table with a covering of green cloth very old; 1 linen cloth for the same. A pewter flagon, a small gilt cup and cover, a handsome silver chalice with the inscription 'The Parish of Manningford Abbots the Gift of the Revd. Chas. Adams, late Rector of this Parish and Elizabeth his wife 1782' and a large silver paten or salver given at the same time. A chest of little use because of the damp. A pulpit and reading desk. A pulpit cloth and cushion of crimson velvet, the gift of Francis Dugdale Astley esq. A large bible of the last translation. 2 large common prayer books. The Ten Commandments in a frame. A font cover, 2 surplices, one very old. 3 register books one beginning in 1539, the other in 1732. The church and the seats in the gallery are repaired by the parish, the chancel by the rector. The churchyard fence on W. and N. sides is repaired by the parish, the E. side by Edward Fowle, the S. side by the rector. The whole quantity of land including the churchyard, paddock and buildings before mentioned is 1a. 1r. and is bounded on E. by land of Edward Fowle, N. and W. by a meadow called the Bury now occupied by Mr. Hooper and S. by the road leading to the meadow.

The allotments of the glebe in the field acre are: A piece of arable land, 5a. 2r. 16p., bounded E. by the common droveway, S. the Packway from Upavon to Pewsey, W. land of Mr. Edward Brown, N. land of Harry Reeves; 3a. at the bottom of the field lately laid down to pasture bounded E. the road to the field, S. by Broadway, W. Mr. Fowle's lower allotment, N. a private road and lands belonging to Mr. Brown. An old enclosure of arable land called the Common ground, 1a., bounded E., W., and S. by lands of Mr. Edward Brown either in possession or in reversion, N. by the common. Timber trees in the above 6 ash, 3 oak, 2 elm, all young trees and at present of little value. An enclosure of arable called the Butt ground, 3a., bounded E. by a road or foot path from Sharcott to Wilcot and in the parish of Pewsey, W. by land of Mr. Edward Brown called the Butt grounds, N. by land in Pewsey belonging to Mr. Goodman, S. by the road leading to the common; wherein are growing at this time 12 ash, 29 oak, 6 elm and a small thicket of underwood with some oaks, etc., interspersed, the timber is most of it small but cannot ascertain the exact value of it probably c. £20. An enclosure called the Peat meadow, part of it planted with wood for fuel the other part for garden ground and pasture, 3r., bounded E. W. and N. by land of Mr. Edward Brown, either in possession or reversion, S. by the river where are growing 18 withy or willows 19 young ash lately planted, 10 Lombardy poplars lately planted and 1 young oak.

No pension, stipend or allowance is received or paid by the incumbent or now payable out of the living except for tenths, taxes and insurance. All tithes predial or mixed are due to the rector and no exemption by modus or otherwise is claimed. No lands are allotted for the repair of the church or utensils thereof. The stock money now in the hands of Mr. Edward Brown, churchwarden is £1 14s. 3½d. The parish clerk is appointed by the minister and paid at Easter yearly £1 by the parish. Right of common for 15 sheep and 5 lambs now of no value.

John Fletcher, rector, Edward Brown, churchwarden, William Robbins, overseer, Edward Fowle [X], William Hooper

514   12 Jul 1808 (D1/24/142/7)
The parsonage house, garden, barn, stable yard, and a small paddock adjoining the churchyard, c. ½a. A piece of arable land on the top of Manningford drove bounded by Upavon road, 6a. A piece of pasture land bounded on E. Pewsey road, on W by a field belonging to F. D. Astley esq., 3a. A garden on N. side of the river and a small willow bed adjoining, together 1r. A piece of arable land called Butt ground by the road leading to the common bounded E. and N. by enclosure belonging to Mr. Goodman on W. by an enclosure belonging to late Mr. Brown, 3a. 1a. of arable land on the top of the common bounded by enclosures belonging to F. D. Astley esq., and the late Mr. Brown. Great and small tithes are held by the rector.

George Smith, rector, John Buckland, churchwarden.

MANNINGFORD BRUCE rectory

515   29 Oct 1671 (D1/24/143/1)
The churchyard, fenced by the parish on the W. and on the N. by the farm, the rest of the bounds maintained by the parsonage. A close of c. 80 lugs adjoining

the churchyard, fenced about by the parsonage. An orchard and 3 little garden plots of *c.* 80 lugs. 2 barns standing in a little backside near the dwelling house, with a little stable at the S. end of the wheat barn, and a fodder house adjoining the churchyard. A plot of ground adjoining the river called By the Moor of *c.* 120 lugs, fenced about by the parsonage except the E. side which is maintained by a tenement called the Hould.

Edward Alexander, William Greene, churchwardens

Nil written in the margin nullifying a practice attempt at his signature by Edward Alexander [Ed. Ederd]

516   6 Jan 1678 (D1/24/143/2)

A dwelling house, 2 barns, 1 stable with backside adjoining. 2 gardens, 1 orchard, 1 close adjoining to the house and churchyard. 1 meadow ground, being *c.* ½a., the ground of Mary Alexander wid. on E. and the river compassing the other parts.

William Barton, curate, John Carpenter, Abraham Newman [X], churchwardens.

517   4 Jan 1705 (D1/24/143/3)

A parsonage house, 2 barns, a stable and outhouses, a backside, a garden and garden, 2 little rickyards and a close fenced on N. E. and W. by the rector and adjoining S. and E. side of the churchyard, which is also the privilege of the rector, the whole containing *c.* 1½a. A little meadow ground called the Moor, *c.* 3yd., abutting on W. end to the ford and having a mill stream on N. and a ground of Samuel Alexander on S.

Great and small tithes except that every parishioner pays in lieu of full tithes 'by received custom' for a calf 6d., for the tithe of milk, commonly called cow white, 2d. per cow, for a garden 1d., for eggs 1d. per house. Yearly Easter offerings of 2d. for every person chargeable. There is due to the rector for burying in the chancel 1 mark and for churching of women 4d.

John White, rector, Samuel Alexander, John Benger, churchwardens, John Alexander, Samuel Burden.

MARDEN vicarage and rectory

518   1588 (D1/24/144/1)

A survey made by the help and assistance of Mr. William Lavington, Roger Lavington, Richard Hamshire, John Moxham, James Clark, Thomas Amer and Richard Moxham, ancient and substantial men of the parish.

To the parsonage belong: 2 [½ *struck through*][1] yardlands leaze on the down for 100 sheep as far forth as the farmer; a barn[2] and a close adjoining it in several; 12 beast leaze and a bull; 19 lugs in the common meadow; 3a. lying in Patneys mead called Wylcott mead; the tithe corn except that which belongs to the vicarage.[3]

To the vicarage belong: the vicarage house with a backside, a barn, and stable; 2 little closes in several, 1 lying next the churchyard[4] which is converted to a garden and orchard by the vicar,[5] and the other lying by the waterside towards the mill, called the Pond close; all the tithe hay, wool, and land of the lordship of Marden, and all other privy tithes.

1. 2 leazes in **519** and in a terrier of 1738 among deeds in Bristol cathedral, *Wiltshire Notes and Queries*, pt. 90, pp. 259-260.
2. This is omitted in **519**.
3. Named as Butlers comprising 9 yardlands in **519**.
4. One additional close in **519** described as next the churchyard [lytten].
5. Mr. [John] Beckingham in **519**.

519   1 May 1609 (D1/24/144/2)
As 518 with amendments in footnotes. Made by Thomas Amer, Nicholas Henton, James Clarke, Richard Smythe, Richard Amer. *Names in the same hand*

520 1704 (D1/24/144/3)
     A true copy taken out of the ancient terrier of what belongs to the vicarage. The vicarage house, a barn, a stable in the backside, 2 little closes in several, one adjoining next the Litten the other by the waterside called Pond close. Tithe corn of 9½ yardlands called Butlers. Tithe hay, wool and lamb of the lordship of Marden and all other privy tithes, viz.; orchards, offerings, eggs, gardens, pigs, geese, turkeys, calves, cow white, honey, wax, hops, agistments. The close next the churchyard is converted to a garden and orchard.
     George Bradford, vicar, Richard Holloway, James Webb, churchwardens.

MARLBOROUGH ST MARY vicarage

521   18 Oct 1698 (D1/24/145/1)
A terrier of the lands and profits exhibited at the triennial visitation of Gilbert bishop of Salisbury held at Marlborough. All manner of tithes. A vicar's house on the Green now rented by John Stent at £3 p. a. but not fit for a minister to live in. The churchyard bounded on the E. side from a yard in the garden of Jeremiah Burgess on the N. by the outer sides of all the dwelling houses to 14ft. within Sheats Lane on the S., including the droppings of the houses with all the penthouses, gardens, outhouses, and a workhouse now in the possession of Mr. Williams; the S. side from Mr. Williams's workhouse on the E. running in a straight line to Mr. Williams's house on the W. where it is bounded 18ft. from within Sheats Lane and 32ft. from the street towards the Market House; the W. side from Mr. Williams's house running in a straight line by Walter Randall's house through the houses of Mr. Fowler and Mr. Benger to the Turn stile inclosure, and from there through the houses of Messrs. Spackman, Kenton, Parsons, and Mr. Thomas Glyde at the corner where it is bounded 20ft. from Kingsbury St. and 20ft. from Silverless St.; the N. side from Thomas Glyde's house to Southey's barn and from 18ft. towards Silverless St. to the ground held by Jeremiah Burgess. Part of the church which runs in a straight line from the E. end of the mayor's seat through the whole body of the church, which is reckoned as chancel ground

where the dues for burial are paid to the vicar viz. 10s. for every grown person and 5s. for every child, except within the rails where the dues are 20s. and 10s.

The library of Mr. White, late rector of Pusey, Berks., given to Cornelius Yeate and his successors, vicars of St. Mary's. and the catalogue of the books, is in the chest of the mayor and magistrates. £5 p. a. bequeathed by Mr. White payable on New Year's Day by his executors out of an estate at Coxwall Berks.[1] on condition that the vicar duly catechizes as more fully appears by the will which is also lodged in the chest of the mayor and magistrates. Easter offerings for all persons who do not subscribe quarterly towards the maintenance of the vicar are of every householder and his wife 12d., of servants 6d. and of every other person in the family of 16 years of age 2d. <Half the perpetual interest of £80 given by Dr. [Edward]Cressett>. The clerk's dues are 4d. of every householder.

This terrier agrees with the church book where it is attested by the most ancient inhabitants who several years together on Ascension day walked the boundaries of the churchyard, and was read 17 Oct at a parish meeting and agreed to by all the parishioners then present.

Cornelius Yeate, vicar, Hugh Blagrave, John Blissett, churchwardens, Henry Stent, mayor, Thomas Fowler, Thomas Glide, Jonathan Austine, Richard Edney.

1. This appears to have been changed on an estate in Bampton, Oxfordshire in the mid. 19th century when a dispute arose over it. (WSRO 871/6).

522   n. d. [1783][1] (D1/24/145/2)
A vicarage house situated on the Green, built with brick and lath and plaster, covered with tiles, containing 4 rooms ceiled, the lower floored with brick, the upper with elm, the walls plastered.

The churchyard bounded as follows: All the E. side from a court or yard within the garden of Daniel Sutton on N. by the outmost sides of the dwelling houses from that place to 14ft. within Sheats Lane or Oxford St., behind a house in the possession of George Hewitt on N. including the droppings of the said houses, together with all the penthouses, outhouses and gardens. All the S. side from the said house occupied by George Hewett running in a straight line to the dwelling house of Richard Luff on W. where it is bounded 18ft. within Sheats Lane or Oxford St. and 32ft. from the Street towards the market house. All the W. side from Richard Luff's house bounded as aforesaid running in a straight line by the dwelling house of Samuel Tucker through the dwelling houses of William Perrin, Mrs Mortimore and George Hewett across the church passage by the dwelling house of Mrs Eeles through the dwelling houses of Nathanial Merriman, John Bailey and Edward Batt at the corner where it is bounded 20ft. from Kingsbury St. and 20ft. from Silverless St. All the N. side from Edward Batt's house bounded as aforesaid to the ground possessed by Daniel Sutton where it is bounded 18ft. from Silverless St. All that part of the Green bounded thus from a mere stone by Daniel Sutton's house at the N. W. corner by the old church way on the W. to a gutter running from the house of Hugh Richardson on S. W. corner, along the said gutter on the S. across the Town gutter on S. E. corner from there on E. to a mere stone by the road on N. to the mere stone by Daniel Sutton's house.

A house situated on the churchyard built with bricks and lath and plaster covered with tiles containing 6 rooms the upper ones not ceiled, floored with elm the walls plastered. All that part of the church which runs in a straight line from the E. end of the mayor's seat through the whole body of the church which is reckonned as Chancel ground where the dues for burials are paid to the vicar: 10s. for every grown person, 5s. for every child except within the rails where the dues are 20s. and 10s. respectively.

All manner of tithes arising and growing within the parish. £8 p. a. from the treasurer of the Queen Anne's Bounty. The perpetual interest of £80 given by Dr. [*Edward*] Cresset. £5 p. a. bequeathed by the Rev. Mr. White payable yearly on New year's day by the executors of Mr. White out of an estate at Coxwell in Berkshire[2] upon condition that the vicar do duly catechise the children and servants of the parish. The library of Mr. White is kept in a room adjoining the church a catalogue of which is annexed to this terrier.[3]

Easter offerings, the ancient dues for which of all persons who do not quarterly subscribe to the maintenance of the vicar of every house keeper and his wife 12d., of servants 6d., of every other person in the family of 16 years of age 2d.

A silver chalice with the inscription 'Thos. Geering, Thos. Wall, churchwardens, A. D. 1658' weight 14oz. A silver plate with the inscription 'Deo & Sacris dedicavit Winifred Wall A. D. 1724'. A velvet pulpit cloth and cushion, 6 bells, a clock with chimes, 2 fire engines. A house and meeting house built on church land situated on the Green, leases of which are renewable every 40 years at £50 each besides a quit rent of £1 1s. p. a. for the house. These fines and rents together with the revenue of that part of the Green specified above are appropriated to the repair of the church. The writings are in the custody of Mr. Colman.

The clerk is appointed by the vicar his dues are 4d. of every housekeeper, his perquisites amount to about £5 p. a. The section is elected by the parish, his fixed salary is £2 12s. p. a. his perquisites amount to about £10 p. a. The churchyard fence is repaired by the parish.

Henry Whinfield, vicar, Thomas White, Thomas Hillier, churchwardens, T. Baverstock, John Ward, Edward Goatley, John Sweeper.

1. The churchwardens were recorded in the bishop's visitation book, Jul 1783 (WSRO D1/50/30).
2. See footnote 1. to **521**.
3. The catalalogue no longer with the terrier.

MARLBOROUGH ST. PETER AND ST. PAUL rectory

523   6 Dec 1677 (D1/24/146/1)
A dwelling house with a woodhouse, 2 gardens, and a close of pasture adjoining, *c.* 1a. in all. All the tithes of meadows or other lands without exception or composition for any, and all other tithes according to the tithing table, together with all the oblations and obventions of the inhabitants.

Joshua Sacheverell, rector, Hugh Row, Henry Coursey, churchwardens.

524   19 Jan 1783 (D1/24/146/2)

Terrier presented at Bishop Shute's primary visitation in Marlborough St. Peter and St. Paul 28 Jul. 1783.

A parsonage house having between it and the street an irregular court fenced therefrom partly by a brick wall but mostly by wooden palisades set upon a brick and stone foundation. Its walls are partly brick partly brick paned partly flemish and partly hung with tiles. Its roof is partly covered with slate and partly with tiles. It contains a parlour floored with deal wainscotted on 3 parts: the 2 cupboards set up by Mr. Meyler on each side of the window serving for wainscotting where they stand: A small kitchen floored with bricks and flagstones and wainscotted chair high on one side and one end: A pantry floored with bricks: 3 small places used as cellars, floored with brick and flints: A brewhouse chiefly paved with flagstones: 2 staircases the best thereof wainscotted in some part. A room over the parlour badly floored with elm and wainscotted chair high on 3 parts and up to ceiling near the chimney; 4 other small low bed places floored as the last and 3 garrets all ceiled and floored as before. A square stable built by Mr. Meyler with brick up to the eves on 2 sides and 1 end and measuring *c.* 12ft.; the upper part of that end and the whole of the other end is closed with boards and parts of it from a wood or straw house whose *c.* 17ft. by *c.* 15ft. On the woodhouse abuts a necessary house built of wood all which buildings are covered with tiles. In the N.W. part of the garden stands another decent necessary house with brick walls, deal floor and tiled. The stable yard is parted from the gardens by palisades; and a pair of gates parts the 2 gardens. The whole of the premises including the gardens, orchard or meadow stand upon or contain nearly 3r. of ground. They are bounded N. by the High St., E. by the river Kennet, W. by a tenement garden and meadow belonging to the wid. Hitchcock who is to maintain a sufficient fence on that side. The quick hedge now growing on the Parsonage land being planted by Mr. Meyler for ornament and a screen against a disagreeable ditch; near the river grow 2 chestnut trees; in a court or garden behind the house 1 fir tree; in a court before the house 7 lime trees trimmed. In the churchyard 2 yew trees none of them of much value.

All manner of tithes of things tithable in the parish together with all oblations and obventions of the inhabitants of the parish amounting to *c.* £8 p. a. 15s. payable at Easter p. a. by the churchwardens in compensation for pulling down a tenement belonging to the rector abutting against the N. wall of the chancel and his not feeding the churchyard. Quarterly dues from certain lands belonging to the rector but have not been paid out of late years; distinct from the occupiers' quarterly subscriptions: In Kingsbury Ward; Samuel Hawkes, 2d.; Samuel Hawkes for late Pages, 4d.; wid. Furnell's house, 1s.; Jasper Cripp's house, 1s.; Benjamin Merriman, Crown Inn, 8d.; wid. Smith, 8d.: In the High Ward, Thomas Warner for Mrs. Smith's, 6d.; Thomas Warner for Mr. Garlick's, 6d.; the earl of Aylesbury for George Taylor's, 1s.; the Rev. Mr. Meyler for his tenement, 2s.; the duke of Marlborough for Mr. Warner's, 10d.; same for Stephen Neate's, 9d.; Benjamin Merriman for George Jones', 4d.; Benjamin Merriman for his own house, 4d.: In the Baily Ward, William Few for Richard Chamberlain's 3d.

In 1693 Dr. Edward Cressett by his will left £80 to trustees for the use of the minister of this parish, but never having been placed out by them or their executors on proper security and descending from the surviving trustees to his executor and so downards who paid the interest thereof regularly. The capital was lately lost and sunk by the last holder's dying insolvent. But a relation of Mrs. Anne Liddiard of Marlborough, that the church should suffer no loss through her family, was graciously pleased on 25 Oct. 1782 to give and pay unto the Governors of Queen Anne's Bounty £80 towards augmenting the rectory and on the same day and year Harborn Hammond gent., of Marlborough gave and paid to the Governors £20 for the same purpose. But the gift becoming void by statute of Mortmain.[1] Mr. Meyler rector, by deed of gift 7 Apr. 1783 replaced that £20 and the honorable trustees of Mrs. Pyncombe's charity; viz. Sir Thomas Dyke Acland, Copplestone Warre Bampfylde esq., and James Bernard esq., allotted and gave £100 of that charity to the Governors for the same purpose, which with God's blessing on the benefactors it is to be hoped will in due time take place.

Yearly rents belonging to the parish church are collected every Easter by the sexton and applied to the use of the church: The earl of Aylesbury, a meadow, 2s.; Benjamin Merriman, the Mount Inn, 10s.; Richard Harris, The Coach and Horses and house adjoining, 16s. 8d.; James Gooding, The Six Bells Inn, 4s.; William Few, Sun Inn, and house adjoining, 4d.; John Hyde, a meadow, 2s. 10d.; George Golduyer, a house and garden, £2; Thomas Warner, a house and malthouse, £2; John Braithwaite, a meadow, 6d.; William Westmacott, 2 houses, 8d.; James Shipton, a house, 2d.; Charles Higham, a house, 6d.; Rev. William Grinfield, the old Greyhound Inn, 1s.; William Francis, a house, 1s.; Thomas Hancock, a malthouse, 6d.; the duke of Marlborough, a house and shop, 6d.; the same for The Three Tuns Inn, 2s.; Samuel Higham, a house, 9d.; the same, 3 houses in Silverless St., 10s.; Thomas Warner, The Bell Inn, 3d.; Jasper Cripps, a house, 1s.

These belong to the church and parish: In the Chancel, which is wainscotted someway up on N. and S. sides and adored with paintings on canvas in panels on the E. with the Ten Commandments thereon, a communion table surrounded with rails at a convenient distance and covered daily with crimson velvet with silk fringe round the bottom and bound round the top with gold lace, a square piece of crimson velvet hanging behind the altar and a fine black cloth with black fringe to hange there in Lent and on fasting days: 2 large brass candle sticks with wax candles therein, a piece of carpetting and floor mats, 3 low benches covered with leather for the communicants to kneel on, 2 crimson velvet cushion stands for the minister. In the church: a pulpit, a desk for the minister and one for the clerk, a crimson velvet cushion with gold fringe and tassles, a black cloth cushion with black fringe and tassles, narrow crimson velvet valences with gold fringe and tassles and narrow black cloth valences with black fringe for the pulpit and desk and a stool in each to kneel on. The King's arms painted in 1778, 2 large brass chandeliers hanging by iron links pointed over the middle aisle, a small chandelier hanging by iron links over the chancel, 2 brass sconces to the pulpit, 2 brass sconces to the desk, a brass sconce to clerk's desk, 4 brass sconces hanging to 4 pillars in the body of the church, 4 brass sconces in the organ loft, an organ, with iron rods and green cloth before it: the organ was erected by subscription in 1776 and the organist has hitherto been paid in the saame method; a time piece afixed to the front of the gallery at the W. end of the church. Books: a large bible of royal paper and gilt covers, a large common prayer book in the desk, a large common prayer book in the clerk's desk; in the chancel 2 quarto common prayer books with red covers, gilt; on the middle of the communion table stands an old folio common prayer book on one end, opened; on each side of the chancel stand chained onto desks 2 Preservatives against Popery in 1738 given by Robert Clavering, late rector; Erasmus' comment on the Gospels and Acts of the Apostles chained to a shelf in the vestry; Bishop Jewel's Defence of the Apologie of the Church of England lacking a title page [caret titulo], Fox's Book of Martyres, 2 vols. folio, one of them greatly torn; a vol. of sermons lacking a title page folio, 6 quarto common Prayer books in the churchwardens' pew. On the N. wall of the church is affixed the Lord's Prayer and a table of degrees on the S. wall the Apostles' Creed, and a painted table signifying that Thomas Ray in 1715 gave the rents of certain tenements in Salisbury for the poor clothiers of Marlborough, Bradford, Trowbridge and Chippenham alternately, which has not been received of late years; that Mrs Anne Pain in 1640 gave to the Goldsmiths' Company in the city of London £300 to pay £5 p. a. to the poor of Marlborough, all in frames. A each end of the churchwardens' pews are iron rods with crimson harrateen[2] curtains.

In the vestry room are 2 chests of oak, one for the writings belonging to the parish whereon are 3 locks, the keys whereof are kept by the minister the other 2 by the churchwardens, the other chest for keeping the plate and vestments which are 2 large pewter flagons, a pewter bason for the font, a pewter plate, 2 pewter plates to collect alms with; a large silver cup with a cover, weight 24oz. 14dwt. inscribed on the side 'I. H. S. hic est sanguio meus'; a large silver bason for the offertory, weight 37oz. 14dwt., inscribed' Deo et Eccle. Sancti Petri Winifreda Wall filia Hu'di Wall hujusce paroc. Generosi pietissime Dedicavit' and in the middle are her arms; a silver plate for the bread, weight 13oz. 4dwt. inscribed 'Robertus Clavering, Rector, D. D. CQ';[3] a silver straining spoon weight 1oz. 8dwt. inscribed 'q t p'; 2 surplices; one silk Oxford Master of Arts hood, in the care of the parish clerk. A long oak table, an oak elbow chair, a small deal table, a case of shelves, a wheel barrow, 50 leather buckets, 6 long ladders, 2 fire crooks; outside the gates and screen are 9 long forms, 2 high stools and 2 low stools to support the coffins. A stone font with a painted covering. In the tower are a large clock with a small bell to strike the hour on and to call the congregation to prayers and 6 larger bells for ringing peals. On outward E. part of the tower is a dial moved and regulated by the clock within.

The parish clerk is chosen by the minister, he has no wages fixed but receives his dues for every wedding 1s., for every christening and registering 6d. and for every parish burial 1s. 1d.; for every other funeral 2s. 6d. at the least. The sexton is chosen by the parishioners, his standing wages are £3 11s. 2d. (he finding thereout the bell ropes) and receives for digging every parish grave and ringing the bell 1s. 9d. and for every other grave 3s. and for every wedding 1s. It is usual for both jointly to collect and equally divide the benevolence of the parishioners at Christmas yearly.

The corporation of Marlborough with their officers til of late years used to meet and go to one of the churches on Good Friday in the morning and between morning and evening services went around the town and distributed certain sums of money at their discretion to certain poor inhabitants, and a certain sum continues to be distributed annually on that day, by their officers to such families in the town as several members of the corporation shall nominate, though not so liberally as in times past. Whether such money arises from certain lands and tenements left to the corporation in trust for such use or proceeds out of their bounty, is not commonly known but custom of distribution has been time out of mind. The chancel is repaired by the rector, the church tower and churchyard fences by the parishioners.

Thomas Meyler, rector, John Wentworth, William Mctier, churchwardens, W. Westmacott, Thomas Warner, George Taylor, James Higham, Benjamin Hancocks, William Fuidge, James Wentworth, Bara[chiah] Joyce, Joseph Rogers, John Brinsden, Henry Goodman, William Hitchcock, D. Dixon.

1. Not the statute of Mortmain of 1279 but the Mortmain Act, 1736, which imposed restrictions on the devising of property to charitable uses.
2. A linen fabric used for curtains, etc.
3. CQ is an unfamiliar abbreviation. Clavering studied at Christ Church, Oxford, and perhaps it should read C C.

MELKSHAM vicarage

525   25 Sep 1608 (D1/24/147/1)
A dwelling house with outhouses, an orchard, and two gardens, which have always been held by the vicars and their assigns, also the churchyard.

By me, John Awdry, vicar; Robert Shewring, churchwarden, John Gerysh, Robert Smythe, Thomas Flower senior, John Small.

526   1 Jun 1619 (D1/24/147/2)
A vicarage house with an orchard and garden adjoining, 1½a. Churchyard, 2a. All manner of tithes and other duties except corn and hay. Sufficient hay to find a horse yearly. A churchyard at Seend, 3a. A house garden adjoining and churchyard at Erlestoke, c. 1a.

Robert Maye, Robert Cooke, churchwardens, Nicholas Ruttye, Thomas Flower, sidesmen.

527   1671 (D1/24/147/3)
By a copy of the Registry and Arches[1] of Sarum it appears that in 1649 an allowance was made to the vicar; that the vicar should receive all the profits and small tithes and all other portions and customs of the mother church of Melksham and the chapels adjoining without any diminution except the tithe of the blade of beans and peas and some rents and customs as described in the copy, which are to remain to the common uses of Sarum. The vicar ought to have a house and orchard and hay enough to keep 1 horse.

Peter Priaulx vicar, William Peirce, Mathew Crine, churchwardens.

1. The name of the court of appeal of the province of Canterbury here transposed to
    the bishop of Sarum's court, probably as a result of the hiatus caused to ecclesiastical
    administration by the Interegnum, 1650–1659.

528   21 Dec 1704 (D1/24/147/4)
A dwelling house with orchard garden and backside adjoining and belonging
with the churchyard. All the small tithes of the parish and the sum of £6 1s. 8d.
p. a. from the parsonage by the owner of the great tithe.

Bohun Fox, vicar, Jacob Selfe, Francis Kington, churchwardens, Thomas Smith,
Thomas Parker, John Harris, Robert Drinkwater, overseer.

529   16 Nov 1721 (D1/24/147/5)
Note of a verdict in a Chancery case Fox v. Rutty that the vicar is entitled to
tithes from lands called Islay and not the rector of Whaddon.

530   31 Jul 1783 (D1/24/147/6)
A vicarage house, c. 56ft. x 28ft. with stone walls covered with stone tiles, consisting
of a parlour with boarded floor wainscotted and plastered walls and ceiled. A
hall, kitchen pantrys, cellar and brewhouse with stone floors plastered walls and
ceiled. 5 chambers and a small chamber with plastered walls and ceiled. A cellar
and woodhouse c. 44ft. x 15ft. with stone floor and plastered walls of chamber
or study over the last with plastered walls and ceiled. A stable c. 19ft. x 15ft. the
walls built of stone and covered with stone tiles. A double necessary house c.
12ft. x 9ft. with stone walls and covered with stone tiles. A chaise or wagon
house c. 19ft. x 15ft. with stone walls and covered with stone tiles. A court and
yard bounded with walls. A garden bounded with walls and hedge. A close or
paddock bounded with hedges, 2 elm timber trees growing value c. 30s. all
adjoining the vicarage house and containing in all c. ½a.

A right of common for 7 cows or 3 horses and 1 cow in Melksham common
during the time of stocking til the Michaelmas following. The vicarial tithes of
the parish of Melksham and of the chapelry of Seend.

Church furniture: 6 bells, a clock with chimes, a silver flagon with the
inscription 'The Gift of Ellinor Long to the parish church of Melksham Anno
Domini 1731', weight c. 3 lb. 7oz.; a silver cup, c. 10oz.; a large silver salver with
the inscription 'Ex dono Petrie Priaulx A. M. huius Eccl.Vicarie donate Jan VIII
Ano Doe MDCLXXXX', weight c. 1lb. 2oz.; 2 small silver waiters, c. 11oz.; a
bible and 2 common prayer books with 2 registers; one of marriages the other
of baptisms and burials.

The church is repaired by the parish, the chancel by John Awdry esq., owner
of the great tithes the N. aisle by Paul Methuen esq., the S. E. aisle by Richard Jenkins esq., Revd. Mr. William Stone and Mrs. York, S.W. aisle by Mrs. Mary Thresher.
The churchyard fence by the parish Richard Jenkins, esq., Revd. Mr. William
Stone and Mrs. York, the executors of the late Thomas Beaven and wid. Phelps.

The clerk is paid by the parish £6 p. a. and appointed by the minister. The
sexton is paid £2 10s. p. a. by the parish and he is appointed by the parish.

T. Bruges, William Stone, curate, William Flower,[1] James Beaven, churchwardens.

1.   William Flower rendered account as churchwarden for this year (WSRO 1368/
     56).

MELSHAM: Erlestoke chapelry

531   n. d. early 17th cent. (D1/24/147/7)
A certificate for the glebe land. As far as we can learn there is 1 close of *c.* 2a. with
a barn. To our knowledge there is no vicarage house for it has been long in the
hands of Sir William Bronker and his predecessors. We have learned that there was
a house, and a serving priest living there, but since then Sir William Bronker made
it a house to keep hawks in, and now the house is clean down and defaced.
     Richard Trimnell [X], Thomas Graunte [X], churchwardens.

532   21 Dec 1704 (D1/24/147/8)
A house with little plot of garden.
     David Thomas, curate, Hugh Tilly, Richard Halliday, churchwardens, Thomas
Alderidge, Edward Cromwell.

533   31 Jul 1783 (D1/24/147/9)
A vicarage house *c.* 20½ft. x 16ft. the walls built with stone and covered with
stone tiles; consisting of a kitchen with stone floor plastered walls and ceiled; a
pantry with stone floor plastered walls and ceiled; 2 chambers plastered walls
and ceiled. A garret.
     An orchard garden bounded with hedges adjoining the vicarage house *c.*
¼a. with 8 elm trees value *c.* 7s. each. 4 pieces of meadow or pasture land lately
enclosed and adjoining to each other on W. side of Stokes marsh, bounded with
hedges, *c.* 44a. The last land was given under the Erlestoke enclosure award[1] in
lieu of all vicarial tithes.
     Chapel furniture: 5 bells; a silver cup and cover, *c.* 14 oz.; a pewter plate and
pewter quart and cover; a bible and common prayer book. The chapel is repaired
by the parish, the chancel by Joshua and Drummond Smith esqs., lords of the
manor. The chapel yard fence is also repaired by Joshua and Drummond Smith:
44 small elm and 2 lime trees, standing in the chapel yard value *c.* 3s. each.
     The clerk or sexton is paid by the parish 10s. 6d. p. a. and collects from the
inhabitants some trifling sum at Easter. He is appointed by the minister.
     John Baily curate for John Newton, vicar, Isaac Axford, chapelwarden, John
Tilly, Joshua Sainsbury, Robert Axford.

1.   Dated 1782. (WSRO EA 21).

MELKSHAM: Seend chapelry

534   26 Sept 1608 (D1/24/147/10)
Within Seend there is neither house nor land, only the churchyard.
     Simon Dalmer, Abraham Self, churchwardens, Edward Michell, John Prittles.
     Churchwardens' names in the same hand

535   20 Dec 1704 (D1/24/147/11)
A churchyard *c.* 2a. All small tithes except of corn, hay, peas and beans.

Bohun Fox, vicar, Ambrose Parridice, Francis Michell, chapelwardens, Ambrose Awdry.

MERE rectory (impropriate)

536   23 Nov 1771[1] (D5/15/1)
Terrier of the rectory held by William Chafin Grove esq., under a 21 year lease granted by Rev. Dr. Thomas Greene, dean of Salisbury. The parsonage house, much out of repair and not inhabited for a great number of years with a backside adjoining situate in Castle Street. A large new tiled house called Dewdneys with a backside, a very small garden, stable, cart house and barn adjoining in Church St. opposite the churchyard. A backside with barn adjoining the churchyard on E. side,

Several parcels of arable land lying dispersedly in the common fields of Mere. In Widdenham field: 3a. in one piece at the upper end of the field, a headland, adjoining to the W. side of Dever Long wood shooting N. and S. yearly value £1 3d.; 2a. in one piece shooting E. and W. next to Stourton hedge except 1a., 13s. 6d. In Westcomb field: a large forked a. shooting up to the down called Old Castle, land in the tenure of William Harding W., a land in the tenure of William Maidment E., 6s. 9d.; A single a. shooting up to the down called Old Castle, William Harding E., land belonging to the White Hill farm W., 6s. 9d.; 1a. lying N. and S. and shooting up to Catherine hedge which divides Stourton parish from Mere, adjoining Dever Long wood 1a., William Wickham W., 1a. John Welch E., 6s. 9d.; 1a. in the same furlong lying N. and S. shooting up to Catherine hedge, 1a. John Welch W., 1a. William Harding E., 6s. 9d.; 1a. in the same furlong lying N. and S. shooting up to Catherine Hedge, single acres of William Harding E. and W., 6s. 9d.; 1a. in the same furlong shooting up to Catherine Hedge, 1a. William Harding W., 1a. John Welch E., 6s. 9d. On Deans hill: a piece of 2a. shooting N. and S. having a footpath only between it and Mrs Ford's hedge on E. Lammas road W., 13s. 6d.; 1a. shooting N. and S., ½a. on E., a land of John Perman W.; 6s. 9d., formerly belonging to a tenement called Sarah Gowers; in the same furlong westwards, ½a. shooting N. and S., John Perman E. and W., 3s. 4½d.; in the same furlong westwards 1a. shooting N. and S., Aaron Dewdney E., John Perman W., 6s. 9d.; in the same furlong 2 lands shooting N. and S. of which one is ½a. and lies on E. and adjoins the Holloway from Mere to Maiden Bradley, the other is 1a. opposite to the end of the last ½a. and shoots down to Pudditch, John Toogood E., the road W., 1s. 1½d.

On the N. side of Castle Hill: A piece of 2a. shooting N. and W., William Maidment E., William Harding W., the Lammas road N., 13s. 6d., n. b. belonged to Morris Maidment's tenement before it fell into hand; a piece of 2a. in the same furlong westwards shooting N. and S., William Harding E., Christopher Dowding W., 13s. 6d. n. b. formerly belonged to a tenement called Sarah Gowers; a piece of 2a., a headland to the same furlong shooting E. and W., to a Holloway on N., 13s. 6d.

In Wetland Gutter: 1a. shooting N. and S. across the gutter, Christopher Dowding E. John Taylor W., 6s. 9d.; in the furlong westwards a piece of 7a. shooting N. and S. and across Wetland gutter, William Maidment E., William Harding W., £2 7s. 3d.; in the same furlong westwards a piece of 2a. shooting N. and S. across Wetland gutter, William Harding E., William Ford W., 13s. 6d.; at the N. end of the last 2a. is ½a., a headland, shooting E. and W., 3s. 4 d.; 1a. shooting E. and W. William Wickham S. which adjoins the little Holloway, William Ford N., 6s. 9d.; 1a. shooting N. and S. on E. side of the Lammas road to Widenham field having Breach on W. side of the road, 6s. 9d.; a piece of 1½a. shooting N. and S. into a land of William Wickham, Wetland gutter E., a great linch W., 10s. 11½d.; a forked piece of 2 yd. on W. side of Wetland gutter shooting nearly E. and W., part shoots upon Wetland gutter, 3s. 4½d.; a piece of 1½a. shooting up to Knowl gate a footpath S., a land of Wickham's N. shooting E. and W., 6s. 9d., n. b. formerly belonged to a tenement called Sarah Gowers.

In the S. side of Castle hill: A piece called Brambly furlong 18a., £6 1s. 6d.; 2 triangular pieces one 4a. the other 2a. separated from each other by a footpath, S. the road to Wood land, N. the turnpike road from Mere to Wincanton, £2 6d.; 1a. on N. side of the turnpike road shooting E. and W. separated from the 2 triangular pieces by the road, 6s. 9d.

In the field between Mere and Burton; 1a. shooting E. and W., a large weal [wale][2] or green road S., 1a. John Perman N., 6s. 9d.; 2 single a. shooting N. and S. upon Hollwell, 1a. Thomas Toogood E., 1a. John Tucker W., 1a. belonging to White hill lying between them, 13s. 6d.; a piece of 2a. shooting N. and S. in the same furlong, John Perman E., John Toogood W., 13s. 6d.; ½a., headland, lying contiguous to the river and opposite to Ivy mead which a. formerly went with the George Inn, 3s. 4½d.

In the field called S. Brook: a piece called Duggarell's acre lying near Mere hill, green ground, 4a., £4; 1a. lying under John Coward's hedge which is in an enclosure of Christopher Dowding shooting E. and W., the hedge S., 1a. of Robert Butt N., 6s. 9d.; 1a. called Green acre northward in the same furlong shooting E. and W., the wid. Maidment's a. S., a footpath N., £1 9s.; ½a. in the same furlong shooting E. and W. on N. of the footpath, 3s. 4½d.; a piece of 2a. in the same furlong shooting E. and W. Richard Sly S., William Ford N., 13s. 6d.; a headland ½a. shooting N. S. towards S. Brook gate, 3s. 4½d.; 1a. of green ground in an enclosure of Henry Clark called Dye house formerly taken out of S. Brook, 6s. 9d.

Several parcels of meadow lying dispersedly in the common meadows: 1a. in Huddles Hearne adjoining to Wood lane, £1; ½a. in the common meadow called Mere mead shooting against the stile of the footway from Mere town to Mapledore hill at the further end of the mead, 10s.; 1a. in the same mead shooting against the gate of the land from Mere town into Mere mead, £1; 1a. in the same furlong, £1. In Lords mead, 7½a. in lieu of tithe of the mead lying dispersedly in the mead, £7; 2 closes of meadow or pasture called Cockershays in Rook St. in Woodland tithing, 8a., £8; 3 closes of meadow or pasture in Rook St. formerly belonging to the tenement called the Black house, 4a., £4; all which above mentioned houses arable lands meadows and pastures are let to farmer James Maidment.

A cottage in Rook St. with garden, orchard, and 3 little plots of ground in the tenure of Thomas Turner, 2a. 1yd., £4; 2 closes of meadow and pasture in the tithing of Woodland formerly belonging to a tenement called Blackhouse now in the tenure of Christopher Dowding, 9a., £10; a ground of meadow or pasture at the end of Boar St. by the W. side of Pitteridge lane now in the tenure of Edward Tucker, 3a., £4; a plot of ground called George paddock adjoining W. end of Dean's orchard and a little plot of ground adjoining called Shitbrook now in the tenure of Mr. Harry Grove, 2a., £2; a house called the George Inn with a brewhouse, stable, small garden in the tenure of William Hallett to be let with the cottage hereafter mentioned, £10 10s.:

Cottage houses: a cottage with a garden in Pettycoat lane in the tenure of Laurence Cox; a cottage with a garden in Pettycoat lane, Joseph Butt; a cottage with garden and backside opposite the S. W. corner of the churchyard, Stephen Butt; a cottage in Church St. with a small garden adjoining a ground belonging to the vicar of Mere, John Griffin; a cottage with a garden and orchard adjoining the last premises, the overseers of the poor of Mere; one with a small garden in the same street opposite the churchyard gates, Joseph Buckett; a cottage with a small garden in the same street adjoining the E. end of the last cottage, William Cousins; a cottage with small garden in the same street divided from the last cottage by a lane to Castle St., Walter Alford; a cottage with small garden in Church St. adjoining the last cottage, John Bowles; a cottage with small garden in the same street adjoining the last cottage, Mary Thick wid.; a cottage with garden in the same street on the opposite side, Thomas Alford; 2 cottages with small gardens on N. side of the same street near the market house, Matthew Barter; a cottage on S. side of Castle next to the George Inn and let with that inn; a cottage house adjoining the last cottage, William Hill; a cottage adjoining the last cottage, Elizabeth Beckett; a cottage with small garden now converted into a blacksmith's shop adjoining the last cottage, Edward Alford; 2 cottages with small gardens in the same street, separated from the parsonage backside by a lane into Church street all joining together and vacant; a cottage at the lower end of the S. side of Salisbury St., John Arnold; a cottage with small in Water St., Alice Lawrence wid.; a cottage in the same street, William Love with c. 5 lugs of garden on the opposite side of the way and near to Martin Toogood's backside; a cottage and garden in Dark lane, Joel Perman; a cottage garden and orchard at W. end of Castle St. and called Rag farm, Robert Down.

Quit rents received from the Dean's copyhold tenants: Thomas Perman for late William Rix's tenement in Church St., 1s. p. a.; the wid. Maidment for part of Perry's tenement 4s. 8d.; same for Howell's tenement, 2s. 4d.; Samuel Butt for part of Perry's tenement, 1s.; Stephen Butt for Knapp's tenement, 8d.; Robert Butt for late Seagrim's tenement, 4s.; same for Barnards ground, 4d.; Thomas Perman for late Traceys tenement in Castle St., 3s.; same for late Traceys tenement in Church St., 1s.; Thomas Alford for late Perry's tenement, 2s.; Edward Alford for a tenement in Castle St., 5s.; Mrs. Pittman for Hedge Pitts, 1s. 2d.; Aaron Dewdney for Plummers, 1d.; Martin Toogood for his tenement in Water St. (lease), 1s.; Thomas Moors for a tenement late William Howells, 1s.; total £2 4s. 8d.

Tithe corn for the whole parish worth £250 p. a.; tithe hay in Mere mead, Huddles Hearne and Whatley and the green ground in S. Brook £2 p. a.; tithe wood in the parish £1; Lammas tenths payable 12 Aug. p. a. in lieu of tithe hay of the enclosed pasture and meadow grounds of the whole parish, £9 10s.; payable yearly out of lord Weymouth's farm at Kingston Deverill on 12 Aug. £4.: total £26 14s. 8d. Total yearly value of the glebe, etc. £83 9s. 7½d. Total £352 4s. 3½d.

Delivered to the dean this is a true terrier, by Mr. William Chafin Grove.

1.   For the history of the proprties in this terrier see *The Dean's Farm* by M. F. Tighe (Mere Papers nos. 12 and 15).
2.   A ridge; but weal used topographically to describe a feature like the mark on a body caused by a lash.

MILDENHALL rectory

537   n. d. late 16th cent.[1] (D1/24/148/1)
A close called Dene field being arable, *c.* 20a. Little Dene close, arable and a coppice of wood adjoining containing together *c.* 6a. A meadow called Dry mead, *c.* 2a. 12a. land in the common field called Thicket field. 8a. in the common field called Middle field. 16a. land in the W. field. 5a. in the wood.

Tenements in Mildenhall: 1 tenement with ½ yardland of 9½a. held by Robert Lovelocke; 1 tenement with ½ yardland of 8½a. held by Philip Lawrence; 1 tenement with ½ yardland of 11a. held by William Gybbes; 1 tenement with ½ yardland of 8a. held by Thomas Lawrence, parson; another tenement of Poulton of *c.* ½ yardland of 13a.

1.   Between 1575-1593 when Thomas Lawrence was rector.

538   n. d. early 17th cent.[1] (D1/24/148/2)
A certain enclosure lying at Woodland called Deanfield, 30a. A coppice of underwood with a little close adjoining called Dean Coppice [Copps] or Little Dean field, 5a. A meadow at Grove one side lying next the river the other next the highway, 3a. A piece of arable land lying in Thicket field joining upon the wid. Hall's land and on the other side on William Plaster's land, 1½a. A piece of land lying on the hill westward from Plumtree bottom between land of William Heale and William Pearce, 1½a. A piece of arable lying in the same field called Bastard hill, between land of the wid. Hall and John Bosher, 7a. A piece of arable lying in the same field eastward from New gate towards Shutthill bottom between land of John Jones and John Boshere, 2a. 1a. in the same field lying by greenway side butting upon William Jones his enclosure.

The Middle field: A piece of land lying by greenwayside, 3a. A piece on Twangley shooting athwart the church path, 3a. In Broad-hanger a piece between John Jones and the wid. Hall, 2a.

The W. field: A piece of arable lying in Hare-den bottom between William Jones and the wid. Hall, 1a. Upon the top W. hill a piece of arable abutting upon the wid. Hall and Thomas Lovelock and between Edward Plaster and the wid. Hall, 2a. A piece called the White land between John Boshere and the wid. Hall,

4a. A piece joining to Raw-down hedge resting upon the highway at Rowdown gate, 2a. A piece adjoining to Drove-land hedge, 1a.

Outside [without] the parsonage bars called the Parsonage Dean, a piece, 7a. In the Ore field butting upon Rowdown and the river 4a. In the same field next to the Drove-lane hedge a piece, 1a. The side of the house, barns, stables, hayhouse, gardens, orchards, hopyards and other ground, 3a.

Tenements belonging to the parsonage: Poulton tenement; in Poulton, 18a. of arable land, 50 sheep leaze in the fields and downs, leaze for 2 kine and a runner, 2 horse leaze, common for pigs as the farmer has both beyond the bridge and otherwise, with a plot of ground enclosed with a house and garden near Poulton bridge, with a little plot of meadow ground lying in Mr. Browne's meadow, ½a.

There are 4 other tenements in Mildenhall village whereof one is in the occupation of Philip Lawrence containing arable pasture and meadow as follows: In Brookfurlong towards Durnsford [Dunsford] mill between Mr. William Jones and Philip Godwin butting upon 1yd. of the wid. Halle's ground, 1a.; in the same furlong a piece having on the one side J. Greenaway's land and on the other P. Godwin's, 1a.; a piece of land butting upon Durnsford leaze having on each side J. Greenaway towards the river and Thomas Lovelock towards Thickett, ½a.; in the same Thicket field in Shuttle furlong, 1a.; in the Middle field in Twanley between William Jones, senior, and John Jones of Mildenhall town, 1a.; Bryer land upon the churchway between the wid. Hall and Robert Gibbes, 1a.; in the W. field, at the Town's end between Geoffrey Golding and William Stainner, 1a.; in the Ore butting upon Rawdown hedge and the river, 1a.; his house, backside, with a meadow and a little plot outside [without] the hedge in the field at his close end, 1½a.

The second tenement occupied by Geoffrey Golding; at Durnsford field gate butting upon the gate along the highway side, 1a.: In the Middle field in Twanley between John Boshere and Thomas Lovelock, 1a.; in Bryerland crossing the churchway, 1a.; in the same Bryerland a piece shooting over the churchway between Philip Godwin and the wid. Hall, ½a.; in Keife land a piece shooting upon Greenway between J. Jones and the wid. Hall, 1a.; upon the W. hill between the wid. Hall and John Boshere a plot, 1a.; in Little Dean between John Boshere and the wid. Hall, 1a.; at the Townsend between Philip Lawrence and John Boshere, 1a.; in the Ore butting upon Rawdown hedge and the river, 1a.; a house, meadow, garden and backside, 1a.

The third tenement in the possession of Thomas Lovelock: In Thicket field butting upon Durnsford leaze between Philip Godwin and P. Lawrence, 1a.; in Twanley between Geoffrey Golding and William Heale, 1a.; in Broad-hanger a piece butting upon William Heale and the wid. Hall, 1a.; in Keifeland butting upon Greenway between the wid. Hall and Edward Plaster, 1½a.; in Bryerland between 1a. of Mr. Jones his copyhold in Mildenhall and John Jones, 1a.; in the Middle field at the end of his close and butting upon the wid. Hall, ½a.; in the W. Hill the head acre, 1a.; at the Towns end between the wid. Hall butting westward upon John Boshere, 1a.; in the Ore reaching from the river to the hedge, 1a.; his housing, backside and meadow close, ½a.

The last tenement occupied by Edward Lewes: In Thickett field westward from Plum tree bottom between the wid. Hall and John Jones, ½a.; westward from thence between J. Jones and the wid. Hall, ½a.; in Shutt-hill next adjoining William Jones senior, his enclosure, ½a.; next to Greenway joining John Boshere's piece, ½a.; in Twanley a piece having John Boshere's land on either side, 1½a.; in the same Middle field in Broadhanger next to the wid Hall's land, 1a.; in the same field butting upon the Churchway and William Heale, s land, ½a.; in Bryerland between William Heale and J. Jones, 1a.; at the Town's end by the enclosures next the churchway, 1a.; In W. field, on the top of the W. hill between William Heale and John Jones, 1a.; a piece next to Conney-lench butting upon Thomas Lovelocke southward, 1½a.; at the Towns end between John Boshere's 2a., 1a.; at Woodlands next to the pond and joining to Rushmoor a piece of enclosure, 1a.; the housing, garden and a close, 1a.

All these 4 tenements in Mildenhall town have each of them 30 sheep leaze, 2 kine and a runner and leaze for 2 horses in the common fields and upon Rawdown together with the lord's tenants.

William Earth, rector, Thomas Costard [X], John Plaster [X], churchwardens.

1. Between 1593-1619 when William Earth was rector.

539 1671 (D1/24/148/3)
The parsonage house, barn, stable and other outhouses. The orchard gardens, barton and a green plot of ground behind the barn, 2a. At the Dean field near Woodlands an enclosed ground, c. 12a. An enclosed ground lying next to the former northwards, 18a. An enclosed ground lying westwards having a small coppice, c. 3a. An enclosed ground lying near Woodlands house northward, c. 2a. At the Down an enclosed ground, c. 10a. c. 40a. of arable land in the common fields. A mead by the river near Grove, c. 2a. 5 tenements having each of them ½ yardland, in all c. 50a. A tenement of recent [late] erection having 4a. of arable land belonging to it. Total 143½a.

Stephen Constable, rector, Thomas Parkins, Francis Chappell, churchwardens.

540 10 Dec 1677 (D1/24/148/4)
The parsonage house, 2 barns and a stable with other outhouses, an orchard, 2 gardens, a backside and a little close adjoining in all c. 2a. 5 small tenements with c. 50a. of land belonging to them. 4 closes of pasture ground at Dean fields, c. 36a. A watermead, c. 2a. A close of pasture called the Down, lately enclosed, c. 10a. c. 40a. of arable land lying in the common fields. All great and small tithes.

Stephen Constable, rector, Ralph Tabor, Robert Smith, churchwardens.

541 5 Apr 1684 (D1/24/148/5)
As 540. Stephen Constable, rector, Francis Chappell, Edward Coster, churchwardens, Ralph Tabor, John Taber, overseers, Lawrence Skeate.

542 8 Jan 1705 (D1/24/148/6)
A parsonage house, barn, stable and carthouse. An orchard, garden, the backside, and a little close behind them all of them containing c. 2a. of ground. A tenement in which Lawrence Skeate lately lived to which belongs a barn, a stable, a little close of c. ½a. of ground and 12a. in the common field lying thus; 1a. in Tonely;

3 x ½a. more in Tonley; ½a. lying by the green way; 2a. above Shettal bottom; ½a. under Squire Nourse his hedge; 2 x ½a. shooting against a pit in Thicket field; ½a. of Tabors lying between them; ½a. on W. side of the green way by the bush; 1a. in Bryerland; 1a. more in Bryer and next to the hedge; 3a. in Whiteland athwart hill; 1a. at the towns end 3 x ½a. in Little Dean Bottom.

½ yardland called that which belongs to the Burnt house to which there belongs a close of near 1a. of ground and 7a. of arable in common field, a picked a. lying along by Thickett way, 1a. shooting on the green way in Bryerland and ½a. shooting athwart Church way in Bryerland, 1a. more in Bryerland, ½a. in Rably field, 1a. called Coneylinch acre, 1a. at the towns end, 1a. in the Owre.

½ yardland more called Browns to which there belongs a close of c. ½a. and 5½a. of arable in the common field viz. 1a. in Shettall bottom, 3 x ½a. in Thickett field below the bottom, 1a. in Bryerland, 1a. at the towns end, 1a. in the Owre.

½ yardland called Alexanders to which there belongs a cottage in which Thomas Pipin lately dwelt, a close of c. 1a. of ground and 9½a. of arable in the common field viz. 1a. in Broadhanger, 1a. in Toncly, 1a. below the way shooting upon Durnsford leaze hedge, 3 x ½a. in Bryarland, ½a. against Brown close hedge, 1a. more in Bryarland, 1 head a. by the great landshoot in Little Deans, 3 x ½a. in Little Dean bottom, 1a. in Owre. 4a. more in the common field formerly belonging to Chappels bargain viz. 1a. lying above Harding bottom, 3 x ½a. in Tonely, ½a. in Shettall bottom, 1a. above Plumtree bottom.

½ yardland lying at Poulton to which there belongs a little close where the house stood, c. ½a. of ground, 2a. shooting against Tabors down, ½a. lying along by the highway shooting on the close where the house stood, ½a. of meadow in Barns close, at the N. corner of it bounded at the W. end by a merestone and going from it straight to the 3 elms next to the backside, ½a. under the Crate hedge, 1yd. at Cowdown gate, ½a. joining to Smock acre, a head ½a. above Bay furlong, ½a. more just above him shooting farther W. than the other, 1a. at the end of the 10a. belonging to Poulton having the butts on the other side, ½a. shooting into the lower 7a. lying W. of him, 1a. in Bay furlong shooting aginst the hedge that parts Bay meads, a head ½a. heading Bay furlong and shooting against Ogbourne hedge, ½a. lying higher in the same furlong and shooting against Ogbourne hedge, 1yd. lying higher and shoting against Ogbourne hedge, 1a. heads Littleworth, 1a. at the bushes, 1a. called Stony acre heading a piece on N. side of him, a. at the W. side of Stony acre heading the furlong that shoots up to the bottom, 1 head a. in the middle of the field heading the furlong that heads Stony acre, ½a. lying along by Rabley hedge, in all 15½a. of arable, ½a. of meadow besides the little close where the house stood. To this yardland at Poulton there belongs commons for 50 couples of sheep and a ram, 2 cows and a runner, 2 horses from the time the field is broke to St. Martins day [11 Nov].

There belongs also to the ½ yardlands in the Mildenhall field 30 sheep commons to each, in all 120, commons for 2 beasts and a runner and 2 horse commons to each. In the common field there are 42a. of arable which are called the glebe, belonging to the rectory, which lie thus: 2a. athwart the hill in Rabley field, 2a. in Broadhanger, 3a. by the green way lying by Squire Nourse's hedge, 1a. heading Squire Nourse's piece, 3 x ½a. in Tonely, 1a. more in Tonely called Vicarage acre, 3 x ½a. shooting against Squire Nourse's hedge on E. side of the green way, 7a. on the brow above Shettall bottom, 3 x ½a. in Plumtree bottom, ½a. shooting upon Durnsford lease hedge, 1a. shooting against the brooks side, 4a. in Whiteland, 1 head a. under Cunnylinch in Little Dean bottom, 7a. in the Dean joining to the home close, 1a. the outmost of that furlong 2a. under the Down hedge, 1a. in the Owre under the hithermost hedge, 4a. more in the Owre lying all in one piece.

There belongs to the glebe 1 cow down containing 9a., 1 watermead, 2a. 3yd., at Dean fields 1 ground, 18a., 1 ground adjoining to it, 12a., 1 ground containing 4a., 1 ground, 2a., 1 coppice c. 4a. All tithe of things titheable within the parish and half of the tithe of wool of Puthall [Puttal] farm.[1]

Dues commonly paid are 2d. for every communicant yearly, for every cow and calf 8d., for a fat milch cow 2d., for a weaned calf 2½d., for a dry cow 1½d., for a calf if killed the left shoulder, eggs 2d. for every hen, 3d. for every cock. Poulton mill pays yearly 10s., Werge mill 10s., Durnsford mill and Stitchombe mill each of them 6s. 9d. p. a.

Edward Pococke, rector, Ralph Taber, William Bayly, churchwardens.

1. In Little Bedwyn.

543   n. d. [1783][1] (D1/24/148/7)
Particular of the rectory in the hands of Revd. Richard Pococke, patron and rector.

The dwelling house is a large building of brick and stone tile which with 4 barns, stables, offices, garden and farm yards contain c. 2a. And as the rector resides on the spot the whole is in his own occupation. The premises are kept in good and substantial repair. There are likewise 2 old cottages belonging to the premises. In the churchyard are 18 elm and ash trees many of the same kind on other parts of the glebe.

The glebe lands lie in different parts of the parish; that nearest to the parsonage house is 5 pieces of meadow ground, c. 5a., the next is that which was common field land and has lately been enclosed by the present earl of Ailesbury who after endeavouring to pass an Act for that purpose without the consent of the rector, which scheme failed, at length obtained his acquiescence to the enclosure by the persuasions of his friend Mr. Penruddock who sent the rector word he might have very advantageous terms. On 18 March 1774 the rector met the earl of Ailesbury by appointment at Mr. Penruddock's house, London, on this business and the purport of their meeting was reduced into writing and signed by both parties but before they parted the rector on recollection told the earl he must have the same number of acres allotted him as the lands then belonging to the parsonage should be found to amount to when measured. These conditions were agreed to in the presence of Mr. Penruddock yet notwithstanding this agreement the rector found on receiving an account of his allotment his quantity of acres reduced from 77 to 61 in consequence of which treatment the rector last year had an opportunity of speaking with the earl on the subject and said that he should expect the 16a. he had lost by the enclosure be immediately restored and received only for answer that the rectory had got quantity for quality which the rector thinks a very unfair way of proceeding and in direct contradiction to their former agreement.[2]

Near to the new enclosed land lies a piece of old enclosure containing *c.* 8a. The next part of the glebe is called Dean field and consists of 3 enclosed fields surrounded with rows of wood and 2 small coppices containing *c.* 40a. 15a. of glebe intermixed among the lands of 2 farms called Poulton farms with ½a. of meadow.

The communion table is covered with a green cloth with other proper linen. 2 small, 1 larger plate for the sacrament bread with 2 cups for the wine without any mark. There are in the tower 4 bells.

Richard Pococke, rector, Thomas Neate, Isaac White, churchwardens.

1. The churchwardens were recorded in the bishop's visitation book, Jul 1783. (WSRO D1/50/30)
2. An agreement was made in 1776. (WSRO 9/20/48, 9/20/143/3)

MILSTON rectory

544 n. d. late 16th cent. (D1/24/149/1)
The parsonage has all the tithes of 25 yardlands of arable land, of tenements, 8 little a. of glebe land, 1a. of meadow, and 38 sheep leaze, common for 1 cow, 1 bull, and 1 horse. 2 parts of the tithes of a farm; the third part belonged to Wherwell abbey [*Hants.*],[1] now let by lease from the Prince (sic) to which belongs the tithing of 120a. of corn one year and 60a. another year, 23a. glebe land, the tithes of 5a. meadow, 1 meadow of 1½a. 100 sheep leaze, and the tithes of wool of 400 sheep, all out of the farm. A great hindrance to the parsonage.

1. Later known as the Horrell tithes see **546**.

545 1671 (D1/24/149/2)
Inquisition taken according to the command of the bishop. All kinds of tithes of Milston and Brigmerston with all offerings and other ecclesiastical duties except a portion of tithe at present paid to Mr. John Munday viz. out of the farm flock the tithe of 400 sheep, the first that run at leet[1]. The tithe of a meadow called the Wirgis and of a meadow called the Mill moor with part of Gudgeon mead and also of 3 meadows adjoining it on E. The tithe of 176a. in the 2 summerfields, 23a. of glebe in the 2 summerfields. 1 meadow, *c.* 1a. 100 sheep leaze in the common fields and downs. Rectorial glebe: 8a. of arable ground with 1a. at the downs hedged in and also a mead adjoining the churchyard. 38 sheep leazes. A mansion house barn, stable yard and garden. 1 cow leaze in the common field and a horse leaze for an unknown number. 13s. 4d. p. a. for a mill.

Lancelot Addison, rector, Leonard Munday, Leonard Lewis, churchwardens.

1. Leet meaning letting go, see also **857** footnote 1.

546 1705 (D1/24/149/3)
Terrier and inquisition according to the command of the bishop.

All tithes of Milston and Brigmerston of all grounds common and enclosed with all offerings duties and customs except on a portion paid at present to madam Coleman. 8a. of arable. 1a. of ground upon the downs to be hedged from the common always which is mentioned in a terrier now in the registry [court] but which ground through the neglect of the late incumbent or his tenants is now thrown open and common but which is now to be enclosed again at the pleasure of the present rector. 1a. meadow adjoining the churchyard. The herbage of the churchyard with the walnut tree and all other trees in or belonging to the fence or rails and all hedges, trees and plantations, only the mounds next to the street are made and repaired by the respective parishioners. 38 sheep leazes.

A mansion house, barn, stable, yard and garden adjoining the house enclosed with a mudwall. A pretty large piece of building that stood joining the S. E. end of the house and fronted to the street and extended c. 40ft. to a pond belong to the parsonage yard, which building is necessary for the convenience of the rectory but was taken down in the late incumbent Dr. Addison's time and if it is ever set up again this is the responsibility of his executor.

A cow leaze and a runner or bullock in the common fields and an unknown number of horses. 13s. 4d. or 1 mark due from Mr. Pinkneye's mill to be paid each Easter Monday and is gathered with the Easter Book.

Tithes of apples, pears, plums and all other kinds of fruit with the tithe of all sorts of corn and grain and grass or herbage arising out of all common, enclosed lands or downs pertaining to the manor of Milston and Brigmerston except the aforsaid impropriation. Tithe of the lord of the manor's pigeonhouse or dovehouse.

Easter offerings· for every cow 2d. and for every calf 4d. that shall become and fall during the year and for every thorough white cow 2d.; for Mr. Hyde's farm 1s. 4d. for his garden and eggs 11d.; for John Mundy's lease and copyhold 8d. for his garden and eggs 5d.; for farmer Lawes of Milston his living 6d. for his garden and eggs 5d.; for the living that is now the wid. Maton of Milston 6d. for her garden and eggs 5d.; for Mr. Pinkneye's freehold garden and eggs 6d.; for Thomas Mundy's leasehold 4d., for his garden and eggs 2d.; for wid. Collier of Brigmerston her living 8d. her garden and eggs 2d.; for the garden of Collier's that was Page's 1d.; for wid. Dorothy Lawes 4d. garden and eggs 2d.; for John Lawes of Brigmerston 6d. and for garden and eggs 2d.; for wid. Hooper's copyhold 6d., garden and eggs 2d.; wid. Anne Lawes 2d. garden and eggs 2d.; wid. Haydon's copyhold 6d. garden and eggs 2d.; wid. Maton's living in Brigmerston oblation money, garden and eggs all 6d.

Those gardens and houses lately built and enclosed which have been excused by the incumbent from payment of Easter dues and tithes: William Hillier; William Castlemane; Edward Biddlecombe's leasehold house and garden lately purchased of the lord of the manor; the house and garden belonging to the mill; wid. Phillips, Phillip Phillips; Thomas Smith; house and garden belonging to the living of Milston called Thorntons; house and garden of wid. Wills' leasehold in Milston; Thomas Peck's house and garden formerly John Cooper's; John Edmunds leasehold; a garden belonging to a living called Sopps in Milston now farmer Lawes'; Richard Patne's leasehold lately purchase of the lord of the manor; all of which houses and gardens are liable to pay the oblations and tithes.

For all young pigs that fall during the year 1 out of every 7 belongs to the rectory; in case fewer fall in one year they are added to the following year or else valued and the tithe paid in money. The tithe pig is paid at Easter. Tithe lambs due on all lambs from sheep bred in Milston and Brigmerston and half tithe due on lambs from sheep wintered outside of the parish, to be paid in money or kind. The tithe lambs if weaned are to be taken up each St. Mark's day [25 Apr] before all who have bred lambs in the parish be they many or few who are to render a just account of them to minister in order that they may be tithed unless they agree to pay in money. Any lambs which fall late and are not weaned by St. Marks day those are to remain with the owners' ewes until ready to be tithed.

Those lands lying in the common field belonging to the rectory to have the tithe and also of those appertaining to the impropriator or said portion of tithe called Horrell,[1] now Mrs. Ann Coleman's as now viewed in the field by the assent of Mrs. Coleman's tenant who rents that portion of the tithes, by those who have lately taken up the rent of the tithes of the parsonage and by the churchwardens. Horrell tithe: The land on which this is due lie in 2 narrow adjoining fields; in the narrow field lying next to Mr. Duke's field 5 reported a. belonging to Thomas Mundy's living leasehold at Milston Townsend; 1a. of the wid. Phillips; 2a. of the wid. Miller; half a piece of Thomas Mundy's leasehold being 5a., the tithe of the other half belongs to the rectory; 5a. of John Mundy's leasehold; 5 reported a. of Mr. Pinckney; 50 reputed a. called Mr. Hyde's farm field; half a piece of ground called the wid. Maton's Ten acres, formerly Bachelors, the tithes of the other half lie alongside Mr. Duke's field; 1 reputed a. of John Edmonds alias Holloway lie upon the hill between a 2a. piece of Horrell glebe[1] and the said wid. Maton's Ten acres; 12a. called Thorntons upon the hill belonging to farmer Lawes and the wid. Maton; 10a. [. . .] the field of farmer Lawes upon the hill being 2 furlongs long.

The tithe of all other a. in the Narrow field next Mr. Duke's field belong to the Rectory namely: 2 separate a. of Horrell glebe; 3a. of the wid. Maton formerly Sopp's; 2½a. of Thomas Mundy's leasehold formerly Heath's; 2a. of the wid. Maton formerly Sopp's which have been encroached away from the parsonage since the last terrier; 3½a. and 2a. of Horrell glebe; 2a. of Horrell glebe lying between the farm field ground; 5a. of wid. Maton's Ten a. formerly Bachelor's being the lower part of the piece; 2½a. Thomas Mundy's leasehold being half of the leasehold (the other referred to in the Horrell tithe section); 20a. of Thomas Mundy's leasehold lying in 2 pieces on the hill, 18a. called Thorntons now the wid. Maton's and farmer Lawes; 1a. of the wid. Collier formerly Pages; 1a. of Thomas Mundy; 1a. of John Edmonds; all which arable grounds are not a. by measure or the lug but reputed a. and total 163a. in the Narrow field next Mr. Dukes field of which 98½a. are Horrell tithes and 65 are Rectory tithes:

In the Narrow field lying close to the former: Horrell tithes: 5a. of Thomas Mundy's leasehold at Townsend in 2 pieces and parted by 1a. of Horrell glebe; 2½a. of Thomas Mundy; 21a. of Thorntons and 10a. called Thorntons both belonging to farmer Lawes and the wid. Maton; 10a. of Thomas Mundy's leasehold; 1a. of Collier's formerly Page's; 1a. of John Edmonds; 10a. of the wid. Maton's formerly Bachelors; Tithes of all other a. in the field belong to the rectory: 1a. of Horrell glebe at Townsend between the said 5a. of Thomas Mundy;

1a. of the wid. Phillips; the wid. Miller's 2a.; 2a. of the wid. Maton called Copps; 3½a. and 6½a. of Horrell glebe; 10a. of farmer Lawes upon the hill next to Mr. Hyde's farm High field which 10a. lie at the end of the Narrow field. Next to this end begins the High field with the said farm High field; this Narrow field comprises 103a. in the common field of which the tithe of 77½a. belongs to the Horrell and 25½a. to the rectory.

The Horrell enjoys the tithe of 400 sheep's wool out of the farm flock that first run at leet.[2] 22a. of Horrell glebe in both narrow fields belongs to the rectory: lands in the second narrow field of which the tithe belong to the rectory *c.* 1a. of meadow of Horrell glebe: 100 sheep leaze on the common fields or downs, the tithe such sheep bred and pastured in any year or past year or lambs bred upon the leaze in the same manner of all sheep or lambs within the manor of Milston and Brigmerston according to the quantity of breeding and the time of abiding and pasturing be it much or little. Tithes belonging to the Horrell of 3a. of the farm mead called Gudgeon mead lying between the river on S. E. and the drowning carriage on N. W. and the part of the mead reaching W. to a little sluice or drawing and a remarkable fall in the ground which is the mark that time out of mind parted the Parsonage and Horrell tithes; a meadow of farmer Lawes formerly Sopps adjoining the said E. part of Gudgeon mead and farmer Lawes adjoining mead called Poynters mead; Poynters mead next adjoining and now John Mundy's which is also unbounded and thrown open into another large mead of John Mundy; that part of the last Poynter's mead for which the tithes belong to the Horrell reaches as far as a little meadow of Mr. Pinckney's freehold called the Paddock; the rest is tithed by the rectory; tithes of a meadow called the Wirgo of John Mundy and a meadow called the Mill moor of Mr. Pinckney; tithe of 98½a. (arable) in the narrow field next to Mr. Duke's field and 77½a. in the other narrow field as described above. The total of land in both narrow fields of which the tithe belongs to the Horrell is 176a. according to a terrier in court made in the late rector's time.[3] All other times belong to the rectory.

William Mundy, rector, John Mundy, John Maton, churchwardens, Richard Rattue, William Castleman, inhabitants, present at the reviewing and adjusting of the parsonage and Horrell rights.

1.　Those tithes of part of the demesne of Milston and Brigmerston held by Wherwell abbey were known as Horrell. They passed into the hands of the lord of the manor. VCH. vol. 15 p. 140.
2.　See **544** footnote 1.
3.　See **545**.

MILTON LILBORNE vicarage

547　　12 Oct 1608 (D1/150/1)
Anthony Whitehart, born in Milton, yeoman, about 99 years of age, testifies that there is a mansion house, a barn, and backside, 2 gardens, an orchard, and the churchyard; 15a. 1yd. of arable land; a little meadow ground of *c.* 1a;[1] and that

the vicars have ever claimed 100 sheep leaze in the heath and common fields; and they have allowance for 6 rother [rudder] beasts on the down. All tithes of the 3 yardlands of the manor of Milton Abbots with all the tenements belonging to it. He has known to be paid a yearly rent of 46s. 8d. allowanced out of the rent of the rectory to the vicar. Another pension of 3 qtr. of corn (a qtr. of wheat, a qtr. of barley, and a qtr. of oats) is yearly paid out of the rectory to the vicar.[2] All tithes of a yardland held by George Banckes with the tenements belonging to it, of ¼ yardland which Geoffrey Benger holds, and of a ½ yardland which Robert Banckes holds. Tithe corn, hay, wool, lambs, and pigs, belong to the rectory, and all other tithes as cow white, calves, etc., belong to the vicarage. He has known to be paid to the vicar tithe hay, cow white, calves, and all other tithes save corn, wool, lambs and pigs which always belong to the rectory, out of from the hamlets of Fifield, Milkhouse Water [Milcot], Clench and Bals.

Henry Wheler alias Franklin,[3] born in Milton, yeoman, being 90 years of age vows that all Anthony Whitehart testified to be true, save except that he doubts whether the vicars have had the tithes of pigs out of the rectory or cows. He has heard the rother beasts were formerly called Benbowes. Richard Winter, born in Milton, yeoman, being 60 years old and above testifies as Henry Wheeler does.

John Cary, born in Milton, yeoman, being about 55 years old, affirms that his grandfather, Robert Cary, had a lease from the abbot of Cirencester of the manor and rectory of Milton Abbots, which came afterwards to John Cary and his brother Richard, and that William Brisley,[4] then vicar, had received all tithes out of the manor, and tenements there. He avows that there was paid yearly to the vicar out of the rent of the abbot, and afterwards of the Queen, 46s. 8d. A qtr. of wheat was paid yearly at Michaelmas, [29 Sep] and a qtr. of barley and a qtr. of oats at the Annunciation B.V. M. [25 Mar],[5] and all other things specified by Anthony Whitehart he avows to be true.

Anne Brisley wid. of William Brisley, late vicar of Milton, dwelling in the vicarage for 30 years testifies that there is 1 mansion house, 1 barn, 2 gardens, 1 orchard, and the churchyard, 1 little several ground[6] of c. 1a., and that there belongs to the vicar also 15a. 1yd. of arable land and 100 sheep leaze in the heath and common fields, and 6 rother beasts leaze on the down. Her husband had all tithes out of the manor or glebe land of Milton Abbots of 3 yardlands and of all the tenements there. [Then as Anthony Whiteheart's evidence.]

Thomas Hamlin, born in Fifield in the parish of Milton, being over 80 years old and Geoffrey Wyot, born in Clench in the parish of Milton, being over 60 years old, affirm that the tithe hay, cow white, calves, and all other tithes of Fifield and Clench to be due to the vicar except corn, wool, lambs and pigs which were in all his time paid to the parson. Anthony Whitehart, Henry Wheeler alias Franklyn, Richard Winter, John Carie, Thomas Hamlin and Geoffrey Wyat all testify that there is 1a. land lying in Staplehurst which always belonged to the church, but of late years has been detained from the church. They have heard George Banckes tell that he knows where it lies, whom they cannot persuade to be examined.

These are the true examinations of every party set down as they delivered their minds. By me George Pynch, vicar, Anthony Whitehart junior, Mark Hamlin [X], churchwardens, Thomas Carie, John Mortimer [X], assistants.

1. c. ½a. in **548**.
2. The rest of Anthony Whitehart's testimony omitted in **548**.
3. Henry Wheeler alias Franklyn's testimony in **548** merely endorses that of Anthony Whitehart with no added information.
4. Vicar between 1564–1595.
5. Omitted in **548**.
6. 5 meadows in **548**.

548   4 Oct 1671 (D1/24/150/2)
*Copy of **547** with amendments in footnotes.* Francis Peckstone, vicar, John Whitehart, Eudas Stagg, wardens, Francis Peckstone, jun., Steven Baning, sidesmen. *Names in the same hand*

549   4 Nov 1704 (D1/24/150/3)
Terrier of the vicarage of Milton Abbotts and Milton Lilborne. The vicarage house consisting of a hall, a kitchen, 3 chambers, a buttery, a well house, a backside, 2 garden plots adjoining the house, part walled consisting of c. 1a.

The herbage of the churchyard and a platt of meadow, c ½a. Pasture in the commonable places for 120 sheep and pasture for 6 cows upon the downs. 18a. of arable land. All tithes arising out of the impropriate rectory of Milton Abbotts and Milton Lilborne now in the possession of John Michell gent.

1qtr. of barley, 1qtr. of oats to be paid yearly by the impropriator on the Ladyday [25 Mar] and 1qtr. of wheat at Michaelmas [29 Sep]. £2 to be paid by the impropriator to the vicar in equal portions on the same feast day. All tithes arising out of 3 tenements now in the possession of John Michell gent., Henry Fruen and William Cooper. All the tithe of hay arising out of the hamlets of Fifield and Clench. All small tithes throughout the parish. All of which tithes lands and payments are valued at £40 p. a.

Joseph Wall, vicar, E. Hungerford, John Batt [X], churchwardens.

550   14 Jul 1783 (D1/24/150/4)
A vicarage house timber pannelled with lath and plaster and covered with thatch containing a parlour with a boarded floor, wainscotted chair-high; 2 other bedchambers and 2 garrets not ceiled and 2 little cellars. A stable and woodhouse adjoining each other measuring c. 18ft. x c. 14ft., built with timber and flakes and covered with thatch.

A little garden before the house and a paddock behind it and churchyard adjoining containing in the whole c. 1a., bounded N. and W. by lands of John Richmond Webb esq., on S. by an orchard and garden in the tenure of John Batt and Stephen Holding, on E. by Milton Street and fenced partly with a mudwall and partly with hedges. A walnut tree, a maiden ash tree and 6 small maiden elms are standing in the paddock and a yew tree in the churchyard all not exceeding the value of £5.

A close of arable land called Wall lands, 7a., bounded on N. and E. by lands occupied by William Naish, W. by lands belonging to Fifield farm, S. by land of John Smith. A close of arable called Walls Croft, between 5 and 6a. bounded N. partly by land of William Naish and partly land of Mr. John Stevens, W. by land of William Naish, E. land belonging to Froxfield almshouse, S. by the highway between Milton and Easton.

It is said there are 4 more a. of arable land belonging to the vicarage but if so they are intermixed with lands of Philip Pulse esq., and having been for a great number of years occupied with these lands they cannot now be described with any degree of accuracy.

Vicarial tithes and Easter offerings from the whole parish with tithe hay from the tithings of Fifield and Clench. A pecuniary stipend of *c.* £6 13s. 4d. paid to the vicarage out of the impropriate rectory and other small payments are said to be due but for a great many years have been let or compounded with the said stipend to the owner of the rectory for the rent of £20 p. a. for the whole.

There is a church clock, 3 bells (one of them cracked), a silver chalice or cup (weight not marked), a pewter flagon, a table cloth for the communion table, 2 napkins, a bible and 2 common prayer books, a pulpit cloth, cushion and linen surplice.

The owner of the rectory repairs the chancel, and the parishioners repair the church and churchyard fence. The clerk's wages are 4d. for every yardland in the parish and 4d. for every inhabited house; he is appointed by the vicar for the time being.

John Swain, vicar, Edward Batt, churchwarden, William Jay, James Warwick, John Moody, John Cannings, William Liddiard, John Batt.

MINETY vicarage [and parsonage from 553]

551   1608 (D1/24/151/1)
A little close of *c.* 2a., and the churchyard adjoining, with the common field on one side, and the parsonage, and the parson's glebe land on the others. The vicar has all tithes except corn and hay.

Richard Munden, churchwarden.

552   15 Dec 1671 (D1/24/151/2)
The vicarage house with a small garden, an orchard and a little stable. The churchyard with appurtenances except that part which the impropriator has made several to enlarge his rick barton. A little paddock[1] and close adjoining the vicarage house, *c.* 1a. A ground lying in Gloucestershire[2] called Flis-Streech, 4a.[3]

Richard Browne, vicar, Samuel Pittman, William Coole, churchwardens. *Names in the same hand*

1. The paddock is omitted in **553** but the acreage is the same.
2. Part of Minety was an outlyer of Gloucestershire until 1844.
3. 5a. in **553**.

553   4 Dec 1677 (D1/24/151/3)
Parsonage. The parsonage house with barn stable garden and orchard. 2 paddocks adjoining the parsonage house, *c.* 2a., with that which was taken out of the churchyard to enlarge it. 3 closes[1] adjoining the parsonage house, *c.* 16a. The

Horse-pool ground, c. 10a.² A common ground, c. 3a.² The Parsonage piece, c. 4a.² The Parsonage Ham c. 3a.² A Ham in the Lammas mead laid out for the tithe of it, c. 3a. Tenements: A tenement called Reads living, c. 6a. 6 other small tenements in all c. 3a.

   Vicarage. As *551 with amendments in footnotes.*
   Richard Browne, vicar, John Frankham, Nicholas Taylor, churchwardens. *Names in the same hand*

1. Now put into 2 closes in **555**.
2. Described as in Gloucestershire in **554** where all other parsonage property and land is described as in Wiltshire.

554   7 Dec 1683 (D1/24/151/4)
Parsonage as 553 with amendments in footnotes.
   Vicarage: *House and churchyard as in 553;* The little paddock and close¹ c. 1a. bounded E. Parsonage close and part of the churchyard, S. the vicarage orchard and part of the churchyard, N. W. the highway² all in Wilts. A ground in Gloucestershire called Flistrick,³ 2a. bounded E. by a common ground now owned by John Norgrove, S. the highway called Flistrick lane, W. Flistrick ground now owned by Robert Taylor, N. Great Cowleaze owned by John Norgrove.
   Godfrey Jenkinson, vicar, John Norgrove [X], George Barrett, churchwardens.

1. The close described as a younger orchard in **555**.
2. N. W. by the common in **555**.
3. Now divided into 2 grounds in **555** bounded in N. ground of George Pitt, esq., W. ground of Mr. Waller, S. road to Tetbury.

555   15 Dec 1704 (D1/24/151/5)
As 554 with amendments in footnotes. Vicarage. The Franktenement or freehold of the church.
   Godfrey Jenkinson, vicar, Thomas Browne, William Parson, churchwardens. George Price, Joseph Nott, Henry Rundel, John Francome, Robert Browne, Henry Welling, John Mason.

NETHERAVON rectory and vicarage

556   24 Mar 1614 (D5/10/2/1)
The Parsonage: The parsonage house, a kitchen adjoining, 2 barns, 2 stables, 1 fodder house, 1 orchard and garden.
   Tenements: 1 cottage in Peasehayes with a garden, 2 cottages at Botchers ditch with 2 backsides and 2 gardens. A barn standing in Tuckers close in Chisenbury.
   Glebe land called Four yardlands: Meadow; Reignolds, 2a.; Peasehayes, 1½a.; Parsonage mead, 5a.; a close of pasture called Withey bed, ½a.; a close adjoining the parsonage barn; a plot of meadow in Corse mead, 3r.; a plot of meadow in S. mead, 1a. Arable land in Outlands fields: In the S. Summerfield; in the furlong called Tothill, 5a.; in Graylands, 9a.; In the S. Homefield; In Long Falshill, 1a.; in

the Barn, 6a.; at Kentes bush, 2a.; in Bellringers, 2a.; in Buttock furlong, 1a.; in Grinknall, 1a. In the Middle Summerfield; In Wexslade, 6a.; in Handripp, 18a.; in Handripp bottom, 4a.; in the furlong above Wadden, 3a. In the Middle Homefield; In Little Falshill, 3a.; In Little Wadden, 1a.; in Crucktaile, 1a.; in Wadden, 2a.; in Great Ditch, 4a.; in Little Ditch, 3a.; in Red lands, 6a. 3r.; in Millballs, 1a.; in Culverland, 3r. In the N. Summerfield: in N. Brache, 6a.; in Newbroke land, 4a.; in Brandier, 9a.; in the furlong shooting upon Dicks head a., 1a.; in Trowbridge furlong, 1a.; in the furlong shooting upon Fifields side, 3r.; in the furlong shooting upon Trowbridge furlong, 2a.: In the Lower Summerfield, 3a. In the N. Home field; in Lanchard furlong, 2a.; in Great Widden, 2a.; in Great Ridge, 2a., in Little Ridge, 1a.; in Whipp Clive, 1a.; at Sladd, ½a. and 1a.; in the furlong against Down, 4a.

Common of pasture for 200 sheep, 8 horses, 12 rother beasts and 36 pigs unto the same 4 yardlands.

Tithes: Tithe of the mill in Netheravon. Tithe corn and grain in Netheravon and Chisenbury, excepting of the above glebe land. Tithe wool and lamb of the farm and farm lease of Chisenbury called Brunyngs farm. All other tithes.

2 parts of 3 of tithe wool and lambs of the farm of Mr. Wardour, the Farm of Mr. Bruen, 4 ½ yardlands of Mr. Bridges, 4 ½ yardlands of John Sutton, and the yardland of Thomas Gyne all in Englands side.

Tithe hay of all common meadows in Netheravon and Chisenbury except the above 4 yardlands of glebe. Tithe hay of the enclosed meadows called S. meadows of 2 meadow called Mills Meads, of all the meadows belonging to the yardlands called Newtons and of 2 closes called Court closes. 2 parts of 3 of all privy tithes of the farm of Mr. Wardour and the farm of Mr. Bruen gent, and of the 4½ yardlands of Mr. Bridges and the 4½ yardlands of John Sutton; exception oblations only.

Vicarage: The vicarage house with a barn, stable orchard and garden adjoining. A meadow called the Vicars close, 3r., lying by the above-named meadow called Reynolds with passage through Reynolds to it.

All manner of tithes from the parsonage glebe land. Tithe wool and lambs with all privy tithes upon Outlands side, upon a yardland of William earl of Bath, upon 2 yardlands of Sir Thomas Flemying, upon 1 yardland of Richard Legg, upon 2 yardlands occupied by Elizabeth Hearne wid. and a cottage occupied by Agnes Hearne wid., all lying in Englands side. Third part of tithe wool and lambs upon the abovenamed cottage, occupied by Henry Lanchard senior, and all the privy tithes belonging to it. Third part of tithe wool and lambs and privy tithes, payable upon the abovenamed farms of Mr. Wardour and Mr. Bruen upon the 4½ yardlands of Mr. Bridges, 4½ yardlands of John Sutton and the yardland of Thomas Gyne all lying in Englands side.

Tithe hay of the orchard of Mr. Bruen's farm in Englands side and of all grounds in Netheravon and Chisenbury except all the closes belonging to the farm of Chisenbury and the 2 closes called Court closes. All manner of tithes coming out excepting the tithes of the farm of Chisenbury, all tithe corn and grain payable out of Chisenbury and the third part of tithe wool and lambs issuing out of the 9 yardlands held by Robert Goodale in Chisenbury which said third part is paid to the vicar of Upavon.

Richard Harper [X], John Hearne [X], churchwardens, Edmund Rumsey [X], Richard Edryg, John Hearne senior, John Daves.

NETTLETON rectory

557   n. d. [1605][1] (D1/24/152/1)
We have belonging to our parsonage house a sufficient dwelling house, with 2 barns, and other necessary houses with a large court; 1 ground on the N. of the parsonage house, *c.* 1a.; 1 little garden; the herbage of the churchyard; 8 beast leaze in our common marsh for the summer time; finding always a sufficient bull for the parish. We have no glebe land but as above, together with the tithes.

Thomas Saintsbery, Thomas Deverill, churchwardens; William Nychols, Thomas Neate, sidesmen *Names in the same hand*

1.   Endorsed: Terriers exhibited 1605.

558   27 Oct 1671 (D1/24/152/2)
The dwelling house, 2 corn barns, a stable, a hay house, a yard, a little close and 2 gardens, the whole containing *c.* 2a., all lying together square, bounded S. churchyard, W. Sainsburys close, N. Notts close and Longs close, E. with the street. Pasture for 8 beasts, a bull during the summer in 2 grounds called the East marsh and the West marsh, the incumbent paying a yearly rent of 12s. 11d. to the lord of the manor. All tithes of the whole parish.

John Fabian, rector, William Wimbowe, John Kinton, churchwardens, George Alborne, Nicholas Beaker, sidesmen.

559   16 Nov 1704 (D1/24/152/3)
A parsonage house, garden and orchard. A rick barton and backside all containing *c.* 1a. A great barn a straw house and a hayhouse all in tenantable repair. A stable and a little barn demolished by the late High wind[1] and not yet repaired. 8 cowleazes and a bulls leaze in the common marshes.

Joseph Reckards, rector, Nicholas Beakar, John Hollis, churchwardens.

1.   The storm of Nov 1703 which affected much of the West Country.

560   n. d. [1783][1] (D1/24/152/4)
The parsonage house is built with stone covered with tile. It consists of 6 rooms above, 1 room is floored with sycamore and papered and ceiled, another is floored with deal papered and ceiled, another is floored with oak, ceiled but not papered, another is floored with oak, papered and ceiled. Rooms below: a parlour papered, a kitchen, a brewhouse, a hall, 2 pantries, a cellar. Outhouses; 2 barns, both are built with stone and covered with thatch, one is 25yd. long and 9yd. wide, the other is 15yd. long and 6½yd. wide. 2 stables, one 8yd. long 5yd. wide, the other 4yd. long 3½yd. wide.

A great garden, ½a.; a small garden, *c.* 2yd. long, 13yd. wide; another little ground, 14yd. long, 9yd. wide; a small spot of ground called the Drying yard,

21yd. long, 21yd. wide; the rick barton, 20yd. long, 13yd. wide; a court before the house, 17½yd. long, 8yd. wide; the yard before the little barn, 18½yd. long, 13yd. wide; the farmyard, 33yd. long, 21yd. wide.

Trees in the churchyard; a sycamore value 8s., a chestnut value 4s., 4 small elms value 1s. each. No other lands belong to the parsonage. 8 beast leazes commonly let at 10s. each. The gardens yards and outlets are fenced with walls.

Furniture of the church: A blue pulpit cloth, 5 bells, the communion plate is silver; a flagon, a chalice, a cup and 2 salvers. The parish is charged with the repair of the edifices and churchyard fence. The clerks wage, 20s., is paid by the parish. The clerk is appointed by the rector.

Daniel Mills, rector, Joseph Hall, James Hatherell, churchwardens, Zachariah Huggins.

1. The churchwardens were recorded in the bishop's visitation book, Jul 1783. (WSRO D1/50/30))

LONG NEWNTON rectory

561   13 Oct 1608 (D1/24/153/1)
N. field: 2a. lying towards the middle of the field on Glosslade furlong butting N. and S.; 1a. more lying on Bocke furlong butting E. and W.; 1a. lying on the Long headland furlong, shooting E. and W.; 1a. at the end of the last a., shooting also E. and W., lying on Vouldowne furlong; 1 head a. on the same furlong shooting E. and W. Total 5½a.

S. field: 2a. butting on the highway and the parsonage orchard, shooting E. and W.; ½a. lying under the hanging of a hill near the Grandge slade shooting E. and W. Total 2½a. The leaze of c. 7a. in the S. field, the highway towards Tetbury on the S., the lord's leaze on the W., and on the N. leaze beloning to a farm called Five acres, and leaze of Robert Weeks called Tedbury leaze on the E.

Richard Escot gent., Robert Weeks, churchwardens, Thomas Weeks, Samuel Myllard, sidesmen. *Names in the same hand*

562   1671 (D1/24/153/2)
A house and garden 2 barns and a stable. A piece of ground called Stars furlong, 3a., lying near the parsonage house and adjoining Trewmans close. Tedbury ground, 7a., lying near the way from Newnton to Tetbury. 5½a. in the N. field. The tithes of between 600 to 700a. of arable and 100a. and upwards of pasture are detained from our minister by Sir Giles Estcourt and those to whom he has let leases of it but by what right we know not. The tithe of all the rest of the parish is paid to our minister.

Walter Davis, minister, Giles Saunders, John Ridley, churchwardens.

563 1704 (D1/24/153/3)
The parsonage house with 2 barns, 1 stable, 1 barton, 1 garden with an orchard adjoining.

A parcel of ground called Stares furlong, 4a. 2 grounds lying near Tetbury called the Parsons leazes, 10a. 5½a. of arable land dispersed in several places in the Upper field. All lands in the parish pay Easter dues and small and privy tithes to the rector, but some particular lands are exempted from paying corn and hay tithe to the rector.

John Giles, rector, Benjamin Harding.

564   n. d. late 18th cent.[1] (D1/24/153/4)
The parsonage house is built of stone and covered with tiles, it consists of 13 rooms. The outhouses are 2 stables and a brewhouse. The glebe consists of 14a. all enclosed with hedges and in 3 separate enclosures of 3a., 4a. and 7a.

The parishioners are charged with the repairs of the churchyard walls. The clerk's wages are by custom 25s. p. a. paid by the parish. He is appointed by the clergyman.

Edward Estcourt, LL. D., rector.

1.   Edward Estcourt was rector between 1775-1803.

NORTH NEWNTON vicarage and Hilcott

565   14 Feb 1705 (D1/24/154)
A true and perfect terrier of all glebe lands and dues as far as we know or have been creditably informed. The churchyard, and a piece of ground of c. ½a. lying between a tenement and ground of Thomas Alexander's on the E., and a tenement and ground of Richard Higgins on the W.; the E. side, and N. and S. ends of it to be bounded by the vicar, and the W. side by Richard Higgins; the churchyard to be bounded by the parishioners. All tithe wool, lambs, gardens, orchards, eggs, calves, cow white, pigeons, pigs, geese, mill composition at 6s. 8d. p. a. and all other tithes except corn and hay which belong to the impropriator. 1 ridge of wheat to be sown yearly in the fields of Cuttenham [Cutnam] farm by the owner for the use of the vicar to the value of 20s. pa. £10 p. a. given to the vicarage by the late earl of Pembroke to be paid by the impropriator.

Luke Sympson, vicar, Thomas Alexander, John Lavington, churchwardens, Richard Green gent., Edward Alexander, Richard Higgons.

SOUTH NEWTON vicarage

566   9 Jun 1609 (D1/24/155/1)
With the hamlets of Stoford, Little Wishford, Chilhampton, Burdens Ball, Ugford St. Giles.

A small thatched dwelling house with a hall, 2 other under rooms, 3 lofts, a kitchen, a hayhouse. Implements in the hall: a bench with locks and keys for the doors. A barton, a garden, a hopyard, c. ¼a., with the herbage of the churchyard, c. ¼a. All tithe hay of all the marshes, home closes and meadow plots named below. All tithe wool and lambs and all other small tithes according to the custom of the parish, i. e. 2d. for every communicant at Easter; 10d. for every marriage; 6d. for every certificate of banns; 6d. for every child christened; 1d. for every customed garden; 2d. for every milch cow; the tenth penny for all foreign agistment [forrayne injoycement] beasts;[1] 16s. from the mill for all tithes arising out of the grist mill, tucking mill, hay grounds and orchard. Custom of the manner of paying tithes of lambs, calves and pigs: of 4 lambs and under ½d. each; of 5 lambs ½d. a lamb; of 6 lambs 3d.; of 7 lambs a tithe lamb allowing back 1½d.; of 8 lambs a tithe lamb paying back 1d.; of 9 lambs a tithe lamb paying ½d.; of 10 lambs a tithe lamb. The like of pigs. For every calf weaned ½d.; for every calf killed the left shoulder; for every calf sold the tenth penny unless there fall out a tithe within the year.[2]

Certain grounds which are usually cut for hay with tithe to the vicar: in S. Newton a close belonging to a bargain called Forest lying from the W. end of the house to the river; a plot called Porters ham; the home close of Richard Daniell which has been accustomed for grazing cattle; a little mead plot of Henry Blake at the E. end of Water acre; Sturton ham belonging to John Plenty; wid. Carpenter's Rey mead close, a plot of ground lying in the farmers Rey mead at the W. end of wid. Carpenter's Rey mead close; 2 meadow plots of John Percye one on the W. side of the mill, the other on the E. side; all the home closes which have been ever accustomed for grazing cattle and not known to pay tithe to the parson, if they shall be cut for hay, ought to pay tithe to the vicar. In Chilhampton the vicar has all the tithes of hay except the common meadow and Portnams. In Burdens Ball all the tithes of hay of the several grounds belonging to the farm, and tithes of 2 plots of ground belonging to a tenement of Mr. Thomas Eyre. In Stoford a close called Culver close, tithe hay to the vicar, and all the dry grounds about the dwelling houses have been accustomed for the grazing of cattle. In Little Wishford Henry Blake his home close and Shailes Island tithe hay to the vicar, also all Robert Sedgewick's mead grounds, marsh grounds and dry grounds in Little Wishford. Moreover these grounds following belonging to Mr. Huzy his farm tithe hay to the vicar: Short hams, Hillmead, and ½a. of mead ground lying between Hillmead and Robert Sedgweeke his mead ground. Also oxen lease with as the dry grounds belonging to the farm which have ever been accustomed for grazing cattle and not known to tithe to the parson ought to tithe hay to the vicar. In Ugford St. Giles John Hayter's Mill ham and 2 other little mead plots tithe hay to the vicar. Also John Whithart his W. close has sometimes been ploughed up and sowed with oats and other grain and paid tithe thereof to the vicar, sometimes it has been cut for hay and paid tithe to the vicar; likewise all the dry grounds which have been ever accustomed for grazing cattle if they shall be ploughed up for corn or cut for hay ought to pay tithe to the vicar.

Thomas Good, vicar; John Percy, Richard Staples, churchwardens, John Plenty new churchwarden.

1. Animals born or weaned outside the parish but which feed on herbage within it; barren not foreign in 1705, probably a mistake.
2. Unless a tenth calf is born.

567   n. d. mid. 17th cent.[1] (D1/24/155/2)
Copy of 566. Leonard Dickenson, vicar, Henry Blake, Robert Lawes, churchwardens.

1.   Leonard Dickenson was vicar between 1630–1663.

568   Not used.

569   15 Jan 1705 (D1/24/155/3)
Copy of 566. Taken out of the old terrier and only varied but where customs and some things have changed since. S. Newton: All the marshes, home closes, meadow plots are to pay tithe hay to the vicar excepting Rye mead and Water acre. The vicarage we reckon is worth £45 p. a.
    Giles Compton, vicar, Robert Horne, Samuel Francis [X], churchwardens.

NEWTON TONY rectory

570   29 Jun 1605 (D1/24/156/1)
An enclosure adjoining the parsonage house and barton of *c*. 3r., half of which was formerly an orchard and has fruit trees growing in it. A garden plot lying between the parsonage house E. and a malthouse belonging to the parsonage W., and paled in on the N. and S. A parcel of meadow in the common meadow of the said town, *c*. ½a., having on the E. a parcel of the same meadow held by Thomas Lavington, and on the W. another parcel held by William Lavington, bounding N. and S. on the arable fields of the town.
    29½ ridges of arable land in the common fields of the town, every ridge in common account going for an acre, as follows: 7½ ridges lie in a field called the Churchfield; a half now enclosed by the consent of the inhabitants, during the time of the present incumbent, butting W. on this enclosure, E. on 2a. arable, part of the glebe, N. adjoining a half of William Lavington, S. on an a. of David Drake; 3a. bounding W. on the last half, E. on 1a. of Peter Judd, S. adjoining 1a. of Peter Judd, N. to 3 x ½a. of Thomas Kent; 2a. bounding E. on 3a. of Christopher Osgood, W. on an a. of Henry Wood, butting N. on an a. of Richard Gauntlet, S. partly on a foreacre of Henry Wood, partly running further with a tongue and becoming headland to several [diverse] acres underneath it, and at last butting on the land of Christopher Osgood; 2a. having E. 3a. of Thomas Kent, W. 4a. of Nicholas Mortimer, butting S. on a foreacre of Thomas Kent, N. on 3a. of Nicholas Mortimer.
    2 ridges in Longdean field, lying E. towards the down, W. being foreland to the furlong adjoining, butting S. on 3a. of Richard Gauntlet, Henry Wood, and Christopher Osgood, shooting N. towards the N. drove.
    4 ridges in Ballange field; 2a. lie near Milborrow, having on the E. 2a. of Christopher Osgood, on the W. 1a. of Thomas Kent butting S. on 4a. of Christopher Osgood, N. upon Choldrington field; 1a. lying next to the Picked ham meadow, E. 1a. of Richard Gauntlett, W. 1a. more of Richard Gauntlett, butting S. on a foreland of Peter Judd, N. on a foreland of Christopher Osgood;

1a. lying somewhat higher in the same furlong having E. 1a. of Robert Carpenter, W. 2a. of Thomas Kent, butting S. and N. on the same forelands.

3 ridges in the Great Hite field; 2a. having N. 1a. of Nicholas Mortimer, S. 1a. of Richard Gauntlet, butting W. on 4a. of David Drake, E. on 1a. of Henry Wood and ½a. of Peter Judd; 1a. more having N. 1a. of Richard Gauntlet, S. 1a. of Thomas Lavington, butting W. on 4a. of Nicholas Mortimer in No Mans furlong, E. on a foreacre of Gilbert Gyne.

4 ridges in the W. field; ½a. having W. 1a. of John Warren, E. ½a. of Gilbert Gyne, butting S. on a crooked half of Thomas Lavington, N. on the highway to Amesbury [Ambrosburie]; 1a. having N. 1a. of William Lavington, S. 1a. of John Grace, butting W. on 2 x ½a. of John Grace and the wid. Kent, E. also on 2 x ½a. of William Lavington, and Thomas Lavington; ½a. having on the N. ½a. of wid. Kent, on the S. 1a. of Robert Carpenter, butting W. on the Three bush field, E. on a foreacre of Gilbert Gyne; 1a. having W. the same foreacre, on the E. 1a. of wid. Perin, butting S. on the way to Allington, N. on 1a. of David Drake; 1 other picked a. having on the S. the same way, on the N. a half of John Smart, and butting E. on the way to Amesbury.

1 ridge in the Garson field having on the E. 3yd. of William Lavington, on the W. 1a. of Robert Carpenter, butting N. on Allington way, S. on 2a. of John Smart.

3 x ½ ridges in Three Bush field; 1 half having on the S. 3yd. of David Drake, on the N. ½a. of wid. Carpenter, butting E. on the W. field, W. on 3yd. belonging to wid. Bevis; another half having on the W. ½a. of William Lavington, on the E. 1a. of wid. Kent, butting N. on a forehalf of wid. Perin, S. on 1a. of William Lavington; another half having on the N. ½a. of John Warren, on the E. 1a. of wid. Aire, butting S. on 1a. of wid. Kent, N. on a. of Richard Judd.

1 ridge in the Church hill field, having on the W. ½a. of William Lavington, on the E. ½a. of wid. Kent, butting S. on the bourne, N. on 1a. of John Grace.

1½ ridges in the Mead field; 1a. having on the S. 1a. of wid. Perin, on the N. the Cleeve field, butting W. on the meadow, E. on the same field; the other half having S. 1a. of wid. Perin, on the N. ½a. of John Smart, butting E. on a foreacre of Richard Judd, W. on a foreacre of John Smart.

6 x ½ ridges in the Cleeve field; 1 half having on the E. and W. 2½a. of William Lavington, butting N. on the meadow, S. on a forehalf of William Lavington; another half lying above the Cleeve, having on the N. ½a. of wid. Kent, on the S. ½a. of Thomas Lavington, butting W. on a forehalf of wid. Perin, E. on ½a. of Nicholas Mortimer; another ½a. having on the S. ½a. of Richard Gauntlet, on the N. ½a. of Nicholas Mortimer, butting W. on the Mead field, E. on ½a. of John Smart; ½a. having on the S. 3 x ½a. of wid. Perin, on the N. ½a. of William Lavington, butting W. on Nicholas Mortimer's butts, E. on the down; another ½a. having on the S. 1a. of William Lavington's, on the N. 1a. of Wid. Kent's, butting E. on the S. drove, W. on a forehalf of Thomas Lavington; another ½a. in the same furlong having on the S. ½a. of John Smart, on the N. ½a. of wid. Perin, butting E. on the S. drove, W. on ½a. of John Grace.

In regard of the glebe land there is common of pasture for 85 sheep and 2 rams of which 60 sheep and 1 ram enter common with the N. flock, and the rest with the S. flock; 1 bull, 3 kine, and 2 bullocks, or heifers, 2 kine and 1 heifer or bullock enter common on the N. side, and 1 cow enters common on the S. side, and the other bullock or heifer likewise every second year. There are due all tithe hay, corn, wool, lambs, and other privy tithes, except a certain portion of tithes of the demesne lands formerly given to Amesbury abbey, now, by the dissolution of the abbey, to the King viz.; the tithe of 20 ridges of wheat and 20 ridges of barley, and all the tithe oats growing on the demesne lands, with the tithe of 110 lambs; and except the tithe of milk for which by custom they pay 2d. for 1 cow white yearly.

Taken by Robert Batt, rector, John Grace and William Lavington, churchwardens, and by other honest and substantial men.

571   13 Dec 1677 (D1/24/156/2)
A mansion house with a stable, barn, cow house, mixton and a croft all *c.* 1a. 4a. of plough land in Baldlinch[1] field of which 2a. are bounded on each side with land of William Chiles;[2] 1a. bounded E. land of wid. Beavois, W. land of Edward Jud 1a. bounded on each side with land of William Chiles; 2a. in Longdean headland bordering on the downs.

7½a. in Church field of which 2a. are bounded E. William Chiles, W. William Phillips; 2a. bounded E. Mr. Hayter,[3] W. John Woods;[4] 2a. bounded N. William Chiles, S. Edward Jud;[5] 1 head a. bounded E. Edward Jud;[5] ½a. bounded S. Robert Beaumond, N. John Cooper.

3a. in Great Height field of which 2a. bounded S. Ann Beavois,[5] N. William Phillips; 1a. bounded S. John Cooper, N. John Jud.[5] 5a. in the W. field, of which 1a. bounded N. Margaret Bundy[6] S. William Perrin;[7] 1a. bounded W. William Smart, E. the highway; 1a. bounded S. John Gyne[8] N. Richard Hobbs; 1a. bounded S. Ann Girle N. Margaret Bundy;[6] ½a. bounded E. Margaret Bundy,[6] W. William Smart; ½a. bounded N. Robert Hillyard, S. William Smart.

1a. in Foxlinch field of which ½a. bounded N. John Dench,[9] S. Edward Rolfe;[10] ½a. bounded W. Margaret Bundy,[6] N. William Chiles; ½a. bounded E. John Cooper, W. John Dench.[9]

1a. in Church hill bounded W. Margaret Bundy[6] E. John Gyne.[8] 1a. in Lampeth field of which 1a. bounded E. Richard Hobbs; ½a. bounded S. Richard Hobbs, N. Margaret Bundy.[6]

3a. in Clevehill field[11] of which ½a. bounded S. Margaret Bundy,[6] N. Mr. Hayter;[3] ½a. bounded N. John Cooper; ½a. bounded S. Richard Hobbs, N. Margaret Bundy;[6] ½a. bounded S. John Woods[12] N. William Phillips; ½a. bounded N. Mr. Hayter,[3] S. John Cooper; ½a. bounded each side Margaret Bundy.[6] 1a. in Broadberry field bounded E. Mr. Hayter,[3] W. wid. Beavois.[5] *c.* ¼a. of meadow. The Churchyard, *c.* ¼a.

All tithe corn, hay, wool, lamb with all the small tithes except that the Great farm, now in the possession of Hon. Mrs. Frances Fiennes, has tithe free, 20 ridges of the first sown wheat, 20 ridges of first sown barley and all oats and 110 lambs. The rector pays to the owner of the Great farm 5s. p. a. for the churchyard. The rectory has 85 sheep leazes, 5 cow leazes and 3 horse leazes.

Joseph Kelsey, rector, John Gyen, William Phillips [X], churchwardens.

1. Baling field in **572**.
2. William Childs and Mr. Kelsey in **572**; bounds of remaining 2a. in Baldlinch omitted in **572**.

3. Richard Dunn in **572**.
4. Mary Carpenter in **572**.
5. Mr. Kelsey in **572**.
6. John Slaymaker in **572**.
7. Joel Rowden in **572**.
8. Zachariah Blake in **572**.
9. John Judd in **572**.
10. wid. Rolfe in **572**.
11. Churchill field in **572**.
12. wid. Carpenter in **572**.

572   31 May 1705 (D1/24/156/3)
Property and land as 571 with amendments in footnotes omitting meadow and churchyard. All tithe corn except 20 ridges [rudges] of the first sown wheat and 20 ridges of the first sown barley and all oats belong to the owner of the land formerly belonging to Amesbury abbey. Easter offerings and all other great and small tithes belong to the rectory.
Joseph Kelsey, rector, John Cooper, Robert Bemont, churchwardens.

NORTON vicarage

573   n. d. late 16th cent. (D1/24/157/1)
1a. of meadow ground in Grenehill and a little rag [rage] of ground behind John, lord Chandos' Arches house called the Farmhouse. The same rights pertain to these lands as pertain to the farm land of Norton which farm was held by Malmesbury abbey. The farm is named as a parsonage because no tithes were paid out of it as long as the monastery stood and so continues to this day.
The style of writing is somewhat convoluted and the meaning is rather unclear. It has been summarised here.

574   16 Dec 1671 (D1/24/157/2)
½a. of pasture in John Driver's ground value 10s. p. a. A parcell of pasture ground value £1 6s. 8d. p. a.
Walter Pitman, vicar, William Milsome, churchwardens.

NORTON BAVANT vicarage

575   6 Jun 1609 (D1/24/158/1)
Terrier exhibited to the registry of Henry bishop of Salisbury.
A dwelling house and a barn, a barton, a garden, and 3 little closes of pasture adjoining of *c*. 2½a. In the W. field: ½a. arable land shooting on the bourne ditch, 1a. of Richard Symes on the E., and ½a. of Roger Dew on the W.; 3 x ½a. above the highway abutting on the highway at the S. end, ½a. of Thomas Langley on the W. and ½a. of John Turner on the E.; a little ½a. under the hill shooting out on the Whiteway; 1a. at the parsonage gate, 1a. of the parsonage land on the W., and Mr. Bennet's Turne furlong on the E.

In the E. field: 1a. shooting on the Meade ditch, ½a. of John Turner, formerly Malin's on the E., and 1a. of the parsonage land on the W.; 1 butt lying between the ways, having a butt of William Dew on the W.; 1a. more having 2a. of John Turner on the E. and 1a. of Richard Symes on the W.; 1 little a. shooting on the Mead ditch, being linched in on both sides, ½a. of William Dew adjoining on the W.; ½a. lying in Somers howse shooting against the hill, ½a. of Thomas Langley on the E., and the great linch on the W.; another little ½a. in Somers howse having ½a. of Roger Dewe on the E. and ½a. of Richard Symes on the W.; 1a. shooting out on the highway to Warminster and on the Lower way, having 2a. of William Dew on the E., and 2a. of the parsonage lands on the W., in a furlong called the Church furlong; 1a. more in the same furlong, having ½a. of John Turner on the E. and 1a. of the parsonage land on the W.; 2a. more heading the 9a. of the farm land on the W. and 1a. of Margaret Mathewes lying on the E.; 3 x ½a. shooting on Broad Barrow way, having ½a. of John Turner lying on the E. and ½a. on the W.; another little a. in the same furlong, ½a. of Thomas Burge on the E. and ½a. of Joan Frowde on the W.; on the beach 1a. lying by the downs side, and 1a. of Amy Edwards on the N.; 1a. more on the Beach, linched in on both sides, 1a. of Amy Edwards on the W.; 1a. more lying by the same a. on the E., being linched in on both sides, shooting N. and S.; 3 x ½a. in Heycoumbe lying between the farm land and the Clieves, also linched in; in Kingeswell ½a. shooting E. and W., being linched in on both sides; 3a. in the same furlong in 1 piece, having a linch on the N. and 1a. of Thomas Chambers on the S.; 1a. more in the same furlong having a great linch on the N. and 1a. of Thomas Langley on the S.; another little a. lying on Thornefolde and shooting out on Hatchburies field, 1a. of John London lying on the S.; 1a. in Rowledge furlong, having 1a. of John Turner on the S. and 1a. of Richard Flowers on the N.; ½a. in the same furlong, being linched in on both sides; 3a. in on piece in the same furlong, being lynched in on both sides, 1a. of Richard Knight adjoining on the S.; ½a. being linched in on both sides, shooting E. on the 40a. of the farm land; 1 little a. lying on the N. hill, shooting out on Middleton green way, being linched on both sides; ½a. adjoining Robert Whitewood's ½a, shooting N. and S. which is head to a furlong called Millers linches; ½a. more in the Lower furlong, ½a. of the parsonage lands lying on the W., and ½a. of Amy Edwards on the E.; 2a. by the white earth pit by Middleton way, ½a. of William Dew on the E. and 1a. of Richard Symes on the W.; 1a. more crossing the bourne, having a linch and 1a. of John Turner's on the W., and ½a. of John Turner on the E.; 1 little a. lying on the N. side of a furlong called Woeland, having a linch on the W., and 1a. of the parsonage land on the E.; 3 x ½a. in Hollope shooting up against Scratchbury, having 1a. of John Turner's on the E. and ½a. of William Bennet gent., on the W.; 1a. in Woeland, 1a. of Amy Edwards lying on the N. and 1a. of Roger Dew on the S.; 1a. more lying in the same furlong, having ½a. of Richard Symes on the N., and 1a. of William Dew on the S.; 1 little head a. shooting on Middleton green way, being head to 2 furlongs; 1a. more lying in Middleton Hoale, being linched in on both sides. All which parcels of land we esteem to be c. 32a.

Common of pasture for 4 great beasts, either plough beasts or kine; with 100 sheep to be depastured and fed in the commons, fields and down. With those of the tenants there, together with the churchyard, and tithe wool and lambs, cow [kine] white and calves, oblations and offerings, with the whole tithes of Butlers and Whislees, together with tithe hay through the parish, and all other duties, tithe corn in the common fields, tithe hay and corn of the farm and the new leases taken out of the fields, certain grounds called the Gowers only excepted.

By me John Whitewood, vicar; William Dew [X], Richard Symes [X], churchwardens, Thomas Chambers [X], John Whatlye, John Edwards.

576   17 Apr 1678 (D1/24/158/2)
A house of four bays with a barton. A barn of five bays and no stable adjoining to it. A garden and orchard *c.* 1yd. A little parrock on N. of orchard, ½a. 2 parrocks of meadow on S. of garden and orchard, 2a.

41½a. of arable as they lie in the common fields of Norton: In that part of Home field, commonly called the W. field; ½a. near the Bourne ditch bounded E. ½a. Richard Symes,[1] W. ½a. of Joseph Dewe;[2] 1½a. lying about the highway leading to Warminster bounded E. ½a. Prudence Edwards wid,[3] W. ½a. John Langley; 1a. in Middleton Hole one end shooting up against Scratchbury hill, the other end reaching over the way that leads into the N. field into Middleton field where it is bounded by a meer stone on N. side; ½a. under S. side of Scratchbury by the cliff [Cleive] from the end of Mrs. Elizabeth Bennet's[4] 4a. to the white way that leads up the hill; 1a. lying outside the parsonage barton scoured on E. with a linch from a furlong of Mrs. Bennet's[4] land, W. with a linch to about the middle of it from an a. of Mr. John Pearce, the other part is bounded by the way leading from the parsonage to the highway.

In that part of the Home field commonly called the E. field: 1½a. in the furlong outside Mrs. Bennet's[4] lower new leaze; ½a. bounded W. ½a. of Mr. John Mervin,[5] E. 1½a,. of the same Mr. Mervin;[5] 1a. in the same furlong bounded W. ½a. Prudence Edwards wid.,[3] E. ½a. Richard Knight;[6] in Church furlong 2a. on W. side where it leads to Mrs. Bennet's[4] 11a. and is bounded E. 1a. Mr. John Mervin;[5] 1a. in the same furlong bounded W. 1a. Mr. Pearce esq., E. ½a. Mr. John Mervin;[5] 1a. in the last furlong bounded W. 2a. of Mr. Pearce, and divided by a linch from 2a. of George Knight on E.; 1a. in Short furlong abutting on the Meadow ditch called Mead ditch which is linched on W. from 1a. of George Knight and E. from ½a. of John Langly; in the Long furlong 1a. at the home side of it bounded W. 1a. of Richard Symes,[1] E. 2a. Mr. John Mervin;[5] 1a. more towards the further side of the same furlong bounded W. 1a. Mr. John Pearce, E. ½a. Mr. John Mervin;[5] 1 little a. amongst the Butts bounded W. 1a. George Knight, E. 1a. of Mr. J. Mervin.[5] 2 x ½a. in Summer Hole one bounded W. 1a. of Richard Symes,[1] E. ½a. Prudence Edwards wid.,[7] the other lying against a high linch on W. and having only ½a. of John Langley between it and Cotley hill on E.

In the N. field: Upon Breach 1a. shooting E. and W. bounded S. the downs, N. 1a. Christopher Moodie;[8] 1a. in the uppermost furlong on Beach linched in from an a. of Christopher Moode[8] on W. and from 1½a. of Mr. Pearce on E.; 1a. in the Middle furlong upon Beech linched in from an a. of Mr. Pearce on W. and from an a. of John Langlie on E.; 1½a. in Heycombe having the cliff on E. is parted with a great linch from the farm land on W.; in Kingswell furlong ½a.

bounded Bourne ditch on S. parted by a linch from ½a. of John Whatlie[9] on N.; 3a. in the same furlong bounded S. 1a. of the wid. Chambers,[10] N. ½a. of wid. Chambers;[10] 1a. in the same furlong bounded S. 1a. of John Langlie, N. the nethermost of the great linches; 1a. on the hill called Thornfold linched on S. from an a. of the wid. Bowers[2] and N. from ½a. of Mr. John Mervin;[5] in Rowlease furlong: 1a. at the upperside of it bounded N. 1a. of John Dew[11] and linched from 1a. of Mr. John Mervin[5] on S.; ½a. in the same furlong linched in from an a. of the wid. Chambers[10] on N. and from ½a. of Mr. John Mervin[5] on S.; a piece of 3a. in the same furlong linched in from ½a. of Richard Symse[1] on N. and from 1a. of Richard Knight[6] on S.; in the farm furlong ½a. linched from ½a. of Mrs. Bennet[4] on S. and from 1a. of George Knight on N.; 1a. on North hill linched from 1a. of the wid. Bowers[1] on N. and from ½a. of John Langlie on S.; 1 long ½a., ½a. of John Whatlie[9] lying between it and the same furlong on E. and ½a. of Mr. Pearce on W.; ½a. in the furlong called Blackland bounded W. ½a. of Mr. Pearce, E. ½a. of Christopher Moodie;[8] in the furlong at the lower end of Blacklands a piece of 2a. having ½a. of George Knight on E. and 1a. of Richard Syme[1] on W.; 1a. abbutting on the lower end of the last 2a. in the furlong that lies athwart the bourne, bounded E. ½a. of Mr. John Mervin,[5] and is linched from 1a. of the same Mr. Mervin[5] on W.

In that part of the N. field called Hollop: 1a. parted by a linch from the White lands on W. and with ½a. of Mr. Pearce[12] on E.; 1½a. in the Short lands lying against Scratchbury hill bounded E. ½a. of Mr. Mervin,[5] W. ½a. Mrs. Bennet;[4] in the Long furlong 1a. bounded E. 1a. of the wid. Chambers,[10] W. ½a. Joseph Dewe; 2½a. in the same furlong bounded E. ½a. of Richard Syme,[1] W. 1a. George Knight;[10] 1 little head a. lying between 2 furlongs that turn out upon it on either side one end of which abuts against London way the other upon ½a. of John Langlie.

Pasture and feeding for 100 sheep at all times upon all the downs common fields and commons that belong to the tenantry flock. Pasture and feeding for 7 cows and 2 runners upon the Cow down and in the common meadows fields or any other commons in Norton at all times with any of the inhabitants. Pasture and feeding for 2 horses in the common plot of meadow called Heathfield and as many horses as the vicar pleases in any other of the commons of Norton.

The tithe of corn sown upon the glebe of the vicarage. All tithe corn and hay and all other tithes payable on the following lands: Daffords woods, Butlers, Whistlchayes and Henfords [Hempsford] marsh. Tithe corn of any down or pasture ground that may be newly broken up and has not been known formerly to yield any tithe to the parson. Tithe hay, wool, lambs, pigs, conies, honey, apples, wood, eggs geese. turkeys, etc. that do shall or may arise. All offerings, oblations, mortuaries with the benefit of breaking ground in the chancel (for burial) and disposing of the seats. Herbage of the churchyard. 1d. p. a. for the tithe of the white of each milk cow kept within the parish. Tenth calf if the vicar please to drive til they come to that number, otherwise he receives the tenth part of the price if it is sold, the left shoulder if killed, and ½d. if weaned. 1d. p. a. for the tithe herb of each garden. 1s. for the fall of each calf. 13s. 4d. p. a. as custom tithe for a grist mill of Mrs. Bennet,[4] occupied by John Pearce. 4s. p. a. custom tithe for a fulling mill occupied by Thomas Goddard.[13] The tithe of a grist mill called Bathe mill occupied by William Bramble[14] for which there is no custom but the vicar and miller agree.

Timothy Thorne, vicar, John Knight, John Whatly, churchwardens.

1. John Symse in **577**.
2. John Compton in **577**.
3. Elizabeth Dew wid. in **577**.
4. John Bennett esq in **577**.
5. William Bennett esq in **577**.
6. John Knight in **577**.
7. John Langlic in **577**.
8. Thomas Robins in **577**.
9. Matthew Wornel in **577**.
10. Thomas Chambers in **577**.
11. Richard Langlie in **577**.
12. Mr. Benet in **577**.
13. Samuel Pierce in **577**.
14. One Love in **577**.

577   8 Jan 1705 (D1/24/158/3)
*As **576** with amendments in footnotes.* The whole value £45 p. a. Timothy Thorne, vicar, John Knight, Thomas Chambers, churchwardens.

578   29 Jul 1783 (D1/24/158/4)
The vicarage house is built with brick and stone all covered with thatch except the brewhouse which is tiled. The ground floor consists of a parlour, floored with elm, whitewashed walls and ceiled, a kitchen, paved with flat stones, white washed walls and ceiled, a small brewhouse and a cellar both neither ceiled. On the first floor 2 good chambers floored with elm whitewashed walls and ceiled, 2 much smaller chambers floored with elm whitewashed walls and ceiled. No garrets. Outhouses; a stable for 2 horses built part with stone lath and plaster and boards, covered with thatch. A barn 16ft. by 42ft. built about 2ft. from the ground with stone, the remainder with boards, covered with thatch.

The kitchen garden, 30 lugs, fenced to S. W. and N. with a live thorn hedge, to E. with pales. The yard which adjoins the garden, 18 lugs, fenced to N. by the stable and a mudwall to E. a dead hedge belonging to Mr. Parry to S. by the barn to W. by the garden pales.

The glebe: 2a. of pasture land adjoining the vicarage garden bounded S. the river, W. Mr. Parry's field, E. partly Mr. Parry's garden and field, partly W. end of the vicarage garden, and part Mr. Knight's ground, N. Hickman's orchard: fenced by a dead hedge and ditch, *c.* 40 very small elms a few withys and pollarded ashes in this ground.

Arable land: In the W. field; ½a. W. of Compton's ½a., N. of Syms' a.; 3 x ½a. above the turnpike, W. of Langley's ½a., N. of Dew's ½a.; 1a. in Middleton Hole, S. of James Knight's ½a., N. of Bayleys lands; ½a. under Scratchbury, S. of the cliff, N. of Edgale's a.; 1a. at Parsonage, S. of the road, N. of Mr. Parry's 18a.

In the E. field in Church furlong; 2a. of headland, S. of Mr. Parry's 11a., N. of Mr. Parry's ½a.; 1a. S. of the glebe 2a., N. of James Knight's 2a.; in Picked furlong; 3 x ½a. N. of Mr. Parry's 3 x ½a., S. of Mr. Parry's ½a.; in this same furlong 1a., N. of Mr. Parry's ½a., S. of Dew's ½a.; 1a. next the mead, E. of James Knight's a., W. of the highway; 1a. in Long furlong, S. Syms'a., N. of Mr. Parry's 2a.; 1a., S. of glebe a., N. of Mr. Parry's 3 x ½a.; 1a. in Buts furlong, N. of Mr. Parry's a., S. of James Knight's a.; Summers hole ½a., N. of Langleys ½a., S. of Wickham's ½a.; ½a. N. of Compton's ½a., S. of Syms' ½a.; in Beach on the hill 1a., E. of the old quarries, W. of Mr. Bayley's a.; 1a. in the Long ground, N. of glebe 3 x ½a., S. of Mr. Bayley's a.; 1a. in the same, N. of Langley's ½a., S. of glebe a.

In Harcombe Bottom 3 x ½a., N. of the cliff, S. of Farm field; in Thornfold 1a., E. of Compton's a., W. of Mr. Parry's ½a.; 1a., E. of Langly's a., W. of Langly's ½a.; 3a., E. of Mr. Bayly's a. W. of Mr. Bayly's a.; ½a., E. of the Bourne, W. of Wornal's ½a.; in Rowlands furlong 1a., E. of Mr. Parry's a. W. of Mr. Bayly's a.; ½a., E. of Mr. Parry's a. W. Langly's (sic) Thomas Benet; 3a,. E. of John Knight, W. of Syms' ½a.; in Farm furlong ½a., E. and W. of John Knight; in N. hill 1a. E. of Langly's ½a., W. Mr. Parry's a.; ½a. by the Bushes, N. of Wornal's ½a., S. of glebe ½a.; in Stone furlong 2a., N. James Knight's ½a., S. of Syms' ½a.; in Bourne furlong 2a., N. of Mr. Parry's ½a., S. of Mr. Parry's 3a.; in Nut furlong 1a., N. of glebe a., S. of Langly's a.; in Winden furlong 1a., E. of Compton's a., W. of Mr. Bayly's a.; 1a., E. of James Knight's a., W. of Syms' ½a.; against the hill in the same field 3 x ½a., E. of Mr. Parry's ½a., W. of Mr. Parry's a.; against Middleton way 1a. of head land between 2 furlongs.

120 sheep leazes in the Tenantry field, none in the Farm field. 4 beast leazes and 2 horse leazes in Heath field. Tithe of grass and all great and small tithes of an estate of Mr. Robert Long at Butlers Combe. No pensions, augmentations, gifts or bequests made to the church (except what is mentioned under the furniture of the chancel) or the minister. No pension payable out of the living or anything established to the expense or charge of the incumbent.

The furniture of the church: A cushion covered with blue cloth, a pulpit cloth of the same colour, a surplice, 4 bells. The furniture of the chancel: an oaken table covered with blue cloth a linen cloth and a napkin; a handsome silver cup inscribed 'The Gift of Patience Bennet wid. to the Church of Norton=Bavant 1710'; no weight on it. A small but hansome silver salver inscribed 'The Gift of Mrs. Eth. [1] Bennet wid. to the Church of Norton Bavant 1756'; no weight on it. A small silver cup inscribed on the lid '1576'; no weight on it. There is only a bible and a prayer book.

No lands or money in stock for the repair of the church or utensils. Church and tower are repaired by the church rates. All the estates in the parish except the vicarage are charged in proportion to their value with the expense of the church yard fence. The clerk's wages are paid by the church rates and he is appointed by the vicar.

Thomas Fisher, vicar, John Knight, John Layland, churchwardens.

1. Etheldred.

OAKSEY rectory

579 13 Jul 1608 (D1/24/159/1)

c. 20a. of glebe land and pasture and *c*. 3a. of meadow in lieu of the tithes of hay of Sideham, Small mead and certain acres and lots of meadow in Park mead, parcel of the farm. Part of the glebe, being inclosed, adjoins the parsonage house, and adjoins on the N. a highway from Oaksey [Woxsey] to Somerford Keynes, and on the S. the S. field. Another part of the glebe, also inclosed, adjoins on the N. the N. field, and on the S. a meadow called Rodwell Moor. The other part of the glebe, likewise inclosed, lies at a place called Moor Cross, and on the S. adjoins a ground of William Playster alias Tucker, and on the N. adjoins the highway to Somerford Keynes, near John Robe's house recently erected at Moor Cross. Common of pasture in the W. wood, and all other tithes, rights and duties accustomed and payable.

Certified by Thomas Earl, rector, John Driver [X], William Baker [X], churchwardens, Francis Bradshaw, William Playster alias Tucker [X], questmen John Pitman senior [X], Edward Fisher [X], William Right [X], John Sheremore [X].

580 16 Dec 1671 (D1/24/159/2)

A parsonage house with barn and stable. 2 gardens in an orchard. A ground adjoining to the orchard called the Home Close,[1] An enclosed land adjoining the last on E. and known as [vulgo] Long croft,[2] An enclosed land a little further E. usually called Moor Cross lees.[3] An enclosed land called the Meadow,[4] lying N. next to a large ground called Knight's meadow alias Radwell moor. An enclosed ground lying among several grounds called the Norwoods,[4] known by the name of Parson's Norwood.[5] A cow's common in Minety moor.[6] All acreages by common estimation.

Robert Dalton, rector, Thomas Sparrow, Thomas Allis [X], churchwardens.

1. Home lees, 4a. in **581**, *c*. 3½a. in **582**.
2. 10a. in **581**.
3. 1½a. in **581**.
4. 6a. in **581**.
5. All tithes great and small except on The Norwoods, 40a., in lieu of which the parson has Parson's Norwood, 4a., in **581**.
6. Omitted in **581**.

581 16 Feb 1678 (D1/24/159/3)

*As **580** with amendments in footnotes.* Robert Dalton, rector, Robert Oatridge, William Mayor, churchwardens.

582 16 Dec 1704 (D1/24/159/4)

*As **580** with amendment in footnote.* Henry Poole, patron of the church, Henry Golsey, rector, Lucian Manby, John Jonson, churchwardens.

ODSTOCK rectory

583   n. d. late 16th – early 17th cent.[1] (D1/24/160/1)

A parsonage house with barn, hayhouse, stable, garden, orchard, and pigeon house with stable within the compass of ½a. ground; the churchyard also of c. ½a. In the common meadow called E. meadow 3a. in one piece butting on the water and a ham of Thomas Clark's at the S. end, on 3a. of John Newman at the N. end, a several ground belonging to Thomas Caster on the E., and 3 x ½a. of Anthony Chub on the W.; 1a. more in the same meadow part of the E. end butting on the marsh, on the W. butting on 3a. of John Newman, on the S. ½a. of Richard Caster, on the N. ½a. of Mrs. Bower wid. 1a. of several ground lying at the end of the W. field, the N. end butting on a like meadow held by Andrew Caster, the S. end on the way leading to Homington, on the E. a little close of the wid. Mowdye, on the W. a little drove to water cattle.

In the common field called the Home field 2a. of arable in one piece in the Lower furlong, on the W. 1a. of Richard Caster, on the E. 1a. of Thomas Clark; 2a. on the W. side of the same field lying by Whitlime Bush; 1a. lying in Short furlong, Richard Caster having ½a. on the S., and on the N. 1 head a. of Thomas Caster's living; a head half, headland to the same furlong; 3a. of ground more lying by the green way; 3yd. more lying by Small Bushes linchet [lincherd]; 1a. headland to Redland furlong; 1 half under a linchet near Peascland Bush.

In the W. field 1a. on the hill on the outside of the field; 1a. in Sheweland between 2 linchets; 2a. more butting on the way to Homington; 2a. in one piece lying between 2 linchets called Dead Man bottom; 1 head a. at the E. end of the same 2a.; ½a. of ground linchet, 1 half of the wid. Mowdye on the E.; in the hill foot 3 x ½a. of ground in one piece in the furlong towards the highway, on the E. 1a. of John Newman, on the W. linchet; ½a. of ground on the E. of the short hedge, and on the E. ½a. ground held by Richard Caster, on the W. 1a. of Mrs. Bowers; 1a. more in the same furlong; 3yd. lying under Bolts Bush; 1a. in the furlong above Bolts Bush, on the W. 1a. of John Newman; 2a. in the furlong butting on the last land both sides linched; 1a. more in Short furlong, Goody Mowdye has ½a. on the S. and on the N. 3yd. held by Andrew Caster; 1a. butting on the Peak, John Newman having 1a. on the W. and Thomas Clarke 1a. on the E. Lastly 100 sheep leaze and 8 beast leaze.

Giles Thornburgh, clerk, Thomas Carter, Thomas Clarke, churchwardens.

1.   Giles Thornburgh was rector 1582-1637.

584   4 Aug 1783 (D1/24/160/2)

The parsonage house is 40ft. x 19ft. built with bricks and flint to the first floor with timber and rough cast to the second floor and is covered with brick tiles. It consists of an entrance with a brick floor and plastered walls and ceiling, a parlour with oak floor wainscotted with deal and a plastered ceiling, a kitchen with an oak floor, the sides plastered upon battens and a plastered ceiling, 2 pantries with oak floors and plastered walls and ceiling, 1 cellar even with the other rooms with a brick floor, walls and ceiling plastered. 3 chambers and 2 closets on the first floor with deal floors and plastered sides and ceiling and 3 garrets, 2 of them with oak floors 1 with ash, 2 of them plastered on the sides and ceiled, the other not.

An outhouse built with brick and tiled with brick tiles consisting of 3 rooms, 2 of them 14 ft. square, the other 12ft. by 11ft.; a coal hole opening into one of them built with brick and tiled. A stable 31ft. by 19ft., one of the sides built with brick the other with brick flints and timber, one end with bricks sidewall high, the other end the ground pinning bricks and flints, both ends with timber and boards to the tops and covered with thatch. A barn 84ft. by 20ft., the ground pinning bricks and flints both ends with timber and boards to the top and covered with thatch. A cart house which stands upon 12 posts and covered with thatch. A yard 130ft. by 50ft., the site of the barn included. The fences around it and the buildings are least wall and dead hedges. A garden, ¼a., fenced round partly with quick and partly with dead hedges.

The church yard adjoining to the garden, ½a., exclusive of the site of the church. The rector maintains the fence above halfway round, the farmer part of it and the parish the remainder next to the road. In the rectory fence are 3 elms topped, worth c. 15s.; in the parish fence, which the rector by consequence of the parishioners has taken care of for many years, are 1 elm topped, 8 young elms and as many Scycamore trees.

The glebe lands consist of 10a. 3yd. in the Home field,[1] 7a. in the Bottom field,[2] 9a. 3yd. in the Hill field,[3] in all 27a. with 80 sheep commons. 4 ½a. of meadow[4] with common of pasture for 8 rother beasts. I need not be more particular because the parish is going to be enclosed.

All kinds of tithes, particularly tithe of 50a. of coppice are due to the minister. The furniture of the chancel consists of a silver chalice and cover which holds a pint, a pewter plate, a napkin a double covering for the communion table, one of tapestry, the other of linen in good condition. The furniture of the church, a surplice, a bible and common prayer book almost new, a pulpit cloth and cushion, old fashioned but decent, and 3 bells. No inscription or mark of weight upon the chalice nor any books belonging to the church. The minister repairs the chancel and all the edifices besides the church and part of the churchyard fence as above. The clerk is also sexton and his wages 1s. 4d. for every lands [yardland], as he says, 36s. p. a. But, besides the glebe there are only 26 yardlands in the parish and the farm which consists of 15½yardlands, pays by custom only 18s. p. a. which makes his wages only 32s. p. a.

John Bedwell, rector, Henry Brown, churchwarden, William Chubb, W. Lucas, principal inhabitants.

1. Land described as follows in a note made in 1731 in the parish register : 3a. in Yedown, W. side of Greenway; ½a. heading Short furlong; 1a. in Short furlong, Mary Chubb N., William Chubb S.; 2a. in Hedge furlong, Mrs. Clark E. and W. 1a. heading Redland; 3yd. on the Linch; ½a. heading Short furlong on the hill; 2a. in the Second furlong next the Bottom field (WSRO 784/2).
2. As n. 1: 1a. in Shoreland, Mr. Chubb E. and W.; 1 head a. at Croft stile; 1a. called Parsonage close or drove; 2a. across the bottom, Mr. Chubb N. and S.; ½a. heading the Bottom furlong; ½a. at Twelve acres corner; 1a. at the top of the Hill field.

3.   As n. 1; 1a. in the Peak, Dr. Ballard E., William Chubb W.; 2a. on the W. side, Mrs.
     Clark W., Mr. Hebbard E.; 1a. heading Shortfurlong; 3yd. in Shortfurlong, Mr.
     Mathews S. Mr. Long N.; 1a. butting on Short hedge; 1a. shooting on Coppice
     furlong, Mrs. Clark W., Mary Chubb E.; ½a. in Coppice furlong, Mr. Mathews E.,
     Mr. Champion W.; 1½a. against the highway, Dr. Ballard E., Mr. Webb W.; 1a. in the
     first furlong called Short furlong, Long S., Wats N.
4.   As n. 1: 3a. in the lowest part of Mill furlong; 1a. in the lower corner, Mr. Champion
     N., Mr. Chubb S.; ½a. in the other furlong.

OGBOURNE ST. ANDREW vicarage

585   20 Sep 1672 (D5/10/2/4)
A vicarage house of *c.* 3 bays, an out house for to lay wood in or the like, a
backside garden and other ground about the house, ½a. A churchyard, ½a. All
tithe wool and lamb in the parish excepting tithes of Poughcombe [Puckham]
farm held by Mr. Bond and of Rockley [Ruckley] farm[1] as they pay no tithe to
the vicar. For calves the left shoulder of every calf killed and the tenth penny of
every one that is sold, for every through white cow 2d. For every cow that has
a calf 1d. For every calf weaned ½d. For every garden 1d., for bees the tenth
penny if they take or sell them. For offerings 2d. a garden. For all other privy
tithes as apples, eggs, pigs, geese and the like according to the custom of other
places. There is £20 p. a. which is given for an augmentation to the vicarage by
the dean and chapter[2] of Windsor and is now paid by the tenant Mr. Edward
Goddard senior.
     Thomas Doverdale, vicar, William Waldron, Thomas Hurlbatt, churchwardens,
William Benger, John Seymour senior, William Haukes.

1.   Mr. William Grinfield's Rockley farm in **586**.
2.   *Recte* canons.

586   31 May 1705 (D5/10/2/4)
*As **585** with amendment in footnote but without the detail of the small tithes.*
Robert Wake, vicar, Philip Seymour, John Pearce, churchwardens, Thomas
Seymour, John Mihill, John Pithoues, Francis Richens.

OGBOURNE ST. GEORGE vicarage

587   23 Sep 1672 (D5/10/2/5)
A house of 4 bays. A barn of 3 bays, a wood house at one end of it and a stable
at the other, of half a bay a piece. The close, gardens, yard with the ground on
which the buildings stand, ½a., which with the houses is worth £3 p. a. The
churchyard, 1yd. of ground, worth 8s. p. a. 120a. of pasture ground of which the
vicar receives tithe in kind or £12 p. a. that is to say 2s. per a. The vicar receives
tithe for Vicarage close belonging to the farm but for no other pasture belonging
to the farm. From the farm in consideration of the close and of other petty dues

the vicar has £1 p. a. or may refuse taking tithe in kind. For every tenth lamb 2s., he has every tenth lb. of wool in the parish except the farm which pays neither lamb or wool to the vicar.

Tithe wood for all woods which are titheable. The parishioners pay 1d. for cow white, ½d. for every calf if it is weaned, the tenth penny if it is sold and the left shoulder if they kill it. 1d. for garden, 2d. a piece for offerings and for bees the tenth if they take them or sell them. Tithe pig, apples and eggs at Easter according to other places. Mr. Edward Goddard of Ogbourne St. Andrew pays £20 p. a. for agistments.

Robert Clements, vicar, William Smith, churchwarden, William Gardner, William Dixsun.

588   Jun 1705 (D5/10/2/5)
£20 augmentation of the church of Windsor. A homestall of 5 bays, a woodhouse, barn and stable of 5 bays. A close and garden adjoining the vicarage house end, c. ½a. All tithes except corn except tithe of the great farm which pay tithes to the vicar, only for cow white, calves, pigs, geese, eggs, garden and offerings.

Robert Clement, vicar, Henry Buckerfield, Henry Brunsden, churchwardens, John Goddard, Richard Brunsden.

ORCHESTON ST. GEORGE rectory

589   n. d. late 16th cent. (D1/24/161)
All the tithes and offerings and 1 yardland of glebe in Chawfield of 24a. arable land with pasture for 40 sheep and leaze for 2 horses or other beasts in the same field, with common for swine as the other inhabitants have. 1 yardland more in Bewdon of 18a. arable land with pasture for 40 sheep and leaze for 2 horses in the same field, with common for swine as the other inhabitants have. Also 3a. arable land in Southborne in Elston field, with a little close adjoining the end of the of the a. and another close of pasture of ½a. lying on the N. of Nicholas Mundaye's barn in Elston, with common and pasture for 3 kine and a bull on Elston cow down called Mugdal.

ORCHESTON ST. MARY rectory

590   13 June 1609 (D1/24/162/1)
A dwelling house with a garden and other edifices. A close of 3 yds. in the middle of which stand 2 barns. 80 sheep leaze in the commons and pastures called Littlecotts, and 4 beast leaze in the same field. The churchyard. 37a. arable land in the field called Littlecotts.

Giles Thornburgh, parson, Edward Downe, William Coker, churchwardens.

591   19 Dec 1677 (D1/24/162/2)
A dwelling house with garden and other edifices. A close, c. 3yd., in the middle of which stands 2 barns, a stavell house, a stable and a vetch house and 2 cottages.

80 sheep leaze in the commons and pastures called Littlecott and 16 lambs leaze. In the same fields 4 beast leaze and for as many pigs as the parson wishes to keep there. The churchyard. 38a. of arable land in Littlecots. The said land to be folded according to the custom of the place or else the parson is to have the fold upon every eighth night or every eighth a. If the farmer has 7a. folded the parson is to have 1a. folded and so proportionally.

Giles Thornburgh, rector, John Elderton, churchwarden, George Stagg, George Whitehorne [X].

OVERTON vicarage

592   13 [. . .] 1588 (D1/24/163/1)
A dwelling house with an orchard, a garden, a court or barton, a barn, a stable, and 2 closes of pasture or meadow adjoining, c. 2½a. A plot of meadow ground lying on the N. of the river Kennet, sufficiently mered, c. 3yd. Arable land lying in the common fields of Overton and Fyfield called Threescore acres as appears by a copy of a composition[1] belonging to the vicarage, the land being dispersed in the common fields among the tenants' land, and not annexed or mixed with the parsonage or farm land. 100 sheep leaze on Hackepen down among the sheep and stock belonging to the manor of Overton held by Richard Kingsmill esq., called Hackpen flock. 13 beast leaze on the N. side of the water on the common downs. Common and pasture for 13 pig hogs. A yearly pension of 38s. 9d. with all Easter duties, lammas duties, tithe wool, lambs, hay, calves, pigs, geese, honey, hemp, apples, and all other small tithes excepting from the vicarage tithes due from the lands of the monastery of Winchester[2] in the parish of Overton. Major tithes, excepting the same land belong to the rectory.

A parcel of woody ground called Prieste's grove estimated to be of [. . .] by our accustomed perambulation, and as our vicar claims in the right of the vicarage. We think it lies in the parish of Overton because we take it in by our perambulation between Atlyes copse on the N., a park recently enclosed on the E., and a ground called Henley on the S., which the vicars have usually held, and cut and taken the wood from time to time at their will. A yearly rent of 13s. 4d. for the feeding of a flock of sheep called the Temple flock at a certain time of the year. We never knew any vicar to have any tithes from the farm in W. Overton where Richard Franklin now lives, other than oblations at Easter, 2d. in money and chrisomes when they happen. The tithes of a farm in Lockeridge sometime belonging to St. Margaret's Priory near Marlborough are now disputed in law between our vicar and Richard Brown who claims to be aquit of the tithes for the yearly payment of 3s. by virtue of the composition. A house and orchard in Fyfield. A little house and a little close adjoining in Alton [Priors]. The tenants and inhabitants of Fyfield and Alton [Priors] pay all manner of duties and tithes as the tenants and inhabitants of Overton do.

William Smith, William Smith, churchwardens of Overton, Robert ?Kyngseman,[3] Thomas Stephens, William Stephens, sidesmen. Richard William, Christopher Streche, churchwardens of Fyfield, John Dymer, Matthew Studley, sidesmen. *Names in the same hand.*

1. The composition referred to probably dates from late 13th-early 14th centuries; see VCH xi p. 200. At several place in the terrier extracts from it in Latin are quoted.
2. St. Swithin's priory.
3. The surname is extremely faint but this reading is supported by the fact that a Robert Kinsman paid subsidy in 1576 (WRS vol. 10).

593   1608 (D1/24/163/2)
A vicarage house with an orchard, garden, a barton a little close a barn and a close of pasture or mead beneath the barn in all c. 3a. A plot of meadow in the N. side of river Kennet, c. ½a. 100 sheep leaze upon Hackpen. Common of pasture upon Estertown downs for 13 kine or oxen. Common or feeding for 13 pigs or pigs in the N. side. A pension from the new countess of Pembroke of 38s. 9d. A yearly payment of 13s. 4d. for the feeding of the Temple flock within the parish of Overton. 46a. 3yd. of arable and meadow in the field of E. Overton namely 10a. of arable land in the S. fields of the church, 14a. of arable land and 3 yds. of meadow land on the E. side of the church towards Lockeridge. 22a. of arable lying in the N. fields beyond the river Kennet.

Thomas Clifford, vicar, Roger Malum, Richard Dismer, Thomas Stephens, William Smyth, Robert Kingesman, Richard Willmott. *Names in the same hand*

594   1 Nov 1671 (D1/24/163/3)
The vicarage house, parlour, hall and kitchen. A barn of 4 bays. A stable ground about the house, the gardens and backside, c. 2a. 2a. in a field called Bittom laying E. and W. bounded N. 2a. of Thomas Clifton. 1a. in Blaksmith laying N. and S., Thomas Clifton at one end, Thomas Smith at the other. 3a. lying athwart Whiteway, Thomas Clifton on both sides. 2a. in the White field laying E. and W., Thomas Stephens on one side John Strech on the other. 1a. laying against White way shooting E. and W., Thomas Clifton laying next. 1a. laying N. and S. which heads Thomas Clifton and John Strech.

½a. in Dean Close field; 1a. laying N. and S. next to Thomas Clifton, 2a. laying E. and W., Thomas Clifton on one side Richard Kingsman on the other; 3a. laying at the lower end of Whitslade laying E. and between 2 laynes [lannes].

In Whitslade field: 1a. laying E. and W., Thomas Strech laying on both sides; ½a. laying E. and W., Robert Browne on one side and Thomas Clifton on the other.

½a. on Redhill laying E. and W., the wid. Stephens on one side and William Trueman on the other. 2a. in the Pound field laying E. and W., Thomas Strech on one side and the wid. Stephens on the other. 1a. in the same field laying E. and W. Thomas Smith on N. side. 2a. in Gibstone furlong laying N. and S. Thomas Strech on one side Mr. Smith on the other, Thomas Stephens on one side Thomas Clifton on the other.

38s. 9d. p. a. is due to the vicar from the earl of Pembroke. 13s. 4d. p. a. is due to the vicar from the Temple down.

In the N. side of the water: 1a. in Cattenborrow furlong, the wid. Mason on one side, Thomas Strech on the other; 1a. in the same furlong Thomas Clifton on one side, the wid. Pobjoy on the other; 1a. in the same furlong Robert Brown on one side; 1a. in the same field laying N. and S. next to wid. Pobjoy.

In Whitehill: 1a. laying E. and W. Thomas Smith on one side, the wid. Pobjoy on the other. 1a. laying N. and S., the farm piece on one side Thomas Clifton on the other.

In the furlong called Paddel drove: 1a. laying N. and S. Robert Browne on one side, [sic] Thomas on the other; 2a. laying N. and S. Thomas Smith on one side Thomas Strech on the other; 2a., Thomas Smith on one side, the wid. Pobjoy on the other; 1a., Robert Browne on one side the wid. Pobjoy on the other.

On the fore hill called the Vicar's Bush: 3a. laying N. and S., William Trueman on both sides; 2 head a. laying E. and W. Thomas Clifton on one side, Robert Browne on the other; 1a. laying E. and W. Thomas Strech on one side, Robert Browne on the other. In Bum furlong: 1a. laying E. and W. Thomas Strech on one side, Robert Browne on the other; 1a. laying E. and W. the wid. Pobjoy on the one side, Mr. Richard Browne on the side; 2a. Thomas Strech on N. side; 1a. laying N. and S. Mr. Richard Browne on one side, Thomas Strech on the other.

13 beast leaze belonging to the vicarage. 100 sheep leaze upon the farm down belonging to Hackpen [Haxpin]. A plot of meadow ground on the N. side of the water, Thomas Clifton on one side William Trueman on the other.

Robert Browne, Edward Franklin, churchwardens.

595   11 Jan 1705 (D1/24/163/4)

In obedience to the command of Gilbert, bishop of Sarum, we present our terrier as follows. The vicarage is endowed having within its precincts 2 chapels of ease, Fyfield and Alton Priors. It has the following tithings: E. Overton, W. Overton, Lockeridge and Shaw belonging to Overton; Alton and Stawell belonging to Alton Priors; and Fyfield a tithing of itself. In Overton: The vicarage house, the barn, the outhouse, the backside, the garden and the meadow adjoining contain in common computation 3a. A plot of meadow in the common mead called Broad Mead, ½a. having the river on S. and the great road on N. A little plot of meadow in Gipson furlong lying upon Stanly at Half Way Bush, ½a. The churchyard. 2 plots of garden one formerly let to William Andrews senior, and the other to Mary Andrew wid., next to the houses they now inhabit.

24a. 1yd. in the several fields on S. side of the river: namely In Bittom 6a. of which 3a. lie in the Shills next to Hatchet Gate field running across the road, 1a. in Blacksmiths furlong, 2a. lie together running up to Long Hedge from W. to E. 4a. in Hatchet's Gate field of which 2a. lie together and run from W. to E. upon the road called Whiteway lying to the S. of farmer Welles, 1 is a head a. running from S. to N. to the other a single a. in the same field. 6½a. in Barrow field of which 3 lie together running from W. to E. having Candle acre on N.; 1a. called Barrow acre, the W. end lying on the N. of the barrow having ½a. between it an the barrow; a head a. running from E. to W. upon 3a. of John Stretch; 1a., separated from the last a. by an a. running in the same way upon the ½a. that belongs to the vicarage; this ½a. runs from N. to S. having another ½a. to W. of Roger Polton being both head ½a.

1½a. in Gypson furlong of which the a. runs from S. to N. upon Stanly having a ½a. of farmer Wells on E.; the ½a. runs the same way upon the abovementioned ½a. of mead in Gipson furlong.

3a. 1yd. in Pound field of which 1a. runs from W. to E. upon the S.W. corner of Stanly, 2a. run from W. to E. upon the last a.; the yd. runs the same way under a linchet on S. side near the middle of Stanly.

2a. and 2 x ½a. in Long field of which 1a. is in Whitslade furlong running from W. to E. upon a ½a. belonging to the vicarage; ½a. of mead in Gipson furlong; 1a. runs from S. W. to N. E. upon Roger Polton having an a. of John Brown upon N. W.; ½a. is on Red hill in Pan furlong running from W. to E. upon a ½a. of Robert Wells senior, having 2a. of Roger Polton on S.

On N. side of the river: 22a. of arable namely 4a. in Cattenbarrow all lying severally 3 running E. to W. 2 of these run up Ten acre hedge, one next to the great road, one with an a. of Roger Polton on S., one with Robert Browne on N. and one with Cattenbarrow layne on W. lying under it. 2a. in White hill, one runs from N. to S. upon 8a. belonging to the farm in E. Overton and it has the same farm field on W., the other is called Pickle Dean acre running E. to W. and separated from Pickle Dean by 1a. of Thomas Smith.

6a. in Vicar's field of which 3 lie together running N. to S. having an a. at each end belonging to the vicarage, the other a. lies nearer Pickle Dean Bottom running from E. to W. having Robert Brown on S.

6a. in Paddle Drove of which 2a. lie together from S. to N. upon Richard Andrew's 3a. having an a. of Thomas Smith on W., 2a. run the same way having Roger Polton's a. on W., the other 2a. are single a. one running the same way having Robert Brown upon W., the other a. runs the same way from S. to N. having an a. of Robert Brown on E.

4a. in the Hitching field, 2 of which lie together running from W. to E. upon 3a. belonging to the vicarage being 2 head a. having on N. ½a. John Brown; a single a. called Bum acre running the same way having 2a. of Mr. Fowle on S.; the other single a. running S. to N. upon Thomas Smith's a. having an a. of John Davis on W.

Tithe hay, wool, lambs, calves, wood, cheese, hemp, flax and all other small tithes throughout Overton except all the tithes of the farm in E. Overton in the possession of John Smith, of the farm in W. Overton in the possession of Michael Cook and of half of the tithe of Thomas Smith's tenement in W. Overton, the tithes of George Brown, Robert Brown and a third of the tithes of 1½ yardlands that were Thomas Churche now in the possession of Hercules Wright, George Church, Robert Church, Scory Hall and Thomas Kingsman.

Memo. there is a 1/2yardland in Lockeridge now joined to the farm in E. Overton in the possession of Thomas Stretch which pays tithe to the vicar.

Benjamin Smith, vicar, Michael Cooke, Robert Brown, churchwardens, Thomas Smith, John Davis, Robert Church, principal inhabitants.

Memo. There is a sheep sleight of 100 sheep that may pasture with Hackpen flock belonging to the farm in E. Overton now in the possession of John Smith. There is a pension of 13s. 4d. p. a. paid by farmer Cooper of Rabson farm for Temple down due on St. James Tide [25 Jul]. There is an augmentation of 38s. 9d. to be paid in 2 equal portions on the feasts of All Saints [1 Nov] and of the apostles St. Philip and St. James [1 May] was paid formerly by the earl of Pembroke then after he bought E. Overton by James Clark esq., and then by John Bowles esq. as trustee of the present John Clark esq. Offerings 2d. from those born in the parish, 4d. from outcomers. Church goings 8d. for each person. Benjamin Smith, vicar.

OVERTON: Fyfield chapelry

596   n. d. early 17th cent. (D1/24/163/5)
15a. lying on N. side of Fyfield, 4 of which are called Priest Craft on which the vicarage house stands and a garden ground. 3a. lying in a field called Rylands on S. side of Fyfield. A piece of Bushie ground called Priest grove, 2a., the wood of which the vicar is to have no more.

Richard Stretch, William Younge, churchwardens, Nicholas Stanmer, Christopher Stretch, sidesmen.

597   21 Dec 1704 (D1/24/163/6)
In obedience to the command of Gilbert, bishop of Salisbury. The chapelry of Fyfield is a parish of itself with one tithing. The chapel has 18a. of arable land, 3a. of which are in the field called Reylands on the S. side of the river, the other 15a. are N. of the river in the N. field; 4a. of these called Priest Croat lie before the church; 2a. and 2 x ½a. in Fore hill; 1a. in E. hill; 2a. in Court Linch; 1a. in Smillans; 2a. run against Hownsell; 1a. in Red lands; 1 head a. shooting out upon Lockeridge field. A paddock by the church next to Mortimer's paddock, more than 1yd. of ground. The churchyard.

Tithe hay, wool, lamb, calf, wood, hemp, flax and all small tithes belong to the vicar of Overton. 7s p. a. paid to the vicar of Overton at Easter. A plot of wood ground called Priests grove next to Ablase down, c. 4a., in lieu of tithe wood in Fyfield lying E. upon Clifford's ground from the ? gate running W. to a mere called the picked stone and then to the rails of Ablase coppice and S. from a stone in Bird's hedge W. to a hillock and then to an ash in Henly hedge, c. 4 lugs, about Henly road.

Benjamin Smith, vicar, Robert Wells, Thomas Whale, churchwardens, Thomas Smith, Christopher Stretch, John Walter (principal inhabitants).

Memo. The vicar sets his hand to what is above only as far Priest grove there being within the Fyfield perambulation c. 120a. of coppice ground. He believes there ought to be more than 5a. in Priests grove and that he has been shown a plot of ground, c. 12a., bounded towards N. on the corner of Ablase close now in the possession of John Smith running W. straight up to a corner in Lockeridge breach and S. to the same mere stone. Tithe cheese due to the vicar because he finds it mentioned in a copy of the ancient composition between the parish of Fyfield and this vicar.

PATNEY rectory

598   1608 (D1/24/164/1)[1]
Rectory house, with garden, orchard, underwood, fishing, barn, and other buildings, c. 2a. Churchyard, c. 1r.

Meadow: a close of pasture adjoining the rectory on the S., *c.* 1a.; ½a. in W. mead, ½a. of William Nash on the E. and 1r. of John Upton on the W. and abutting on Calves Leaze ditch on the N.; 1r. there next to a pond at the corner of William Gylberd's close, ½a. of William Nash on the E., and 1r. of Brian Manning on the W. and abutting on a stitch of Brian Druett on the S. 3 separate butts, *c.* 3r., in Normead of which the first towards the E. lies between the land of William Nash on the E. and John Upton on the W., the second is also between the land of William Nash and John Upton, the third between the land of John Upton on the W. and wid. Miles on the E. In E. mead in the common meadow or Lot mead [prato customario seu vicissitudinario] called Scotchfolde 2 men's day works at mowing in English 2 mens mowths[2] according to the custom of the tenants of the lord there.

Arable, 1 virgate: in Sandhills ½a. having ½a. of Brian Nash on the N. and 1r. of wid. Miles on the S.; in Staffordland ½a. having ½a. of William Nash on the N. and ½a. of Brian Manning on the S.; ½a. there having 1r. of Brian Nash on the N. and ½a. of William Gilbert on the S.; ½a. there having ½a. of Brian Manning on the N. and ½a. of Lionel Walter on the S.; in Westshortland 1r. between ½a. of Brian Nash on the W. and 1r. of wid. Miles on the E.; ½a. there between ½a. of Brian Nash on the W. and ½a. of William Gylbert on the E.; ½a. there between ½a. of wid. Miles on the W. and ½a. of William Nash on the E.; ½a. there between ½a. of Brian Manning on the W. and 1r. of William Nash on the E.; ½a. there between ½a. of Richard Nash on the W. and ½a. of Brian Hayward on the E.; ½a. there having ½a. of Brian Nash on the W. and ½a. of wid. Miles on the E.; ½a. in Middleshortlands ½a. between ½a. of Brian Nash on the W. and ½a. John Upton on the E.; ½a. there between ½a. of William Nash on the W. and ½a. of Wid. Miles on the E.; ½a. there between ½a. of Brian Hayward on the W. and ½a. of William Nash on the E.; ½a. there between ½a. of William Nash on the W. and ½a. of Richard Nash on the E.; in Eastshortland ½a. between ½a. of William Gilbert on the W. and ½a. of William Nash on the E.; ½a. there between ½a. of William Nash on the W. and 1r. of Richard Nash on the E.; in Woland 1r. between ½a. of William Nash on the N. and 1r. of Brian Hayward on the S.; in Pyzbreech 1r. between 3r. of William Nash on the E. and ½a. of William Gilbert on the W.; ½a. there between ½a. of Brian Manning on the E. and 1r. of Lionel Walter on the W.; in the Clay in Garfurlong ½a. between ½a. of William Nash on the N. and 1r. of Brian Manning on the S.; in the Foreclay ½a. between 1a. of Brian Hayward on the N. and ½a. of William Gilbert on the S.; in the Sands in Underborowe furlong ½a. between ½a. of Lionel Walter on the W. and ½a. of William Nash on the E.; 3r. there between 1r. of William Gilbert on the W. and ½r. of wid. Miles on the E.; in Wandike ½a. between ½a. of Lionel Walter on the W. and ½a. of William Gilbert on the E.; in Netherfurlong land ½a. between ½a. of Brian Hayward on the E. and 1r. of Wid. Miles on the W.; 1r. there between ½a. of Richard Nash on the W. and 1r. of Brian Manning on the E.; in Bessells ½a. between ½a. of William Gilbert on the W. and ½a. of Brian Nash on the E.; ½a. there having on both sides ½a. of William Nash; in Broadlands ½a. 1r. between ½a. of wid. Miles on the E. and ½a. of William Nash on the W.; in Stockfurlong ½a. between ½a. of Brian Hayward on the S. and ½a. of Lionel Walter on the N., and abutting on the green way on the W. Tithe hay in Bellarts ham lying beyond the path near the Allens gate [yate] in the parish of All Cannings. Common of pasture for 6 cattle [averiis] 3 oxen [affris] and 1 bull.

Geoffrey Bygge, rector, William Nash [X], Thomas Humphrey [X], church-wardens, Brian Hayward [X], William Gylbert, Richard Waterman.

1. The document is in Latin.
2. In a survey of Patney made in 1567 the meadow, comprising 12 acres, was described as being divided by lots each year among 8 tenants and the rector. Presumably the rector's allotment was measured as the area of grass which 2 men could cut in a day. (Pembroke survey vol. 1 p. 250; Roxburgh Club, 1909).

599 n. d. late 17th cent.[1] (D1/24/164/2)
A fair dwelling house in sufficient repair. A barn consisting of 6 bays and a cut end at each end. A barn of 2 bays, a stable, a cowhouse, a pig sty, all in good repair. A garden, an orchard, 2 withy beds, a little meadow all on S. side of the dwellinghouse all c. 1½a. A close, 1a., bounded E. parsonage orchard W. a close of John Sweet. Hall close, c. 4½a. bounded N. side the highway, S. side a close of Nicholas Nash. N. mead, c. ½a., bounded W. a ground of John Manning, E. a ground of Thomas Manning. Heath ground, c. 1a., bounded S. side a ground of Abraham Harding, N. side a ground of Joan Nash.

Arable land: In Hall field; ½a. in Sandells furlong bounded S. side a yd. of John Amor N. side a ½a. of Brian Nash butting on a headland of Richard Heyward on W. end, a headland of Nicholas Nash on E. end; in Staffirlane furlong ½a. bounded N. a ½a. of Richard Heyward, S. ½a. John Manning; ½a. bounded N. side ½a of Nicholas Nash, S. ½a. of Thomas Manning; ½a. bounded N. ½a. John Manning, S. ½a. Lionel Walter; in Shortland 1yd. bounded W. ½a. Nicholas Nash, E. 1yd. John Amor; ½a. bounded E. ½a. Thomas Manning, W. ½a. Thomas Stretch; ½a. bounded E. Richard Heyward, W. ½a. John Amor; ½a. bounded W. ½a. John Manning, E. ? ½a. Richard Heyward; ½a. bounded W. ½a. Nicholas Nash, E. ½a. Richard Heyward; ½a. bounded E. ½a. John Amor, W. ½a. Thomas Stretch. In the Little Sand belonging to the same field: In Underborough furlong ½a. bounded W. ½a. Lionel Walter, E. ½a. Thomas Stretch; 3yd. bounded W. 1yd. Thomas Manning, E. 1yd. John Amor. In Wansdyke [Wandike] furlong ½a. bounded W. ½a. Lionel Walters, E. ½a. Thomas Mannings.

In Cannings Path field ½a. bounded N. ½a. Richard Heyward, S. ½a. Thomas Manning. In Shortland belonging to the same field ½a. bounded W. ½a. Bryan Nash, E. ½a. Abraham Harding; ½a. bounded E. ½a. John Amor, W. ½a. Thomas Stretch. In the little Sand belonging to that field; ½a. bounded W. ½a. John Amor, E. ½a. Richard Heyward. In the same furlong 1yd. bounded W. ½a. Nicholas Nash, E. 1yd. John Manning.

In Bessells field ½a. bounded W. ½a. Thomas Manning, E. ½a. Brian Nash. In the same furlong ½a. bounded W. ½a. Lionel Walter, E. ½a. Thomas Stretch. In Broadland furlong ½a. and a single yd. bounded W. ½a. John Amor, E. ½a. Thomas Stretch. In Stokeway furlong ½a. bounded N. ½a. Lionel Walter, S. ½a. Richard Heyward.

In Nightlease field: In Peasebreach furlong ½a. bounded W. 1yd. Lionel Walter. E., ½a. John Manning. In Oland furlong [furland] 1yd. bounded N. and S. Richard Hayward; ½a. bounded N. ½a. Richard Heyward, S. 1yd. John Manning. In Shortland belonging in the same field ½a. bounded E. and N. Thomas Stretch; ½a. bounded W. ½a. Thomas Manning, E. ½a. Thomas Stretch; ½a. bounded ? W. Nicholas Nash, E. ½a. Thomas Stretch; ½a. bounded E. and W. Richard Hayward.

Nicholas Shorter, rector, Richard Hayward, Brian Humphry, churchwardens.

1. Nicholas Shorter was rector between 1662-1682.

600   1 Jan 1705 (D1/24/164/3)

A dwelling house, barn, stable and other outhouses, a garden, orchard, withy beds and ponds all *c.* 2a. A close of meadow ground at the lower end of the orchard, 1a. ½a. meadow in W. mead near Calves leaze. A close of ground adjoining the barn, 1½a. The churchyard, *c.* 1yd. 2 closes of meadow ground by the wayside near Hall bridge, 5a. A close of sheep meadow called Heath, 1a.

Arable land in the common fields: In Sandals ½a. lying between ½a. Brian Nash N., ½a. John Amor S.; in Stafford land ½a. between ½a. Margery Hayward wid. N., ½a. Brian Nash S.; ½a. between ½yd. Nicholas Nash N., ½a. Edward Noyes S.; ½a. between John Manning N., Lionel Walter S.; in W. Shortland 1yd. between Nicholas Nash W., wid. Hayward E.; ½a. between Nicholas Nash W., Edward Noyes E.; ½a. between John Amor W., John Manning E.; ½a. between John Manning W., wid. Hayward E.; ½a. between Nicholas Nash W., wid. Hayward E.; ½a. between 2 x ½a. John Amor; in Middle Shortland ½a. between Bryan Nash W., Brian Humphrey E.; ½a. between 2 x ½a. John Amor; in E. Shortland ½a. between 2 x ½a. of wid. Hayward; ½a. between John Amor W., Nicholas Nash E.; ½a. between wid. Hayward W., Edward Noyes E.; ½a. between wid. Hayward W., John Amor E.; in Woland 1yd. between 2 x yd. of wid. Hayward; in Pys Breach 1r. between wid. Hayward E., Edward Noyes W.; ½a. between John Manning E., John Amor W.; in the Clay in Garforland ½a. between wid. Hayward N., John Manning S.; in the Foreclay ½a. between wid. Hayward N., Edward Noyes S.; in the Sands in Underborough furlong ½a. between Lionel Walter W., John Amor E.; 3yd. between John Manning W., John Amor E.; in Mandike [*prob. Wansdyke*] furlong ½a. between John Drewet W., John Amor E.; in Nether Long lands ½a. between wid. Hayward E., John Amor W.; 1yd. shooting down to Piggs paddock; in Bessels furlong ½a. between Edward Noyes W., Brian Nash E.; ½a. between 2 x ½a. of wid. Hayward; in Broad land ½a. between John Manning W., John Amor E.; 1yd. of arable land next adjoining (i. e. the last mentioned land); in Stoke furlong ½a. between wid. Hayward S., Lionel Walter N. In all 15a. more or less.

Tithe corn, hay, lambs, wool, pigs, geese, apples, pears, hemp, peas, etc., are all due and payable in kind by the customary tenants of the parish. Tithe hay growing in Billarts-ham in All Cannings. Tithe of 3a. of meadow in W. mead belonging to the rectory of Marden, of 4a. these belonging to Overton farm, and of 8a. so called now belonging to Brian Nash all in W. mead. Customary tithes as the sum of 3s. 4d. payable yearly at Easter by the occupier or owner of the mill in lieu of tithe for the same.

Custom 6d. for every calf, 1d. for every colt, 2d. for every cow. Every yardland pays 2d. for eggs and 1d. for garden herbs. Each parishioner over 16 years is bound by law to pay 2d. for offerings. These are all yearly duties and are to be reckoned for at every Easter.

Commons of pasture for 4 cows, 3 horses and 1 bull in the fields and meadows when they are broken.

James Cobham, rector, John Manning, Brian [Bryant] Humphrey, churchwardens, Nicholas Nash, Edward Noyes, parishioners.

PERTWOOD rectory

601   5 Dec 1677 (D1/24/165/1)
A dwelling house with a barn and stable adjoining; 1 meadow; a garden; 1½a. arable in the E. field; 2½a. in the Middle field; 3½a. in the W. field.

Robert Olden, rector, John Mervyn.

602   18 Jan 1705 (D1/24/165/2)[1]
2½a. in the E. field. 2½a. in the Middle field, 2½a. in the W. field. 1 close of meadow, 1a. The value of the land and the tithes amounts to £25 p. a.

Robert Olden, rector, Enoch Williams.

1.   Written on the back of part of a final concord.

PEWSEY rectory

603   24 Jun 1609 (D1/24/166/1)
The parsonage house with 2 barns and a stable standing in the barton adjoining, also a garden lying on both sides of the house. A little close lying right before the parsonage house which was once an orchard with a pond in it. A close of meadow or pasture on the E. of the house, c. 1½a. A close of meadow or pasture called Sinberryes, c. 2a., lying in the tithing of Down Pewsey between the tenement and ground of the lord of the manor, now held by Edmund Cook, formerly by William Amor deceased, on the S., and a cottage with a close belonging to the rectory on the N. A close of meadow or pasture called Coxhill, c. 3a., lying near a house and grounds called Bucklies held by John Benger gent. on the N. and the house and ground of the lord of the manor now held by Edmund Amor on the S. Another close of meadow or pasture, c. 4a., called Broad mead or Broad Marsh mead, lying in the tithing of Down Pewsey and abutting on the W. side of the river that comes from Bucklies house or mill and the close called Coxhill, and on the E. on the arable field called Broome Croft field, allotted to the rectory for ever out of the demesnes of the farm of the manor to be occupied from Ladyday [25 Mar] yearly until St. Giles's day [1 Sep] about harvest, and afterwards to the copyhold tenants of the tithing for pasturing their beasts and cattle until the following Ladyday, in lieu of tithe grass and hay on the farm meadows, grass or hay places; which meadow now, by mutual

agreement between the present parson, Mr. Meredith Morgan, and the copyhold tenants of the manor, belongs to the rectory all year long. There are also adjoining 2a. more newly inclosed and allotted to the parsonage out of the beasts common of the tithing of Down Pewsey, in lieu of 15 beasts pasturage from Holy Rood day [3 May] until the eve of St. Martin the bishop [10 Nov] and far more beneficial.

2 several cottages in Down Pewsey with 2 gardens, and a little close of meadow or pasture of ½yd. belonging to them, one held by John Jeney, carpenter, and the other held by Katherine Rose, wid. 3½a. arable in Down Pewsey in the field called Hither Blacknell or E. Blacknell; 7a. arable land in the W. Blacknell; 1a. in Shorthedge furlong; 1a. arable land in Shercott field; 3a. in the E. Hitching field near to Fifield; 1a. arable land in Down Pewsey Hitching in the W. of Wickham hedge, ½a. arable land at Mill Croft gate; 4½a. in the E. Clay in Southcott field; 3a. arable land in Down Pewsey Hitching; 6a. in Southcott W. field beneath Longe burrow; 2a. in the same field above Long Burrow; 3a. arable land at Mouchers croft end. Pasturing of 12 kine and a bull on the farm pasture called Weastbury bounded on the W. with a meadow called Long moor, and on the N. adjoining the highway to Devizes, abutting on the W. on the Broad field of Sharcott, and on the E. on the grounds of Andrew Harding gent. and the grounds of the tenants of Down Pewsey. The pasturing of 100 wether sheep to go continually all the year with the sheep of the workmen on the downs and common fields as in the past. 2 ridges of arable land of 3yd., 1 of which shoots down on Edmunds Chrouch and the other on Parsons bush.

Thomas Bybie, curate, Edmund Sommersette, Timothy Pynckney, churchwardens, Richard Paple [X], Henry Wattes [X], Cuthbert Cole and William Allen [X], sidesmen.

Endorsement: Exchequer case (between John Thorpe clerk plaintiff and John Neate, gent. defendant.)

At the execution of a commission in this cause at the Rose and Crown in Everleigh 24 Sept 1724 this writing was (produced to Thomas Baden gent. as witness on the part of the defendant) before us John Powell, M. Foster, John Gilbert.

604   6 Nov 1671 (D1/24/166/2)

In the E. field next Fifield 3a. above Docke Furlong way a linchet on E. side and land of Richard Harding on W. side. 1a. in a furlong shooting against Emit hill, land of George Allin on E. side, land of Ralph Smith on W. side. 1½a. in a furlong shooting against Weedhill, a linchet on E. side and land of William Allin on W. side. 1a. shooting against Titcombe bottom shooting against the last 1½a., land now of Eleanor Allin on E. side, land of Richard Lewes esq., on W. side. 1a. in a furlong shooting against Short Hedge furlong, land Roger Coleman on W. side, land of Sarah Dyke on W. side. 1a. in Short Hedge furlong land of Amor Summerset on W. side, land of Roger Oram on E. side. 3a. which head Short Hedge furlong shooting on Short Hedge, land of Eleanor Allin on N. side.

3a. in the W. field outside [without] Wanbridge in a furlong shooting against the water lake, linchets on E. and W. sides. ½ head a. shooting against Millcroft gate the way on S. side. 1a. in Longborrow among the White earth pits, land now of Eleanor Allin on S. side, land of Richard Clarke on N. side. 1a. shooting against Edmonds Crutch, lands now of John Stratton on N. side, a linchet on S. side. ½a. on the farm hill between 2 linchets shooting against the Quar pit. 7a. in Blakenill shooting against Sharcott field, land of Roger Oram on E. side and a linchet on W. side.

1a. in Sharcott field shooting on the way a linchet on W. side, land now of John Godman on E. side. 1a. shooting on Upavon way, land of Ralph Smith on E., land now of Edward Munday on W. side. 3a. on E. side of the green way as goes to Longborrow and shooting on the farm land at the S. end and land of William Allin on N. end. 3a. shooting on Park way and upon the last 3a., farm land on S. side and a linchet on N. side. 100 sheep to depasture with the work flock 10 beasts and a bull to go and feed in the farm grounds called Westberries from 3 May until Holy Cross being the 14th Sep.

A meadow ground called Cinberies, c. 3a., with a cottage belonging to it in N. E. corner, the dwelling house of Amor Summerset on S. side. A pasture ground called Broad Marsh, 5a., joining to Bromcroft on E. side and Cotshill on W. side. A pasture ground joining to the farm grounds called Inlands, c. 1½a. The parsonage house with 2 barns, a stable and outhouses, the backside gardens and orchard joining it, c. 4a.

Thomas Pyke, Richard Hardinge, churchwardens, Anthony Godman, overseer, Ralph Smith, John Winter and William Allin, assistants.

Endorsement as 603.

605   15 Dec 1704 (D1/24/166/3)
An old dwelling house with offices thereunto belonging at present in good repair with a garden adjoining. An old barn S. from the yard of 5 bays of building, a garden adjoining in the W. end and a new barn of 4 bays contiguous to the E. end of it. Another new barn on the E. side of the yard of 4 bays having a stable for saddle horses with a hay loft over it adjoining the end of the stable. 2 stables for carthorses on W. side of the yard with a carthouse at the other end and a lodging room for servants over it all these several outhouses are in good repair.

An orchard and kitchen garden and fish pond at the lower side of the orchard. Home close, 2a., bounded partly by Thomas Poulton and Jasper Marchment on W. side. A close called St. Bury's, 4a., bounded N. by Humphrey Tarrant and Thomas Banks and by itself, E. and W. by 2 highways, S. by Edmund Somerset and by itself. A ground called the Gore, c. 14a., bounded E. by the farm cowlease, W. by the grounds of the tenants now in the possession of John Glass, the wid. Tucker and Edward Sheppherd, S. by itself and the farm grounds, N. by the highway.

2 grounds called Cotswold and Broad marsh, c. 13a., separated by the river. Broad marsh bounded S. the wid. Pyke's grounds on other sides by itself. Cotswold, bounded S. by William Amor, W. the highway leading to Buck lease, N. by itself.

Several parcels in the common fields, c. 35½a. 1r.: In E. field; in Dock furlong 3a.; at Lamb pits 1a.; at Weedhill 2a.; in Sawers Hedge furlong 1a.; in Short hedge 1a.; at Mouchers croft 3a. In W. field at Parkway, in 2 pieces, 6a.; above Long Borrough 1a.; near Farm hillway alias Edmunds Crouch 1a. In Down Pewsey field 3a.; near Milcroft gate ½a.; on the W. side at Wickham hedge 1a.; at the hill linchets ½a. 1r. In Sharcott field 1a.; at W. Blackenell 7a.; at the Quar pits 3a.; all being by estimation.

The right to feed 100 sheep upon W. down and in the common fields called E. and W. Blacknell. The right to all tithes in Pewsey except what has been formerly in compositions between the farm and the rector.

John Hersent, rector, Ralph Winter, Ralph Smith junior, churchwardens, Ralph Smith senior, George Allen, Edmund Summersett.

Endorsement as 603.

PLAITFORD chapelry

606   18 Sep 1608 (D1/24/167/1)
We present that the glebe land in Plaitford belonging to the rectory of West Grimstead is 1 close of meadow, woodland and pasture of *c.* 4a. and is bounded with the highway on the N., the farm meadow on the S., the churchyard [litton] on the E. and the farm barton on the W.

Richard Wall, rector, William Sanders [X], Richard Russell [X], church-wardens, John Read, Edward Barter, sidesmen.

607   n. d. [1704x1705][1] (D1/24/167/2)
Terrier of the chapel of Plaitford annexed to the rectory of W. Grimstead. A dwelling house containing 2 rooms being skilling on 1 side. A barn, a stable 2 grounds adjoining *c.* 5a. Tithe in kind of all sorts as corn, grass, wood, cow white, calves, pigs, honey, hops, wool, lambs, geese all to the value of £30 p. a. We have heard that formerly these was aid out of the Melchet [Milchwood] park £4 p. a. but not to our knowledge.

John Foot, rector, Thomas Pinhorne, churchwarden.

1.   The churchwardens were recorded in the bishop's visitation book, Oct 1704 (WSRO D1/50/6).

608   1783 (D1/24/167/3)
A small brick and thatched dwelling consisting of a little kitchen and buttery below stairs, and 2 chambers over them plastered and ceiled. A small garden with a hedge fence adjoining the glebe land of 4½a. on which 3 oak trees are standing. Great and small tithes of the whole parish. The wages of the clerk are 20s. p. a. The communion plate consist of a ½ pint silver cup and cover weighing *c.* 10½oz., a pewter flagon and small pewter dish.

Neville Wells, rector, Roger Pope, John Hinton, churchwardens.

POOLE KEYNES rectory

609   2 Oct 1622 (D1/24/168/1)
2 yardlands, and pasture and feeding for all manner of sheep and cattle in the fields and commons as far as the freehold or any of the tenants of 2 yardlands.

8½a. in Woodfield of which there are 5½a. butting on the ground called Littmoore in the parish of Kemble; 1a. butting on the drove lane; 1½a. butting on Shurmoore Corner; and ½a. butting on Kents mead. 5a. in Toms field: 1a. and 2 x ½a. butting on Millome; 2a. in Crow furlong, one butting on a ground of Edward Hales, the other on a ground of John Blanford's; and 2 x ½a. butting on the drove lane. In S. field: 4a. butting on the drove lane called Rickes lane; and 1 farndell butting on Sir Nevill Poole's ground in the moor. A dwelling house, a barn and a ground about the house, c. 2a. Tom field ground, c. 4a., William Sparrow's ground on the S., the field on the W., and Millome on the E. A ground called Shurmoor, c. 4a., Hawkins having a ground on the E. and Hinton on the W. A ground called Southill on the S. of Shurmoore, c. 4a., Hawkin's ground on the E., Beechie on the W. and Allis on the S. A ground called the Rickes, c. 2a., Blanford having a ground on the N. and Hinton on the S. A ground called Goulditch, c. 4a., the S. field lying on the E., Longford having a ground on the N. and William Birt on the S. There belongs to it certain lots in the Lottmead for 2 yardlands. A ground called the Moore ground of 22a., Skidmoure and Richard Allis having grounds on the S. and Christopher Munden N.

All the tithes of all the grounds and enclosures of Poole moor, both the tithes of the tenements and freeholds and of all the grounds of Sir Nevill Poole recently enclosed. The tithe of Pilsmoore lying between Oaksey [Oxie] and Poole, being part of the farm of Poole. And generally all tithes, oblations, and mortuaries of the farm, and also of the freehold and tenements and all probate of wills within the parish because it is a peculiar.[1] Every customary tenant that holds any living by the yardland is to pay 4d. a yardland p. a. rising to 5s. p. a. with the 15th yardland. The tithe of 2 coppices [coops] woods, one called N. wood held by Sir Nevill Poole, and the other called Park wood held by the tenants of Poole, and it is lawful for the parson to put in his feller and to cut and carry away the tithe drift with the tops and lops of the trees that are within the tithe drift as often as it shall happen.

John Ferebe, rector, William Hall, churchwarden, John Blanford, William Sparrow, sidesmen, Thomas Hawkins, William Birt [X], William Hintone, John Fisher [X], William Goulden [X], Thomas Skidmoore [X], Francis Hartright [X], Richard Longford [X].

1.   There is no evidence that this was ever the case.

610   25 Sep 1677 (D1/24/168/2)
A house, garden, barn, homestall, and a little close adjoining, c. 1a. Several grounds: the Moor, c. 15a.; Golding, c. 4a.; Reeks, c. 2a.; Santhill, 4a.; Shurmoor, 4a.; Thoms field lease, 2a. In the S. field 4a. of arable lands in Stan furlong; 1 farndell by the Goldage. In Thoms field, 5a. of arable lying dispersedly. In Wood field, 8a. lying dispersedly and 1 farndell. Tithes great and small.

Thomas Myles, rector, William Sparrow, Thomas Blanford, churchwardens.

611   15 Dec 1704 (D1/24/168/3)
A house and garden, a barn and stable and home stall and a little close adjoining, c. 1a. Several grounds: The Moor, c. 18a.; Goldige c. 4a.; Rix, c. 2a.; Santill, 4a.;

Shurmore, 4a.; Thomsfield, c. 2a.; Wood lease, c. 2a.; Frogmore, c. 4a. In S. field 4a. of arable in Stan furlong and a farndell by the Goldiges. In Thoms field 5a. lying dispersedly. In Wood field 8a. of arable lying dispersedly. Sheep pastures in the common fields proportional to 2 yardlands.

Elias Carteret, rector, Henry Blandford, William Pitt, churchwardens, William Sparrowe, Thomas Blandford, sidesmen.

612   18 Jul 1783 (D1/24/168/4)

Before we enter upon a description of the houses and lands etc. belonging to the parsonage it is proper to observe that the parsonage has lately undergone a great alteration by an enclosure in the parish which took place by authority of Parliament in 1772 whereby allotments of lands have been made to the rector in lieu of tithes, lands exchanged and the whole parish exonerated from tithes except a few grounds which will hereafter be described for which money payments are fixed, payable half yearly, Ladyday [25 Mar] and Michaelmas [25 Sep], amounting in the whole to £5 14s. 4d. A copy of the award is ordered by the Act to be enrolled in one of his majesty's courts of record at Westminster or with the clerk of the Peace of Wiltshire[1] and having been so enrolled to be lodged with the lord of the manors of Kemble and Poole for the perusal, use and benefit of all interested parties.

1. A dwelling house, built with stone, timbered part with elm and part with oak and covered with slate, containing on the ground floor a parlour, a hall and kitchen, 2 pantries and a small cellar and a brewhouse adjoining all ceiled except the brewhouse. The parlour floored with deal and wainscotted chair high, the rest paved with stone. Above stairs 4 chambers and 2 closets, the floors oak, elm and ash all ceiled except the chamber over the kitchen and 2 garrets over the hall and parlour chambers. A barn and stable under roof divided by a partition wall c. 56ft. in length, the walls stone the timber elm and covering thatch, also a pig sty and necessary covered with slate and a coal house.

2. The rectory has c. 213a. including the churchyard, whereof 164a. are arable and 48 meadow and pasture, with right of feed in the lanes within the parish; Namely: A plot of land near the house, c. 11a., bounded W. by W. field and Frogmoor, N. by Selby's wood, E. by Court fields, and the lane leading thereto all belonging to Charles Coxe esq., S. by the road leading to the church, including within it the dwelling house and other buildings, 2 gardens communicating with one and other by an arch over a pool, 2 small courtyards, one within the other, and 3 meadow or pasture grounds; the first to the S. called William's close, 2a. 11p., the second to the N. called the Home close, c. 2½a., the third having Selby's wood on N., 6a. The courts are enclosed with stone walls and the gardens on 3 sides the same, and on the remaining side with a quickset hedge faced with stone.

An arable ground called the Parsonage wood, c. 5a., bounded W. by Wood lane, E. by the Breach, N. by a ground called Myles wood, both belonging to Mr. Coxe. A pasture ground called the Parsonage moor, 22a., bounded E. Tadpole lane, W. Mr. Cripse's grounds in the parish of Oaksey, N. Wilkin's moor now Mr. Coxe's. An arable ground called Goulditch, nearly 4a., bounded W. Tadpole lane, N. and S. Mr. Coxe's grounds called Goulditches. An allotment of arable land in

Gravel furlong in S. field, 19a. 1r., 7p. abutting on Brick lane on E. and lying between Mr. Coxe's lands in the same field. A meadow ground called Sant Hill, 4½a., lying behind Shurmoore to E. and bounded to W. by it. A large field of arable called Woodfield, 68a. 1r., 27p., bounded N. and W. by lands of the parish of Kemble, S. by Court fields and Kent's mead, divided into 2 by a quickset hedge which runs across it from S. to N. from N. E. corner of Kent's mead. A large field of arable called Tomsfield, 67a. 1r. 10p., bounded S. and W. by Broadlane and the road leading to Ewen, N. by Mr. Hinton's and Mr. George's lands in the tithing of Ewen; the public quarry is within this field but not included in the measure of it and contains 2r. 27p. A meadow ground called Quay Pool, 3a. 2r. 29p., having Tomsfield on W., Millham in the parish of Somerford Keynes on E.

2 small pieces of meadow now formed together namely: Tomsfield leaze and Goosehay, c. 3a. lying between the foresaid Millham on E. and Tomsfield on W.

N. B. There were formerly certain lots in Lot mead for 2 yardlands which was what the glebe was estimated at as appears in [609], but this Lot mead having long since been divided and enclosed, by what authority is not known, either no allotment was made to the rector for them, or which is more probable, the allotment that was made is now through the length of time fallen into the hands of the lord of the manor.

3. Money payments in lieu of tithe: £3 2s. 10d. p. a. payable half yearly in lieu of tithe of Moor's moors lying at S. E. part of the parish, bounded N. Elmoores, S. W. by Mr. Coxe's moors, S. E. and N. E. by lands in the parish of Somerford Keynes. £2 1s. 6d. p. a. payable half yearly in lieu of tithes of the Elmoores bounded N. by S. field, S. Moon's moors. 10s. p. a. payable in the same manner, in lieu of tithe of a ground belonging to Robert Adamson esq., lying between the most westerly of W. fields and the Ridings. Oblations and mortuaries are due by terrier and reserved by the Act [*enabling the Enclosure*].

4. No trees of any kind growing in the churchyard, neither any timber fit for use or of any great value on any part of the glebe the whole having been cut down from time to time for repairs.

5. The church and chancel have lately been rebuilt from the foundation and neatly pewed with deal, the church by the parishioners, the chancel, except the communion table and rail by the rector. The furniture is a bell, a bible, 2 prayer books, a surplice, a pulpit cloth and cushion, a cloth and proper linen for the communion table, and a pewter flagon and a silver chalice with 'Henry Blandford, churchwarden 1692', inscribed on it.

6. The front wall of the churchyard is repaired by the parishioners, the other 3 sides by Charles Coxe esq., lord of the manor.

7. The churchwardens are chosen yearly at Easter, one by the rector, the other by the parishioners.

8. The clerk, who is also sexton, is appointed by the rector but his customary wages, 10s. p. a., are paid by the churchwardens.

George Green, rector, Henry Blandford, Henry Stevens, churchwardens, Thomas Stevens.

1. Transferred to the clerk of the Peace of Gloucestershire in 1897. Now held in the Gloucestershire Record Office.

POTTERNE vicarage

613 10 May 1588 (D1/24/169/1)
Terrier made by William Rook, Mark Sartayen, churchwardens, John Long senior, John Long junior, sidesmen, John Flower, the farmer and Robert Pryor.

A close behind the vicarage barn abutting on the Hollow way, c. 2a. arable. Another close beyond the grove abutting on the highway, c. 3a. arable. A close called the New lees shotting on Mr. Burley's brook, c. 6a. arable. 1a. arable lying in the Claye by the mere side on the E. and William Bristow on the W. 4a. meadow in Cadley mead, Mr. Burley on both sides. A pasture close called Dolls, 2a., William Long having a plot on the W. An orchard and a garden within the mud wall of the vicarage, and a barton.

Tithes due to the parson from the following lands. Old Park, the New Park and the Park mead held by John Dauntsey [Dantyssy] of West Lavington gent. Hurst: held by John Dauntsey, and a meadow called Iselee.

Cadley: Land owned Richard Burlye gent.; 8a. in the Field held by William Rooke; 2a. at E. Well and 1a. in held by John Long lying in the Clay by Swaynes; another 2a. held by Philip May lying in the Clay; 2a. more held by Richard Prictwo lying in the Clay; 1a. arable held by Richard Smith on Chillesbury; a meadow at his house called Whistley held by Mr. Burlye; the end of Sanfordes mead from the mere stone upward held by Mr. John Dauntsey, and a parcel of underwood lying in Lymilles

Land of Mr. Drew: land held by William Hill and John Barenes. Land of Mr. Rodgers; Philip May of Pudding's portion whole tithe. Nicholas Bond's portion; Thomas Collins's portion; whole tithes of James Newman's portion; John Stuckle junior for a close called Tankers land, another pasture close by the lane side, and another close at the end of Little barn; Mr. Lamborne's portion; Robert Pirree's portion held by John Long of Woodbridge.

Stephen Stuckle's home close, John Bristow's close by his house, and John Luffe's close by his house. Thomas Ellington's portion of the land of Mr. Rodgers; 2a. in Kytmere at the lower end of the close by the vicarage.

Spray tithe; in the tenure of John Bartlett with 2½a. of arable lying in the tenure of Nicholas Bond. Byde; in the tenure of William Lavington, farmer. Tithe of all the mills. The kine white, 6d. for a cow tithe and the calves. Canhill; in the tenure of < John *struck through*> Thomas Busschell; John Drew gent., a meadow shooting upon the marsh lane; John Wheeler, a meadow lying in Rokes marsh and another pasture ground in Fylford croft.

614 28 Mar 1609 (D1/24/169/2)
Tithe wool, lamb and calves, consideration for cow white. The profits of the churchyard. Whole tithe of ½ yardland which Ralph Nash now holds from Mr. Trew and tithe hay of Broadmead adjoining the marsh from the gate to the oaks which grow towards the upper end. The whole tithe of John Harvest's land. The whole tithe of Mr. Rogers' land except certain grounds which are now occupied by James Newman and Dovies' mead, Linchils piece and Little Kitmoor now held by John Stuckle senior. The whole tithe of Spraye. Tithe of Spray acre. The whole tithe of Bide. The whole tithe of the Park and Hurst now occupied by Sir

John Dauntsey [Danteseye]. The tithe of *c*. 2a. in Sandford at the hither end of the mead. The vicar has quietly possessed the tithe of a certain ground called Abbats Ball for the space of 14 or 15 years, but John Harvest a sworn man with us says he remembers that John Long, sometime parson, gave this tithe to the vicar so that to whom in right it appears with we cannot suppose.

Tithe of all the mills and of a close adjoining Rushfords mill. Tithe of a meadow called Woodfine mead. Tithe of a meadow taken from Spray lying by Potterne wood, now occupied by wid. Trippett.

Isley mead now occupied by Sir John Dauntsey. The tithe wood of Limehill. A ground called Doles, 5a., joining the Crosslanes to the vicars own use, tithe free. A ground called Frogwell, 8a., to the vicars own use without tithe. A meadow by the Park gate, 5a., to the vicar's own use, tithe free. 5a. of meadow by Devizes way to the vicar's own use, tithe free. 1a. in the Clay by the bushes to the vicar's own use, tithe free. 1 close of arable joining to the vicar's barn, 3a., to vicar's own use tithe use. An orchard, a barn, a cowhouse a kitchen, a garden and a dwelling house.

The whole tithe of Canehill appertains to the vicar as appears by a judgement given against John Long, sometime parson, for Mr. Noies who bought the tithes of the vicar and is ready to confirm upon oath. If there appertains any other profits to the vicar by which we now remember not we will upon further instruction give information thereof.

Nicholas Stranguidge, vicar, Philip Maye [X], William Rook, churchwardens, Philip Wheller, John Harvest, Thomas Smyth, John Pierce [X]

615   16 May 1638 (D1/24/169/3)
A dwelling house, orchard, garden, backside, barn and hay house, a close of arable, *c*. 3a., a ground of arable, *c*. 5a., 2 arable grounds called Frogwell, *c*. 8a., a ground called Doales, *c*. 4a., Cadly mead, *c*. 5a., 1a. in Potterne Clay, the profits of the churchyard, the vicar keeping the bounds all in the occupation of John Northey, vicar of Potterne.

Tithes due to the vicar on the following lands: Potterne Park and Hurste occupied by Sir John Danvers; 4 grounds called Knowlakers, *c*. 20a., part of a ground called Sanforde Two acres at the upper end of it and a ground of arable called Abots Bale, *c*. 6a., occupied by John Grubbe esq.; Canehill occupied by Mr. Richard Steevens of Stanton; one arable ground called the Furlong, *c*. 5a. occupied by William Hunte; one arable ground called Cheriehill occupied by Nicholas Cremues, *c*. 5a.; Lipstreet Leaze, *c*. 2a., the Marsh mead, part of the meadow called Wineslade, *c*. 3a., occupied by Philip Harveste.; Wineslade, *c*. 3a., occupied by Edward Bayley of Devizes; Tanckerland, *c*. 3a., a ground called Keetmoor, *c*. 3a. occupied by Michael Paradise except 3 rudges in Keetmoor; a ground called Keetmoor, 2a., occupied by William Rooke; E. Brooke leaze, *c*. 6a., occupied by Thomas Collans; Lymehills wood, *c*. 10a. in Potterne Clay, 3 arable grounds called Eyres Closes, *c*. 18a., a ground called Chilbury, *c*. 4a., occupied by John Hitchkocke; Byde occupied by William Maundrell gent., and William Chappell; 2 grounds called Potterne Wood leazes, one other meadow ground lying by Potterne wood occupied by Robert Longe; Spray grounds occupied by John Meriweather of Lavington; a ground called Roomoor, *c*. 5a., occupied by John Meriweather; ½ yardland occupied William Harvest; 2 grounds called Blackborough, *c.* 8a., a ground lying by Thomas Payne's house, *c.* 2a., 1a. in John Blandford's leaze, ½a. in the Clay field occupied by John Harvest.; a ground called Woodfinemead, *c.* 5a. occupied by Rebecca Harvest wid.; ½ yardland occupied by John Harvest; a ground called Barme, *c.* 2a., occupied by Philip Smyth; a ground called Blackborough leas, *c.* 4a., occupied by William Lye; Spray acre, 1a. in Potterne Clay occupied by Elizabeth Mogridge wid.; a meadow ground called Rushford mead, *c.* 3a., occupied by John Pearse; the orchard in Cadeley, *c.* 4a., Square mead, 4a., and the Younder mead nigh to the Grove, 4a., and the String by Fidington, *c.* 2a., occupied by John Grubbe esq.; 1a. in the Clay fields occupied by Philip Wheller; a close occupied by Richard Wikes.

The tenth calf due to the vicar. If the owner has but 7 the vicar is to have 1 and to repay the owner 1½d. If there be but 6 or under if the owner sells them the vicar is to have 6d. a calf, if the owner kills them the vicar is to have the left shoulder and for every weaned calf ½d. throughout the parish except the farm. In consideration of cow white tithe due to the vicar 1d. a cow: wool and lamb. If it be not a whole tithe of lamb [*i. e. less than 10 lambs*] then the vicar is *?*to have one and to repay the owner 1½d.; if it be under 7 the owner is to pay 1½d. for the fall of every lamb to the vicar except the farm. For suckling [stucling] pigs the tithe due to the vicar if it be but 7 is to have one and to repay the owner 1½d. If it be 6 or under the owner is to pay the vicar ½d. for the fall of every pig except the farm. The vicar ought to keep a boar.

1d. a garden and tithe of apples throughout the parish except the farm. Mills occupied by William Longe of Marston, tithe due 2s. p. a.; by John Harvest, 1s. p. a.; by John Blanford 8d. p. a.; Roger Bredmore 20d. p. a. Byde mill occupied by Edward Marchant. A ground called Lymehiles occupied by Roger Wheller, tithes due to the vicar. For the sale of every calf 1d. except the farm. For geese tithe throughout the parish except the farm.

William Rooke, John Merewether [X], Christopher Long, William Bristo, John Huden, Robert Gorge, William Hunt, sidesmen.

616   25 Apr 1676 (D1/24/169/4)
Whole tithes of the following lands: The Park in the possession of James Harris gent. Bide occupied by Stephen Browne, tenant to James Harris. Hurst occupied by Ambrose Brown, tenant to Dr. Yeats and Islemead owned by the same Dr. Yeats. 4 grounds called Knowle acres formerly Philip Whellar occupied by wid. George, tenant to Mr. Walter Grubbe. 2a. at the upper end of Sanford occupied by James Still, tenant to Mary and Martha Pitt. 2 grounds in the possession of William Smyth one called Abots Bale the other Barme. The grounds called Cane hills owned by John Sloper of Devizes gent. A ground called Chery hills owned by Richard Vince of Devizes. A ground called the Furlong occupied by Gabriel Cromwell, tenant to William Hunt gent. A ground called Lipstreet, part of a ground called Broad mead from the gate to the oaken tree towards the upper end, a ground called Winislade, a ground called Baylies mead, a ground called Woodfine mead all owned by Philip Harvest gent. A ground called Gooseham occupied by Gabriel Cromwell, tenant to William Hunt gent. 2 grounds called Tankerland and Wedland, a close called the Croft, except 1 rudge

in Wedland, all occupied by Walter Coleman, tenant to Jane Rainger. A ground
called Little Keetmoor in the possession of Richard Rooke. A ground called E.
Brook lease lately Collinge's now in the possession of John Munday of Devizes.
Limehills, formerly wood now destroyed, in the possession of William Wayling.
A piece of land in Potterne Clay, 10a. 3 grounds called Eyre closes, a ground
called Sheephouse lease, a ground lying by Limehills formerly coppice now
destroyed all in the possession of William Wayling. 3 grounds called Potterne
wood leases formerly Christopher Long's occupied by wid. George alias Edwards,
tenant to Mr. Walter Grubb.

There are 2 grounds in Potterne wood formerly coppice now destroyed that
have been ploughed and sown. Mr. John Northey, then vicar of Potterne,[1]
demanded the tithes of these grounds. Robert Longe desired the tithe whereupon
Mr. Northey commenced a suit against Robert Longe and received the tithe. A
meadow called Tripets mead now in the possession of James Harris gent. Spray
grounds in the possession of Francis Meriwether of Easterton. A close adjoining
Raingborn mill occupied by William Baylie, tanner.

Spray lying in Potterne Clay near Coxtall piece. A ground called Roomers
in the possession of Richard Meriwether. ½ yardland, lately William Harris' of
Imber, 3 grounds occupied by William Coopar and 8a. occupied by Thomas
Wats and Richard Smyth tenants to Mrs. Harris of Imber.

Hoder close occupied by Richard Smyth, tenant to Mrs. Harris of Imber.
Land of John Harvest of Keevil occupied by John Cookesey. ½ yardland, lately
John Harvest's, namely 1 ground called Devizes way leaze, 1 ground called
Riley, 3 grounds called Weeke leazes in the possession of Mrs. White and William
Hunt. A ground called Little Blakeburie in the possession of William Lye, tenant
to Mrs. Jane Grubb. A ground called Parsonage Grove in the possession of William
Lye. Rushefords mead occupied by Thomas Purchas. Orchard mead, the Square
mead, the Yonder mead and the Strings near Fiddington common occupied by
John Cooksey, tenant to John Hayward. Hartmore occupied by John Munday
and Roger Powell, tenants to Mrs. Salter. 1a. in the Sands near Coxtal occupied
by wid. George, tenant to Mrs Grubb. A close part of Collingses land occupied
by Daniel Church.

The profits of the churchyard. Tithe calves, wool, lamb, and all other privy
tithes in the parish. For cow white 1d. for every cow in the parish. For every calf
weaned under 7 if the vicar will not deny he is to have ½d. a calf, if we have 7
the vicar is to have one paying the owner 1½d. Every garden 1d., and the tithe
of all orchards in the parish. Tithe of all geese. For the sale of every colt 1d. Tithe
of Hurst mill [...], Worton mill 2s. 6d. Rushfords mill 8d., Whislie mill 12d., the
little mill 8d., Raingbourne mill 1s. 8d., Byde mill 3s. 4d.

Glebe all tithe free [*i. e. of rectoral tithes*]: 2 grounds called Frogwell, 8a.;
grounds called Devizes Way leaze, 5a. and Doales, 5a.; a meadow adjoining to
Potterne park, 5a.; 1a. of arable near the Claybush. A dwelling house, garden,
barn, stable, hay house and backside. If anything else comes to our knowledge
which at present we remember not upon further instruction we shall be able to
give information.

Richard Bowman, vicar, Robert Poape, William Lye, churchwardens, John
May, Thomas Parsons [X], sidesmen.

1. John Northey was vicar between 1629 and 1668.

617   8 Jan 1705 (D1/24/169/5)

Glebe land: 2 grounds called Frogwells 5a. A ground called Doles or Five Lanes ground, 5a. A meadow by the Park gate called Cadley or Vicarage mead, 5a. 1a. of arable in the Clay by the Bush. 1 close adjoining to the vicar's barn, 2a. A dwelling house, gardens, orchard, barn, hay house, 2 stables. The profits of the churchyard.

Whole tithes due on the following lands: Potterne park in the possession of Mr. Harris of Salisbury. Hurst in the possession of the earl of Abingdon. 3 grounds called Knowl acres, c. 2a., in the occupation of Walter Grubbe esq. 2a. in Sandford in the possession of Edward Nicholas esq.: these 2a. lie at the upper end of the mead. Abbots Ball, 5a. in the possession of Edward Nicholas esq. Certain grounds called Cane Hills, c. 35a., in the possession of Edward Nicholas esq. 2 grounds the Furlong and Goosham in the possession Mr. Thomas Hunt. An arable ground called Fursehill in the occupation of Richard Vince. 2 grounds called Lipstreet, 2a., and Marsh mead from the upper end to the oak or the mere stones in the possession of Mr. Palmer. 2 grounds called Hartmore meads, 5a., in the possession of Robert Pope. 3 grounds, one called the Croke, the other 2 called Kitmoors that were formerly Ranger's now in the possession of Richard Rook. Little Kitmoor lying by the side of Long Kitmoor, 2a., in the possession of Richard Rook. A ground lying along New lane brook, 6a., in the occupation of Mr. Benjamin Street. The Three Hills in the possession of Edward Nicholas esq. 7a. in Potterne Clay in the occupation of Robert Wailing. 4 grounds called Eyers closes in the occupation of Robert Wailing. Chelsbury, 4a., in the possession of William Pitt. Byde in the possession of Mr. Harris of Salisbury. 3 grounds called Potterne wood leases, 14a., in the possession of Walter Grubb esq. Spray ground in the possession of Francis Merweather. Roomer, 6a. in the possession of Mr. Long of Salisbury. 2 grounds called Riley and Sand ground, 8a., in the possession of Mr. Thomas Hunt. Woodfine mead from the orchard to the ditch in the possession of Robert Harvest. Spray acre in the Clay in the possession of Thomas Parsons. 2 grounds besides 3 x ½a., the 3 x ½a. lying under Lyme Hill wood, all c. 11a., in the possession of John Cooksy. Blackborough, 2½a., in the possession of Mrs. Jane Grubbe. 3 grounds called Rushy leaze with a little ground adjoining to it, a ground of 3½a. adjoining to Oars lane all in the possession of John Pope. 6a. in the common field adjoining to Coxtal lane in the possession of Thomas White. 4 grounds, one above Croke mill, the other 3 adjoining to Park mead, 8a., in the possession of Mr. Thomas Hunt. The Grove, c. 6a., in the possession of Edward Nicholas esq. Hartmores, 28a., in the possession of Edward Nicholas esq. ½a. at the upper end of Coxtal piece in the possession of T. Watts. 2a. lying the foot of the Three hills in the possession of Mr. ? Eyles. Little Barny, 1½a., in the possession of Robert Smith. In Cadley; Orchard mead, Square mead, the Yonder mead by the grove, and the String by Fiddington, 14a., in the possession of John Cooksy. 1a. in the Clay field in the possession of Walter Grubbe esq. 1 close, c. ½a., in the occupation of Benjamin Street.

Other dues: Every tenth calf in the parish if the owner has but 7 the vicar is to have one. 1d. for every cow white. Tithe of all wool and lambs in the parish.

1d. for every garden. Tithe of all orchards and of all geese. For the fall of every colt 1s. Tithe of Worton mill 2s. 6d., Roger Jourdan's mill 8d., Whistley mill 1s., Thomas Parsons's mill 8d., Mr. Neate's mill 1s. 8d., Bide mill 1s. 8d.

Charles Mutel, vicar, Anthony Curtis [X], one of the churchwardens, Robert Pope [X]. Philip Smith, Robert Harvest, Robert Whitt, Thomas Edwards, Nathaniel ?Alexander.

POULSHOT [POLLESHOTE] rectory

618   28 Dec 1608 (D1/24/170/1)
A dwelling house, a barn, an outhouse, an orchard, a garden, a barton, a home close, a close called Taullers, a close called Moses, and a meadow called Sandford. All the rest of the arable glebe land which lay in the common fields, was exchanged about 30 years ago by Mr. John Bowe, then parson, with the freeholders and copyholders of the manor of Poulshot, with the consent of the lords, and laid in 4 places by measure, and is now enclosed: a close called Eastnolle; another close called Marsh furlong; another close called Headland; and a plot of meadow in Swilly mead not inclosed. A plot of 2a. of tithing meadow in Inne mead, called Two acres; a plot of tithing meadow in Swilly mead called Two acres and the tithe of Little Crane mead. All tithes offerings and duties due in all the parish, with all the tithes of rectory ground called Bushy marsh held by Edward Crew and others; a little parrock lying by Spye Park; 2 x ½a. of meadow in Slayds mead; a little meadow and coppice [coopes] held by one Paradise; all of which grounds are between Blackmore forest and Chittoe wood. Common of pasture for 80 rother beasts in the common called the Marsh. Common of pasture for 12 rother beasts in the common called the Hay, of which 2 belong to the parsonage, and the other ten are due to the parson and his successors for the tithe hay. Tithes of milk paid every tenth day in kind or agreed for in all other parts of the parish from 3 May to 1 Aug. Common of pasture for 4 horses in the Haie from 1 Aug to 1 Feb., and common of pasture for the same 4 horses in the Marsh at all times and as long as the freeholders and copy holders keep or ought to keep any horses in the Marsh. Common of pasture for 90 sheep in the commons, the Marsh and the Haie, from St. Andrew's Eve [29 Nov] to 1 Feb. Common of pasture in the Launes for horses and sheep at all times of the year without oppressing.

By me Christopher Dugdale, rector; William Mayo, William Ranger, church-wardens, John Bishop [X], Thomas Richards [X], William Hill, sidesmen.

619   26 Oct 1671 (D1/24/170/2)
The parsonage house or tenement with a barn and stable together of 6 bays of building and a cut, with a garden, orchard and backside and a close of meadow or pasture adjoining E., c. 4a. 2 closes of arable lying at the E. end of the last close, c. 11a. 2 closes of pasture called the Hay leaze adjoining N. side of the last close bounded N. the street or highway called Hay lane, c. 23a. A close of arable or pasture called Marsh furlong lying in Marsh lane bounded E. side by that lane N. end with a close called Hook's, c. 13a. A ground or close of arable or pasture

called Headlands lying in Byde mill lane bounded N. that lane, S. Inmead, c. 16a. A close of meadow called Sandford mead, c. 2a., bounded W. the river, N. another close of the same name belonging to Mr. Edward Pierce. A close of meadow or pasture called Trullyes, c. 3½a., in Mill lane or Trully lane bounded E. by that lane. A close of meadow or pasture called Moyse's, c. 3a., lying in the street bounded S. that street. A plot of meadow called an Acre lying in Swilly mead at E. or upper end.

Charles Pickering, rector, William Somner, John Steevens, churchwardens.

620   3 May 1705 (D1/24/170/3)
Terrier taken by churchwardens and sidesmen with the advice of the rector. A dwelling house, barn, granary upon stavells with a pigeon loft over it. A garden and orchard, and a barton. The churchyard. One home close, closes called Trullys and Moyses. A meadow called Sandford. 2 closes (supposed formerly to have been one) called E. Knolle. Closes called Marsh furlong and Headlands. A plot of tithing meadow in Inn mead, called Two Acres. 2 plots of meadow, c. 3a., in Swilly mead. 2 closes formerly one called the Hay grounds.

Tithe of Little Crane mead. All tithes, offerings and duties except cow white in all the Hay grounds which were enclosed in 1635, and in 2 little meads called the Hay meads lately in the possession of Thomas Ellington and now Thomas White of Potterne, supposed formerly to have been Lammas meads. All tithes of certain grounds called Bushy marsh and of a little parrock lying by Spye Park, of 2 x ½a. of meadow in Slades mead and of a little meadow and coppice [coopes]. All the last 'rehearst' lands are lying and being between the forest of Blackmore and Chittoe wood in Poulshot.

Isaac Walton, [*rector*], Simon Pierce, John Cooke, churchwardens for 1704, Daniel Mayo, John Jones [X], sidesmen for 1704, William Mayo, John Cook senior [X], Richard Bellwell, William Winnell.

621   27 Aug 1785 (D1/24/170/4)
The area of the site of the parsonage house together with the garden, outhouses and yard measures on W. side 228 ft. where it is bounded by the street or highway, on N. side 270ft. bounded by a yard and close, the property of Soloman Hughes esq., and occupied by George Vince; on E. side 204ft. bounded that part of the glebe called the Home close and S. side 300ft. bounded by an orchard and garden belonging to William Noyes, carpenter, and by 2 small tenements, one of which is the property of William Pierce, now inhabited by John Mills, the other the property of the same William Noyes, at present uninhabited.

The parsonage house is chiefly built with brick, but the W. front is partly brick, partly lath and plaster, rough cast and measures in length 72ft. The whole is covered with tiles. It contains the following rooms: A parlour 20ft. by 16ft., ceiled and floored with boards, but not wainscotted. It has a stucco dado with surbase and plinth. A parlour, 14ft. 8in. by 13ft. 2in., ceiled and floored with boards. It has a dado of board with surbase and skirtingboard on 3 sides. A parlour 14ft. 8in. by 13ft. 2 in., ceiled and floored with boards, a stucco dado with surbase and skirtingboard. A kitchen 19ft. by 15ft., ceiled and laid with brick. A back kitchen or brewhouse, 14ft. square, ceiled and laid with stone. 2

cellars, a servant's pantry, a dairy with other convenient offices. Above stairs are 7 lodging rooms, ceiled with boarded floors.

Outbuildings: A barn and stable under one continued roof covered with thatch and in breadth 22ft. The stable is walled with brick in panes and ceiled. It measures 27ft. in length. The barn is walled with elm boards and is c. 55ft. in length. A granary of brick in panes covered with tiles. The upper chamber of it is a dovecote, 15ft. by 13ft. A coach house built with brick walls, ceiled and thatched, 12 ft. in front 19 ft. in breadth. A wain house upon timber posts and thatched, 36ft. by 12ft.

Glebe: Home close, 3a.; Six acres or Middle ground, 6a.; Peaked ground, 6a., all occupied by the rector. Great ground, 14a.; Ten acres or Lower ground, 10a.; both occupied by wid. Marshal and son. These grounds are bounded round in succession as follows: By Stephens close and Bottom ground, part of the estate of Soloman Hughes esq., now rented by George Vince; by Hay ground belonging to Mr. Chandler of Devizes Green and occupied by him; by Hay lane as far as Hay ground, the property of Charles Simpkins esq., rented by Mr. John Gilbert; by the said Hay ground and by the Six acres also owned by Charles Simpkins and rented by John Gilbert; by Butchers close and Home close, 2 grounds belonging to an estate of Walter Long esq., now occupied by Mrs. Elizabeth Godwin, by an orchard belonging to William Noyes, carpenter, as far as S. E. corner of the Parsonage yard and lastly by the parsonage yard and garden. Marsh furlong, 14a., now let to Mr. Thomas Waite, bounded E. by Marsh lane, N. by a ground called Hooks, part of the estate of J. Powel esq. deceased, and rented by Mr. Thomas Waite, W. by a piece of arable called Little Hooks, part of an estate of Walter Long, esq., occupied by Mr. John Cooper and by 2 grounds called N. fields, owned by Mr. William Trimnel occupied by himself as his brothers, S. by a ground also called Marsh furlong, part of an estate of Soloman Hughes esq., rented by the wid. Burbidge and son. Headlands, 14a., now occupied by [. . .] Pritchard of Seend, bounded N. by Bide Mill lane, W. by a ground called Headlands and by Headlands mead, part of the estate of Philip Carteret Webb esq., rented by William Fox, S. by Inn mead, E. by a ground called Brock furlong, part of an estate of William Long esq., rented by Mr. Giles Newman. A lot in the said Inn mead of 1a., now let to Mr. John Cooper bounded W. by the said Headlands mead, S. by the brook, N. by the said Headlands, E. part of the glebe. Moys's close, 3a., let to Mr. John Cooper bounded E. by the street or high road, N. by a ground also called Moys's close, part of an estate of Walter Long esq., occupied by Robert Wilson and by another ground called Chapel's close, part of an estate of Mr. John Tuck occupied by Mr. William Trimnel and his brothers, W. by a ground called Home close, part of an estate of Charles Simpkins esq., occupied by Mr. John Gilbert, S. by an orchard owned by Mr. James Glass rented by Mr. Jacob White of Worton and by a ground called Ellington, part of an estate of Soloman Hughes esq., occupied by the wid. Burbidge and son. Tullies, 2a. let to Mr. John Cooper bounded N. by Mill lane and a small tenement owned by William Pierce, W. a ground called Bowdens close, part of an estate of Walter Long esq., occupied by Mr. John Cooper, E. by a narrow lane leading from Home close to Mill lane. The churchyard, c. ½a., rented also by Mr. John Cooper. Sandford mead, 2a., now rented by Mr. John Cooper, is separated on N.

by a double ditch and a row of willows on the farther bank from another mead
of the same name, part of the estate of Charles Simpkins, esq., occupied by the
said Mr. Gilbert, W. by the brook from 2 grounds called Wallons part of an estate
of Walter Long, esq., occupied by the said Mr. John Cooper, bounded S. by a
ground also called Wallons, said to be owned by Mrs. Draper of Potterne and
now rented by Mr. John Glass of Potterne, E. by a mead part of an estate of
James Sutton, esq., now occupied by Mr. John Glass. N. B. Mr. Sutton's mead
and Mrs. Draper's ground are in Potterne.

A lot of 2a. in Great Swiller or Swallow mead rented by the duke of Somerset
for 2 guineas p. a. But in what part of the mead it lies is has been for some time
unknown. Total 77a.

Tithes of all kinds are due in kind without any modus or exemption except
that for Great Swiller or Swallow mead no tithe is paid on a supposition that the
above lot in Great Swiller was assigned in lieu of tithe.

In the church are 3 bells and a tinkler, a pulpit cloth and cushion, a crimson
cloth fringed for the communion table, a white linen cloth for the same, a flagon
of pewter, and a chalice and plate of silver. The chalice has no inscription but on
the top of the cover 1576. On the plate round a sun in the middle are the words
'The Gift of the Rev. Is. Walton, Rector of Poulshot'. The clerk, who is also
sexton, has no settled stipend as such, but is paid for certain services and receives
occasionally certain customary fees.

The chancel is repaired by the rector, the church by the parishioners. The
rails of the churchyard, which commence in Mr. Webb's ground now rented by
Mr. William Fox, from a point nearly opposite to the N. W. end of the chancel
and proceed on E. as far as Mr. Cooper's cowhouse, which stands almost opposite
the S. E. corner of the chancel, are maintained by the parishioners at large, the
remainder of the mounds by the owners of the adjoining lands respectively.

Benjamin Blayney, rector; John Cooper, John Gilbert, churchwardens, James
Burt, Abraham Marshall, William Ballinger.

PRESHUTE vicarage

622   1608 (D1/24/171/1)
We present that the vicar holds a dwelling house with a garden and little close of
meadow adjoining on the S. the whole of c. 1/2a., and no other land.

By me John Hitchcock, vicar; Richard Dymer [X], John Smith [X[1]], churchwardens.

623   25 Sep 1677 (D1/24/171/2)
£25 p. a. from the master of the choristers.[1] 20 marks p. a. from the impropriator
(not received for the last ten years). The Vicar's close, ½a. A garden plot and as
much ground as the vicarage house was set upon. The churchyard (not enjoyed
since Mr. Hitchcock renewed the lease). The tithes of Clatford, a hamlet in the
parish, and oblations.

Thomas Myles, vicar, Edward Greenaway, churchwardens, Nicholas Greenaway.

1.   Of Salisbury cathedral see **624**.

624   22 Jul 1783 (D1/24/171/3)
The terrier, a duplicate whereof (God willing) will be delivered to the registrar
of Shute, bishop at his primary visitation to be held at Marlborough on 28 Jul.
   1. In the oldest register book beginning in Apr 1607 it is recorded by rev.
John Hitchcock, vicar 'The other, which I made for many years before remaining
in my house, was consumed by fire with the rest of my goods' No house appears
to have been erected ever since in its place.
   2. The vicar, by original endowment, as appears from ancient terriers, enjoys
a meadow called the Vicar's close, c ½a., bounded E. by a meadow belonging to
the rectory, S. by a land leading to the Castle mill, W. by a lane leading to the
churchyard, N. at present only by mere stones from a meadow to John Brathwaite,
esq., occupied by Mr. Clark. N. B. when there was a fence between the vicar's
close and Mr. Brathwaite's meadow, a moiety was maintained at the expense of
the vicar or his tenant, the other moiety at Mr. Brathwaite's or tenant's expense.
In the bank on W. side grow 2 elm trees worth 8s. In the bank on S. side grow 2
others worth 8s.
   3. The vicar receives from the master of the choristers of Salisbury cathedral
(by his office rector and proprietor of the tithes of Preshute) a yearly pension
payable quarterly by way or name of augmentation. The quarterly payment is £8
9s., when the Land Tax is 4s. in the £ and £8 15s. 6d., when it is at 3s. in the £.
   4. In 1634, John, bishop of Salisbury, with the consent of Edward Thornburgh,
then master of the choristers, as appears by an instrument already lodged in the
bishop's registry, by way of augmentation endowed the vicarage with all the
profits of the churchyard, Easter offerings, customary offerings of women at
their purification after childbirth, mortuaries and all other oblations. He further
endowed it with all great and small tithes, mixed and minute, arising and accruing
within the hamlet of Clatford. But after a modus or composition for the tithes
of 8 yardlands called Demesne lands in Clatford was pleaded by the owner and
after several trials in the Court of Exchequer in the reign of William III a verdict
was given and a sentence pronounced at an Assize at Salisbury; namely 20s.
payable at the font every Easter Sunday and the produce of the best acre of
wheat growing on the Demesne land.[1] However, at the same verdict and sentence
the tithes of Coney-berry and Pricket Leap contended to belong the Demesne
lands were confirmed to the vicar as likewise the tithes of the following coppices
of underwood: namely Short Oaks, c. 5a. 2r.; Aston coppice, 10a. 10p; Foxbury
33a. 1r. 12p.; and Bottom coppice, c. 21a. 30p.
   5. No other pension or gift appears to have been made to the church nor has
any custom established any expense or charge on the incumbent by distribution,
entertainment or otherwise. Memo: It is since discovered that a cottage and
garden and 4a. 2r. of land called Moses in Manton occupied by John Brathwaite
esq., at £6 p. a. is left for the repair of the church forever.
   6. To the church and chancel belong a large oaken communion table with
rails of the same before it. 2 oak chests, a deal box to hold the utensils, vestments
and ornaments belonging to the parish. A crimson velvet covering for the
communion table, a large damask table cloth and a damask napkin. A small silver

cup and cover, a pewter flagon and pewter plate. A surplice, a crimson velvet cushion and a crimson velvet covering for the pulpit, and a crimson velvet valence in the front of the reading desk. 2 brass sconces affixed to the pulpit, a remarkably large font of jet, noted by Camden in his Britannia, lined with lead with a high oaken covering, the upper edges of the font being a little defaced by the tools of profane workmen. 5 bells in the tower, a gallery in the S. E. corner of the church. The King's arms over the arch leading to the chancel.

7. At the W. end of the church stands a handsome gallery belonging to what is now called the Castle Inn, formerly the seat of the dukes of Somerset. Books belonging to the church are a large folio bible, a common prayer book for the reading desk and a common prayer book for the clerk's pew.

8. The chancel is upheld and repaired by the rector or his lessee, the church and tower by the churchwardens at the expense of the parish. The churchyard is bounded and fenced on N. by the river Kennet, W. by the rectory garden wall, S. by part of the same wall, a gate and a stile maintained by the churchwardens and a hedge and ditch belonging to Mr. Brathwaite's meadow, E. by a hedge and ditch belonging to the rectory. In the churchyard grow 12 chestnut trees worth 3s. each, and 3 ash trees worth £1 10s.

9. The present clerk, does the sexton's office likewise, as his grandfather did for many years, was nominated by the vicar in 1748 and no custom or usage appears to the contrary. He received 40s. wages from the churchwardens for finding bell ropes, washing the surplice and oil dressing the church and keeping it clean. His customary fees are: for every banns published 1s.; for every wedding 1s.; for registering every christening 4d.; for digging every parish grave and bell ringing 3s. 4d.; for digging every other grave and bell ringing 4s. 6d.; it has been customary likewise for the wealthy and well disposed inhabitants to give him some benevolence at Easter.

Mr. John Coleman of Dinton gave 20 marks to the parish the interest to be expended in apprenticing poor children belonging to it. But the parishioners having in 1750 entrusted the 20 marks into the hands of Mr. John Neate senior, then of Barton farm, who in 1782 died insolvent, so that the principal money and interest from 20 Apr 1762 are likely to be lost forever.

Thomas Meyler, vicar, Edward Vaisey, Thomas Canning, churchwardens, John Brathwaite, James White.

1. A verse written in the Preshute parish register after the burial of Lewis Morse, vicar, extolls his successful effort in recovering these tithes which were then valued at £35 p. a. (WSRO 1298/5). See also WAM vol. 30 pp 107-8.

PURTON vicarage

625   1588 (D1/24/172/1)

Tithe corn and hay belonging to the vicarage of Purton with the names of the fields and places where the said tithes do lie and the names of the ancientest men of the parish which reduced the same into writing, viz. Robert Masyling, Adeline Elbrow, Henry Swegar, John Weaving, Anthony Dowdswell, Adeline

Gillam, Richard Bathe senior, George Browne, John Sadler, William Helliar, William Cox and Thomas Carter, sidesmen, and Edward Ryman and Michael Ryman, churchwardens [. . .][1]

Tithes of [*the following lands*] Come field: 4a. of Edmund Ryman under Edmund Parnell's hedge; 1a. of Edmund Ryman lying on Lyne hill, 1a. more on Hobbs mead; 1a. of Anthony Dowdswell lying on Lyne hill; 1a. held by Edmund[2] Digs in Pytt furlong, 1a. of his on Lyne hill being parted between Edmund Ryman and him, 1a. of his at W. hill[3] held by Edmund[2] Diges.[4] Batellfield: 2a. of Edmund[2] Diggs, one lying towards Jeffries close end and the other towards Edmund Ryman's close end. Spresfolde field: the Parsonage piece, *c.* 6a. Churchfield: 1a. of Richard Brewer being the next a. of the 'twaine' toward the church lying hard by the vicar's piece; 1 head a. formerly held by Philips now by Henry Masling; ½a. held by Nicholas Skillinge. Cobhill: the tithe of Cobhill lying in Stepstones and held by Anthony Gleede. Sparsfold field: 1a. of Robert Maslinge lying under Phillips hedge being 3 ridges; 1 head a. held by Anthony Glede at Priest mead;[5] 3a. of land and mead at Hoorewell held by Robert Smythe; 1a. of Edmund[2] Digs at Sparsfold hedge end; 1a. of Richard Bathe in the same furlong; a meadow called Phillips ham, *c.* 6a., lying at Locknun[6] and Brymill held by Henry Masling; 1a. of John Shurmer lying at Brymhill; 1a. of Edmund Ryman; 1a. of John Gleede, 1a. of Michael Ryman, all last 3a. shoot down towards Wroughton's mead; ½a. of Robert Smythe in Brymhill.[7] Bearfield: the Parson's piece next to Wollen lane *c.* 3a.; 7a. at Elderne Stubb, being arable; 1a. of arable of Edward Sadler lying in the Slade hill; 1a. of Edmund[2] Diggs shooting down the Slade hill; 1a. of George Browne in Puckpit furlong; 1a. of John Gleed in the same furlong; 1a. of Joan Scyssel in the same furlong; 1a. of Marian Ryman at Hobrucks way end; 3 laynes in Waterfurlong held by Joan Scyssel being below the bush next to Smyth mead; the head a. in Waterfurlong held by John Lane; 2 hams in Smyth mead held by Robert Masling and Robert Smythe; 1a. in Smyth mead held by Anthony Glede called the Crown acre; a ham, 2a., called Weavings Goars [Goers] held by John Weaving; 1a. of arable held by Christopher Gleede[8] at Barwaie; 1a. of Robert Smythe, 1a. of Joan Scyssel, 1a. more of Anthony Glede all these 4a. lie end to end. Clarden: 1a. of arable of Robert Masling in Clarden beyond Hobrucks ways hedge; 1a. of Joan Scyssel in the same furlong; 1a. held by Edmund Digs in the same furlong; 2a. of Edmund[2] Digs shooting down on Little mead; ½a. of John Weaving next to the last; 1a. of George Browne in the same furlong; the Gylden, ½a., at Heskins close end held by Joan Scyssell; 1a. of Robert Smythe; 2a. being 5 ridges held by William Helliar at Heskins close end. The Down: 1a. of Henry Sengar;[9] 1a. in the Hurne being 3 ridges held by Marian Ryman; 1a. in the Hurne called the Lamp acre held by Joan Masling; 1a. of Olive[10] Kybellwhite called the Maglen[11] acre; 1a. of John Ryman shooting on the last; 1a. being 3 ridges of Nicholas Skilling shooting down towards Hursteed; 1a. held by Christopher Glede[8] near John Weaving's piece shooting down on Little mead; 1a. being 3 ridges of Edward Sadler in the same furlong; 2a. of Joan Scyssell lying hard by the Down pits; 2a. of laynes at the Down pits of Joan Scyssell shooting down towards Hernes hedge. Woodwards craft;[12] Shillings being *c.* 6a. of laynes held by Henry Senger;[9] 1a. of laynes of Joan Masling called the Lamp acre shooting on Twenty Acre ditch; 1a. of laynes

of Joan Masling lying in Gossye mead; 2a. of laynes of Edmund[2] Diggs shooting
down on Twenty acre ditch; 1a. of arable of Henry Sengar[9] in the hither
Woodwards craft[12] at Hernes hedge. The Prye: 3a. of arable of John Weaving,
one lying at Wroughton's mead; one in the middle of the Prie and the other in
Longhams; 2 x ½a. of his one at Mawvers cross the other on the Prie side; 2a. of
Robert Maslin, one shooting down on Long hams the other at Shelvinche; 2a.
of Robert Smythe, one lying in the Shelvinche next to Robert Masling the
other shooting down towards Fawkners bridge being meadow called the Crown
acre; 1a. of arable of John Masling; a ham of his, *c*. 4a.; 1a. of meadow of his
shooting down toward the Ree;[13] 1a. of meadow of Michael Ryman in Hilly
mead; 1a. being 3 ridges of Edward Sadler shooting on Small way; 1a. being 3
ridges of Edmund[2] Digs [Dix]) shooting on the Prie way.

1. This title section only appears in **627** but not in **628–630**.
2. John in **627–630**.
3. In W. leaze in **627–630**.
4. 1a. of John Richens added in **627 630**.
5. Priest mead omitted in **627–630**.
6. Hockman in **627-630**.
7. 1 yd. of John Aketts added in **627–630**.
8. Joan Burgess wid. In **627–630**.
9. Swegar in **627–630**.
10. Oliver in **627–630**, possibly a misreading here.
11. Naglet in **627–630**, possibly a misreading.
12. Croft in **627–630**.
13. In Hilly mead added in **627–630**.

626   30 May 1609 (D1/24/172/2)
A dwelling house, barn, stable, oxhouse, 2 gardens and home bartons. A close of
meadow called Prist mead, 5a., adjoining on S. side a ground of William Webb
called Sparsalls, N. side highway. An enclosed plot of pasture ground called the
Down plot, 6a., joining E. side upon a ground of Leonard Pridy S. side Smith
mead. An enclosed plot of pasture ground called the Coniger, 2a. joining N. side
upon Henry Maslin's home barton, S. side Windmill hill. A piece of arable land
in the Church field, 5a., joining on W. side land of the wid. Jefferies, E. side land
of Anthony Baker. A piece of arable land in Bathfield, 1a., joining on N. side
land of Giles Diggs, S. side the farm land. A piece of arable in the Sladehill, 1a.,
joining on N. side land of the wid. Cicil, S. side land of Reeves farm. A piece of
arable land lying in Clarendon, 1a., joining on E. side land of the wid. Sadler, W.
land of Henry Maslin. A piece of arable land, ½a., lying joining on E. side of
land of Edmund Brown, W. side land of the wid. Harfatt. A piece of arable land,
1a., lying on the top of Clarden joining N. land of wid. Cicill. A piece of meadow
ground lying in Smith mead, 1a., joining N. side upon the enclosed meadow of
Leonard Pridy, S. side land of Edmund Maslin. 3 tenements belonging to the
vicarage: The first occupied by Kellon Moulden, a dwelling house, stable, garden
and backside adjoining the house, on W. side of the house 2 paddocks of meadow
ground, 1a., on N. side of the house a plot of meadow, 5a., and bounded on W.

side by land of Edmund Diggs: A piece of arable land lying in the Down joining on E. side land of wid. Weaving, W. land of Michael Ryman. The second tenement occupied by John Ritchings is situated in Paven Hill [Pivenhill]; a dwelling house, barn, stable, cowhouse and other outhouses, a garden and backside and a little paddock of meadow, ½a., joining on S. side of the house on W. side the highway. Another little paddock of meadow, ½a., joining on N. side land Benett Gleede, S. on the home arable ground: The home close of arable ground, 8a., joining on the S. side land of the wid. Cuffe, N. the last paddock: A plot of ground called Stonehey, 10a., joining on N. side land of Robert Blake, E. land of Edmund Morgan: A piece of arable land lying in Bettle field, 1a., joining on E. side land of Edmund Diggs W. land of John Bathe. The third tenement occupied by Thomas Mayle is in Restrop [Resthrop]: a dwelling house, stable garden and backside: A home close, 2a., joining on N. side Bettle field on S. side the highway: A piece of arable land lying in Bettle field, 2a., lying both N. and S. between land of Giles Diggs.

James Hemerford, vicar, Michael Ryman [X], William Waker [X], churchwardens; Henry Maskelyne, Thomas Sadler, John Sherman [X], John Gleede, Robert Gleede, George Maskelyne [X].

627   1671 (D1/24/172/3)
The dwelling house, barn, backside, garden and the churchyard. A close called Collingham, 2a. Priest [Prist] mead lying in Sprasholds[1] field, c. 5a. 5a. of land and mead lying in the Church field. 1a. of arable land in the Slade lying in Barefield. ½a. of arable land lying in Packpitts in the same field. ½a. of arable land in Waterfurlong in the same field between John Gleede of Pavenhill and John Weaving.[2] ½a. in the same furlong. 1½a. of arable land shooting down upon Smith mead in the same field.

1a. of arable being 3 ridges in Clardon shooting down upon Horebrookes way. ½a. of arable in the same furlong. 1a. of arable upon the top of Clardon. 1yd. of arable in the same Clardon shooting down upon Heskins close.

1a. of arable in the Down at Heskins close end. 1a. in the same furlong and ½a. arable lying next John Weaving's[2] piece. ½a. of arable shooting up towards the Down pitts.

1a. in the Prye in 2 sundry places namely; ½a. of arable at Mavers Cross hedge shooting down upon Small way; ½a. at Wroughtons mead lying between the lands of John Sadler and John Weaving.[2]

All manner of oblations, tithe honey and wax, tenth penny of the sale of a colt and a calf, tithe wool, lamb, calf, cow white, pig and goose of the parish and the farm and parsonage except 3 tenements occupied by Robert Blake senior, Robert Hawkins and William Read.

The vicar has a tenement lying in Paven Hill [Peevenhill] occupied by John Ritchens[3] with 2 several paddocks, 1a., and a close of arable, c. 6a., 10a. of arable in Stonehay, 1a. in Comefield,[4] 1yd. in Barrfield. A tenement lying in Restrop occupied by John Akett,[5] with a close of arable, c. 2a., 1a. in Waterfurlong and 1yd. in Brimhill. A tenement in Bentham occupied by Kellen Moulden[6] with 2 several paddocks, a close, c. 5a., a close of arable lying in Common croft. The vicar has tithe hay and corn out of these tenements as well as all other tithes. *The remainder of the terrier is a copy of 625 including the title missing in the original; amendments in footnotes to 625.*

William Bathe, vicar, John Telling, Thomas Moulden, churchwardens.

1. Sprasfeld in **628**, Sprassells in **629-630**.
2. Wavering in **628** and **629**, Weaving in **630**.
3. Daniel Osborn in **628**, no tenant in **629** or **630**.
4. Combe field in **629** and **630**.
5. John Littel in **628**, William Mayson in **629**. No tenant in **630**.
6. Thomas Moulden in **628**. Robert Moulden in **629**, the vicar in **630**.

628   13 Apr 1678 (D1/24/172/4)
Copy of 627 with amendments in footnotes to 627 and 625. William Bathe, vicar, Richard Diggs, Anthony Saunders, churchwardens.

629   8 Jan 1705 (D1/24/172/5)
Copy of 627 with amendments to footnotes to 627 and 625. William Bathe, vicar, John Jewell, Charles Spencer, churchwardens.

630   11 May 1711 (D1/24/172/6)
Copy of 627 with amendments in footnotes. Presented at the visitation at Marlborough.

W[*illiam*] Bathe, vicar, James Hilliard, Richard Read, churchwardens.

630A   1725 (303/2 p. 199)[1]
An account of the glebe lands; Bentham grounds rented by Joseph Gray at £7 p. a.; the Down Grounds rented by John Manfield at £6 p. a.; the Stonris, with a ground by Mathew Iles, and 3 beast leazes rented by John Jefferis at £18 10s. p. a.; 12 leazes in Momislease rented by Richard Scutts at £3 p. a.; Church field french grass ground rented by Humphry More at £9 9s. p. a.; the ground at Common plat and a piece by the home barn in the vicar's own hands value £7 p. a.; 7 more beast leazes value £3; 39 p. of ground in Battle field value 5s.

Measured 16 Mar 1726 the vicar's enclosure in Church field, 6 ¼a. 33lugs (within the hedges) by John Hilliard.

1. This note is in a tithe account book among the Purton parish records.

630B   23 Dec 1728 (303/2 p. 214)[1]
Note by Richard Glasse, vicar. It was the misfortune of my father, my predecessor, to succeed a gentleman from whose executors he could obtain or hear of no true account (either by books or otherwise) of the great tithes belonging to the vicar, so that he and I since have been obliged to find out our own great tithes by enquiry by which means (I fear) a great many acres will be entirely lost, however I have set down underneath what acres now pay tithe which are far short of the acres mentioned in the terrier: 3a. in Gardners field lying on the N. side on Purton farm; 1a. called Quor acre lying in the N.W. part of Back field; ½a. in Battlefield in the possession of John Jefferis; ¼a. in the possession of

Robert Holliday, tenant, Mr. Goddard's estate of Standing; 2a. in Smith mead occupied by Anthony Bathe; 2½a. called the Butts in Clardon occupied by Anthony Bathe; the great tithe of the Hurn's (I cannot tell what the measure) occupied by Anthony Bathe; 1a. in Brimnel occupied by James Hilliard; 7a. in Backfield called Bayleys ground occupied by Timothy Patey; the great tithes of Cobhill occupied belonging to Mr. Goddard's estate; ½a. in the Slade, Mr. Herring's, occupied by Thomas Roberts; 1a. called Woodwards Craft occupied by John Packer; 12a. on the N. side of the Down, the estate of Mr. Nevil Maskelyne, occupied by farmer Osburn; 2a. in Rickets mead, Mr. Maskelyne's estate, occupied by farmer Osburn; 2a. in Clardon, late John Guttridge's, occupied by Thomas Moulden; 6a. called Shillings in the possession of Thomas Moulden; 1a. in the Coniger belonging to Dr. Clarke, occupied by Edward Morgan; 2a. in Brimnel belonging to Dr. Clarke, occupied by Edward Morgan.

1. This note, in a tithe account in the Purton parish records, emphasises the problems of relying on the 1588 terrier (**625**) for so many years. It had become totaly inaccurate as a result of which those lands owing great tithes had been considerably reduced.

RODBOURNE CHENEY vicarage

631   13 May 1588 (D1/24/173/1)
Terrier taken by Edmund Webb, William Morsse, churchwardens, John Wareman, Roger Morsse, sidesmen. A mansion house [...], a stable, a cowhouse, a dovehouse, an orchard, a garden, [...], 3 grounds all of less than 1a. [...], 8a. 3yd. Arable, 1a. 1yd. Meadow, 2a. [...] and pasturing in the common fields for 4 beasts and 20 sheep [...] yearly out of the parsonage of £5. The tithe corn and hay of the glebe land of the parsonage. The tithe hay of the meadow on both sides of the brook from the church wall to Alesford bridge. All other tithe hay of the rest of the parish belongs to the parsonage (being impropriate).

632   1 Jul 1608 (D1/24/173/2)
A mansion house, a little orchard, a small garden ground, the churchyard, 8a. 3yd. of arable land, 1a. 1yd. of meadow ground lying in the comm fields of Rodbourne. A close of c. 2a. and feeding, pasturing and going in the same common fields for 3 rother [rudder] beasts, 1 horse and 20 sheep. A pension of £5 p. a. out of the parsonage. The tithe corn and hay of the glebe land of the parsonage. Tithe hay of the meadow on both sides of the brook extending from the church unto Alesford bridge. All other tithes except tithe corn and hay of all the residents of the whole parish.
    By me Anthony Ellis, clerk; John Morsse junior [X], William Tinson [X], churchwardens, John Morsse senior [X], Thomas Wekes [X], sidesmen.

633   1677 (D1/24/173/3)
Terrier delivered into the registry of bishop Seth. A large house, barn, stable, pigeon house and gate house all adjoining together.[1] The churchyard, walled, c. 1a. A little garden adjoining S. side of the house, being c. 1 p. in breadth. An

orchard garden or hopyard, c. ½a., having the Gastern on the S. and the highway N. A ground called the Vicarage marsh, c. 4a. A close enclosed out of the common fields, c. 14a., having the linch on S. A pension of £5 p. a. paid to the vicar out of the parsonage after this manner; £3 p. a. paid by Edward Hill as tenant unto Sir Edward Baynton, out of the parsonage; 40s. p. a. paid by the tenants of Robert Oldsworth esq., out of that part of the parsonage in Haydon and Haydon Wick. All great and small tithes from the lands within the parish anciently belonging to Hales abbey. All tithes of corn and hay and herbage for dry and barren cattle paid out of the Dowls, Dowlsham Five acres and Marsh belonging to Sir Edward Baynton now occupied by Edward Hill, his tenant, 2 other little grounds now occupied by John Cole and Robert Wilks and out of all the lands called Griggorys now occupied by William Road, that is to say a little close at Morden, 2a. on N. side of Church hill, 1a. against Wick Hill, 1a. in Barke furlong, ½a. of meadow joining unto the house all of which lands belong to Sir Edward Baynton.

All the great and small tithes from lands or grounds called Bayleys hill, the Goose moor and the Little Coppiced mead, belonging to Edmund Webb esq., occupied by Thomas Mills, his tenant; the Goose ham, the Combs and Slatters close belonging to Sir William Halcroft now occupied by Samuel Burge, his tenant. The vicar received an ancient accustomed payment of 18d. by the pound according to the pound rent in lieu of tithes of all pasture grounds that are fed or depastured with fat or 'fating beasts' or such cattle as are not profitable for the plough or pail throughout the parish. Also some reasonable composition for the latter moweth or yea mead where such fat or unprofitable cattle are depastured and after the same manner for the herbage of dry and barren cattle. The vicar received by ancient custom only 2d. for every cow milk where only dairy cows are kept. Also tithe calves, colts, wool, lambs, pigs, geese, eggs, hops, hemp, flax, honey, wax, apples, pears and other fruit, gardens and all oblations and Easter offerings.

Nicholas Adee, vicar, Francis Steevens, William Jacob, churchwardens, Thomas Heath, Thomas Wildey, sidesmen.

1. A certificate of completion to the wall, gate and gate house recorded that they had been 'better rebuilt and repaired then they have been since the memory of Man', 22 Mar 1678 (WSRO D1/14/1/3/49).

634   29 Sep 1708 (D1/24/173/4)
Terrier made by Edward Hill, Edward Jenner, churchwardens, Portman Thatcher,[1] John Wort, sidesmen, Thomas Webb, Harold Tuckey, Henry Evens and Richard Strange.

A mansion house, a little orchard, a small ground, the churchyard. A close of meadow, c. 3½a., called the Vicarage marsh, tithe free, having the marsh of Thomas Webb esq., Serjeant at law, on E. and the marsh of John Baynton esq., on W. A ground partly arable, partly meadow, c. 14a., tithe free, bounded lands of the same Thomas Webb on W. and N., land of the same John Baynton on S., and land of Richard Weston on E. The vicar has a pension of £5 p. a. of which £3 is paid by Edward Hill, tenant to the same John Baynton, out of that part of the parsonage belonging to John Baynton; 40s. p. a. paid by Gregory Gerring, esq., or his tenants out of his part of the parsonage in Haydon and Haydon Wick. Tithe corn and hay of the glebe land of the parsonage belonging to the same John Baynton occupied by the same Edward Hill, Susanna Cole wid., and Margery Read wid. Tithe hay of some closes of meadow lying on each side of the brook between the church and Alesford bridge, and tithe hay and corn out of a ground called the Dowles belonging to the same John Baynton. No other tithes due other than the following: 2d. for every cow white, 4d. for every through milch cow, tithe calves and sheep, which if kept the whole year, then he receives tithe wool only, but if kept less time than a whole year he received ¼d. a month. Tithe lamb to be taken at St. Mark's day yearly [25 Apr]. Tithe herbage, where no tithes have been paid before either to the parson or the vicar in the same year. Tithe for fatting or unprofitable cattle which are not bred or used to the plough or pail (saddle horses excepted). Tithe of fruit, eggs, sucking pigs, colts if not worked a season, offerings and gardens. The vicar is not entitled to any tithes out of the closes called Great Sowbrooke, Little Sowbrooke, Bottom mead and Twenty Swathes, being lands of the same Thomas Webb, nor of any cattle therein depasturising for it is believed that by a decree of Chancery upon the enclosure of the common field those are exempted and that satisfaction was given to the vicar for the same by the said ground of 14a. The vicar has not demanded any such tithes of those lands for nearly 40 years.

1. Portman Thatcher is the only one of the compilers of the terrier who did not sign the terrier.

ROWDE vicarage

635   14 May 1588 (D1/24/174/1)
We the parishioners having advisedly considered of and uprightly scanned the inquisition directed to us from your lordship, have reduced into writing to be presented at this visitation at Devizes.

We have an impropriate parsonage and a vicarage endowed so that the impropriator has 35a. glebe land lying dispersed in the fields, and 1a. in Sewlow mead, with 4 tenements and 1 newly erected, a barn, and a close of 1a. by the churchyard wall, with all tithes of corn and hay, pulses, and suchlike, and common in the Marsh for 4 beasts, and in the fields for 12 with the tenants. The vicar has only 1 mansion house, messuage with a curtilage and a ?ltilag and all small tithes, rights, duties, customs, and profits and ecclesiastical emoluments, according to a composition ordained and dated at Potterne 9 Apr [5 Ides Apr] 1326 by Roger, bishop, in the 11th year of his episcopacy. By virtue of which composition we find also that the vicar is to have, together with the premises, tithes of the demesne lands of the rectory, and the tithes of 4 crofts in a plot of ground called the Clyf or Clyffeld ? enclosed to tillage in some part, and moreover should be discharged by the rector of all other ordinary burdens chargeable for the church, of procurations to the archdeacon, Hilary money, and all other extraordinary payments except that the vicar should pay out of the benefice 3s. 2d. yearly, and he is to have the whole herbage of the churchyard. But our vicars now contrarywise are charged with tithes to his majesty, procurations to the archdeacon, Hilary, and all other ordinary payments at the visitations, and besides that the impropriator has withheld the tithes of the demesne lands and the 4 crofts very wrongfully as we think, without any consideration, time out of mind. There was paid 30 years ago an annual pension of 40s., as the lease termed it, from the impropriator [proprietary] to the vicar for the term of a lease granted by old Sir Edward Baynton and the vicarage with the bounds and other premises were repaired from time to time at the proper cost and charges of the impropriator, which has now long been withheld sythens likewise except that the vicarage and bounds are still slenderly repaired by the impropriator. We hope in tender consideration of the small portion of the vicar your Honours will think of it accordingly and put your helping hands to restoring it conveniently, according to the good meaning and right determination of the old composition, which if it please your good lordship to endeavour, with some careful and fatherly pains, we think you shall do a very good deed, and bind us, your poor diocesans, still to pray heartily for you.

By me, Robert Maundrell;[1] Thomas Sertch, Richard Tolyns, churchwardens, Robert Fylk [X], Peter Coxhed, sidesmen, Edward Bayntun, Richard Hues, William Hope, William Harper, John Waters [X], Robert Sumner.

1.   Maundrell was lessee of the manor of Rowde. (VCH vol. 7, p. 219)

636   1 Oct 1608 (D1/24/174/2)
A mansion house with a messuage or curtilage, a backside, a barn and the churchyard, *c.* 1a. all adjoining the church.

All the personal and predial tithes and all profits, rights and duties, except tithe corn, hay and pulses. A real composition dated 1326 lies in the registry.

John Tyes, vicar, John Hwlat [X], Robert Flower [X], churchwardens, Robert Sumner [X], Richard Bollen [X].

637   21 Dec 1671 (D1/24/174/3)
A piece of ground, 27yd. in breadth by 31yd. in length lying on N. side of the churchyard on which piece stands a house containing 10 rooms, small and great, with a stable or outhouse. There is no glebe land, the vicar has privy tithes of the whole parish. A custom of paying mortuaries which is for every person dying in the parish who is worth £10, 10 groats; if worth £20, a noble or 6s. 8d.; if worth £40, 10s., paid to the vicar.

Thomas Jekyll, vicar, Samuel Webb, John Compton [X], churchwardens, Zachariah Pattrick, sidesman.

638   9 Apr 1705 (D1/24/174/4)
To bishop Gilbert. the presentment. Rowde is a vicarage presentative in the gift of John Baintun esq.,[1] To it belongs a dwelling house with a outhouse, namely a stable and a washhouse or brewhouse both on a piece of garden ground belonging to the vicarage. The last garden ground is bounded S. side, the churchyard, W.

side partly by a garden belonging to the George Inn and partly by a house and garden belonging to John Hope, N., partly by a garden belonging to the George Inn and partly by a tenement belonging to Roger Brewer,[2] E. side by Church lane. The bounds of the garden are to be maintained by the vicar for the time being except where houses abutt on the same. The garden contains in length from N. and S. measuring W. side of the garden 98ft. and in breadth from E. to W. 79ft. 9in.

The churchyard, 1a.; its bounds are maintained and upheld at the charges of those persons whose grounds adjoin to or abutt on the churchyard, except the S. side and gate and wicket or door leading into the churchyard out of Church lane, which are to be maintained at the charge of the parishioners.

Small or minute tithes, that is to say all the tithe of all things except corn and hay. But it is to be noted that of late years there has been a sort of composition between the vicars and parishioners that the parishioners shall pay in lieu of small tithes to the vicar 6d. in the pound for all lands half yearly at the feasts of St. Michael [29 Sep] and Ladyday [25 Mar]. The composition was first made when Mr. Thomas Syms was vicar, about 1663 and the rate made according as lands were then valued and assessed to the church and poor, nevertheless, the composition may be broken or altered by the vicar and parishioners as they shall see cause. It amounts at present to the yearly value of £34 5s.[3]

All the great tithe (of corn and hay) arising out of land, c. 33a., at Rowde hill now in the possession of John Stevens gent., by purchase from John Wicks, late of Chippenham, gent. The last Mr. Wicks gave these tithes to the vicarage for ever by his will.

Mortuaries for all persons who die in the parish payable as follows: 3s. 4d. where the inventory amounts to £10, 6s. 8d. when £20 and 10s. when £30.

We humbly desire that our presentment and certificate may be recorded in your lordship's registry and there preserved In futuram rei memoriam.

Latimer Crosse, vicar, Francis Ellyot, John Webb, churchwardens, Samuel Webb, jun., Humphrey Buckler, John Hisock, Thomas Maslen, Thomas Hope.

1.   Sir Edward Bayntun in **639**.
2.   No owner named in **639**.
3.   £50 in **639**.

639   30 Jul 1783 (D1/24/174/5)
*As **638** with amendments in footnotes.* The vicarage house is a brick building the great part of which has been taken down being very ruinous, and rebuilt at the expense of the present vicar: 2 stories high, 3 rooms on each floor, the roof partly tiled and partly thatched. The outhouses are thatched. In the churchyard are a few lime and elm trees. In the tower of the church are 5 bells. Belonging to the communion table is a small silver salver and cup containing about ½ pint. The clerk is appointed by the minister and paid by the parishioners by custom, 4d. a house.

W[*illiam*] Higginton, vicar, Walter Post, Thomas Miles, churchwardens, John Goodman, B. Stephens.

RUSHALL rectory

639 1588 (D1/24/175/1)
1a. in the Bose field called Beggars acre and another head a. in the same furlong next to Osmund Plant. 1a. [. . .] in the N. field next to the ? greenway, Thomas Hurle has ½a. next to it; 2a. more in the same field shooting along the green way, and the farmer has 1a. next; a head a. on Blackehell; and 1a. more in the same furlong next to the farmer's a. and William Pinkney's ½a. 2a. in Sharppe hill next to John Sidnold's a. and on the other side William Pinkney's ½a.; 2a. in Flat furlong, John Butt has 1a. on the N. and ½a. on the S. side; 4a. more lying together in the same field, the mere on the S. side and William Pinkney's a. on the N. side; 2a. more shooting on the E. side on the 4a., ½a. of Osmund Plant on the N. side and another ½a. on the S. side. 4a. on the Port way mered in on both sides; 2a. more between the lands shooting on Milies butts; 1a. more in Thornelinche furlong, Thomas Hurle on one side, Elizabeth Bewley's ½a. on the other; 1a. more in Mide furlong, John Chandler has 1a. on the S. side and Hurle on the N. side; 1a. more in the same field, William Long on the N. side and the farmer on the S. side; 1a. on the S. hill, John Chandler has ½a. on the N. side and Baldwin has ½a. on the S. side. A head a. on Green way, Anthony Sidnold on the W. side; 2a. in Whitway furlong, Thomas Sidnold has ½a. on the S. side and Baldwin on the N. side; 1a. in Alfones ditch, Thomas Sydnold's half on the S. side and the farmer on the N. side. Between the two 3 x ½a. headland. A plot of meadow at Parsines Ball in 2 closes adjoining the parsonage, one called the Pidgine close, and the other called the Orchard close. Pasture and feeding for 72 sheep in Werdenfolde.

641 n. d. early 17th cent.[1] (D1/24/175/2)
29a. arable land. Commons of pasture for 72 sheep feeding in the flock called Worden flock. A meadow, ½a. of ground, lying by the water side near the house. 2 closes, one on N. side, the other on S. side of the house, containing ½a. a piece.

Richard Pinckneye, parson, William Mortmore, John ?Merewether [Mwrthre].

1. Richard Pickney was rector between 1580-1623.

642 1671 (D1/24/175/3)
33a. in the several fields as follows: In the Shepherds Patch field 10a.: 2a. in Lockeway furlong bounded N. side ½a. of John Rutt, S. ½a. of John Coster: In the furlong above it 4a., bounded N. side 1a. Mr. Michel S. side a linchet: 2a. in the second furlong above bounded N. side 1a. lately belonging to Thomas Rutt, S. side ½a. of the last Rutt; in Shepherds Patch furlong 2a. bounded N. side 1a. late William Mortimer, S. side ½a. Mr. Michel.

In the Middle field 9a.: 1a. in Pening furlong bounded N. side 1a. William Coster, S. side 1a. Mr. Chaundler: 1a. in Midfurlong having 1a. on N. side of Mr. Mundye and on S. side 1a. of Mr. Chaundler: 1a. shooting upon the end of the 4 lawns bounded N. side ½a. Robert Rutt, S. 1a. Mr. Mundye: 2 hill a. between the lawns shooting upon William Tyler, having Mr. Michel's land on E. and W.:

4a. shooting upon Portway bounded with 2 lawns, bounded N. and S. with single a. of Mr. Chandler.

In Whitesse Foot field 5a.: 1a. in the bottom, having 1a. Mr. Chaundler N., ½a. William Tyler S.: 2a. in the bottom shooting athwart Whitesse Foot way bounded N. side 1a. Baldwin,[1] S. ½a. William Tyler: 1a. upon the hill in Greenway furlong having 1a. lately of Thomas Rutt on E. side, 3 x ½a. Robert Moxham W.: 1a. in Piggs Tayle furlong, having ½a. Mr. Chaundler N. side, ½a. Matthew Aymer S. side.

In the N. field 7½a.: 1a. called Beggars acre bounded E. 1a. wid. Hutchins and lying headlands on W. to several of the tenants: 1a. in the same furlong, having E. and W. single a. of Edmund Aymer: 1½a. having Wood way N., ½a. Mr. Mundye S.: 2a. having Wood way W. side, 3 x ½a. Mr. Chaundler E.: 1a. heading Blacken hill furlong on S. side having 3 x ½a. Stephen Rutt N.: 1a. in the same furlong having S. ½a. Mr. Michel, N. 1a. Mr. Chandler.

In Tween Town 1½a. lying along the path on E. side and headlands to several of the tenants on S. side. A little enclosure called the Hop yard, c. 4 lugs. c. ½a. of meadow ground shooting upon the parsonage orchard and joining a meadow of Mr. Pinckney.

The parsonage house containing a porch, a parlour, hall, kitchen, a middle room between the hall and kitchen, 2 butteries, a wash house[2] and a milk house, with convenient upper rooms all in good repair, having a fair backside with 2 courts before the house walled in and a little court on the back of the house paled in. A barley barn containing 6 bays and a threshing place with a little skilling for cows on one side of it. A wheat barn joining the barley barn containing 3 bays and a threshing place. A horse meat barn[3] containing 3 bays. A stable with a partition for the cart horses and hackney horses with a pig sty at one end and a cart house at the other all in good repair.

An orchard with a rick yard joining it, c. 1 yd. of ground. A kitchen garden, c. 4 lugs, with a pigeon house standing on it, in good repair. A little garden for flowers taken out of the back side with a mud wall about it except where it is fenced with the barley barn.[4] Beside the tithes of the whole parish, the tithe of a little meadow called Bacons mead lying on the other side of the N. river in Upavon and of another little mead now held by Edmund Aymer of this parish, lying on the same side, belonging this parsonage and hitherto always peaceably enjoyed. The tithe of 2a. of the Priory land[5] counted in Upavon so the tithe thereof has been lost for many years.

William Baxter, rector, John Chandler, Robert Moxham [X], churchwardens.

1. Late Baldwin in **643**.
2. Wash house described as lately taken down and about 2 bays of building added for a brewhouse and coal house of great use and convenience erected at the great cost of the present incumbent in **643**.
3. Horse meat house now joined to the end of the barley barn in the rick yard which lately stood before the house being a great annoyance and ready to fall and now a fair court walled in where it stood at the great cost of the present incumbent, in **643**.
4. A wood house added in **643**.

5. Described in **643** as heretofore part of Rushall but by the ploughing up of a linchet laid now to part of the same land in Upavon.

643   17 Dec 1677 (D1/24/175/4)
As 642 with amendments in footnotes. William Baxter, rector, John Coster, Edmund Aymer [X], churchwardens.

644   17 Jan 1705 (D1/24/175/5)
A parsonage dwelling house of *c.* 4 bays, partly tiled partly thatched with 2 gardens and an orchard and 2 courts, a large garden and a stable of *c.* 2 bays with a carthouse at the end of it, a wheat barn of *c.* 3 bays and a barley barn of *c.* 7 bays and a pigeon house in one of the gardens and a little close behind the stable.

A piece of meadow ground lying in Tweentown at the upper end thereof bounded N. side by a meadow and the upper end of an a. of arable land belonging to the farm and S. side by an orchard belonging to Robert Carpenter. The churchyard, of which the gate is to be repaired by the minister, 4 p. of rails on the right hand of the gate to be repaired by the parish and all the rest of the mounds to be repaired by those who hold the farm.

In the N. field the W. side of the highway leading to Woodbridge 1a. called Great Beggars acre, arable land, bounded S. side 1a. of Richard Ford. Another a. of arable land called Little Beggars acre bounded on each side by an a. of John Amer. On E. side of the highway leading to Woodbridge 2a. of arable land lying together bounded W. side by the highway, E. side by 3 x ½a. of John Chandler. 3 x ½a. of arable land bounded on one side by the last highway and on the other by ½a. of Robert Munday. A head a. on Blackenhill furlong of arable land bounded by 3 x ½a. of John Tyler. 1a. of arable land in the same furlong bounded on one side by 1a. of John Chandler and on the other by ½a. of Richard Chandler.

In Tweentown 1 head a. and ½a. of arable land lying by the side of the highway. In Whitefoot furlong 1a. of arable land bounded by 1a. of John Chandler and by ½a. of John Tyler. 2a. together crossing the way bounded by 1a. Thomas Andrews and ½a. John Tyler.

Upon Whitefoot hill in Greenway furlong 1a. bounded by 2a. Thomas Andrews and 3 x ½a. of William Dyke. On the same hill 1a. bounded by ½a. of Robert Carpenter and ½a. John Chandler. In the furlong above Portway 4a. lying together bounded by linches on both sides. In the place called Four Launes, 2a. bounded by a lawn on each side. In Whiteland furlong 1a. bounded by 1a. of Robert Munday and ½a. of the wid. Rutt. In the Midd furlong 1a. bounded by 1a. Robert Munday and 1a. of John Chandler. In Penny furlong 1a. bounded by 1a. John Costerd and 1a. of John Chandler.

In Shepherds Path field in Lickway furlong 2a. lying together bounded by ½a. of James Oram and ½a. of Stephen Rutt. In the next furlong fieldward 4a. bounded by a lawn and 1a. of Richard Chandler. In the middle of the bottom 2a. lying together bounded by ½a. and 1a. both of Thomas Andrews. In Whiteland furlong 2a. lying together bounded by 1a. of Thomas Andrews and ½a. of Richard Chandler.

The whole tithe of all grass and corn or grain that is cut. 72 sheep leaze. The tithe of Bacons mead and of a little plot of ground of John Amer lying in

Upavon field by the river side. 3 cow leaze. A plot of ground called the Hopyard at the upper end of Tweentown.

Charles Francis Gifford, curate, Thomas Andrewes, Richard Chandler, churchwardens, John Chandlor, Peter Ford.

SALISBURY ST. EDMUND rectory

644A   31 May 1705 (D1/24/176)
An Easter book commonly called Easter dues valued at the yearly rent of £12.
Thomas Naish, rector; Nicholas Minty, Thomas Aboren, churchwardens.

SALISBURY ST. MARTIN rectory

645   7 Jul 1705 (D1/24/177)
Tithe corn and hay belong to the dean and chapter of Salisbury or their tenant. All other tithes, dues, obventions, oblations, customary payments from marriages and burials, and the churchyard belong to the incumbent minister or rector.

Peter Terry, rector, Richard Rumsey, Thomas Stoddart, churchwardens, Daniel Floyd, Bartholomew Case [X], sidesmen.

SEAGRY vicarage

646   n. d. late 16th cent. (D1/24/178/1)
A house in which our late minister dwelt called the vicarage house, with a garden, orchard, and a little court. As for glebe land or terrier we know none, but we have diligently enquired of the ancient men of our parish, and they say it is a parsonage and vicarage, and that the corn only belongs to the parson, and the other tithes to the vicar, but whether it is so we do not know.

Richard Box [X], John Weldon, sidesmen, Edward Blackmore, William Hebard [X].

647   1671 (D1/24/178/2)
A dwelling house, barn, stable, a small orchard garden, 1/3a., bounded E. and S. by the river, N. and W. by Sir Edward Hungerford. A pension of 9 marks p. a. and a ground which is kept from the vicar by the owners of Bradenstoke abbey which was presented at the bishop's last visitation.

Christopher Simon, vicar, William Sparrow, James Grinaway, churchwardens.

648   1704 (D1/24/178/3)
A house garden barkside and churchyard. Christopher Simons, vicar, Robert Hollis, John Wheeler, John Hibbard, John Hibbard, churchwardens.

SEMLEY rectory

649 1588 (D1/24/179/1)

A presentment of the glebe lands to be delivered to the bishop's officers at his visitation held at Salisbury. A pasture ground called the E. wood, 6a.; a coppice adjoining, 3a., both bounded by the highway. A close of pasture called Brache, 6a.; a meadow adjoining, 5a.; a close of pasture adjoining, 8a.; another close called Chethayes adjoining, 2a., which 4 grounds are encompassed by the highway.

A close called Culverhayes, 4a.; a close called Rooke wood, 1a.; a close called Shepeland, 8a.; a meadow called Gorehayes, 7a.; a plot of ground, c. 1a. all of which 5 grounds adjoin the parsonage house. A tenement, 4a.; a tenement, 2a.; a coppice called Inox, 1a.; a coppice called Lesells, 8a. which he holds as parcel of his glebe land for which he rebates us one offering day. We pay to the parson whatever tithe is due to him according to our custom.

John Grey senior, John Edwards, churchwardens, Walter Thorne, Thomas Hayne, Steven Burden, sidesmen. *Names in the same hand*

650 11 Nov 1614 (D1/24/179/2)

The parsonage house, the backside and orchard, 1½a. A close called Shiplande, 14a., abutting on the grounds of John Abbott and the land of Edmund Bennat on E. and ground of John Bodman on W. A close called Culverhay, 6a., abutting on the ground of John Bodman on W. and on a way called Semlane on S.W. A close called Rookewood, 1a., abutting on the ground of John Bodman on W. A meadow called Goarehay mead and a little meadow, 8a., abutting upon the highway called Semlane upon W. and a ground of Thomas Pulley on E. A parcel of ground called Applehay, 9a. A close called Chethay, 3a. A meadow called Breach Meadow, 8a. A close called Breach Close, 10a., all which grounds lying in one compass bordering upon the highway called Semlane on N.W. and the highway from Shaftesbury on S.W.

Inockes mead and the coppice [coppis], 7a., bordering upon ground of George Bragg called Collis on S. and the last highway on W. Liffields coppice and pasture, 16a., bordering upon the grounds of William Browne alias Clement upon W. and the last highway on E. Southwood coppice and the pastures adjoining, 14a., bordering upon the ground of Robert West on W. and ground of Anthony Daines on S.

A cottage and meadow, 2a., bordering on the churchyard on N. and the highway from Shaftesbury on W. Another cottage with an orchard and a meadow, 1a. bordering upon the last highway on E. 1a. of ground in Hook farm called Parsons acre of which the parson had only the first share, namely the hay; a third part of hay in another meadow made to his hand, which we cannot say whether they be glebe or not only that the parsons of Semley have had these rights for the space of 50 or 60 years and never out of the parson's hand saving within this 3 years last past have been detained by the farmer of Hook and is now in controversy which we leave to the judgement of law.

Thomas Lawrence, rector, Henry Blanford, Walter Hayne, churchwardens, John Thorne [X], William Hascoll [X], Robert West, George Haskoll. *The churchwardens names are in the same hand.*

651   1671 (D1/24/179/3)

The names of the rooms in the parsonage house and outhouses; a parlour, a kitchen, a dairy house, a buttery, a chamber below stairs, a study, a parlour chamber, 3 other chambers, a barn, a stable, a woodhouse and a washhouse.

Around the houses are 5 closes of pasture and meadow beside the barton orchard and garden namely: a close called Sheplands, 8a.; another meadow called Goory meadow, 8a.; a close called Culverhay, 7a.; another called Rookhay, 2a.; another called Pondes, 1a.; all which grounds are bounded W. side by Sem river and a meadow of Mr. Coles[1] belonging to a tenement called Amberleas, N. side by a meadow called Sheplands and a meadow belonging to Mr. Lawes,[2] E. side with a close of Richard Knight,[3] called Fords and 2 closes of Henry Lambert,[4] S. side by Sem lane. 4 other closes called Applehay, 8a.; another called Chetty, 2a.; another called Brach meadow, 7a.; another called Brach close, 8a., all which grounds are compassed about with the highway except a close called Chetty on W. side of Brach close belong William Gray[5] of Sem. A close and small coppice, 6a., bounded E. side with a close called Pond[6] close on S. side Long meadow both belonging to Mr. William Bennett,[7] W. side bounded by the highway, N. side with Long meadow belonging to Mr. Pinkney.

A meadow called Blackhouse meadow, 2a., bounded with the highway and the churchyard. A close and coppice called S. wood, 10a., bounded E. side with a close called Reads belonging to Mr. Joyce,[8] S. side with a close of the wid. Ambrose[8] and a meadow belonging to the tenement called Oysters, W. side with Hayell[9] meadow belonging to the last tenement, N. side with a ground belonging to Samuel West[10] and the highway.

A close of coppice and furze called Liffiels,[11] 4a.,[12] bounded on E. side with the highway, S. and W. with 2 grounds belonging to Mr. William Knipe,[13] N. with a close of Henry Strong.[14] Hook farm pays in lieu of tithe £3 and the fore shear of 1a. of ground on the farm called the Parson's acre bounded N. side with a close belonging to the same farm, called Hook woods and the third of the fore shear of another meadow called Cranne meadow bounded N. side with a close called Hooke wood, S. side with a coppice called Aldernwood coppice.[15]

The rest of the parish pay the tenth pook of corn, the tenth pook of grain, the tenth calf, tenth lamb, tenth fleece of wool, tenth pig, tenth goose, tenth fruit of the orchard and 3d. for cow white for a cow, 1½d. for offerings, 4d. for churching of women, 10d. for marriage.

Thomas Smith, rector, Walter Blanford, John Lush, churchwardens.

1. Mr. Powell in **654**.
2. William Ogden esq. in **652** and **654**.
3. Peter Browne in **652**, John Benett in **654**.
4. Late Lamberts now Mr. Powell in **654**.
5. Thomas Blanford in 652, John Phelps esq. in **654**.
6. Pound close in **654**.
7. John Bennett in **654**.
8. Robert Hyde esq. in **652**, Hyde Parker and [—] Strode in **654**.
9. Hazell in **654**.
10. Farmer Rixsen in **654**.

11. Liffields in **654**.
12. 10a. in **652** and **654**.
13. Mr. George Knype in **652**, Mr. Edward Knipe in **654**.
14. Roger Strong in **652**, John Benett in **654**.
15. Reference made to the custom as recorded in manor court presentment 2 Oct. 1672 together with **650**, **651** and **652** in **654**.

652   1704 (D1/24/179/4)
As 651 with amendments in footnotes. Thomas Smith, rector, Thomas Gray, Isaac Blanford, churchwardens.

653   1 Aug 1783 (D1/24/179/5)
The parsonage house was entirely new-built by Dr. Gregory, late dean of Christchurch [*Oxford*], of stone and covered with slate; contains 4 rooms on a floor, namely a hall and a kitchen ceiled and bricked, 2 parlours floored with oak, the larger wainscotted, the other half wainscotted and papered. The barn measures 85½ft. by 18½ ft., the stable 41½ft. by 22ft.

c. !00a. of land; 60 arable, 20 pasture, 10 coppice wood and the rest furze and waste ground, enclosed and abutted chiefly by the common; has no right of common.

The garden, orchard and court contain *c*. 2a., partly paled, partly hedged. In the churchyard are 10 elm trees each valued £1. 10s. On the glebe a number of young oaks, value uncertain.

The rector receives great and small tithes by composition at so much in the pound. 2a. of land were formerly given, when and by whom unknown (no deed in being), for repairing the church.

4 bells in the tower. The pulpit has a cushion and furniture of crimson velvet, the communion table of purple velvet. A silver flagon holding *c*. 3 pints inscribed, 'The Gift of Mrs. Ann Willesford of the ancient family of Woodwards of Gloucestershire'. A chalice inscribed 'Semley Wilts 1714'. A patten inscribed 'Semley Parish, Wilts. 1769, Thos. Powell, Church Warden' each of silver. No mark of weight on either utensil.

The church is repaired and the fence kept by the parishioners; the chancel by the rector. The clerk and sexton (both in one) paid by the parish £3 p. a. appointed by the rector.

L[*ewis*] Stephens, rector, Thomas Powell, churchwarden.

654   25 Jul 1803. (D1/24/179/6)
The parsonage house rebuilt in the incumbency of Dr. Gregory is a neat substantial dwellinghouse and with offices which were much improved by Rev. Lewis Stevens, late incumbent. Land and tithes as **651** with amendments in footnotes. 'And because the memory of the same custom in part or in all may be continued in times to come and unimpaired we the churchardens and overseers of the poor [...] with the inhabitants enclose names are herein subscribed do request and direct that the presents may be also deposited in the registry of the Bishop.

John Bracher, churchwarden for the rector, John Merchant, churchwarden for the parish, James Bracher, John Bracher, overseers, John Benett, John Goddard, John King, Mary Marsh, John Maidment, Thomas Andrews, John Rixsen, William

Hacker, John Pond, Samuel Baker, Thomas Powell, George Parham, James White, Anthony Targett senior, Thomas Brockway, John Sanger, Vincent Harris, Edward Knype, Sarah Baker, Thomas Baker, Isaac Blandford, Anthony Targett junior.

SHALBOURNE vicarage

655   6 Jun 1628 (D5/10/2/8)
3½a. in the E. end field upon Cutton hill. 2a. in the field at E. End Townsend. 4a. 1yd. in Shalbourne N. field. 1a. upon the barrows in E. field. ½a. at the vicarage gate. Vicars croft by Newtown common, 6a. Church lands: 2a. of arable lying in Rowlands within the gate, the hedge on the one side and Edward Ranger's land on the other. Parsonage land: 1a. of arable in the E. end field at Townsend. 1a. of arable in the W. field at W. end.

Rowland Hyll, vicar, John Tallmage, (X), William Crpener[1] (X), church-wardens.

1. Probably Carpenter. The marriage of a William Carpenter was recorded in the parish register in 1625.

656   6 Aug 1639 (D5/10/2/8)
A dwelling house, a barn and stable, an outhouse, a pigeon house lately taken down, an orchard, a garden. 3½a. in the E. end field upon Cuttonhill, 2a. in the field at E. End Townsend; 4a. in Shalbourne N. field; 1½a. in E. field; 6½a. in the Vicar's Croft by Newtown; ½a. of Lammas meadow in W. End Gore mead.

Benjamin Some, vicar, Thomas Mundy, Thomas Pearse, churchwardens. Christopher Denman, John Tallmage, [X], sidesmen, John Smith.

SHERRINGTON rectory

657   n. d. late 16th cent. (D1/24/180/1)
A tenement held by John Daniel with a little close, backside, and garden, part of which, with a garden and backside, is now held by John Edridg, all at the will of the parson. 27a. land in the field among the tenants land, besides 120 sheep leaze to common with the tenants and a little close of pasture of c. ½a. called Cox heys. Common for the parsons rother [rudder] beasts, horse and swine as far forth as the tenants. Tithe corn, wool, and hay, and all other tithes within the manor, none excepted. Finally all the offerings with the privy tithes of the mill the manor and paid yearly in the Easter book.

Thomas Adams, Humphrey Edridg, churchwardens, George Imber, John Marshman, sidesmen. *Names in the same hand*

658   24 Jun 1609 (D1/24/180/2)
Terrier delivered to the registry of bishop Henry by the churchwardens 10 Jul 1609. The parsonage house with a kitchen adjoining. A barn, a garden, a backside, 120 lugs [loogs]. A tenement with a little close, backside and garden, c. 60 lugs,

occupied by Henry Whitte, part of which is occupied by John Furnell, all at the will of the parson. A close of pasture called Cox hayes, c. ½a. 27½a. of arable land in the fields amongst the tenants lands in diverse and several places namely: 1a. in Lanchyeard furlong [furland] lying E. and W. between lands of George Imber S., John Edridge N.; 1a in the same furlong between lands of the said George Imber on both sides; 1a. in the same furlong between lands of George Sidnam S. side, William Cilye N. side; ½a. called the Parson's stitch being a headland lying N. and S.; ½a. in Lanchyeard furlong between land of Thomas Harvye S. side, William Whitte N. side; 1a. in the same furlong between land of Thomas Harvye on S. side, Thomas Adams on N. side; 1a. in the same furlong between land of George Imber S. side and Joan Kinge wid. on N. side; 1a. in the same furlong lying land of Richard Pashen on both sides.

7a in Stornehill field namely: 1½a., headland to the farm land lying N. and S.; 1a. lying N. and S. between land of George Imber on W. and Richard Pashen on E. side; 1½a. in Cunniger Bottom lying E. and W. between land of Joan Kinge wid. on both sides; 1a. lying E. and W. between land of George Imber on S. side and Thomas Adams on N. side; 2a. in the same field lying E. and W. between land of George Imber on N. side and John Edridge on S. Side.

7a. in Cunnygar field namely; 1a. lying N. and S. between land of George Sidnam E. side and John Edridge on W. side; 1a. lying E. and W. between land of Tristram Crouche on N. side, George Sidnam on S. side; ½a. lying E. and W. between land George Imber on S. side, George Sidnam on N. side; ½a. lying E. and W. between land of George Sidnam on S. side and Joan Kinge wid on N. side; 1a. lying E. and W. between land John Edridge on S. side and Thomas Admas on N. side; 1a. lying E. and W. next under the cliff [cleeve] having the cliff on S. side and land Thomas Harvye on N. side; 2a in the same field lying E. and W. between land of Richard Pashen on S. side and Joan Kinge wid on N. side.

6½a. in the W. field namely; 1a. lying N. and S. between land Richard Pashen on N. side and George Sidnam on E. side; 1a. lying N. and S. between land of George Imber on E. side and Thomas Martin on W. side; 1a. lying N. and S. between land of George Sidnam on E. side and Joan Kinge wid on W. side; ½a. lying E. and W. next the way on N. side and land of Thomas Harvye on S. side; 1a. lying N. and S. between land of Richard Pashen on E. side and Thomas Adams on W. side; 2a. lying E. and W. between the land of John Edridge on S. side and Joan Kinge wid on N. side.

120 sheep leaze to common in the fields and down and elsewhere with the tenants. Commons for the parson's rother beasts, horses and swine as far forth as the tenants. All tithes within the manor of corn, wool, lambs, hay with all other tithes none excepted. All offerings with the privy tithes of the mill within the manor, paid yearly in Easter week.

Henry Gregorie, parson, Thomas Adams, John Edridge senior churchwardens, George Imber [X], Thomas Hibberd [X], Mathew Burbage [X], Richard Pashin, Thomas Harvye [X], William White [X], George Sidman [X].

658A 1671 (D1/180/3)
The parsonage house, 2 barns, a stable, a hay house, a cart house, all in good reparation. An orchard and garden, backside and as little pasture ground, c. 1a.

27½a. in the arable fields. 2 small cottages at the yearly rent of 12s. 8d. 100 sheep leazes in the common fields. 1 horseleaze. 6 beast leazes.

Samuel Squire, curate, John Pashen, Henry Bath, churchwardens, Thomas Harvy, Edmund Thick, sidesmen.

659 21 May 1705 (D1/24/180/4)

A mansion house and backside; 3yd. of ground; a garden, 12 lugs; 2 barns, a stable, a cart house, a cow house and a pigsty. 2 tenements, one occupied by Mary Flower wid., the other occupied by Susanna Grey wid., each with a garden plot of *c.* 30 lugs. A close of pasture, *c.* ½a.

27½a. of arable in the fields amongst the tenants ground: 7a. in the E. field; 1a. butts on the way from Codford St. Mary to Hindon and lies between land of George Imber on S. side and Edmond Thick on N. side; 1a. in the same furlong lands of George Imber on both sides; 1a. in the same furlong between land of Ambrose Paine on S. side. Thomas White on N. side; ½a. called the Pin Butt lying N. and S. in the same field; ½a. in the same field lying between land of Richard House on S. side and Joan White wid. on N.; 1a. in the same furlong lying between lands Richard House on S. side and Avis Davys wid. on N.; 1a. in the same furlong lying between land of George Imber on S. side and the lady Wallop on N.; 1a. in the same furlong between land of William Patten on both sides.

6½a. in the W. field called Borough field: 1a. lies N. and S. between land of William Pashen on W. side and Ambrose Pashen on E.; 1a. lying N. and S. between land of George Imber on E. and Thomas White on W.; 1a. lying N. and S. between land of Ambrose Pashen on E. side and the lady Wallop on W. side; ½a. called Colliers Hare lying E. and W. next to the way on N. side and land of Richard House on S.; 1a. lying N. and S. between land of William Pashen on E. and Avis Davys wid. on W.; 2a. lying E. and W. between the land of Edmund Thick on S. side and the lady Wallop on N.

7a. in the Coneger field: 1a. lying N. and S. between lands of William Pashen on E. and Edmund Thick on W.; 1a. lying E. and W. between land of Joan White wid. on N. side and Ambrose Pashen on S.; ½a. lying N. and S. between land George Imber on S. side and Ambrose Pashen on N.; ½a. lying E. and W. between land of Ambrose Pashen on S. side and the lady Wallop on N.; 1a. lying E. and W. between land of Edmund Thick on S. side and Avice Davys wid. on N. side; 1a. lying E. and W. next under the cliff and Richard House his a. on N. side; 2a. in the same field lying E. and W. between land of William Pashen on S. side and the lady Wallop on N.

7a. in Stornehill field: 1. ½a. at the upper end of the field lying N. and S. bounded E. ½a. of William Pashen; 1a. lying N. and S. between land of George Imber on W. side and William Pashen on E.; 1½a. in Coneger Bottom lying between land of the lady Wallop on both sides; 1a. lying E. and W. between land of George Imber on S. side and Avis Davys wid. on N.; 2a. in the same field lying E. and W. between land George Imber on N. side and Edmund Thick on S. side.

Commons, tithe and offerings as **658**.

Thomas Lambert, rector, George Imber, Edmund Thick [X], churchwardens, Robert Short, John Collens, Richard House [X].

660   n. d. [1783]¹ (D1/24/180/5)

1. The parsonage house is built with stone and covered with thatch. It contains three rooms on the first floor and three on the second. The parlour is floored with oak and wainscotted with deal, painted. The hall is floored as the parlour, not wainscotted. The kitchen is neither floored nor wainscotted. The parlour and hall have the same kind of ceiling, the same lathing, plastering and whitewashing. The guisses of the upper floor make the ceiling to the kitchen. We have no third floor.

There is a back kitchen, two butteries and a cellar, and on a floor over, once chambered. All thatched. There is a small stable joined to the back kitchen, thatched. A wood house, thatched, at a small distance from the parsonage house. Two small gardens, a flower garden before the house and a small kitchen garden at some distance from it. A small orchard, newly planted. The parsonage yard contains two barns, a large one and a less one. A stable, a cart house, all thatched and a rick barton.

2. The glebe: *c.* ½a. with two small cottages, thatched with a small garden to each house, near to the churchyard. Over right this ½a. is a small pasture ground called the Paddock *c.* ½a. 100 sheep leaze on the sheepsleight. In Lower field 2a. in the Hookland only 1a. of Mrs. Imber between them, bounded N. by an a. of Mrs. Snow and S. by an a. of William Imber senior, measures 1a. 1 r. 1p.; 1a. bounded N. by an a. of Thomas Mussell, S. by an a. of John Patient, measures 2r. 30p.; ½a. at Stitch bounded N. by an a. of James White S. by 1½a. of Mrs. Viney, measures 1r. 35p.; 1a. at Stornal bounded N. by an a. of Mrs. Snow, S. by an a. of Mrs. Viney, measures 2r. 20p.; 1a. above Stornal bounded N. by an a. of Thomas Mussell, S. by a linchard, measures 2r. 20p.; 1a. at Fields End bounded N. by an a. of William Patient, S. by ½a. of William Patient, measures 2r. 20p.

3. Tithes: Due on Edmund Lambert esq. 's estate 9½ yardlands; Mrs. Viney 2 yardlands; Thomas Mussell 3 yardlands and 1½a.; William Patient 1½ yardland; Mr. Rowden 1 yardland; Mrs. Snow 1½ yardland; William Imber junior ½ yardland and 4a.; John Patient 1 yardland; James White ½ yardland; Thomas Felthem ½ yardland; Humphrey Imber ⅓ yardland; Mrs. Lambert 1 yardland; Thomas Alford 1a.; William Imber senior 1 yardland; Codford meadow, 1 yardland. Tithes of the mill, a composition there is 1a. in the field and a small bit of meadow belonging to the mill; tithes of underwood computed at £6 p. a.

4. and 5. Nothing.

6. Furniture of the church: A large bible and common prayer book. A crimson cloth for the reading desk, fixed. A green cloth for the pulpit. Cushion covered with the same. Two large linen communion cloths. A large silver flagon marked 'Ex Dono Tho. Lambert S. T. P. Rector Ecclesiac Sherrington'. A silver patten. A silver cup. Three napkins. A large new green cloth for the communion table. The parish chest old. Two joint stools for funerals. A bell.

7. Nothing.

8. Edifice and churchyard fence. The body of the church is kept by the parish; the chancel by the minister. The fences of the churchyard are maintained by the minister and the farmers. No timber on it or elsewhere.

9. The clerk's wages paid by custom by the farmers according to their estates. Appointed by the minster. No sexton.

Thomas Wilmot Case, rector, John Trowbridge, churchwardens, Thomas
Mussell, James White.

1.   The churchwardens were recorded in the bishop's visitation book, Jul 1783. (WSRO
     D1/50/30)

SHERSTON MAGNA vicarage

661   n. d. late 16th cent. (D1/24/181/1)
A close of pasture, c ½a. lying between a tenement of Thomas Clarke on the E.
and Litton way on the W. In the N. field 1a. lying in Milfurlong between the
land of Roger Drewe on the E. and a land of Robert Davis on the W.; 1a. in a
furlong called Scilands furlong between the land of John Seaborne on the E. and
a land of Ivies Hold on the W. [. . .] lying between a leaze of Edward Busshell on
the N. and a land of John Lyne on the S. ½a. lying in Rowborowe furlong
between the land of Thomas Soore gent. on the E. and a land of Roger Long on
the W. [. . .] lying in Windmill field between the land of Roger Long on the E.
and of Rowland Aylif on the W. ?[In the S.] field: ½a. lying at Noble Cross lane
between a lease [. . .]ong on the S. and a land of Francis Neale on the N.; [. . .] a.
shooting by Cranmore way on the E. and heading [. . .]ong on the W.; 1a. lying
on Easton Townes hill between a land of Richard Goodinge on the E. and a land
of Roger Drewe on the W. A little plot of meadow ground lying in Short mead
between the plot of Robert Bailif on the S. and a plot of Roger Drewe on the N.
      In the S. field of Pinkney: 1a. lying in Purnell hill furlong between the land
of Thomas Geering on the E. and a way on the W.; ½a. in Walles Hill furlong
between a land of Robert Farre on the N. and a land of Nicholas Isgare on the
S.; ½a. in the same furlong between Isgare's lands on both N. and S.; ½a. lying in
a leaze which Robert Farre has enclosed; ½a. lying in Malmesburies Thorne
furlong between a land of Nicholas Briant on the S. and Malmesburies way on
the N.
      In the N. field of Pinkney: 1a. lying in water furlong between a land of
Robert Pharre on the N. and Hide house land on the S.; 1a. lying in Hornes
Hill furlong between the land of William Wilkes on the E. and Hide House
lands on the W.

662   10 Oct 1609 (D1/24/181/2)
The mansion house, garden, orchard and courts adjoining near to the church. A
little close or parrock adjoining to Lydden Way, ½a. A farndell of meadow in a
common meadow called Shortmead between a plot of meadow of Robert Bailie[1]
on N. side and meadow of Roger Drewe[2] on S. side.
      In Sherston's N. field 3a. three farndells at Wootton Way between a piece of
2a. of William Prater gent[2] on W. side and ½a. John Seaborne[3] on E. side; 1a. in
Milfurlong near to Chessells gate between an a. of Thomas Davis[4] on W. side and
½a. Roger Drewe[2] on E. side. 1a. in Windmill field between a piece of 2a. of
Roger Longe[5] on E. side, ½a. of Joan Ailiffe wid.[6] on W. side. ½a. upon
Rowburrowe between an a. of Roger Longe[5] on N. side and ½a. of Philip

Warne[7] on S. side. A farndell lying at Willesley Lane end under the hedge of Edward Bushell[8] on N. side and land of John Hall[9] on S. side. 2½a. in Sherston's S. field, one lying by the highway leading to Cramer lane called the Picked acre. 1a. lying on Eastontowne hill between land of Richard Goodynowe[10] on E. side and Roger Drewe[2] on W. side.[11] 2½a. in Sherston Pinkney's N. field namely: 1a. lying on Hornehill between land of John Danvers gent. on E. side and John Franklynon on W. side; 1a. in Waterfurlong between land of Thomas Geeringe on N. side and John Seaborne on S. side and ½a. lying E. of the forenamed ½a. between an a. of Thomas Gerring on W. side and ½a. of John Bryan on E. side; this ½a. came to the vicarage by exchange made by Robert Farre for ½a. in the S. field.

2a. 1 farndell in Sherston Pinkney's S. field namely: 2 x ½a. lying upon Pinkney Hill, ½a. of Nicholas Isgar running between them; 1a. lying by Isgors way land of Thomas Geringe on E. side, Isgar's way on W. side; 1 farndell lying by Malmesbury way, land of John Brian on S. side and Malmesbury way on N. side.

Richard Woodroff, vicar, John Haye, William Gosemore [X], Roger Drewe [X], John Hyll, Walter Gastrell [X].

1. Alice Hobbs in **663**.
2. Richard Escourt esq. in **663**.
3. William Powell in **663**.
4. Robert Davis in **663**.
5. Alice Holborough wid. in **663**.
6. William Cove in **663**.
7. Philip Manning in **663**.
8. Giles Marsh in **663**.
9. An a. of the parsonage in **663**.
10. Goodenogh in **663**.
11. The following lands in Sherston Pinkneys N. and S. fields not described in detail in **663**, but the vicar receives £1 p. a. for them as has been paid for divers years.

663   30 Oct 1671 (D1/24/181/3)
As 662 with amendments in footnotes. ½a. lying at Aldertons lane end under a hedge of Elizabeth Howells

Henry Hayes, vicar, John Cook, Peter Jaques, churchwardens, Robert Davis, Richard Davis. *Names in the same hand; signature of vicar only.*

664   5 Jan 1705 (D1/24/181/4)
Terrier delivered to the bishop's registry. The dwelling house with barn, stable, court and gardens situate on W. side of the churchyard. A close, ½a., between Lidden way on W. side and a close of Joyce Clerk wid., on E. 1 farndell of meadow in a common called Short mead between a plots of meadow of Mrs. Elizabeth Estcourt on N. and S. sides.

In the N. field: 1a. near Wootton way between 2a. of Mr. Estcourt on W. and ½a. William Powell on E.; 1a. in Mill furlong between 1a. of William Powell, on W. and ½a. Mrs. Elizabeth Estcourt on E.

1a. in the Windmill field between an enclosed ground of Mrs. Elizabeth Estcourt on E. and ½a. of Sarah Cove wid. on W. ½a. upon Rowborrow between 1a. of Mrs. Elizabeth Estcourt on N. and a land of Isaac Manning senior on S.; 1 farndell lying near Wilsley lane between 1a. belonging to the parsonage on S. and an enclosed ground of Mrs. Elizabeth Estcourt on N.

In the S. field 1a. lying by the highway between Easton Grey [Eston] town and Creamore called a picked a., 1a. lying on Eston Town hill between an enclosed ground of Mr. John Goodenough on E. and a land of Mr. Estcourt on W. ½a. lying at the end of a lane which is the highway between Sherston and Alderton between an enclosed ground of the wid. Howell on S. and a land of the wid. Neal on N.

4½a. and 1 farndell lying in Sherston Parva at Sherston Pickney. The churchyard belongs to the vicar but the bounds that belong to the churchyard are to the kept in repair by the churchwardens at the expense of the parish.

Out of the profits of the impropriate parsonage of Sherston Parva at Sherston Pickney there is due to the vicar of Sherston Magna £3 p. a.: that is to say 40s. of that £3 which we believe was constantly without any interruption paid to the vicar from the time whereof the memory of any man living is not to the contrary until Michaelmas [29 Sep] 1691 and 20s. of the same £3 was which was also constantly paid without any interruption before 1620 until Michaelmas 1691 and which 20s. ought to be paid for the said 4½a. and 1 farndell in Sherston Parva and belonging to the vicarage of Sherston Magna. But from Michaelmas 1691 the £3 has been unjustly withheld from the vicar. We have heard and do believe that when John Adye purchased the rectory of Sherston Pickney of John Cooper in or about 1689-1690 Cooper acquainted Adye before they bargained that £3 p. a. was charged on the rectory payable to the vicar and whoever did buy the rectory must pay that sum as Ladyday [25 Mar] and Michaelmas in two equal portions and Adye before the bargained was concluded said this was an argument to beat down the allowed price, that it was charged with the payment of £3 p. a. and for that reason Cooper allowed and abated Mr. Adye above £65 in the purchase. And Adye, after he had purchased and was in possession paid the vicar £3 p. a. until Michaelmas 1691. But we have heard that Adye did not cause any mention to be made of the said £3 p. a. in his deed of purchase.

There is due and payable to the vicar for officiating as minister of Alderton £30 p. a. which sum is usually paid by the dean and chapter of Gloucester cathedral by the hands of their treasurer in two equal portions at Ladyday and Michaelmas. This ought to be paid out of the profits of the impropriate rectories of Sherton Magna and Alderton.

Tithe for pasturing all unprofitable cattle according to a modus called the Penny Shilling, which is the twelfth part of the value of the grass eaten by such cattle. If a foreigner, that is an inhabitant of another parish, is occupier of any titheable enclosed land or ground in the parish he is to pay the vicar tithe according to a modus called the Penny Shilling, that to say, he is to pay the twelfth penny of a third of the yearly value of every enclosed ground mowed or sowed. If a parishioner shall not let his land to a foreigner but shall agist his land with the sheep of a foreigner there is usually paid 3d. per lamb which is 2s. 6d. for every tithe lamb and then is payable in lieu of tithe wool for every such sheep ½d. by the quarter of the year and for every such sheep that shall be depastured only 30 days in only one quarter the said ½d. ought to be paid as it should have been if the sheep had continued in the parish the whole quarter.

Tithe wool of sheep of parishioners to be taken in kind and their tithe lambs to be taken on St. Marks day [25 Apr]. The present vicar commonly taken 3d. per lamb, which is 2s. 6d. for every tithe lamb. For tithe wool of every sheep of parishioners not shorn in this parish ½d. is payable per quarter of a year. If the sheep are kept only 30 days in any quarter, the said ½d. is to be paid.

For every water mill for grinding corn 2s. p. a. Mortuaries have been paid to the vicar for the time being from the time whereof the memory of any man now living is not to the contrary according to the Statute for mortuaries. Every inhabitant that has a titheable garden is to pay for pot herbs consumed [spent] only in his own family 1d. p. a. But if the fruits of his garden are not spent in his own family but are sold or are otherwise disposed of out of his family, tithes are to be paid in their proper kind.

In lieu of tithe calves and tithe milk every calf, except for the first calf of a heifer, 8d. which is 6s, 8d. for every tithe calf. For every first calf of a heifer 6d. which is 5s. for every such tithe calf. For the milk of a heifer, for the first year that she is a milk beast 2d. and for the tithe milk of every other milk cow or milk heifer 3d. p. a. But the vicar cannot tell whether he is bound by custom to take these sums of money in lieu of tithe calves and tithe milk. All offerings are due to the vicar. Tithes apples, pears, eggs of hens, colts, pigs, geese, ducks, honey, wax, pigeons, flax and hemp, and all other tithes in the parish except for tithe corn, hay and wool in Silkwood which belong to the rectory. The vicar is not paid for any small tithes arising on the glebe of the rectory of the parish.

Richard Weeksy, vicar, George Guest [X], Francis Hobbs [X], churchwardens, Alex Holborrow, John Hale, William Wallis, Daniel Bennet [X], Giles Hitchings, Charles Gale. Inhabitants of Sherston Pickney: Richard Millsum, John Neale, Timothy Shipton [X], James Chappell, Richard Jones, John Weeks senior[X].

SHORNCOTE rectory

665   30 Nov 1671 (D1/24/182/1)

We present upon our oaths a true terrier of all the glebe lands and tithes so far as we know or have credibly heard by conference with our honest neighbours.

A dwelling house, a barn, a stable, a pigeon house, a court. A little ground called the Hopyard, c. 3 farndells. 2 little grounds called the Capses, c. 5a., lying S. from the House. Three little grounds called the Farr leeses lying N. from the house, c. 10a., the hedge on the N. standing on the wayside belongs to the parsonage. 3a. meadow in Aishton meadow, 2a. of which are at the upper end shooting on Sheerditch, and 1a. is at the lower end shooting on the Thames. 9½a. arable in common fields, 8a. of which in Westtom field, and 1½a. in the N. field lying as follows: 1a. shooting on Tudmor; 3a. and a farndell in the Short furlong adjoining Mr. Hawkin's piece; 3 farndells lying between a piece of 7a. and 1 head a. of the farms; 1a. lying in Larke furlong; 1a. on the down in Riie furlong; 2 x ½a. shooting on Portway. In the N. field 2 x ½a. shooting on Portway lying on the E. side of the way; 1 farndell on the down toward Cerney lying between 2 farndells of Mr. Barned. The glebe is rated at 2 yardlands with commons in commons and common fields as the rest of the parish have. All tithes are paid in kind according to custom.

There are certain acres of land in Ashton field and meadow in Ashton meadow which pay whole tithe to the parson of Shorncote. In Ashton field: 4½a. in the N. field held by Mary Pierce wid. or her under-tenants, 4a. of which lies shooting on Portway, the other ½a. in Herring furlong; the same Mary Pierce has 3 farndells in the W. field shooting on the Ricksons near the Downmead gate; John Hawkins esq. has 1a. in the W. field in Long linke furlong; Edmund Hinton has 2a. lying in the Long furlong that shoots on Sheerditch lying in the N. field; Edmund Carter has 2a. lying in Blacklands furlong; Edmund Maslynes or his undertenant has 2a. in the long shooting on Sheerditch and 1a. more in Blacklands. In Ashton meadow Mrs. Ann Masters or her undertenants have 21a.: 7a. at Hulliston Corner; 9a. lying on the E. of Ditch dooles; 4a. not far from there; 1a. called Norcut acre; there is a certain parcel of meadow being a Hiping ham; c. 2a. held by Edmund Hinton which pay only half tithe (to the parson). There is a little ground adjoining Friday's ham and held by Edmund Hinton of c. 2a. which pays whole tithe.

Henry Munden, William Hawkins, churchwardens.

666   7 Dec 1677 (D1/24/182/2)

A dwelling house, barn, stable, pigeon house, garden and backside or court adjoining the house. All manner of commons in the common fields for 2 yard-lands. A little close called the Hopyard, 2 farndells, lying S. of the dwelling house bounded E. part of the farm, S. by Henry Munden, W. by Thomas Ford.[1]

A ground called the Caps, 5a., lying S. of the house, bounded E. common field, S. and W. Thomas Ford,[1] N. Henry Munden; the hedges on E., S. and W. quarters belong to the parsonage. Three little enclosed grounds lying together called the Fare[2] Leeses, 10a., lying N. of the house, bounded E. and S. by part of the farm, W. and N. by the highway; the hedges on W., N. and E. quarters belong to the parsonage. 3a. of meadow in Ashton Keynes[3] mead namely: 2a. shooting on Sheerditch,[4] bounded[5] W. Thomas Ford,[1] E. Ashton farm meadow; 1a. shooting upon the Thames, bounded[5] W. by Shornecote farm mead, E. John Parker's ground. 9a.[6] of arable land lying in common field namely: 1a. called the Thoroushute lying in the midst of a piece of 10a. belonging to the farm; 3 farndells lying between a piece of 7a. and a single head a. of the farm; 3a. 1 farndell lying in a short furlong joining Mr. Hawkin's piece; 1a. lying in Larke furlong bounded W. a piece of 2a. of Shorncote farm, E. an a. of John Giles of Ashton; 1a. lying on the Down; 2 farndells shooting upon Portway having a farrundell of Edward Hinton between them; 1 farndell lying in Cocked furlong between 2 farndells of Thomas Ford; 2 single ½a. shooting upon Portway from Baggers Bush; 1 farndell lying on E. side of Portway in the N. field.

All manner of tithes to be paid in kind according to the custom of this place. Certain a. lying in Ashton field and meadows whose tithes belong to the parsonage: John Say has 5a. 1 farrundell[7] in the field; 4 of the a. lie in a furlong that shoots upon Portway in the N. field; ½a. lies in Herring furlong in the N. field; 3 farndells[8] lie in a furlong that shoots upon the Ricksons[9] in the W. field. John Hawkins esq. or his undertenants have 1a.[10] in Longlinck furlong. Edmund Carter has 2a.[11] in Blacklands furlong; Edmund Hinton has 2a.[12] in a furlong that shoots upon Sheerditch in the N. field; Mr. Richmond[13] has 2a. in a furlong upon Sheerditch in the N. field and 1a. in Blacklands furlong; Mrs Ann Masters wid.[14] or her undertenants have 21a. of mead in Ashton meadow namely; 7a.[15] at Hallston corner;[16] 4a. not far from it; 9a. lying in a furlong called Ditch dole; 1a. called Northcutt acre. 2a. of meadow in Ashton mead being on Hiping Ham in the possession of Edmund Hinton, lying one year by Kibbs Ham and the other year shooting upon Wickway;[17] 1a. lying in an enclosed meadow ground[18] in the possession of Edmund Hinton which lies under the hedge joining to Ashton meadow.

Mr. John Turner, rector, Henry Munden, churchwarden, William Hawkes, sidesman. *Names in the same hand.*

1. John Truby in **667** and **668**.
2. Farther leases in **668**.
3. Ashton mead in **667** and **668**.
4. Sheerditch and Shireditch in **667** and **668** respectively.
5. No bounds given in **667** and **668**.
6. Described as 6a. in the W. field, 1a. upon the Down, 2 x ½a. and 2 single farndells shooting on Portway; 1 farndell in the N. field on Portway, 1 farndell on the Down shooting on Chaplins ground in **667** and **668**.
7. 4½a. only in **667** and **668,** the three farndells being omitted. In **668** the land is held by George Ferris when the 4a. as described as bounded N., the rector, S. John Truby and the ½a. N. Charles Farindon, S. George Ferris.
8. Held by George Ferris in **668**.
9. Described also as near Down Mead gate in **667**.
10. Mrs. Alice Chapman in **668**, in **667** and **668** described as being in the W. field.
11. These 2a. described as 1a. in Blackland furlong and 1a. shooting upon Sheerditch in **667** and **668**. Held by Olive Carter **668**.
12. Also described as the Long furlong in **667** and **668**.
13. Olive Richmond in **667** and **668**.
14. Dr. Masters in **668**.
15. Called Badgers Ham in **667** and **668**.
16. Hailstone in **667** and **668**.
17. Described as in the N. land doles in **667** and **668**.
18. Also described as adjoining Fridays ham in **668** and **667**.

667   17 Oct 1698 (D1/24/182/3)
As **666** with amendments in footnotes. John Turner senior, rector, John Truby, Robert Hawkes, churchwardens.

668   20 Oct 1704 (D1/24/182/4)
As 666 with amendments in footnotes. John Turner, rector, Jonathan Hawkes, churchwarden.

669   29 Jul 1783 (D1/24/182/5)

Terrier made pursuant to the directions of the bishop and deposited with the registrar at the primary visitation. A parsonage house, built of stone, covered with tiles,
3 rooms on the lower floor, one of which is ceiled and 3 bed chambers on the upper
floor, none of which is ceiled or wainscotted. A barn c. 40ft. x 18ft., a stable c. 30ft.
x 12ft., a cart house at the E. end of the barn c. 18ft. x 10ft. all thatched with straw.

A little close called the Hopyard which with the garden and court measures
1a., bounded E. part of Mrs. Baker's farm, W. Mrs. Amoson's farm; the hedges on
the W. side belong to Mrs. Amoson, all the rest to the parsonage. A close called
the Capps, 5a., bounded N. and S. Mrs. Baker's farm, W. Mrs. Amoson's farm; the
hedges on E., S. and W. belong to the parsonage. 2 grounds called the Far leases,
10a., bounded N. and W., highways, E. and S. Mrs. Baker's farm; the hedges W.,
N. and E. belong to the parsonage. A ground 4a. 1r. bounded all sides Mrs.
Amoson's farm; hedges on S. belong to Mrs. Amoson, the rest to the parsonage.
A ground, late in the common field but now enclosed by an Act of 1777, and
granted to the rector in lieu of tithes, and some small parcels of land in Ashton
Keynes, 15a. 3r. 11p.; hedges on E. belong to Mr. Whorwood, the rest to the
parsonage. A little ground 1a. 2r. 16p., adjoining the said Hopyard, late Mr. Whor-
wood's, but granted under the said Act to the rector; hedge on N. belong to Mrs.
Baker, the rest to the parsonage. The churchyard, c. 2r., the glebe contain 38a. 27p.
and is all arable except for the Hopyard and Mr. Whorwood's late little ground.
There is no timber of any value on the premises. The hedges are chiefly quickset.

All manner of tithes payable in kind according to the custom of the place. 2
cow pastures and a quarter in a common called Tudmore. There are no
augmentations of any kind.

There is a table and chest in the church; a chalice and patten weighing
together c. 9oz., a surplice, a small bell, a bible and common prayer book. The
chancel is kept in repair by the rector, the church and churchyard by the
parishioners. The clerk who is likewise sexton is paid by the parishioners.

John Davies, rector, William Stephens, churchwarden, William Kimber,
William Weeks, principal inhabitants.

SHREWTON vicarage

670   n. d. late 16th cent. (D1/24/183/1)

All manner of offerings and tithes, corn only excepted, which is impropriate to
the parsonage. Also 1 yardland of 24a. of arable wheat field with pasture for 40
sheep and leazes for 2 kine on the cow down and leazes for 2 horses in Netfeeldes
with other common for swine as the inhabitants have. There is an annuity of 20s.
to be paid to the vicar out of the parsonage, but it has been detained for about
20 years.

671   1609 (D1/24/183/2)

Terrier taken by the churchwardens and ancient men. A dwelling house containing
four fields of building, a barn and stable of four fields. A garden, backside and
building c. ½a. A pigeon or dove house standing in the backside.

1 yardland in Net field bounded as follows: Net field next to Rollestone [Rowstone] field, 1½a. shooting near to the pound of Rolleston, Amesbury way on one side, land of Sir Edward Escourt on the other; 1a. more in the Upper furlong, land of Thomas Tooker on one side, land of Robert Wansborough on the other; 1a. in the Lower furlong, land of Robert Gilbert alias Netton on one side, land of Richard Munday on the other; 1a. in Upper furlong, land of Richard Munday on the home side, land of Sir Edward Escourt on the field side; 1a. in the Lower furlong, land of Sir Edward Escourt on the field side, land of Richard Munday on the home side; 1a. in the Upper furlong, land of Sir Edward Escourt on the home side, land of Robert Wansborough on the field side; 1a. called the Pit acre in the Lower furlong, land of Sir Edward Escourt on the home side, land of Robert Wansborough on the field side; ½a. shooting against Amesbury way, land of Sir Edward Escourt on the home side, land of Thomas Tooker on the field side; ½a. shooting against Corne Borowes being linched on both sides, land of Thomas Tooker on both sides.

The Middle field: 1a. in Broadland, land of Thomas Tooker on the home side, land of Richard Munday on the field side; 1a. shooting E. and W., land of Richard Munday on one side, two stitches or butts on the other side; 1a. more shooting on Amesbury way having a linchet at the upper end of the home side and land of Sir Edward Escourt on the home side, land of Thomas Tooker on the field side; 1a. more shooting on the headland that shoots on the end of the last a. having two stitches or butts on one side, land of John Godwin on the other; 1a. lying near the plot of layne, land of Thomas Tooker on the field side, land of John Kelloway alias Longe on the home side; 1a. more above the plot of layne having a linchet on the field side, land of Thomas Tooker on both sides; ½a. shooting right at the end of the ½a. in the other [?Hurst] field, being linched on both sides, land of Thomas Tooker on both sides; 2 great a. being linched on both sides, land of Thomas Tooker on one side, Hurst field on the other; 1a. in the new broke land, land of Mr. Thornell on one side, land of Richard Munday on the other.

The Hurst field; 1a. shooting on Amesbury way, land of John Godwin on the home side, land of Richard Munday on the field side; 1a. more shooting on Amesbury way, land of Robert Wansborough on the field side, land of John Longe on the home side; ½a. shooting athwart the S. bottom, land of Thomas Tooker on the home side; 1 picked a. lying upon the Hurst, land of Sir Edward Escourt on one side, land of Thomas Tooker on the other; 1a. more upon the Hurst being at one end headland to the picked a., land of Sir Edward Escourt on one side, land of Robert Wansborough on the other side; 1a. lying in the N. W. Bottom being headland on one side, land of Thomas Tooker on the other side; a long ½a. shooting S. and N. being headland at the N. end, land of Richard Munday on the other side; 1a. shooting on the Down, W. and N. and of Thomas Tooker, S. and E., land of Sir Edward Escourt.

All manner of tithes and offerings except tithe corn to the parsonage. 4 sheep leaze in the common flock of Net, 2 kine leaze upon the downs of Shrewton, 2 horse leaze in the fields of Net according to the custom there, with all commodities for 1 yardland.

By me Giles Thornborough, deputy of the vicar; Robert Goldisborough, Robert Wansborrowe [X], churchwardens, John Smyth, John Keloway [X].

672   9 Oct 1671. (D1/24/183/3)

In all 25a.: 7a. in the field next Rolleston (Rowstone); ½a. in the Lower furlong, Nicholas Munday W.; 1a. in the Upper furlong, Robert Wansbury E., Thomas Chartwrite W.; 1a. in the Lower furlong, Alice Payne W., Thomas Netton E.; 1a. in the Upper furlong, Robert Hughes W. Alice Payne E.; 1a. in the Lower furlong, Humphrey Giles W., Richard Shope E.; 1a. in the Upper furlong, Henry Shope E., Richard Shope W.; 1a. in the Lower furlong Alice Payne W., Robert Wansbury E.; ½a. shooting on London way, Nicholas Coaker W.

In Middle field, 11a.; 1a. shooting on London Way, Charles Gilbert E., Nicholas Coaker W.; 1a. lying by Middle way; 1a. in Broad land, Robert Wansbury W., Thomas Netton E.; 1a. in Pechole, James Langly on both sides; 1a. shooting fieldward Henry Shope N., James Langly S.; 1a. by the plot of layne, James Langly W., Thomas Chartwrite E.; 1a. above the plot of layne Humphrey Giles E., Robert Wansbury W.; 1a. shooting up hill and down hill Charles Gilbarte E., Robert Wansbury W.; 2a. lying by the outside Charles Gilbert E.; 1a. in the new broke land Thomas Netton W.

Middle Hurst field, 7a.; 1a. shooting on London way, Robert Hughes E., Thomas Netton W., 1a. on London way, James Langly W., Robert Wansbury E.; 1a. athwart the bottom Robert Wansbury E., Alice Collett W.; 1 head a. on the bottom Robert Wansbury S.; 1 picked a. upon the Hurst, Edmund Sutton S., William Alexander N.; 1a. athwart the Hurst, Edmund Sutton W., Robert Wansbury E.; 1a. in the new broke land, Alice Pane S., Robert Wansbury N.

Housing belonging to the vicarage: A hall, a kitchen and buttery, 3 chambers overhead; a barn of 3 rooms, a pigeon house, orchard and garden, 1yd. of ground. Valued [rated] at yearly: lambs 150 at £3; wool £14; hay £3; glebe land £7; paid out of the parsonage £1; the churchyard 10s.

Richard Bigge, vicar, Nathaniel Costard, Robert Goldesborough, churchwardens.

673   3 Jan. 1705 (D1/24/183/4)

1 yardland of glebe with its appurtenances viz. pasture for 40 sheep and 10 lambs in the common fields and downs called Net or Netton, pasture for 2 kine and 2 runners or young beasts going in the common herd of the parish, pasture for 2 horses in the common fields and meadows at the usual times; feeding for [. . .] swine in and after the harvest.

The arable part of the glebe has dispersed in the fields of Nett or Netton viz. in the field next Rolleston [Rolston]7a.; ½a. in the Lower Homeward furlong, James Elderton W., Salisbury way E.; 1a. in the Upper furlong, Mr. Wansborough E., Mr. Hart W.; 1a. in the Lower furlong Thomas Payn W., Thomas Netton E.; 1a. in the Lower furlong, Humphrey Giles W., Richard Sopp E.; 1a. in the Lower furlong, Humphrey Giles W., Richard Sopp E.; 1a. in the Upper furlong Robert Kello W., Thomas Payn E.; 1a. in the Upper furlong, Henry Sopp E., Richard Sopp W.; 1a. in the Lower furlong, Thomas Payn W., Mr. Wansborough E.; ½a. in the Short furlong at the upper end of the field Nicholas Coker W. [. . .] E.

In the Middle field, 11a., 1a. shooting or abutting against London way Mr. John Gilbert E., Nicholas Coker W.; 1a. lying by Middle way, part of John

Munday's barn being built on it; 1a. in Broad land, Mr. Robert Wansbrough W., Thomas Netton E.; 1a. in Pecksole, James Langley on both sides formerly now [. . .]; 1a. shooting fieldward Henry Sopp N., William Read S.; 1a. by the plot of laine Mr. Green now Elias South E., Thomas Kello W.; 1a. above the plot of laine, Humphrey Giles E., Mr. Wansbrough W.; 1a. shooting uphill and downhill, Mr. John Gilbert E., Mr. Wansbrough W.; 2a. on the outside of the field bounded with great linchets on both sides, Mr. John Gilbert S.; 1a. in the new broke land, Thomas Netton W., linchets on both sides.

In the Middle Hurst field, 7a.; 1a. shooting on London way Robert Kello E., Thomas Netton now Thomas Pierce W., linched in with 2 great linchets commonly called the Five yards; 1a. crossing the S. bottom, Mr. Wansbrough E., Henry Law W. linched on both sides; 1 head a. in the Bottom shooting fieldwards and homewards ending homewards in the middle of Mr. Sopp's a., Mr. Wansbrough and a great linchet S.; 1 picked a. upon the Hurst, Edmund Sutton S., John Alexander N., having a short linchet on the fieldward end and on N. side; 1a. crossing the Hurst headland to the last a., Edmund Sutton W., Mr. Wansbrough E.; 1a. in the new broke ground, Thomas Payn S., Mr. Wansbrough N. Tithe hay of all the meadows, downs and fields in Shrewton and of Small mead in Winterborne Stoke.

The mansion house contains a parlour, a hall, a buttery and kitchen all lately rebuilt and covered with reed or brick tile, 4 chambers, 2 garrets. Outhouses: a barn of 3 rooms, a pigeon house, and coalhouse, all in good repair with a garden, 1yd. of ground, the yearly value of ground and housing £2; the yearly value of the yardland with appurtenances £7; the yearly values of tithe hay £3, of tithe wool £14 and of tithe lambs £3. £1 paid out of the parsonage by those who enjoy tithe corn at 4½d. a yardland. The churchyard with offerings cow white tithe honey, etc. £1. 5s., total £31. 5s.

Thomas Browne, vicar, Robert Wansbrough, Samuel Gilbert, churchwardens, Robert Gouldisborough, John Munday, Henry Soppe.

GREAT SOMERFORD rectory

674   4 Oct 1608 (D1/24/184/1)
A dwelling house with garden and orchard and other ground, butting on the streat way on the E., the churchyard [litton] on the N., a close of John Winckworth on the S., and the Avon [Haven] running on the N., c. 1a. A tenement at Startley [Starkly] with a close adjoining, c. 2a., formerly called the Parson's ground. A parcel of ground lying in the Vervells of John Yew gent. on the S. and the running brook on the N. side of c. ½a. A close of pasture within the town of Somerford, c. 1a., the ground of Thomas Leonard on the S. and on the N. a close of William Knape. 1a. meadow in the W. end of Horsam one part of which lies in Avon running on the W., in which part of the Avon the rector has an interest and right in any benefit from the Avon so far as his ground reaches it. 2a. of meadow at E. end of Horsam, the Avon bounding on the N., and on the S. his own bounds. Pasture for 9 beasts and a bull in the New lease. 1½a. meadow in the S. mead. 1½a. meadow on the Inner Nithie, butting on ½a. of

Thomas Sely which lies on the S. and ½a. of Humphrey Mayo which lies on the N. 1a. meadow in Warrames, John Comly butting on the N., and William Baily on the S. ½a. meadow in Warrames, William Baily butting on the [E.], and William Knapp on the W. [. . .] of lot meadow in Rodde mead; [. . .] ½a. of lot meadow in Rodde mead butting on [. . .]ford; [. . .] ½a. of land meadow butting on Rithy ford [belonging] one year to the parsonage and the next to a tenant of [. . .] Mumparsons. 6 beasts leaze in Mr. John Yewe's marsh called Lammas ground from Holyrood day [14 Sep] to Lammas [1 Aug]. 4 beasts leaze in the W. marsh called Lammas ground.

In W. field: 1a. arable land lying in Sand Hill furlong, William Yewe lying on the N. and Thomas Pockerage on the S.; 1a. of land in Four acre furlong, William Browne lying on the N. and Thomas Hoskins on the S.; 3a. more in the same furlong, William Knap lying on the S. and John Sely on the N.; ½a. lying in Green Way furlong, John Mayo lying on the N. and the green way on the S.; 1a. in Hastreat furlong, Gabriel Lovell on the N.; 1a. lying in Long hedge furlong, Mr. John Yewe on the N. and Thomas Heskins on the E.; 1a. more in the same furlong, Thomas Lennar lying on the W., and Thomas Winckworth on the E.; 1a. shooting on Thomas Sely's lane end, William Mayo lying on the W. and William Browne on the E.; 1a. on the Seetch furlong, Humphrey Mayo lying on the E. and Thomas Pokeridge on the W.

In the Broad Field: ½a. lying on Long hedge furlong, Francis Wood lying on the E. and Richard Comly on the W.; 2a. in the same furlong, John Comly on the W. and Thomas Winkworth on the E.; 3a. in the same furlong, Richard Comly lying on the W., William Knappe on the E.; 1a. lying under Long Hedge, Robert Knowles on the N., William Yewe on the S.; 1a. lying in Hucklands, Humphrey Mayo on the W., Robert Knowles on the E.; 1a. lying in Odnill furlong, William Yew lying on the S., Thomas Pockeridge on the N.; 1a. in the same furlong, Thomas Sely on the S. and Mr. John Yewe on the N.; 1a. in the Moor furlong, William Browne on the N., Mr. John Yewe on the S.; ½a. lying in the same furlong, Mr. John Yewe on the S., William Knappe on the N.; 1a. in Inland furlong, William Mayo on the N., William Yewe on the S.; 1 close of pasture of c. 5a. in the same field, adjoining the way on the W., and Thomas Hoskins on the E.

In the Down field; 1a. in Copped thorne furlong, William Yewe on the W., Thomas Sely on the E.; 1a. in Shadwell furlong, William Yewe lying on the S., Richard Pitman on the N.; 1a. lying in the Moor furlong, William Yewe lying on the S. and N.; 1a. in the same furlong, Richard Pitman on the S., Francis Wood on the N.; 1a. in the same furlong, Richard Pitman on the N., William Browne on the S.; 2a. lying in Middle Down furlong, William Pitman lying on the S., Thomas Lennar on the N.; 1a. in the same furlong; William Yewe lying on the S., Mr. John Yewe on the N.; 1a. lying in the Shilfe Acre furlong, Thomas Sely on the N., William Yewe on the S.; 1a. in the same furlong, Mr. John Yewe on the N., Thomas Northway on the S.; ½a. lying in Long Down furlong, William Yewe on the N., Humphrey Mayo on the S., ½a. in Middle Down furlong, Mr. John Yew lying on both sides; 1a. lying in the Moor furlong near Shelf yeat, Thomas Heskin on the S., Mr. William Baily on the N.; 1a. in the furlong next to the New Lease yeat, William Knap on the E., Richard Pitman on the W.; 1a. in the same furlong, Thomas Northway lying on the E., William Yewe on the W.; ½a. lying in Catbraine furlong, Richard Pitman on the S., Thomas Sely on the N.; ½a. lying by Horsam hedge, the hedge bounding on the N., William Pitman on the S.; ½a. lying in Horsame furlong, Richard Pitman on the S., William Mayo on the N.; 1a. lying behind Shelf yeat, Thomas Heskins on the E. side, Richard Pitman on the W.

    Richard Pitman, Thomas Winworth.

675   6 Nov 1671 (D1/24/184/2)

A dwelling house containing, below stairs 5 rooms and a cellar, above stairs, 1 storey high, 6 rooms and a closet, up another pair of stairs 2 storey high, a study and an apple loft built by the present incumbent. A brew house, or bakehouse by itself on S. side of the house, a bay of buildings containing a stable, a cowhouse and a hogsty on W. side, a barn containing 10 fields of building, one of which is taken up in it by an oxhouse on W. end with a wain house and a new wainhouse built by the present incumbent on E. side of the house; on N. side of the house is a pigeon house with a house of office on the E. end; also a hen house adjoining the brewhouse, built by the present incumbent. Garden and pasture ground about the dwelling house c. 1a.; a flower garden on N. side bounded with a stone wall, a court on S. side between the house and the brewhouse, a small court adjoining the flower garden bounded with a stone wall and a plot of ground pailed round for brassicas [coleworts] and such like necessaries.

    A close at Startley [Starkly], c. 2a.; a parcel of ground in the Fermer fields of Sir Robert Jason, c. ¼a.; a close of pasture within the town, c. 1a., bounded S. land of John Leonard, N. Sir Robert Jason; ½a. pasture ground on W. end of Horsham bounded N. the Avon; the rector has the right of any profit arising from the Avon as far as his ground extends along it.; 2a. of meadow ground on E. end of Horsham bounded N. the Avon and by his own bounds on S.; an enclosed ground, 3½a., on S. side of the last land, arable or pasture, bounded S. the Down field. Pasture for 9 cows and a bull in New Lease. 1½a. in S. mead. ½a. of meadow in Inner Nythy bounded S. Deborah Sealy, N. Jonas Lawrence. ½a. of meadow ground in Warham; bounded N. Jasper Wheeler, W. Sir Robert Jason. 2 x ½a. in Rodmead. A picked ½a. in Rodmead butting upon Whiteacre ford. ¼a. butting upon the Mead Headenford. In the moor 2 swaths or one-fifth a. from Hollyrood day [14 Sep] to Lammas Day [1 Aug]. 6 beast leaze in Sir Robert Jason's marsh [marrish] called Lammas ground and 4 beast leaze in the W. Marsh called Lammas ground. Whether the last beast leaze be in lieu of tithe we know not, by the report of our predecessors it was so.

    In the Broad field: ½a. lying upon Long Hedge furlong bounded W. side Thomas Davis, E. side Sir Robert Jason; 2a. more in the same furlong, W. side Deborah Sealy, E. Isaac Knap; 1a. under Long hedge N. William Knowles, S. John Yew; 1a. in Hucklands W. Rebecca Mayo, E. William Knowles; 1a. in Odnill furlong S. Peter Aland N. Mr. Thornbery; 1a. in the same furlong S. John Mayo, N. Sir Robert Jason; ½a. in Moor furlong Sir Robert Jason on both sides; 1a. in the same furlong N. Sir Robert Jason, S. John Mayo; 1a. in Brick mead corner adjoining to Seagry heath; a close of pasture, c. 5a., in the same field; 2a. shooting upon Long Hedge towards Vinslade corner E. Sir Robert Jason, W. Thomas Davis.

In the W. field: 1a. of land lying in Four acres furlong, N the wid. Bridges, S. James Yew; 3a. more in the same furlong, S. Sir Robert Jason, N. Deborah Sealy; ½a. in Apple furlong, N. Samuel Knap, S. the greenway; 1a. in Hay Street furlong, N. John Lea; 1a. in Long Hedge furlong, Sir Robert Jason on both sides; 1a. in the same furlong, W. John Yew, E. Sir Robert Jason; 1a. shooting upon Deborah Sealy's lanc end, W. John Mayo, E. Jeffrey Broune; 2 x ½a. lying in Smith Marrish furlong, E. Peter Aland, W. John Mayo.

In the Down field: 1a. in Copped thorne furlong, W. Peter Aland, E. Richard Hibberd; 1a. in Moor furlong S. Peter Aland, N. John Yew; 1a. in the same furlong N. the wid. Arch, W. John Rummin; 1a. in the same furlong N. John Rummin, S. Jeffrey Broune; 2a. in Middle Down furlong S. John Rummin, N. John Leonard; 1a. in the same furlong S. John Yew, N. Jasper Wheeler; ½a. in Long Down furlong Sir Robert Jason on both sides; ½a. in Middle Down furlong S. Jasper Wheeler, N. Sir Robert Jason; 1a. in Moor furlong near Shaile Yat N. Jasper Wheeler, S. John Leonard; 1a. in the furlong next to New Lease Yat E. Sir Robert Jason, W. John Rummin; 1a. in the same furlong E. Mr. Thornbery, W. Peter Aland; ½a. in the furlong called Catsbraine S. John Rummin, N. Richard Hibberd; 1a. upon New Lease furlong N. Richard Hibberd, S. Richard Yew; ½a. in Long down furlong N. Richard Yew S. Rebecca Mayo. A messuage, being church land, with ½a. adjoining; 1 beast leaze in New lease; 1a. in the W. field in White Land furlong; c. 3a. in the corner Vinslade all which are let for 3 lives under the rent of 6s. 8d. p. a.; the present incumbent has no profit thereof and therefore although it be no part of the glebe yet by our oaths we think ourselves obliged to insert it.

John Knappe, Samuel Knappe, churchwardens, William Knowle, John Leanard, sidesmen. *Names in the same hand*

676   11 Dec 1677 (D1/24/184/3)
Glebe enclosed: The Home stall i. e. the dwelling house, brewhouse, barn and ox house adjoining, stable, cow house, pigeon house, with all other ancient buildings of less note, together with the backside, gardens and close in all 2a. A close called Kinnard's leaze 1¼a.; Seagry heath leaze, 5a.; Burnt House close, 3½a.; Verrell ham, ½a., Horseham leaze 3½a.: Whereof ½a. was anciently of the glebe, the other 3 reputed a. were laid together upon exchange and enclosed by Mr. Aske[1] viz. 1½a. of Mr. John Romane, the 1a. bounded N. the said glebe ½a., E. New leaze, S. lands of Mr. Thomas Davies, W. Mr. William Greenfield. The ½a. bounded N. and W. land of Mr. William Greenfield, E. New leaze, S. Horsham furlong. Exchanged for 2a. of glebe, 1a. of which lies in Shadwell, bounded N. land of Mr. John Romane, E. Mr. Romane's Shadwell leaze, S. John Yewe, W. Mr. Jonas Laurence, all which are now in Mr. Romane's new enclosure in Shadwell; the other a. lies on Sandhill in the W. field, bounded N. land of Mr. John Romane, E. the Mead lane, S. the Wid. Christine Serjeant, W. the Heath or Sandhill way, now in Mr. John Romane's new enclosure on Southill. 1a. of Mr. Thomas Davies bounded N. Mr. John Romane, E. New leaze, S. and W. Mr. William Greenfield, exchanged for an a. of glebe in the Broad field having N. Long Hedge way, E. 2a. of glebe, S. Venslade, W. the wid. Comlye's leaze.

½a. of John Mayow (now Mr. William Greenfield) bounded N. with the said

a. of Mr. Thomas Davies, E. New leaze, S. Mr. John Romane, W. Mr. William Greenfield, which ½a. together with 2 other ½a. adjoining Seagry Heath leaze, was exchanged with Mr. John Mayow for 1a. in Inland furlong in the Broad field, bounded N. Mr. William Greenfield, E. Mr. John Romane, S. Richard Winkworth, W. Barrow acre.

Glebe in common. In Horsham: A reputed ½a. situate at the gate at W. end of the said meadow. Horsham mead plot, c. 3a., at E. end of the said meadow. In S. mead 1a., called one of the short a. bounded N. with the Ten stitches, E. the Syndram acres, S. Dock ham, W. Isaac Knapp's short a. ½a. in the W. end of the same meadow near Mr. John Shadwell's leaze by lot. In the Moor one-fifth a. called Five acre, about the middle of the Moor by lot.

In the Nythe: ½a. bounded N. land Richard Hybberd, E. Broad leaze, S. John Yewe, W. Mr. William Greenfield.

In Broad mead: ¼ part of one of the a. called Goose acres by lot. William Torcham's 1a. bounded N. Richard Yewe, E. the river, S. Dockham, W. Courseham. ½a. bounded N. E. Dockham, S. E. Mr. Jonas Lawrence, S. W. Mr. Thomas Davies, N. W. Courseham. In Rodmead 2 x ½a. by lot. One of the picked ½a. near White acre ford by lot.

In the Down field 14a.: ½a. in Cattsbrain furlong bounded N. land of Richard Hybberd, E. New leaze, S. land Mr. John Romane, W. Mr. William Greenfield. 2a. in New leaze gate furlong, one bounded N. Mr. William Greenfield, E. Jasper Wheeler, S. the way to New leaze, W. Mr. John Romane, the other bounded N. Mr. William Greenfield, E. Mrs. Aske,[1] S. the highway to New leaze, W. wid. Aland. 2 x ½a. in Long down furlong; one bounded N. William Knapp, E. Mr. William Greenfield, S. Mr. John Mayow, W. the highway to New leaze; the other bounded N. Richard Yewe, E. Mr. William Greenfield, S. the Wid. Rebecca Mayow, W. the said way. 1a. in New leaze furlong bounded N. Richard Hybberd, E. New leaze, S. Richard Yewe, W. Jasper Wheeler. 3½a. in Middle Down furlong: ½a. bounded N. John Mayow, E. the highway crossing the field, S. Jasper Wheeler, W. Richard Hybberd; 2a. together bounded N. John Leonard, E. John Gaby part of the glebe and Mrs. Aske S. John Romane, W. the way; 1a. bounded N. Jasper Wheeler, E. the wid. Rebecca Mayow and Richard Yewe, S. Richard Yewe again, W. the way. 1a. in Shadwell furlong, N. John Gaby, E. Mrs. Aske's Shadwell leaze, S. Mrs. Aske's a., W. the glebe. 1a. in Copped Thorne furlong, N. Mr. William Greenfield, E. Richard Hybberd, S. John Wheelers leaze, W. Wid. Aland. 4a. in Moor furlong, the first from Copped Thorn having N. John Yewe, E. the way, S. Wid. Aland, W. the Moor; the second having N. [...] Arch, E. the way, S. Mr. John Romane, W. the Moor; the third having N. Mr. John Romane, E. the way, S. Mr. Geoffrey Broune, W. the Moor; the fourth, being 2 x ½a., having N. land of Jasper Wheeler belonging to the Grove living exchanged and now enclosed by William Knollys, E. ½a. of William Knollys, S. John Leonard, W. Geoffrey Broune.

11a. in the Broad field: 1½a. in Moor furlong, the ½a. bounded N. land of Jasper Wheeler, E. the Moor, S. John Mayow, W. the way crossing the field; the a. bounded N. John Mayow, E. the Moor, S. Mr. William Greenfield, W. the said way. 2a. in Adnel furlong, one bounded N. Mrs. Aske, E. the way leading to Seagry, S. wid. Aland, W. William Yewe; the other N. John Mayow, E. the said way, S. Mr. William Greenfield, W. the same footpath to Seagry leazes. 1a. in Seagry

Way furlong lying in 2 x ½a., one of them being a headland, N. highway to
Seagry, E. William Knappe, S. Seagry Heath leaze belonging to the glebe, W. the
highway, exchanged by John Mayow with Mr. Aske. 1a. in Huckland furlong, N.
a headland of Mr. William Greenfield, E. William Knollys, S. William Knollys
leaze, W. the wid. Rebecca Mayow. 1a. near Long Hedge way N. William Knollys,
S. John Yewe, E. John Yewe's new enclosed leaze, W. Jasper Wheeler's headland
belonging to the Grove. 2a. together in Vinslade furlong, W. Long Hedge way, E.
Jasper Wheeler, S. the mead plot in Venslade, W. an a. of Mr. Thomas Davies esq.
which was exchanged by Mr. Aske for an a. in Horsham leaze. 2½a. in the Little
field; the 2a. bounded N. the Long Hedge way, E. Isaac Knappe, S. Samuel
Knappe's new enclosure, W. Samuel Sealy; the ½a. bounded N., the Long Hedge
way, E. Jasper Wheeler, S. wid. Arch, W. Mr. Thomas Davies.

9½a. in the W. field: In Long Hedge furlong 2a.; 1a. bounded N. the way
between Smith mead and Long Hedge furlong, E. William Knapp, S. Long
Hedge, W. John Yewe; the other N. the said way, E. William Knapp, S. Long
hedge, W. John Mayow. 1a. in Clay Corner furlong lying in 2 x ½a., N. John Lea,
E. Whiteland way furlong, S. the wid. Comlye's new enclosure, W. Haw Street
hedge. ½a. in Queen Bush furlong, N. Samuel Knappe, E. Mr. Jonas Lawrence, S.
the Greenway, W. Mr. James Comlye. 1a. in Smith marsh lying in 2 x ½a. N.
Smith Marsh furlong way, E. wid. Aland, S. Long Hedge furlong, W. Mr. William
Greenfield; this a. was formerly exchanged by Edward Mayow with Mr. Kinaston
for an a. of the glebe lying in the Lower Seech bounded N. Broad mead headlands,
E. Rebecca Mayow, S. Hollow street way, W. wid. Serjeant. 1a. in White Ash
furlong called the Pigeon acre, N. White Ash way, E. Thomas Browne, S. Hollow
Street way, W. Mr. William Greenfield. 4a. in the Four acres furlong; 3a. together,
N. Mrs. Aske, E. Sandhill Way, S. Mrs. Aske, W. William Bedford's enclosure; 1a.
N. wid. Bridge's enclosure, E. Sandhill way, S. William Knollys, W. Startley heath.

Beast leazes: 9 cow leazes and a bull leaze in the New leaze; 4 beast leaze in
the Bushy Marsh; six in the Lower Marsh; in the Broad mead six beast leaze, a
quarter stint.

Richard Browne, rector, Samuel Knapp, John Hyargett.

1. The document clearly refers to Mr. Aske and Mrs. Aske as they appear in this calendar.

SOMERFORD KEYNES vicarage

677   1605 (D1/24/185/1)
We the churchwardens and sidesmen present upon our oaths a true terrier of all
the glebe land so far as we know or have credibly heard by conference with our
honest neighbours.

The vicars or their farmers until Mr. Harpe[1] was instituted vicar have received
all the tithes of corn growing both in the farm fields and in all other fields, and
for the other tithes of the farm they received them, or money for them as we
have heard, and the vicars have received all tithes of corn and hay and privy
tithes of the other parisioners. Because there is a parsonage and a vicarage we
have heard that there was only 40s yearly due to be paid to the parson and

impropietor [proprietary] in lieu of the parsonage and we do not know neither have heard that any one in the right of the parsonage received any tithes, but Mr. Michael Strange and his father challenged the parsonage tithes of the farm and receives them in his own demesnes since Mr. Harp[1] was vicar.

There belongs to the vicarage a dwelling house with a barn, stable, edifices, buildings and court now occupied by Mr. Sneade,[2] the vicar, and there is a barn adjoining the vicarage called the parsonage barn, but we have known and have heard said that it was always held by the vicar. There belongs to the vicarage a close of c. 7a. near Barrow Hill; a close of c. 7a. in the N. field; 1a. there called Nunacre; a several meadow in the meadows of c. 10a.; a plot of arable land in the Farm field of c. 7a. and pasture and feeding in the common meadows for as many cattle as may be kept on 2 yardlands, and we have known that vicar Ferris[3] for a long time had 4 beasts pasturing and feeding in a herd on the farm moors from Whitsunday until Michaelmas [29Sep] and the herd was to have from the vicar 1d. when he received the beasts and his Sunday dinner, and 1d. at Michaelmas when he gave up the beasts. The certainty of this report we do not know, but refer it unto any certain evidence which remains upon record.

Henry Neale, Robert Usold, Thomas Litton, William Emetts, Richard Kemseford, William Burge. *Names in the same hand*

1. There is no record of the institution of Mr. Harpe to the vicarage but presumably he preceded John Sneade, see footnote 2.
2. John Sneade, vicar 1596-1619.
3. Bartholomew Ferys was instituted in 1547.

678   1671 (D1/24/185/2)
A mansion house, stable, barn and other edifices now occupied by Mr. John Turner, vicar. A court, a garden and a close, c. 7a. near Barrow hill. A close, c. 7a. in the N. field. 1a. called Nunacre in the middle of the new enclosure of Edward White. 1 several mead, c. 10a. in Somerford meads. A close of arable of c. 7a. in the farm field to be sown every other year. £10 from the demesnes. Tithes in kind except from the following grounds taken out of the farm: A pasture ground of c. 3a. at Stonestitch occupied by William Hauks: A pasture ground of c. 1a. adjoining Broadleas occupied by Garrett Redding; a meadow ground of c. 6a. occupied by William Parsloe of which 1a. is tithable; 12a. of meadow ground occupied Edith Jordgone wid.

24 beast pastures and 60 [3 score] sheep pastures. John Wilkins, John White, churchwardens, William Usill, sidesman. If there be any more to this present we refer ourselves to the ancient terrier at Salisbury bearing date 1605.

679   1677 (D1/24/185/3)
A mansion house, stable, barn and other edifices occupied by Mr. John Turner[1] vicar. A court and garden, a close of pasture ground of c. 7a. called Barrow hill bounded S. William Hawkes,[2] E. and W. the highway, N. Common Barrow hill and part of the farm ground; the hedges all around, except against the farm ground, belong to the farm ground; a close of c. 7a. in the N. field bounded S. and E. the highway, N.[3] part of the N. field, W. ground belonging to the farm

called Shuters hill, hedge all around belong to the vicarage; 1a. called Nune acre lying in the middle of a new enclosure belonging to Edward Whit's living[4] in the N. field; a several meadow in the meads c. 10a., bounded N. the Mead lane, E. William Stephens,[5] S. the river, W. by Mary Taylor wid.,[6] the hedges on N. and W. quarters belong to the vicarage; a piece of land in the Farm field of c. 7a. lying near to the old coppice shooting from the Ridge way down to the river.

All manner of tithes to be paid in kind to the vicar excepting the lands following: All the lands belonging to the farm occupied Richard Southby and Edward Fowell esq.[7] or their undertenants; a close called Stone Stitch in the possession of William Hawkes;[8] 2 little closes lying in the meads in the possession of Margery Jordan;[9] a little close or meadow in the possession of William Parslow; a little close in the possession of Garrett Reading esq.[10]

There are certain hams and parcels of meadow in the farm and other grounds which pay tithe to the vicar; a ham in a meadow called Pillsmor, Constables ham, c. 4a. in S. E. corner of Pillsmor, 1a. in William Parslow's mead on E. side of the meadow joining to George Uzold's[11] hedge; St. John ham, c. 3a., in Lower Stedham lying by the river near to Pooll Moor; Wells acre in Lower Stedham on E. side of the ground joining to John Whit's close.[12] Constables ham in Pillsmore, St. John's ham and Welles acre in Lower Stedham are in the possession of Richard Southby[13] or his under tenants.

24 beast leazes pasture and 60 sheep pastures in the commons and common fields according to the custom of the parish. Memo.: The terrier of 1605 [**677**] in the office at Salisbury certified that the vicars received all great and small tithes arising from the farm without denial until Mr. Harp was insituted vicar. We present that the farm pays £10 a year to the vicar.

John Turner, vicar, William Stevens, George Ussold, churchwardens, Thomas Blackford, sidesman.

1. Mr. John Turner junior in **680**. As **679** in **681**.
2. Elizabeth Hawkes wid. in **681**.
3. Bounded N. ground of Jonathan White and William Tayler in **681**.
4. Jonathan White's living in **680** and **681**.
5. John Prince in **681**.
6. Richard Tayler in **681**.
7. Edward Foyle esq. only in **680**. Mr. Edward Southby added in **681**.
8. Anne Hawkes in **681**.
9. Thomas Barns in **680** and **681**.
10. Edward Foyle esq in **680** and **681**.
11. The wid. Ussold in **680**. Anne Ussuld in **681**.
12. Thomas Blackford in **681**.
13. Mr. Edward Southby in **681**.

680   18 Oct 1698 (D1/24/185/4)
As 679 with amendments in footnotes. John Turner, vicar, John Hoskins, Richard Blackford, churchwardens, Thomas Blackford, William Stevens.

681   1704 (D1/24/185/5)

As 679 with amendments in footnotes. John Turner, vicar, William Tayler, Jonathan Westmecutt, churchwardens.

LITTLE SOMERFORD PARVA [ALIAS SOMERFORD MAUDETTS]
rectory

682   13 Jul 1608 (D1/24/186/1)

The ground lying about the house with the building there, c. 10a.; the New leaze, c. 6a.; the Ham, 1½a.; the Nurnehill, c. 4a.; the Breach, c. 6a.; 2 lots, one in Haye mead, the other in Kinge mead, c. ½a. The tithe of 5a. of Steen mead in Rodbarne meadow. Richard Andrews, rector, William Bailey, William Woodroff, churchwardens, John Seely, Richard Thorner, sidesmen. Names in the same hand.

683   1671 (D1/24/186/2)

The dwelling house[1] containing 10 rooms great and small, a brewhouse, barn, stable under the roof of the barn, a barton [barken], an orchard, a garden all lying together square, c. 2a. 2 home grounds lying together on S. side of the dwelling house, c. 8a. A very small parcel of ground called the Woodhayes, c. ½a., on N. side of the dwelling house.[2]

A ground called the New Lease, c. 6a., with a lane to go into the same. A little meadow called the Ham, c. 1½a.; 2 grounds lying together called the Breach, c. 7a.; a ground called the Nurnill, c. 4a.; a half lot lying in Little King mead; a half lot in Haymead. 4 beasts' feeding with the parish for a yardland in the common of Braydon; 4½ beasts' feeding with the parish for a yardland in the common meads; 4 beasts' feeding for a yardland with the parish in the common meadow called Balsay; 2 beasts' summer feeding in the meadow called Balsay.

John Palmer, rector, Daniel Powell, Robert Hibberd, churchwardens, John Hibberd, Jeffrey Bayly, sidesmen.

1.   No buildings mentioned in **684**.
2.   The Home grounds Woodhayes garden and orchard estimated at c. 10a. in **684**.

684   18 Oct 1698 (D1/24/186/3)

The tithe of 5a. of stean mead in Rodbourne meadow. John Callowe, rector, John Sloper, Giles Simpkins [X], churchwardens, John West, Richard Allaway, sidesmen.

685   n. d. [1783][1] (D1/24/186/4)

The parsonage house consists of a hall, parlour, kitchen below stairs, 5 bed chambers. The house is built of stone and tiled, the hall and kitchen are paved with freestone, the parlour is floored and wainscotted with oak halfway, the remainder is papered, all the rooms are ceiled. The outhouses are a brewing – kitchen, cellar, barn and stable. The quantity of ground in the garden with an orchard adjoining may be 3a.

The glebe is 26a.: There are no houses on it; the whole is enclosed and divided in 6 enclosures: 6a., 6a., 2a., all pastures; 5a., 1½a., 5½ all ploughed land. The minister in common with the rest of the parishioners has a right of commoning; there is no regulation with respect to the number of beasts, sheep. Tithes amount to *c.* £120 all due from the parish of Little Somerford.

There have been no pensions etc. made to the church. In the church are 3 bells and a clock. The communion plate consists of a cup or chalice and a small plate, by the inscription upon them, to belong to this church of Little Somerford which is all the information the inscriptions give. The weight is specified.

There is no money in stock for the repairs of the church. The parish collectively is charged with the repairs of the body of the church and churchyard and fence. The minister is charged with the repairs of the chancel. The clerk's wages, who is also sexton, is £1 6s. He is appointed by the minister.

John Morgan, curate, Matthew Robertson, Henry Ady, churchwardens, William Reynolds senior, John Reynolds, William Reynolds junior.

1.   The churchwardens held office in the year up to Easter 1783 (WSRO 1149/16).

SOPWORTH rectory

686   22 Oct 1608 (D1/24/187/1)
Adjoining to the dwelling house, the churchyard, an orchard and garden, a meadow and an arable close, in all *c.* 10a. In the W. field at Verncroft end 2½a. between the land of Robert Clarke on W., the land of John Hay on E; ½a. in the same furlong, Robert Chanlor E. and John Shipwey W; 1a. upon Chilborowe hill John Shipwey N. and Thomas Toghill S.; 1a. upon Hordown hill Thomas Toghill E., Richard Cullimer W.; 1a. in the same furlong of Richard Cullimer E., Agnes Neale W.; 1a. in the same furlong Robert Chanlor W., Agnes Neale E.; 2a. in the same furlong Robert Shipwey E. and land of Richard Cullimer W.; 1a. upon Smyth hill John Shipwey E and John Hay W.; 1a. on the same furlong John Shipwey E., John Clarke W.; 1a. in the same furlong John Clarke W. and Francis Watts alias Martin E.; 1a. upon Smith hill Richard Cullimer S., John Clarke N.; 1a. in the same furlong John Clarke S. and Agnes Neale N.; 1a. in the same furlong Agnes Neale S., John Clarke N.; 3 x ½a. in a piece there John Clarke S., Agnes Neale N., ½a. upon the same hill John Clarke on both sides; ½a. in Horedowns bottom John Clarke S., Agnes Neale N.; 2a. in Sands furlong Richard Cullimer W., John Hay E.; 1a. in the same furlong John Shipwey W., Agnes Neale E.; ½a. in Black Readinge Agnes Neale W. and John Hay E.; ½a. in the same furlong Richard Cullimer E. and Agnes Neale W.; 2½a. on N. side of Chilborowe hill Richard Cullimer S. and William Bailey N.; 2a. in Verslande Thomas Toghill S. and the Millway N.; 2 x ½a. in Verslande Richard Chanlor N. and Thomas Toghill S.; 1a. shooting upon Chapples hedge John Clarke N. and John Shipwey S.; 2a. above Chapples hedge John Hay N. and Richard Cullimer S.; ½a. by the Millway Robert Shipwey S. and John Hay N.; ½a. in the same furlong John Hay S., John Clarke N.; 2a. upon Sopworth hedge, one of them John Hay S., Agnes Neale N.; the other Agnes Neale S., William [...] S., a piece

of 3 x ½a. John Clarke S. and John Shipwey N.; 3a. in the Slough John Shipwey S., John Clarke N. 1a. at Forked bush William Bailey E., John Clarke W.; ½a. on [. . .] hedge George Chanlor E., Agnes Neale W.; ½a. in the same furlong John Hay W., Agnes Neale [E.]; 1 farndell in the same furlong William Bailey W., John Shipwey E.; 1. ½a. at Deacons Close end 1a. shooting upon [. . .] John Clarke W., John Shipwey E.; 4a. in one piece shooting upon Deacons Close end John Shipwey W., Agnes Neale E., 1a. shooting upon Deacons Close end Agnes Neale W., John Clarke E.; ½a. shooting upon Deacons Close end John Clarke W., William Bailey E.; 2a. shooting upon the Parsons Quarre William Bailey W., John Shipwey E.; 2a. at the Parsons Quarre John Clarke N., Agnes Neale S.; 1a. in the same furlong Agnes Neale N., John Hay S.; 1a. shooting upon the Millway John Salte W., Thomas Toghill E.; 1a. in the same furlong John Shipway E., Agnes Neale W.; ½a. in the same furlong Thomas Toghill W., John Shipway E.; 1a. in the same furlong Richard Cullimer E., John Hay W.; 1a. at Marlens, John Hay N., Robert Shipwey S.; 1a. in Pistle furlong John Salte W., John Shipwey E.: 1a. in the same furlong Agnes Neale E. and Thomas Toghill W.

In the E. field; ½a shooting upon the new wall a farndell running down from the end of the last Richard Cullimer S. and Thomas Toghill N.; ½a. at Ockly bush Robert Clarke N., John Shipwey S.; ½a. in the same furlong, John Shipwey N., Agnes Neale S.; 1a. in the same furlong John Clarke N., Robert Clarke S.; ½a. crossing Clatterbridge way John Clarke S., Agnes Neale N.; ½a. in the same furlong John Shipwey S., William Bayley N.; 1a. in the same furlong called Well acre John Shipwey S., Francis Martyn N.; ½a. of meadow in Ashden bottom; ½a. in the same bottom Didmarton field N. the brook S.; 1a. upon Ashdens hill, Didmarton field W., John Hay E.; ½a. in the same furlong Agnes Neale E., John Shipwey W.; ½a. in the same furlong Robert Clarke W., William Bailey E.; ½a. crossing the Horse way heading the above lands S., John Shipwey N.; 1a. at Madgetts Bush Robert Chanlor S., William Bailey N.; ½a. in the same furlong William Bailey S., Thomas Toghill N.; ½a. in the same furlong John Shipwey N., Thomas Toghill S.; 2a. in Cock Piece in the same furlong Agnes Neale on both sides; 1a. shooting upon Clatterbridge John Shipwey W., Francis Martin E., ½a. in the same furlong John Clarke W., Agnes Neale E.; ½a. in Wall furlong John Clarke E., Agnes Neale W.; a piece of 3 x ½a. in Rushmeere John Hay S., John Shipwey N.; ½a. in the same furlong John Shipwey S., William Bailey N.; 1a. in the same furlong Agnes Neale S., John Clarke N.; 1a. in the same furlong Francis Martin N., Thomas Toghill S.; 1a. in the same furlong Robert Shipwey N., John Shipwey S.; a head a. upon the down between Robert Shipwey and Richard Cullimer; a piece of 4a. shooting upon Tetbury way John Clarke N., Francis Martin S.; ½a. in the same furlong John Shipwey N., John Clarke S.; ½a. upon Tetbury way Thomas Toghill on both sides; 1a. in the same furlong John Clarke S., Francis Martin N.; 1a. in the same furlong John Clarke N., John Hay S.; 1a. at Sampsons Bush John Clarke N., John Shipwey S.; 1a. in the same furlong Robert Chanlor S., Thomas Toghill N.; 1a. in the same furlong Francis Martin N., Robert Chauler S.; 1a. at Howse Bush Robert Shipwey N., John Clarke S.; 1a. in the same furlong Agnes Neale S., John Hay N.; 1a. at Agnes Neale's short hedge Agnes Neale S., John Salt N.; 1a. in Little furlong William Bailey N., Francis Martin S.; ½a. in the same furlong John Clarke N., John

Shipwey S.; ½a. in the same furlong John Shipwey N., John Hay S.; 1a. upon Roughbarrows William Bailey S., Robert Chanlor N.; 2a. in one piece in the same furlong John Clarke N., the head S.; 1a. upon Wheat down John Clarke on both sides; 2 x ½a. at Symons Pits one of them John Shipwey E., John Hay W., the other the head W., John Hay E.; ½a. upon Wheat down John Shipwey N., Robert Chanlor S.; 2a. in the same furlong Robert Chanlor N., John Shipwey S.; 1a. upon Wheat down George Chanlor E., Agnes Neale W.; ½a. in the same furlong Agnes Neale E., William Bailey W.; ½a. in the same furlong William Bailey E., John Shipwey W.; ½a. under the hedge at Crowden gate; 1a. in Crowden hill John Shipwey E., John Clarke W.; ½a. in the same furlong John Shipwey on both sides; ½a. in the same furlong John Shipwey E., Thomas Toghill W.; 2a. in the same furlong John Clarke on both sides; ½a. there John Shipwey W., Agnes Neale E., ½a. in the same furlong, John Shipwey E., Richard Cullimer W.; ½a. in the same furlong Richard Cullimer E., John Shipwey W.; 1a. in the same furlong John Shipwey E., Richard Cullimer W.

By me Robert Mason, rector, and by me Robert Clarke [X], Robert Shipwey, churchwardens, Thomas Toghill, John Shipwey.

687   16 Dec. 1671 (D1/24/187/2)
The mansion house, 2 gardens, 1 orchard, 1 court and a close of meadow, c. 3a., and a close of arable, c. 5a., all adjoining near unto the church. 59a. and 3 farndells of arable in the W. field, 52½a. of arable in the E. field.

Charles Kingscote, Stephen Lewis, churchwardens.

688   10 Nov 1704 (D1/24/187/3)
A good and large parsonage house the greatest part of it lately built by the present rector, standing near the church and churchyard containing 5 large bays, one kitchen, 2 pantries, a parlour, 4 chambers whereof 1 is to be made a study, the roof being low and covered over with tiles made of slate; 1 little garden between the house and churchyard; 1 large barton the S. end thereof adjoining to Church lane, Mr. Robert Gore having a piece of land called Kingscots orchard on W. side; a large yard or backside between the barton and the dwelling house; a stable at the N. end of the barton; a cart or waine house at the E. end of the great court; a little house adjoining the dwelling house being some time an oast house for drying of malt and at other times used to hold wood and coal; a piece of ground adjoining the great court being c. 1 farndell and called the Old orchard, having a few old apple trees growing there, 1 meadow adjoining to the churchyard having been heretofore divided by an old broken wall and hedge but now lies open together and undivided containing 5a.; a pasture ground adjoining to the last meadow abutting at the lower end of it on a field of Sopworth called the N. field and sometimes called the Oate Leasow, c. 5a.

The arable land in the W. field lying and being dispersed in divers and sundry places: In Luckley furlong a piece of 2½a. butting on the Rowlearow hedge Mr. Robert Gore on S. W. side, Mr. William Hodges W.; ½a. in the same furlong butting on Luckley stile, Stephen Lewis E. side, Mr. Robert Gore's enclosure sowed with french grass on W. side: In Chilbury Hill furlong 1a., Mr. Robert Gore on S. side, Mr. William Hodges on N. side and butting on Luckley furlong; In Badminton Hill furlong 1a., Mr. Robert Gore E. side, Mr. William Hodges, W. side, abutting on the highway from Sopworth to Sadbury; 1a. Mr. William Hodges W. side, Mr. Robert Gore (sic) W. side, butting on the last highway called Sadbury way; 1a. Mr. Robert Gore on both sides, butting on the same road; 2a. Mr. Robert Gore E. side, Mr. William Hodges W. side butting on the same road: In Black Riding furlong ½a. Mr. William Hodge E. side, Mr. William Hodge W. side, butting on Badminton Hill furlong; 1a. and ½a. both with Mr. Robert Gore on both sides, butting on Badminton Hill furlong; 2a. Mr. Robert Gore E. side, Mr. William Hodges W. side, butting on Badminton Hill furlong: In Smith Hill furlong 1a. Mr. Robert Gore on both sides, butting on Sopworth hedge; 1a. Mr. Robert Gore S. side, Mr. William Hodge N. side, butting on Sopworth hedge; A piece of land of 3 x ½a. lying under Sopworth hedge: In the Upper furlong above Chapel hedge 2a. Mr. William Hodges S. side, Mr. Robert Gore N. side adjoining to a furlong next Mr. Gore's french grass wall [. . .] near Chapel hedge, Stephen Lewis S. side, Mr. Robert Gore N. side: In Clarkes Bush furlong near the middle of the field 2 x ½a. Stephen Lewis having 1a. of land belonging to Jordens tenement between them: A piece called the Pecked piece land belonging to Mr. William Hodges' farm S. side, Mr. Robert Gore N. side and comes up to the end of the green meres: a piece 2a. on N. side of the Mill way, Stephen Lewis S. side, Mr. William Hodges W. end: In Stony Pitts furlong 1a. butting on Mill way Mr. Hodges' farm land E. side, Mr. Robert Gore W. side; ½a. butting on Mill way Mr. William Hodge E. side, land belonging to Jordens tenement W. side; 1a. butting on Mill way Mr. Robert Gore on both sides; 1a. butting on Mill way and called the Tump acre Mr. Robert Gore on both sides: In Slow Bere furlong ½a. Mr. Robert Gore on both sides; ½a. Mr. Robert Gore S. side, Mr. William Hodge N. side; a piece of 3a. called Slow Piece, Mr. William Hodges both sides: In Sopworth Hedge furlong butting on that hedge 3½a. Mr. Robert Gore N. side, Mr. William Hodges S. side; 2 separate a. butting on the last hedge, Mr. Robert Gore on each side: a piece of 2a. at Persons Bush, Mr. William Hodge N. side, Mr. Robert Gore S. side; 1a. at Kenhill Thornes butting on Manscroft, Mr. Robert Gore on both sides: In Little furlong 1a. Mr. Robert Gore on both sides; a piece of 3½a. Mr. Robert Gore on both sides: a piece of 2½a. Mr. Robert Gore on both sides; 1a. near Persons Bush, Mr. Robert Gore on both sides; 1a. and 2 x ½a. Mr. Robert Gore on each side; 1 farndell Mr. Robert Gore E. side, Nicholas Iddell W. side: In Marlens furlong butting on Didmarton closes ½a. Mr. William Hodges E. side, Mr. Robert Gore W. side; 1a., 3a. and 1a. Mr. Robert Gore on each; 7 farndells near Didmarton closes heading the same furlong; 4½a. butting on Badminton hedge was some time enclosed into the park or great enclosure of the duke of Beaufort. 60a. of arable in the W. field together with the last 4½a. enclosed into the park of the duke.

Arable land lying dispersed in divers and sundry places in the N. field: ½a. by the side of Mr. William Hodges 5a. butting on the highway from Sopworth to Didmarton and under Mr. William Hodges 6a. hedge; 1 farndell butting on the last ½a. on W: In Long Okley furlong 2 x ½a. Mr. Robert Gore having ½a. between them; 1a. the wid. Clarke S. side, Mr. William Hodges N. side; ½a. Mr. William Hodge S. side, Mr. Robert Gore N. side; 1a. called Well Splat acre Mr.

Hodges' hedge on both sides; ½a. by the brook side butting at W. end of it on Mr. Gore's Ashton Bottom meadow: In Short Okley furlong 1a. butting on Mr. William Hodges' Eight a. hedge, Stephen Lewis S. side, Mr. Robert Gore N. side; 2 x ½a. Mr. Robert Gore having ½a. between them and butting on the same hedge; piece of 2. ½a. butting on the same hedge, Mr. Robert Gore's land on both sides: ½a. in Didmarton field on the N. side of Mr. Gore's Ashton Bottom meadow hedge: In Clatterbridge Hill furlong 4a. viz. 1a. being a head a. to a furlong in Didmarton field, 2 x ½a. and 2 x 1a. butting on the brook: In Rushmeere furlong adjoining to Didmarton field 5½a. viz: 1 x ½a. being a head ½a., a piece of 3 x ½a., 1 x ½a. and 3 single a.: 1a. butting on Mr. Gore's french grass leaze called the Down leaze that heads the last furlong having Mr. Hodges' new enclosure on E. side: In the furlong butting on Rushmeere furlong 7a. viz. a piece of 4a., 2 x ½a., 2 x 1a., the piece called White piece being between them: In Honey Bush furlong and butting on the highway from Sopworth 3 x 1a. lying apart from each other: In the Down furlong 2 x 1a., one butting on Mr. William Hodges Little Down hedge, the other on S. side of a piece of land of Mr. Gore which butts on the Sadbury highway: In the furlong above the last furlong 2a. 3 farndells viz. 1 single a., a piece called 3 farndells, 2 x½a., being apart from each other: In the furlong butting on Coney Warren wall on S. side of Mr. William Hodges' little enclosed down 3a. viz. 1a. and a piece of 2a. butting on the last wall: In Wheat Down furlong 1a. Mr. William Hodges E. side, Mr. Robert Gore W. side: In a furlong adjoining to Nicholas Iddolls Rowbres hedge 2 x ½a. Mr. Robert Gore's having a ½a. between them. In a furlong which butts on Sherston hedge which parts Sherston field and Sopworth field but which belongs to Sopworth 2a. viz. 2 x ½a. and 1a.: In Crowdown Hill furlong on Crowdown brook 7½a. viz. a piece of 2a. 2 x 1a. apart from themselves and 7 x ½a.

The rate, tithes, pensions and portions of tithes called Easter dues are as follows: offerings paid at Easter; cow white and calves, sheep's wool and lambs, eggs and garden pence, apples, pears and plums; also tithe grain, hay, pigs, etc.

John Cooke, rector, Richard Amos, William Wickes, churchwardens, William Hodges.

689   25 Jul 1783 (D1/24/187/4)
Terrier intended to be delivered to the registrar of the bishop at his primary visitation at Chippenham 30 Jul.

The parsonage house, a very ancient building adjoining the churchyard, is built of such common wall stones as the quarries in this country generally produce and is covered with stone tiles. It is 57ft. by 21ft. and 12ft. high in the side walls. It contains 4 rooms on a floor viz. the kitchen, 19ft. by 16ft. in the clear, is not ceiled, is floored with stones and has base walls plastered; a pantry 9ft. by 8ft. and 6ft. high in the side wall, floored with stones covered with tiles; a parlour 15½ft. by 13½ft. 7ft. high is not ceiled, floored with stones base walls plastered; another pantry or cellar (no underground cellar) 12ft. by 10½ft., 8ft. high, ceiled to the boards floored with stones. A passage leading from the parlour to the kitchen 11ft. by 3ft. and another passage from the outer door to the staircase is 6ft. by 3½ft. 4 lodging rooms above stairs not ceiled, with boarded floors, 16ft. by 10ft., 10ft. by 7½ft., 19ft. by 16ft. and 16ft. by 11ft. An outhouse annexed to one end of the dwelling house, 12ft. by 11ft., 7ft. high covered with thatch. A necessary house 8ft. by 8ft., 4ft. high in the side wall, covered with tiles.

A barn 71ft. by 22ft., 13ft. high, built with stone walls and the roof covered with thatch; the threshing floor is of oak planks; a porch to the barn 13ft. by 16ft., 11½ft. high, also a sloping piece of building added to one side of the barn lately erected by the present rector, Mr. John Perfect, to keep the barn healthy and dry and to put straw etc. into it, 27ft. x 10½ft., 6ft. high, commonly called a skeeling, stone walls roofed with tile. At one end of the barn is an adjoining stable 21½ft. by 17ft., 9ft. high, stone walls, floored with stone, covered with thatch. Beyond the stable on the same side of the barton or barnyard is a wainhouse 27ft. by 15ft., 7ft. high, stone walls and roofed with thatch. The barton or barnyard measures c. 42. ½ square lugs, i. e. 1r. 2½p., fenced with dry walls (i. e. stone walls without mortar).

The parsonage garden is a very poor and ordinary piece of ground 41 ¾ lugs or 1r. 1 ¾p., fenced with dry walls, 2 young elm trees growing there. A narrow strip of ground adjoining the barn on W. side exactly the length of the barn and stable, 7 lugs or c. 1½p., fenced with a dry wall. A small elm tree growing there.

The churchyard measures 62p., fenced for the most part with dry walls. 2 young growing elms there planted by the present rector and a walnut tree of middling size. A close of glebe land (pasture) adjoining to the churchyard, 3a. 2r. 11p., inclusive of bounds, is bounded W. by land belonging to the duke of Beaufort and the parsonage garden, S. by the churchyard and land belonging to the duke, E. and S. E. by the duke of Beaufort, N. glebe land. A close of pasture (at present) but not many years ago has been ploughed, adjoining to the last close, 3r. 27p., bounded N. and W. by the Duke of Beaufort, S. by the last close. Fences for the most part consist of hedgerows, partly dry walling. On the hedgerows and other parts are growing 5 young indifferent oak trees, 20 young elms and 12 young growing ash trees.

At the further end of the parish bearing N. E. from the village is a piece of glebe land (arable) called the Twelve acres, 10a. 3r. 39p., bounded N. E. by the Duke of Beaufort, E. Thomas Estcourt Cresswell esq., S. glebe land. Fences are partly dry walls and partly hedgerows. In the hedgerows are standing 2 or 3 ordinary oaks, 22 elms, most of them young and of different sizes, and 2 ash trees in other parts of the ground.

A piece of glebe (arable) adjoining to the last called the Thirty acres, 31a. 15p., bounded N. and E. by glebe land, N. W., S. W. and S. by the duke of Beaufort. In the hedgerows are standing 62 young ash trees planted some years ago by Mr. Melksham[1] the then rector. Fences partly dry wall, partly hedgerows.

A piece of glebe (arable) adjoining on N. to the last called Roughborows Fourteen acres, 12a. 20p. bounded N. W. and S. by glebe, E. by Mr. Creswell. Fences for the most part dry walls, w. part hedgerow. No trees.

A piece of glebe (arable) adjoining to the last called Roughborows Twelve acres, 12a. 3r. 31p., bounded N. and E. by Mr. Creswell, S. almost wholly by glebe, and part the duke of Beaufort, W. and N. by glebe land. Fences partly dry walls, partly hedgerow. In E. hedgerow are standing 23 elms of different ages and sizes.

A piece of glebe (arable) adjoining to the last called Roughborows Eight acres, 4a. 3r. 2p., bounded N. by the last, E. and S. by Mr. Creswell, W. the duke of Beaufort. Fences dry walls and hedgerows. No trees.

Total of statute a. etc. inclusive of bounds as measured in 1753 by the direction of Mr. Payne,[2] then rector. 2 home closes of pasture 6a. 3r. 4p., 6 pieces of arable contiguous to each other, 92a. 2r. 33p. Total 99a. 1r. 37p.

The chancel is repaired by the rector, the church by the parish or the rest of the proprietors who also keep up the churchyard fence.

The rectory of Sopworth claims all tithes, both great and small, within the parish but from no township or or any other place. There is a customary demand of every housekeeper of 5d. p. a. at Easter. It is customary for the churchwardens to allow the rector 5s. p. a. for attending visitations.

N. B. There is a farm rent called a pension of 40s. p. a. due to the crown on old Michaelmas day[3] and paid out of the rectory.

It does not appear that any modus has ever been established in lieu of tithes except the composition which has been paid to the rectory by the Beaufort family for many years past for land taken into the duke's sheep leys, maybe so. The clerk's salary is paid by custom by all the proprietors in general. We have no sexton.

The good books, furniture and utensils belonging to the church and chancel: A pewter flagon for the use of the communion table, containing in measure c. 1 quart. A small thin silver cup with a loose lid or cover for administering the sacrament wine holding about ½ pint. It has no inscription or weight marked upon it. An oaken communion table and a fine linen cloth and 2 napkins. An oaken chest in the chancel for locking up the books etc. in. A pulpit cushion covered with an ordinary stuff and an ordinary fringe round it of the same colour. A fine surplice of holland. 2 common prayer books in folio. A large bible of the last translation in folio.

2 bells in the tower with their frames, the one larger sort commonly called a sermon bell, the other a small one called a saints bell. 2 stools to rest the corpses upon in time of the funeral service.

John Perfect, rector, John Comly churchwarden, John Witchell, overseer, John Harris, Samuel Witchell.

1. John Milsum was rector 1727–1743.
2. Thomas Payne was rector between 1752–1757
3. 29 Sep but here the reference is to the date before the alteration to new style in 1752 in which year 11 days were lost to allow for the adjustment thus Old Michaelmas day would be 10 Oct.

STANTON ST. BERNARD vicarage

690   16 Oct 1671 (D1/24/188/1)

The vicarage house with a kitchen distant from it by c. 20 ft. A garden on W. and S. of the house adjoining the churchyard and extending to it eastwards. A plot of ground on E. of the said houses held by the exchange of ½a. of arable in Little Mead furlong with the lessee of the parsonage. On the last plot the present vicar erected a barn containing 3 rooms with a stable on W. end. An orchard on N. of the vicarage house severed from it by a common way bounded E. and N. with a common ditch, W. with a hedge from the end of parsonage barn in a direct line towards the common field. A cut end or stable joined to the parsonage barn. A ground of pasture called the Upper Vearnes,[1] a ground called the Lower Vearnes[1] with 2 withy beds containing 10a. A ground of meadow called Whitepott mead or Milkham containing 3½yd. These grounds were added to the vicarage above 60 years since, about the time of the last enclosure. At the same time was added the whole tithe of the ground then enclosed (to whatsoever use converted) called the Vearnes, the Night leases, or Wihickes,[2] the Moors and Hassells which before the said enclosure were commons for kine and sheep.

The lands lying dispersedly in the common fields as follows: In the Upper F. field next Alton field; ½a. in Fochirs[3] Combe shooting up to the hill between 1a. of Richard Lavington[4] on E. and 1yd. of Thomas Walters[5] on W.; 3a. in Woodway shooting upon Alton field eastwards and the end of the great farm westward between 2 lanes on N. and S.; ½a. between lands of the great farm shooting upon 1 head a. of Michael Smith[6] on N. and S.; ½a. in Blackland between ½a. of Thomas Walters[5] on S. and the land of the little farm on N.; 2a. in Blackland between the lands of Michael Smith[6] on W. and a laine[7] on S.; ½a. in Born[8] shooting upon Hairpath way between ½a. of Samuel Hamen[9] eastwards and ½a. of Thomas Walters[10] westward; ½a. in Kenard between ½a. of Robert Pile E. the way on W.

In the Middle field below: ½a. in Old Dower between ½a. of Samuel Hamen[9] westward and ½a. of wid. Godwin eastwards; 2 butts near Little Mead tree between ½a. of William Lydall[11] on N. and a laine[7] on S.; 1a. in the Sands between 1yd. of Thomas Walters on S. and 1a. of Henry Vowle[12] on N.

In the Middle Upper field: 2 picked a. in the White land, called the Goores, between ½a. of the wid. Godwin Northwards and a laine southward; 1 head a. in Outworth, 1a. in the same furlong between ½a. of William Liddall[11] on N. and Thomas Walters[5] on S.; ½a. in the same furlong between 3yds. of Thomas Walters[5] on N. and head ½a. of Robert Pile[13] S.; 1a. in Nell furlong between ½a. of Edward Vowle[12] on W. and lands of the Little farm E.

In the E. field below Bicken laine;[7] 1a. in Short-rudgeway between ½a. Robert Pile[13] westward and 3 x ½a. Thomas Walters[5] eastward; ½a. in Hedgwick between ½a. Thomas Walters[5] W. and E. mead on E.; 2½a. in Clay furlong shooting upon the E. meads between lands of the Little farm on S. and 1a. of Thomas Walters[5] on N.; ½a. in Short Buttocks between ½a. of Robert Pile[13] on W. and a laine[7] on E.; ½a. of Lammas meadow next to the E. meads between the Tithingman Plot on N. and Thomas Walters[5] on S.

In the Upper field next All Cannings field: From 1a. in Nettlebed between 1a. of Richard Lavington[4] on S. and the hill on N.; ½a. in Nettlebed between ½a. of William Liddall[11] on S., 1a. Samuel Hamlen on N.; 3yd. in Rough hole between 1a. of William Liddall[11] on E. and 1yd. of William Liddall[11] on W.; 3 x ½a. in Blackwell near Tanne hillway between ½a. of Christian Smith wid.[14] on W. and a laine[7] on E.; 1a. in Shooters furlong between 3 x ½a. of Henry Vowle[12] on E. and ½a. of John Ring[15] on W.; 2a. in Short Cannings land between lands of the Little farm on N. and ½a. of Samuel Hamlen S., the N. ½a. shoots upon the lands of the Great farm, the other 3 x ½a. upon 1 head a. of Thomas Walters.[5]

In the W. field below the town: 3 x ½a. in Inlands between ½a. of Christian Smith wid. on N. and ½a. belonging to the Little farm on S.; 1 butt shooting upon John Ring's little mead[16] between a butt of the Little Farm eastward and 2 butts of William Cromwell[17] westward.

For the manuring of the said lands the vicar has 100 sheep leaze in the Town down for which he pays to the lessee of the parsonage 50s. p. a. The said lands laying in the common fields were added to the vicarage in consideration of an augmentation made to it in 1383, of 13 qtr of corn, half wheat, half barley, which has ceased from the time that the vicar has enjoyed the said lands. There belongs to the vicarage tithe of the glebe lands of the parsonage and vicarage excepting that ½a. of arable in Little Mead furlong above mentioned which the parsons holds by exchange with the vicar. The tithe of the Home grounds and of Whitpot mead or Mill mead. Tithe sheep excepting only those that are depastured on the S. part of Milk hill for which they say there is nothing due to the vicar for the time they are depastured there. Tithe lamb except those that happen to fall and are bred upon Milkhill. But if the ewes depastured Tithe egg, every yardland pays 5d. p. a. Tithe of rods, the Great farm pays 4d. p. a.; the Little farm pays 4d. p. a. The customary tenants for every yardland pays 1d. p. a. There belongs to the vicar offerings, tithe calves and 2d. for every milk cow; tithe apples, pigs, bees, geese, pigeons, cherries and hops. Feeding of the churchyard and a seat or pew in the chancel upon S. side.

Thomas Crapon, vicar, Henry Foule, William Willy, churchwardens, Michael Smith.

1. Ferns in **691**.
2. Withicks in **691**.
3. Fochers in **691**.
4. Mr. Thomas Lavington in **691**.
5. Richard Walters in **691**.
6. Mr. Michael Smith in **691**.
7. Lawn in **691**.
8. Bourn in **691**.
9. Samuel Hamlyn in **691**.
10. Wid. Walters in 691.
11. George Tydoll in **691**.
12. Henry Fowle in **691**.
13. Wid. Pile in **691**.
14. William Smith in **691**.
15. Mr. Daniel Dyke in **691**.
16. The Little Mead in **691**.
17. John Cromwell in **691**.

691   15 Jan 1705 (D1/24/188/2)
*As **690** with amendments in footnotes.* John Shorthose, vicar, Richard Walter, Thomas Godwin, churchwardens.

Memo. The lessee of the parsonage has a power to enter again upon the parcel of ground at the E. end of the vicarage house at his pleasure.

STANTON FITZWARREN rectory

692 n. d. late 16th cent. (D1/24/189/1)

The churchwardens and sidesmen present that there is only a parsonage and no vicarage. The parsonage has a several close of 1½a. on which the parsonage house stands of 6 bays or spaces being ?stalled, a barn of 6 bays and a stable of 1 bay being covered with thatch with a garden and backside adjoining all on the W. side of the high street of Stanton [Staunton], the common lane leading from the street to the W. field on N. side, a tenement of Walter Hungerford esq. on S., a close occupied by Richard Cole on W.

All manner of tithes in their several kinds are due to be paid to the parson or his deputy. 2 yardlands [yards] of glebe in the common fields called Stean mead and Lot meads in common with other inhabitants' lands in the parish. 13 beasts and 60 sheep common leazes belonging to the same 2 yardlands and for horses the parson may keep as many as for a yardland as any other may do. The custom of the parish for tithing of sheep is as follows. If any man buys 10 ewes at Michaelmas [29 Sep] and keep them until St. Marks tide [25 Apr] and then of these 10 ewes have 7 lambs, the parson has the third best of the lambs and gives the owner 3d. and so makes even at St. Mark's tide. But if of these ewes there arise 6 lambs at St. Mark's tide then the owner gives the parson 3d. and so makes even for the whole year. If under 7 or above 10 [...] St. Mark's tide is given and taken. If any have above 17 as 40 and upwards then at St. Mark's tide [...] draws 2 lambs the parson the third ending his tithe with the last. And if the owner keeps these even until shear time then he pays for 4qtr. of tithe wool. If he keeps them the whole year then he pays the whole tithe but if he buys them but 6 weeks before shear time and then he shears them then he pays the tenth of the tenth, if under 6 weeks then he pays no tithe wool. And if after shear time he sells them before St. Marks tide then at Easter the seller pays the parson ¼d. a piece. If after St. Martins tide [11 Nov] but before shear time then at Easter next following the seller pays ½d. a piece. And so in like manner for the tithe wool and selling of dry sheep as hogs and wethers.

Tithe corn as wheat, barley, rye, beans, peas, oats, vetches, lentils and hay, the tenth sheaf and tenth cock making use of it as we do our own. If any man has mares that fold in the parish and if he sells the foal before it be 1 year old he pays the parson the tenth penny at Easter next after the sale: If he weans him then he pays 1d. at Easter and no other tithe for colts.

For offering all housing people that receive communion pay 2d. a piece at Easter for the whole year but the first time they receive they pay ½d. When a woman is purified she pays a chrisom.[1] When a man is married he pays to the parson 8d. and 2d. to the clerk.

If any man have 10 kine and 7 calves or above then the owner pays 1 of the 7, if he be above 7 weeks, and the parson pays the owner 1½d. If any have 1, 2, 3, 4, 5 or 6 kine and of the 6 calves or under and if he sells them, or any at Easter, he pays the tenth penny to the parson. If he kills any of them then the owner pays the right shoulder or shoulders to the parson for his tithe of that calf or calves if he weans them then at Easter he pays ½d. for each one weaned. Tithe white according to the custom of every new milk cow 2d. and thorough milk cow 1½d. and so much for a heiffer. For young tithe pigs: If the owner has 7 the parson has 1 paying to the owner 1½d. If under 7 the owner pays to the parson ½d. a piece for the odd. And if he will wean them the owner must keep the tithe pig for 5 weeks. Tithe geese to be paid at Lammas [1 Aug] saving ¼d. a piece for the odd. Tithe for every garden in the parish 1d. Tithe onions, garlick, kemp and honey are due to the parsonage.

1. A chrisom cloth worn by a child at baptism.

693   2 Jul 1608 (D1/24/189/2)
Terrier taken by the advice of William Edwards parson of Stanton Fitzwarren according to the 56th. canon by William Waterman, William Bacon, Nicholas Jackson and William Akerman.

The parsonage house containing 3 space of housing with a kitchen and a little space of housing thereunto adjoining. Another house containing 3 space of housing. A barn and stable containing 8 space of housing. A garden plot and 2 out bartons, c. 2a. 13 other beast leazes, 80 sheep house beast leazes without stint.

W. field: ½a. in Long Yard furlong shooting E. and W. lying between land of Hercules Burges in S. side and land of William Akerman in N. side; 3yd. in Myssel Yard furlong shooting E. and W. William Watterman S. side and John Strainge N. side; 1a. in Marsh furlong between William Waterman W. side and Robert Ringe E. side; 3yd. more in Marsh furlong, John Ryme W. side, John Colle E. side; ½a. in Stife furlong shooting E. and W. Robert Ring S. side, John Colle N. side; ½a. in Stiffe furlong shooting E. and W. William Waterman both sides; a double butt shooting upon the marsh William Waterman bounding in every side; ½a. in Long Small [Smale] land William Waterman S. William Akerman N.; ½a. in Long Small land shooting E. and W. William Akerman S. side, William Bacon N. side; a headland a. in Pisse furlong shooting N. and S. William Akerman E. side; ½a. in Short Small land shooting E. and W. Hercules Burgis S. side, John Colle N. side; ½a. in Short Small land shooting E. and W. William Watterman S. side, William Bacon N. side; ½a. in Coombe furlong shooting E. and W. William Akerman S. side, Robert Ringe N. side; ½a. shooting upon Rooves lying N. and S. William Akerman E. side, Nicholas Jackman W. side; ½a. in Howles furlong shooting N. and S. William Watterman E. side, Nicholas Jackson W. side; ½a. in Howles furlong shooting N. and S. Hercules Burgis E. side, John Ryme W. side; ½a. in Howles furlong shooting N. and S. William Akerman, E. side, Robert Ringe W. side l; ½a. in Howles furlong shooting N. and S. William Watterman W. side, William Akerman E. side; ½a. in Rensecombe furlong shooting N. and S. John Colle E. side, William Watterman in the over side; 1 headland ½a. in Rensecombe furlong shooting N. and S. William Watterman E. side; 1a. in Rensecombe furlong shooting E. and W. Hercules Burgis in every side; 1yd. more in Rensecombe furlong shooting E. and W. William Watterman S. side, Robert Benjamyes N. side.

S. field: ½a. in Ryve furlong shooting E. and W. William Johnson S. side, William Bacon N. side; 1a. in Cats Brayne furlong shooting E. and W. William Akerman S. side, William Watterman N. side; ½a. more in Cats Brayne furlong shooting E. and W. William Akerman S. side, John Ryme N. side; 1yd. more in Cats Brayne furlong shooting E. and W. William Akerman S. side, Robert Ringe N. side; 1yd. in Deane furlong shooting N. and S. William Watterman E. side, William Bacon W. side; ½a. more in the same furlong shooting N. and S. William Akerman in every side; 3yd. (yarden) more in the same furlong shooting N. and S. Hercules Burgis W. side, John Strainge E. side; ½a. in Broad land furlong shooting N. and S. Joan Barrat W. side, Nicholas Jackson E. side; 1yd. more in Broad land furlong shooting N. and S. William Akerman W. side, the King's highway E. side; 3yd. shooting E. and W. in Nether Cross furlong William Akerman S. side, Robert Ringe N. side; ½a. more in the same furlong shooting E. and W. William Akerman S. side, William Watterman N. side; 3 yd. [yarden] more in the same furlong shooting E. and W. William Akerman S. side, Deane hedge N. side; 3yd. in over Cross furlong shooting E. and W., William Watterman S. side, Hercules Burgis N. side; ½a. in the same furlong shooting E. and W. William Akerman S. side, Robert Ring N. side; 3yd. in Cotham furlong shooting E. and W. William Watterman S. side, Hercules Burgis N. side; ½a. in the same furlong shooting E. and W. William Akerman S. side, Nicholas Jackson N. side; ½a. in the same furlong shooting E. and W. Hercules Burgis S. side, William Bacon N. side; ½a. in the Hytchin shooting E. and W. William Watterman S. side, William Akerman N. side; 3yd. more in the said Hitchin furlong shooting E. and W. William Bacon S. side, Hercules Burgis N. side; ½a. in Over Hitchin shooting E. and W. William Watterman both sides; ½a. in the same Hitchin shooting E. and W. [. . .] Savidge N., John [. . .] S. A head laine in the same Hitchin [shooting] E. and W. Hercules Burgis [. . .].

East field: [. . .] in Barfurlong shooting N. and S. William Watterman both sides; ½a. in the same furlong shooting N. and S. Robert Ringe W. side, Nicholas Jackson E. side; 1[. . .] in the same furlong shooting N. and S. William Akerman W. side, William Watterman [E.] side; 1 head land ½a. in Sand furlong shooting E. and W. John Ryme S. side; ½a. in the same furlong Robert Ring N. side, William Watterman S. side; ½a. in Over Dean furlong shooting N. and S. William Watterman W., Hercules Burges E.; 1yd. in the same furlong shooting N. and S. William Akerman W. side, Robert Ring E.; ½a. in the same furlong shooting N. and S. William Watterman W. side, John Colle E. side; 1 headland ½a. in the same furlong shooting N. and S. William Bacon W. side; 1 butt in Rawe lands end shooting E. and W. William Akerman S. side, Hercules Burgis N. side; ½a. in Hovestone furlong shooting E. and W. William Watterman both sides; ½a. in the same furlong shooting E. and W. Robert Ring S. side, John Ryme N. side; ½a. in Rawe lands shooting E. and W. William Akerman S. side, Joan Barrat N. side.; ½a. in the same furlong shooting E. and W. Robert Ring S. side, William Akerman N. side; ½a. in the same furlong shooting E. and W. Robert Ring S. side, Hercules Burgis N. side; ½a. in the same furlong shooting E. and W. William Watterman S. side, William Bacon N. side; 1 butt in Sheepst[. . .] furlong shooting E. and W. Hercules [. . .] S. side, William Akerman N. side; ½a. in [. . .]alstane furlong shooting N. and S. William Watterman both sides; ½a. in the same furlong shooting

N. and S. William Watterman W. side, Hercules Burges E. side; ½a. in Wooland shooting E. and [W.] William Watterman S. side, [. . .] Bacon N. side; ½a. in the same furlong [. . .] William Bacon [. . .] Akerman; 1yd. in the same furlong William Bacon S., [. . .] Akerman N.; a headland ½a. [. . .] in Luggingsham shooting N. and S. William Bacon E., Nicholas Jackson W.; ½a. in Lower Santhils shooting N. and S. William Akerman E. side, John Strainge W. side; ½a. in Upper Santhils shooting E. and W. Robert Ringe N. side, William Bacon S. side.

Meadow lands: 1yd. of meadow upon Purnell shooting N. and S. William Akerman W. side, the Haywards ham E. side; [. . .] by N. called the Fleets, William Akerman E. side, William Watterman W. side; 1a. in the same Eastrene furlong shooting E. and W. William Bacon N. side, Aldam Rime S. side; ½a. of meadow in the same furlong shooting E. and W. William Bacon N. side, William Jackson S. side; 1a. in the same furlong shooting E. and W. William Bacon both sides; 2 parts of lot meadow lying with William Bacon and William Akerman yearly and every year in the common lot meads of Stanton.

Meadow ground lying in the moors: 2a. of meadow ground in N. side of Moreford way shooting E. and W. William Akerman every side; 2a. of meadow on S. side of Morefords way shooting E. and W. William Akerman every side; 3 x ½a. S. side of the said moors shooting E. and W. William Akerman S. side, John Colle N. side.

Pigs, geese, ducks and hens so many as have been kept without stint according to the custom there that is to say as many as the parson is able to keep in the common fit for that purpose or elsewhere.

694   1 Nov 1671 (D1/24/189/3)
Terrier presented to the court at Salisbury by the minister, churchwardens and sidesmen.

A rectory with tithe corn or grain and hay, the tenth sheaf and cock making it and using it as they do their own. [see memo. at end]. Tithe wool, hemp, hops and of honey the tenth pint and if it be sold the tenth penny. The tenth calf to be taken up when 40 days old. The tenth lamb to be taken up at Markstide [25 Apr] The tenth pig, the tenth goose. Tithe apples, pears and coppice woods. There is due for the sale of every sheep if sold before St. Martins day [11 Nov], a ½d. if sold afterwards a penny and for the sale of a colt the tenth penny but if not sold, 1d. only is to be paid for the fall thereof. There is due to the minister at Easter from every communicant every woman when churched 6d. for every marriage 12d. to the minister, 6d. to the clerk. For the mill there has been usually paid 4s. p. a. There is due for every milk cow to be paid at Easter 2d. and for every heifer 1½d. and likewise for a thorough milk cow. There is due for grazing or fatting cattle and also for poultry what the law of the land does require in that behalf. There are 2 yardlands of glebe land belonging to the Parsonage: A parcell of ground, c. 1½a., upon which is situated the parsonage house containing 7 bays of building, a barn and stable of 8 bays, a turf house of 1 bay, with a cow house and cart house, the dwelling house lying on W. side of the High Street of Stanton, it being also covered partly with slate and partly thatch. An enclosed ground, c. 14 or 15a., Mr. Edward, Hippisley N., Horswell S.

Arable grounds and layes in the E. field: Lower Hitchin:[1] 3 yds. Mr. John Hippisley N., Richard Waterman S.; ½a. William Wild N., Richard Waterman S.; ½a. Mrs. Stibs N., John Hippsley S.; ½a. Richard Jackson N., Thomas Savage S.; 3yd. Mr. J. Hippsley N., Mrs. Stibs S. Over Hitchin:[1] ½ headland a. Jeffrey Rime N.; ½a. Richard Savage N., wid. Strange S.; ½a. Richard Waterman S., Mr. Edward Hippisley N. Over Cross furlong: ½a. Giles Head N., Thomas Savage S.; 3yd. Mr. John Hippisley N., Mr. Edward Hippisley S. Deane furlong: ½a. Richard Waterman W., J. Hippisley E.; 1yd. Giles Head E., William Wild W.; ½a. Mr. Edward Hippisley W., wid. Strange E.; 1 headland ½a. Mrs. Stibs W. Whorstone furlong: ½a. Richard Waterman S., Mr. Edward Hippisley N.; ½a. Giles Head S., Jeffrey Rime N. Rawlands Butts: 1yd. Giles Head S., Thomas Savage N.; 1yd. Thomas Savage S., Mr. J. Hippisley N. Rawlands: ½a. William Wild S., Thomas Savage N.; ½a. Giles Head S., Thomas Savage N.; ½a. Giles Head S., Mr. John Hippislcy N.; ½a. Mr. J. Hippisley S., Mrs. Stibs N. Barth[2] furlong: 1yd. Mr. Edward Hippisley E., William Wild W.; ½a. Richard Jackson E., Giles Head W.; ½a. Mr. Edward Hippisley on both sides. Horstone furlong:[3] ½a. Mr. Edward Hippisley on both sides; ½a. Mr. Edward Hippisley W., Mr. John Hippisley E. The Sandes: 1 headland a.; Jeffrey Rime S.; ½a. Mr. Edward Hippisley S., Giles Head N. Woolands Buts: A double butt Mr. Edward Hippisley on both sides; 2 single butt Mrs. Stibs N., Mr. J. Hippisley S. Woolands: 1yd. Mrs. Stibs S., Richard Waterman N.; ½a. Thomas Savage N., Mrs Stibs S.; ½a. Mrs Stibs N., Mr. Edward Hippisley S.; ½a. that heads Woolands and Crooked yards. Crooked yards: 1yd. William Wild S., Mr. John Hippisley N.; 1yd. Mr. J. Hippisley S., Giles Head N. Billensome furlong: 1yd. William Hawkins N., Mr. J. Hippisley S.; ½a. Richard Waterman S., William Wild N.; 3yd. Mr. Edward Hippisley both sides. Corne Bush:[4] ½a. Mrs. Stibs E., Mr. J. Hippisley W.; ½a. William Wild E., Mrs. Stibs W. Pumhil:[5] 1yd. the Haywards ham E., William Wild W.[6] Lugginsome: 2 butts Richard Jackson W, Mrs. Stibs E.; 1 headland ½a. William Wild N.; ½a. Mrs. Stibs S. wid. Strange N.; ½a. Richard Waterman S., wid. Strange N. Stanton Mead: 1a. in the over mead Mrs. Stibs on both sides; ½a. that runs across the highway Nicholas Jackson S., Mrs. Stibs N.; 1a. in the Lower mead Mr. J. Hippisley S., Mrs. Stibs N.; a double fleate Mr. Edward Hippisley W., Thomas Savage E.; a parcel of mound betwixt Westrop and Stanton, Mrs. Stibs on one side, William Wild on the other.

Arable ground and layes in the W. field: S. field Cross furlong:[7] 3yd. William Wild S., Deane hedge N.; ½a. Mr. Edward Hippisley N., Thomas Savage S.; 3yd. Giles Head N., John Rime S. Broadlands: 3yd. the highway S., William Wild N.; ½a. Nicholas Jackson S., Thomas Savage N.; 3yd. William Strange S., Mr. J. Hippisley N. Deane Gap furlong: 1yd. Mr. Edward Hippisley S., Mrs. Stibbs N.; ½a. William Wild on both sides. Catsbraine: 1yd. Giles Head N., William Wild S.; ½a. Jeffrey Rime N., Thomas Savage S.; 1yd. Mr. Edward Hippisley N., William Wild S. Ryveacre: ½a. Mrs. Stibs S., Nicholas Jackson N. Renchcombe:[8] 1 headland ½a. Richard Waterman N.; 1yd. under Hide hedge Richard Waterman on S. E.; 1a. Mr. J. Hippisley on both sides; ½a. Mrs. Stibs on both sides. Holes:[9] ½a. Richard Waterman N. E., Thomas Savage S. W.; ½a. Giles Head S. W., William Wild N. E.; ½a. Jeffrey Rime N. E., Mr. J. Hippisley S. W.; ½a. Richard Waterman N. E., Nicholas Jackson S. W. Upon the top of the hill: 1 headland ½a. Thomas

Savage E. Rooves: ½a. Giles Head N., William Wild S.; ½a. Mr. Edward Hippisley S., Mrs Stibs N.; ½a. Mr. J. Hippisley S., Mr. Edward Hippisley N. Pisse furlong:[10] 1a. that heads Rooves William Wild E. Long yards:[9] ½a. Mr. J. Hippisley S., William Wild N. Short Small land: ½a. William Wild S., Mrs Stibs N. Long Small land: ½a. William Wild N., Thomas Savage S.; ½a. Mr. Edward Hippisley S., William Wild N. Stiffe furlong: ½a. Giles Head S., William Hawkins N.; ½a. Mr. Edward Hippisley on both sides. Marsh furlong: A double butt William Wild on both sides; 3 yd. Jeffrey Rime W., Mr. Edward Hippisley E.; 1a. Mr. Edward Hippisley W., Giles Head E. Buttocks: 3yd. wid. Strange N., Mr. Edward Hippisley S.

The Moors: 2a. in Vany William Wild on both sides; 2a. on S. side of the moor ford way William Wild S., Thomas Savage N.; 3 x ½a. upon the plain of the Moors Mr. Edward Hippisley N., Thomas Savage S.

Lotmead: Half of 1 lot both in the E. field and the W. field with 14 swarths of grass at the corner of Witherslades[11] and 2 swarths of grass at Kingsdown style. Leazes: These belong to the glebe 13 beast leazes, 4 horse leazes, 80 sheep leazes.

Thomas Hotchkis, rector, William Hawkins [X], William Avenell, churchwardens, Nicholas Strange [X], Thomas Orchard [X] sidesmen.

Memo.: That the meant and meaning of that expression concerning hay (making and using it as they do their own) is not that it be made perfect hay before it be tithed but that it be tithed at what time the owners of the hay do draw their cocks together as generally they have been wont to do.[12]

1. Lower and Over Hitching in **695**.
2. Bath furlong in **695**.
3. Horsestone furlong in **695**.
4. Combush in **695**.
5. Pomell in **695**.
6. 2 x ½a. in Santhills added in **695**.
7. Lower Cross furlong in **695**.
8. Renchcombe Bottom in **695**.
9. Holds furlong in **695**.
10. Omitted in **695**.
11. Witherslades corner in **695**.
12. 'to be summer ricked' added in copy in parish register (WSRO 1999/1).

695   1704 (D1/24/189/4)
As **694** with amendments in footnotes. Bounds of lands in E. and W. fields and the Moors not given. Henry Green, rector, Giles Head, Thomas Head, churchwardens, Agraman Selby, Jeffrey Rime, sidesmen, John Head.

696   16 Jul 1783 (D1/24/189/5)
The parsonage house is built with stone and covered with slate; has a small hall ceiled, stone floor; a parlour ceiled, deal floor, wainscotted chair high and papered above; a kitchen, stone floor, not ceiled; a chamber not ceiled; a garret; a barn walled and thatched 36ft. x 23ft.; a stable 24ft. by 20ft.; a cart house. The glebe land consists of a garden walled, 1r. 16p.; a rick yard, walled, 36p.; a farmyard

walled, 1r. 16p.; an arable field, 4a.; an arable field 3a. and a meadow 13a., all enclosed in 1732 and 1s. 6d. settled in lieu of tithes p. a. by Act of Parliament.[1] No timber on the glebe; 1 pollard elm in the churchyard. The living is £131 p. a. In the church chest is a small silver cup and cover; 1698 is the only inscription. The rector repairs the chancel and the churchwardens the church and churchyard wall. The rector appoints the clerk.

Edward Clarke curate, Jacob Matthews, John Tye, churchwardens, Robert Hiett, Joseph Hiett.

1.   Private Act 5 G. 2 c. [1731-1732]. No copy of the award can be traced.

STANTON ST. QUINTON rectory

697   12 Mar 1678 (D1/24/190/1)
A dwelling house, 2 barns, 1 pigeon house, 1 orchard, garden, and backside, a close of arable and pasture adjoining the barn, c. 6a. 6a. of arable on the Little common field, Mr. Thomas Power's land lying on the S. Inclosed grounds: Little field and Green close, 2a.; Broad field, 14a.; Faledowne, c. 10a.; Cowsley, c. 2a., furzy ground; Pucksie, c. 8a., meadow or pasture; Marigod's bower, 5a., arable land; Cliff hill, 8a., arable land; W. field, 7a., arable land; New leaze, 5a., arable land; 4a., arable land. lying near Leigh post. A little leaze at the Lower Stanton and 1a. arable belonging to it. 18a. arable land lying dispersed in the Broad field. 9a. arable in the Little field; 3a. of which lie in Bafurlong, 2a. in Cowleseelie furlong, 2a. in Short furlong, 2a. in Freath furlong. An inclosed ground called Twinwood, 3½a. formerly exchanged with Mr. Thomas Hubbert for a ground called Faledowne, c. 6a., arable, and 120 lugs of wood in the Park for which the owner of the Park in Stanton is to pay 40s. annually to the rector.[1] Tithe hay and corn of all sorts, and all small tithes such as wool, lambs, cows, calves, orchard fruits, and oblations due and payable to the rector.

Daniel Salway, curate, Humphrey Sparrow [X], Richard Horte [X], churchwardens.

1.   An undated and unsigned note in the archives of the earl of Radnor, probably by this Thomas Hulbert, refers to an agreement made by his father James, owner of the Park and [Robert] Merrick, rector for this exchange which would have been made during Merrick's incumbency between 1609-1639 (WSRO 490/1073).

698   11 Dec 1704 (D1/24/190/2)
A mansion house, 3 barns, 2 stables and an oxhouse. The churchyard, gardens, orchard, barton, 3 home closes, all containing 10a. Little field formerly one ground now divided into two, one of which is still called Little field and the other Green hill, 30a. A little field, formerly common now enclosed, c. 6a. A ground called Mariam's Bower, c. 4a. Grounds: New leaze, c. 5a., W. field, 7a. Leigh post, c. 2a. Little W. field c. 3. ½a. Clift hill c. 9a. road field now divided into 2 grounds, c. 12a. A ground called Outward Falldown piece, c. 8a. 3 other Falldowns, c. 8a. Cowseley, c. 20a. Pucksey, c. 8a. In the Common Great field

18a. In the Common Little field 10a. A little house in Lower Stanton with a ground containing c. ½a. All the great and small tithes.

John Byrom, rector, William Reape, William Earle, churchwardens.

STAPLEFORD vicarage

699   n. d. late 16th cent. (D1/24/191/1)

We the churchwardens and sidesmen present that our parson has 55a. land: 4a. in [. . .]; 4a. at Swyld Ford [Fored]; 1a. lying [. . .] end of Long Labinese; 6a. lying at the Eight [. . .] end; 1a. at Calahays; 2a. at Beryr marsh; 1 head a. at Hupedowne; 1a. above Conigere acre in Thorne land; 4a. under Longlabinch; at Lower end 2a. shooting on Thisly furlong; [. . .]a. in Mowsse furlong; 2a. at the lower end of the same furlong; 3a. in Not furlong; 1a. in the E. furlong; 3a. on Chayinhill; 3. ½a. called the Creves; 1. ½a. in Locke Way; 1 single a. in Locke Way; 2a. together in Locke Way; 2a. in Wortfalles; 1 single a. called the Parsonage [Parsonedge] craft lying at the town's end; a close adjoining the same craft; 6a. of meadow at the lower end of W. mead. Also 2 [. . .] leaze, 12 kine and a bull, 2 cows with the farmers. All manner [. . .] to this parsonage. The vicar has a croft of 2a. of [. . .], a pigeon house and a ham of pasture ground, ½a. of ground, and £8 paid by the parson, and the offerings of the parish at Easter, and the churchyard, and a tenement adjoining the vicarage.

Our ancient custom is and has been that the parson should have a lamb from 7, a calf from 7 and a pig from 7 and from 7 to 10, but under 7, ½d.; but now the parson will not drive till it comes to the sheaf tithe which is contrary to our custom, and we wish to have your judgement in this matter without any trouble of law.

700   10 May 1628[1] (D1/24/191/2)

A mansion house containing a hall, parlour, little buttery, a kitchen and 3 chambers over the same rooms and a study. An outhouse containing 3 rooms, a dovehouse and 2 gardens. An outhouse of no use lately taken down by Mr. Wall, vicar, containing 2 rooms.

1 plot of arable land called the Craft, c. 2a. on E. side of the churchyard and a close of mead called the Vicars ham, c. ½a. on S. side of Serrington [Southampton] bridge. A stipend from the impropriate rectory of Stapleford of £12 p. a. A pension of £3 p. a. given by the dean and canons of Windsor in augmentation of the same stipend. The impropriate rectory has tithe corn, hay, wool and lambs. All the rest of the tithes with all duties for offerings, marriages and churching or purifying of women belong to the vicarage.

Humphrey Wall, vicar, Thomas Corne [X], Henry Milward [X], churchwardens, Thomas Luke, Tristram Pearson, sidesmen, Tristram Harris [X], William Collyns [X], Augustine Burges [X], Thomas Baker, Thomas Byges, John Richards, William Harris [X], John Helme [X].

---

1. The vicarage and rectory were assessed c. 1625. The vicarage was valued at £24 8d., which included the pension of £3 mentioned in **700**, together with the following

perquisites:Vicars ham, 20s.; the dovehouse and its ground, 23s. 4d.; the herbage of the chuchyard over and above the charges for the vicar, s fences, 25s.; arable land in the field, 16s.; the vicarage house, garden and barn, if the vicar was otherwise provided with a habitation and could by law let it out, it were all worth to be let, above charges for reparations, 10s.; tithe of the grist mill, 3s. 4d.; privy tithes with Easter dues and other oblations and offerings, £5. William Burges [X], William Pavy [X] (WSRO D1/41/4/25).

701   20 Jan 1705 (D1/24/191/3)
Terrier taken the churchwardens, overseers and others. An old thatched house on E. side of which is a plot of ground, c. 8 lugs, on N. side of which is a little garden, c. 4 lugs. An outhouse, the churchyard with a garden adjoining, c. ½a. of arable land called the Crate. A little ground by Serrington [Southerton] bridge called the Ham, c. 40 lugs. All privy tithes of apples, pigs, honey, pigeons, cow white, eggs and offerings. The churching of women 1s. For every calf sold the tenth penny; for every calf killed the left shoulder. For every calf weaned 3s. 4d. For every agistment beast 3d. For every garden 1d. Due from the mill 3s. 4d. p. a. Due for a ground called Port ham 8d. p. a. £34 with 2 loads of straw paid by the tenant of the parsonage by order of the dean and chapter of Windsor to whom the parsonage belongs. Deducting for tenths and for procuration money paid to the archdeacon and for taxes we compute our vicarage to be worth but £34 p. a.

Benjamin Hope, vicar, John Rattew, Charles Saph, churchwardens, William Collins, John Adams, Thomas Street.

STOCKTON rectory

702   n. d. late 16th cent.[1] (D1/24/192/1)
We have belonging to the parsonage 48a. of glebe land, 14a. in the W. field, 14a. in the Middle field, 17a. in the E. field, with 2 butts of ground of c. 1yd., and 1a. meadow, and a butt in the W. meadow, and a close of c. ½a. Our parson, Mr. Symnell, is to keep 120 sheep, 12 beasts and 2 runners on the W. end of Stockton. He has 3½a. of arable land and a little close of pasture of c. 1a. in the E. end of Stockton. He is to keep 2 geldings, 2 kine, and 6 hogs at the breach of the field on the E. end of Stockton. The farmer of the E. end of Stockton pays 3d. p. a. to the parson for his tithes of hay. He pays 3s. 4d. p. a. for tithes of wood. The farmer has out of his farm flock 200 sheep for which he does not pay tithe. The parson receives tithes for all the lordship of Stockton except that before excepted.

1.   John Symnel was instituted in 1557 (WSRO P1/1Reg).

703   28 Sep 1608 (D1/24/192/2)
3a. of arable land in the E. field lying between the E. of the parish and the arable field of Bapton commonly called Old Lands. 16a. in the hithermost part of the W. field. 8½a. in the middle part of the same field. 15. ½a. in the furthermost part thereof. 1 close of pasture lately taken out of the W. marsh, c. 4½a., having

Mr. Top's close on E. and William Knight's on W. 1 close, *c.* ½a., between a tenement now occupied by Abraham Langley and another tenement appertaining to Thomas Tylly.

John Terry, rector, John Percy, John Bennett, churchwardens. *Churchwardens' names in the same hand.*

704   1671 (D1/24/192/3)
In the E. end of Stockton so much ground consisting of gardens, orchard and backside on which the dwelling house, barn, stable and outhouses are, as contains by estimation 2a. (plus or minus) with a backway for the harvest out the same backside into the fields thereunto belonging.

3½a. of arable lying betwixt the E. marsh of Stockton and the arable field of Bapton commonly called Old Lands. 1 close of *c.* ½a. lying betwixt a tenement now occupied by Robert Edwards and another tenement belonging to Francis Munday with a little cottage thereunto adjoining.

In the W. end of Stockton 45a. of arable land: viz. 11a. in New Hedge field; 12a. in E. middle field; 13a. in W. Middle field; 9a. in the W. field next Sherrington.

1 meadow, *c.* 4½a., taken out of the W. marsh upon its enclosure, having Mr. Topp's close on E. side and a close belonging to Robert Edwards on W. side. In the W. Sheepsleight the parson has the right to keep 80 sheep at summer and 60 at winter. Upon the breach of the E. Tenant's field the rector has the privilege to keep 2 geldings and 6 hogs there. From the farm at the E. end of Stockton for the hay of the same farm, which is not titheable is payable 3s. p. a. Also for the woods of that farm being not titheable, likewise, is payable 3s. 4d. p. a. Also out of the flock of the same farm 200 sheep are exempted from tithe. Lastly the parson receives tithes for all the lordship of Stockton, except before excepted.

Samuel Tyler, rector, William Mascoll, John Helme, churchwardens.

705   24 Jul 1783 (D1/24/192/4)
Terrier of all the glebe etc. taken and made according to old evidences and the knowledge of ancient inhabitants by the appointment of bishop Shute and delivered to the registrar, Mr. [*Joseph*] Elderton, at the visitation at Sarum held 4 Aug 1783.

The parsonage house built with stone and tiled, an entrance room and 4 others on the ground floor and a pantry. 2 of the rooms have board floors, are ceiled and wainscotted chair high. The others are brick or stone floors and one of them is not ceiled. 4 bed chambers and a closet papered and ceiled, one chamber not ceiled and 2 small garrets plastered and ceiled. There is adjoining the above at the S. end a wood house standing upon posts tiled and thatched. A barn with a stone wall 4ft. high with timbers and weather board above 78ft. x 35ft. including 2 oak thrashing floors, a continuance of the same building is a stable 16ft. long, at the end of which is a cart house the width of the barn, all thatched. 2 gardens, one enclosed with a mud wall, one orchard and one barton, all including the land on which the buildings stand upon *c.* 2a. and is fenced by the rector all around, except W. side of the S. garden, joining an orchard belonging to William Wh. Pinchard[1] which is made by him and the hedge from N. end of the W. garden to the street is made by Rebecca Price.

The rector has a right to a back harvest way leading through an orchard called lay close directly into his barton. The churchyard, *c.* ½a., the fence to S. is a brick wall and quick fence made by William Wh. Pinchard [1]; the N. side is a barn, from which the owner or occupier has a right to through a part of the churchyard with his draught horses in time of harvest, a stable, a wall and quick fence made by Rebecca Price; the W. side is a brick wall is made by the parish from the end of William Wh. Pinchard's [1] wall to the gates leading to the church, the gates and the brick wall leading N. joining the barn are made by the rector; and the E. side is the parsonage and a mud wall made by the rector.

c. 3a. of arable land in the E. end of Stockton lying between the F. mead of Stockton and the arable land of Bapton commonly called Old Lands; the hedge at E. and N.W. side is made by the rector, the other side is open. It is fed with the sheep, when the common field is fed, belonging to the occupiers of the land at E. end of Stockton. 1 close, ½a., lately converted into a garden, lying between a tenement and garden belonging to William Ball and John Wheeler and another tenement and garden belonging to Thomas Humphreys; the hedge at E. side is made by Thomas Humphreys; the W. side by William Ball and at the ends by the rector. 1 meadow, *c.* 4a., in the W. end of Stockton, the W. fence is made by Henry Biggs esq., the E., N. and S. by the rector. 1a. of underwood lying in a coppice joining Funthill Bushes, bounded with stones at N. and S. fence and running through a coppice belonging to Henry Biggs esq. A piece of arable land called the Bumbeak, *c.* 4a., lying upon the hill near the above wood, the S. side and W. end fence made by Henry Biggs esq.; the N. side and E. end by the rector. A triangular piece of furze land joining Chilmark down 3a.; the N. fence made by Henry Biggs esq., the other 2 by the rector. 47 ¼a. of arable land lying dispersed over the open fields of Henry Biggs esq. and separated from his land by lynchets and bound stones, which land was measured by the order of David Price, rector, in 1750 by John Gardner and found to contain 33a. 2r. 1p.

The rector has a right to keep upon the W. Sleight 80 sheep in the summer and 60 in the winter, 6 pigs in the stubble after harvest. Upon the breach of the E. Tennants mead he has a right to keep 2 geldings until it is laid up for a spring crop. From the farm at the E. end of Stockton called the Lower farm, there is payable for the hay that is not titheable 3s. 4d. at Easter and for every cow milked in the parish of Stockton 1d. at Easter. There is payable to the rector 2d. by every person of age to communicate, 1d. for every garden, 2 eggs for a cock and 1 for a hen or duck at Easter. The rector has a right to 3d. at the fall of every calf to be paid by the owner, the rector keeping a bull; it has always been the custom as the rector does not buy rams for him not to take the tithe of ram fleece. The tithe lambs have always been delivered to the rector to his order or paid for 3 weeks after old Ladyday, which is 26 Apr. The parson receives tithes for all the lordship of Stockton except that which is before excepted. There is paid to the rector 6d. at every churching of women, for a wedding by banns 5s. and by a licence half a guinea, nothing for christenings or funerals. The clerk's due at a wedding by banns is 1s. by licence 2s. 6d. The clerk is chosen by the rector and paid by custom viz. the rector pays 12s., the great house at the W. end 10s., the Upper farm 7s., the Lower farm 3s. and every house 3d. at Easter. The sexton is chosen by the parish. Every year £5 is paid out of the rectory to the Hospital of St. Cross near Winchester.

Belonging to the parish is, first, the parish Church, an old building covered with lead, a tower, and 4 bells; belonging to which is a communion table covered with blue cloth, also a linen cloth and 2 napkins, 2 silver chalices, 'The gift of Jn. Top the Elder Esq. son of Jn. Top 1640', a silver cup and a plate, 'The gift of Jn. Top Esq.', a large cut velvet carpet to cover the communion table, a blue velvet pulpit cloth fringed, date 1681, cushion for the same, a large bible, 2 large common prayer books, a chest to hold them and a chest to hold the vestry accounts, a bier, a font where children are baptised and a surplice. The N. aisle is seated and floored and kept in repair within by the lord of the manor, all the rest of the church, by the parish. The chancel belongs to the rector and is repaired by him; it is built of stone and tiled.

Edward Innes, rector, William Wh. Pinchard,[1] churchwarden, H. Biggs, B. Rebbeck, overseer of the poor aged 70, Edward Dyer, 64 years old and collected the tithes more than 30 years for the different occupiers, Thomas Humphery aged 70, Thomas Humphery junior, Nicholas Fleming, William Fleming.

1.   William Wanborough Pinchard was married in Stockton in 1759 (WSRO 203/4).

STOURTON rectory

706   n. d. late 16th cent. (D1/24/193/1)
There is of glebe lands 32a. pasture and arable and 8a. of meadow so there is one the whole 90a. It is all enclosed and no one has any common within them.

707   n. d. late 16th cent. (D1/24/193/2)
The tithe of all duties of all parishioners belongs to the parsonage. 6a. of meadow and pasture. 4a. of wood ground encompassed with bushes. 40a. of arable land in several. 7a. of arable in eastover in the open field. The feeding of 200 sheep upon the down in Donhead [Dunhed]. The tenants [tenements] of the parsonage: Mathew Fewell of pasture and meadow 8a. and 10a. of arable land in several; James Burdele of pasture and meadow 6a.; Edmund Buctler of pasture and meadow 7a. and of arable land in several 6a.; Richard Hayme has a little house sometimes was lodging for the serving priest with a backside containing 30 lugs.

708   1608 (D1/24/193/3)
A ground called Innockes, 29a.; a ground called Cockrede, 28a.; a little meadow, 4a.; a ground called the Parsonage barton (barken) with the orchard and a little meadow and a barn standing there upon, 3a.; a ground called Sommerpole close, 16a.; a ground called Cribbes with an old cottage standing there upon, 3a.; a ground called Hill close, 7a.; a little ground lying by Bonham grounds, 2a. Total 92a.

John King, parson, Robert Sandel [X], John Rial [X], churchwardens, William Rose [X], William Kennisom [X], sidesmen.

709 20 Mar 1663 (D1/24/193/4)
The orchard, the gardens, the rick yard, the yard, 2 courts and a little paddock, 2a. A little mead, 1½a. The Great Meadow, 6a. 2 grounds called Innach, 30a. 2 grounds called Cockreade, 26a. A ground called Somerpole close, 16a. A ground called Hill close, 6a. A mead called Cribbes with a little hop yard, 4a. A ground called Bonham close, 3a.

Nathanial Field, rector, Robert Gapper, Robert Candell, churchwardens, Francis Joup, Thomas Stile, Robert Jaye, Thomas Stone, Leonard Suter, Thomas Barnarde.

710 7 Dec 1677 (D1/24/193/5)
The housing, garden and orchard, 2a. The Great Mead next to Broome lane, 5a. 55 lugs. The Little mead next to Pound close, 1½a.; Cribs mead near the Millpond, 2a. 3yd 4 lugs; Hill close, 5a.; Sumeper close next to Bonham ground, 14½a.; Cockread, 17a.; The Hop yard, 20 lugs; Little Cockread, 7a.; Great Innocke, 12a., next to Broom wood; Long Innoke, 8a ; Innocke next to the cross lanes in the road to Mere, 9a. In the county of Somerset: Candle close next to Bonham grounds, 3a.[1]

John Drew, rector, Robert Adams, John Bucher, churchwardens, William Poore, Thomas Stile, measurers. *Names of churchwardens and William Poore in the same hand*

1. In that part of Stourton in Somerset.

711 2 Aug. 1783 (D1/24/193/6)
The house, garden and orchard, 2a. The Great Mead next to Mere lane, 5a. 55 lugs. The Little mead next to Pound close, 1½a.; Cribbs mead adjoining to and partly in Mr. Hoare's water, 2a. 3r. ½p.; Hill close, 5a.; Somaper close, 14½a.; Cock road, 18a.; Little Cock road, 7a.; Great Innock, 12a., next to Broom wood; Long Innock, 8a.; Innock next to the cross lanes in the road to Mere, 9a. The above grounds are all enclosures and contiguous, no other ground intervening and are all bounded by grounds belonging to Henry Hoare esq. In Somerset, Candle [Crandle] close next to Bonham ground, 3a. This last close only is detached from the others and separated from the above mentioned Somaper close by a ground of Mr. Hoare's called Bushey leas, by which it is bounded N. and E. and by Bonham grounds S. and W. belonging to lord Stourton. Total 87a. 3r. ¼p.

Buildings: The parsonage house built with stone and covered with brick tiles, 78ft. by 24ft., containing a parlour, 18ft. by 16ft., 7½ft. high, ceiled, wainscotted and floored with deal; a small hall or entrance 16ft. by 8ft.; a little parlour 15ft. by 12ft. 7½ft. high, stuccoed and terrace floor; a kitchen 16ft. square 9ft. high, the floor Kinton stone,[1] ceiled; a pantry and cellar adjoining, the size of the kitchen, another cellar under the first parlour 16ft. by 3ft. 3 bed chambers over the two parlours and kitchen and of near the same size with the rooms below, all ceiled, papered and floored with board. 3 garrets whitewashed with board floors.

Outbuildings: a stone built brewhouse and landing over it covered with brick tile and ceiled; a well house; a wood house and coal house under the same

thatched roof; a barn and 5 stalled stable under the same thatched roof, stone
built the extreme length 63ft. and 30ft. wide; a second barn and stable for 6 cart
houses extreme length of both 87ft., barn 18ft. wide, stable 12ft. wide, both
thatched.

Church and churchyard, 2r. 12p. In the church, a communion table with
covering of red cloth, a linen cloth for the same, with a napkin, a silver gilt
flagon containing 2 bottles, a silver gilt chalice containing near a quart, a large
silver gilt plate for the offertory, a silver gilt small plate, a silver gilt patten, a
silver chalice used in the visitation of the sick; all and every one of the above
pieces of plate have the inscription 'The Gift of Henry Hoare Esq. to the Parish
Church of Stourton in the County of Wilts. 1723'; A pulpit and reading desk, a
red velvet cushion for the pulpit, a folio bible and prayer book, a quarto ditto for
the clerk, the Book of Homilies, the Ten Commandments, The King's arms, a
bier and cloth, 5 bells and 2 surplices.

Montague Barton, rector, Edward Hiscock, William Read, churchwardens,
Edward Card, David Boyte, overseers, Francis Faugoin, William Breecher, Felix
Faugoin, John Charlton, Thomas Ryall, John Child, John Hicks, Henry Upward,
Thomas Evele, William Chaffen, Francis Shepherd, inhabitants, Robert Taber,
clerk.

1. Paving stone from Keinton Mandeville, Somereset.

712   15 Sep 1827 (D1/24/193/7)
Terrier of the glebe made after an exchange made under several Acts of Parliament
and according to the evidence and knowledge derived from ancient terriers and
old inhabitants.

A substantial parsonage house erected in 1820 at the joint expense of the
patron and rector, built with stone, faced with brick and covered with blue slate,
extending in front from E. to W. 66ft. 6in. and in depth from N. to S. 40ft.
comprising within the walls sundry attached offices and a small court over the
entrance door to which in the centre is a tablet bearing the following inscription
'Domus Ecclestastica constructa 1820 R. C. Hoare patrono, Gulo Partridge,
rectore'.

The house comprises in the front a suite of 3 rooms, library, drawing
room, dining room and at the back, divided by a passage, housekeeper's room,
kitchen, pantry, back kitchen, brewhouse, coal and wood house; on the upper
floor 8 bedrooms and dressing rooms with vaulted cellars beneath the ground
floor about 42ft. by 15ft. The dimensions of the rooms are as follows: library
18ft. by 15ft., drawing room 24ft. by 15ft., dining room 18ft. by 15ft.,
housekeeper's room 16ft. by 12ft., kitchen 16ft. by 12ft., pantry 8ft. 2in. square,
all 10ft. high, back kitchen 13ft. by 10ft., dairy 16ft. by 10ft., brewhouse 17ft. by
10ft., coal and wood house 16ft. by 10ft., bedroom no. 1, 18ft. by 15ft., nos. 2
and 3, both 12ft. by 15ft., no. 4, 18ft. by 15ft. 9in., no. 5, 12ft. by 10ft. 8in., no. 6
12ft. 2in. by 11ft. 8in., no. 7 11ft. by 8ft. 6in., no. 8 11ft. 4in. by 12ft. 4in. all 9ft.
high.

Attached to the house are 2 water closets adjoining each other, and near
thereto is a house 15ft. by 18ft. 6in. built of brick and slated over the well of

water having therein a crank pump with cisterns and pipes complete for supplying the dwelling house and offices with water. The fixtures throughout the house and offices and sundry articles of furniture and a collection of books in the library all, with the exception of a few volumes of books, the gift of the present patron, belong to the rectory and are to descend from the present rector to his successors in the nature of heirlooms, the whole of which will be found particularised in a book kept for registering benefactions and donations in the parish.

A garden and plantation encompasses the house and north-westward of the latter are the following buildings of stone covered with thatch· stalled stable, coach house, and saddle or harness room 66ft. by 43ft., barn and wheel house 63ft. by 34ft. also granary weather boarded 24ft. by 16ft., waggon house on posts 38ft. 6in. by 18ft., stalls and straw house 59ft. by 48ft. with a pigsty near thereto. The whole adjoining to an enclosed barton abbutting N. to the road.

The glebe lands, since the recent exchange, lie compact around the parsonage house and are as follows: (1) House, garden, plantation and barton, 3a. 2r. 24p. (2) Pound close (lately taken in exchange), pasture, 3a. 4p. (3) Great Cock Road, arable, 19a. 1r. 21p. (4) Little mead in front of house, meadow, 4a. 32p. (5) Little Cock Road, arable, 7a. 23p. (6) Little Innock, arable, 9a. 11p. (7) Great Innock, arable, 11a. 1r. 33p. (8) Long Innock, including Berretts on S. W. end and lately taken in exchange, arable 9a. (9) Broom Wood, also lately taken in exchange, meadow, 5a. 3r. 17p. 10. Lower Broom Wood field, arable, 18a. Total 90a. 3r. 5p.

Tithe corn, grain, pulse, hay, wood, wool, lamb, calves, cow, pigs, milk, eggs, poultry, gardens, orchards and all other titheable matters to be rendered in kind. Offerings at Easter, fees for banns, marriages, mortuaries and other surplice fees. The population is supposed to be from 600 to 700 souls. The parish church lies in a valley to the W. of the parsonage house and has been lately put into a complete state of repair and the interior thereof painted. It is a turreted building of stone with a square tower on the W. and consists of a nave extending from the turret and belfry 43ft. 6in. and from the choir to the alter 28ft. 9in. From the N. door its breadth is 31ft. There is a side aisle to the N. and the family pews of Sir Richard Colt Hoare projects to the S. There are sundry monuments in the church also a table of the Ten Commandments gilt lettered in the chancel and of the royal arms affixed in front of the gallery. A communion table and covering and the following plate: A flagon to contain 2 bottles; chalice, c. 1 quart; plate for the offertory, large; plate of smaller size; paten. All silver gilt and bearing the inscription 'The Gift of Henry Hoare Esq. to the Church of Stourton in the County of Wilts., 1723'.

R. C. Hoare, patron, Henry Hoare, William Partridge, rector, Richard Hoare R. N., Philip Crocker, Henry King, churchwardens. James Booth, Robert Davis, Thomas Scammell, John Small, James Green, C. P. Charlton, Stephen Brown, James Holmes, James Winter, Abraham Wintle, William Perry, William Shephard, Fraser Shepherd, Thomas Charlton, William Charlton, N. and G. Messiter, stewards to Sir R. C. Hoare.

STRATFORD SUB CASTLE rectory

713   30 Dec 1614 (D1/24/194/1)

We have a very fair dwelling house with 2 fair barns covered with tiles, a fair garnard house also covered with tiles, a stable, and an oxhouse. A barton adjoining the stable and garnard house of *c.* ½a. Another barton adjoining the oxhouse and barne of *c.* ½a. A garden adjoining the E. side of the dwelling house. Another garden or orchard lying on the W. of the dwelling house, on the W. of which lies a close of pasture or meadow of *c.* 1a., and on the N. a close of pasture or meadow of *c.* 2a., on the N. Mill lane. 7a. in one piece lying in Gryffins mead, the broad stream running on the E. end, and on the W. the common field called Stratford Layne. 3 x ½a. in the same meadow bounded as before. 4a. in another meadow called Mill mead, the mill pond running on the E. and the main river on the W. 2a. meadow lying in Chinnhames mead, and the shear of a meadow called Cables of *c.* 2a. A little paddock adjoining the common street on the W. and a field called Home field on the E. of *c.* ½a. Another paddock, bounded as before. Another close of meadow or pasture of *c.* 2a. abutting E. on the common street, and W. on the main river, S. on a piece of meadow or pasture belonging to Leonard Moggeridge gent. and N. on a close of meadow or pasture held by Edward Godfrey gent. and parcel also of the parsonage. Common of pasture for 14 rother beasts and 2 horses from Lammas [1 Aug] according to the custom, and common of pasture also for 120 sheep.

Arable land: 15a. lying in the Home field; 15a. in a field lying on the N. of the old castle; 10a. in a field adjoining Little down; 19a. in St. Johnes field; 5a. in Powles Dean field; 16½a. in S. field; 6. ½a. in Marsh furlong; 13½a. in Stratford Layne field. A tenement held by Edward Godfrey with a garden and orchard of *c.* 1a.; a close of pasture of 1½a.; another close of meadow or pasture of *c.* 2a. adjoining a close belonging to the parsonage on the S., on [. . .] a close belonging to John Lowe esq., parcell also of [. . .]; also belonging to the tenement a [. . .]; another messuage or tenement held by [. . .] with 2 closes of meadow or pasture [. . .] S. side to a close of mead [. . .] the parsonage. Another messuage [. . .] barn and stable and [. . .] of *c.* [. . .]. Another tenement held by Gabriel Kydd with a garden and backside; a close of arable belonging to it of *c.* 1a. adjoining on the W. to a close or croft called Welchnutt belonging to Mr. George Jerrington, abutting on the N. on Bonnes Lane [field]; 1a. arable belonging to the tenement, lying in the same field 1a. arable in the field adjoining the N. side of the old castle. 1a. arable in the field adjoining Little down. 1a. arable in Powlse Deane field.

Anthony Davis, Robert Edmunds, Christopher Merrivale [X], Henry Axford [X], Robert Dybbyns [X], Oliver Parham.

714   1704 (D1/24/194/2)

The parsonage is appropriated to the cathedral of Sarum and the dean and chapter or their tenant are in possession of the parsonage house, glebe lands, tithes and all profits arising from the same, they nominate a person to serve the cure to whom they allow £80 p. a.

Thomas Henchman, curate, William Townsend, Samuel Pavy, churchwardens.

STRATFORD TONY rectory

715   3 Apr 1605 (D1/24/195/1)

A perfect note of all the arable land meadow and pasture delivered into the bishop's office of record. The patron of the parsonage as we do take it is Mr. Robert Hyde, son to Mr. Laurence Hyde deceased of Hatch. There belongs to the rectory 1½ yardlands of arable land pasture and meadow. In the Southfield on the hill there are 8a. of arable land, 2 of which lie in the parsonage hedge furlong, 2a. at the Over Eight acres, 2a. lie at Greenes hedge, 1a. on the path to the Bottom field, and 1a. on the path called the Broad acre. In the Bottom field there is 1 head a. adjoining a piece called Milland. An enclosed close called Great Gaskyn of 11a. which is to be sown with the N. field and also to lie open and be common with the N. field. Another enclosed close called Little Gaskyn of 6a. which is always in several. A little meadow called Warr mead of 1a. which is always in several. Another little meadow called Long mead of 1a. which is always in several. Biggin Hill close of 2a. which lie always in several. Churchlands close of c. 1a. which is always in several. A little ham which was allotted to the parsonage in respect of the tithe of other hams thereabouts. A little meadow by the parsonage house called Culverheye of c. 1a. which is always in several. Orchard ground about the house of c. 1a. lies always in several. 1a. in Lumberds mead allotted to the parsonage in respect of the tithe hay there only to cut and carry away.

There is common for 80 sheep to go over all the downs and common fields with the town flock. Common for 18 lambs from Ladyday [25 Mar] until Michaelmas [29 Sep]. Common for 4 horses and 4 beasts to go with the town horses and beasts. Furse growing on the common down to be taken in proportion and rate with the tenants of the town. There is going out of the parsonage yearly a pension of 30s. to the King always payable at Michaelmas. All that part of the E. end of Homington which belongs to Kings College, Cambridge belongs to the parish of Stratford and pays all tithes to the parson of Stratford and are to bury, marry, and christen there.

Davy Naylor [X], Thomas Clark [X], churchwardens; William Mills senior [X], William Mills junior [X], sidesmen.

716   26 Sep 1671 (D1/24/195/2)

All tithes that ever shall become one or payable within the parish except hereafter in this terrier excepted. The full tithes of 9½ yardlands in the tithing of Homington and whatsoever church dues or offerings shall become due from any persons living in that part of the same tithing which belongs to Stratford Tony.

A mansion house, a brew house, a wood house, a barn, a stable, a fodder house besides some skillings, an orchard, 2 gardens. An enclosure called Biggen hill c. 1a. 1yd.; an enclosure called Churchlands in which is a tenement belonging to the parsonage; an enclosure called Culver close, c. ½a.; an enclosure called the Fishpond close, c. 1½a.; an enclosure called the Long mead c. ½a.; an enclosure called Little Gascoyne c. 4a.; a ham, c. ½a.; in lieu of the glebe and tithes of 11 other hams as they now are divided; c. 1a. or more in Lombards mead in lieu of the glebe and tithe of the whole mead and this a. is to be changed yearly for the next adjacent, so that the parson is to have one one year and the other the next, of which 2a., the longer, is to be a lug, r. or p. narrower than the shorter; the parson has in that mead common of feeding proportionable for his a. when it is fed.

A parcel of arable ground called Great Gascoyne, c. 7a., lying in N. side of the river and belonging to the N. field, to be sown in course with that field; to be common every year with that field when the corn is carried off the ground and to lie still or rest every third year and be common with that field.

In the S. fields lie dispersedly, c. 9a. of arable ground belonging to the parsonage as glebe, to be sown and lie still or rest in course with those fields in which they lie. Common of pasturage in all the commons of the parish for the number of commonable cattle belonging to 1½ yardlands in the herd or herds of kine or flocks of sheep; and the cutting of furzes "in stem or course" for 1½ yardlands.

Edward Ward, rector, Edward Hill, John Barter [X], churchwardens, Thomas Coffin, Thomas Coffin★ [X], sidesmen.

★'and what relates to Homington he know, th'other not. '

717   21 May 1705 (D1/24/195/3)
*An acknowledged copy of 714.*William Fawconer, rector, John Blethman, Edward Bodenham, churchwardens.

STRATTON ST. MARGARET vicarage

718   13 Oct 1608 (D1/24/196/1)
Terrier of the parsonage and vicarage belonging to Merton College, Oxford. The parsonage has a mansion house with 2 barns, a stable with a backside and a close; 1½ yardlands of 30a.; common for 60 sheep, 7 rother [rudder] beasts one year and 8 the next, also common for 3 horse beasts one year and 4 the next; a cottage with a backside and 1a. arable lying in the Roiall field, and a little plot of ground by Fars land.

The vicarage has a mansion house,[1] a backside,[2] the churchyard, and all tithes of wool, lambs, cow white, calves, pigs, geese, with other diminute tithes.

William Fouler, vicar, Thomas Barret, William Surgood, churchwardens, John Bennet, John Welch, sidesmen.

1.   Described as an ancient house and also with a garden in **719**.
2.   In **720** and **721** this is described as 43p, bounded N. house and garden Richard Jordan E. highway S. house and garden of John Gilman, W. a field called the Clays.

719   14 Nov 1671 (D1/24/196/2)
As 718 relating to the vicarage only with amendment in footnote. John Lea, John Gray, churchwardens, Thomas Reade, Thomas Jackson, sidesmen.

720   6 Nov 1677 (D1/24/196/3)
As 719 with amendments in footnote. Godfrey Jenkinson, vicar, Edward Champ, Humphrey Coke[1], churchwardens, Thomas Sargent, Richard Gillman, sidesmen.

1. Cook in 1678.

721   13 Mar 1678 (D1/24/196/4)
As **720**. *Witnesses as* **720**.

722   19 May 1705 (D1/24/196/5)
A vicarage house out of repair with a small building adjoining to it which is propped up, a small garden and the churchyard. As for glebe we know not of any and we believe that the tithes of the whole parish amount to £12 p. a. and some years £16. They are as follows: Sale of sheep 20d. a score; agistment sheep 5d a score by the month; wool the tenth part according to the time the sheep have been in the parish; lambs 2s. for the tenth one and the odds 2d. each; cows 2d. each; calves 8d. on the fall; poultry 3 eggs for a cock and 2 for a hen; each garden 1d.; colts [. . .]; pigs 2s. for the tenth, sometimes one pig out of 7; fruit the tenth part; geese, if any, 1s. at Lammas [1 Aug] for the tenth; hops, if any, the tenth part; grazing beasts 1s. each; Welch beasts the tenth part. 3 little grounds which were given by Sir William Hedges to the vicar and for the vicar's widow after him and their value is £7 p. a.

William Palmer, vicar, Henry Read, Nicholas Jackson, churchwardens, Thomas Cook, John Lewis, overseers, Francis Kemble, Richard Read, John Sprat, Nicholas Smith, John Salt, John Tuft.

723   18 Dec 1712 (D1/24/196/6)
A mansion house with backside and orchard, 40p., bounded N. house and garden of Charles Looker, E. the highway, S. house and garden of Richard Gillman, W. the field called the Clay. The churchyard. *Tithes as* **718**. A pasture ground called Harnell Lease and the ham adjoining all *c.* 11½a. purchased by Sir. William Hedges of London in 1693 from Thomas Butcher of Stratton St. Margaret for the use of the vicars and their widows during their widowhood. When there be no widow to return to the use and behoof of the vicar for the time being.

William Palmer, vicar, Robert Gillman, churchwarden, Nicholas Smith, overseer, Francis Kemble, Henry Read, Richard Read.

SUTTON BENGER vicarage

724   14 May 1588 (D1/24/197/1)
We the churchwardens with the consent [codecent] of 4 of our honest neighbours do this said as touching your bill concerning what appertains to the parsonage and to the vicarage.

Our parsonage has a close adjoining the parsonage house of 1a. and all the tithes of corn and hay except the tithe of the glebe land of the vicarage, and the vicar can, upon the freedom of the parsonage, keep nothing upon the common beyond his several. Our vicarage has a close of 3a. and the vicarage bounds the S. end and the other side; he has 5a. 1 farndell of arable land in the S. field; 6½d. in the Middle field; 1a. in Barratts; 7a. 1 farndell in Wortheis N. field and Penbroucks; also 1 farndell in Longs park and 1 farndell in a ground called

Pucemire and a little earnell more in the same Pucemire the which 2 farndell and little earnell are witheld from our vicar being his own right by Mr. Long of Draycot and his tenant Mr. Robert Ernelye dwelling in Sutton Benger; also in the common meadow he has 1yd. mead as it falls by lot, and 1a. as it is rated in the same mead and a little parting lot in Sindroms of which portions he has most years 3 loads [lodds] yearly; a garden with a little plot which the vicarage house stands in. All the tithes of cow white, calves, pigs, geese, wool and lambs etc. and the offering days quarterly.

All these things above mentioned we have with our churchwardens William Boxe and Valentine Mapatt set our names Richard Lovell, John Geell senior, Edward Box senior, Richard Coller senior. [*Names in the same hand*]

725   13 Dec 1671 (D1/24/197/2)
Terrier of the glebe in the possession of the present incumbent William Aust. A close of pasture called the Hill leaze, c 4a. A close of arable or pasture called Berrycraft leaze, c. 2a. 2 beast leazes at the Hird and through the mead at the Breach. 1yd. mead in the common mead and pasturing at the breach for 6 beasts with 1a. of land mead and 1a. farndell and in the same meadow. 5½a. in a field called N. field Penbrokes and Worthyes; 1a. of arable in the Basset field; 6a. 1 farndell of arable in the Middle field; 5a. of arable in the S. field all lying dispersed in several furlongs. A vicarage house.

Richard Messiter, Ralph Barnard, churchwardens.

726   14 Mar 1678 (D1/24/197/3)
A dwelling house, garden plot adjoining of 6 lugs lying next unto the churchyard. 1yd. mead in the common mead being 1 part of ¼ of a lot called the Four Quarters. 2 x ½a. of land mead in the common mead one lying on a place called Salie, the other at a place called Vinchester and part of a lot at a place called Collers post. 5a. of arable land in the S. field whereof 3a. lie in Mayfurlong, ½a. in Clefurlong and the other (sic) 3a. lie dispersedly about the field. 5a. of arable lying dispersedly in the Middle field. 4½a. 1 farndell in the N. field and Worthies whereof ½ lies at Pembrokes, 1a. at Puckmore and the rest dispersedly in the field. 1a. of arable in a field called Barret. 1 enclosed ground of 3a. called the Hill leaze. 1 enclosed ground of arable of 2a. called Worthis leaze, Sir James Long's Berricraft lying on W. Worthis field on E.

The small tithes as cow white, calves, wool, lamb, pigs, orchard fruit etc. and oblations. An augmentation granted by the dean and chapter of Sarum of £10 p. a.

William Auste, vicar, John Pierce, John Barnard, churchwardens. [*Names in the same hand*]

727   29 Oct 1783 (D1/24/197/4)
A short history or account of the original endowments of the vicarage with copies of 2 ancient terriers and the state of the living as at present enjoyed by Rev. Charles Davies, vicar.

The vicarage appears to have been endowed by Walter de Wylye, bishop of Salisbury in 1256 by virtue of a papal bull, with all great and small tithes, reserving a pension, or clear annual payment of 30 marks, to the dean and chapter of

Sarum and the patronage of the church was thereby transferred from Malmesbury abbey to the bishop and his successors (see the original in the chapter of Sarum). The vicars appear to have been in quiet possession of the tithes for above 200 years, when on account of the supposed non-payment of the pension the dean and chapter appear to have seized the great tithes and to have held them by their bailiffs and tenants with some small alteration until 1716. In 1716 vicar Thomson,[1] collated in 1694 and died in 1742, applied to the dean and chapter for the restitution of the great tithes and after some struggle obtained, through the mediation of the then bishop, the following terms: The chapter, on the bishop resigning to them the patronage of the living, oblige themselves to convey the great tithes to the vicar by lease at the reserved rent or pension of 30 marks or £20. They further contribute £100 which in addition to Colston's benefactions,[2] induced the Governors of the Queen Anne's bounty to contribute £200 more for the augmentation of the living and with which the small estate at Brinkworth was purchased for £400.

In 1729 the parish, then chiefly common field and arable was, by common consent, enclosed and the glebe lands exchanged, by what authority is not said, and by which enclosure the possessions of the church were much altered and the value of the tithes lessened in a very considerable degree. The material circumstance seems to have been unnoticed by and probably unknown to the vicars Miles,[3] Watkins,[4] Atkinson[5] and Rand[6] who immediately succeeded Thomson[1] nor would it be an easy matter now to propose any remedy as the situation and almost the names of the several fields are forgotten. The vicar however not knowing what opportunities may hereafter offer to himself or successors of recovering any latent or dormant claim begs to be excused from giving any account of the present possessions of the church as a perfect terrier, lest such terrier should operate as a bar to all future pretensions. The following statement will give every necessary information to his successors and as such he conceives answer the lord bishop's intention and meet with his lordship's approbation though somewhat deficient in form. [*There follows summaries of* **724** *and* **725**]. The vicar at present is by the original endowment as well as by virtue of the dean and chapter entitled to, and in actual possession of all the great and small tithes, subject to modus, particular custom or prescription and is bound to the annual payment of 30 marks or £20 to the dean and chapter. His glebe consists of the Parsonage close, barn with 2 thrashing floors, stable for about 6 horses, churchyard, vicarage house and small garden all adjoining the church. 1 close of 3a. in N. hill, N.W. of the church; a close of 6a. in Barret to E. of the church; a close of 4a. in Newland E. S. E. of the church; a close of 5a. called Hoddy pit[7] having a few small elms in the S. hedge, a yd. lot in the common mead, a reputed a. on Gally, ½a. under new lands, a long ½a. on Winchester, an undivided piece or yd. under new lands and all in the same mead; and a ½ acres' end likewise under new lands disputed by Sir James Long and his late tenant Thomas Messiter, which the present vicar has not been able to recover.

Commons for 3 horses or 6 beasts at the breach of the mead for this Lot mead, and 6 sheep viz. 1 for each ½a. when the corn has been taken out. The Queen's Bounty was disadvantageously laid out on a small farm in Brinkworth called Windmill farm about 1 mile to the N. of Brinkworth Church, consisting of a cottage, beast hovel, 3 closes of 12a., and an unstinted right of common on the large or other commons in the parish.

The vicarage house which was a mean, small, ill-constructed thatched hovel, having fallen down while under repair, is now rebuilt and will consist, when finished, of a large cellar or wood and coal house 36ft. by 14ft, 2 kitchens 15ft. by 15ft., parlour and hall each 15½ft. by 15½ft., 2 common bedchambers 15ft. by 15ft., 2 others 15ft. by 14ft., a light closet 8ft. by 10ft.; 2 attics 15ft. by 15ft. It will cost the vicar over £600 exclusive of old materials, who found the profits of the living under £80 exclusive of repairs of house, chancel, barn, stable, etc., nor can it, he conceives, be raised so as to make it a decent maintenance for a resident vicar.

The parish consists of about 80 families, little farmers and labourers amongst whom are a few Quakers and Methodists, but neither of whom have any meeting house in the parish. The church is large and tolerably well built but in very bad repair internally. There is a small piece of ground called Church piece left for ornamenting the church but which has produced very little of late; it now lets for c. 30s. p. a. The tower contains 5 small unmusical bells; the pulpit cushion is old and mean, the communion plate consists of a small silver cup and cover a plate and pewter flagon.

The parish is computed in Dugdale's Montasticon[8] at 10 hides and may consist of 1,000a.; a great part of which lying at a great distance from the village is very poor. The fee simple of the whole belongs to Sir James Tilney Long and most of the tenants, on small farms, are at rack rent. It stands mostly on gravel soil, is bounded N. and N. E. by Seagry brook, E. partly by Avon river and partly by meadows belonging to Draycott, on S. by Langley brook, on W. by Draycott parish and Sir James Long's park but which boundary is not well defined. It is situated 4 miles N. of Chippenham, 24 miles E. from Bristol, 7 miles from Malmesbury, about 10 miles S.W. from Wootton Bassett and 17 miles from lime and coal. It may be about 3 miles long and 1 mile broad but great part of it to the N. is very meadow. The land tax at 4s. is £63, the poor rate at 2d. is 4d. the vicar. The vicar pays an eighth of the rates which amount to c. £25.

1. Thomas Thompson was vicar between 1696 -1742.
2. A gift by Sir Edward Colston in 1710 to the Governors of the Queen Anne's Bounty.
3. Ezekial Mills was vicar in 1742.
4. Edward Watkinson was vicar between 1743-1744.
5. William Atkinson was vicar between 1744-1765.
6. Brock Rand was vicar between 1765-1774.
7. Hoary Pit in a plan of an exchange of glebe with Sir James Tilney Long in 1790 (WSRO D24/18/2).
8. *Monasticon Anglicanum* by William Dugdale.

SUTTON MANDEVILLE rectory

728   n. d. late 16th cent. (D1/24/198/1)
16a. of arable in the common fields. 17½a. of pasture ground in several. 1½a. of meadow in the common mead. 60 sheep leaze. Freedom of herbages as well as

of the common meadows and common fields at the days of breaches accustomed, for such cattle as the parson has, according to the ancient orders of the parish. Total 36a. of land.

Customs for Lammas tithe: 1d. for cow white; ½d. for the fall of a calf; 1d. for the fall of a colt; if there be 5 calves the parson is to have calf in this order; the owner [honer] is to value [praise] and the parson to choose so is it in likewise manner of pigs and lambs; if there be 10 lambs or 10 calves or 10 pigs the parson is to have the tenth; if there be 9 lambs the parson is to have a lamb paying to the owner ½d.; of 7 the parson is to have 1 paying the owner 1d.; of 6 lambs the parson is but to have of his parishioner 3d.; of 8 lambs the parson is to have 1 paying the owner 2d.; under the fall of 5 lambs at season the parson is but to have for the fall for each one but ½d.; that in the like manner and course is it of calves and pigs accustomed to be paid. The parson is to have of every ancient householder 6 eggs or 1d. at the choice of his parishioners on Good Friday; the parson is to have the tithe of geese in manner as follows of 10 or 9 one paying ¼d., of 8 one paying ½d., of 7 one paying 3s. 4d. of 6, the parson is but to have 1½d, of for half a goose.

General Customs: The parson is to have the tithe sheaf of wheat, rye, and other grains as it falls as also the tenth pooke as it falls of all manner of grain; so likewise tithe of all meadow grounds being mown and not otherwise; the tenth lb. of wool grown within the parish of every several parishioner; our custom is that it shall happen that any parishioner to kill in his house 1 calf or more then the parson is to have a shoulder of every calf so killed, also the tenth lug of all coppice sold within the parish and not otherwise; our custom is to have a sufficient and lawful bull and boar found by the parson for the service of the parish at all times; as also our custom is at the parson's hands to have a sufficient drinking with bread and cheese to serve the whole parish on Easter Day; that all the tithes of the farm of S. Ugford[1] now in the tenure of Thomas Hawle gent., is belonging and appertaining to the parson of Sutton Mandeville.

1. In Burcombe.

729   10 Jun 1609 (D1/24/198/2)
Terrier taken by the churchwardens and others. The parsonage house with a stable adjoining, the barn and backside,[1] orchard, garden adjoining, a little parrock called Piggs close, the Long parrock, the Yonder parrock and the Long mead adjoining the house and lying together, 8a., having on S. side the highway, on E. the land of George Staples of Fovant, on N. grounds of Stephen Seymour and a meadow of the Hardings called Dalmers, and on W. grounds[2] of John Barter and Thomas Rendoll.

A close of arable or pasture ground taken and enclosed out of the common of Sutton called the Heath, 9a., having a ground of John Cudrington gent. on N. side, Swallowcliffe common at W. end, a close of Agnes Androwes wid. on S. and the highway that leads to Sutton W. field on E.

A close of pasture or arable land called the Field close,[3] 6a., having the highway on S., the ground sometime Hentons land on E., the ground of Thomas Jones[4] and the wid. Androwes on N., and a close of John Bealinge[5] on W.

A close sometime parcel of the farm of Sutton Mandeville, 10a., exchanged for a close of meadow sometime appertaining to the parsonage lying in a meadow sometime common called Man mead,[6] having the river on N., the land sometime William Ley esq. called Gauntes ham on E. and part of the land of John Cudrington gent. on W., divided from the same parsonage a. with rails and posts and also exchanged for common of all animals if cattle in Hill mead,[6] Broad mead[6] and Man Mead;[6] the close is bounded on N. with a close of Richard Biddlecombe called Pitclose, the ground of the Hardings, John Needle, the wid. Androse and the wid. Scamell[7] on E., a close of Richard Biddlecombe, on S. and the ground of the farm of Sutton on W.

Common of pasture for 60 sheep to feed and pasture in all the common fields, downs and droves of Sutton and commons of pasture for all manner of commonable cattle in the fields of Sutton at stubble time.

16½a. of arable land lying in the common fields of Sutton: In the S. field 4a. viz.; 1a. in the Combe which shoots E. and W., land of Richard Biddelcombe N., John Needle S.; 1a. in Stowe furlong, land of Thomas New E., Thomas Rendall W.; 2a. in Waterfurlong, the N. a. whereof has land of Thomas Jones on N., Martha Imber on S., the S. a. has land of wid. Scamell on N. and Thomas New on S. In the W. field 9½a. viz.; 1a. under drove hedge that leads to Buckes barrow; a piece of 3 x ½a. in Whitewood furlong, lands of John Needle on E. and W.; 1a. in the same furlong land of Richard Biddlecombe on W., and ½a. of Hentons lands on E.; In W. Sandhill furlong 2½a. viz.; 1a. land of Thomas Rendoll on W. and Robert Harding on E.; 1a., land of John Bealing on W., Robert Harding and John Harding on E.; ½a. land of John Cudrington gent. on W., John Bealing on E.; in the Hare furlong which shoots N. and S. 3. ½a.; 1a., land Thomas and Robert Jones E. and W., 1a. land of Martha Humber wid. on W., John Bealing on E.; 1a., land of Thomas Rendoll on W., a piece of 3a. of the wid. Scamell on E.; ½a. land John Cudrington gent. on E. and John Needle on W. In the field next Delawares Cross 3a. viz.; in Waterfurlong 1a. land John Cudrington gent. on N., Frances Best wid. on S.; in Peasedean 1a., land of Richard Biddlecombe on W., the wid. Androwes on E.; 1a. at Delawares cross that shoots E. and W. having land of Stephen Seymour on S. and Thomas and Robert Jones on N.

All manner of tithes yearly renewing and arising within the parish saving the tithe hay of Gauntes Ham[8] sometime the land of William Ley esq., which appertains to the parsonage of Teffont Evias. A portion of tithe corn and hay of the farm of S. Ugford[9] now in the possession of William Hall gent. viz. tithe corn and hay in the Great field of the farm, tithe hay of Cothey ham, tithe corn and hay of the Long croft on W. part of the barn, saving tithe hay and corn of about 3 x ½a. of E. end of the same close which appertains to the vicarage of Bulbridge, tithe hay of the Great meadow of the farm, saving tithe hay of 3a. belonging to the hospital St. John near Wilton, now Mrs. Saunders' and saving the tithe hay of c. 1a. at E. end of the same meadow which belongs to the vicarage of Bulbridge.[10] All tithe corn and hay of the Pound Close belonging to the same farm.

Tithe of 11a. of arable in the open and common field of Bulbridge[10] but now enclosed into divers several closes in the occupation of divers men; tithe of a close of 7a. now in the possession of Richard Togood adjoining the farm field of S. Ugford,[9] the highway on N.; tithe of 2a. in a close adjoining the last close in the possession of the same Richard Togood which shoots N. and S.; in the same close tithe of 1a. which lies *c.* 8p. from the N. hedge of the last close, also in the possession of Richard Togood and which shoots E. and W.; tithe of 1a. in 2 several closes in the occupation of Henry Blake and George Hayter, *c.* 8p. from the N. hedge of the same closes and which shoots E. and W. which a. lies most part in Blakes close and scarcely the twevelth part of the said a. in Hayters close. Witnesses as above.

Thomas Sanger; Thomas Jones, Henry Younge, churchwardens. *Church-wardens names in the same hand*

1. With an ox stall and wainhouse in **730**.
2. Described as of the wid. Barter and Robert Lucas called Georges in **730**.
3. Described as enclosed out of the Judas field in **730**.
4. The Joneses in **730**.
5. Ralph Bealing in **730**.
6. Described as now owned by Thomas lord Arundell and John Cudrington in **730**.
7. Wid. Scamell not mentioned in **730**.
8. This exception is not mentioned in **730**. See also **744**.
9. In Burcombe.
10. In Wilton.

730   29 May 1613 (D1/24/198/3)
*As **729** with amendments in footnotes and land in the common fields and tithes as follows:*
    In the common fields of Sutton 16½a. of arable land: In the E. field next de la Wares Cross 3a.; 1a. next de la Ware's Cross, having 1a. of Stephen Seymour on S., the Joneses on N.; 1a. in Peasdean having 1a. of Richard Biddlecombe on W., 1a. of Agnes Androse, wid. on E.; 1a. in Waterfurlong having 1a. of John Cudrynton gent on N. and a piece of 3 x ½a. of Frances Best wid. on S.
    In the W. field 9½a.; 3½a. in Whitewood furlong; 1a. next Buckes Barrow drove having a piece of 3 x ½a. of Richard Biddlecombe on E.; a piece of 3 x ½a. having 1a. of John Needle each on E. and W.; 1a. under Whitewood having ½a. of Richard Bidlecombe on W. ½a. of Hentons land on E.: In Hare furlong 3½a.; 1a. having 1a. of the Joneses each on E. and W.; 1a. having 1a. of Philip Humber on W., ½a. of [. . .] Bealing on E.; 1a. having a piece of 3a. of Richard Livelong on E., 3yd. of Robert Lucas on W.; ½a. having 1a. of John Cudrinton gent. on E., a piece of 3 x ½a. of John Neadle on W.: In W. Sandhill furlong 2½a.; 1a. having 1a. of Robert Lucas on W., a piece of land of Robert Harding on E.; 1a. having ½a. of [. . .] Bealing on W., a piece of 2yd. of the Hardings on E.; ½a. in Butterslade Hay ½a. of [. . .] Bealing on E., ½a. of John Cudrinton gent. on W.
    In the S. field 4a.; in Coombe 1a. having a piece of 3a. of Richard Biddlecombe on N., John Needle on S.; 1a. in Stowe furlong having ½a. of Robert Lucas on W., ½a. of Thomas Newe on E.; 1a. in Water furlong having ½a. of Richard Livelonge on N., ½a. of Thomas Newe on S.; 1a. in the same furlong having 1a. of Philip Humber on S., 1a. of the Joneses on N.

A portion of tithe corn and hay out of the farm of S. Ugford [*in Burcombe*] occupied by William Hall[1] gent. viz. tithe corn of the Great field lying on S. of the road from S. Burcombe to Wilton containing *c.* 150a. of landshard land; tithe corn of 7a. shooting N. and S. in a close adjoining the last field, in the occupation of Richard Toogood yeo.;[2] tithe corn of 3a. in the same close shooting E. and W. about the distance of 8 lugs from the hedge of the same close next the highway; tithe corn of *c.* 1a. lying in a close in the occupation of Henry Blake[3] adjoining the close of Richard Toogood[2] about the distance of 8 lugs from the hedge of the same close next the highway; tithe corn of 10 lugs of land in a close of George Hayter[4] next the close of Henry Blake on E. part; tithe corn and hay of Pound close sometime parcel of the same farm in the occupation of Christine Hayes, wid. of Wilton;[5] tithe corn and hay adjoining the close of the same farm on W. part saving the tithe corn and hay of *c.* 1a. of the same close at the E. end appertaining to the vicarage of Bulbridge from a tree in the S. hedge of the same close over right against the cart gap or shard[6] that comes out of the same farm great field and so direct westwards to a gulley in the same farm great mead; tithe hay of a meadow called Coathy ham lying at the W. end of the same close; tithe hay of the farm great meadow and of all the rest of the meadows saving out of the same great meadow ½a. from the gulley in the Great meadow eastwards the tithe hay which appertains to the vicarage of Bulbridge.

Thomas Sanger, rector, Robert Harding, Walter Biddlecombe.

1. Mrs. Anne Coward in **731**, Mr. Richard Barford, rector of Wilton in **733**.
2. John Twogood gent. in **731** and **732**.
3. John Rendoll in **731**. [. . .] Rendoll in **732**.
4. John Hayter in **731**. George Hayter in **733**
5. George Sadler gent. of Wilton in **731**. Mrs. Twogood of Wilton in **732**.
6. Dialect word for a broken gap in a hedge or wall.

731   14 Nov 1671 (D1/24/198/4)
The dwelling house with a stable, barn, and carthouse adjoining. At the N. side of the house there is an orchard of *c.* 30 lugs of ground. At the E. end of the house are 5a. of pasture. Long meadow adjoining the moor belonging to Henry Bracher on N. side containing 2a. wanting 40 lugs. Upon the hill in the In ground, Broome close, 10a., adjoining E. side to a ground belonging to William Long on W. side to a ground of Henry Bealing. Barne close adjoining the highway leading to the common fields of Sutton adjoining on E. side to a ground of John Foote. Heath close, 8a., adjoining on W. end to Swallowcliffe common and on N. side Mrs. Mary Codrinton's 2 common grounds.

16½a. in the three fields: In the field called Ballyard Cross 1a. at the end of the drove shooting E. to the hedge and W. to an a. of William Long on N. side adjoining an a. of Henry Bracher. In the bottom of the same field called Peasedeane 1a. shooting N. and S. adjoining to W. side of an a. of William Long; 1a. in Water furlong shooting E. and W. adjoining an a. of Mrs. Mary Codrinton on N. side.

In the S. field 1a. in Water furlong shooting E. and W. adjoining on S. side of an a. of Thomas Lucas; 1a. in the same furlong shooting E. and W. on N. side adjoining ½a. of Henry Bealing: In Slow furlong 1a. shooting N. and S. adjoining on W. side to ½a. of Thomas Simmons: In Combe Hole 1a. shooting E. and W. adjoining on S. side to 3 x ½a. of William Long.

In the W. field 1a. shooting N. and S. adjoining to Buxberry hedge in Whitewood furlong; 1½a. shooting N. and S. adjoining on the E. side 1a. of William Long; 1a. in the same furlong shooting N. and S. adjoining to a yd. of Dorothy Purdy wid.: In Butter slade ½a. shooting N. and S. adjoining on W. side to ½a. of Mrs Codrinton: In Sandhill 1a. shooting N. and S. adjoining on W. side to ½a. of Henry Bealing; in the same furlong 1a. shooting N. and S. adjoining on W. side to an a. of Thomas Simmons: In Hare furlong 1a. shooting N. and S. adjoining on W. side to 1a. of William Marshman; in the same furlong 1a. shooting N. and S. adjoining on W. side of 1a. of Thomas Lucas; in the same furlong 1a. shooting N. and S. adjoining N. side to 3yd. of Thomas Simmons; in the same furlong ½a. shooting N. and S. adjoining W. side a piece of land of William Long.

Tithe corn, pasture and meadow and tithe of all orchards, coppice, garden and all other things. *The portion of tithes on the farm of S. Ugford as 730 with amendments in footnotes.*

Augustine Hayter, rector, Henry Bealing, William Adlame, churchwardens. *Names in the same hand.*

732   3 Jan 1705 (D1/24/198/5)
House, garden, orchard, barn, stables, backside and out houses. The Horse leaze, Cow leaze and Long mead all adjoining the house, being *c.* 8a. Barn close and a barn standing in the same being *c.* 5a.; Broome close *c.* 10a.; Hearth close *c.* 10a.; in the Little field *c.* 3a.; in the Upper field *c.* 4a.; in the Great field *c.* 9a.

John Ring, John Selward, churchwardens, Robert Long, Henry Bealing.

733   23 Jan 1705 (D1/24/198/6)
The dwelling house with a barn at the S. end, a stable and barton containing 40 lugs; a garden on S. side of the house; an orchard on N. side *c.* 40 lugs; 1a. of pasture ground adjoining the orchard; 3a. of pasture adjoining E. a meadow of Mr. Westfield; a meadow, 2a., adjoining N. to the moore of Thomas Feltham; 10a. of arable on the hill of the said parish called Broom close adjoining E. to a close of Robert Long; 5a. of arable in a close next the highway that leads to Shaftesbury with a barn at the S. end of the close; 2 grounds called Heath closes, 10a., viz. the close next the highway leading to Swallowcliffe, 6a., the close lies by the highway leading to the common fields, 4a. 16½a. in the 3 fields of Sutton viz. 4a. in the field under the plain, 3 in the field adjoining E. to the field of Fovant, 9½a. in the Great field adjoining W. to Swallowcliffe. *Tithe portion of the farm of S. Ugford as in 730 with amendments in footnotes.*

Augustine Hayter, rector, Thomas Feltham.

SUTTON VENY rectory

734   n. d. late 16th cent.[1] (D1/24/199/1)[2]
A close and an orchard [. . .]; 140 sheep leaze feeding together [. . .], 8 oxen, 1 bull and 1 horse feeding [. . .]; 6a. of arable [. . .]; 3a. without tithe hedge [. . .]; 3a.

shutting N. and S. [. . .]; ½a. in the North field [. . .]; ½a. more at Larkesborrowe [. . .]; ½a. more at Rubbers layes; 1a. at Laynsdeane [. . .]; 2a. upon Sandhill shooting [. . .]; 2a. more in the same furlong shooting [shutting] upon [. . .]; 1a. at Pattens on the East field [. . .]; 1a. on Long land lying in the W. ?field [. . .]; 2a. more in the same furlong lying [. . .]; 2a. more in the same furlong lying [. . .]; ½a. in Batted land lying upon [. . .]; ½a. more in the same furlong [. . .]; 1a. in Woodcombe lying in the N. side of S [. . .]; ½a. in Wetland lying in the W. ?field; 2a. in Woodcombe lying in the E. side [. . .]; 1a. in same; 2a. in Whitland lying in the S. side [. . .]; 2a. at Lucas Pich; 1a. at Weane Shard; 1a. at Abbots corner; 3a. in Hichcombe lying in the S. side of at Ladder Foot; 2a. shooting to Copthorne lying upon the S. side of [. . .]; 4a. shooting N. and S. upon the same; 1a. in the whole of Hichcombe in the E. side of Sir [. . .]; 1a. more in the same furlong lying in the S. side [. . .]; 2a. in Hichcombe N. and S. upon the same; 1a. in the whole of Hichcombe in the E. side of Sir [. . .]; 1a. at Waitting hill shooting upon the W. side [. . .]; 1a. more at Waytting hill lying in the E. side of Sir Walter [. . .]; 2a. above Winkers Cliff in the N. side of Sir Walter [—]; 1a. more in the same furlong upon the hill in the N. [—]; 3a. at Gospel Ball shooting upon the way; 1a. above Heycombe by the cliff [cleaft]; 1a. in Heycombe bottom in the N. side of Sir Walter Hungerford; 1a. more in the same furlong by the cliff; 1a. above Ladder Foot.

Steven Hinton senior, John Ghrist, churchwardens, William Diet, Steven Longe, Thomas Hill, Thomas Gilbert, sidesmen. [*Names in the same hand*]

1. Sir Walter Hungerford died in 1596.
2. The document is defective along its right hand side.

735　7 May 1705 (D1/24/199/2)
5a. butting on N.W. side of the house; 5a. shooting against Richard Compton's hedge at E. end of the same field; 2a. in the same field at W. side of 3 x ½a. of lord Weymouth occupied by Richard Compton; ½a. in the N. field on E. side of 3 x ½a. of James Thatcher; ½a. at Larksborough on N. side of John Hinton's a.; ½a. in Rubbers Lays on W. side of Mr. Bilstone's 5a.; 1a in the same field on E. side of Mr. Leonard Bilstone's land occupid by Henry Garrett; 2a. on Sand hill on N. side of John Hinton's ½a.; 2a. in the same furlong on W. side of Jane Due wid.; ½a. in Woll lands on W. side of Thomas Foster; 1a. at Patten on E. side of John Hiscock; 1a. at Long lands on E. side of Madam Bronker occupied by Stephen Long; 2a. in the same furlong on E. side of lord Weymouth.; ½a. in the same furlong on N. side John Franklin; 1a. in Wood combe called Pit acre on N. side of James Thatcher; 2a. in Wood combe on S. side of Jane Dew wid.; 1a. in Wood Combe Hole on W. side of John Weecks;. 1a. in Waiting hill shooting along by the highway; 1a. in the same furlong; 3a. at Gospel Ball; 1a. by Weycombe Cleeve on S. side of John Hiscott; 1a. in Heycombe Bottom on S. side of Mr. Thomas Buckler; 1a. in the Cliff on S. side of John Hiscock.

1a. on the Hither hill on S. side of lord Weymouth; 2a. on the same hill on N. side of Richard Collier.; 1a. in the same hill on S. side of Lord Weymouth; 2a. at Lader Foot on S. side of Mr. Bilstone; 1a. in Hick-Combe on N. side of Mr.

Thomas Buckler; 2a. in the same furlong on S. side of John Franklin; 1a. called Butt acre on N. side of lord Weymouth; 1a. in the same field shooting against the highway; 2a. at Lucas Pitch; 2a. in Hich-combe furlong shooting by the way side that goes up to Copthorn; 4a. shooting upon the last 2a.; 1a. amongst the linches; 3a. in White land on N. side of Richard Collier. The garden, orchard, and backside, 1a. 1 close of pasture, 1½a. Pasture and feeding for 140 sheep pasturing and feeding with one of the farmer's flocks. Pasture and feeding in the fields downs and commons for 8 oxen, 1 bull and 1 horse.

Richard Bayly, rector, John Winton, John Wrench, churchwardens.

736   1 Aug 1783 (D1/24/199/3)

1. The parsonage house built with free stone and covered with stone tile contains 2 parlours, kitchen, cellar and pantry; both parlours have oak floors, are papered and have plain ceilings; the kitchen has a brick floor, plain walls and ceiled; the cellar and pantry have brick floors and are not ceiled. 5 chambers, 3 with elm floors and 2 with deal floors all ceiled; 4 papered, 1 not. A study ceiled and papered and a deal floor. No garret. Brewhouse and fuel house 30ft. by 15ft.; brick walls covered half with brick, half with thatch.

2. On the glebe are 2 barns, stable for 5 horses, cart house, farm yard and rick yard. The barns and stable stone walls 4ft. high, the rest elm all covered with thatch, the farm yard fenced with the buildings. The rick yard fenced with a dead hedge, one of the barns has 2 floors. Pigeon house, stone walls and stone tile. The whole ground is 59 reputed a., of which 6 are pasture, garden and orchard; the garden and orchard are c. ½a. fenced part dead, part quickset hedge; adjoining is a pasture field of c. 4½a. fenced with a quickset hedge on N. side and bounded by the common fields on S. side and fenced with a dead hedge. It is bounded with 2 fields each c. ½a. bounded by the turnpike road on S. and both fenced with a dead hedge.

53 reputed a. in the common fields: In Great Hitchcom 1a. bounded W. Mr. Buckler, E. Mr. Bennett; 2a. bounded N. Mr. John Long, S. Mr. Buckler; 1a. a headland at the end bounded S. Mr. Halliday; 1a. bounded S. Mr. Buckler, N. Mr. Bennet: In Hitchcom 2a. bounded W. Mr. Randall, E. Mr. Axford; 4a. bounded W. Mr. Randall, E. Mr. Hinton; 2a. bounded N. road to Hindon: In Copthorn linchetts 1a. bounded E. Mr. Buckler, W. Mr. Hinton: Under Emms Lader way 2a. bounded S. the hill, N. Mr. Hinton: Upon Emms Lader hill 1a. bounded Mr. Long of S. Wraxall [Raxall] S. Mr. Axford; 1a. bounded S. Mr. Buckler, N. Mr. Axford; 2a. bounded N. Mr. Collier, S. Mr. Samuel Long; 3a. shooting out against Hindon road bounded N. Mr. Buckler, S. Mr. Randall; 1a. this side of Hawkem on the top bounded S. by the cliff [cleave], N. Mr. Hughs: In Hawkem bottom 1a. bounded N. Mr. Buckler, S. Mr. Hinton: In Hawkem 1a. under the cliff bounded S. by the cliff, N. Mr. Randall: Upon Wayton hill 1a. bounded E. Hindon road, W. Mr. Collier; 1a. bounded W. Mr. Buckler, E. Mr. John Long: In Whiteland 2a. bounded S. Mr. Collier, N. Mr. Long of S. Wraxall: In Woodcom 1a. by the turnpike bounded E. Mr. Buckler, W. Mr. Hughs; 1a. in Longland in Woodcom bounded E. Mr. William Randall, W. Mr. Buckler; 2a. same bounded E. Mr. Randall, W. Mr. Halliday; ½a. in Woodcom by Batter'd Half belonging to Mr. Buckler on N., Mr. Randall S.; ½a. in Woodcom by Ripe acre belonging to

Mr. Randall on N., Mr. John Long S.; 1a. in Pit land furlong (in Woodcom) bounded S. Mr. Hinton, N. Mr. Collier; 2a. in the Bottom (in Woodcom) bounded E. Mr. Collier, W. Mr. Bennett; 1a. in the Hole (in Woodcom) bounded E. Mr. Bennett, W. Mr. Buckler; ½a. in Wetland furlong (in Woodcom) bounded N. Mr. Randall, S. Mr. Buckler: 2a. upon Sand hill bounded E. Mr. Buckler, W. Mr. Randall: 2a. at Dimmicks lane bounded W. Mr. Buckler, E. a hedge: 1a. at Lays lane enclosed with a thorn hedge on W. belonging to Mr. Hinton and E. belonging to the parsonage: ½a. in Lays bounded E. Mr. Hinton, W. Mr. Buckler: ½a. in Slade bottom bounded N. Mr. Randall, S. Mr. Buckler: ½a. in Hither N. field bounded E. Mr. Randall, W. Mr. Samuel Long: 3a. at Marshes corner bounded N. by the road, S. Mr. Buckler.

There are 12 beast leaze, 1 horse leaze and 140 sheep leaze. On the enclosed pasture are 40 elm saplings, 12 large chestnut trees, 12 young ones lately planted. In the churchyard are 5 old elm pollards, 1 young elm sapling and 4 lately planted.

3. The minister has great and small tithes of the parish.

4. There are 2a. of water meadow and 1a. 1r. of arable land belonging to the church. There is no pension or stipend payable out of the living.

5. This is answered by the last question.

6. There are 2 surplices, a velvet cushion for the pulpit, a large linen cloth for the communion table and a small one, a pewter chalice, a silver cup and cover, 2 prayer books, a bible and 6 bells.

7. There is no money in stock for the repair of the church.

8. The minister keeps the chancel in repair and the parish the other part of the church. The S. and E. side of the churchyard are repaired by the parish the N. side by Walter Long of N. Wraxall and the W. side partly by William Buckler and partly by the minister.

9. The clerks wages are 40s. p. a. paid out of the church rates and he is appointed by the minister.

B[rouncker] Thring, minister, Stephen Long, Samuel Long, churchwardens, John Long, Richard Randall, Stephen Best, inhabitants.

SWINDON vicarage

737   1 Jun 1588 (D1/24/200/1)
Touching the inquisition given us in charge to consider of between the vicarage and parsonage there.

We present the parsonage there is an impropriation and has belonging to it all the tithes of corn and hay, and also a yardland, the tithe of which is due to the vicarage. The vicarage has a yardland belonging to it, and all other tithes, corn and hay excepted, and as to this day they are in that manner quietly enjoyed, so to our uttermost knowledge they have been time out of mind all other things we present to be good and fair.

James Lord [X], Thomas Spencer, churchwardens, William Stichall, John Hethe, Thomas Heathe [X], Henry Cuffe [X], John Stychall [X], Roger Ewyn [X], John Smythe [X], William West [X], William Dyer [X], Thomas Eyres [X], Henry Farmer [X].

738   13 Oct 1608 (D1/24/200/2)

1 yardland with appurtenances as other yardlands usually have in the same tithing with the free tithe of the same yardlands and the tithe of 1 yardland belonging to the parsonage and occupied by John Barnald. The parson has tithe hay and corn except from the farm of Mr. Martyn in the tithing of Eastcott the most part of the tithe is withheld under right 'now gotten' from the Crown. Mr.Vilet, parson of Swindon, claims tithe hay and corn from that farm. Mr. Kendall, vicar of Swindon, claims tithe lamb, wool and all privy tithes from that farm if the tithes hay and corn are due to the parson.

All other tithes due to the vicar in kind unless they bargain or compound for them save only the farm of Broome, the tithe hay for which the parson has in kind. If there should be any corn tithe the parson ought to have it or no we refer that to the trial by the law. We do not know the tithe of lamb or wool from Broome farm to be paid in kind but there is in the parish a book of prescription which shows it has been paid in kind unto the vicar of Swindon, Walter Stichall yeo., then being farmer of the vicarage. We know and find by certificates made into this court out of this parish that the farmers and occupiers of that farm and the vicars been have compounded and agreed sometimes for more and sometimes for less as they could agree concerning the tithe of that farm.

Miles Kendall, vicar, William Stichall, Robert Tuckye, churchwardens.

Endorsement: In Exchequer Thomas Smith, D. D. plaintiff v. Ambrose Goddard esq. William Bay senior 1 Oct. 1777.[1]

1. For papers in this case see WSRO 1461/1131.

739   17 Oct 1671 (D1/24/200/3)

A meadow and a pasture field, *c.* 20a., in Nether Swindon marsh. 3r. 24p. of meadow ground in Mr. Martyn's meadow in the tithing of Eastcott allotted by a decreee in Chancery in lieu of a beast leaze belonging to the vicar. The vicarage house with a kitchen and woodhouse near adjoining and a garden on W. side and another on E. side with a paddock *c.* ½a. and a dove house there.

A composition[1] of £20 p. a. to be paid to the vicar of Swindon by Thomas Goddard esq. for the tithes of his manor of Nether Swindon. The whole tithing of Walcot is tithable in kind, £5 p. a. according to an ancient composition to be paid to the vicar for the tithe of Broome farm.

W. Swindon fields are tithable for sheep, wool and lamb. W. Swindon closes are titheable in kind. Okus [Okess] farm titheable in kind. Mandown consisting of 18 beast leazes paying 8d. p. a. for every beast leaze to the vicar. Siddown consisting 88 [4 score and 8] beast leazes pays 4d. p. a. for every beast leaze to the vicar.

The tithing of Eastcott is all titheable in kind except so much which is called farm land whereof as yet we could never have a just account.

Henry Thomson, vicar, John Hughes, Thomas Mill, churchwardens, John Smith, Thomas Heath, sidesmen.

1. For a copy of this composition following an enclosure agreement in Lower Swindon in 1650 see WSRO 1461/620.

739A   n. d. mid 17th cent.[1] (WSRO 1461/1329)

In arable: In the Lower field 1a. and 1a. 1yd.; 1a. in the field called Tismead; 1yd. upon Berry hill; ½a. upon Louse hill; ½a. over Broome path; 1yd. near Oxenlease; ½a. at Thomas heath Close end; ½a. at the old quarry; ½a. by Windmillelme; 1 head yd. and ½a. by the Park; ½a. shooting upon Newhams; ½a. in the Middle furlong shooting upon Brind's lease.

In grass which is steane mead: 1a. 1yd. in Newhams; 5 lugs in the Lot mead that is 1a. 1yd.; ½a. in Smale mead; ½a. in Tismead.

In grass which is laines: 1a. in Walcot laines; ½a. in Rodbus; ½a. of laines towards Coate high upon Whettington; 1yd. of laines shooting upon the bush above Floodwel.

Tithe of the parsonage yardlands, both of corn and hay and tithe of 4 beast leases in the Marsh. Lastly the vicarage has 4 beast leases and 30 sheep leases in the Town field.

1. This document is endorsed 'Mr. Gallimore's schedule' which probably refers to William Gallimore who was vicar from 1623 and who was party to an agreement to enclose land In Lower Swindon in 1650 (WSRO 1461/62).

740   30 Dec 1704 (D1/24/200/4)

Between19 and 20a. of lay land valued at £15 p. a. The vicarage house and garden. Value of the tithes p. a.: East Cot and Westcourt £15 3s. 3d.; Nether Swindon, £20; Broome farm £5; Walcot £12 5s.; Siddown and Mandown £3 1s. 10d.; tithe wool £1 10s.; about the town some closes 13s. 6d. Total p. a. £71 13s. 7d.

John Neate, vicar, Richard Yoke, Christopher Herring, churchwardens.

741   25 Jul 1783 (D1/24/200/5)

The vicarage house is built chiefly of stone with some brickwork and is covered with slate. It has 2 underground cellars and a small vault, a ground floor and upper storey. The ground floor consists of a kitchen and pantry adjoining, each floored with stone, 2 parlours floored with boards, the larger with deal, the smaller with ash. The larger is wainscotted more than chair-high and thence papered to the ceiling which, with the ceilings of all the other rooms in the house, is common plaster whitewashed. Over the cellars are 2 rooms, a servants room and a pantry with separate passage to it, all floored with ashen boards. Up a pair of stairs are 4 bed chambers, 2 closets and a very convenient study. Adjoining to the kitchen is a brewhouse, 14ft. by 10ft., covered with slate, to which adjoins a coal house covered with tile. In the orchard of c. ¼a., bounded N. by a common road, E. by Mr. Goddard's yard and stables, S. the vicarage garden, W. Mr. Vilet's yard and garden, is a stable of 3 stalls, a pigeon house and a woodhouse, all covered with tile. On E. side of the house is a garden 84yd. by 21yd. 2ft., on W. side is another garden bounded on S. and W. by a common causeway, N. by Mr. Vilett's garden, E. the vicarage house; its breadth from the parlour side to the W. wall is 15½yd. by 24yd. 1ft.

The glebe consists chiefly of 2 meadows adjoining to each other. The larger is 15a. 2r. 18p., the smaller is nearly 5a. The larger is bounded E. and N. and W.

sides by Mr. Goddard's property, on S. side which is 345yd. 1 ft., is bounded for 275yds. 1ft. by the smaller of the vicarage meadows and the remaining 75yd. by Mr. Goddard's property. The smaller meadow is bounded E. S. and W. by Mr. Goddard's property, N. by the larger meadow of the vicarage.

Vicarial tithes are due from the parish in general. Broome farm is covered by a modus and pays only £5 p. a. 8 ox gangs of land, formerly the property of the priory of Southwick, Hants., are in the opinion of Mr. (now chief Baron) Skynner exempt from the tithes to the vicar. Mr. Goddard and predecessors have for a number of years paid £20 p. a. for the estate called Lower Town: but whether this estate is or not duly exempt from any further payment or tithe has not been determined by any legal decision.

The churchyard limit, determined by a trial at the Assizes, from the land mark stone inscribed P. G. at the distance of 4yd. 18 in. from Mr. Goddard's wall running on the W. side to the S. wall is 60yd. 2ft. and from the land mark stone on E. side of the churchyard inscribed P. G. at 3yd. 18in. from the house wall is 51yd. 1ft. The measure of the churchyard from E. to W. wall is 56yd. The walls terminating Mr. Goddard's property are repaired by Mr. Goddard, the other walls by the parish. In the churchyard are 11 elms and 1 elm in the smaller meadow of the vicarage and no other trees on any part of the glebe.

The church has a handsome pulpit with a crimson velvet cloth and cushion and the chancel a decent green cloth to the communion table there are 3 pieces of plate for the communion service: viz. a paten weighing 13oz 1 dwt. the gift of Mr. Day; a flagon marked 47 and a cup marked 19. 10. Both having this inscription 'The gift of Mrs. Millicent Neate, daughter of the Rev. Mr. John Neate' (the Flagon) 'late minister of this church 1738'.

Books belonging to the church, a bible, and common prayer book for the use of the vicar and clerk and the Book of Homilies.

In the tower are 6 bells. The following estates left for the repair of the church: An estate in Upper Stratton (in Stratton St. Margaret) let to William Adams at £5 19s. p. a.; a cow common let to Ambrose Goddard esq. 8s. p. a.; a house in Newport St., Swindon let to Samuel Webb at £2. 5s. p. a.; a ground in Swindon let at £9 p. a., total £17 12s., money at interest £100; interest paid 30 Mar 1783 £4 10s.: Total £122. 2s. Writings concerning these are kept in the church box under 3 locks and keys.

The clerk (upon a vacancy is nominated by the vicar), receives wages from the parish £2 12s. p. a., customary payments at Easter and fees for marriages and for opening graves for burial.

Thomas Smyth, vicar, William Kemble, Richard Farmer, churchwardens.

TEFFONT EVIAS rectory

742   19 May [. . .] late 16th cent. (D1/24/201/1)
Taken by Leonard Androwes, Thomas Strowd, Thomas Bownd and Henry Dave.

A close called Copped Bush close or New close, 6a.; a close called Prest Croft, 5a.; Twenty acres close, 3a.; ½a. in the common mead. Commons of pasture in common mead and in the common fields for 7 rother beasts, for 2 horses, 1 bull and 60 sheep. Every second year 1 plot in Fovant mead with common of pasture for 4 rother beasts the same year containing 1/8a. Arable land: In South field 10a. of linchet [lanchett] land; 7a. of linchet land in the W. field; in the Mill field and Hold Copts furlong 5½a. of lanchet land.

743   17 Sep 1608 (D1/24/201/2)
The Home close, 1a.; the close called Prestcrate, 5a.; New close alias Coppid Bush close, 6a.; Twenty acres close, 3a.; ½a. in the common meadow. In the S. field in the piece called Twenty acres a piece of arable, 9a.; 1a. by Crafte stile; 1a. in Wooldinge furlong. In Sonde field 4a. by Coppid Bush close. In Holt Copes field 1a. 3yd. In the Quarr field at Whatlye Gap, 3a.; 2a. by Linkhorn Bushes; in the same field Picked acre, 1a.; in the same field 1a. lying next the way.

Gabriel Estgatt, rector, John Jarvis, Henry Bownd [X], churchwardens, Henry Andrews [X], John Pitman [X].

744   n. d. early 17th cent.[1] (D1/24/201/3)
A parsonage mansion house, a garden, backside, curtilage, barn, stable and kitchen. 5 several closes which the parson has or maintains with hedges or ditches. c. ¼a. in the common mead and 3 beast leazes. Tithe of a piece of meadow called Gauntes Ham[2] lying on the other side of the great river [Nadder], the lands of William Ley parcel of the manor of Teffont. The profit or share of 1 year every other of a plot of c. ¼a. of meadow adjoining the last; John Pittman, tenant of William Ley, having the other year. The year the parson has that share of grass he has 4 beast leazes in Fovant mead which William Ley, tenant of Fovant and, so John Pitman, hath the like common of pasture when he has the share of the meadow.

Gabriel Esgat, rector, William Thurley, Richard Trewland, churchwardens, Henry Androwes [X], Henry Bownd [X], sidesmen.

1. Gabriel Eastgate was rector 1604–1638; William Ley died in 1624.
2. In Sutton Mandeville, see **729**.

745   19 May 1705 (D1/24/201/4)
The parsonage house, barn, stable, orchard garden and paddock adjoining, 1a. 51 lugs. A ground called Priest Craught, 6a. 37 lugs. A ground caled Five acres adjoining on E. side to a ground called Longfield or Combs ground, 6¼a. 15 lugs. A ground called Eight acres, the lower end of it adjoining a ground called Pater Noster, the upper end adjoining to the lane that goes to the freestone quarry, 9 ¼a. 31 lugs. A ground called Little Twenty acres, the lower corner to E. adjoins the Great Twenty acres, 2¼a. 15 lugs. A little plot of meadow in Fovant common mead which belongs to the parsonage and another living, the parsonage has it one year and the living the next and so alternately mown by the rector and the owner of that living. There was a plot of 60 lugs called a Half which lay in the common mead alias Broad mead and 3 or 4 cow leazes after the breaking it at Lammas day [1 Aug] for feeding which was exchanged for a plot of meadow in Fovant common meadow and 10 beast leazes. The tithe of ½a. of meadow in

Sutton Mandeville meadow. The parishioners pay 8d. a cow and 3d. for every lamb and all other things that are titheable they pay in kind as they arise.

Thomas Mills, rector, Richard Dominicke, churchwardens, Edward Davys, Henry Goodfellow, overseers.

746   28 Jul 1783 (D1/24/201/5)
The parsonage house is 69ft. by 21ft. built with stone and covered with thatch; it consists of a small entrance with a stone floor walls and ceiling plastered, 2 parlours with oak floors, one papered on the sides the other wainscotted with oak both with plastered ceilings; a kitchen with stone floor, the sides plastered the ceiling not; a brewhouse, the ceiling plastered the sides not; a cellar even with the other rooms with a brick floor the sides and ceiling not plastered.

A stable 41ft. by 20ft. with 2 divisions, stone walls on the sides and partly stone walls and timber and boards at each end, covered with thatch. A barn 37ft. by 21ft., the ground pinning stone, timber and boards above and covered with thatch. A small carthouse adjoining, one side and end upon posts and boarded and covered with thatch. The yard, c. 20 lugs of ground; the fences around it are the barn, stable and stone walls maintained by the rector. The garden, c. ¼a., the house on one side a dead hedge on the other and quick hedges at each end maintained by the rector. A paddock above, ½a., adjoining, the garden on one side a dead hedge on the other, a quick hedge at one end and a woody bank at the other, all maintained by the rector. An enclosed field called Great Twenty acres, 9a. with c. 80 lugs of quick hedge belonging to it. An enclosed field called Little Twenty acres, 2½a. with c. 40 lugs of quick hedge. An enclosed field of 8a. with c. 50 lugs of quick hedge. An enclosed field of 5a. with 100 lugs of quick hedge. An enclosed field called Priest Croft, 4½a., and ½a. of woodland with c. 60 lugs of quick hedge. The rest of the quick hedges are maintained by the lord of the manor or his tenants.

The churchyard is c. ¼a., exclusive of the site of the church, with a yew tree on it. The wall next to the street is maintained by the parish, the remainder of the fence is maintained by the lord of the manor or his tenants who rent the farm.

There are growing on the glebe lands 60 young trees most of them elm and some oak which do not measure a foot round, except 2 or 3 which are a little larger.

All kinds of tithe are due to the minister. The furniture of the chancel consists of a silver wine quart flagon washed with gold, a silver half pint chalice with a high foot and a silver salver with a plate on it about 7in. over dated 1693. A linen cloth covering for the communion table and a napkin to cover the sacred elements in good condition.

The furniture of the church; a surplice, a bible and common prayer book, a pulpit cloth, and cushion in tolerable condition and 3 bells. No books left or belonging to the church. The minister maintains the chancel. The clerk is also Sexton and his wages 20s. p. a. payable out of the church rate.

John Bedwell, rector, James Evans, curate, Henry Macey, churchwarden, Henry Goodfellow, John Goodfellow, George Macey, Henry Macey junior, Harry Larkam, James Leaver, James Targett, substantial inhabitants.

TIDCOMBE rectory (747-8) and curacy (749)

747   nd. late 16th cent. (D1/24/202/1)
50a. arable with the commons belonging to it for 60 sheep and 7 horses or beasts.

Thomas Sier, John Tamage, churchwardens. *Names in the same hand*

748   n. d. late 17th cent.[1] (D1/24/202/2)
13a. in the E. field: 8a. in the N. fields; 10a. 1yd. in the W. field; 2a. in Fosbury field; a mead adjoining to the parsonage barn. Commons in the downs and fields for 4 beasts and 60 sheep.

Edmund Holford, curate, Edward Marten, Thomas Norris, churchwardens, William Rumsey, Thomas Plott, Edward Randall, Thomas Fidler. *Names of the curate and churchwarden in the same hand*

1.   Edmund Holford was curate between 1660-1689.

749   nd. late [1704x1705][1] (D1/24/202/3)
Nothing is found withheld from the curacy. A stipend of £38 p. a. is paid to the curate by the dean and canons of Windsor.

William Meaden, curate, William Rumsey, William Livlocke, churchwardens.

1.   The churchwardens were recorded in the bishop's visitation book, Oct 1705 (WSRO D1/50/6).

NORTH TIDWORTH rectory

750   22 Feb 1672 (D1/24/203/1)
A dwelling house containing divers rooms, a pigeon house, a lesser barn containing 5 bays, a larger barn containing 5 bays likewise, a stable under the same roof being 1 bay of the same building, a barn yard, a rick yard and garden ground the whole homestall containing in all ¾a. and 20p. Herbage of the churchyard. 4 field a in Mr. Maton's field below the hill; viz. 2 in his N. field, 1 in his S. field, 1 in his Middle field, the W. part of Mr. Maton in the late times of trouble enclosed as part of a new made meadow but allowed and set forth to the rector as much of the farm land on E. part of the last a. as he took from him in the W. part.

In the fields of Tidworth Moyls as follows in the E. part of the E. field, 3a. and in the W. part of the same field, 2a. and a short headland called a Yard. In the S. field, 5a. In the W. field a piece called Three halves and 3 other distinct a. whereof 1 lies on W. side of Quarr hill. In all the said fields immediately after harvest each year there pertains to the rector common for all the rectors or his tenants' pigs or for 2 horses and for 2 cows and also common in the summer fields and downs for the said 2 cows when the farmer shall put his own cows in the said fields and downs. Also common for the said 2 horses on the lay banks or summer fields if the farmer shall feed any horse of his own before the harvest.

Common for 60 dry sheep during the whole year on all the fields and downs of Tidworth Moyles the farmer first breaking the downs or fields.

By ancient custom for garden herbs growing in any garden in the parish 1d.; for every calf killed by the first owner the left shoulder and for every other calf not amounting to a tithe the tenth of the worth or price; for the milk of every milk cow or heiffer, 1½d.; the tithe corn, hay, wool and lamb and all other things titheable in any place in the parish excepting a portion of tithes appertaining to Winchester cathedral in the name of which portion of tithes all manner of tithes arising from a certain farm in the E. end of the parish in the occupation of Mr. Walter Pouse are reserved for some years past from the rectory. But upon our inquiry we are credibly informed by such as do remember that all the tithes of that farm were received by the rector except the tithes of a parcell of land called the Piks, 3a.; of a long headland so called, 2a.; a piece of poor land upon Ravens hill, c. 10 field a.; and 2 fleeces of the tithe wool all which were part of the said portion of tithes. But the greater part of the portion was payable out of the farmlands of Tidworth Zouch [Souch] sometimes called Bery farm; namely the tithe of 400 sheep, the tithe of Bush Mead and the N. part of the common mead from the lower end of ?Denmead upwards; also tithe out of that part of Windmill field which lies directly from the said lower end of ?Denmead and to Collingbourne down and is bounded E. by the common mead; also tithe out of Short furlong in the N. E. corner of the said Windmill field adjoining to the highway eastwards and to Collingbourne down N.; tithe out of a piece of land in the Middle field lying between Parston and Tides way and the highway which crosses the said Elderway; tithe out of a lesser parcel of land at [. . .]; tithe out of that part of the S. field which lies directly S. from the great [. . .] parcells of land no tenants lands lay intermixed. But it is not remembered that Winchester cathedral or its tenants did receive the portion of tithe in kind but that the rector of the parish [. . .] received the portion. In consideration thereof he paid the yearly sum of £6 [. . .] to Winchester cathedral or its tenants but that Mr. Sherrill sometimes tenant to Winchester cathedral for the portion contended with Mr. Vaughan, then rector of the parish, [. . .] the rector holding and paying for it as aforesaid.

Edward Northey [*rector*], Robert Butler, churchwarden.

751   4 Aug 1783 (D1/24/203/2)
Rev. Thomas Fountaine rector. The dwelling house containing a hall, kitchen, brewhouse and buttery floored with bricks, 2 parlours wainscotted and floored with boards, a cellar, a small pantry with boarded floor, 5 chambers ceiled, a barn containing 5 bays, a stable under the same roof containing 1 bay of the same building, another stable built with stone containing 4 stalls, a coachhouse and woodhouse adjoining the same a small court on N. side of the dwelling house and a small court at the S. side of the house, a backside and garden fenced partly by a wall and partly by a hedge, the whole homestall containing 3r. 20p. The herbage of the churchyard.

In Mr. Hughes farm fields are 4 field a. viz. 2 in the Upper croft, 1 in his Middle croft and 1 in his Lower croft. *Land in the fields of Tidworth Moyles and rights of common as* **750**.

Tithes as **750**.[1] The portion due to Winchester cathedral is described as arising from part of a farm in the E. end of the parish occupied by Mr. Thomas Northeast[2] and part of the farm owned by Mr. Hughes in the Park field[3] which parcels are bounded and staked out distinctly from the other lands.

Henry White, curate, Robert Amor, Thomas Northeast, churchwardens, Edward Poore, John Cooper.

1. A suvey of the tithes made in 1790 describes the land as c. 1a. of arable dispersed in late Matons farm lying in Picked Pit field, Middle Croft and Upper Croft and 12a. dispersed in the land of Tidwoth Moyles farm lying in the Twenty acres, N. Piece, S. Piece, Upper Piece, Home field, S. field and N. field (WSRO 2159/24).
2. Called N. Tidworth farm in 1790 (WSRO 2159/24).
3. Called late Matons farm in 1790 (WSRO 2159/24).

TILSHEAD vicarage

752　　n. d. late 16th cent. (D1/24/204/1)
A house of 3 fields of building thatched. A barn of 2 fields and a cut which is thatched also. A little croft, garden and barton containing 1a.

753　　n. d. early 17th cent.[1] (D1/24/204/2)
A dwelling house, and a stable and backside, ½a. All other tithes corn only excepted. The churchyard, ½a.

Henry Moore, vicar, William Coxe, Humphrey Coxe.

1. Henry Moore was vicar between 1598 and 1623.

754　　17 Dec 1677 (D1/24/204/3)
As **753** but also *mentioning oblations offerings and mortuaries.* Anthony Delacourt, vicar, Ambrose Naish, Humphrey George.

TISBURY vicarage

755　　n. d. late 16th cent. (D1/24/205/1)[1]
The parsonage was sometime belonging to the abbey of Shaftesbury and since the suppression of abbeys passed into the king's hands and after that to the dean and chapter of Bristol who have demised and granted it to Sir Mathew Arundell. All such rights duties and tithes appertaining to the rectory have been yielded and paid to the vicarage.

Touching the register book of christenings marriages and burials the same is contained and kept under [. . .] .

Endorsement: In the Exchequer between Thomas Prevost clerk,[2] complainant and John Benett, Joseph Trim and Joseph Day, defendants this paper writing was shown to Edward Davies gent., witness 1 Oct. 1812.

1.   As the document is illegible in parts and rather verbose, it has been summarised.
2.   Thomas Prevost was the vicar of Tisbury.

756   n.d. early 17th cent.[1] (D1/24/205/2)
A dwelling house of divers rooms in the same, a kitchen and bakehouse, a barn and stable under 1 roof. A little close hedged in several with an orchard and garden adjoining being 1¼a. The churchyard and all the trees growing lawfully to be used by the vicar for the time being.

Vicars of old and time out of mind lawfully usually received for their due portions of living and maintenance all oblations due to the church as in wax money and other things. Also mortuaries of all the parishioners when they die although they be (sic) tenants of the church or person of the same. Also tithe of hemp and flax growing in gardens and other places which are dug [digged] by feet of men or have been used to be dug. All tithes in money which rises of odd lambs being of the number of 6 or under, for every such lamb ½d. All tithe of geese, pigs, calves, colts, mills, dovehouses, eggs, roots and herbs growing in gardens as onions [vunions], garlick, beans, peas and hops. Tithe of gains and wages which artificers of the parish receive for their labours and arts. Tithe of all woods and coppices[2] titheable throughout the parish except such as grow upon the lord's demesne or lands of the parsonage. Tithe of bees and honey throughout the parish except the lord's demesne and the parson's tenants. There are moreover belonging to the vicar the tithes of certain small closes and garden plots as they call them as well meadows as arable, mainly 2 little plots in a meadow in the tenure of Alice Combe wid., a piece of mead called Church mead in the tenure of Leonard Farnell, a piece of mead called Bishop's mead in the tenure of Edward Cotten, a little plot in a mead in the tenure of John Fezard, a little plot in the mead by Kebells well in the tenure of Lawrence Fezard, a little mead in the tenure of John Abbot near his tenement all in the village of [Tisbury].[3] Tithe of a little plot in the tenure of William Michell alias Thresher in the hamlet of Haselden. Tithe of a small close called Chapel close in the tenure of Thomas Grey; of a little plot [...] close of Margaret Scammell wid. and of another plot of meadow now in the tenure of the said Margaret; of a plot of arable ground in the tenure of John Rose adjoining to his orchard; of 3 plots of meadow in the tenure of Edward Fryker called Upper mead, Nether mead and Upper House; of 2 plots of ground in the tenure of William Trubridge alias Wyks joining to his house; of a little plot in the tenure of John Oborn near his house; of a plot of mead in the tenure of Edward Sanger; of a little plot in the tenure of Thomas Snooke joining to his orchard; of 3 small plots of meadow and arable in the tenure of Thomas Joye, of a little plot of meadow in the tenure of William Grey joining to his garden, of a plot of arable in the tenure of the said William near to the house of John Case; of 2 little plots of meadow in the tenure of John Case; of a little plot of mead in the tenure of Margaret Sanger wid., lying in a mead of the said Margaret called Cutheyes, all these in the village of E. Hatch.

Furthermore besides these old and accustomed tithes there was a new augmentation and increase to the vicars made by Ralph Ergham,[4] bishop of Salisbury, that the vicars should receive in all times to come for ever, over and above the said portions all manner of tithe of corn, hay, lambs and wool coming from the hamlets and villages of Billhay [Bynley], Lynley, W. Hatch and Farnell [Farnhull], and tithe of cheese and cow white and of all fruits of trees in the parish, except that shall arise from the cattle of the lord of the manor and parsonage. There are also excepted generally from the vicars all such things as did sometime appertain to the chantry and chapel of the Blessed Virgin Mary in Tisbury.

John Boles, vicar, Edward Fricker, Henry Fricker [X], churchwardens. *Endorsement as* **755**.

1. These churchwardens signed the bishop's transcript for 1608/9.
2. Wood growing on the waterside called Water wood not excepted as some have claimed added in **757**.
3. Tisbury in **757**.
4. In 1380: see VCH vol. 13, p. 241.

757   5 Jun 1705 (D1/24/205/3)
Terrier given into the bishop's court in Salisbury. *Details of vicarage and churchyard as* **756**. All oblations due to the church. 15s. 4d. for all persons buried in the chancel. *Tithes as* **756** *omitting the wages of labourers*. Tithes of certain small closes or garden plots, meadow and arable: a little plot in the tenure of Edward Carde; tithe of the herbage of Mathew Combe's orchard, 1a.; a little plot of meadow near Kebbles well in the tenure of John Grey, an orchard plot in the tenure of John Feazard; a little plot called Church mead in the tenure of John King[1]; Bishops mead in the tenure of John Cotton;[1] an orchard plot in the tenure of John Cotton near his house; a plot of meadow in the tenure of Albinus Martin gent. or his tenant; all in the village of Tisbury. Tithe of a plot in the tenure of John King, another plot in the tenure of Mrs. Baseley both in the hamlet of Hasledean. Tithe of 2 plots in the tenure of William Turner junior; 2 small plots in the tenure of William Turner, uncle to the last William; a plot in the possession of William Turner senior; 2 plots in the tenure of William Bracher lying near his house; 2 plots in the tenure of John Steevens of Chilmark adjoining to his house; a plot in the tenure of John Scamell called Mappell Close near the tenement he lately bought of John Fricker; 2 plots adjoining to the house of the said John Scamell; a small plot of arable joining to the house of Eleanor Obern[2] wid.; 2 plots in the tenure of Thomas Scammell; a plot in the tenure of William Bracher lying in the mead called Cutheys, all in the village of E. Hatch. Tithe of 2 plots belonging to lord Arundell's farm joining to the house of Nicholas Scamell; 2 plots belonging to William Scamell, one near his own dwelling house, the other joining to the house called Creatures; a plot in the tenure of Anne Dyar wid.; a close and orchard plot in the tenure of William Grey; 2 plots in the tenure of Mary Scammell wid.; a plot in the tenure of Israel Target; a plot belonging to James Lambert, miller, all in the village of Bridzor. Tithe of a little plot belonging to the farmer of Mrs. Mayne[3] of a little [. . .] in the tenure of Francis Haylock adjoining to his orchard; of a piece of mead adjoining to the house of William Parret of Totterdale, all in the tithing of Chicksgrove.[4]

As the final paragraph of **756**. Thomas Marchant, vicar, Richard Doig, William Bracher, churchwardens.
Endorsement as **755**.

1. Occupier not named in **758**.
2. Obourn in **758**.
3. Mr. Mayne in **758**.
4. Chickens Grove in **758**.

758   5 Aug 1783 (D1/24/205/4)
*As **757** with amendments in footnotes.* 6 bells and chimes belong to the church. The communion plate consists of 2 silver flagons, one given by Mathew Davis, the other by Philip Davis; 2 silver salvers without the names of donors; 2 silver chalices, one given by Robert Hyde, the other purchased by the churchwardens. The walls of the churchyard are repaired by the parish. The clerk and sexton's wages are paid by the parish. Each receives £3 p. a.
William Nicholson, vicar, Edward Bracher.
*Endorsement as **755***.

TOCKENHAM [Tockenham Wick in 759-761] rectory

759   12 May 1588 (D1/24/206/1)
A view taken by Thomas Bawdry, George Odye, churchwardens, William Jacobb, John Zely, William Wallop, William Gregory, Humphrey Bocher, John Newenton, Robert Stampford, William Edwards, and Richard Odye.
    A parsonage house containing 3 fields or spaces, a kitchen, containing 2 fields or spaces, a barn, an oxhouse, formed to both containing 5 fields or spaces, a garden court and backside containing in the whole 1a. The churchyard [lytten] on N., highway on E., ½a. A close of pasture ground called the Home [Whom] ground with a ground called the Hook adjoining, the whole containing 8a., the highway W., and S. a field called the Yander field E., a pasture of Thomas Bawdry called Wylkins on N. A pasture ground called Smaleangers, 6a., a field called Padmead S., a pasture ground called Shawood N. and a pasture ground of Isabel ? Soertt E. 2a. of arable land in the W. Lye whereof one lies adjoining to a several ground of William Gregory N., a ½a. of Robert Bocher S., the other a. lies between a ½a. of William Wallop on N. and ½a. of William Edwards S. A plot of arable ground, 4a., in Broadmead furlong between an a. of Robert Bocher W., ½a. of William Edwards E. A plot of arable land in Little mead, 3a., between 1a. of Thomas Gregory W., ½a. William Edwards E.
    In the Yander field, 1a., between ½a. of Meadow ground of William Gregory E., ½a. of Isaac Beysant W., 1 plot of arable in the Yander field above Middlebrook 4a, 1a. of arable of John Walter W., ½a. of John Newenton E. A plot of arable in the Yander field lying at Little mead knap, 2a., between a plot of John Newenton S., land of the demesnes called Home [Whome] piece N. 1a. of arable in W. Tockenham field between land of Henry Bartlett S., land of Thomas Landefer N. 1a. in the same field between land of Henry Bartlett on both sides. Common of pasture in the commons and fields for 2 rother beasts, 1 horse beast and for 30 sheep and the pasturing and feeding for 2 rother beasts in Little Vasterne from 3 May until Michaelmas [29 Sep]. The rector's predecessor did put in certain beasts in W. Tockenham by what title we know not. The

parsons have enjoyed all kinds of tithes within Tockenham Wick according to the custom there.

Sir Edward Bonde and Sir Raphe Wyck, clerks,[1] last parsons, their premises as above specified.

1. Edward Bond was rector between 1546-1570; he was succeeded by Ralph Wycke. The bishop's register recording institutions to benefices is lost for the years 1584-1594. Presumably Wycke left between 1584 and 1588, by the use of the phrase 'last parsons there' to describe Bond and Wycke. Thomas Penidge appears as rector in 1594 and probably was the successor to Wycke. The title Sir is a translation of the latin Dominus, here meaning Father, a title used for Pre-Reformation clerics.

760   19 Sep1662 (D1/24/206/2)

Terrier taken at the visitation of bishop Humphrey. A dwelling house, 2 barns, an orchard, a garden and the churchyard. Parsonage close, 8a., pasture. The Two acres near the last close and late enclosed out of the common field. Smallinges, part arable, part pasture, 10a. 15a. of arable in the common fields. Common for 15 beast and a bull after the breach of the field and feeding for 60 sheep in the common field all the year. All the meres adjoining to any of the glebe land in the common field belong to the parsonage. The feeding of 2 beasts in Little Park in Wootton Bassett.

Theophilous Quintin, rector, Thomas Smyth, Richard Church, church-wardens, Richard Coales [X], John Butcher, sidesmen.

761   30 Oct 1671 (D1/24/206/3)

A parsonage house, an outhouse or woodhouse, newly built on the W. side of the dwelling house. A great barn, a lesser barn with a stable at the N. end of it. A large backside and a churchyard, an orchard and a garden.

A close of pasture containing above 8a. adjoining to the great barn on S. and ascending along the highway on the W. called the Cow lease. A close called the Two acres, c. 2a., on E. side of the Cow lease divided from it by a little lane. A close of arable or pasture called Small acre, 7a., adjoining northward to a great ground called Shaw wood on W. side to a field called Pad mead. A little paddock of meadow belonging and adjoining to the same, c. 2a., abutting on the N. a ground of Richard Pinegar on the E. to a ground of Mr. Smith, and on the S. and W. to the said common field called Pad mead.

1a. of pasture in Little Mead called the Shells adjoining to Middle brook. In several fields 14a. of arable land viz.: in Middlefield, 3a. adjoining to the Lammas way on the W. and to the land of Mr. Smith on E. and on the N. to another parcel of glebe, 5a., which 5a. are bounded W. by the same Lammas way, E. by land of Mr. Say, N. (where c. 1a. of it is meadow or mowing ground) with an enclosed ground called Broad Mead: In the far field beyond Middle brook 4a. abutting eastwards on a parcel of arable called Ship Lands Piece, N. the land of Mr. Wallis, S. on land of Mr. Smith, where there is a broad mere belonging to the said 4a., W. with Middle brook: In the common field called the W. Ley 2a., one northward adjoining to an enclosed ground of Mr. Wallis, the other lying within 2 x ½a. of the same, one belonging to Mr. Wallis the other to Mr. Smith.

Right of pasturage for 2 beasts for the summer feeding in a ground called Little Park belonging to the manor of Vasterne for which is usually paid yearly by the lord or owner to the rector £1 6s. 8d.

Note that wherever the parson has land in the field and a mere or way adjoins thereto the whole mere or way belongs to the parson.

Theophilus Quintin, rector, Charles Freeth, Thomas Smith, churchwardens.

762 31 Mar 1678 (D1/24/206/4)

Terrier returned into the bishop's registry. The dwelling house with an orchard, garden and backside adjoining. A great barn, another large building in which is contained a wheat barn, a hay barn and a stable. A little house called the Mill house and a wood house. A close of pasture adjoining to the dwelling house, 8a., called Cow lease. A close of pasture adjoining to that called Two acres, 2a. An enclosed ground part pasture and part arable called Small acres, 8a. 15a. in the common fields viz.; In the W. Ley 2a. of arable in 2 several parcels. In the Home field, 5a. in one parcel, 3a. in another parcel, 4a. beyond Middle brook; 1a. of pasture called the Shells.

A portion of tithe to the yearly value of £1 6s. 8d. which is paid out of Little Park in Wootton Bassett in lieu of summer feeding for 2 beasts.

Theophilous Quintin, rector, Charles Freeth, Richard Garlicke, churchwardens.

763 1704 (D1/24/206/5)[1]

A dwelling house with an orchard and garden adjoining. 2 barns and a stable, a wood house and a cart house. A ground called the Cow lease, 8a., adjoining to the former. Another ground, 2a., which lies by a ground called the Peak belonging to the farm and which leads to the Cow lease. 1a. in a ground called the Shilles in the form of a triangle that borders upon Little mead between 2 pieces of ground of Mr. William Wallis, the one lying eastwards the other northwards before the enclosure. 4a. in the Further field that heads upon a little stream called Middle brook between 2a., one of Mr. Mathew Smith, the other of Mr. William Watly. 5a. in another field called the Further field which heads upon a ground called Broad mead between Mr. Smith's land on E. and John Reeve's on W. before the enclosures. 3a. in the same field that heads upon a ground called Little mead between Mr. Smith's land on W. and John Reeves on E. before the enclosures. A piece of ground called Smallingrass, c. 9a., that butts upon a ground called Shaw wood and heads upon another ground called Pad mead. 2a. in the W. Lyes the one next the hedge that butts upon Wicks close the other butts upon a piece of ground called Gibbes. 2 x ½a. being in the same between them, the one Mr. Wallis' the other Mr. Smith's before the enclosure. 15 beast leazes in the common fields and 60 sheeps pastures. Right of common in the grounds called the Marsh adjoining to Tockenham Wick. 2 beast leazes in a ground called Little Park in Wootton Bassett in lieu whereof by a long standing composition there is paid yearly and confirmed by the rectory of Tockenham £1 6s. 8d.

Benjamin Barkley rector, Thomas Smith [X] churchwarden, Cornelius Butler, George Skuse, Robert Smith [X].

1. In his return to the bishop's visitation queries, 1783 Algernon Frampton, rector, reported that he would not be able to make a new terrier as he disputes the validity of an enclosure agreement of 1699 as a result of which the value of the living was considerably reduced. (WRS vol. 27 p. 217)

TOLLARD ROYAL rectory

764   1677 (D1/24/207/1)

c. 53½a. of arable lying in the three fields. c. 3a. of meadow adjoining the garden next to the house. A small cottage at the lower end of the street next to the pond. Pasture for 140 sheep belonging to the glebe in the Sheep down. 5 cow leazes in the common of pasture for rother beasts with 4 or 5 horse leazes in the same being linchets [launchets] or breach of the fields.

Samuel Beadle, rector, John Evemy, George Samwaes, churchwardens, William Monday, Thomas Lucas, Francis Newhook.

765   1783 (D1/24/207/2)

The parsonage house is built with brick in front with stone and flint in other parts; it is covered with red tile; it contains on the ground floor a parlour, wainscotted, plastered above, floored with deal, ceiled with plaster; another parlour chair high wainscotted, plastered above, floored with deal, ceiled with plaster; a kitchen floored with brick, the walls and ceiling plastered; a little pantry at the back of the kitchen finished the same as it. On the chamber floor are 4 rooms, the first on the left from the landing place and lighted from the N. is floored with deal, the walls and ceiling plastered, the second room to the left is floored with deal, the walls papered and ceiling plastered; the first on the right hand from the landing place is floored with deal, the walls papered and ceiling plastered; the second room to the right is floored with deal, the walls and ceiling plastered. There are 3 garrets floored and ceiled. There is an outbuilding close to the principal one covered with red tile and divided in 3 parts, the first containing a well and chimney is floored with brick and ceiled against the roof; the second not floored but a little room over it floored and ceiled; the third not floored but a room over floored but not ceiled or plastered. Adjoining to the principal building and outhouse is a little garden walled against the road. The farmyard or curtilage has on E. side next the little garden an open hanging cowhouse covered with thatch and a very little stable enclosed only with hurdle work and also a chicken house; on N. side of the curtilage and ranging along the public road is a barn with a threshing floor in it and is c. 86ft. by 20ft.; on W. side and next the rickyard is a very little barn with a lime and sand threshing floor and between it and the great barn a stable with hay loft over, the whole thatched and joined to the great barn by one angular roof; the curtilage is bounded on S. and S. E. by the quickset hedge of the new garden and the road that leads up to it. Adjoining the curtilage and buildings on W. side of it is the rick yard containing c. ¼a. of ground. All the fences belong to and are repaired by the rector; the fence next the road, a dead fence, that next the meadow, quick and that next the garden, quick. The new garden is situated above the rickyard and contains c. ½a. of ground; all the fences of it belong to and are repaired by the rector and are quick fences; the entrance to this garden is from the road which leads to Tollard Green. The old hanging garden is situated on S. side of the parsonage house on the oppposite side of the road, it contains a little more than ¼a. of ground, all the fences belong to and are repaired by the rector except the fence on E. side which, although there is a quick set hedge for ornament, is a dead hedge and belongs to and is repaired by the occupier of the adjoining hanging ground.

There is a little garden at the bottom of the parish near the pond, c. ¼a. of ground, where, as is reported, formerly stood a cottage; the fences of this garden belong to the rector and are repaired by him except the fence on N. side which is repaired and kept by the occupier of the ground adjoining on N. side. Behind the rick yard and new garden the fences of both which now range in a straight line, is situated the remaining enclosed pasture ground belonging to the parsonage containing c. 4 or 5a., bounded S. by the road leading to Tollard Green and by Ashmore field, W. ground occupied by William Bennet, N. W. by a little meadow belonging to a wing called Newhooks, N. by the public road leading to Shaftesbury, E. by the rickyard and new garden, all the fences belonging to this ground are kept and repaired by the rector except the N. W. fence against the little meadow of Newhooks ground which belongs to and is kept and repaired by the occupier of that ground.

The arable ground belonging to the parsonage is situated in the 3 common fields called Ashmore field, Rushmore field and Middle field: in Ashmore field are 13 different pieces of ground in all nominally said to be 25a., but are only 13 statute a. In Rushmore field are 6 different pieces of ground in nominally said to be 15a. but are 13 statute a. In the Middle field are 7 different pieces of ground in all nominally said to be 12a. but are 10½ statute a.

The rector has and repairs the following fences; the hedge between the 8a. in Ashmore field and Marle, being the S. hedge; also W. and N. hedges and gate of the said 8a. against the down; at the bottom of 1a. on Langdon against the down; also at Gaprishade c. 12 paces abutting against the S. W. part of the enclosed pasture ground of the parsonage; on Tollard Green against the Gunville down; in Middle field against the down so far as 2 of the parsonage pieces come close to the down and no farther; a little piece of hedge at the bottom of Rushmore field in Monday Bottom.

A common right to stock 140 sheep on the several downs common fields and grounds. Right to stock 7 cows on Tollard Green and of browsing [brousting]. Right to stock all sort of stock in the stubble fields as soon as all the corn is carried away and to bait horses on all the linchets and other places where grass grows that is not enclosed.

There are 3 bells in the tower and there is a very ancient little cup and a little modern plate for the communion service. The church, tower and all belonging to them are repaired by the parish. The chancel alone is repaired by the rector. The churchyard fences are made of dead wood and new done as often as needful by the occupier of the Higher field, except the gates which are repaired by the parish. The same person is clerk and sexton and is appointed by the rector but receives no stated wages.

Henry C[*hurley*] Manley rector, Josiah Rabbets, Henry Rogers, church-wardens, George Green, John Green.

TROWBRIDGE rectory

766   25 Nov 1671 (D1/24/208)
In Trowbridge, Studley and Trowle Parva: The chancel of the mother church of Trowbridge which is to be kept in repair by the rector. The parsonage house with the gardens and orchards. A cottage and garden adjoining in the possession of Robert Lansdowne. A tiled barn with a stall at the end of it. A dovehouse and pigsty adjoining. A thatched barn with stable at the end of it. Another pigsty and a henhouse. A cottage and garden occupied by Edward Veale. An adjoining garden occupied by Margery Boide wid. and another adjoining garden occupied by William Martin, all of which are in Adcroft lane and contain ½a.

The churchyard, the bounds of which are to be maintained by the inhabitants whose houses and outlets adjoin it and the 2 gates at the entrances into it by the parish. The 3 Home closes of meadow or pasture, 9a.; the Conygere Paddock ½a. near to the 3 Home closes; the Adcrofts 4 grounds of meadow or pasture, 16a.; the Down-lease, lately enclosed, containing, beside the bounds, 14a., which were lately taken in exchange[1] for commons of pasture (belonging to the Rectory) for 18 beasts and 1 bull in the Down of Trowbridge from Whitsun to Michaelmas [29 Sep]. 10½a. of arable dispersed in the E. field with Meadsplats at the ends of several of them. A close called Budlease at the further end of the W. field (near the lands of Edward Flower), 3 or 4a. The W. mead newly enclosed out of the Meadsplats in the W. field, 3a. Common of pasture without stint in the common fields of Trowbridge and in Ashton and Drineham commons and all the commons of vicarage in the parish.

The tenth cock of all hay within the parish except in two little meads lying between Trowle bridge and Ham mead, one of which belongs to the farm of Trowbridge (lately the estate of Henry Willet), the other to the estate of John Rogers. The tithe of these two meads is, by a certain prescription, paid out of part of that meadow belonging to Rogers which part the Rector is to mow and carry away in lieu of the tithes of the two meads.

The tenth sheaf of all wheat, beans and whatsoever corn is sheafed and the tenth cock of all barley, oats, peas, vetches and all other grain.

For the cow white of every cow summerfed within the parish or by any parishioner in the commons belonging to it, 4d. at Michaelmas.

For all sheep kept within the parish till shearing time the tenth fleece of wool or if less than 10 fleeces the tenth lb. of weight or, if sold off before shearing time, for each sheep 1s. 4d. for each month they have been kept in the parish and so for all sheep taken in as agistments (joystments) to be paid at Lady day [25 Mar]. The tenth of all lambs fallen within the parish to be paid at St. Marks Day [25 Apr]

The tenth of all calves fallen within the parish to be paid at Whitsuntide and in case they be 4 rather than 10 for every calf sold the tenth of the price, if killed by the owner a shoulder of the calf so killed, if weaned 1½ per calf. The rector may choose the calves of 2 or more years together and so take his tenth (which they call driving) and the same in lambs and pigs.

If calves are weaned and kept by the owner until they are to be milked or yoked no tithe is paid for their feeding. If they are sold before they come to be milked or yoked, the tenth of the money which they are sold for is to be paid to the rector.

For every ground fed with unprofitable cattle such as grazing beasts, horses, etc. the tenth of the rent or yearly value of the ground is to be paid in lieu of tithe. If such cattle are put into a ground with others on which tithes are payable, the tenth penny of the cost of the weekly feed is paid. Every man who pays tithes is allowed to keep his market horse tithe-free. Cattle that are only used to plough the land no tithe is to be paid. Cattle kept for carriages on the road are reckoned as unprofitable cattle.

If a ground that is mowed is let after to another person, that person is to pay the tithe of after feeding.

The tenth or seventh pig, the tithe of apples, pears and other fruit, of turkeys, geese. For every hen an egg and for every cock 2 eggs paid at Easter.

The Easter offering of every communicant, 2d. For every garden of herbs 1d. paid at Easter. Larger gardens of peas, beans, etc. and nurseries of fruit to be paid in kind.

For the two mills of Trowbridge, 10s. to be paid at Easter. For every parishioner married, either within or outside the parish, by a licence, 5s., by banns 1s. For every woman at the time of her churching 4d. at least. For the breaking of ground for burial in the chancel 10s. for every funeral sermon 10s. at least and the mourning cloth if any. For every back door which opens into the churchyard, hithertofore granted upon suffrance to some neighbouring inhabitants, 6d. p. a.

In Staverton [Staffordton]: The tithes of this hamlet are paid by ancient composition or custom viz.: For demesnes the greater tithes are not paid to the rector. For lesser tithes the customary payment to the rector is £1 13s. 4d. For tenements 13s. 4d. p. a. out of every half yardland and out of every Mundays hold (which is a ¼ of the yardlands) 3s 8d. p. a. All of which is to be paid quarterly. There are 24 half yardlands and 3 Mundays holds. The annual total is £17.

For the mills 9s. to be paid at Easter. By custom the herbage of the chapel yard belongs to the rector. The bounds of it are to be made good by the owners of the demesnes and others whose lands bound on the chapel yard.

On the N.W. side of Ashton common called Slowgrove are 6 grounds called Polebarne grounds and Singers-grounds in the possession of Joseph Holton, James Singer and Eleanor Singer wid. On the S.W. side of the said common 8 grounds called Footpath-grounds, Blackball grounds and Arnolds Meads now in the possession of the said Joseph Holton, William Slade, Robert Beach senior, Harry Wallis and William Yerbury. By a certain custom or prescription have been paid to the rectors of Trowbridge who have always paid in lieu the annual rent of 4s. to the vicars of Steeple Ashton. This right was recently disputed by the vicar of Steeple Ashton but the rector was able to show the bishop and the vicar that he could prove the custom by witnesses, occupants of the said grounds, for the last 50 years.

Robert Hawkins rector, Robert Witchell, Edward Martyn, churchwardens.

1. Note in margin that this exchange was recorded in the court rolls of the manor of
    Trowbridge, Michaelmas 1671 in **767**. The court roll for 10 Oct 1671 includes a
    letter from Robert Hawkins, rector, to Robert Beach asking him to confirm this
    exchange which was made in 1667 and three other exchanges of land in Meadsplats
    in the W. field held by Thomas Chepman of Studley (2) and Robert Witchell of
    Trowbridge (1). (WSRO 2203/3)

767   18 Dec 1704 (D1/24/208/2)
As *766* with *amendment in footnote*. Robert Keylway rector, William Clarke,
Andrew Willett, churchwardens, Edward Davis jun., Edward Martyn, Samuel
Watton.

TYTHERINGTON chapelry

768   n. d. mid 17th cent.[1] (D5/10/2/13)
In the E. field: 8a. shooting against 1a. of Thomas Ball and John Ball on E. end
and ½ of Mathew Wornell on W. end with linchets on both sides. In E. Hill: 8a.
shooting against Corton field on E. end and against Long Borg on W. end with
linchets on both sides. In Shortborg: 8a. shooting against Long Borg on E. end
and 1a. of Mathew Wornell and Walter Marsh on W. end. In Down hedge: 4a.
shooting against the furlong called Three linchets on E. end and ½a. of the wid.
Bishop on W. end and with lynchets on both sides. In Old Drove: 4a. shooting
against E. old drove on E. end and 3 linchets furlong on W. end and with linchets
on both sides. In Whi[. . .]land: 8a. shooting against Hayfurlong on E. end and
Waterland on W. end with linchets on both sides. In Water land: 4a. shooting
against Wills hedge on E. end and E. Broad on W. end with linchets on both
sides.
    In Chickhedge: 4a. shooting against W. Broad on E. end and 1yd. of Edward
Baylie on W. end, with linchets on both sides.
    Philip Hunton, minister, William Langley, John Chamberlen, churchwardens.

1. Philip Hunton was collated to the prebend of Horningsham and Tytherington in
    1631 and was succeeded in 1686.

UPAVON vicarage

769   n. d. late 16th cent. (D1/24/209/1)
There is no glebe pasture or commons. There is a little house standing on a
piece of ground of ½a. Tithes of wool and lambs and hay are shared with the
impropriate rector. The small tithes belong to the vicarage.
    Edmund Bayley, Jeffrey Tipper, churchwardens. John Seward, Robert Pyke,
Thomas Lacey, sidesmen. *Names in the same hand*

770   1 Apr 1609 (D1/24/209/2)
Terrier of the tithes. All small tithes namely calves, pigs, geese, swans, eggs, fruits
of the orchard and gardens, tithe in money for the milk cows [milch kyne]. All

tithe hay, wool and lambs of and from all copyholders and freeholders except the great farm or manor out of which farm is paid to the vicar a third part of tithes of a flock of sheep going on E. side of the water (i. e. the river Avon). Tithe hay of certain parcels of meadow ground viz. of the Hook lying in Haymead, of a parcel of meadow lying in the mead called Sherford and of a parcel of meadow lying in the lower end of Broad mead, with all the small tithes arising or increasing out of the said farm. Also is paid to the vicar out of the prebend there all tithe wool and lands and tithe hay of certain parcels of ground viz. Whiddich, Long close, 3 little closes lying by the side of Long close, the close called Blarenes, a little piece of ground lying by the house called Amottes and of a piece of meadow ground at the upper end of Mylmeads with all other small tithes arising or increasing out of the prebend. A third part of all tithe wool of Robert Goodale's flock of Chisenbury[1] lying in the parish of Netheravon; he has 360 sheep leazes or commons.

The vicarage house yard and backside with the churchyard.

Thomas Taylor vicar, John Seward, Robert Bessem [X], churchwardens, Richard Seward, Thomas Oram.

1. W. Chisenbury in Netheravon see **772**.

771   31 May 1614 (D1/24/209/3)
Terrier of the lands. 4½a. now in the occupation of Maurice Jarvis demised by lease by the parishioners, of which land 1a. lies in Beggers Bushfield in Shefford fulong shooting E. and W. between the land of Jeffery Tipper on S. side and Leonard Oram on N. side; 1½a. in Sleafield shooting E. and W. between 2 linchets, Jeffery Tipper's land on S. side and Leonard Oram's land on N. 1a. lies upon Slea hill shooting N. and S., land of Eleanor Button wid. on both sides. 1a. in Loose-come field shooting E. and W. and lies on N. side of 3a. of Eleanor Button wid.

½ yardland in the use of John Staynar or his assigns for which ½ yardland he has and does yearly pay to the churchwardens of Upavon 9s. rent and 2s. for the chief rent. But how the occupier holds the same that is not well known neither is any of the land known except Church close. A plot of ground at the S. end of Docke mead in the occupation of Eleanor Button wid. or her assigns for which she pays yearly to the church 3s., but it is esteemed a great deal more worth.

Thomas Taylor, vicar, Jeffery Tipper [X], William Bayly, churchwardens, James Pyle [X].

772   1671 (D1/24/209/4)
A dwelling house with a small backside and garden worth £1 10s. Tithe of orchards, gardens, dove houses, turkeys, geese and eggs worth £1 10s. Tithe of hay, wool and lamb of all the tenants, as they are called, and also the sum of all freeholders gave those excepted following worth £10; all tithe hay, wool and lamb of Buttons farm worth £3. Tithe wool and lamb of Bacons farm[1] and tithe hay of 2 closes lying under Barly hill, of a close lying by the Horn field, of a hook [hoocke] of meadow at Mill mead called Peirces mead and of a hook of meadow at Hay mead worth £3 10s; all tithe hay, wool and lamb of the Priory. Tithe hay of 2 closes lying beside the Ham field, of a close next to White hedge

and of White hedge mead and of a hook of meadow at Mill mead, worth £3 15s. Tithe corn and hay of Long close being formerly all of it meadow, worth 10s.; tithe corn of ½a. of ground next to Mill mead that was formerly meadow belonging to Benger's living, worth 1s. 6d.; a third part of tithe wool and lamb of the lady Hungerford's farm, tithe hay of Kings close, a plot of mead at Broad mead, a plot of meadow next the waterside at Hay mead, a plot of meadow at Sheffords mead and of all the meadow hereto belonging at Mill mead only a little hook next to the flood gates excepted, worth £1 10s.; tithe hay of a hook of meadow at Hay mead and 2 distinct portions of meadow at Shefford in Upavon but belonging to Herds farm at W. Chisenbury [2] and likewise a third of the tithe wool of the same farm.

Richard Wyatt, minister, Andrew Biffen, Henry Long, churchwardens.

1.   Batons farm in **773**.
2.   In Netheravon.

773   1704 (D1/24/209/5)
*As **772** with amendment in footnote.* John Shorthose, vicar, John Oram, Robert Tarlton, churchwardens, Roger Bonner, John Green, sidesmen, Thomas Oram [X].

UPTON LOVELL rectory

774   n. d. early 17th cent.[1] (D1/24/210/1)
2a. in Upper Newton on E. side of Robert Hillman's 2a.; ½a. in the same furlong on E. side of wid. Mogge's a.; ½a. in the same field shooting upon Longdole. ½a. in Lower Newton on W. side of Hillman's a.; 1a. in the same field on E. side of Imber's yd. 3a. shooting upon Hillman's backside; 1a. shooting upon William Hayward's backside; ½a. lying upon N. side of Mr. Reelye's half in Minford field; ½a. W. side of Hillman's 3 x ½a. in Marsh furlong.; 1a. in the same furlong on E. side of Richard Millard's a.; ½a. in the same furlong on W. side of Mr. Reeleye's ½a.; 1a. in the same furlong on W. side of Mr. Reeleye's ½a.; 1a. in the same furlong on W. side of Sparye's a.; ½a. shooting upon Smale way; 1a. in Pitt furlong on W. side of Richard Millard's a.; 2a. in the same field linched out on both sides.

2 x ½a. in Culverland field shooting on each other; ½a. in the same field shooting upon the highway; ½a. in the same field shooting upon the highway lying on E. side of Hillmans ½a.; 1yd. in the same field shooting upon the same way; 1a. in the same field on W. side of Robert Stevens' a.; 3a. shooting upon Robert Stevens' barn.; ½a. in the same field on W. side of wid. Slye's ½a.

1a. in the West Field called Bellalinch acre; ½a. in Short linch on E. side of Mr. Hillman's 2a.; 1a. in Short linch on W. side of Robert Stevens' a.; 1a. in East Hedway shooting upon the green hedge; 3a. upon the brow of the hill on W. side of wid. Mogge's ½a.; 1a. on the hill shooting upon the Green way; 1a. in the bottom on E. side of Andrewe's ½a.; 1a. in the bottom lying in the same furlong. 1a. upon Bageburrowe; 1a. in the bottom on S. side of William Hayward's ½a.; ½ head a. in the same field.

1a. in the Hole in the Little field. 1yd. in the garden between 2 linchets; ½a. of meadow in Langdole; 2 x ½a. in Nether mead; 2 lugs in W. mead.; 1a. called Startle mead. Pasture for 120 sheep. Cow leaze for 6 kine and 1 bull. 5 fields of dwelling house. 9 fields of barn room and a field of stable room. ½a. of ground about the house with the gardens and orchard. 2 gelding leazes.

John Gordon, rector, James Manninge, minister, William Gilbert [X], Richard Moore [X], old churchwardens, Robert Hillman, William Hayward [X], new churchwardens.

1. John Gordon was rector between 1608–1619

775 8 Jan 1672 (D1/24/210/2)

A dwelling house of 4 bays with a porch on the E. side. A greater barn of 5 bays with a porch on the E. side. A lesser barn of 4 bays with a porch on the N. side and a stable adjoining of 2 rooms. The garden, barton and close adjoining to the houses.

Arable lands: 1a. in Baggberry lands of John Hodder clerk S. side, Humphrey Newman clerk N. side; ½a. in the same field being a headland, Humphrey Newman E.; 1a. in the Bottom the land of John Moody on both sides; 1a. in the same field land of Mrs. Mary Realy wid. E., John Stephens gent. W; 1a. in the same Bottom, John Holder clerk E. side, Mathew Best W. In Culforlands 3a. together shooting on the town having a linch on N.; ½a. abutting on the last 3a., John Moodie on W., Humphrey Newman clerk on E.; 1a butting against the highway, John Stephens gent E., Thomas Mogg W.; 1yd. Humphrey Newman clerk W., John Jackman E.; ½a. in the same furlong John Hodder clerk W., Abraham Langley E.; ½a. over there, John Hodder clerk E., Mrs. Mary Really W.; ½a. in that furlong, Mrs. Mary Really on both sides; ½a. shooting upon Smale way, John Hodder clerk W., John Jackman E.; 1a. in the furlong called E. Headway John Hodder clerk S., John Stephens gent. W.; 1yd. in the Yeardens, Timothy Farley W., John Godward E.; 1a. in Little field William Blake W., Richard Gilbrid E.

In the Marsh field 1a. in the furlong shooting towards the town Humphrey Newman clerk S., Christopher Turner N.; 3a. together in the same furlong Mary Really N., John Stephens gent. S.; ½a. in the furlong upon Marshedge John Hodder clerk E., Timothy Farly W.; 1a. in the same furlong William Blake on both sides; ½a. shooting against Mineford John Hodder clerk N., Mrs. Mary Really S.; ½a. shooting against Marshedge Richard Powell W., Timothy Farley E.; 1a. butting on Marshedge John Moodie E., Abraham Langley W.; ½a. shooting on Smale way John Moodie W., Mrs. Mary Really E.; 2a. together in Upper Newton John Hodder clerk W., Thomas Mogg E.; ½a. in the same furlong Thomas Mogg W., Timothy Farly E.; ½a. in the same field John Stephens gent. N., Timothy Farly S.; 1a. in Lower Newton bounded with a linch W. and a hedge E.; ½a. John Hodder clerk E., John Godward W.; 3a. together in Pit furlong abutting on the highway bounded with a linch on both sides; 1a. in the furlong on Smale way John Moodie W., John Ettyly E.; 1a. in Short Lynch William Blake W., John Stephens gent. E.; ½a. in the same furlong John Hodder clerk W., Thomas Parker E.

1a. in W. field lying on a linch Mathew Best N.; 3a. together on the brow (brough) of W. hill William Blake W., Thomas Mogg E.; ½a. on W. hill, Humphrey Newman N., Timothy Farly S.

½a. of meadow in Longgold John Stephens gent. E., Richard Pachine W.; ½a. in Nether mead, Mrs. Mary Really W., John Moodie E.; ½a. in the same mead. John Ittyly N., Catherine Ember S.; 1yd. in the same mead Mathew Best N., John Moodie S.; a little plot of ground in the same mead Thomas Mogg N., Christopher Turner S.; Startle mead wholely by estimation ½a. adjoining to Buckles Mead.

All these several parcels of arable and meadow land are to be measured for length and breadth with the land of other men lying next unto them, except where they are bounded by some ancient linchet or mere stone. The tithe of all things tithable in kind save cow white [milk kine] which is a 1d. or 2d. of the parishioners and ½d. for each calf weaned in the parish. Commons and feeding for 120 sheep and for so many horses and rother beasts as other men might keep upon 2 yardlands.

Edmund Sly, rector, William Bishop, Abraham Langly, churchwardens. *Churchwardens' names in the same hand.*

776   8 Jan 1705 (D1/24/210/3)
A mansion house, 2 barns, a stable, garden and orchard and ½a. of pasture adjoining. 35½a. of arable land lying in the common fields. 2½a. of meadow ground lying in the common meads. 120 sheep leazes belonging to the common fields and downs. 10 beast leazes in the commons. Tithe wheat, barley, peas, oats, vetches, lentils [tills] and all other grains. Tithe hay. Tithe lamb, wool and pigs. Easter offerings, cow white 1d., for a calf sold the tenth penny, for a calf killed the left shoulder.

Henry Muselwhit churchwarden, William Barsley, Thomas Mogg, John Moody, inhabitants.

777   n. d. [1783] and 1786[1] (D1/24/210/5-6)
Lands in Maish field: 3a. shooting against Raxworthy's orchard, Clare's 3 x ½a. N. and S.; ½a. shooting E. and W. Clare's ½a. N. and S.; ½a. shooting against Longdole, Barley's ½a. W., Raxworthy's 3 x ½a. E.; 1a. shooting against Maish stile, Miss Lewis or Revd. Brewer E. and W.; 1a. against Maish hedge, Langleys ½a. now Clare's a. W., Clare's a. E.; Long furlong against Small path ½a. Clare's 3a. E. Cumer, now Moody's a., Pit furlong against Small path W.; 1a. shooting against Small path, Miss Lewis or Revd. Brewer's a. E., Clare's a. W.: Pit furlong against turnpike road; 3a. headland, Clare's 2a. E.: Little Field Hole next to Aiston field: 1a. Ralph Dyer E., Miss Lewis or Revd. Brewer's a., Cross field shooting against Small path W.: ½a. Barton's now Robert Moody's ½a. E., Bailey's a. W.; Cross field shooting against Bailey's barn: ½a. Bailey's ½a. E., Clare's a. W.; Cross field shooting against Pound Lane: 3a. headland Edmund Imbers now Revd. Crowch's a. N.; Cross field shooting against Horn Castle;: 1a. lying under Clare's tyning shooting N. and S. Clare's a. E.; Long furlong in Cross field against the turnpike; ½a. Baily's ½a. W. Langely now Clare's ½a. E.: Cross field against turnpike; ½a. Bailys 3 x ½a. W., Clare's ½a. E.

W. field under the turnpike road: 1a. upon a green linch shooting E. and W. Baylys 3a. N. under the turnpike road. Bagbary; 1a. shooting E. and W. Baker's ½a. N., Raxworthy's a. S. 1a. in the same furlong shooting E. and W. Clares a. N., Bayly's a. S.: In the Bottom shooting against Little field; 1a. shooting N. and S. Clare's ½a. W. Bayly's 2a. E.; 1a. in the same furlong shooting N. and S., Clare's a. W. Clare's 2a. E.; 1a. lying N. side of the Bottom shooting N. and S. lying close by Shelf furlong S. Raxworthy's 3 x ½a. E., Bayly's ½a. (sic)E.: In Yarnes so called; 1yd. shooting N. and S., Bayly's yd. W., Raxworthy's ½a. E.: E. Headway: Head ½a. shooting N. and S. Butchers ½a. now Crouch's in Shelf furlong lying E. side of the head ½a.; 1a. in the same furlong shooting E. and W. against the drove at W. end, Clare's 2a. N., Raxworthy's ½a. S.: Short linch against the turnpike road; ½a. shooting against the turnpike road, Raxworthy's 2a. W., Sharp's ½a. now Clares E.; 1a. in the same furlong shooting against the turnpike road Miss Lewis or Rev. Brewer's 3 x ½a. W., Clares a. E.

W. Hill: ½a. shooting against the drove Butcher's ½a. now Crouch's on S., Raxworthys 3 x ½a. N.; 3a. shooting into the quarry W. end of the drove Bayly's outside ½a. E., close against the drove and Miss Lewis or Rev. Brewer's ½a. W.

Pasture land: An enclosed hedge round pasture water meadow called Parsonage Newton, 2½a.; a dry ground lying by the water side between Upton and Knook called Startle mead, ½a.; ½a. lying in the common meadow called W. mead; Butcher's now Crouch's yd. on one side, Miss Lewis or Rev. Brewer's yd. on the other; ½a. lying in the common meadow called Longdole Clare's yd. E., Clare's ½a. W.; 2 x ½a. in the common meadow called Nethermead; ½a. at the upper end where the wagons enter the meadow, Clare's a. called Hatch acre W., Clare's yd. E.; ½a. in the same meadow shooting N. and S. Clare's yd. E., Bayly's ½a. W.

Right of commoning for 12 beasts and 120 sheep.

Parsonage house with a green court before it built with brick and covered with brick tile contains 2 rooms in front, a hall with a stone floor and a parlour with an oaken floor both plastered. Above stairs 2 rooms in front and 2 garretts. A back kitchen behind and a pantry and a cellar, a study and 2 small lodging rooms over. A court before the house with an orchard at the left side. 2 thatched barns in the yard and a court house. A rickyard. A stable and a woodhouse joining to one of the barns. Another small house formerly called a school house. Behind the house is a pleasure garden mudwalled around and near it a kitchen garden with a small paddock joining and hedged round.

The fences around the churchyard are kept in repair in proportion to the several estates in the parish. 35 horse chestnut trees and a yew tree in the churchyard. The clerk's wages £1 10s. p. a. paid by the churchwardens at Easter and appointed by the minister at the same time. The furniture of the church is a scarlet pulpit cloth and cushion, a scarlet cloth to cover the reading desk, a green cloth to cover the communion table, a black cloth to cover the corpse and a surplice and 4 bells. Communion plate is a silver paten, and a silver chalice with an inscription 'Upton Lovell Five Pounds was given towards this cup by Sarah Benson Anno 84'. No inscription on the paten.

John Crowch rector, George Ingram, John Bayly, churchwardens, John Raxworthy, John Patient, churchwardens, John Dyer, Charles Gamblin [X], Richard Mogg, William Dyer.

1. The terrier is in 2 parts, the first section, witnessed by the rector the first two
churchwardens is dated 1786, and covers enclosed glebe land and meadow; the
second, a repeat of the meadow land with beast leazes, parsonage house, church and
churchyard, was witnessed by Mogg and Dyer and the second pair of churchwardens
who appeared as the new churchwardens at the bishops primary visitation, Jul 1783
(D1/50/30).

UPTON SCUDAMORE rectory

778   n. d. late 16th cent. (D1/24/211/1)
The orchard and backside, 1a. A parrock of 1yd. A close called Chappel at
Thurlstone [Throlson], 3a. <4a. 1yd.>. 2a. on Beare hill. 1½a. on Henford mead,
2a. in Gassons. 4a. 3yd. in the E. field. 8a. in the S.W. field. 1½a. at One Barrow.
2½a. on the churchway in the S.W. field. Total 2a. 2yd.
　　Christopher Hill, Christopher Cabell, churchwardens, Christopher Daniell,
Robert Greene, sidesmen. *Names in the same hand*

779   25 Sep 1608 (D1/24/211/2)
½a. shooting up to Oddington; 1a. bounding upon Palmersland; 1 head yd.
bounding upon the farmland under Oddington; 1a. in the same field bounding
upon the Chylkhils piece; 3yd. in the same field bounding upon Chylkhils
piece; 1yd. under Sydnams Banks, one end bounding upon the land of Heytesbury
almshouse; ½a. lying under Oddington bounding upon an a. of Thomas Hill;
3yd. upon Holloways land ¹; a single yd. shooting upon Copthorne way; ½a. in
the same furlong shooting towards the same place.; ½a. in the same furlong
bounding upon the land of Heytesbury almshouse; 1a. in Bucks furlong bounding
upon Christopher Greens 2 x ½a.; 1a. shooting upon the 5a. of farm land; ½a.
shooting upon Gallards piece; 1a. in Gallards piece; ½a. shooting up to Spring
bush; 2a. in Waterside; 3yd. headland to Lock furlong; ½a. bounding upon Lock
furlong; 1a. crossing Portway; 3yd. upon Portway; 1yd. shooting upon Portway;
½a. in Crane a.; 2a. in Gaston.
　　In the W. field: 3yd. in Reddfurlong; a single yd. in the same furlong; ½a. by
Church way; ½a. by the Wood way; ½a. shooting upon Broad mead; 1a. by
Hensters mead; ½a. shooting upon Hedgecroft way; ½a. at Hedgecroft headland
to Thomas Hill's 3a.; 1a. upon Beare hill; ½a. joining to the way that goes from
Oldberis elms.
　　Chappell close in Thurlstone [Thoulston], 3a. A little parrock called the
Vicarage, ½a. A close in the backside of the house, 1a. An orchard and garden
contained in the same area. 5 beast leazes upon the common. 80 sheep leazes in
the common fields.
　　Thomas Hill, Christopher Hiscot, churchwardens, Robert Greene, John
Hustis, Christopher Hill. *Names in the same hand*

1. All the land before this described as being in E. field bottom in **781**.

780   14 Feb 1705 (D1/24/211/3)

1a. of pasture joining to the house whereof being of late years turned into an orchard and garden. Vicarage parrock, ½a. Chapel close[1] for layes, 3½a. Arable land in the E. field:[2] ½a., 1a., 1yd. 1a., 1yd., ½a., 3yd., 3 yd.; 2a. in Gasson. Arable land in the W. field: ½a., 1a., ½a., ½a. running out of Hedgecroft way; 1a. running out upon Hensters mead. In other fields: ½a. running out upon Broad mead; ½a. lying by Wood way; ½a. lying in Short furlong; 3yd. lying in Red furlong; 1yd. lying in the same furlong; ½a. lying by Bristol cross; 1yd. running out upon Portway; 3yd. running athwart Portway; ½a. going from New close hedge across Portway; ½a. running out upon Portway piece;[3] 3yd. lying in a furlong called Waterside; 2a. lying in the same furlong; ½a. running out upon Springer's bush; 1a. lying in Galery piece;[4] 1a. lying in Buck's furlong; 1a. leaning towards Whitehouse down way;[5] 1yd. running along the same way.

Richard Barry rector, William Seaman, Giles Green, John Daniell, John Hooper.

1. Chapel hayes in **781**.
2. In E. field bottom in **781**.
3. Porters piece in **781**.
4. ½a. called half and ½ shooting upon Galery piece added in **781**.
5. ½ shooting on White House Down way added in **781**.

781   1 Aug 1786 (D1/24/211/4)

As 780 with amendments in footnotes. This was transcribed from an old terrier written by Lionel Seaman, son of William Seaman who was rector in the reign of King William.[1]

Thomas Owen M.A. rector, Jonathan Pearce, Andrew Pearce, churchwardens.

1. In fact William Seaman was rector between 1628-1681.

URCHFONT vicarage

782   n. d. late 16th cent. (D1/24/212/1)

There is no glebe apart from a close of pasture adjoining the vicarage and 1a. of meadow in Small mead in the hamlet or lordship of Stert. The herbage of the churchyard. The prebend and parsonage are appropriated to the Dean and Canons of Windsor and have 20a. in the common field called Dunfurlong.

William Hoode, Robert Collett, churchwardens, Mr. Robert Noies, Mr. John Titcombe, William Hoode, Robert Edwards, sidesmen. *Names in the same hand*

783   10 Dec 1677 (D1/24/212/2)

The vicarage house consisting of 4 bays which consist of 5 lower rooms and 3 higher rooms. A barn consisting of 4 bays and a small cut at the end which is a stable to contain 2 horses. A garden, 27 lugs. A close of land, 1½a.

Thomas Combes vicar, Robert Noyes, Richard Amor, churchwardens.

784   n. d. [1704x1705][1] (D1/24/212/3)

Terrier of Urchfont and the free chapelry of Stert. For use and feeding the churchyard. A certain proportion or quantity of great tithes arising in the tithing of Urchfont valued c. £40 p. a. for the specialities whereof are found in a former terrier delivered into the venerable court in 1671[2] by Revd. Thomas Annes. Some damage and improverishment to the vicarage has occurred due to the alteration of tenure or employment of the lands on which these tithes arose since then.

Offerings, personal oblations and obventions and small tithes from the tithing viz. gardens, orchards, pigs, calves, cow white, pigeons, mills and whatsoever property comes under the name of small tithes. Small tithes from the tithing of Wedhampton excepting some 10 yardlands as before. Small tithes of Eastcott [Escott] as before.

Stert Chapelry: Great and small tithes belong to the vicarage of Urchfont, as rector of it, except arising from the farm and certain messuages appertaining, to the yearly value c. £20.

Offerings personal from the farm and tithing. Use and feeding of the churchyard. No house barn or stable.

We the churchwardens and inhabitants of both places do of our own especial motion and for ourselves (on behalf of the present incumbent) humbly offer present and declare that the constant and incidental service of the church and chapel in consideration of the distance and passage between them and of his personal bodily infirmity is very laborious difficult and heavy.

John Swallowe vicar and rector, John Pierce, Richard Dowse, church-wardens. Edward Alexander, William Pearce, Robert Crooke, Philip Noyes,[3] John Salmon.[3]

1. The churchwardens were recorded in the bishop's visitation book, Oct 1704. (WSRO D1/50/6)
2. Thomas Arne was rector between 1662-1671. This presumably refers to a lost terrier.
3. Noyes and Salmon signed at the end of the section on Stert and not as the others after the first section suggesting that they were from that chapelry.

WANBOROUGH vicarage

785   12 Jan 1672 (D1/24/213/1)

A mansion house with outhouses, garden and orchards, a small tenement with a garden plot called Lynges house near the churchyard.

Pasture land: 3a. of meadow ground in the E. Nithe shooting upon Marston brook land of Mr. Gooding on both sides; 2a. in the W. Nithe shooting N. and S., Mr. Hodge E., John Blisset W. of 1 of the a., the wid. Plummer E., the wid. Brown W. of the other a.; 1a. in the Swanhill shooting N. and S., John Blissett E., Mr. Chamberlane W.

Arable land: 1a. in the Ham shooting N. and S., John Herring E., John Wake W.; 1a. in the bottom of Ham shooting E. and W., John Blisset and John Smith S., a bayting land N.; 1 throughout ½a. shooting through 2 furlongs (that is 1a.)

Thomas Elton E., Thomas Elton, John Gardiner W.; ½a. more shooting N. and
S., Mr. Gooding E., William Elliott W.; 2a. of Hitching land in the W. field
shooting upon Iccleton way, Mr. Gooding E., John Bond W.; 2a. on Berrycombe
shooting N. and S., Daniel Wells E., Mr. Gooding W.; 1a. below Standlinch in
the W. field, Mr. Brind S, the wid. Plummer N.; 1a. butting up to Ridge way
shooting N. and S., Henry Phillips E., the wid. Plummer W.; 3 x ½a. in Gally hill
shooting N. and S., Mr. Gooding E., Thomas Edwards W.; 1a. butting upon
Thomas Edward his Pickes shooting E. and W., John Wake S., Mr. Gooding N.;
1a. butting upon Butcher way shooting N. and S. Mr. Gooding S., John Gardiner
and Edward Morecocke N. In the E. field: 1½a. shooting E. and W. above Hinton
Marlborough way, Mr. Gooding S., John Blisset N. 1a. athwart Butcher way
shooting E. and W., John Haggard S., Mr. Gooding N.; 1a. shooting on W. laines
shooting E. and W. Mr. Gooding S. the wid Reade N.; 3 x ½a. shooting E. and
W., the wid Baull S., the wid Coventry N.; 2a. shooting upon Middle way E.
and. W., Thomas Elliott S., Henry Phillips N.; 1a. shooting upon W. way, John
Haggard S., John Smith N.; 1 butt a. above Standlinch shooting E. and W., Mr.
Gooding S., the wid Reade N.; 1a. shooting up to Standlinch shooting N. and
S., the wid Reade both sides; ½a. at W. furrow shooting E. and W., Edward
Warman S., Mr. Chamberlayne N.; ½a. in the same furlong Mr. Chamberlayne
S., the wid Reade N.; 1a. shooting on W. way E. and W., Mr. Gooding S., the wid
Reade N.

Pensions, tithes and other yearly profits: A yearly pension of £1 p. a. paid by
the impropriator or rector of the parsonage of Wanborough on Michaelmas day
[29 Sep]. Tithe of all the glebe land of the parsonage. Whole tithe of Earlescourt
farm [1] of William Glanvill esq. now in the possession of William Lancton. Whole
tithe of a close called the Pills on E. side of the furlong shooting on Eldernes
furlong. Whole tithe of 8 closes called the Hides or Hides closes (excepting only
part of a close lying westwards called Cockatrils, c. 3a., which belongs to the
parsonage). Whole tithe of the Hide field on E. side of the town joining to
Hinton field lying between Iccleton way and Ridgeway being c. 1 furlong in
breadth and a mile in length. Whole tithe of 4 x ½a. and a butt on W. side of the
Hides butting at the lower end of the Pills. Tithe of ½a. called Picketts Butts
adjoining the said close called Pills in the occupation of Mr. John Harward.
Tithe of 1a. in Heycroft on E. side of a ground of Mr. Goodings called Ambrose.
Tithe of the said Ambrose. Tithe of 1a. in the Corn marsh called Hooked acre
lying W. side of the Hides. Tithe of 1a. 1yd. called Hemland on W. side of the
Hide closes towards N. end thereof. Tithe of 11a. belonging to the Great Bargain
which also belong to the said Hide field, Mr. Gooding being grand landlord,
lying in the Breach viz. 2a. lying in a place called Puppills, 3 x ½a. shooting E.
and W. upon the Oare, 3 x ½a. lying about the Middle furlong all in the upper
breach, ½a. shooting N. and S. the S. end butting upon the highway, 3 x ½a.
shooting upon Middle hedge, 1a. shooting E. and W. lying by the Brook on N.
end and upon Portway on S. end, 1a. shooting E. and W. lying by the Brook side,
1a. lying E. and W. shooting upon Hinton mead on E. end and Portway on W.
end all in the lower breach. Tithe of a small part of a close lying on S. end of
Earlescourt field in the possession of Mr. John Whipp belonging to Earlescourt
farm. [1] Tithe of a ground called Bidecroft belonging to Warnage [Warnidge]

farm in the possession of Mr. Chamberlayne. Tithe of Ambrose Dockham, Mr.
Gooding being grand landlord, lying near and adjoining the said Bidecroft a
brook only parting the said places. Tithe of the Mill acre belonging to Warnage
farm shooting N. and S. upon Ambrose Dockham. Tithe of the Mill way adjoining
to the Lot mead belonging to Warnage farm. Tithe of all grazing grounds and all
the privy tithes. Tithe of all coppices. Note by William Henry that John Gardner
gave them an account of the glebe.

John Bourne, vicar, Richard Warman, Edward Warman[X], Thomas Brind,
churchwardens. John Brind.

1. In Little Hinton.

786   21 May 1705 (D1/24/213/2)
The vicarage house, garden, orchard, backside, barn, stable, cowhouse, woodhouse,
etc. Another little house and garden near the church. Arable: 2a. at Berry combe;
1a. shooting on Marlborough way; 1a. shooting on Ridgeway; 1a. shooting on
Thomas Edward's Picts; 1a. shooting on Butcherway; 1½a. at Gallow hill; 1a. at
Wet furrow; 1a. shooting on Standich; 3a. shooting on Middle way; 1a. shooting
on W. field; 1½a. above Ridgeway; 1a. shooting on the laynes; 1a. shooting on
the W. field; 1a. shooting over Butcherway; 1½a. shooting on Mr. Phillips's piece;
2a. shooting on Ickleton way; 1a. in the bottom of the Ham; 1a. at Coney-Berry
end; ½a. shooting on Ickleton way.

Meadow: 3a. by Merston brook; 2a. in the W. Nithe; 1a. at Swanhill; 1a. in
the bottom of the Ham; 1a. shooting on Clublane end.

5 W. side leazes at Holy Rood day [14 Sep] 2 more at Lammas [1 Aug] and
60 sheep leazes. All the tithes of the parsonage land with 20s. p. a. augmentation.
All the vicarage land tithe free. All great and small tithes of Eastcourt farm, [1]
Upper and Lower Hide and the Hide field. Tithe of Mr. Elliot's Platt, meadow.
Tithe of the wid. Haggard's Platt, meadow. Tithe of 10a. in the breach called the
Bargainers land. Tithe of the mill 3s. 4d. p. a. Tithe wool; lamb 2d.; honey; hops;
pigs every seventh; for offerings 2d.; for cow white 2d; for a calf 6d.; for a colt
2d.; for a garden 1d.; eggs for a cock 3, for a hen 2.: Tithe apples, pears, plums,
walnuts, etc. Marriage fee 2s. 3d.; churching a women, 6d.; agistment sheep, ¼d.
per month.

Thomas Gray, vicar, Thomas Edwards, Richard Herring, churchwardens.
John Brind, William Goodinge, John Haggard.

1. In Little Hinton.

WARMINSTER vicarage

787   n. d. late 16th cent. (D1/24/214/1)
The first 10 lines are illegible. The parsonage barns and c. 2yd. of ground lying
about [them]. A land in the tithing of Boreham [Borton alias Borame], the
ground about the barn containing about 1yd. 18a. of arable lying in the fields of
Warminster.

788   10 Jun 1609 (D1/24/214/2)
A dwelling house with hovel or stable and a close of 1a. in which they stand, bounded on S. the highway, N. land of Sir Edward Hungerford decd., E. and W. land of Corpus Christi college, Oxford.

All manor of tithes and other duties except corn and hay belong to the vicarage.

George Richardson, vicar, Edmund Pirrie, John Allen [X].

789   27 Sep 1671 (D1/24/214/3)
Terrier exhibited at the visitation of bishop Seth. The vicarage house lies in the W. end of Warminster, containing 5 bays with some small appendices. To which adjoins a garden and parrock, c. ¼a., bounded E. and W. land of Corpus Christi college, Oxford now in the possession of William Slade or his assignes, S. the street, N. land of Lady Hungerford now in the possession of Giles Wright.

Tithe wool and lambs, tithe of the underwood of 6 coppices of Sir Edward Hungerford and 9 coppices of Thomas Thynne esq. in Norridge wood and also of Adlam's coppice Easter dues viz. 2d. by way of offering for every person above 16 years old in the parish; 2d. for each garden in composition for herbs; 2d. from everyone that keeps hens; 2d. in composition for the tithe of the milk of each cow; ½d. for every calf that is weaned; for every calf that is killed by the owner a shoulder; for every calf sold tenth penny of the price. Tithe pigs and geese, apples, pears and other fruit. The herbage of the churchyard. 10s. from everyone that buries any person in the chancel. Mortuaries from them that are chargeable by statute. The seats on the S. side of the chancel. 6s. 8d. per quarter from the rector or vicar of Corsley. Tithe of 100 sheep from the farm of late called Seamans farm in Upton Scudamore because part of the sheep feeding is in Warminster parish. 6d. by way of offering for the churching of every woman. As to the tithe of great parcels of ground occupied by gardeners and the tithe of grounds summerfed by unprofitable cattle the improprietor does at present receive the same though the vicar looks upon himself as wronged thereby.

There is a church house belonging to the parish lying at the S. side of the churchyard and bounded on the other side with the street. It contains 3 fields of building and is at present in good reparation. There belongs to the parish an almshouse seated upon the bridge called the Alms house bridge but not endowed.

Paul Lathom, vicar, Edward Middlecott, William Adlam, churchwardens, Richard Carpenter, sidesman.

790   1 Jan 1705 (D1/24/214/4)
The vicarage house containing 4 rooms on each [of a] floor together with a pump house, stable and coal house with a garden and paddock abutting against a street called W. End on S. and against a water course on N., lands of Corpus Christi college, Oxford in the possession of William Slade gent. on E. and W.

The herbage of the churchyard with profits of burying in the chancel. A pension of 4 nobles[1] p. a. payable by the rector of Corsley. Tithe of 15 coppices called Norridge wood belonging to viscount Weymouth and Green coppice lately adjoining Longleat park but now within it. Tithe of Adlam's coppice.

454 WILTSHIRE GLEBE TERRIERS

Tithe wool, sheep feeding and of lambs at the rate of 3d. a lamb or 2s. 6d. for the tenth one. Cow white at the rate of 2d. a cow, 6d. or the left shoulder for every calf killed or sold. All private gardens, 2d. per garden p. a., all orchards. Poultry 2d. from each inhabitant that keeps them. Tithe pigs, geese and pigeons. Offerings, 2d. a head. A composition tithe for the after grass and winter feeding of Norridge grounds. Mortuaries are also payable according to the statute.

Edward Chubb, vicar, William Slade, William Bleeck, churchwardens.

1. A noble was the equivalent of 6s. 8d. [33p.]

791   25 Jul 1783 (D1/24/214/4)

1. There is a vicarage house built of stone and tiled. It contains 7 rooms upon the first floor, all of which are ceiled, 5 rooms upon the second floor, ceiled, and 2 garrets. The walls are papered except the kitchen, pantry, cellar, china closet and long room which are plastered. There is a large brewhouse and a stable for 5 horses. There is a barn with 2 thrashing floors for wheat and barley and a large shed.

2. The glebe land cannot precisely be ascertained at present. An Act of Parliament[1] was lately passed to give land in lieu of great and small tithes, but the award is not yet made out by the commissioners which being done most of the tithes will be extinct.

3. There is a pension of £1 6s. 8d. p. a. due from the rector or incumbent of Corsley paid at Ladyday [29 Mar]. There has been a pension of 10s. paid by the vicar to the impropriator as specified in the vicar's endowment. Whether this will be continued after the exoneration of lands from tithes seems to be doubtful.

4. There is a velvet cushion and cloth for the pulpit, gold trimmings; 6 bells, a cloth for the communion table; a flagon, 72oz., containing 1 gallon; 2 cups, a pint each, one with the inscription 'Warminster 1750'; the other with the inscription 'John Langley Thomas Potticary churchwardens 1682 Warminster'; 4 dishes or plates one with the inscription 'Warminster 1761'; another 'Warminster 1766'; another 'John Slade Edward Larkham churchwardens Warminster 1779'; and another 'Sacrum Deum et Ecclesie Parochiali de Warminster Donum Edward Chubb J. B. Vic. anno Dom. 1706'; these are all of silver.

5. The parishioners repair the church and churchyard fence. The impropriate rector repairs the N. side of the chancel, the vicar repairs the S.

6. The clerk has no salary. He has Easter dues and fees at weddings. He is appointed by the vicar. The sexton has a salary paid by the churchwardens viz. 40s. p. a. for keeping the church clean. He has a fee at a wedding and is paid for graves and knells. He is appointed by the parishioners.

M[illington] Massey, vicar, Thomas Williams, George Lye, churchwardens.

1. The Warminster and Corsley enclosure award, 1783 settled great and small tithes (WSRO EA 23).

WESTBURY rectory and vicarage

792 12 Apr 1614 (D1/24/215)
Parsonage: One mansion house with adjoining small backside and little garden, 1yd., next to the churchyard. 2 barns, a pigeon house, a hay house and 2 grounds adjoining called Bittames close, 5a. which include a tenement and garden. A little tenement with small backside and little house called the stable. 3 pasture grounds, 26a., called Chaunters lease. Pasture, 6a., called Parsons croft. A tenement occupied by Robert Linche with a barn, orchard, garden, backside and little house all containing 1a.; 2 pasture grounds, 1½a.; 45a. of arable land in the fields with 1a. of laines. A tenement occupied by Jeffrey Whitaker with barn, stable, orchard, garden, backside and other edifices, 1a., with 8½a. of arable land in the fields and 1a. of meadow. A tenement occupied by Edward Wilcox with barn, stable, garden, orchard and backside, ½a.; 1a. of laines and 4a. 1r. in the arable fields. A tenement occupied by Richard Garnesey with little garden measuring 1yd. A tenement occupied by Thomas Reason with small garden measuring 1yd.; 4a. of arable and 1a. of meadow in the common mead occupied by John Reason. A tenement occupied by Robert Kington with barn, stable, orchard, garden, backside and other edifices measuring ½a. with 5½a. of arable in the fields. A tenement occupied by Andrew Painton with barn, orchard, garden and backside ½a. with 4a. of arable in the fields and ½a. of meadow in the common meadow. A tenement in the use of John Moorefoote with barn, garden, orchard and backside with 3 x ½a. of meadow. A tenement in Hawkeridge occupied by William Gawen with barn, garden, orchard and backside with 5a. of meadow adjoining the house; 1a. of meadow and 14½a. in the arable fields. 1 little close of pasture occupied by Goodwife Boutcher, whereunto pertains 28a. of arable in the fields of Bratton and 2a. of meadow in Withie Meads Barrow. 6a. of laines occupied by Thomas Edwards, Richard Edwards and wid. Cutbert.

The vicarage: A mansion house with stable, pigeon house, backside and a little green court between the said mansion and pigeon houses with other edifices measuring 3yd. 1a. of laines by Withie mead. The churchyard, 1a. At Dilton, a house with garden and the chapel yard, 3yd.; 23½a. of arable in the fields of Dilton. At Bratton, a little house with garden and orchard measuring ½a. The ground wherein the chapel stands, ½a.

William Thomson, vicar, Nicholas Amylls, John Greenhill, churchwardens, Rafe Selfe, Thomas Reason [X], Nicholas Pearce [X], Henry Phippe, Hugh Wats, William Gawen, Robert Tucker [X], John Mo[or]fote [X], Nicholas Bugward [X].

WESTPORT with Charlton and Brokenborough vicarage

793 23 Nov 1671 (D1/24/216/1)
Houses and glebe land in the parish of Charlton: An old barn or house which time out of mind has been used only as a barn containing 2 fields of building standing in Barn close.[1] The said Barn close, 2a., and a close called Drylease adjoining Barn close 3a., both on one side of the lane called Perry Green. 2 closes called Hay leases, 8a., on the opposite side of the said lane. 2 closes, 8½ or 9a.,

called Graunden[2] grounds lying between Hicks-hays and the Heath. In the Home field of Charlton: 1a. in Withy mead; 1½a. in Long furlong; ½a. shooting upon Long furlong path; ½a. in Black land; ½a. on thwart of Cricklade way [Creedkladway];[3] and ½a. of Lot mead. In Middle field: 2a. in Shawfords Hill under the wall; 1a. in the same place and another 1a. adjoining this; ¼a. at the Wells; 3a. in a piece of Middle Hill; 1a. in Small Lands; 1½a. upon the hanging of Merce Hill; 1a. under the hedge next to Hankerton field in the Ham; 1a. more on the top of Merce Hill being the third a. from the ground of Mr. Henry Martin; 1a. shooting upon Wallow hedge; 1a. more on top of Merce hill next to Simon Outridge's[4] piece.[5] In the W. field: 1 piece of 3a. under S. Hill wall; 3 x ½a. more in the furlong shooting upon Hill wall; 1a. lying on thwart of Tetbury way beyond the windmill; 2 x ½a. at the windmill; ½a. on thwart of Woodway; 1a. on the other side of Woodway; ½a. shooting along S. Hill path, being the second from the path; ½a. in Slat furlong; ¼a. shooting upon the Park wall; ½a. near the Stone Style bushes; 1a. near the same place, 1a. at the Holy bushes; 1a. more in the same place next to Capt. Web; 1a. adjoining a piece of Mr. Wyke; one two rudged ½a. near the same place; ½a. in Fern furlong.[6] Being in all 3 fields 33½a. 1a. of ground at the Quarries in the Graundon[2]; c. ½a. called the Paddock at the Lype between the grounds of Mr. Kinaston and [. . .] Tuck.

Richard Beswick, vicar of Westport with Charlton and Brokenborough, Henry Martyn, Edward Horrell, churchwardens.

1. The barn is omitted in **794**.
2. Granden in **794**.
3. ½a. in Coves leaze at the gate lying under Mr. Waters hedge added in **794**.
4. Simon Oatridge in **794**.
5. 1 farndell of Lot mead in **794**.
6. 1 farndell under Mr. Tyler's in the mead added in **794**.

794   22 Dec 1704 (D1/24/216/2)
As **793** *with amendments in footnotes.* Richard Beswick vicar, Henry Martyn, Richard Young, churchwardens. Richard Young, Thomas Panting, Thomas Webb, Robert Long.

795   n. d. [1783][1] (D1/24/216/3)
A schedule of parochial lands belonging to the parishes of Westport, Charlton and Brokenborough. Upper Barns close, 3a.; Lower Barns close, 2a.; Great leaze, 7a.; Small leaze, 2a.; Lords leaze, 2½a.; Webbs leaze, 7a.; Hay ground, 5a.; Parsons ground, 8a.; The Parsons Patch near Lipe, ½a.; the Clergymans mere up Cricklade Piece as a wagon road to Barn close. No timber fit to cut, a few young trees, but most pollards in the hedgerows. An unlimited right of common. No vicarial house in any of the parishes.

John Hollinworth, vicar, Richard Young, churchwarden, James Lea, John Stump, William Millard, Michael Shipton.

1. The churchwarden was recorded in the bishop's visitation book, Jul 1783 (WSRO D1/50/30).

WHADDON rectory

796 18 Oct 1608 (D1/24/217/1)
2a. in an orchard and close, a garden, a barton with a dwelling house, a barn, a stable, ox house and a pigscit[1] in good repair. 6a. in a close called the Lane, Mr. Henry Longe W., William Brunker E.; 2a. in a close of Mr. Henry Longe called All Marsh, Mr. Long N., highway S.; 1a. shooting upon All Marsh between John Fennell W., William Brunker E.; 2a. in Mardyland between John Weale S., Gabriel Spender N.; 1a. in the same furlong between Mr. Longe of Whaddon and John Brunker junior; ½a. at Green way between Richard Swayne W., John Brunker senior E.; ½a. at Holeham between John Brunker senior W., the furlong called Buttes E.; 1a. in Ryelands between John Smith of the March [*recte Marsh*] W., Richard Swayne E.; 1a. at Three Thornes between John More E., John Brunker junior W.; 1a. in the same furlong between John Moore and John Brunker senior; 2a. in ?Jellum land between John Brunker E., John Slade W.; 1a. at the Railes, the Sands S., John Moore N.; 1a. shooting upon Long land, John Moore on both sides; 1a. at the Pittes between John Brunker senior E., William Brunker W.; 1a. in Bittom between John Moore N., John Slade S.; 2a. in Aven mead John Fennell E., John Serten W.; 1a. at Whetthill between John Brunker senior S., Mr. Henry Longe N. And so much in the Lower field.

Now those lands in the Higher field: 2a. in Dockwaies Bush furlong between the highway E., John Slade W.; 2a. shooting upon Dockwaies furlong between John Gollage W. and the highway; 1a. at Dockways Bush between the rector of Hilperton E. and the highway; 1a. in the Higher furlong between Mr. Longe E. and the highway; 1a. shooting upon Slades Rails between John Moore E. and John Fennell W.; 1a. in the same furlong between William Selfe and John Brunker senior; 1a. upon the top of the hill in Nayler, John Brunker senior on both sides E. and W.; ½a. in the same furlong between Richard Gravener W., John Brunker E.; 1a. in Hillhedge furlong between the rector of Hilperton S., John Moore N.; ½a. on the top of the hill in the further field between John Brunker junior E., John Serten W.; 2a. at the Pittes between Mr. Edward Longe W., John Smith E.; 1a. in Flexland Mr. Henry Longe on E. and W. sides; ½a. at Moonelight furlong John Moore S., (sic) John Brunker N.; 2a. at the Lower Moonelight furlong between John Selfe E. and Lower Moonlight furlong W.; 2a. in Packamillway furlong between George Smith N., the highway S.; 1a. in Mannixmoor furlong between John Serten E. and John Slade W; 1a. in the same furlong between John Hiscocks W., Thomas Marchaunte E.; 1a. at Lippyeate between John Fennell W. Robert Graunte E.; 1a. in S. field Thomas Smith S., the highway N.

And so much is the glebe and now there are the tithes. Tithe of 1a. of meadow in the Higher field in the furlong called the Heed of Short Buttes occupied by John Moore, Richard Swaine and Gabriel Spender. Tithe of all the Lower field above the High Pack way except that belonging to the rectory of Hilperton and 1a. lying next to the Breach. Tithe of all the meadow belonging to the parish of Whaddon lying in Aven mead. Tithe of all the glebe lying in the Upper field. Tithe of all the Ingrounds enclosed by the hedge compassing Dollmead, Homeground, the Lane, Goares furlong and Allmarsh. Tithe of 1a. of Mr. Henry Longe and another of John Brunker senior in Dollmead corner.

Tithe of a ground called Ilely from Candlemas [1 Nov] till Michaelmas [29 Sep] in the occupation of Mr. Longe and of 1a. of Richard Swayne in Hollbrook field and of all the ground within the river on S. from Ilely bridge to the end of a ground called Innmead together with the mill belonging to Mr. Longe. Tithe of all the In grounds of Paxcroft [Pascroft] belonging to Henry Friar and John Weele on this side of the brook. All sort of tithes 'publique and privie' due out of the livings of these parishioners; Mr. Henry Longe, Richard Swaine, William Brunker, John Brunker senior, John Moore, John Brunker junior, Gabriel Spender, Elizabeth Brine wid. and Henry Friar of Paxcroft.

Thomas Thompson, parson, Gabriel Spender [X], John Moore senior [X], churchwardens.

1.   A dialect form of pigs cot, a pen.

797   23 Feb 1705[1] (D1/24/217/2)
2a. for an orchard, garden, backside and a dwelling house, barn and stable. 6a. in a close called the Laynes, Sir Walter Long E., Thomas Witchall W. 12 lug a. lying in the Lower field in 3 several grounds lying at the end of one another, Sir Walter Long E., Isaac Wiltshear and Sir Walter Long W. In the fields both below and above the elm: 3a. in Dockways furlong John Foot W., Thomas Witchell E.; 1a. at Marlin Pool Thomas Witchell E., the rector of Hilperton W.; 3a. shooting up to Hunts hedge John Merryweather E., the rector of Hilperton W.; 1a. in Mannocks Moor Giles Brown on both sides; 2a. at Lower Moon-light James Smith E., the furlong of Moon-light W.; 1a. at Flaxland, Mary Fryer wid. E., Thomas Steevens senior W.; 3a. at Flaxland, Semington field E., William Alloway W.; 1a. at Flaxland, Semington field E., William Knight W.; 1½a. shooting upon Short butts Thomas Witchell S., Giles Brown N.; ½a. at Upper Moon-light Giles Brown N., Joseph Terrill S.; 2a. at Haywards Cross Thomas Witchell W., Giles Brown E.; 3a. in Pack-mill way furlong James Matravers N., the highway S.

Tithe of 1a. of ground called Therendale acre in a small enclosure lately made belonging to the farm at Pitts adjoining to Hilperton field. Tithe of 1a. in the Water meadow belonging to James Matraver's living. The tithe of 2 several ½a. in the last meadow, the one called Selfs Half and the other Browns Half. There is to be paid by the lord of the manor of Whaddon unto the rector 5 marks p. a., half at Lady day [25 Mar] half at Michaelmas [29 Sep]. The rector is to have going and depasturising of 4 cows from 3 May unto 14 Sep yearly in all those grounds commonly called Court leaze, Oakley leaze and Oat leaze and New mead. There is to be paid by the lord of the manor to the rector £5 11s. p. a. as above in lieu of the tithe of Longlands, Monkwood, the Lower field grounds, belonging to the lord of the manor, the Mill meads and 2a. in Dollmead. Tithe of Swains parrock, Moor close, Buckels and Taunton's home leaze and orchard, of James Slade's orchard and a ground called Gibbes and of Cutters, Terrils and Witchels Home close. Tithe of grounds on W. side of the church and going by the names of the Lower field grounds except those belonging to the lord of the manor for which he pays composition on the Avon mead, the Green ways, the Breaches, the Balls and of the swayth lying on S. side of the highway leading to Staverton. Tithe arising out of the laines, Goore furlongs, the Nine acres and All marshes. Tithe of all the ancient enclosures belonging to Edward Capp and Christopher Gardner of Paxcroft [Pastcroft] on N. side of the brook that parts the common called Sloegrove from those grounds. Tithe of all the ancient glebe land belonging to the rectory of Whaddon lying in the parish of Hilperton.

Benjamin Lewis, rector, Isaac Willsher, churchwarden, Edward Capp, sidesman, Gabriel Spender, Christopher Gardiner [X], Joseph Terrell [X].

1. A survey of the rectory made in 1783 valued the tithes at ?23 15s. 5d. and the glebe, which was rented out, at £69 18s. 5d. including interest of £3 13s. 7d. on a loan by the Queen Anne's Bounty. (WSRO 3228/65)

797A 31 Jul 1783 (669/6)[1]
A parsonage house, c. 50ft by 22ft, with stone walls and covered with stone tiles, consisting of 2 parlours with boarded floors, plastered walls and ceiled; a kitchen and pantry with stone floors, plastered walls and ceiled; 3 chambers with plastered walls and ceiled and 2 garrets. A stable, c. 31ft by 16ft, the walls built with stone and covered straw. A court and gardens bounded with pales and hedges, also an orchard with hedges, containing in the whole together c. 1a.

(1) a piece of arable land called The Four acres, 4a., lying near Haywards cross, against Semington field, having land of lord Rivers on E. side, Edward Eyles esq on W. side, and the lane on N. end. (2) A piece of arable land, c. 32p., lying against Semington field and the road or lane leading from Whaddon through Madling Pit[2] towards Paxcroft on W. side. (3) A piece of arable land called Madling Pit, c. 6a., on W. side of the road leading from Whaddon to wards Paxcroft. (4) A piece of arable land called Little Madling Pit, c. 2½a., lying on lying on E. of Great Madling Pit, Edward Eyles esq N. and E. (5) A piece of arable land, c. 2a., lying in a ground belonging to Mr. Tubb having the field called Great Madling Pit on E. (6) A piece of pasture land called The Little Ground, c. 2a., lying on S. side of the road or lane leading from Whaddon to Hilperton Marsh, James Slade on W. (7) A piece of pasture land called The Twelve acres, c. 12a., Walter Long E. and W. (8) A piece of pasture land called The Six acres, c. 6a., having the same lane to Hilperton Marsh on S. end (9) 2 pieces of pasture land, c. 6a., in the foot road leading from Whaddon to Semington, lord Rivers W., Edmund Lewis E. Nb all these lands are bounded by hedges except nos. 2 and 5. (10) A piece of land lying in W. meadow in the tithing of Semington with a small strip to the same that leads to the river, together c. ¾a.

The great and small tithes. The furniture of the church: 2 bells; a silver cup, plate or stand with the inscription 'This belongs to the Church at Whaddon in Wilts', weight c. 1lb 6oz; a bible, 2 prayer books. The church and churchyard fence is repaired by the parish, the chancel and aisle by Walter Long esq. The clerk is paid [. . .] p. a. and is appointed by the minister.

1. An unsigned copy in the parish records.
2. Marling Pit in a survey of the glebe, 1770 (WSRO 947/958).

WHITEPARISH vicarage

798   n. d. late 16th cent. (D1/24/218/1)
We present that our parsonage is impropriate. It has 4½a. of glebe land and tithe corn, hay, wood, hemp and fruit except the fruit of gardens. Great and privy tithes of Whelpley chapel, except offerings. The parsonage holds half the tithe wool and lamb of St. James chapel;[1] the other half with privy tithes belongs to the vicar. We present that the vicarage has a guillet of land of 1a. with the house standing on it with a little mead plot of 20 lug with the churchyard and 2 little cottages. The vicarage has all the privy tithes, except Whelpley, with wool, lamb, calf, pig, geese, weddings, churchgoings, burials and mortuaries.

1. Probably the chapel at Abbotstone and Titchbourne which was dedicated to St. James. See WAM vol. 10, p. 318.

799   1677 (D1/24/218/2)
Terrier of the church lands for the upholding and repairing of the fabric of the church. White Poyne, 4a., in the possession of Giles Eyre esq., Phillipp's garden and St. Mary ham formerly in the possession of one Freeman. The clerk's house or the buildings lately repaired situate in the green called Hilgroves in the Fursegoe. The church house in the street. Woodwells and Abers formerly in Edmund Fox's possession. A stitch of land in Maplefield. A plot near Titchborne. A parcel of ground not long since in the possession of the wid. Downing. Tristram Lights etc. Recorded in the register book of Whiteparish.[1] Grays Eye given by James Lynch gent. to maintain a free school £9 p. a.
Samuel Stone, vicar, Robert Leach [X], James Barnes [X].

1. This copy gives the date of gift by James Lynch as 1642. It was 'taken out' by Francis Green, vicar, 10 May 1674. (WSRO 830/2)

800   1705 (D1/24/218/3)
The tithe wool, lamb, calves, cow white, offerings, gardens, eggs and carrots. The vicarage house and orchard, garden, churchyard and little mead. Yearly value £30.
Francis Wallace, vicar, Thomas Relph, Henry Rogers, churchwardens.

WILCOT vicarage

801   n. d. early 17th cent.[1] (D1/24/219/1)
A house, little garden and orchard containing about ½a.
By me W[illiam] Palmer, vicar, Thomas Chandler, Michael Church, church-wardens. *Churchwardens names in the same hand*

1. William Palmer was vicar from 1605.

802   1671 (D1/24/219/2)

A vicarage house with an outhouse or stable[1] and a backside and garden, c. ½a. and the churchyard with all customary dues for christenings, marriages and burials. Offerings at Easter of all persons from 16 years old and more [upper]. The small tithes; wool and lambs,[2] geese, pigs, turkeys and eggs, carrots, turnips, vetches [fretch], beans and cabbages, of hops, honey and rabbits. Tithe of many other small things if they are there growing of which all the parishioners pay except the farm of Francis Wroughton esq.[3]

It is reported that the vicarage was worth £50 p. a. before the enclosing of the grounds in Oare [Woer] hill and the enclosing of the grounds of Stowell lying between Draycot and Pewsey. But since it is scarce worth £30 p. a. The parishioners pay no tithe grass, corn to the vicarage nor wood: the wood has been in controvery but they refuse to pay any.[4]

Samuel Greenebury, vicar, James Bowden, John Chandler, churchwardens.

1. A coal and wood house and 2 other outbuildings in **804**.
2. Tithe calf and for tithe white a composition of 1½d. for every cow payable at Lammas [1 Aug] and 1s. for the fall of every calf added in **803**.
3. The exceptions in **803** and **804** are as follows: The estate of Roger and John Gale (Roger Gale in 1677 terrier (see **803**); Henry Reeves in **804**), 2½ yardlands, pay two parts of the tithe wool and lamb to the vicar of Wilcot and the third part to the rector of Huish. The wid. Pontin's estate (Michael Pontin in 1677 terrier (see **803**); John Pontin in **804**), 1½ yardland pays two parts to the rector of Huish and the third part to the vicar of Wilcot. They pay all other small tithes to the vicar of Wilcot. The farm of Francis Wroughton gent (occupied by Mr. William Coles except a part reserved to Mr. Wroughton in **804**), 10 yardlands, refuses to pay any tithe but the vicar has had heretofore £3 p. a. out of the farm whether as a composition for tithes or as a gratuity we know not.
4. The note about tithe wood, omitted in **803** and the 1677 terrier.

803 22 Dec 1704 (D1/24/219/3)

*As **802** with amendments in footnotes.*

This terrier is recorded in an old register[1] and was first made 16 Dec. 1677. But the customs of paying tithes at present is as follows: The inhabitants of Wilcot and Stowel pay 10s. p. a. for each yardland in lieu of all the predial tithes mentioned above and proportionably for a quarter or lesser quantity except Francis Wroughton gent. who pleads an exemption for tithe for his farm. The inhabitants of Oare belonging to this parish pay 14s. p. a. for each yardland in lieu also of their predial tithes and proportionably for a quarter or lesser quantity which is due and payable quarterly. Draycot farm pays all the fore-mentioned dues in kind unless the vicar and possessor otherwise agree. There is likewise due to the vicar 6s. 8d. for every person buried in the church and 20s. for every person buried in the chancel. All which scarce makes the vicarage worth £30 p. a., tenths and visitation fees deducted.

John Astley, vicar, John Deacon, William Brinsdon, churchwardens, Richard Stratton, overseer, Francis Wroughton, Hodges Durnford, John Andrewes.

1. (WSRO 1739/1); amendments to this terrier are noted in footnote to **802**.

804   18 Oct 1785 (D1/24/219/4)

As 802 with amendments in footnotes. There is also belonging to the vicarage an estate in the hamlet of Stert. It cost £400, of which £200 was given by the governors of Queen Ann's bounty and £200 by Francis Wroughton esq. We never saw the title deeds nor do we know what is become of them.

The vicarage house is brick and timber built and wholly thatched except the brewhouse (which is tiled) and consists of 5 rooms on the ground floor, 5 on the second storey, 2 garrets and a cellar. The ground rooms are a kitchen floored partly with board and partly with brick and ceiled, the sides partly plastered and partly boarded; 1 parlour floored with board, papered on the sides and also overhead in order to conceal (as we apprehend) the defects of the ceiling which is uneven; another small parlour floored with board, wainscotted and ceiled; a pantry paved with brick and ceiled, the sides partly plastered and partly boarded and a brewhouse floored with stone neither plastered nor ceiled. The rooms on the second storey are papered and ceiled, the garrets are plastered and ceiled. The cellar is paved with brick and plastered. The outhouses are brick and timber built and thatched. The length of the stable is 15ft. and the breadth 14ft., the length of the wood and coal house (adjoining the stable) is 34ft. by 11ft. The length of the building adjoining to the back part of the dwelling house is 11ft. and the breadth almost 6ft. The length of the other outbuilding 18ft. and breadth 7ft. The stable, wood and coal house, a brick wall and pales are a fence to the garden next the street and a brick wall and quick hedge on E. side. The fence on S. side not belonging to the vicarage is a staked hedge and ditch.

The estate in Stert consists of a dwelling house brick and timber built and thatched, a barn and stable adjoining timber built and thatched and lands which according to a survey that has been made contain 15a. 1r. 34p. are as follows: Enclosed lands: Matcham's orchard, 2r. 16p.; Top's orchard, 1a. 2r. 28p.; meadow heading Mr. Warriner's Long Lands, 1a. 3r. 24p.; a close of withy below the same, 1a.; meadow on N. side of Mr. Warriner's meadow, 1a. 2r. 29p.; meadow below the aforesaid, 1a. 2r. 16p.; meadow below sand ground, 1a. 2r. 1p.; the sand ground (arable), 1a 25p. Total 10a. 3r. 19p. In the common field: Shoot acre, 3r. 6p.; 1a. in Upper furlong W. side of Fry's 7yds., 3r. 2p.; a. W. side of Mr. Warriners picked a., 3r.; 1a. in Lower furlong between Mr. Warriner's a. and 3a., 3r. 7p.; 1a. E. side of laynes, 7yds. 3r. 4p.; 1a. in Upper furlong E. side of Mr. Warriner 3a., 2r. 36p. Total 4a. 2r. 15p.

There are on the estate 31 elms valued at £7 10s.; 4 oaks valued at 14s.; 2 ashes valued at 8s.; besides Pollards and saplings. In the churchyard of Wilcot there are 13 elms valued at £5 besides 4 pollards.

There are belonging to the parish church 3 bells (one of which is cracked), a font and pewter bason, a chest, a bible and common prayer book, a surplice, a pulpit cloth and cushion, a communion table with a green cloth, a linen cloth and a napkin, a pewter flagon, a silver chalice or cup with a cover and a silver paten or plate. On the cup is inscribed 'This Communion Cup and Cover was given by the Parishioners of Wilcot to the Parish Wilcot for ever John Chandler William Pyke churchwardens, 1664'. On the cover is this inscription 'He that eateth my flesh and drinketh my blood hath eternal life. Luke ye 6th verse the 54th.' The paten has no inscription.

The parish is charged with the repair of the church, the impropriator with the repair of the chancel and certain estates and the parish with the repair of the churchyard fence. The clerk who also performs the office of a sexton, is appointed by the minister. His wages, besides his perquisites, are c. £45 p. a. and are paid by the occupiers of the several estates in the parish.

Thomas Markes, vicar, William Coles, Richard Edmonds, churchwardens, Joseph Wild, John Pontin, Roger Stratton, John Hazeland.

WILSFORD AND MANNINGFORD BOHUN vicarage

805   n. d. late 16th cent. (D1/24/220/1)[1]
The vicarage house and orchard adjoining, a garden and backside. A stable with a hay house. 8qtr. corn to be paid out of the parsonage, viz. 3qtr. wheat and 5qtr. of barley. All tithe hay of Wilsford and Manningford Bohun. Tithe wool and lamb and all other privy tithes except that which belong to the parsonage of Dauntsey.[2] Paid out of the mill 7 bushells of corn, 3 bushells of wheat and 4 bushells of malt.

Endorsement: The composition remains in the hands of Mr. Hayward who married with Mrs Teshe[3] who was the vicar's wife of Wilsford.

1. The document is incomplete and this section concerning the vicarage is preceded by a fragment of the end of a section presumably about the parsonage.
2. The rector of Dauntsey acquired the right to certain great and small tithes for part of the Wilsford Dauntsey estate in the late 13th century. (VCH vol. 10, p. 212.)
3. George Tashe was succeeded as vicar on his death in 1582.

806   13 Oct 1705 (D1/24/220/2)
A true terrier in as far forth as we whose names are hereunto subscribed do know or have been credibly informed as follows. A dwelling house, stable and wood house with backside, garden and orchard containing ¾a. and the herbage or agistment of the churchyard.

All the tithes in the two tithings except tithe corn and hay belonging to the impropriator and moiety of the tithe of Lower farm in the possession of Madam Evans widow of George Evans esq. late of Goarly in Hampshire which moiety belongs to the rectory of Dauntsey. The vicar of Wilsford has the tithe of hay on the dry ground of Lower farm namely the two crofts extending from the hedge which joins the common field towards the hill to the orchard of the farm; the croft next to the field being now ploughed up. The tithe of the 2 Hams; of the headlands in Cadbin; of 1a. in North Brook called Dreadaway; of Nethton, when mowed and not sown with corn; the tithe of 2 closes called Downes and Hankes together with the tithe of all clover and other grass sown at any time on any part of Lower farm except such part whereof the tithes belong to the rector of Dauntsey.

We present the tithe of lambs, calves, pigs, geese, turkeys, pigeons, bred upon Lower farm together with tithe of eggs, honey, gardens and orchards on the said farm.

We present the tithe wool due from the occupiers of the said farm to be paid as follows when the sheep are sheared 340 are to be let run freely from the field without any choice or interruption as are due to Dauntsey. The tithe wool of the remainder is due to be paid to the vicar of Wilsford. 8qtr. of corn clean winnowed and fit for use to be paid yearly at proper and convenient times by the impropriator or his tenant to the vicar namely 4qtr. of wheat, 2qtr. of barley, 2qtr. of oats to be measured by the usual and customary measure of the said village.

We present to be paid yearly by the owners or occupiers of the mill in Wilsford now in the possession of Edward Springbatt 4 bushells of good malt, namely 1 bushell each Quarterday and 3 bushells of good wheat namely 1 bushell each at Michaelmas [29 Sep], Christmas and Ladyday [25 Mar]: To be measured as above.

All persons over 16 residing within the 2 tithings to pay 2d. to the vicar at Easter offerings. 2d. for every cow white, 2d. per yardland for eggs, 12d. for the fall of a colt, 6d. for a calf from the two farms at Wilsford and 4d. from the tenants, 8d. for a calf at Manningford together with the tithe of the agistment of sheep and cattle depastured in the two tithings.

Thomas Twining, vicar, Mary Quintin daughter of Mr. Samuel Quintin, above 40yrs vicar of Wilsford, Robert Frith, William Benger, churchwardens, Michael Springbet, Richard Hiller, Richard Greene, William Longcraff, William Frith.

807   23 Jul 1783 (D1/24/220/3)
A vicarage house c. 50ft. by 19ft. The front is partly brick and partly lath and plaster. The back part and sides are composed of timber frames filled up with lath and plaster and the covering throughout is thatch. In it are contained 2 parlours floored with elm the largest has a plastered wall and the small one a deal wainscot. It has likewise a small kitchen pantry and brewhouse. There are 3 bed chambers with plain white plastered walls and elm floors, a little room called the study, a small lumber room and a closet. The ceilings are plain and in good repair. The outhouses are a stable in good repair sufficient for 3 horses and a boarded loft over of proportionable dimensions. Behind the stable is a small woodhouse. There is a court before the house surrounded by a mud wall which together with the garden is c. ½a. The garden is bounded by 40 pollard elms a ditch and a stake fence. The churchyard is bounded by a fence of railing repaired at the parish expense and round it grew 12 pollard elms and 6 pollard ashes.

In the church are 5 bells and the communion plate consists of a small salver with this inscription 'Deo & Ecclesiae de Wilsford Maria Quintin, Sam. olim ejusdem Vic. Fil. DDD 1715'. The cup or chalice is a handsome piece with this inscription 'Wilsford 1733 Thomas Twinning, vicar, Sam. Springbat, Wm. Holloway, churchwardens'. The flagon is pewter. The church is repaired at the expense of the parish and the chancel by Mr. Hayward, the impropriator, of that part of the parish called the Wilsford part. The parish is divided into 2 parts viz. Wilsford and Manningford Bohun; each of which pays tithes to the vicar. In that part called the Wilsford part are contained 49 yardlands all of which pay tithes to the vicar except 9 yardlands which pay tithes to the vicar of Dauntsey.

In Manningford Bohun are 34¼ yardlands, all of which without exception pay tithes to the vicar of Wilsford. The tithes consist of hay and grass of all kinds together with tithe of sheep, lambs, cows, cow white, calves, colts, pigs, poultry, potatoes, apples, fruits and garden stuff of all sorts and whatsoever else is or may be deemed small or vicarial tithes.

There is no glebe land belonging to the vicarage, but the impropriator of Wilsford pays annually to the vicar 2qtr. of oats and the impropriator of Manningford Bohun pays likewise annually to the vicar 2qtr. of wheat, 1 of barley and 1 of oats. The vicar has furthermore a right to all customary dues for christenings, churchings, marriages, burials and offerings at Easter of all persons of 16 years old and upwards. The clerk has besides his other perquisites a customary payment of 4d. p. a. out of every yardland. There is a horse leaze but no cow leaze belonging to the vicar.

Richard Trickey, vicar, John Alexander, John Hayward, churchwardens, William Alexander, overseer.

WILTON rectory

808   1609[1] (D1/24/221/1)
A backside and orchard adjoining the parsonage house, ½a. for which the quit rent is payable to the earl of Pembroke. A backhouse or stable with backside or garden, ¼a., W. an orchard held by John Everleye, E a tenement of Robert Bruer deceased. A plot near the Magdelen, ¼a., E. land of the earl of Pembroke, W. land of John Everleye. A plot, ¼a., W. little ground of John Everleye, N. ground of Mr. Hues, S. a backside or hopyard of John Kengington, E. Water lane. A little plot of ground or orchard, 6r. [roads], W. Water lane, E. a tenement of Mr. William Grey, N. the garden of John Smythe, S. the river. 1a. of meadow in Custom mead called Tythinge acre. A close, ¾a., W. lands of the hospital of St. John, N. and E. the highway. A little ground or hopyard, ½a., W. a tenement belonging to John and Thomas Hayes, E. a tenement of John Hulett. A barn with backside and little hopyard at Bulbridge, ¼a., W. lands of Mr. Redman, E. a hopyard of Mr. Hues, N. the river, S. the highway. 2 closes, 2a., with a pigeon house, W. the highway, E. Green Hayes belonging to the earl of Pembroke, S. lands of Thomas Hayes. A close of pasture, 3a., near Bulbridge Marsh, W. leazes belonging to the earl of Pembroke W., the river N., lands of the earl of Pembroke occupied by John Hortington E. 5a. of arable in the W. field of Bulbridge, S. lands of the earl of Pembroke occupied by Robert <Henry *struck through*> Blaake and Walter Northest, N. ground of Thomas Hayes. 5a. of arable in the Middle field of Bulbridge, E. and W. lands of the earl of Pembroke occupied by Walter Northest. 2a. of arable in the E. field of Bulbridge E. lands of the earl of Pembroke occupied by Robert Blaake, W. lands of the earl of Pembroke occupied by Henry Blaake. Meadow, 3a., in Ditchampton, W. the river, E. Burton Ball, S. lands of the earl of Pembroke occupied by Robert Strugnell, N. Oxen lease belonging to the earl of Pembroke occupied by John Haies.

Terrier of such land as pertains to the Church of St. Mary in Wilton. A little house or tenure with garden, orchard or backside near Little marsh, N. the river,

S. the lands of Thomas Greye, W. land of Christopher Potticary occupied by John Hais.
Robert Parker, rector, Christopher Bells [X], William Phillips [X].

1. A survey of the manor of Washerne in 1567 notes that tithes due to the rector and vicar of Bulbridge before the dissolution of Wilton abbey which appear to have been lost by 1609. *The First Pembroke Survey*, ed. C R Straton, vol. 1 pp. 17-18 (Roxburghe Club 1909).

WILTON: Netherhampton vicarage

809   n. d. early 17th cent.[1] (D1/24/221/2)
A vicarage house with an orchard and garden, ½a. on W. side thereof lies the house of William Smyth, on E. side thereof lies the ground of Judith Randall. A general ground enclosed called the Marsh, 1a., E. Henry Randall's ground, W. Roger Shropsheer's ground. In the W. field 1a. of arable land, N. William Smyth, S. Margaret Ovell; ½a. of arable land, W. Margaret Ovell, E. Goldwale. In the Middle field, 1a. of arable land, S. Maud Lyght, N. Sibel Thring; ½a. of arable land, S. Roger Shropsheer, N. Sibel Thring. In the E. field 2a.; ½a. W. Roger Shropsheer, E. Edmund Woodward; ½a. of arable W. Thomas Hankock E. Elizabeth Smyth; ½a. of arable land S. Margaret Ovell N. John Randall; ½a. of arable land E. Edmund Hibberd, W. John Randall senior.
     All other duties belonging to the vicarage amount to £13 4s. The vicarage house with backside, garden and the Marsh Close and 20 sheep leaze amount to 46s. 8d. Total £15 10s. 8d.
     Robert Parker, rector, William Smith [X], Steven Sharlock [X], Henry Randall [X], Steven Bacon [X], Steven Randall.

1. Robert Parker was rector of Wilton between 1593-1611.

810   1671 (D1/24/221/3)
There is but only a vicarage house, 1½a. of pasture ground, 5a. of arable ground in the fields and 20 sheep leazes in the common fields let for £4 p. a. The parish duly pays the minister £13 4s. p. a. Total £17 4s.
     John Merriott, Jacob Pasmor, churchwardens. *Names in the same hand*

WINGFIELD rectory

811   29 May 1588 (D1/24/222/1)
The parsonage house and garden and 6a. of meadow adjoining. 2a. of pasture in W. field. 2a. of pasture in Sheep mead. 9½a. of arable in Stovards field. 7a. of arable in Westwood field. 4½a. of pasture in the common mead. Total 31a. All the tithes. Feeding in the common for a mare and a colt.
     John Smethe, William Wydden, churchwardens, Christopher Nott, John Notte, sidesmen with others of the parish.

812   18 Jun 1608 (D1/24/222/2)

Terrier taken according to the Canon.[1] The grounds lying in the S. and S. E. side of the parsonage house and adjoining to the same with the orchard, garden, the barton or backside, 8a. bounding on the E. side the lane or drove of John Baylie gent., W. side upon a ground of the same John Baylie called Doollemead with a parrock called Germans, N. the common; Marshcraft, an arable ground, 4a., lately enclosed lying in Stoofford field, N. highway, S. a ground of Thomas Crooke and a ground of Alice Clemante wid.; Ponbury close, an arable ground, 2a., enclosed in the W. field, W. a ground of Robert Baylie gent., E. a ground belonging to Stooford. A plot of ground called the W. field in the W. field not enclosed, E. the end of the lane, W. the ground of Robert Baylie gent.; 2a. in Sheepmead, W. a ground of Christopher Morrisse, E. a ground of Toby Horton gent.; 1a. of pasture lying in Vellease enclosed in the ground of Edward Rundell mill carpenter, E. the wid. Pypp, W. Edward Rundell; Stoones acre, 1a. of arable, in Vellease lying enclosed within a ground of William Walters yeo. E. Thomas Reed, vicar of Bradford, W. the ground of William Walters; a meadow ground lying in the Moor, 3yd., S. ground belonging to St. Margaret's almshouse, Bradford, N. ground of Thomas Crooke of Wingfield; 3yd. of meadow in the Moor Grype, S. a ground of Edward Rundell, N. a ground of Richard Busey of Pomeroy [Ponbury]; Moor Grounds, 3a., lying in the new enclosed grounds of Henry Long of Southwick gent. in Stofords field; WholeLands <S. ?Lynes Piece *struck through*>, 1½a., an arable ground in Stofords field, and a ground in the same furlong, 3yd., both shooting westwards upon Goormead ditch and ½a. called the Headland, E. the hedge of Henry Long of Southwick gent., W. the land's end; a short butt lying next the highway and the same furlong, 1yd.; an arable ground, 3yds., lying in Freshfords moor, S. the [. . .]licke arable land of Alice Clemante wid., N. land of Toby Horton of Iford gent. An arable ground butting Westwood field near the moor gate, 2a., with the ground or short butt within the moor hedge, N. William Seele [Seeld], S. John Notte; 3yd. of ground in the same furlong with the end of the same, N. John Nott, S. Thomas Reade, vicar of Bradford; 1a. of meadow in Wheatmores bottom, N. William Seele, S. John Howell and shooting upon the highway; 3yd. of ground in Westwood field lying next the ground of the said Thomas Reade on W. and next the ground of William Walters E.; a ground in the same furlong W. William Walters, E. land John Nott next the upper end and Richard Redman of Westwood, next to the lower end; a land of arable in the same field but the upper end is mead N. John Renald, S. Toby Horton of Iford gent.

1.   87th canon in **813-815**.

813   13 Dec 1671 (D1/24/222/3)

The parsonage house, the barn and the stable, 2 gardens, ¼a. An orchard, ¼a. The chancel. The churchyard, ½a. The Home grounds, 6½a.; a ground called Lipeate, 4a.; W. close, 2a.[1] In Stoford field[2] a little arable land, ¼a. arable, shooting against Slow hedge[1]; ½a. near Slow hedge; 1½a. and ¾a. arable shooting on this side the gutter. In Lower Slowe 1a. of pasture ground lying in the uppermost furlong shooting against the lower hedge. In Sheepmead, 2a. of meadow ground lying

next the gate. In Westwood field, 1a. of meadow in Wetmead bottom shooting at
the highway; ¾a. of arable land in the middle of the field;[1] 2 arable lands,
containing 3yd. a piece, one lying on the upper side and the other on the lower
side of the farmer of Rowleys 25a.;[1] 3yd. of arable land shooting at Crooke
mead;[1] ½a. and 1a. of arable shooting against the way near the moor. In the
moor 1yd. and 1a. of arable near the hedge dividing the moor and Westwood
field; 3yd. of meadow in the middle of the Moore near the willows. In Vellease
1a. of pasture ground shooting against Vellease lane; 1a. of pasture adjoining on
the one side to Walter's Vellease and on the other to the vicar of Bradford. In
Trowle mead ditch 3yd. of meadow lying next the hither hedge. In W. field a
little parcell of arable pasture ground, almost ¼a., lying on the uppermost part
of W. close.[1]

Edward Cornelius, rector, John Baylie, John Mathews, churchwardens.

1. Omitted in **814** and **815**.
2. Land in Stoford described as pasture in **815** in the following amounts ½a., 1½a.,
   1½a.

814   20 Dec 1672 (D1/24/222/4)
*As **813** with amendments in footnotes.* 2a. of pasture ground in Trowle mead
ditch lying next the hedge dividing the Moor and Trowle mead ditch. 2a. of
pasture ground lying next Blacklease hedge the hedge parting it and shooting
against the lane against Westmead bottom. A little parcel of pasture ground, ¼.a.,
next the highway near Black lease and Howells ground against the highway and
against Westmead bottom.

Edward Cornelius, rector, John Baylie, Joseph Barnard, William Seele, Henry
Noble, John Tily senior, churchwardens and sidesmen. Confirmed by Edward
Lowe, chancellor [*of the diocese*], saving the right of bishop Seth and his suc-
cessors.

815   17 Oct 1704 (D1/24/222/5)
*As **814** with amendments in footnotes to **813**.* Robert Hyett, rector, Benjamin
Cooke, churchwarden, John Baylie, John Seele [Seeld], sidesmen.

816   4 Jan 1811 (768/2)[1]
The grounds fronting the parsonage house to the S. E., 6a. The garden, old
orchard, cow barton, etc. The paddock now a kitchen garden, 1a. The ground
called Lypeats on S. side of the road leading from the common to Stowford, 5a.
Inner Sheep mead, 2a., now occupied by Isaac Moore. The ground called Trowle
Mead ditch on E. side of the road leading to Bradford, 6a. 1a. of land in Vellease
lane. 4a. intermixed in the estate of Henry Shrapnel esq. Certain lands mentioned
in an old terrier of which the pariculars are not at present ascertained. Be it
therefore remembered that these lands as described above as glebe lands are no
part of the estate purchased by me of the executors of the late Mr. John Wadman.

Edward Spencer, rector, Thomas Spencer.

1. This terrier is written in a parish register.

WINTERBOURNE BASSETT rectory

817 19 Sep1662 (D1/24/223/1)
A dwelling house, a barn, an orchard, a garden and a close adjoining, ½a. The churchyard. 2 pasture grounds by the W. field lying both together, 13a. In the common fields 29a. of arable land. Pasture for 40 sheep in the common field. Robert Hopkins, Tarrant Reeves,[1] Ralph Ady [X].

1. The names are disfigured by ink blots and are not very legible. Tarrant Reeves was surmised with the assistance of an indexed transcript of the parish register by Wiltshire Family History Society.

818 1671 (D1/24/223/2)
c. 11a. of pasture grounds E. Edward Brunsdon his land, W. Thomas Shepherd's. c1½a. of pasture ground adjoining to the churchyard S. John Reeves. Arable land: In the S. field or the field next the town: 1½a. of land near the hill shooting upon Lamborne way E. and W. William Davis; 1yd. in the same furlong E. John Marsh, W. William Davis; ½a. in the same furlong E. William Davis, W. John Marsh; ½a. in the same furlong Thomas Shepard's land on both sides; ½a. in the same furlong E. Thomas Shepard, W. John Marsh; 2½a. in the same furlong E. William Davis, W. Edward Brunsdon; 1a. in the same furlong part of it belonging to Longland E. John Marsh, W. Thomas Shepard; ½a. in Longland furlong E. William Davis, W. Thomas Shepard; 1a. in the same furlong E. Edward Brunsdon, W. William Davis; 1yd. in the Short furlong E. John Marsh, W. Harepath furlong; 3yd. upon Harepath furlong, Thomas Shepard on both sides; ½a. shooting upon Harepath furlong N. John Marsh, S. Thomas Shepard; ½a. in the same furlong N. Edward Brunsdon, S. John Marsh; 1a. in the same furlong N. Edward Brunsdon, S. Lamborne way.
In the N. field: 1a. in Wet yards E. Thomas Shepard, W. John Marsh; 1a. at Nettle hill, N. William Davis, S. Edward Brunsdon; ½a. adjoining to a hedge that parts the fields E. John Marsh.; 1a. that shoots upon Harepath N. the farm, S. William Davis; 1a. 1yd. in the same furlong N. Thomas Shepard, S. William Davis.; 1a. 1yd. in the same furlong N. Edward Brunsdon, S. William Davis; 2a. that shoot upon the brook N. Edward Brunsdon, S. Thomas Shepard; ½a. in the same furlong N. John Marsh, S. Edward Brunsdon; ½a. in the same furlong shooting upon the Harepath N. John Marsh, S. Thomas Shepard; 1½a. in White-hill N. William Davis, S. John Mars; 5½a. in the same furlong John Marsh on both sides.
A fair parsonage house about 4 bays with a barn of 4 bays and a stable adjoining to it with a garden and backside, 1a.
William Davis, Edward Brunsdon, churchwardens.

819 1677 (D1/24/223/3)
Land in the E. fields beginning towards the hill: 1½a. E. and W. sides William Davis and butting against the hedge between the field on N. and butting against Lamborne way on S.; 1yd. E. James Barens, W. Thomas Shepard; 1a. E. Thomas Shepard, W. William Davis; ½a. E. Thomas Shepard, W. John March; ½a. E. and W.

Thomas Shepard; ½a. E.Thomas Shepard,W.John March; 2½a. E.William Davis, W. Edward Brunsdon; 1a. E. John March, W.Thomas Shepard,; ½a. E. Edward Brunsdon,W.Thomas Shepard, all butting against the hedge on N. and Lamborne way on S.; 1a. in Longlands E. Edward Brunsdon, W. William Davis, butting against the hedge on N. and Lamborne Way on S.; 1yd. E. John March, W. Harepath furlong butting on William Davis on N. and James Barens on S.; 3yd. above Harepath N. and S.Thomas Shepard butting on E. on the glebe W. on Harepath way; ½a. below Harepath N.John March, S.Thomas Shepard butting on Harepath way on E. and Thomas Barnet on W.; ½a. below Harepath N. Edward Brunsdon, S.John March butting on Harepath way on E. and Thomas Barnet on W.; 1a. below Harepath N.Thomas Shepard, S. Lamborne Way butting upon Harepath way on E., Thomas Barnard on W.; 10a. of pasture ground E. Edward Brunsdon,W.Thomas Shepard, John Reeves on N. side, Rabson farm on S. side; the ground about the dwelling house 1a.

Lands in the N. fields: 5½a. upon Wheatell N.William Davis, S. John March butting upon Thomas Shepard on E. side, John March on W. side; 1½a. upon Wheatell N. William Davis, S. John March butting on John Reeves on E. and John Marsh on W.; 2a. below Harepath N. Edward Brunsdon, S.Thomas Shepard butting upon Harepath way on E. and the brook on W.; ½a. below Harepath way N. John March, S. Edward Brunsdon butting upon Harepath on E., the brook on W.; ½a. below Harepath W. John March, S. Thomas Shepard butting upon Harepath on E., John March on W.; 1a. above Harepath N.Thomas Barnard, S.William Davis butting upon Harepath on W. and William Davis on E.; 1a. 1yd. above Harepath N.Thomas Shepard, S.William Davis butting on Thomas Barnard on E. and Harepath on W.; 1a. 1yd. above Harepath N. Edward Brunsdon, S. William Davis, butting on Thomas Barnard on E. and Harepath on W.; 1a. upon Nettel Hill E. Edward Brunsdon,W.William Davis butting upon William ?Voke on N. and Edward Brunsdon on S.; 1a. in Wheat Yards E.Thomas Shepard,W. John March, butting George Franklin on N. and Thomas Barnard on S.; ½a. laying between the fields E.John March and lying under the hedge between the fields.The parsonage house has 5 fields of building, the gardens, orchards thereunto belonging contain 1a.The barn has 5 fields, the stable, 1 field.Tithe corn, hay, wool, lambs, calves, cow white, pigs, geese, apples and offerings.

George Elweke, rector,John March,Thomas Barnard, churchwardens,Thomas Baskervile, Sampson Cooper.

WINTERBOURNE GUNNER rectory

820   8 Sep 1608 (D1/24/224/1)
Taken by William Reeves,William Jude,Thomas Thorneton, Richard Bowles, John Haydon.

First and foremost in the N. field 1a. lying between the lands of William Reeves on E. and Thomas Thorneton on W. 1a. between the lands of William Reeves on N. and Richard Bowles on S. bounding E. and W. 1a. between Mr.John Sutter's lands on S. and Thomas Thorneton's on N. bounding E. and W. 1a. between the lands of Mr.John Sutter on W. and Richard Bowles on E. bounding N. and S.

In the Middle field 2a. between the lands of William Reeves on N. and Richard Bowles on S. bounding E. and W.

In the third field adjoining Winterbourne Dauntsey 1a. between the lands of Mr. John Sutter on E. and Richard Bowles on W. bounding N. and S.; 1a. between the lands of Mr. John Sutter on N. and Leonard Browne on S. bounding E. and W. 60 sheep may be kept on the fields and downs. Also for the In ground we judge it to be in quantity an acre of ground and somewhat better.

Ralph Pickhaver, rector, Charles Swerynge, William Reves [X], John Haydon, Thomas Thornton [X].

821   30 Oct 1671 (D1/24/224/2)
Winterbourne Cherburgh [Sheerborough] and Gunner.

Terrier taken at the appointment and by the command of bishop Seth. In the W. side of the parish are *c.* 8a. of arable glebeland viz.: In the N. field next to Gomeldon [Gumbleton] 4 single acres of which 1a. lies between 2a. belonging to the farm in the possession of Mrs. Comfort wid. on the upper side and *c.* 2a. on the nether side belonging to wid. Boles; 1a. abutts on 2a. belonging to George Thornton yeo. 1a. butts on 2a. belonging to wid. Boles; 1a. abutts on the roadway which leads to Amesbury and Great Durnford.

In the Middle field 2a. abutts on 4a. belonging to Mrs. Comfort wid.

In the S. field on the W. side of the parish, 1a. abutts on Longhead acre belonging to Mrs. Comfort wid.; 1a. abutts on the roadway leading to Salisbury and lies near the gate leading to the house belonging to wid. Boles.

60 sheep leazes in the common fields and downs of the abovesaid part of the parish (*i.e. the west side*) that is called Winterbourne Sheerborough. 2 cow leazes and a leaze for 1 horse at the breach of the fields. 1a. of pasture of which ½a. lies at the upper end of the orchard and ½a. on the W. side of the parsonage house. 1a. of ground on which stands the house, barn, stable and other housing. The other part consists of the orchard, garden, court, barton, etc. All tithes predial and personal, greater and smaller within the parish.

John Burnley, rector, William Judd, John Knowlton, churchwardens, George Thornton, William Bowiles, assistants, William Browne, sidesman.

822   25 Jan 1705 (D1/24/224/3)
All tithes little or great. Glebe on W. side of the parish: 2a. in the field against Winterbourne Dauntsey of which 1a. bounded with 2a. of Mr. Helliot and 2a. of William Boles and 1a. bounded with 1a. of George Thornton and 1a. belonging to the living lately in the possession of T. Brown; 1a. in Middle field; 2a. together bounded with 2a. of William Boles and 1a. of William Reeves. 4a. in the field next to Gomeldon [Gumbleton]; 1a. the upper a. bounded with 2a. of George Thornton and 1a. of William Reeves.; 1a. bounded with 2a. of Mr. Helliott and 2a. of George Thornton; the lower a. bounded with 2a. of Mr. Helliot and 2a. of William Boles; 2a. of pasture on which stands a dwelling house, barn, stable, outhouses all in good repair and an orchard. The feeding or leaze of 60 sheep, 2 horses, 2 cows and the running of pigs in the fields and common at the usual times as the neighbours. Henry Dampney, rector, William Bowles, (sic) Godwin Godwin,[1] churchwardens.

1. Probably Goddin, a family name that appears in the parish registers. Confusingly though the burial of Goddin Goddin was recorded in 1710.

WINTERBOURNE MONKTON vicarage

823   1671 (D1/24/225/1)

The churchyard for the sepulture of the dead, ½a. In the Homestall containing the mansion house, and barn, garden, barton and close, c. 1a. A close called Long Meadow c. 4a. Pasture for 4 cows upon the cow downs at Hackpen. Pasture for 1 horse and 30 sheep in the fields. Arable in the E. field: ½a. in Town furlong lying 2 acres' breadth from the N. side of that furlong; 1yd. or r. being the southernmost of those 2 short butts at the E. end of Hawn furlong by Marlborough way; ½a. upon S. side of Chinkhill furlong shooting along by the N. side of Marlborough way; ½a. in N. E. Chinkhill lying 2 acres' and a half breadth from the W. side of that furlong; 2yd. or ¾a. in the furlong called Wat Harding's house lying 2 acres breadth from the W. side of Harepath; 1yd. or r. upon the E. side of Wat Harding's house adjoining to Mear furlong; 1a. upon the S. side of Broad Linch furlong adjoining to Shills furlong; 1yd. or r. in Broad Linch furlong lying upon the S. side of the small linchet in the same furlong; a head ½a. upon the E. side of Picked stone furlong lying against the W. end of Broad Linch furlong; ½a. in Picked Stone furlong shooting northward from the Picked Stone; 3yd. or ¾a. upon Barwick side furlong lying 1 acre's breadth from the N. side of Snugged lands and lying against the W. side of the other 3yd. next before mentioned; ½a. in Mear furlong lying 3¼ acres' breadth from the W. side of that furlong; 2 single yd., called the Vicarage Short yards, towards the E. side of the same Mear furlong; 1a. in Hackpen Long furlong lying 1½ acres' breadth from the S. side of that furlong; 1 head a. upon the N. side of Chinchester furlong lying against the S. end of Midfurlong; ½a. in Midfurlong lying 2 acres' breadth from the E. end of Chinchester head a. last mentioned; ½a. in Smithlands lying 1 acre's breadth the N. side of that furlong; 3yd. or ¾a. in Shaftesbury 1 acre's breadth from the E. side of Harepath; ½a. in White furlong lying ½ acre's breadth from the N. side of that furlong; 1a. in White lands lying 3 acres' breadth from the E. side of that furlong. Total 13½a.

Arable in the W. field: 1a. called Galley acre lying upon the N. side of Crofts; 1a. lying upon the S. side of Crofts; 1a. in Buttockes lying ¾ acre's breadth from the N. side of that furlong; 1yd. or r. in Westminster furlong lying 1 acre's breadth S. from the One Legged acre in the same furlong; ½a. in Westminster furlong lying 3 acres' breadth from the N. side of that furlong; 1 head yd. or r. lying against the N. E. end of Westminster furlong; 1yd. or r. in Long Oare shooting from the end of the head yd. last mentioned to Barwick hedge; 1a. in Midfurlong lying bestride the Gripfurrow; ½a. in Drove furlong shooting down upon the Court acre and lying 11 acres' breadth from the E. end of that a; ½a. in Cob furlong lying 7 acres' breadth from the S. side of that furlong; ½a. in Cob furlong lying 12½ acres' breadth from the N. side of that furlong; ½a. in Gosborne Long furlong lying 2 acres' breadth from the W. side of that furlong; a head ½a. upon the N. side of Bane furlong lying against the S. end of Apple furlong; 1yd. or r. in

Bane furlong lying 1½ acres' breadth from the N. side of that furlong; 3yd. or ¾a. in Bane furlong lying 1 acre's breadth S. from the ½ linch in the same furlong; 3yd. or ¾a. lying 2½ acres' breadth south from the last half linch in the same furlong; 1 head ½a. upon the E. side of Short Oare lying against the W. end of Bane furlong; ½a. lying 1½ acres' breadth from the W. side of that furlong; ½a. lying 1¾ acres' breadth from the W. side of that furlong.; ½a. lying 1 acre's breadth from the E. side of the same furlong. Total 12½a. Arable in the S. field: A head ½a. that lies upon the N. E. side of that field.

Tithe corn growing upon Cobbins Upright lands, Juggins piece, ½a. of the Lower farm called Lambornes half; ½a. of Eatwells copyhold lying in Smithlands above Harepath in the E. field. Tithe corn growing upon Crofts in the W. field. Tithe corn growing upon all the lands belonging to the Mill hold except the 2 Court acres. Tithe hay growing in the whole parish except Sir Francis Popham's farm of which only the tithe of the Goose close and the W. side of Broad Meadow belongs to the vicarage. Tithe wool and lambs in the whole parish except Sir Francis Popham's farm. Tithe milk and calves in the whole parish for both which a custom is pleaded by the parishioners to pay 3d. a cow and 4d. a calf. Tithe pigs, geese, hops, honey, herbs, apples, eggs, etc. and oblations in the whole parish. A pension of 40s. p. a. from his Majesty usually paid by the lord of the manor of Avebury and allowed him again by his Majesty's auditors at Malmesbury. A composition of £8 p. a. made by Richard Long, vicar, about 40 years ago with Mr. Duns[1] then lord of the manor of Avebury for a quantity unknown to the present incumbent of wheat and barley to be paid out of his farm at Avebury. By me John Brinsden, vicar.

1.   William Dunche who sold the manor in 1640. VCH vol. 12, p. 91.

824   3 May 1678 (D1/24/225/2)
The churchyard, c. ½a. The Homestall containing the vicarage house, barn, stable, barton, gardens and home close, c. 1a. An enclosure lying next to a meadow called Southend at the S. end of the village, c. 4a.

Arable land in the E. field: ½a. in Headdens furlong lying 2 acres' breadth from the N. side of that furlong; 1yd. or r. lying upon the N. side of Hawn furlong shooting E. and W. by the S. side of Marlborough way; 1yd. or r. being the southernmost of those 2 short butts lying at the upper end of Hawn furlong by Marlborough way; ½a. lying upon the S. side of Chinkhill furlong shooting E. and W. along by the N. side of Marlborough way; ½a. in N. E. Chinkhill furlong lying 2½ acres' breath from the E. end of the ½a. next before mentioned; ¾a. or 3yd. or r. lying in a furlong called Wat Harding's house 2 acres' breadth below Harepath; a head ½a. upon the N. side of Shills furlong lying against the S. end of Picked Stone furlong; 1a. lying upon Broadlinch furlong under the broad linchet; 1yd. or r. lying upon the S. side of the small linchet in the same furlong; a head ½a. upon the E. side of Picked Stone furlong lying against the W. end of Broadlinch furlong; ½a. in Picked Stone furlong shooting N. and S. from the Picked Stone to Barwick field; 1yd. or r. in Barwick Cross furlong lying 3 acres' breadth above Harepath; ½a. in the same furlong lying 3 acres' breadth eastwards from the yd. next before mentioned; ¾a. lying in Barwick furlong shooting E. and W. being 1 acre's breadth from the S. side of that furlong; 3yds. or r. or ¾a. being a headland lying against the W. end of Barwick furlong and shooting northward upon the broad linchet above mentioned; 2 single yd. or r. being 1 acre's breadth apart and lying towards the E. side of Mear furlong called the Vicarage Shortyards; 1a. in Hackpen–Long furlong 1½ acre's breadth from the S. side of the same field; ½a. in Midfurlong lying 2 acres' breadth below the E. end of Chinchester head a. and shooting northward upon Marlborough Way; 1 head a. upon the N. side of Chinchester Furlong lying against the S. end of Midfurlong; ½a. in Smith lands furlong lying 1 acre's breadth from the N. side of that furlong and shooting down westward upon Harepath between 2 linchets; 3yd. or r. or ¾a. in Shaftesbury furlong near Goare piece lying 1 acre's breadth above Harepath; 1a. in White furlong on the S. side of Chinkhill lying 3 acres' breadth westward from Harepath; ½a. in White furlong lying ½ acre's breadth from the S. end of the a. next above mentioned and shooting eastward upon Harepath.

Arable land in the W. field: 1a. in Crofts called Gally acre adjoining to Barwick Common; 1a. in Crofts adjoining to the Farm field; 1a. in Buttox furlong lying ¾ acre's breadth from the N. side of that furlong and shooting westwards upon Nollands; ½a. in Westminster furlong lying 1 acre's breadth southwards from the One legged acre in that furlong; 1yd. or r. in Westminster furlong lying 3 acres' breadth from the N. side of that furlong; 1 head yd. or r. of land lying against the E. end of the yd. next before mentioned.; 1yd. in Long Oare shooting from the N. end of the head yd. next before mentioned up to Barwick field; 1a. in Midfurlong lying before the gripfurrow or draining furrow; ½a. in Drove furlong shooting upon the W. end of the Court acre; ½a. in Cob furlong lying 7 acres' breadth northward from Drove way.; ½a. in Cob furlong lying 5 acres' breadth northwards from the ½a. next before mentioned; ½a. in Town furlong lying 1½acre's breadth from the S. end of Gosborne long furlong; ½a. in Gosborne long furlong lying 2 acres' breadth from the W. side of that furlong.; a head ½a. upon the N. side of Bane furlong lying against the S. end of Apple furlong; 1yd. or r. in Bane furlong lying 1 acre's breadth southward from the head ½a. next before mentioned; 3yd. or r. or ¾a. in Bane furlong lying 1 acre's breadth southward from the ½ linch in the bottom of Bane furlong; 3yd. or r. or ¾a. in Bane furlong lying 3 yards' breadth southward from the 3yd. next before mentioned; 1yd. or r. in Bane furlong lying 2 acres' breadth southward from the 3yd. next before mentioned; a head ½a. upon the E. side of Short Oare lying against the W. end of Bane furlong; a ½a. in Short Oare lying 1 acre's breadth westward from the head ½a. next before mentioned; 1yd. or r. in Apple furlong lying 1 acre's breadth from the W. side of that furlong and shooting the S. end upon the head ½a. upon the N. side of Bane furlong; ½a. in Apple furlong lying ½ acre's breadth eastward from the 3yd. next before mentioned; ½a. in Apple furlong lying 1 acre's breadth from the E. side of that furlong.

Arable in the S. field a head ½a. lying upon the N. E. side of the field shooting N. and S. along the W. side of the furlong called Upright-Lands.

Tithe corn growing upon Cobbins, Upright Lands, Tuggins piece, Martha's half, ½a. of Eatwells Copyhold lying in Smith lands above Harepath in the E.

field and 5a. belonging to the Milhold in the E. field. Tithe corn growing upon all crofts lands and 1½a. of land in Drove furlong belonging to the Milhold in the W. field. Tithe corn growing upon 3a. of land belonging to the Milhold in the S. field. Tithe hay growing in the whole parish except the farm belonging to Alexander Popham esq., of which farm only the tithe of the Goose close and the W. side of Broad mead belong to the vicarage. Tithe wool and lambs in all the parish except the farm above mentioned. Tithe milk and calves throughout the whole parish for both which a prescription is pretended viz. to pay 3d. a milk cow and 2d. a dry beast in lieu of all milk and 4d. for every calf. Tithe pigs, geese, apples, hops, herbs, honey, etc. Common of pasture for 4 cows upon the cow downs and for 1 horse and 40 sheep in the common fields. A pension of 40s. p. a. paid by the lord of the manor of Avebury. A composition of £8 p. a. made by Richard Long, vicar, about 40 years ago with Mr. Duns[1] then lord of the manor of Avebury for wheat and barley (of unknown quantities) to be paid out of his farm there. Both the composition and the pension are now paid yearly at Michaelmas [29 Sep] and our Lady day [25 Mar] by equal portions by Robert Bainton esq. now lord of the manor of Avebury.

John Brinsden, vicar, Ambrose Spencer [X], John Purnell [X], churchwardens, Richard Hunt [X], William Axford [X].

1. William Dunche who sold the manor in 1640. See VCH vol. 12, p. 91.

WINTERBOURNE STOKE vicarage

825   10 Jun 1609 (D1/24/226/1)
A house for the vicar to dwell in with garden plot, backside and barn. 3a. of arable in the Parsonage field enclosed with linchets [linchyardes] on each side. The trees growing in the churchyard and the herbage of the same. The tithe of corn or any other grain or pulse of arable rudge[1] lying below Grymst-cleeve in the tenure of Richard Makrel.[2] The tithe of an arable plot called the Shoulder of Mutton in the tenure of Richard Makrel.[3] The tithe of an arable plot or rudge called Stilche lying in Shortsdeene bottom in the tenure of Martin Snow.[4] The twentieth pook or half the tithe hay with the rector throughout the whole manor or parish as well of lord or tenants with the tithe of the grist mill and all the tithe of wool and lamb growing or bred in the manor or parish and rectory. All the lesser tithes as hops and all oblations, offerings, marriage money and for purifying or churching of women, cow white, calf, pig, goose, guinea fowl [genneys], pigeons, eggs, apples, pears, cherries, honey, wax, hops, garden, except on Adam Snow's[5] farm for which the vicar has 3 fleeces of wool, 3 lambs and half the tithe hay with the rector of 2 little meadows called Woollume and Stoples together with the lesser tithes as above. The vicar has tithe wool and lamb and half tithe hay with the rector and he has the same lesser tithes on 7 yardlands in Bourton[6] in the occupation of Giles Tooker esq., Maud his mother, Mr. Thomas Eaers and Henry Myells.[7,8] Tithe of hay on a plot of meadow ground by the Kings Meads belonging to Sir Giles Eastcourte deceased[9] and his heirs now occupied by mother Sheepherde.[10]

John Wican, vicar, Richard Grenne, Robert Downton, old churchwardens, Robert Bird, Thomas Collins [X], new churchwardens, Adam Snow, John Gilbert, Nicholas Kelloe.

1. Ridge in **827**.
2. Nicholas Green in **826**. No name stated in **827**.
3. Walter Kellow in **286**. No name stated in **827**.
4. John Snow in **826**. No name stated in **827**.
5. Mr. Edward Duke in **826**. This exceoption is not mentioned in **827**.
6. In Maddington.
7. Henry Miles and Thomas Repton in **826**. The whole sentence is omitted in **827**.
8. Half tithe [hay] on a plot in Coniegar in the occupation of Sir Walter Ernley and Lady Gore added in **826**.
9. Sir William Earscourt in **826**. No name in **827**.
10. Rachel Miles in **826**. No name in **827**.

826   2 Feb 1678 (D1/24/226/2)
As **825** with amendments in footnotes. Benjamin Culme, vicar, Walter Kellow junior, William Reeves, John Collier, churchwardens, Walter Ringman.

827   1783 (D1/24/226/3)
A small thatched dwelling house with walls partly of flint and partly of lath and plaster: A kitchen bricked but not ceiled, a parlour boarded and ceiled with sides of plaster and a little buttery on the ground floor. Over these are two small chambers with sides of plaster and ceiled and a wool loft. It is surrounded by a little barn and garden with a mud wall fence.

1a. in Parsonage Field adjoining on E. and W. with Mr. Hely's. 1a. in Parsonage Middle Field adjoining on N. with Mr. Hely's and S. with Parsonage Field. 1a. on the outside of Parsonage Middle Field adjoining Mr. Hely's. Other tithes as **825**. Clerk's fees: 4d. for each yardland payable each Easter and the Clerk's Place given by the vicar. Communion plate: silver cup weight ¾lb., a small silver bread plate weight ½lb.

Neville Wells, rector, George Kellow, Henry Chalke, churchwardens.

WINTERSLOW rectory

828   7 Dec 1628 (D1/24/227/1)
In the Middle field 14a., whereof 3a. lie at Deep halve, 4a. at Damsens bushes, 3 x ½a. below the Windmill, 3 x ½a. and a head ½a. shooting upon Pitton field, 2a. shooting upon the head ½a. and 3 x ½a. upon the hill near the church. In the Wood field 15a. whereof 4a. shooting upon Burdnes Copse. 4a. shooting upon the Wood lawn and 7a. in the middle of that field. In the field below the hill c. 11a. whereof 9 lie in a piece near to the down side, 1a. under the hill and 1a. shooting against that one under the hill.

An orchard and 2 bartons, 2a. ¼a. of ground moor whereupon the smith's house stands with its garden joining to the place barton. A mansion dwelling house with 3 barns, 1 fodder house and 2 stables.

16a. measured out by Andrew Hillyarde in 1628 in the presence and by the approval of Mr. Alexander Thistelthwayt, lord of the manor and patron of that benefice, the parts whereof the Corte mead joining to the parsonage orchard and the Bouling close joining to the churchyard and so most of the Hilly close as was then bounded and set out by the said Hillyard and lies on the W. side of the other part of the Hilly close allotted unto Alexander Thistelthwayt of Middle Winterslow gent. for his right of (tithe) corn. This presentment was grounded upon these reasons following: Whereas the common of Winterslow has been enclosed in 1628 in which common the parson had had the right to put up as many beasts as he did usually winter, and had allotted unto him 16a. of the common for his right of herbage, which Mr. Nicholas Elie, the present incumbent, has exchanged with the lord of the manor of Winterslow being the patron of that benefice for so many a. lying near unto church and parsonage house. The patron has conveyed all those a. to the said Nicholas Elie for the right of his parsonage by his deed dated 9 Sep. 1628 which deed describes the a. by the names Cortes mead, Bowling close and for so much of Hilly close as was set out and bounded to and for the use of the parson by Andrew Hillyard of the Close, Salisbury, a man appointed by the lord of the manor. The land was bounded out in the presence of the patron of the benefice with 4 stakes athwart Hilly Close from the N.W. hedge of that ground unto the stake at the N. corner of the Cort mead next the oat barn. The grounds were handed over to Nicholas Elie in the right of his parsonage by Alexander Thistelthwayt in the presence Mr. Alexander, his son, and John White. The lord of the manor has accepted the residue of Hilly close after the allotment had been made by his agreement registered in the manor court book 11 June 1628 and Mr. Alexander Thistelthwayt of Middle Winterslow gent. and his son Edward have accepted the residue of the land being c. 14a. bounded out and served from that part of Hilly close allotted to the parsonage by their deed of 12 Aug. 1628.

John Redman, Alexander Newman [X], churchwardens at the bishop's visitation 1628, James Feltham, John Webb [X], sidesmen at the bishop's visitation 1628. Alexander Thistlethwaite, Peregrine Thistlethwayte, Giles Ingram, Henry Edwards.

829   27 Dec 1671 (D1/24/227/2)
A parsonage house, garden and orchard, 3 barns, 2 stables, a cart house with a henhouse and 6 pig sties thereunto belonging.

A tenement with a garden and a smith's shop lying between the parsonage, lower backside and Mr. Thistlethwayte's backside, the rent whereof is 6s. 8d. p. a. c. 15a. of arable or pasture called the Little close and the Hilly close adjoining the churchyard. 11a. in the field below the hill. 14a. in the Middle field. 15a. in Whiteway field. Common of pasture for 120 sheep with the tenants of W. Winterslow. All great and small tithes in the parish, payable in kind.

Geoffrey Thistlethwayte, rector, Henry Dench, James Linton, churchwardens, Alexander Thistlethwayte esq., Giles Ingram, William Best, John Gilbert, inhabitants of Winterslow. *All but the rector's and churchwardens' signatures in the same hand.*

830   27 Dec 1677 (D1/24/227/3)
As **829**. Geoffrey Thistlethwayte, rector, William Reeves, John Hooker, church-wardens. Alexander Thistlethwayte, William Best, Giles Ingram, James Linton, Thomas King, Alexander Ingram, inhabitants. *All but the rector in the same hand.*

GREAT WISHFORD rectory

831   11 Jun 1609 (D1/24/228/1)
Made with the advice of Mr. John Bower, parson, together with the consent of the best of ability most ancient honest and substantial men there dwelling whose names are hereunder written and delivered the 13 of June next following by the hands of the churchwardens into the registry of the bishop.

A dwelling house with a kitchen near the said house, a barn and stable under one roof, a garden and an orchard beneath the said kitchen.[1]

20a. of arrable with the common fields viz. 4a. in the S. field, 9a. in the Middle field, 7a. in the W. field. 1a. of meadow in Kingsmead, ½a. of meadow in the lower end of Steart mead. A little paddock or ham of meadow near Great Wishford bridge. The parson has commons of pasture for 2 kine, 2 runners, a bull, a boar and pigs at his pleasure and 4 horses from Lammas [1 Aug] until Michaelmas [29 Sep] to bring in his harvest. A duty paid out of a living in Little Wishford occupied by Robert Sedgwick[2] for 2a. of dry ground. The just due is not known but his predecessor William Wagland paid Mr. Hurde[3] the old parson and Mr. Bower the parson that now is, 6d. each Easter. Tithe of the wood[4] called Bonsam Bushes in the manor of Great Wishford occupied by Sir Richard Grobham being under the growth of 21 years. Tithe of a corner of meadow, ½a., in a certain meadow near the Ramhole.

Tithes: Of wheat the tenth sheaf; of barley and other grain the tenth cock; of hay the tenth grass cock. 1d. at Easter for every thorough milk cow and 2d. for every new milk cow. For calves if the parson will drive, the tenth calf, otherwise for every calf weaned, ½d. For every calf killed the left shoulder. For every calf sold the tenth penny. The tenth lb. of wool of all sheep kept in the parish. Otherwise if they have not gone there all year but a part of the year then to give after the rate according to the time that they have gone there. The parson is to have the tenth lamb that is bred on each man's leaze within the parish.

If any man breeds but 5 lambs then the parson is to have half a lamb; if 6 lambs then to have 3d; if 7 lambs or upwards to have a lamb, the parson paying ½d. for every lamb that lacks of 10, the parishioners paying ½d. for every lamb under 5 and in like sort for their pigs as for lambs. For geese and young cygnets in the parish the tenth for young pigeons the tenth, for eels the tenth eel.[5] On Good Friday yearly for every hen 2 eggs. Bees the tenth of their honey or the tenth penny that they make of them. For apples, hops and all small tithes, the tenth.

John Bower, rector. John Hampton junior, Edmund Kingman, churchwardens. Robert Joytea, Walter Kingman senior, Walter Kingman junior, John Deare senior [X], John Hampton senior [X], John Coudrie [X], John Blaake [X].

1. This section omitted in **832-835**.
2. Sir Richard Howe in **834**.
3. William Hurd was rector 1550-1574 and was succeeded by John Bower.
4. Not named in **834** but described as the woods of Sir Richard Howe. Mr. Bonsams his wood in **832**.
5. The tenth eel which they catch at their weirs in **832**. Tenth bales in **834** an obvious misreading from **832**.

832   19 May [. . .] mid 17th cent.[1] (D1/24/228/2)
Terrier presented by the best of ability and most ancient there dwelling at the visitation of bishop John on 21 Mar. As **831**; including the tithes of a corner of Asserton mead occupied by John Maton of Berwick St. James. Tithes for bees if they beak[2] or sell any the tenth penny otherwise if they beak any the tenth part.

Those who made the inquisition Thomas Bonham gent., John Love, Henry Hetherne, Richard Browne, Walter Kingman, Nicholas Kingman, Robert Heyter, Leonard Catcate, Nicholas Kinge, John Pyrrye, Edmund Eve, William Hetherne, William Kingman. *Names in the same hand*

1. Presented at the visitation of John Davenant whose episcopary ran from 1621-1641.
2. Probably a mistake for make, see **831**, or take, see **585**.

833   1671 (D1/24/228/3)
A dwelling house, 2 barns, a stable and a cart house, an orchard and a little garden. 1a. of meadow in Kings mead and a ham, ½a., near Stoford bridge. 4a. in the S. field, 9a. in the Middle field, 7a. in the N.W. field.

Robert Parker, rector, Thomas Haiter, Thomas Deer, churchwardens. *Names in the same hand*

834   10 Jan 1705 (D1/24/228/4)
*As **831** with amendments in footnotes.* William Sealy, rector, John Lock [X], churchwarden, William Cowdrey, Walter Kello, overseers.

835   1 Aug 1783 (D1/24/228/5)
*A certified copy of **833**.* Made by Thomas Frome, notary public; with the following addition: The parsonage house consists of 4 rooms on a floor built of brick stone and flint, thatched and in good repair, a garden walled to the N. Barns and stables and out offices in good condition. £700 and more having been laid out upon it within these 7 years.

James, Birch, rector, Walter Eve, John Henwood, churchwardens and overseers.

WOODBOROUGH rectory

836   27 Dec 1608 (D1/24/229/1)
The parsonage house being the dwelling house with all the rooms fit in as ample manner and sort as it has been in ancient time heretofore with a barn of

5 rooms with a stable and cow house thereunto and also the orchard, garden and barton or backside, 2a.

There belongs to the parsonage commonly called by the usual term of the country 3 yardlands of glebe land: In the W. Sands: A ground called the Parsonage Alders, 2a. between 1yd. of ground of Edward Hooper gent. S. and 1yd. of Philip Francklen gent. N. both shooting E. and W. In the Little Clay adjoining unto the same W. Sands between a croft of Philip Francklen gent. N. and 2a. of William Dowlies S.; 1a. shooting N. and S. in the furlong that lies along the highway between ½a. E. and 2a. 1yd. W. both belonging to Philip Francklen gent.; 1a. of land shooting E. and W. down to the steane mead lying between ½a. of Philip Francklen gent. N., 3a. of John Miles S.; 4a. of land shooting W. and E. upon the mead towards the brook between 1a. of Sir William Butten S. and ½a. of Philip Francklen gent. N.; 1a. shooting W. and E. upon Temead towards the brook lying between ½a. of Sir William Butten S., ½a. of Edward Hoopper gent. N.; 1a. shooting W. to the highway and E. to the brook between ½a. of Richard Noyse S., ½a. of Philip Francklen gent. N.; 1a. shooting W. and E. between 1yd. N., ½a. S. both belonging to Philip Francklen gent.; 1a. shooting W. and E. towards the brook between ½a. of Philip Francklen gent. N., ½a. of Edward Hoopper gent. S.; 1a. shooting W. and E. thoroughly to the brook between 1yd. of Philip Francklen gent., S. 1a. of Sir William Butten N.; a ground called a Craft lying by the side of the common called Woodborough Hurst shooting N. and S., 2a. on E. lies a craft of Philip Francklen gent.

In the field called Broome hill: In the S. side thereof lies 4a. of land shooting E. and W., 4a. of John Miles lie together N., a craft of Sir Ambrose Butten S.; 1a shooting E. and W. thoroughly with the Mead between 3yd. N. and 3 x ½a. S. both of Sir William Butten; at a place called Splottbooshe lie 2a. shooting E. and W. between 2a. of John Miles N. and 1a. of Philip Francklen gent. S.

In the field called W. Clay: 6a. shooting W. and E. to the brook on N. side shoot the lands of Alton called Alton Hedge and on S. side lie 3a. of John Miles; in the Moor furlong lie 2a. shooting N. and S. between 2½a. E. and 2½a. W. both of Philip Francklen gent.; in the second furlong 1a. shooting N. and S. between 1a. of Sir. William Butten E. and 1a. of Philip Francklen gent. W.; in the same furlong 3 x ½a. shooting N. and S. between ½a. of Edward Hoopper gent. E., ½a. of John Miles W.; in Long Wood furlong 1a. shooting E. and W. between 1a. of Edward Hoopper gent. N., 1a. of Philip Francklen gent. S.

In the field called E. Clay: Adjoining the mill in the Moor furlong 3yd. shooting N. and S. between 2. ½a. W. and 3yd. E. both of Sir Ambrose Butten; in Coombe furlong 1a. shooting N. and S. between 1a. W. and ½a. E. both of Sir Ambrose Butten; in the same furlong 2a. shooting N. and S. between ½a. of Sir Ambrose Butten W. and the Windmill hedge on E.; in the upper end of the same furlong 4a. shooting E. and W. between 1a. of John Miles S. and a piece, 7a., of Philip Francklen N.; in Tosemead furlong 2a. shooting N. and S. between 5a. of Edward Hoopper gent. E. and 3yd. Sir William Butten W.; in the same furlong 2a. shooting N. and S. between 3yd. of Sir William Butten E. and 3a. of John Miles W.; in the same furlong ½a. shooting N. and S. between 3yd. of E. and 1a. W. both of Philip Francklen gent. In the field called the Hill land: 1a. shooting N. and S. between 1a. E. and 1a. W. both of Philip Francklen gent.; 3 x ½a. called

Three Half acres shooting E. and W. between 3yd. of Philip Francklen gent N. and ½a. of Sir William Butten S.; upon the top of the same hill 1a. shooting E. and W. between ½a. of Richard Noyse N. and 3a. of Sir William Butten S.; 3yd. shooting E. and W. between a piece, 4a., of Edward Hoopper gent. S. and 1a. of Philip Francklen N.

In the field called the E. Sands: 2a. shooting S. and N. to the grounds called the Horse leazes between 1a. of Edward Hoopper gent. W. and 3 x ½a. of Philip Francklen gent. E.; in the same furlong 1a. shooting N. and S. beteeen ½a. of Philip Francklen gent. W. and ½a. of John Mills E.; ½a. shooting N. and S. between ½a. of William Dowlies W. E. and 1yd. of Philip Francklen gent. W.; in the Heath furlong ½a. shooting N. and S. between a ground of Philip Francklen gent. called a Craft E. and 5yd. of Sir William Butten W.; in the same furlong 5yd. shooting N. and S. between 5yd. of Sir William Butten E. and 3yd. of Edward Hoopper gent. W.; 1 head a. shooting E. and W. lying along the Heath hedge commonly called Manningfords heath or common on S.; in Flax furlong 1yd. shooting N. and S. between 1yd. W. and ½a. E. both of Philip Francklen gent.; in the same furlong 1yd. shooting N. and S. between 1a. of Philip Francklen gent. E. and 1a. of William Dowlies W.; the E. Sands has a ground called Not mead, 6½a., shooting E. and W. between 1yd. of Sir William Butten N. and Manningfords heath S. or common S.

Adjoining into W. Sands and W. Clay lie 1 ground of pasture called the Parsonage Horse leaze, 3a., shooting E. and W., W. Clay lies on N. and W. Sands S. W.

Pasturing and feeding in the common and common fields for 15 rother beasts and a bull at such times of the years according to the usual use as the rest of the parishioners. 60 sheep leaze as the rest of the parishioners have.

The ground land meadow and pasture appertaining to the 3 yardlands of glebe amounts to 70a. and 1yd. with orchard, garden and backside. All tithes that ought to be paid from 37 yardlands, the Easter book and the churchyard.

Adam Noyes, rector, Martin Hoselande, William Banfield, churchwardens, Henry Smith senior, William Weeckes, William Chandler, sidesmen. *Signature of the rector, the others in the same hand.*

837 30 Oct 1671 (D1/24/229/2)
The dwelling house of 5 bays viz. a parlour, hall, kitchen, a room called the broadhouse, and another bay of building standing on posts. A barn of 6 bays, a stable adjoining to the end of it, a garden, orchard, court yard and rick yard, *c.* 2a.

A small cottage or tenement now in the possession of Nicholas Watts which with its garden and ground belonging, *c.* 30p.

In the E. Sand field 2 Not mead grounds lying together both 8a. 2r. 31p. In Bromhill[1] mead 1 ground, 2a. 16p. A ground called Bromhill Craft, 3a. 1r. A ground called the Hurst Craft, 1a. A Hurst ground called the Cow pasture, 14a.

In the W. Sands a ground called Barwick mead together with a small withy bed adjoining and a drove leading to it, 2a. 3r. 30p. In the Upper furlong of the W. Sands a ground, 2a. 2r. 30p. In the lower furlong of the W. Sands, a ground called the Six acres, 6a. 3r. 20p.

In the E. Clay field in Tosmead furlong a piece of land lying between the lands of William Chandler E. and Richard Chandler W., 2a. 2r. 13p. A piece above the drove over against the former piece Mrs Francklen[2] E. and S., the drove N. and W. 6a. 1r. 20p. A piece on the side of the hill Thomas Stratton[3] N., Thomas Dyke[4] S., 1a. 1r. 10p. In the W. Clay a piece 3 furlongs in length Alton field N., Simon Stratton[5] S., 8a. 23p. A pasture called the Horse leas Mr. Lawrence E. and Jane Lavington W., 3a.

William Conyngesbye, rector, Thomas Dyke [X], Adam Smith [X], church-wardens.

1. Brumwell in **838**.
2. Mr. Francklen in **838**.
3. Now Sir Robert Button in **837**.
4. Dykes land in **838**.
5. Sir Robert Button commonly called Strattons land in **838**.

838   3 May 1678 (D1/24/229/3)
*As **837** with amendments in footnotes.* William Conyngesbye, rector, John Franck-lin, Thomas Bradfield, churchwardens.

839   Dec 1704 (D1/24/229/4)
The dwelling house of 5 bays, garden and orchard. The barton backside and stable of 9 bays.

The Hust, 15a. and the Hust Craft, 1a. and Bromell Mead, 8. ½a. In the W. sands 3a. in the upper furlong, 6a. in the lower furlong, 3a. at Long mead end and the Alder mead, 2a. In the E. Clay, 11a. In the W. Clay 8a. near Alton field. The Horse leaze, 3a. A tenement in the possession of Roger Watts.

The whole tithes of the parish taken in kind. The churchyard.

William Conyngesby, rector, Edward Hazeland, Richard Amore, church-wardens.

WOOTTON BASSETT vicarage

840   20 Oct 1671 (D1/24/230/1)
The churchyard for burials. A parcel of land about the vicarage house in yards, gardens and orchards and fishponds,[1] 1½a. 14p. An enclosure called Pond close, 1½a. 12p.[2] An enclosure called Sharp close, 8a. 73p. An enclosure called High mead 13½a. 15p. A parcel of arable land called Barelands, 9a. A parcel of arable land in a field called Cockstalls, 2a. 10p. An enclosure called Parsons Croft mead, 5a. A great enclosure in the E. field hitherto called Rudlands, now called the New enclosure being divided into 3 fields, 53½a. A right of common for feeding cattle in the commons of Wootton Bassett and also in the forest of Braydon.

As to the queries concerning hospitals almshouses, churchhouses, free schools, we know none in our parish nor any endowments.[3]

John Skeate, vicar, Gabriel Cruse, Edward Burchall, churchwardens.

1. Fishponds omitted in later terriers; the land described as N. of the dwelling house in **841**.

2. 1a. 92p. in **841-843**. Pound close in **842-843**.
3. This sentence is omitted in **841-843**.

841 1 Nov 167[?1 or 7] (D1/24/230/2)
As *840* with amendments in footnotes. Tithe wool, lamb, calf and for grazing cattle and all other privy tithes.
John Skeate, vicar.

842 Oct 1698. (D1/24/230/3)[1]
As *840* with amendments in footnote. A copy of a terrier made 4 Dec 1625 in the time of Thomas Lloyd, vicar.
William Pleydell, vicar, John Hollister, Charles Brimsden, Thomas Kington, William Waite.

1. Written in Latin

843 24 Nov 1704 (D1/24/230/4)
As *840* with amendments in footnote. There is £210 belonging to the poor of Wootton Bassett for ever to be disposed of to the poor at the discretion of the vestry.
William Pleydell, vicar, John Gollimore, John Taylor, churchwardens, H. Harding, Charles Hollister.

844 28 Jul 1783 (D1/24/230/5)
1. The vicarage house built with stone and covered with thatch. A hall on the first floor with stone pavement. Kitchen with board floor cellar with stone pavement. Pantry with earth floor, sculery with stone pavement. In the first storey a dining room wainscotted chair high, a drawing room and 3 bed chambers all ceiled. In the second storey 3 garrets. Brewhouse 27ft. by 14ft., a coal house 14ft. by 13ft., a stable, 19ft. by 17ft., all three with stone walls covered with thatch. A barn 47ft. by 17ft. weather boarded covered with thatch.
2. The glebe: A parcel of ground near the mansion house, ½a. 14p. Pound close, 1a. 2r. 12p. Sharp close, 8a. 1r. 30p. A close called High mead, 13a. 15p. A parcel of arable ground called Barelands, 8a. Barelands close, 1a. A parcel of arable land called Coxtalls, 2a. 10p. Another close called Parsons croft, 5a. 3 enclosed grounds, part of the common field, 53½a. Pasture in the common belonging to the parish. In the hedgerows on the glebe are 169 trees value £59.
3. All tithes except corn and hay.
4. Furniture of the church: 5 large and 1 small bells, a clock, 1 silver chalice and cover gilt weight 32oz. the gift of Mr. William Joburn the Parish Church of Wootton Bassett in the year 1631. On the cover is engraved the letters 'WJ'. 1 small chalice and cover weight 11oz. 1 silver salver weight 11½oz. Another silver chalice weight 8oz. 2 pewter flagons. 1 chandelier. 2 sconces to the minister's desk, 1 sconce to the clerk's desk, the gift of Mrs. Jane Hollister of Wootton Bassett.
5. The churchyard: the fence on N. E. side belongs and is kept up at the expense of Mrs Ann Butler. The fence on the S. W. side belongs and is kept up at

the expense of William Arnold. The fence on N.W. is kept up at the expense of the parishioners and the fence next the High Street is kept up at the expense of the lord of the manor.

6. The clerk's wages is £5 p. a. and is paid by the parishioners and the clerk is appointed by the vicar. And there is £20 belonging to the poor of the parish of Wootton Bassett, the interest thereof to be given to the poor at the discretion of the vestry. The interest and the principal now amount to £40 which is now at interest on bond in the hands of Mr. William Cripps and Mr. Edward Robbins of Wootton Bassett. The interest is now disposed of at the discretion of the vestry. Land belonging to the poor: 7a. in Brinkworth let to John Mathews of Brinkworth, rent £8 p. a.; 11a. of land in Brinkworth let to Abraham Young of Brinkworth rent £7 7s. p. a.: Land at Badbury in Chisledon belonging to the poor of Lyneham and Wootton Bassett, let to Jeremiah May of Badbury, rent £11 p. a. the moiety of this and the other rents are disposed of at the discretion of the vestry.

There are certain parcels of land as described in a deed[1] in the hands of Lewis Long esq. of Wootton Bassett which lands were purchased at the expense of William Jones esq. of Iuxta Chew Magna, Somerset and given for the perpetual maintenance of free school for the education of male children belonging to inhabitants of the borough of Wootton Bassett all of which lands are at Haydon and Haydon Wick in Rodbourne Cheney and are now let at the rent of £14 p. a. Also an annuity of 30s. p. a. out of lands described in a deed[1] in the hands of Lewis Long esq. and purchased at the expense of the said William Jones esq. and given for the same use as the above lands.

Timothy Meredith, vicar, George Robbins, John Eacott, churchwardens, Edward Homes, John Mayris, overseers.

1. This deed, dated 7 Oct. 1696, related to Yoster close and a messuage created on it, 1a. 8a. of arable, 6a. of meadow ground and a close of pasture called Blackwell, 9a. (*Endowed Charities Wilts.* 1908 vol. 1. p. 1024-1025).

WOOTTON RIVERS rectory

845   n. d. early 17th cent.[1] (D1/24/231/1)
The parsonage house containing 3 fields of building, the barn containing 4 rooms and 2 cuts, a stable built on posts. 8 beast leazes, 60 sheep leazes. Orchard with garden, ½a. of ground. 15½a. of arable. 8a. of meadow and pasture within either besides a certain ground lately enclosed, 13a. 1yd. The parson has the hay of 1a. of meadow but no after feeding. Leonard Pile pays 16d. p. a. to the parson for a vicarage which hithertofore has belonged to the parsonage as it is reported. The most that this parsonage is worth as it has been valued by the parish is £30 the year the cure and other payments discharged.

John Cooley, parson, Thomas Taichentr [X], Ralph Bainninge [X], John Bainton [X], Peter Rawlings [X].

1. Before 1629 when John Cooley was succeeded as rector.

846 n. d. late 17th cent.[1] (D1/24/231/2)
A fair chancel with a communion table with rails and baluster, a spacious churchyard railed around. A dwelling house containing 7 rooms [roomeths], a backside and garden with a close of meadow adjoining, 1a. 3r., a barn containing 5 bays, a close of meadow caled the Moors, 1a. An enclosed ground called the Search, 13a.; an enclosed ground called the Lawn, 8a.; 2 enclosed grounds called the Clench grounds, 10a. and 2a.; 2 enclosed grounds called the Priest Craft, 4a.; enclosed gardens adjoining the common field, 1a. 1a. in the field called Sowbrooks acres. A piece of land in Little N. field lying over Marlborough Way, 4a.; 1a. in the same field at Gobling hole. In the Great N. field a piece of land against the hill adjoining to the great linchets end, 3a.; 1a. more against the hill adjoining to William Oatridge on W. side. All manner of great and small tithes.
Alexander Forbes, rector, Daniel Tomson, George Hellier, churchwardens.

1. Between 1671-1682 when Alexander Forbes was rector.

847 1684 (D1/24/231/3)
As 846. Jeremiah Williams, rector, Edmund Blake, Anthony Bonning, churchwardens.

848 1704 (D1/24/231/4)
As 846. Jeremiah Williams, John Jennings [X], Anthony Mist, Thomas Flory, Thomas Crook, churchwardens.

849 17 Jul 1789 (D1/24/231/5)
The house built with brick and tiled. On the ground floor 2 parlours with deal floors, one wainscotted entirely with deal, the other with deal chair high and papered above, 2 pantries, kitchen and brewhouse with brick floors, on the first landing place on the stairs, a small room, aspect N. E. with cellar under and brick floor, lately built by the present rector, 4 chambers, 2 wainscotted chair high, 2 papered, a study, 4 garrets, all rooms ceiled and floored with deal.
An old cottage in Parsonage drove way, homestead including the garden and yard, 3r. 36½p. The mead adjoining, 1a. 1r. 1½p. The withy bed adjoining to the mead, 1r. 14½p. A barn, 5 bays, 71ft. by 29ft., the chaise house adjoining the barn, 27ft. by 13½ft. thatched and boarded. Woodhouse, thatched and boarded, a stable brick wall, 27ft. by 16½ft. Garden boundaries in the front of the house pallisades on brick footing 18½yd. A brick wall next the road 27½yd., an earth wall thatched and plastered, 35yd., all erected by the present rector in the room of a dead hedge. The other part of the garden is bounded with a quick set hedge.
A piece of moor, Lammas grounds, bounded on each side with a quick set hedge, 1a. 3 ¾p. An enclosed ground called Parsonage Search, 13a. 2r. 15¼p. An enclosed field called Clinch ground, 11a. 1¾p. An enclosed ground called Priest croft, 3a. 3r. 4¾p. An enclosed ground called the Lawn, 7a. 3r. 8p.
In S. brook field, 1a. 8½p. In N. field a piece crossing Marlborough way, 3a. 2r. 2p. bounded on each side by lawns or linchets. In Golden Hole furlong a piece called One Half but measures 1r. 36½p.

Parsonage piece in Long lands near Marlborough way, 2a. 2r. 15p., bounded E. by a linchet and W. by Hard Land furlong.

In the Hill furlong a piece of land called an acre but measures only 3r. 28p. bounded by a linchet W. and Warners acre E. Common of pasture for 120 sheep. 2 of the principal farmers say they have heard of a small modus for cows. There has never been a perambulation within the parish, it being surrounded by a ring fence. There is another piece of land called Drove acre, 3r. 4p.

Trees standing on the glebe: 2 sapling oaks in Priest Croft. In the Moor 1 oak, 12 sapling oaks, 1 elm, 7 ash. In the Withy bed 3 oaks in the church ground 4 sapling oaks. The parish clerk is appointed by the rector and his wages are 20s. p. a. payable by the parish.

William Mayo, rector, Richard Francis, Isaac Wheeler, churchwardens, William Scriven, Philip Neale, Richard Higgins, other inhabitants.

Memo.: The communion plate consists of a silver cup and cover and a pewter flagon no inscription. The communion table is covered with fine crimson cloth given by Mrs Francis Ernle of Brimslade (in Savernake Parish) and the pulpit is hung with the same. William Mayo, rector.

NORTH WRAXALL rectory

850   12 May 1588 (D1/24/232/1)

Concerning an answer to the general inquisition for the glebe land and other duties we know and do know and understand no wrong to be denied by any man to be denied to the parsonage but that the parson hath time out of mind had his glebe land with all kind of tithes, customs oblations emoluments according to the Queen's highness ecclesiastical laws of this realm of England and honourable order of the same to the comfort every and all which say good save our queen Elizabeth.

Thomas Hatherill, John Cocks, churchwardens, John Webbe, William Brewar, sidesmen. *Names in the same hand.*

851   25 Sep 1608 (D1/24/232/2)

Terrier of all the a. (both arable and several). Arable in the S. field: At Newwood, 5a., at Nuttscocke, 1a.; Prest Grove hill, 1½a.; at the wooden bridge, 1½a.; above Broadland over Colerne [Cullernes] way, 1½a.; at the little bush, 1a.; at Nuttscocke above the way, 1½a.; at Black Cross, 1a.; at the Park end, 1a.; at Horte grove and over rudge way, 1½a.; upon Liggrove hill, 2a.; upon Horte grove, 1a.; upon Gorryes hill, 1¼a.; above Shutt mead, 1½a.; above W. mead, 1a.; upon the moor, 1a.; at Lypyate, 1½a.; shooting upon Waine way, 1½a.; the Parsons brake and the land at Wain way shutt, 2a.; at Pokridge path above Kitle, 3½a.; upon Kitley hill, 1½a.; upon White Cross, 3a.

Arable in the N. field: upon the moor, 1½a.; upon Moor hill, 3a.; in Abden 2½a.; by Coomes footpath, 1a.; over Churchway, 1a.; at the Croft end, 5a.; in Butt furlong, 2a.: Under the footway; upon the Fosse [Force], 3a.; upon Green Mead end, 1a.; in Small furlong, 1a.; over Mill way, 1a.; upon the Fosse Way, 2½a.; upon Mountons Bower, 1a.; upon Burford way, 1a.; over the Fosse way in

Frogdens Bottom 1a.; upon Wheat rudge along by Marsh field way, 2a.; upon Fox Grove end, 3a.; below Bayles bushes, 1a.; 1¼ head a. above Baylies bushs; above Innocks, 3½a.; at Innocks Corn, 5a.; behind Dorwes Stile, ½a.; above the Laund, 3a.; beyond Barelegged bush, 5a.; in Cadley, 7a.

Severall [*fields*]: Shutmead, 1a.; Coule croft, 1a.; the Cheese, 1a.; the Hammes, 1a.; Lipyate, ½a.

Thomas Coren, parson, John Bruer, churchwarden, Thomas Wodam, William Wodam, Richard Colteart, Benedict Jaksenes. *Names in the same hand.*

852   2 Dec 1704 (D1/24/232/3)
The dwelling or parsonage house with 2 barns, an oxhouse, a stable, 2 gardens and an orchard adjoining. In the N. field in several parcels, 53½a. In the S. field in several parcels, 36¼a. Enclosed land: a large close called Prestgrove, *c.* 12a.; a close called Four acres; a small close called Shootmead, *c.* 1a.; a close called Lippeat leaze, *c.* 1a.; a close called the Tining, *c.* 5a.; a close called Coldcroft, *c.* 1a. A portion of tithe paid out of the mills; Hennards mill, 4s. p. a., Doncomb mill, 4s. p. a.; Ford mill, 3s. 4d. p. a.

Thomas Goddard, rector, Mark Davis, John Nicholls, churchwardens, Thomas Parry, Daniel Hawker, overseers.

853   29 Jul 1783 (D1/24/232/4)
The parsonage house which is built with stone and tiled, consists of 2 parlours, 7 lodging rooms, 4 papered, 2 not papered, 1 hung with green stuff, 2 pantries, kitchen and back kitchen which serves for a brewhouse, a cellar under the largest parlour. Outhouses or 2 barns built with stone and covered with thatch, one 57ft. by 18ft., the other 38ft. by 17ft. 3 stables, one 3 stalled, the other 2 stalled, the other an old one and has not been used as a stable for many years; all built with stone and covered with thatch. A coach house and granary over built with stone and covered with tile. A cart house covered with thatch. The ground on which the house stands together with the farm yard and garden is *c.* 1¼a. The glebe land which is all enclosed: Press grove, 12a.; Four acres at Ford; Shute mead, 1a.; the Parsons Tyning, 5a.; Larish, 1a.; Goreys hill, 13a.; Spy park, 3a.; over the Bristol road 7½a.; the Ham, 2a.; Tyning going to Combe, 13a.; Middle Way Tyning, 9½a.; New Tyning, 6a.; Westmead hill, 17½a.; Parsons, 4a.; Lypeer Leese, 1a. A portion of tithe paid out of 3 mills, Hennard mill, 4s. p. a.; Doncomb mill, 4s. p. a.; Ford mill, 3s. 4d. p. a.; £5 p. a. paid by Paul Methuen esq. for the tithe wood. But that is no modus; for it was but £3 p. a. before I demanded more. The whole with what I have in hand is let for £190 p. a. There are timber trees of any value as the glebe is enclosed with walls.

In the Church a bell, communion plate, 2 cups, no mark on them but 1746. One of the cups are real and the other french plate. 2 small salvers, one real, the other french plate. The clerk is elected by the rector and the stipend is paid by the parish out of the church rate. The churchyard wall is at the expense of the parish.

Henry Still, rector, Isaac Holborow, Daniel Parker, churchwarden, Isaac Holborow, John Willton, inhabitants.

WROUGHTON [alias Ellingdon] rectory and vicarage

854   n. d. early 17th cent.[1] (D1/24/233/1)
Rectory: 6½a. of arable land in Hackpin field. 44a. of arrable in the Upper
Fields. 3r. of meadow. 29a. of arable. 9a. of laynes and a plot of 3a. of marsh
ground divided in the E. field. 6a. of meadow, 4a. of laynes and 12a. 3r. of arable
in the field called Lot meadow. 4a. of pasture in several.
    Vicarage: ½a. of meadow called theVicarage close adjoining the churchyard.
By me Oliver Brunsell, [rector].

1.   Oliver Brunsell was rector from 1612 possibly to 1622.This terrier may date possibly
    from 1613 after the visitation of the archbishop of Canterbury.

855   1671 (D1/24/233/2)
An old mansion house, 2 barns with a stable, cow house, cart house, a garden
and orchard. 2 little pasture grounds of several, 5a. 2 grounds lying by them
which are 26½a. In the Lower field, 42a., whereof 3 parts are yearly ploughed
and a fourth lies unploughed. In the Upper field, 75a. of poor land whereof half
is yearly ploughed, the other lies common.
    Several farms in the parish belong to Sutton's hospital[1] and pay an amount
for small composition for their tithes; which is particularly to be seen in their
survey of the hospital.The remainder of the parish pay their tithe in kind except
some tithes which arise out of Elcombe, belonging to Eton College and are in
the possession ofThomas Coulman who pays to the college a yearly rent according
to the price of corn.
    Dr. Robert Newlin, president of Corpus Christi College, Oxford is now
parson who has granted to his tenant then a lease for 3 lives; rent £50 p. a. to be
paid on Ladyday [25 Mar] and Michaelmas [29 Scp].
    The vicar, Mr.Thomas Newlin, has the small tithes with a mansion house,
garden, orchard, a little close adjoining, 1a., with the feeding of the churchyard,
a stable and a woodhouse with an annuity of £45 p. a. paid out of the parsonage
by Dr. Newlin's tenant which makes his vicarage worth £80 p. a.
    The parsonage with the glebe is rated to payments at £2, 600 p. a. pays
yearly to Winchester[2] a pension of £5 to the vicar, £45 to Dr. Newlin of this
place, the tenths £3 2s. 5d., procuration, 7s. 9½d., besides reparations of the
parsonage house, chancel and other payments.
    Thomas Newlin, vicar, John Goldingham, curate, Anthony Lidiate, Edmund
Cope, churchwardens.

1.   The London Charterhouse founded by Thomas Sutton d. 1611.
2.   The dean and chapter Winchester cathedral held the manor of Wroughton.

856   1678 (D1/24/233/3)
The rectory: 6½a. of arable in Hackpin field. 44a. in the Upper fields and 3r. of
meadow. 29a. of arable, 9a. of laines and a plot of moor [marish] ground of 3a.,
divided in E. field. 6a. of meadow, 4a. 3r. of laynes and 12a. of arable in a field
called the Lot mead. 4a. of pasture in several.

The vicarage: 1½a. of meadow called the Vicarage close adjoining into the churchyard.

Thomas Newlin, vicar, Richard Geale, John Tarrant, churchwardens.

WYLYE rectory

857 21 May 1588. (D1/24/234/1)
Survey by John Kent and John Ailes, churchwardens with the help of Robert Bellye, Robert Lock, John Tailor, Oliver Herys, Henry Kent, the most ancient and substantial presented at the bishop's visitation at Salisbury.

Tithe: All the tithes except tithe wool of 300 sheep belonging to the farm of Wylye to be deducted from the whole farm flock in this manner: The farmer is accustomed at shear time to have his whole flock in a penning and 300 of the flock must run forth out of the penning at aventure or at leat[1] as they commonly call it and of the 300 so running forth the farmer must pay no tithe wool but go free for the same.

Arable: 5a. in the E. field and 3 x ½a. lying above a little close belonging to the parsonage. In the W. field 5a. lying upon Hindon's way in a piece and 3 x ½a. above the farm hide in another piece.

Meadow: 1½a. in the W. meadow by the water side called Prestnam whereof the rector has no the after leaze any longer than until the meadow be rid and every tenant has carried away his hay.

Pasture: A little several close lying in the midst of the town. Another little portion of pasture called Scotland in the E. part of the parish abutting upon Hanging Langford ground by the riverside. Another close above the parsonage house *c.* 1a.

Sheep down: Pasture for 60 sheep, a ram and a barge going as far forth as the farmer's flock in the E. field.

Commons for beasts: Pasture in Horse Castle, the moor and common fields for 6 kine and a bull as far forth as the farmer and, by the testimony of Robert Belly an ancient man of 80 years and the parson's man 60 since, 3 hauliers [halliers] more going as the rest.

A parcel of tithe out of the parish: There lies in the parish of Little Langford a meadow called Dutnam, 14a., of which the parson of Wylye has in his right to cut and go and of that part of the farm of Wylye the parson has ever had the tithe.

1. See **545** footnote 1.

858 n. d. early 17th cent.[1] (D1/24/234/2)
A parsonage house upon London roadway in Wylye betwixt the tenement of William Poticarie on N. and the tenement of one Barnes on S., with a garden, orchard and meadow, nearly ½a.

5a. of arable land by Hindon way. 2a. lying in the E. field by the Parsonage hedge. A little tenement wherein James Best <Hill *struck through*> dwells with a garden plot. 3 x ½a. of arable lying on Hindon way.

A meadow ground called Presnam in the common meadow called W. mead abutting on the waterside called Three halves. But it is at the least 2a. by length [longge] which lie from the Sunday after Ladyday [25 Mar] and then it is the parsons to mow, cut and carry away and then his hay being gone he has no longer for that year feeding thereon. A little plot of meadow called Scotland, *c.* ½a. Pasture for 6 kine and a bull and 3 horses to feed with the farmer in Horse Castle the moor and the fields as far forth as the Farmer. 60 sheep, barge and ram going with the farmers flock in the E. end of Downsfield as far forth as the farmer.

Tithe of 10a. in Dutnam part of Dutnam mead, *c.* 13a. in Little Langford. Tithe of all corn, wool, lamb, meadow, pasture, oblations and all other kinds of tithe due by law, both in Wylye and Deptford, only the farmer of Wylye claims and has as long as we remember gone free of 300 sheep of the whole farmer's flock running out at the leat.[2]

Thomas Bower [*rector*], James Gullifer [X], John Oliver, churchwardens and sidesmen, Edward ?Smyth.

1. Thomas Bower was rector between 1582-1619.
2. See **545** footnote 1.

859   6 Dec 1677 (D1/24/234/3)
A parsonage house with barn, stables, pigeon house and other outhouses near London roadway betwixt a tenement of William Potticary on N. and William Barnes on S. with gardens and orchard, *c.* 1a.

5a. of arable land lying by Hindon highway. 3 x ½a. of arable land lying on Hindon's way. 5a. lying in the E. field by the Parsonage hedge. A meadow formerly called Comb-Stocks now called Bisses close or the Hay close, *c.* 1a. 3 x ½a. of arable land above the last close of the same breadth as the close is. A plot of meadow called Presnam or Parradice adjoining to the W. meads and abutting on the water side being above 2a. by a lug. A little plot of meadow called Scotland lying at the E. end on the water side near Hanging Langford meadows, *c.* ½a.

Pasture for 6 kine and a bull to feed with farmers on the Cow down and in the fields as far forth as the farmers. Pasture for 60 sheep, barge and ram going with the farmers' flock in the E. end down and fields as far forth as the farmers. *Tithes and exception as* **858**.

John Stevens, rector, William Pashen, William Pottiakrey, churchwardens, William Potticary, William Musell, John Lock, Bridget Poticary, William Barnes.

860   1783 (D1/24/234/4)
Arable land 1a. by Hindon road, 2r. 6p.; 3a. head piece by Hindon road, 1a. 3r. 20p.; 5a. by Dinton road, 3a. 2r. 26p.; 3 x ½a. adjoining to the pasture, 1a. Meadow land: Priests mead bounded by the river, 2a.; Scotland plot (hay only) bounded by the river, 2r.; pasture joining to the road 2a. 10r. 63 sheep leaze. 28 trees little and great besides 24 elm and ash in the orchard. The above account given by farmer Christopher Fricker.

The parsonage house and premises bounded on E. by the street, on S. by the Hindon road, on W. by Neither way and on N. by Mr. Poticary's premises. The house is built with stone and flints interspersed and covered with slate or tile. A cellar under the great parlour divided with board and lathes, a stone floor. Ground floor, great parlour wainscotted, boarded and ceiled 16ft. 4in. by 19ft.: Hall wainscotted and papered, ceiled and the floor earthen, 15ft. 2in. by 16ft. 4in. N.B. a little butler's pantry opening into the hall; another pantry by the cellar divided from the passage under the stairs by boards 9ft. by 9½ft.: Little parlour wainscotted, boarded and ceiled 9½ft. by 11½ft.: kitchen ceiled, a stone floor 16ft. by 15ft. N. B.; the rooms were measured by a carpenter and the board contents of the chambers and garrets may be pretty well known from their respective situations. Upstairs study over pantry papered; room over great parlour with a closet, both papered; room over hall, papered; room over kitchen, wainscotted and closet within likewise; room over little parlour, papered. N.B.; a back staircase from the little parlour to this room, garrets consisting of 5 rooms, 1 over study, 1 over best chamber, 1 over the little parlour and the other over the kitchen; a little lathed up place, all the rest open and making passages to the rooms; they are mostly ceiled.

Outhouses: Washhouse and pigeon house, slated or tiled all the rest thatched, a covered open place adjoining to the washhouse, then a range of building divided into 3 parts and built with different materials: A coach house with a stable adjoining; a barn with a 3 stalled stable adjoining: another behind fronting the house; a necessary house adjoining; a cart house; a necessary house in the garden and a pigeon house built with stone and flint, situated in the orchard.

The court before the house is fenced on each side with mud walls, thatched and fronting the house with a stone wall and coping. The garden is fenced with a quickset hedge towards the orchard on all the other sides with walls and buildings of earth and stone of one sort or other and covered with thatch and much the same are all the walls about the yard. The orchard on all the other sides with a dead hedge.

The plate of the church: A silver tankard with this inscription on it 'Dabit Deus his quoque quartam' and 'Deo Trin-uni optima maximo Poculum hoc argentum dat dicat consecratque Johannes Stevens Huius Ecclesiae de Wyly Rector in Usum Sacramentalem in Caena Domini Anno Domini 1686'. A gilt cup with curious devices upon it. A silver large plate for the bread with this inscription 'Deo Trin-uni optimo maximo Patinam hanc argentam dat dicat consecratque Johannes Stevens hunius Ecclesiae de Wyly Rector in usum Sacramentalem in Caena domini 1686'. A silver font basin with this inscription 'Wyley Church 1781'. 4 bells and a clock, a scarlet cloth, cushions and furniture with fringe and tassels of the same colour for the pulpit. The same for the front of the desk and a cloth of the same sort and colour for the communion table, 2 large wooden frames in the chancel on each side of the E. window containing the Belief,[1] the Lords Prayer and Ten commandments and a wooden frame on the N. side specifying Mr. Willoughby's charity.[2]

J[ohn] Eyre, curate, Edward Fricker, Christopher Fricker, William Small, Thomas Hayter, churchwardens, George Patient, William Potticary.

1. The Nicene Creed.
2. Established by Christopher Willoughby in 1678 for the benefit of the poor of the parish.

YATESBURY rectory

861   n. d. late 16th cent.[1] (D1/24/235/1)
A note of such lands as are held by Mr. Good, parson.
   In the Foreign [Fearine] field: ½a. of arable land shooting upon Cherrills
field. 4a. of arable in the same furlong shooting upon the Town field. 1a. of arable
lying against the last 4a. 1a. shooting upon the Town field. 4a. in the middle of
the Fearine field. 2a. and 2 other a. shooting uon Cherill field 6a., 6a. and 7a. A
close of pasture, ½a., whereupon the house is situated all which are in the lordship
of Mr. Michael Ernly esq. who is patron of the same. In the Town field: 2a. of
arable shooting upon the B[. . .]e mead. 1a. shooting upon the Home meadow.
1a. shooting upon a place there called the Barrows.
   All manner of tithes are due to the parson.

1.   Thomas Good was rector up to 1598, John Good from 1545.

862   1613 (D1/24/235/2)
Terrier delivered at the visitation of George, archbishop of Canterbury.[1] Dwelling
house, 2 barns, a hayhouse and a stable. A little garden, a close adjoining the
parsonage house and an orchard, c. ½a.
   32a. of arable land of which 16a. lie (to be sowed) for one year in the E. field
of the farm occupied Mr. John Daniel viz: 3a. on the Knowle against the Parsonage
house; 2a. shoot upon Church acre; 4a. join the Church acre on the S. side; 1a.
shoots from the S. corner of the said 4a. E. upon the Town field; 4½a. in one
piece in the same furlong abutts the Town field; ½a. on S. side of the said piece
towards Cunning barrow; 1 head a. at the E. end of the said 4. ½a.; 2a. in the
Town field to be sowed in the same year of which 1a. shoots on the Town mead
and the other lies above it shooting towards the 2 great barrows.
   14a. to be sown in the other year of which 12a. are in the W. field viz.: 7a. at
the furthest end of the Thirty acres westwards from the farm; 3a. up the Knowle
by Devizes way [the vizeway]; 2a. shoot upon the way between Cherhill [Cherrills]
field and the farm field southwards; 2a. in the Town field shooting upon
Sheepestead towards the Windmill which are to be sowed in the same year.
   All tithes to be paid 'in specie and in their kynde'.
   Peter Ritch, rector, John Chilfester, Thomas Smyth, John Good, Henry
Renolds [X], Thomas Seyneye [X].

1.   George Abbot.

863   30 Oct 1671 (D1/24/235/3)
A dwelling house, 2 barns, 1 oxhouse and stable. The churchyard, a close and
garden, c. ½a. 32a. 1yd.[1] in all the fields as follows and that the rector has had no
feeding in our knowledge in the lambs in the fields; 7a. in Sir George Hungerford's
field bounded on the W. with Thomas Whit's land; 3a. shooting E. and W.; 3a.
shooting E. and W.; 2a. shooting towards Cherhill [Chirrall] field, ½a. shooting
towards the Town field; 5a. shooting towards the Town field; 1a. shooting towards
the Town field; 1a. shooting N. and S. all of it bounded on each side with Sir

George Hungerford's land; 4a. bounded on the one side with Sir George Hungerford's land and on the other side with the Church acre; 2a. shooting N. and S. bounded with Sir George Hungerford's land; 3yd. shooting against the Meads; 1a. shooting against the Town field; 2a. lying by the Borne meads in the Town field. The rector has all the tithes in the parish according to the custom of the place.

Thomas Johnson, rector, Anthony Elton, Michael Pope, churchwardens.

1. 31a. 1yd. in **864**.

864   22 Dec 1704 (D1/24/235/4)
As 863 with amendment in footnote. Henry Hindley, rector, William Neatte, John Pope, churchwardens, Robert Bullock, Michael Pope, Thomas Brodfield.

865   2 Jun 1808 (D1/24/235/5)
A coppice, 6a. occupied by Revd. Money: N. Cains, pasture, enclosed, 8a. occupied by Robert Caswell: New Ground, arable, enclosed, 7a. occupied by Robert Caswell: In the field by Barrow way, arable, 1a. 1r. occupied by Robert Caswell: In Barrow field, arable, 1a. occupied by John Washbourn: In Mr. Tanner's Home field, arable, 1a. occupied by John Tanner: Ochard adjoining the garden, barn and parsonage barn occupied by Robert Caswell. These are the estimated quantities, the corn being on the land at present prevents measurement.

William Money, rector, Robert Caswell, churchwarden.

YATTON KEYNELL rectory

866   n. d. [1671][1] (D1/24/236/1)
A parsonage house, outhouses, barn, stable, cowhouse all in good repair with gardens, orchards. 2 pasture grounds called the Upper and Lower crates, *c.* 12a.: A meadow adjoining called Poole-Crate, *c.* 6a.; likewise another meadow called Moor mead, *c.* 2a.[2] Certain pasture or arable grounds called the New Inclosures, 16a.[3] all which several grounds lie adjoining to the house and orchard eastward bounded N. by certain grounds of Samuel Reade, and by a ground of the wid. Bishop called Gores close, E. by a ground of Thomas Wild called New Leaze and a certain ground of Mr. John Taylor called the Groves, S. certain closes of Nathanial Light called the Wood closes, W. the highway to Chippenham.[4]

A pasture ground called Great Halls Moors, *c.* 10a.[5] bounded out by certain grounds of Samuel Read called the Moors and Mr. John Taylor's ground called the Filmeads on W. and N., grounds of Nathanial Light and Samuel Read called Halls moors on S. and E. Another ground called Little Halls Moors, *c.* 4a. bounded out by Mr. John Taylor's Filmeads on N. and E., a little ground of James Hill. called Filmead on W. and Nathan Light's Great Halls Moors on S.

A pasture ground called Little Filmead, *c.* 3a.,[6] John Harris having ½a. in the midst of it, bounded E. Samuel Read's[7] Great Filmead, W. by a meadow of Thomas Cullimore[8] called Filmead.

1½a. of meadow ground enclosed in a meadow of John Bishop[9] called the Yonder Filmead having a merestone on each end bounded out on W. Thomas

Wild, E. a meadow of the earl of Kent[10] now occupied by John Light, S. the N. field of Biddestone.[11]

A meadow ground called the Groves, c. 4a., adjoining N.W. meadow of John Harris called the Groves, a meadow of Samuel Read called Sheephouse mead, E. Samuel Read's Lower Groves and a meadow of Thomas Bell of Allington.

In the S. field which lies common 5a.: 1½a. adjoining to a ground of John Harris called Biddistone way leaze N. and the highway to Biddestone E.; 2 x ½a., one at the end of another, running up under Cullimores Green pitts and a hedge that parts Yatton's S. field from Biddestone's N. field.; ½a. that shoots upon John Bishop's hedge S., a piece of 3a. of the earl of Kent, E.; ½a. that runs under Bishop's hedge along by the wayside that leads to W.Yatton on W., part of which is enclosed ground of Thomas Wild called Long Wall leaze; 1a. that lies between John Bishop's ½a. under Long wall and 1a. of Thomas Wild on S. side; ½a. that lies under William Ast's hedge southwards and adjoins 2a. of John Bishop north-eastwards.

In the N. field 25a.: 1a. upon W.Yatton hill called the Head acre bounded by 1a. of the earl of Kent S. side[12] shooting on the churchway; 1½a. called Hammer land running along the away that leads unto Long Dean mill; the ½a. or butt shoots up the hillside by ½a. of John Bishop; ½a.[13] under the Quarre hill on N. shooting down upon a close of Richard Riley W., the highway adjoining along by the S. side of it to Long Dean; a little piece of meadow lying between 1a. of the earl of Kent, being meadow, and a close of Augustice Clerke enclosed out of the field;[14] a freestone quarry and the hillside by it with 1½a. of arable land above the hill bounding upon 2a. of Richard Riley[15] on W. and 5a. of Samuel Read esq. on E.; ½a.[16] in the same furlong called the Long half adjoining to 1a. of Mr. John Tayler on E. and a piece of 6a. of Samuel Read on W.; 2a. in the Court furlong adjoining to 1½a. of John Harris[17] on S. and ½a. of Nathanial Light on N.; ½a.[18] lying between 2a. of John Harris on E. and ½a. of James Hill on W.;[19] Upon Catlands hill there lies a piece of 6a. adjoining to 3a. of Mr. John Tayler on S. and 3a. of Mr. Thrifts on N.W.;[20] 2a. adjoining to a ground of John Harris called Half Penny leaze and another of Richard Riley on N. and 1a. of the wid. Bishop on W.; a little ½a. thereby in the same furlong between 1a. of the wid. Bishop on E. and 2a. of Samuel Read on W.; 1½a. shooting upon 3a. of Mr. John Tayler on N. and lying between 1a. of William Tayler on E. and 1a. of the earl of Kent on W.; 1a. that shoots against 3a. of Mr. Thrift on N.; 3a. upon Warre hill near adjoining to John Moody's 2a. N.; 2a. by the Stump upon Common hill; 1a. of John Bishop lying between the earl of Kent's land on N. and John Bishop on S.; ½a. called the Butts, ½a. adjoining on N. there is a piece of James Organ of Castle Combe on W. and S. John Bishop's land on S.

A little piece of meadow ground lying under Collam hill by the brook containing c. ½a.; ½a. on W. side of the brook in the occupation and possession of Thomas Flower of Castle Combe and the other ½a. lies under the Common hill now enclosed and possessed by Thomas Wild the earl of Kent's ground being at the W. end of it. Another pasture ground called Broomefield leaze, c. 6a., adjoining the highway called Broomefield way on S. and a ground of Samuel Reade on W. and Jacob Woodman's ground on N. A pasture called Bunniards, c. 8a., adjoining the highway leading to Easton Piercey on N. side, a ground of Mr. Bull in Easton Piercey on E. and Ashwood piece on W.

True copy. George Child, rector, John Harris [X], Thomas Cullimore, church-wardens.

1. Endorsed Wilts. Terr. 1671/2 File G. The same churchwardens signed the 1671 bishop's transcript.
2. 3a. in **867**.
3. 18a. in **867**.
4. 1a. of mead enclosed more or less the hedge running along the highway in **867**.
5. 12a. in **867**.
6. 2½a. in **867**.
7. The wid. Read in **867**.
8. The wid. Wastfield in **867** the meadow not named.
9. Arthur Ven in **867**.
10. Tenant not named in **867**.
11. See **867** for variations after this point.
12. Bounded by 4a. of the earl of Kent on W. side and shooting on the churchway from W. Yatton in **867**.
13. This plot omitted in **867**.
14. Clarkes leaze tenant John Light pays 3s. 6d. in **867**.
15. Mr. Tayler in **867**.
16. This land omitted in **867**.
17. William Harris in **867**.
18. 2a. of arable in **867**.
19. 3a. of William Harris on W. in **867**.
20. See **867** for variations in N. field from this point.

867   20 Oct 1698 (D1/24/236/2)
*As **866** as far as to footnote 11 except that the S. field is not named.*
½a. that runs up under Bishop's hedge along by the way that leads to W. Yatton on W., whereof is enclosed in a ground of Thomas Wilde called Long way leaze. 1a. that lies between Bishop's ½a. under Long Wall and 1½a. of Thomas Wilde on S.; ½a. that lies under William Ast's hedge southward and adjoins 2a. of John Bishop N. and Giddy Hall ½a. E.; 3a. up Warre hill lying by land of Thomas Kent N., John Light N. and S. near Mr. Wild's leaze enclosed on S. W. near Graynes Quarry 2a.

In the N. Field. *As **865** to footnote 20.* 3a. running under Richard Riley's hedge and abutting on N. on ground of Richard Riley; 1a. called the Butts; part which head 3a. of Mr. Thrift on E. and other part heads the Long half; 1½a. abutting on 3a. of John Tayler N. and William Tayler E.; 1½a. of the earl of Kent on W.; 1a. called Broad acre abutting N. on land of Mr. Thrift; 2a. by the Stump on Common hill *as **866**.* A little piece of meadow under Collum hill by the brook side, *c.* ½a., now enclosed, part whereof lies on the other side of the brook in Castle Combe, the earl of Kent on W. A ground of pasture ground called Broomfield leaze, *c.* 6a., land of Samuel Read on W. and Jacob Woodman on N. A ground called Bunnyard, 8a., near the highway leading to Easton Piercey and abutting on N. upon land late of Mr. Bull and on W. upon the land of Sir Adam Wortley.

George Child, rector, Mr. Francis Child, Charles Broom, churchwardens, Gorges Scrope gent., John Browning, Thomas Mills senior, Thomas Mills junior, Richard Pitt, Henry Freme, John Light, Isaac Hawkins, Augustice Clerk. *Signatures of the rector and churchwardens the others in the same hand.*

868   1704 (D1/24/236/3)

According to Gilbert bishop of Salisbury here is a true terrier.

A parsonage house, outhouses, barn and stable with gardens, orchard and backside. 2 pasture grounds called the Upper and Lower Crates, *c.* 12a.; a meadow ground called Pool Crate, *c.* 6a.; a meadow called Moor mead, *c.* 2a.; 3 certain pasture or arable grounds called the New Enclosures, *c.* 18a., with a little a. of meadow by them adjoining to the highway to Chippenham, all these grounds lie adjoining together onto the house and orchard east and south-eastward on arable ground called Great Hall moors, *c.* 12a., adjoining to a ground of Mr. John Tayler called the Field meads; another arable ground called Little Hall moor, *c.* 4a., 'asideing' by a ground of James Hills called the Hall moors southward and a meadow ground called the Groves; *c.* 4a., adjoining a meadow ground of George Harris called the Grove on N.; another meadow called Little Field mead, *c.* 2½a., in which ground lies ½a. now belongs to William Harris, now living in our parish; this ground lies by the highway that leads to Biddestone [Bestone]; a piece of meadow, *c.* 1½a., enclosed in a meadow of Arthur Ven called the Yonder Fieldmead, ½a., which runs along the wayside that leads to W. Yatton on W. is an enclosed ground of Mrs. Wild called Longway leaze.

In the field there is 1a. that lies between Bishop's ½a. under Long Wall; ½a. enclosed with 2a. of John Bishop by Giddy Hall. 3a. upon Warhill lying by the lands of Thomas Kent near Grayns quarry. 1a. upon W. Yatton hill called the Head acre abutting on the churchway from W. Yatton. 1½a., called the Hamer land running along the way to Long Dean mill, one part of it shoots up the hillside by ½a. of John Bishop. A piece of ground enclosed in a meadow of the earl of Kent in the bottom between the fields joining to a meadow of Augusten Clarke on W. side for that butt of meadow the tenant pays 3s. 6d. p. a. A quarry of stone and some waste ground by it, with 4a. of arable land above it abutting on 1a. of Mr. Tayler on W. and *c.* ½a. of William Drinkwater on N. 2a. in the Court furlong 'asideing' by 1½a. of William Harris S., and ½a. of William Drinkwater N. 2a. in the furlong by 1a. of William Harris between them, called the Fatch lands. Upon Catlands hill is 6a. joining to 3a. of Mr. John Tayler on S. 3a. running under Richard Ryle's hedge called Cattland leaze. 1a. called the Butts part whereof heads 3a. of Mr. Thrift on E. 1½a. abutting on 3a. of William Taylor northward. 1a. called Broad acre butting northwards on the land of Mr. Thrift. 2a. by Stump on Common hill, 1a. of John Bishop lying between them, land of the earl of Kent on N. and John Bishop on S.

A little piece of meadow lying under Collum hill by the brookside, *c.* ½a., now enclosed, part of it in the ground of the wid. Wild (sic) gent., the other part has on the other ground of pasture called Broomfield leaze, *c.* 6a., adjoining to the highway that leads to Broomfield. A pasture ground called Bunyards, *c.* 8a., lying by the highway to Easton Piercy and adjoins northward to a ground of farmer Smith, and a ground of Mr. Francis Giles on W.

John Light, Henry Drinkwater, churchwardens, Charles Broom [X], Richard Pitt, overseers, Elizabeth Wild, Mary Read, William Harris, William Drinkwater, Richard Ryly, James Freeme senior, Thomas Messeter, George Harris.

869 1783 (D1/24/236/4)
Terrier to be presented at the primary visitation of bishop Shute at Chippenham 30 Jul 1783.

A parsonage house now divided in 2 parts; one of which is sufficient for a clergyman with a small family, the other, by the addition of a new dairy in 1764, for a tenant to rent the glebe and tithes, with outhouses, barn, pigsties, wagon house and stable, milking yard and shrubbery at the front of the house. The minister's garden and orchard behind the house contain more than 1a. of ground and are enclosed with a good wall.

2 pasture grounds called the Upper and Lower Crate, c. 8a.; Pool Crate, c. 6a.; Marc mead, c. 3a.; 2 pasture grounds called the New Inclosures, c. 7a. and c. 5a., with 1a. of pasture adjoining to the highway that leads to Chippenham, at present known as the Withy Ground. All these grounds lie together adjoining to the house, garden and orchard E. and S. eastward, containing together c. 30a.

An arable ground called the Great Hallmores, c. 9a., adjoining to 2 grounds of Mr. William Beard on E. and S., and to a ground of Edward Sparrow on N.W.; Lesser Hallmores, c. 6½a., adjoining 2 grounds of Mr. Richard Taylor on N.W.

A pasture ground called the Grove, c. 4a., adjoining a ground of Mrs. Browning on S., John Witchell W., Mr. Gale N.; ½a. which runs along by the way side that leads to W. Yatton, bounded on the opposite side by a ground of Mrs. Drewett; in the midst of Mrs. Drewett's in the field there are c. 2a. of arable for which her tenant pays a yearly rent to the rector.

In the field an arable ground called Start Bush, ¾a., below it and adjoining to it another piece of arable land, 5¼a.; another piece of arable land adjoining it called the Wall Tining, c. 7a. A quarry of freestone and some waste ground by it with ¾a. of arable land above it called the Quar ground abutting on 1a. of Mr. Taylor on W. and some of Mr. Beard on N. An arable ground called Court piece, c. 3a., adjoining to a ground of Mr. Beard on S. side and W. end and to Wid. Harris on N. side. A ground of pasture called Broomfield lease, c. 6a., adjoining the highway that leads to Broomfield. 2 other pasture grounds called Bunyards, c. 9a., situate by the highway to Easton Piercy [Priory] and adjoining northward to a ground of farmer Thomas Smith and E. to some land of Kingsman Jaques.

In the Neale's estate at W. Yatton the following grounds are said to be titheable, the rest tithe free: Home close, c. 7a.; Rough furlong, 7a.; 2 New leases, each 8a.; Smiths mead, 8a.; Bean acre, 8a.; Wilds Fillmead 7a.; Middle Fillmead, 7a.; Lower Fillmead, 5a.; Upper Bean acre, 3a., and Middle Bean acre, 4a.

There is belonging to the church and chancel 1 green cloth, bound, to cover the communion table when there is no service and one crimson cloth with a cushion of the same cloth bound with worsted fringe and going to cover the table when there is a service, likewise a large white linen cloth and a smaller one for use when the sacrament is administered; a silver chalice and a smaller one for use when the sacrament is administered; a silver chalice with cover dated 1657 and 2 pewter plates marked 'YK 1783'. 2 candlesticks plated with silver and glass lamps resembling candles. At the upper end of the chancel over the communion table the Ten Commandments are written on 2 tablets of stone dug in the parish, placed in the wall at the E. end of the chancel; each table one single stone excepting the circular ornamental part and on either side of the window; the letters written with white paint, the ground of sky blue; these were set up in 1773.

In the body of the nave of the church distributed around at convenient distances are 21 brass sconces with glass lamps as in the chancel; 2 shorter ones under the gallery with flat tin lamps in the gallery 9 tin lamps, in form like the glass ones, round the lower part of the church.

The pulpit in the N. E. angle has for use in service time, a crimson cloth, bound round in the same manner with 4 tassles. There is a quarto Common Prayer book to be used in the chancel; besides a folio one for the reading desk and one for the parish clerk; a large folio bible and a small book of offices: The King's arms is painted and drained in the compass of about 1yd. square, and hung up against the E. end of the nave of the church over the arch that separates it from the chancel. The Belief[1] is at present painted on canvas, framed and hung up against the wall by the S. door. The Lord's Prayer, of later date, is painted on the wall by the N. door, in short or long lines, agreeable to the separate petitions. In the tower are 3 bells with the following inscriptions: On the treble 'Michael Darbie made me 1675 JW RL CW': on the second 'T. Wild, Richard Rylie, churchwardens 1658', same single letters but no word at length; on the tenor, the same as the second. The church and churchyard fence (which consists of a stone wall) are kept in repair by the parish in general, exclusive of the rector who is at the charge of keeping up the building of the chancel.

The parish clerk has an annual salary of £1 11s. 6d. and is chosen by the minister and parishioners.

This is a true terrier of the glebe lands, containing in the whole c. 89¼a.

James Pidding, rector and patron, William Beard, churchwarden and overseer. Joseph Holborrow, churchwarden, John Witchell.

1. The Nicene Creed.

INDEX OF PERSONS AND PLACES

This index refers to entry, not page, numbers (Roman figures refer to the introductory pages). It includes all parish and minor place names, but not the names of individual fields and agricultural units. Places are in Wiltshire unless stated otherwise. A selection of field-name elements of particular interest to archaeologists, agricultural or landscape historians is included in the separate subject index. References to terriers devoted to a specific parish are printed in bold. All personal names have been indexed, but it has not always been possible to distinguish between homonyms, or collocate individuals who may be styled differently even in the same documents. Variant spellings of surnames are grouped together and cross-referenced. Common forenames are abbreviated. Bishops of Salisbury and other office-holders are indexed under their generic titles.

Derby, Thos, vicar, 243
Derham, Thos, vicar, 391
Derrington, Jn, 396n; Wm, 396–8
Desmore, Hen, 183
Devera(i)ll, Rich, 384; Thos, 557
Devizes St John, **269–70**; purchase of parsonage house, 270
Devizes St Mary, **271–2**
Dew(e), Due, Dwe, Chris, 370; Eliz, wid, 576n; Fras, 32; Jane wid, 735; Jn, 471, 575; Jos, 576; Roger, 575; Walt, 457; wid, 138–40; Wm, 575
Dewdney, Aaron, 536
Dewell, Tim, rector, 501
Dicke, Jn, 238; Wm, 380
Dickenson, Leonard, vicar, 567, 569
Dier, see Dyer
Diet, Wm, 734
Dig(g)(s), Edm, 625–6; Giles, 626; Jn, 625n, 627–30; Rich, 628
Dike, see Dyke
Dilton, chapel and priest's ho, 792
Dinton, **273–6**
Diper, Jn, 391; Wm, 203
Dismer, Rich, 593
Diston, Jn, vicar, 414
Ditteridge, **278–9**
Dixon, Dixsun, D, 524; Wm, 587
Doa(w)le, Hen, 156; Jn, 149; Phil, 149
Dobson, Jn, vicar, 265B, 475
Dobbs, Dan, elder, 495, jun, 495, sen, 495
Docker, Launcelot, vicar, 425
Doel, Jn, 92A
Doig, Rich, 757
Dolman, Jn, 380A; Walt, 122
Dominick(e), Jas, 441–2; Mr, 441–2; Rich, 745
Donhead St Andrew, xiv, xvi, **280–3**, 284–5; Barkers street, 283; Berry Court, farm ho, 282, 284, 286; Easton Bassett, farm, 282; Flitmore lane, 282; Ludwell, 280; Lyes Court, farm, 284; Pigstrough(trow) lane, 282–3; Red cross, 280, 283
Donhead St Mary, **284–6**, 280, 282; Whitson cross, 284–5
Donn, see Dunn
Donnell, Jn, 8
Donney, Hen, Mr, 471

Dorrell, Thos, 18
Doughty, Joel, vicar, 338–9
Dove, Peter, 188–90
Doverdale, Thos, vicar, 585
Dowdeswell, Anth, 625, 627–30
Dowding, Chris, 536
Dowland, Edw, Mr, 471; Jn, vicar, 177, 182
Dowle, see Doale
Dowlies, Wm, 836
Dowlinge, Sam, Clerk, 6; Wm, 493
Down(e)(s), Elias, 118; Edw, 590; Jn, 472; Robt, 536; Wm, 224–5
Downam, Ambrose, 495
Downing, wid, 799
Downton, ix, **287–9**, Charlton, 288; Church lane, 287
Downton, Mich, 243–4; Robt, 825
Dowse, Fras, ir, 203; Rich, 784, Mr, 203
Drake, David, 570
Draper, Gabriel, 89; Mrs, 621; wid, 89; Thos, 89
Drax, esq 144
Draycot, Cerne, **291–3**, 727
Drew(e), Drue, Jn, 91, gent, 613, rector, 710; Mr, 613; Roger, 661–2
Drewet(t), Druett, Brian, 598; Jn, 600; Mrs, 869
Drinkwater, Hen, 868; Robt, 529; Wm, 868
Dri(y)ver, Geo, 19–23; Giles, 18; Jn, 574, 579
Druc(s)e, Anth, 330; Rich, 81; W, 91; wid, 330
Drue, see Drew
Druett, see Drewett
Duckett, Mr, 122
Ducye, Ducey, Edw, 265B; Thos, 91
Dudds, Wm, 8n, 9
Dudley, Hen, vicar, 401
Due, see Dew
Dugdale, Chris, 618; Wm, 727
Dugmore, Jn, vicar, 217
Duke, Edw, Mr, 825n, 826; Mr, 546
Dunch(e), Duns, esq, 20–1; Mr, 823–4; Wm, 823n, 824n
Dun(n)e, Donn, Eliz, 353n; Rich, 571n, 572; Sam, 467; Wm, 353
Dunford, Rich, 89
Dupin, –, 362

Escot, Rich, 561
Essington, Robt, 96
Es(t)court, Earscourte, Eastcourte, Edw,
    rector, 564, Sir, 671; Giles, Sir, 562, 825;
    Mr, 664; Rich, esq, 662n; Wm, Sir,
    825n, 826
Estgatt, Esgat, Gabriel, rector, 743–4
Etchilhampton, 128
Eton college, 415, 855
Etwald, Thos, 31
Etwall, Thos, 152
Eve, Edm, 832; Walt, 835
Evele, Thos, 711
Evemy, Jn, 764
Eve(a)ns; Geo, Esq, 806; Hen, 634; Jas,
    curate, 746; Madam, 806
Everad, Jos, 472
Everleigh, 324–7; Rose and Crown inn,
    603
Everlye(ie), Guy, 458; Jn, 808
Ewyn, Roger, 737
Exton, Roger, 408
Eyles, Edw, esq 400, 797A; Hen, 337; Jn,
    342; Mr, 617; Mrs, 175; Rynalde, 337;
    Wm, alias Hix, 338–9
Eyre(s), Eyer, Eaers, Aire, Chris, 191, 22,
    Mr, 195; Giles, esq, 799; Hen, rector,
    454; J, 454; J M, 454; Mr, 196; Thos,
    105, 737, 825, Mr, 105, 566–8

Fabian, Jn, rector, 558
?Faindr, Thos, 280
Falker, Edw, 319
Fane, Thos, 466
Farewell, Geo, 241
Farindon, Chas, 666n, 667
Farley, hospital, 372
Farl(e)y, Tim, 775
Farmer, Hen, 737; Rich, 741; wid, 464
Farnell, Hen, alias Gouldney, 164; Leonard,
    756; Robt, 441; wid, 441n, 442
Farner, Chas, 290
Farr(e), Pharre, Jn, 167; Robt, 661–2
Fast, Jn, 465
Faugoin, Felix, 711; Fras, 711
Fawconer, Nich, rector, 291, vicar, 434;
    Wm, rector, 717
Fay, Avis, 206–7
Feltham, David, 354; Edw, 353; Jas, 828;

Jn, 84, 363; Thos, 83, 733
Fenner, Rich, Mr, 270
Fenill, Fen(n)ell, Grace, wife of Phil, 443;
    Jn, 395, 397, 796; Phil, 441–2; wid, 396,
    398
Ferguson, Wm, 134n, 136
Fernice, Thos, 164
Ferribe(e)y, Ferebe, Jane, 466n, 467; Jn, 466,
    rector, 609
Ferris, Ferrers, Ferys, Anth, 19,20, Mr, 18;
    Bart, vicar, 677; Edw, Mr, 18–20; Geo,
    18, 666n, 668, Mr, 18; Jn, 19, 21, 185–
    7, rector, 52, vicar, 435; wid, 18
Few, Wm, 524
Fewell, Math, 707
Fey, Edgar, 106n, 107
Fe(a)zard, Jn, 756–8; Lawrence, 756; Rich,
    281–2
Fidler, Thos, 748; Wm, 203–4
Field, Nathan, 709
Fiennes, Fras, Mrs, 571
Fifield Bavant, 334A; Fifield farm, 141
Figgens, Math, 270, Mr, 269
Figheldean, 334; Ablington, 334;
    Choulston, 334; Knighton, 334;
    Syrencott, 334
Fildowne, Hen, 122
Filkes, Fylks, Jacob, vicar, 69; Robt, 635;
    Sam, Mr, 272
Fisher, Edw, 579; Fras, 324; Jn, 391, 609;
    Thos, 61, vicar, 578; Walt, 213
Fisherton Anger, 335–6; Cole harbour, 336
Fisherton Delamere, xiii, 337–42; Bapton,
    337, 339, 704–5; Fisherton mill, 339
Fittleton, xiv, xvi, 343–7; Haxton, 343, 345,
    347, chapel, 346, portionary tithes, 346;
    Odd lands, 345-6
Fitzherbert, Andr, Mr, 494; Hen, Mr, 494,
    rector, 494; Hump, esq, 494
Fitzhugh, Robt, 222
Flem(y)ing, Nich, 705; Thos, Sir, 556; Wm,
    705
Fletcher, Jn, rector, 513
Flewell, Hen, 486–8; Jn, 488
Flodd, Jn, curate, 231, vicar, 236
Flookes, Robt, 281
Flory, Thos, 848
Flower, Chas, Mr, 180n, 182; Edw, 776;
    Geo, esq, 372; Hen, 199; Jonathan,

SUBJECT INDEX

The nature of glebe terriers does not lend them to detailed subject indexing, since they are essentially lists of land, property and tithes. Of these only detailed examples of tithe customs, which illustrate the complexities of the system, have been included. Only by reading the text in its entirety can one fully appreciate the historical value of glebe terriers. This index then is a very selective one dealing mainly with incidental details the reader might not readily associate with these documents. The numbers refer to documents not pages.

P· 205 no. 398 + index Arthur mt Archibald Buckeridge

WILTSHIRE RECORD SOCIETY
(As at April 2003)

President: PROF. C.R. ELRINGTON, F.S.A.
General Editor: DR JOHN CHANDLER
Honorary Treasurer: IVOR M. SLOCOMBE
Honorary Secretary: JOHN N. D'ARCY

Committee:
D. CHALMERS
DR D.A. CROWLEY
S.D. HOBBS
M.J. MARSHMAN
MRS S. THOMSON
MRS I.L. WILLIAMS
K.H. ROGERS, F.S.A., representing the Wiltshire Archaeological and Natural History
Society

Honorary Independent Examiner: J.D. FOY
Correspondent for the U.S.A.: CHARLES P. GOULD

PRIVATE MEMBERS

ADAMS, MS S, 23 Rockcliffe Avenue,
Bathwick, Bath BA2 6QP
ANDERSON, MR D M, 8 Edwin Jones
Green, Northlands, Southampton
SO15 2RY
APPLEGATE, MISS J M, 55 Holbrook Lane,
Trowbridge BA14 0PS
ASAJI, PROF K, 5-35-14 Senriyama-nishi,
Suita, Osaka, Japan 565-0851
AVERY, MRS S, 33 Cardigan Street, Oxford
OX2 6GP
BADENI, COUNTESS JUNE, Norton Manor,
Norton, Malmesbury SN16 0JN
BAINES, MRS B M, 32 Tybenham Road,
Merton Park, London SW19 3LA
BALL, MR S T, 19 The Mall, Swindon SN1
4JA
BARNETT, MR B A, 17 Alexandra Road,
Coalpit Heath, Bristol BS36 2PY
BATHE, MR G, Byeley in Densome,
Woodgreen, Fordingbridge, Hants SP6
2QU

BAYLIFFE, MR B G, 3 Green Street,
Brockworth, Glos GL3 4LT
BENNETT, DR N, Hawthorn House, Main
Street, Norton, Lincoln LN4 2BH
BERRETT, MR A M, 10 Primrose Hill Road,
London NW3 3AD
BERRY, MR C, 9 Haven Rd, Crackington
Haven, Bude, Cornwall EX23 0PD
BISHOP, MRS S M, Innox Bungalow, Market
Place, Colerne, Chippenham SN14
8AY
BLAKE, MR P A, 18 Rosevine Road,
London SW20 8RB
BLAKE, MR T N, Glebe Farm, Tilshead,
Salisbury SP3 4RZ
BOX, MR S D, 73 Silverdale Road, Earley,
Reading RG6 2NF
BRAND, DR P A, 155 Kennington Road,
London SE11 6SF
BRITTON, MR D J, Overbrook House, The
High Road, Ashton Keynes, Swindon
SN6 6NL

BROOKE-LITTLE, MR J P, Heyford House, Lower Heyford, Bicester, Oxon OX25 5NZ

BROWN, MR D A, 36 Empire Road, Salisbury SP2 9DF

BROWN, MR G R, 6 Canbury Close, Amesbury, SalisburySP4 7QF

BRYANT, MRS D, 1 St John's Ct, Devizes SN10 1BJ

BURGESS, MR I D, 29 Brackley Avenue, Fair Oak, Eastleigh, Hants SO5 7FL

BURGESS, MR J M, Tolcarne, Wartha Mill, Porkellis, Helston, Cornwall TR13 0HX

BURNETT-BROWN, MISS J M, Lacock Abbey, Lacock, Chippenham SN15 2LG

CAREW HUNT, MISS P H, Cowleaze, Edington, Westbury BA13 4PJ

CARR, PROF D R, Dept. of History, 140 7th Ave South, St Petersburg, Florida 33701 USA

CARRIER, MR S, 9 Highfield Road, Bradford on Avon BA15 1AS

CARTER, DR B J, JP PHD BSC FSG, 15 Walton Grange, Bath Road, Swindon SN1 4AH

CAWTHORNE, MRS N, 45 London Road, Camberley, Surrey GU15 3UG

CHALMERS, MR D, Bay House West, Bay House, Ilminster, Somerset TA19 0AT

CHANDLER, DR J H, Jupe's School, The Street, East Knoyle, Salisbury SP3 6AJ

CHARD, MR I, 35 Thingwall Park, Fishponds, Bristol BS16 2AJ

CHURCH, MR T S, Mannering House, Bethersden, Ashford, Kent TN26 3DJ

CLARK, MR A G, Highlands, 51a Brook Drive, Corsham SN13 9AX

CLARK, MRS V, 29 The Green, Marlborough SN8 1AW

CLEGG, MS R, 12 Brookes Road, Broseley, Salop TF12 5SB

COBERN, MISS A M, 4 Manton Close, Manton, Marlborough SN8 4HJ

COLCOMB, MR D M, 38 Roundway Park, Devizes SN10 2EO

COLE, MRS J A, 113 Groundwell Road, Swindon SN1 2NA

COLEMAN, MISS J, Swn-y-Coed, Abergwili, Carmarthenshire SA32 7EP

COLES, MR H, Ebony House, 23 Lords Hill, Coleford, Glos GL16 8BG

COLLINS, MR A T, 11 Lemon Grove, Whitehill, Bordon, Hants GU35 9BD

CONGLETON, LORD, West End Farm, Ebbesbourne Wake, Salisbury SP5 5JW

COOMBES-LEWIS, MR R J, 45 Oakwood Park Road, Southgate, London N14 6QP

COOPER, MR S, 12 Victory Row, Wootton Bassett, Swindon SN4 7BE

CORAM, MRS J E, 38 The Parklands, Hullavington, Chippenham SN14 6DL

COULSTOCK, MISS P H, 15 Pennington Crescent, West Moors, Wimborne, Dorset BH22 0JH

COVEY, MR R V, Lower Hunts Mill, Wootton Bassett, Swindon SN4 7QL

COWAN, COL M, 24 Lower Street, Harnham, Salisbury SP3 8EY

CRIGHTON, MR G S, 68 Stanford Avenue, Springfield, Milton Keynes MK6 3NH

CROOK, MR P H, Bradavon, 45 The Dales, Cottingham, E Yorks HU16 5JS

CROUCH, MR J W, 28 Kinh John Road, Gillingham SP8 4PQ

CROWLEY, DR D A, 16 Greater Lane, Edington, Westbury BA13 4QP

D'ARCY, MR J N, The Old Vicarage, Edington, Westbury

DAVIES, MRS A M, 283 Longstone Road, Iver Heath, Bucks SL0 0RN

DIBBEN, MR A A, 18 Clare Road, Lewes, East Sussex BN7 1PN

DRAPER, MISS R, 12 Sheep Street, Devizes SN10 1DL

DYSON, MRS L, 1 Dauntsey Ct, Duck St, West Lavington, Devizes SN10 4LR

EDE, DR M E, 12 Springfield Place, Lansdown, Bath BA1 5RA

EDWARDS, MR P C, 33 Longcroft Road, Devizes SN10 3AT

ELRINGTON, PROF C R, 34 Lloyd Baker Street, London WC1X 9AB

FALCINI, MS L, Old Forge Cottage, North Lane, West Tytherley, Salisbury SP5 1JX

FAY, MRS M, 40 North Way, Porton Down, Salisbury SP4 0JN

FICE, MRS B, Holt View House, 9 Rosemary Lane, Rowledge, Farnham GU10 4DB

FIRMAGER, MRS G M, 72b High Street, Semington, Trowbridge BA14 6JR

FLOWER-ELLIS, DR J G, Swedish Univ of Agric Sciences, PO Box 7072 S-750 07, Uppsala, Sweden 1972

FORBES, MISS K G, Bury House, Codford, Warminster

FOSTER, MR R E, The New House, St Giles Close, Gt Maplestead, Halstead, Essex CO9 2RW

FOY, MR J D, 28 Penn Lea Road, Bath BA1 3RA

FREEMAN, REV DR J, 1 Cranfield Row, Gerridge Street, London SE1 7QN

FROST, MR B C, Red Tiles, Cadley, Collingbourne Ducis, Marlborough SN8 3EA

FULLER, MRS B, 65 New Park Street, Devizes SN10 1DR

GALBRAITH, MS C, Box 42, 17 Gill Street, Coldwater, Ontario L0K 1EO, Canada

GALE, MRS J, 169 Spit Road, Mosman, NSW 2088, Australia

GHEY, MR J G, 18 Bassett Row, Bassett, Southampton SO1 7FS

GIBBS, MRS E, Home Farm, Barrow Gurney, Bristol BS48 3RW

GODDARD, MR R E H, Sinton Meadow, Stokes Lane, Leigh Sinton, Malvern, Worcs WR13 5DY

GOODBODY, MR E A, Stockmans, Rectory Hill, Amersham, Bucks

GOSLING, REV DR J, 1 Wiley Terrace, Wilton, Salisbury SP2 0HN

GOUGH, MISS P M, 39 Whitford Road, Bromsgrove, Worcs B61 7ED

GOULD, MR C P, 1200 Old Mill Road, San Marino, California 91108 USA

GOULD, MR L K, 263 Rosemount, Pasadena, California 91103 USA

GRIFFIN, DR C J, School of Geographical Sciences, University of Bristol, University Road, Bristol BS8 1SS

GRIFFITHS, MR T J, 29 Saxon Street, Chippenham SN15

GRUBER VON ARNI, COL E E, 11 Park Lane, Swindon SN1 5HG

GUNSTONE, MR L, 29 Dorset St, Bath BA2 3RA

HAMILTON, CAPTAIN R, 1 The Square, Cathedral Views, Crane Bridge Road, Salisbury SP2 7TW

HARE, DR J N, 7 Owens Road, Winchester, Hants SO22 6RU

HATCHWELL, MR R C, Cleeve House, Rodbourne Bottom, Malmesbury SN16 0EZ

HAYWARD, MISS J E, Pleasant Cottage, Crockerton, Warminster BA12 8AJ

HELMHOLZ, PROF R W, Law School, 1111 East 60th Street, Chicago, Illinois 60637 USA

HENLY, MR H R, 99 Moredon Road, Swindon SN2 2JG

HERRON, MRS Pamela M, 25 Anvil Crescent, Broadstone, Dorset BH18 9DY

HICKMAN, MR M R, 184 Surrenden Road, Brighton BN1 6NN

HICKS, MR I, 74 Newhurst Park, Hilperton, Trowbridge BA14 7QW

HICKS, PROF M A, King Alfred's College, Winchester SO22 4NR

HILLMAN, MR R B, 18 Carnarvon Close, Chippenham SN14 0PN

HINTON, MR A E, Glenside Cottage, Glendene Avenue, East Horsley, Surrey KT24 5AY

HOBBS, MR S, 63 West End, Westbury BA13 3JQ

HOLLEY, MR R J, 120 London Road, Calne SN11 0AH

HORNBY, MISS E, 70 Archers Court, Castle Street, Salisbury SP1 3WE

HORTON, MR P.R.G, OBE, Hedge End, West Grimstead, Salisbury SP5 3RF

HOWELLS, Jane, 7 St Mark's Rd, Salisbury SP1 3AY

HUGHES, PROF C J, Old House, Tisbury, Salisbury SP3 6PS

HUGHES, MR R G, 60 Hurst Park Road, Twyford, Reading RG10 0EY

HULL, MR J L F, Sandown Apartments, 1 Southerwood Drive, Sandy Bay, Tasmania 7005, Australia

HUMPHRIES, MR A G, Rustics, Blacksmith's Lane, Harmston, Lincoln LN5 9SW

INGRAM, DR M J, Brasenose College, Oxford OX1 4AJ

JACKSON, MR D, 2 Byways Close, Salisbury SP1 2QS

JAMES, MR & MRS C, 18 King Henry Drive, Grange Park, Swindon SN5 6BL

JAMES, MR J F, 3 Sylvan Close, Hordle, Lymington, Hants SO41 0HJ
JEACOCK, MR D, 16 Church Street, Wootton Bassett, Swindon
JELLICOE, RT HON EARL, Tidcombe Manor, Tidcombe, Marlborough SN8 3SL
JOHNSTON, MRS J M, Greystone House, 3 Trowbridge Road, Bradford on Avon BA15 1EE
KENT, MR T A, Rose Cottage, Isington, Alton, Hants GU34 4PN
KING, MR S F, Church Mead House, Woolverton, Bath BA3 6QT
KIRBY, MRS H, 209 Covington Way, Streatham, London SW16 3BY
KITE, MR P J, 13 Chestnut Avenue, Farnham GU9 8UL
KNEEBONE, MR W J R, 20 Blind Lane, Southwick, Trowbridge BA14 9PG
KUNIKATA, MR K, Dept of Economics, 1-4-12, Kojirakawa-machi, Yamagata-shi 990, Japan
LANSDOWNE, MARQUIS OF, Bowood House, Calne SN11 0LZ
LAURENCE, MISS A, 1a Moreys Avenue, Oxford OX1 4ST
LAURENCE, MR G F, Apt 312, The Hawthorns, 18-21 Elton Road, Clevedon BS21 7EH
LAWES, MR G, 48 Windsor Avenue, Leighton Buzzard LU7 1AP
LEGGATT, MR A, 48 High Street, Worton, Devizes SN10 5RG
LODGE, MR O R W, Southridge House, Hindon, Salisbury SP3 6ER
LUSH, DR G J, 5 Braeside Court, West Moors, Ferndown, Dorset BH22 0JS
MARSH, REV R, 67 Hythe Crescent, Seaford, East Sussex BN25 3TZ
MARSHMAN, MR M J, 13 Regents Place, Bradford on Avon BA15 1ED
MARTIN, MR D, 21 Westbourne Close, Salisbury SP1 2RU
MARTIN, MS JEAN, 21 Ashfield Road, Chippenham SN15 1QQ
MASLEN, MR A, 8 Alder Walk, Frome, Som BA11 2SN
MATHEWS, MR R, P O Box R72, Royal Exchange, NSW 2000, Australia
MATTHEWS, CANON W A, Holy Trinity Vicarage, 18a Woolley St, Bradford on Avon BA15 1AF

MATTINGLY, MR N, Freshford Manor, Freshford, Bath BA3 6EF
MILLINGTON, MRS P, Hawkstone, Church Hill, Lover, Salisbury SP5 2PL
MOLES, MRS M I, 40 Wyke Road, Trowbridge BA14 7NP
MONTAGUE, MR M D, 115 Stuarts Road, Katoomba, NSW 2780, Australia
MOODY, MR R F, Fair Orchard, South Widcombe, East Harptree, Bristol BS40 6BL
MORIOKA, PROF K 3-12, 4-chome, Sanno, Ota-ku, Tokyo, Japan
MORLAND, MRS N, 33 Shaftesbury Road, Wilton, Salisbury SP2 0DU
MORRISON, MRS J, Priory Cottage, Bratton, Westbury BA13
MOULTON, DR A E, The Hall, Bradford on Avon BA15
NAPPER, MR L R, 9 The Railway Terrace, Kemble, Cirencester GL7 6AU
NEWBURY, MR C COLES, 6 Leighton Green, Westbury BA13 3PN
NEWMAN, MRS R, Tanglewood, Laverstock Park, Salisbury SP1 1QJ
NOKES, MR P M A, Wards Farm, Ditcheat, Shepton Mallet, Somerset BA4 6PR
O'DONNELL, MISS S J, 42 Wessington Park, Calne SN11 0AU
OGBOURNE, MR J M V, 14 Earnshaw Way, Beaumont Park, Whitley Bay, Tyne and Wear NE25 9UN
OGBURN, SENIOR JUDGE ROBERT W, 317 First Avenue, Monte Vista, CO 81144, USA
OSBORNE, COL R, Unwins House, 15 Waterbeach Road, Landbeach, Cambridge CB4 4EA
PARKER, DR P F, 45 Chitterne Road, Codford St Mary, Warminster BA12 0PG
PARROTT, MRS M G, 81 Church Road, Christian Malford, Chippenham SN15 4BW
PATIENCE, MR D C, 29 Priory Gardens, Stamford, Lincs PE9 2EG
PERRY, DR S H, Priory Cottage, Broad Street, Bampton, Oxon
PERRY, MR W A, Noads House, Tilshead, Salisbury SP3 4RY
POTTER, MRS J, 6 Round Chimneys, Glanvilles Wootton, Sherborne DT9 5QQ

POWELL, MRS N, 4 Verwood Drive, Bitton, Bristol BS15 6JP

RADNOR, EARL OF, Longford Castle, Salisbury SP5 4EF

RAYBOULD, MISS F, 20 Radnor Road, Salisbury SP1 3PL

REEVES, DR M E, 38 Norham Road, Oxford OX2 6SQ

ROGERS, MR K H, Silverthorne House, East Town, West Ashton, Trowbridge BA14 6BE

ROOKE, MISS S F, The Old Rectory, Little Langford, Salisbury SP3 4NU

SHELDRAKE, MR B, 28 Belgrave Street, Swindon SN1 3HR

SHEWRING, MR P, 73 Woodland Road, Beddau, Pontypridd, Mid-Glamorgan CF38 2SE

SIMS-NEIGHBOUR, MR A K, 2 Hesketh Crescent, Swindon SN3 1RY

SLOCOMBE, MR I, 11 Belcombe Place, Bradford on Avon BA15 1NA

SMITH, DR C, 2 Wesley Villas, Church Street, Coleford, Frome BA3 5ND

SMITH, MR P J, 6 Nuthatch, Longfield, Kent DA3 7NS

SNEYD, MR R H, Court Farm House, 22 Court Lane, Bratton, Westbury BA13 4RR

SOPP, MR G A, 23952 Nomar Street, Woodland Hills, California 91367, USA

SPAETH, DR D A, School of History and Archaeology, 1 University Gardens, University of Glasgow G12 8QQ

STEELE, MRS N D, 46 The Close, Salisbury SP1 2EL

STEVENAGE, MR M R, 49 Centre Drive, Epping, Essex CM16 4JF

STEWARD, DR H J, Graduate School of Geography, 950 Main Street, Worcester, Mass 01610-1477, USA

STEWART, MISS K P, 6 Beatrice Road, Salisbury SP1 3PN

SYKES, MRS M, Conock Manor, Conock, Devizes SN10 3QQ

SYLVESTER, MR D G H, Polsue Manor, Ruanhigh Lanes, Truro TR2 5LU

TAYLOR, MR C C, 11 High Street, Pampisford, Cambridge CB2 4ES

TAYLOR, MRS J B, PO Box 3900, Manuka, ACT 2063, Australia

THOMPSON, MR & MRS J B, 1 Bedwyn Common, Great Bedwyn, Marlborough SN8 3HZ

THOMSON, MRS S M, Home Close, High St, Codford, Warminster BA12 0NB

TIGHE, MR M F, Strath Colin, Pettridge Lane, Mere, Warminster BA12 6DG

TOMKOWICZ, MRS C, 2 Chirton Place, Trowbridge BA14 0XT

TSUSHIMA, MRS J, Malmaison, Church Street, Great Bedwyn, Marlborough SN8 3PE

TURNER, MR I D, Warrendene, 222 Nottingham Road, Mansfield, Notts NG18 4AB

WAITE, MR R E, 18a Lower Road, Chinnor, Oxford OX9 4DT

WALKER, MR J K, 82 Wainsford Road, Everton, Lymington, Hants SO41 0UD

WARNEFORD, MR F E, New Inn Farm, West End Lane, Henfield, West Sussex BN5 9RF

WARREN, MR P, 6 The Meadows, Milford Hill Road, Salisbury SP1 2RT

WELLER, MR R B, 9a Bower Gardens, Salisbury SP1 2RL

WENDEN, MRS P, 21 Eastern Parade, Fareham, Hants PO16 0RL

WHORLEY, MR E E, 190 Stockbridge Road, Winchester, Hants SO22 6RW

WILLIAMS, MRS I L, 7 Chandler Close, Devizes SN10 3DS

WILTSHIRE, MRS P E, 23 Little Parks, Holt, Trowbridge BA14 6QR

WOODWARD, A S, 28-840 Cahill Drive West, Ottawa, Ontario K1V 9K5, Canada

WORDSWORTH, MRS G, Quince Cottage, Longbridge Deverill, Warminster BA12 7DS

WRIGHT, MR D P, Haileybury, Hertford SG13 7NU

YOUNGER, MR C, The Old Chapel, Burbage, Marlborough SN8 3AA

UNITED KINGDOM INSTITUTIONS

Aberystwyth
  National Library of Wales
  University College of Wales
Bath. Reference Library
Birmingham
  Central Library
  University Library
Brighton. University of Sussex Library
Bristol. University Library
Cambridge. University Library
Cheltenham. Bristol and Gloucestershire
    Archaeological Society
Chippenham. Wiltshire College
Coventry. University of Warwick Library
Devizes
  Wiltshire Archaeological & N.H. Soc.
  Wiltshire Family History Society
Dorchester. Dorset County Library
Durham. University Library
Edinburgh
  National Library of Scotland
  University Library
Exeter. University Library
Glasgow. University Library
Leeds. University Library
Leicester. University Library
Liverpool. University Library
London
  British Library
  College of Arms
  Guildhall Library
  Inner Temple Library
  Institute of Historical Research
  London Library
  Public Record Office
  Royal Historical Society

Society of Antiquaries
Society of Genealogists
University of London Library
Manchester. John Rylands Library
Marlborough
  Memorial Library, Marlborough College
  Merchant's House Trust
  Savernake Estate Office
Norwich. University of East Anglia Library
Nottingham. University Library
Oxford
  Bodleian Library
  Exeter College Library
Poole. Bournemouth University
Reading
  Central Library
  University Library
St Andrews. University Library
Salisbury
  Bourne Valley Historical Society
  Cathedral Library
  Salisbury and South Wilts Museum
Sheffield. University Library
Southampton. University Library
Swansea. University College Library
Swindon
  English Heritage
  Swindon Borough Council
Taunton. Somerset Archaeological and
    Natural History Society
Trowbridge
  Wiltshire Libraries & Heritage
  Wiltshire and Swindon Record Office
Wetherby. British Library Document
    Supply Centre
York. University Library

INSTITUTIONS OVERSEAS

AUSTRALIA
Adelaide. Barr Smith Library, Adelaide
    University
Crawley. Reid Library, University of
    Western Australia
Melbourne
  Baillieu Library, University of Melbourne
  Victoria State Library
Sydney. Law Library, University of New
    South Wales

CANADA
Halifax, Nova Scotia. Dalhousie University
    Library
London, Ont. D.B. Weldon Library, Univ-
    ersity of Western Ontario
Ottawa, Ont. Carleton University Library
Toronto, Ont
  Pontifical Inst of Medieval Studies
  University of Toronto Library
Victoria, B.C. McPherson Library,

University of Victoria

EIRE
Dublin. Trinity College Library

GERMANY
Gottingen. University Library

JAPAN
Osaka. Institute of Economic History,
Kansai University
Sendai. Institute of Economic History,
Tohoku University
Tokyo. Waseda University Library

NEW ZEALAND
Wellington. National Library of New
Zealand

UNITED STATES OF AMERICA
Ann Arbor, Mich. Hatcher Library,
University of Michigan
Athens, Ga. University of Georgia Libraries
Atlanta, Ga. The Robert W Woodruff
Library, Emory University
Baltimore, Md. Milton S. Eisenhower
Library, Johns Hopkins University
Bloomington, Ind. Indiana University
Library
Boston, Mass.
Boston Public Library
New England Historic and Genealogical
Society
Boulder, Colo. University of Colorado
Library
Cambridge, Mass.
Harvard College Library
Harvard Law School Library
Charlottesville, Va. Alderman Library,
University of Virginia
Chicago.
Newberry Library
University of Chicago Library
Dallas, Texas. Public Library
Davis, Calif. University Library
East Lansing, Mich. Michigan State

University Library
Eugene, Ore. University of Oregon Library
Evanston, Ill. United Libraries, Garrett/
Evangelical, Seabury
Fort Wayne, Ind. Allen County Public
Library
Houston, Texas. M.D. Anderson Library,
University of Houston
Iowa City, Iowa. University of Iowa
Libraries
Ithaca, NY. Cornell University Library
Las Cruces, N.M. New Mexico State
University Library
Los Angeles.
Public Library
Young Research Library, University of
California
Minneapolis, Minn. Wilson Library,
University of Minnesota
New Haven, Conn. Yale University Library
New York.
Columbia University of the City of
New York
Public Library
Notre Dame, Ind. Memorial Library,
University of Notre Dame
Piscataway, N.J. Rutgers University
Libraries
Princeton, N.J. Princeton University
Libraries
Salt Lake City, Utah. Family History
Library
San Marino, Calif. Henry E. Huntington
Library
Santa Barbara, Calif. University of
California Library
South Hadley, Mass. Williston Memorial
Library, Mount Holyoke College
Stanford, Calif. Green Library, Stanford
University
Tucson, Ariz. University of Arizona Library
Urbana, Ill. University of Illinois Library
Washington. The Folger Shakespeare
Library
Winston-Salem, N.C. Z. Smith Reynolds
Library, Wake Forest University

LIST OF PUBLICATIONS

The Wiltshire Record Society was founded in 1937, as the Records Branch of the Wiltshire Archaeological and Natural History Society, to promote the publication of the documentary sources for the history of Wiltshire. The annual subscription is £15 for private and institutional members. In return, a member receives a volume each year. Prospective members should apply to the Hon. Secretary, c/o Wiltshire and Swindon Record Office, County Hall, Trowbridge, Wilts BA14 8BS. Many more members are needed.

The following volumes have been published. Price to members £15, and to non-members £20, postage extra. Available from the Wiltshire and Swindon Record Office, Bythesea Road, Trowbridge BA14 8BS.

1. *Abstracts of feet of fines relating to Wiltshire for the reigns of Edward I and Edward II*, ed. R.B. Pugh, 1939
2. *Accounts of the parliamentary garrisons of Great Chalfield and Malmesbury, 1645-1646*, ed. J.H.P. Pafford, 1940
3. *Calendar of Antrobus deeds before 1625*, ed. R.B. Pugh, 1947
4. *Wiltshire county records: minutes of proceedings in sessions, 1563 and 1574 to 1592*, ed. H.C. Johnson, 1949
5. *List of Wiltshire boroughs records earlier in date than 1836*, ed. M.G. Rathbone, 1951
6. *The Trowbridge woollen industry as illustrated by the stock books of John and Thomas Clark, 1804-1824*, ed. R.P. Beckinsale, 1951
7. *Guild stewards' book of the borough of Calne, 1561-1688*, ed. A.W. Mabbs, 1953
8. *Andrews' and Dury's map of Wiltshire, 1773: a reduced facsimile*, ed. Elizabeth Crittall, 1952
9. *Surveys of the manors of Philip, earl of Pembroke and Montgomery, 1631-2*, ed. E. Kerridge, 1953
10. *Two sixteenth century taxations lists, 1545 and 1576*, ed. G.D. Ramsay, 1954
11. *Wiltshire quarter sessions and assizes, 1736*, ed. J.P.M. Fowle, 1955
12. *Collectanea*, ed. N.J. Williams, 1956
13. *Progress notes of Warden Woodward for the Wiltshire estates of New College, Oxford, 1659-1675*, ed. R.L. Rickard, 1957
14. *Accounts and surveys of the Wiltshire lands of Adam de Stratton*, ed. M.W. Farr, 1959
15. *Tradesmen in early-Stuart Wiltshire: a miscellany*, ed. N.J. Williams, 1960
16. *Crown pleas of the Wiltshire eyre, 1249*, ed. C.A.F. Meekings, 1961
17. *Wiltshire apprentices and their masters, 1710-1760*, ed. Christabel Dale, 1961
18. *Hemingby's register*, ed. Helena M. Chew, 1963
19. *Documents illustrating the Wiltshire textile trades in the eighteenth century*, ed. Julia de L. Mann, 1964
20. *The diary of Thomas Naish*, ed. Doreen Slatter, 1965
21-2. *The rolls of Highworth hundred, 1275-1287*, 2 parts, ed. Brenda Farr, 1966, 1968
23. *The earl of Hertford's lieutenancy papers, 1603-1612*, ed. W.P.D. Murphy, 1969
24. *Court rolls of the Wiltshire manors of Adam de Stratton*, ed. R.B. Pugh, 1970
25. *Abstracts of Wiltshire inclosure awards and agreements*, ed. R.E. Sandell, 1971
26. *Civil pleas of the Wiltshire eyre, 1249*, ed. M.T. Clanchy, 1971
27. *Wiltshire returns to the bishop's visitation queries, 1783*, ed. Mary Ransome, 1972
28. *Wiltshire extents for debts, Edward I - Elizabeth I*, ed. Angela Conyers, 1973
29. *Abstracts of feet of fines relating to Wiltshire for the reign of Edward III*, ed. C.R. Elrington, 1974
30. *Abstracts of Wiltshire tithe apportionments*, ed. R.E. Sandell, 1975

31. *Poverty in early-Stuart Salisbury*, ed. Paul Slack, 1975
32. *The subscription book of Bishops Tounson and Davenant, 1620-40*, ed. B.Williams, 1977
33. *Wiltshire gaol delivery and trailbaston trials, 1275-1306*, ed. R.B. Pugh, 1978
34. *Lacock abbey charters*, ed. K.H. Rogers, 1979
35. *The cartulary of Bradenstoke priory*, ed.Vera C.M. London, 1979
36. *Wiltshire coroners' bills, 1752-1796*, ed. R.F. Hunnisett, 1981
37. *The justicing notebook of William Hunt, 1744-1749*, ed. Elizabeth Crittall, 1982
38. *Two Elizabethan women: correspondence of Joan and Maria Thynne, 1575-1611*, ed. Alison D. Wall, 1983
39. *The register of John Chandler, dean of Salisbury, 1404-17*, ed. T.C.B. Timmins, 1984
40. *Wiltshire dissenters' meeting house certificates and registrations, 1689-1852*, ed. J.H. Chandler, 1985
41. *Abstracts of feet of fines relating to Wiltshire, 1377-1509*, ed. J.L. Kirby, 1986
42. *The Edington cartulary*, ed. Janet H. Stevenson, 1987
43. *The commonplace book of Sir Edward Bayntun of Bromham*, ed. Jane Freeman, 1988
44. *The diaries of Jeffery Whitaker, schoolmaster of Bratton, 1739-1741*, ed. Marjorie Reeves and Jean Morrison, 1989
45. *The Wiltshire tax list of 1332*, ed. D.A. Crowley, 1989
46. *Calendar of Bradford-on-Avon settlement examinations and removal orders, 1725-98*, ed. Phyllis Hembry, 1990
47. *Early trade directories of Wiltshire*, ed. K.H. Rogers and indexed by J.H. Chandler, 1992
48. *Star chamber suits of John and Thomas Warneford*, ed. F.E. Warneford, 1993
49. *The Hungerford cartulary: a calendar of the earl of Radnor's cartulary of the Hungerford family*, ed. J.L. Kirby, 1994
50. *The Letters of John Peniston, Salisbury architect, Catholic, and Yeomanry Officer, 1823-1830*, ed. M. Cowan, 1996
51. *The Apprentice Registers of the Wiltshire Society, 1817- 1922*, ed. H. R. Henly, 1997
52. *Printed Maps of Wiltshire 1787–1844: a selection of topographical, road and canal maps in facsimile*, ed. John Chandler, 1998
53. *Monumental Inscriptions of Wiltshire: an edition, in facsimile, of* Monumental Inscriptions in the County of Wilton, *by Sir Thomas Phillipps*, ed. Peter Sherlock, 2000
54. *The First General Entry Book of the City of Salisbury, 1387-1452*, ed. David R. Carr, 2001
55. *Devizes Division income tax assessments, 1842-1860*, ed. Robert Colley, 2002

VOLUMES IN PREPARATION

Wiltshire farming during the seventeenth century, edited by J. H. Bettey; *Marlborough probate inventories*, edited by Lorelei Williams; *Wiltshire papist returns and estate enrolments, 1705-87*, edited by J.A. Williams; *The Diary of William Henry Tucker*, edited by Helen Rogers; *Early vehicle registration in Wiltshire*, edited by Ian Hicks; *Crown pleas of the Wiltshire eyre, 1268*, edited by Brenda Farr; *The Hungerford cartulary, vol.2: the Hobhouse cartulary*, edited by J.L. Kirby; *The Parish registers of Thomas Crockford, 1613-29*, edited by C.C. Newbury; *Index to the Salisbury Diocesan probate records*; *Andrews and Dury's Map of Wiltshire, 1773 and 1810 new edition*; *The Wiltshire hearth tax returns*, edited by Lorelei Williams; *Wiltshire rural industry organiser surveys and reports, c. 1938 - c. 1957*, edited by John d'Arcy. . The volumes will not necessarily appear in this order.

A leaflet giving full details may be obtained from the Hon. Secretary, c/o Wiltshire and Swindon Record Office, County Hall, Trowbridge, Wilts. BA14 8BS. Details may also be found on the Society's website: www.wiltshirerecordsociety.co.uk.